THE INTERPRETATION OF
FREGE'S PHILOSOPHY

MICHAEL DUMMETT

THE INTERPRETATION OF FREGE'S PHILOSOPHY

Harvard University Press

Cambridge, Massachusetts

1981

Copyright © 1981 by Michael Dummett
All rights reserved

Library of Congress Cataloging in Publication Data

Dummett, Michael A E
    The interpretation of Frege's philosophy.

    Bibliography: p.
    Includes index.
    1. Frege, Gottlob, 1848-1925—Linguistics.
2. Languages—Philosophy. I. Title.
P85. F7D8 1981   401   80-14537
ISBN 0-674-45975-x

Printed in Great Britain

Contents

To the memory of my father

Preface

THIS IS A book which I wrote without meaning to. I had intended to devote this academic year (1978-9) to completing the second volume of my study of Frege, that on his philosophy of mathematics, and to revising for publication my 1976 William James lectures at Harvard, *The Logical Basis of Metaphysics*. However, since *Frege: Philosophy of Language*, originally published in 1973, had gone out of print, the first priority became to bring out a second edition of that book, hereafter referred to as *FPL*, with subscripts 1 and 2 where necessary to distinguish the first and second editions. Ideally, I should have chosen to rewrite the book from start to finish, but this was not possible. A complete revision would have held up the reissue far too long, as well as preventing me during the two or more years that it would have taken from finishing *Frege: Philosophy of Mathematics* and the revision of the William James lectures; and only by issuing the second edition with no more than the most restricted and pressing textual changes was it possible to keep the printer's costs within limits. Two additions were essential, to meet justifiable criticisms expressed, sometimes with vehemence, by every single reviewer. First, a fuller index had to be compiled: being exceptionally inept at the making of indices, I am fortunate to have had the help, in this matter, of Dr Mark Helme and of Mr Charles Donahue. Secondly, it was necessary to insert references to Frege's text. I owe readers of FPL_1 an apology for the paucity of the references given in it, an omission that was not intentional, but an oversight. I found it easier to write the book without having to pause to locate passages to which I was alluding; it was therefore composed almost wholly from memory. My intention was, having completed it, to go through the book, inserting references; in a way I cannot now account for, I allowed this to slip my mind when doing all the many other things necessary to complete the book for publication. If readers find this hard to believe, I do not blame them; it now seems nearly incredible even to me. For the new edition, I have remedied the defect by adding references in the margin, and hope that they will be found helpful; I again owe many thanks to Dr Helme for greatly helping me in this task also.

All this has occupied a certain amount of time; but, before I had completed this work, my publisher suggested that I should write a 100-page introduction to the second edition, explaining the few alterations made in the text, elucidating passages that had been misunderstood, answering criticisms and recording second thoughts. The suggestion was welcome to me because I was conscious that the alterations I was able to make were not always as explicit as I should have wished, owing to the need to respect the lineation of the text; and, further, that there were passages which, as not being actually wrong, I was forced to leave unchanged, but which, if a full revision had been possible, I should have expressed differently. I therefore began to compose such an introduction. In the course of composition, its orientation altered. In his critical notice of FPL_1,[1] E.-H. W. Kluge complains that I refer to very little of the secondary literature on Frege.[2] I did discuss certain interpretations and criticisms of Frege by Church, Marshall, Grossmann, Geach, Tugendhat, Kripke and others, which had come to my attention and appeared to me interesting but mistaken; but, by and large, I naively expected that my exposition of Frege would speak for itself, without the need for elaborate justification of the manner in which I interpreted his writings, or detailed comparison, point by point, with other commentaries. I confess that this hope, sanguine in itself, would have had a firmer basis if I had supplied textual references; but, as already explained, this omission was unplanned. As for the secondary literature, I found myself in disagreement with much that had been written about Frege, but thought it sufficient to let such disagreements appear implicitly in what I had to say.

In writing the introduction to FPL_2, I looked up some of the reviews of the first edition which I had not previously read; this led me, in some cases, to look up other writings about Frege by the reviewers. This process combined with two other factors to make me much more aware of the diversity of interpretation of Frege that is prevalent in the literature about him. One of these other factors was a controversy in which I had engaged in *Inquiry* with Hans Sluga, a former student of mine, now at the University of California, Berkeley, on the way Frege should be understood; I had been prompted to respond to two articles of his, both vehemently attacking me, and both embodying what appeared to me a perverse interpretation of

[1] *Dialogue*, vol. XVI, 1977, pp. 519–33.
[2] P. 521.

Frege. The other was the coincidence that, at just the time that I was composing my introduction, Dr Gordon Baker and Dr Peter Hacker held a seminar in Oxford, advancing their own interpretation, again very much opposed to mine. On some points they advocated views highly similar to Sluga's; on others, they expressed opinions contrary to interpretations on which Sluga and I were in agreement. In one case, ironically, they attributed to Frege a view which Sluga quite falsely accused me of also attributing to him, a view I regard it as demonstrable that he did not hold; that view, namely, labelled by Sluga 'epistemological atomism'. Where Drs Baker and Hacker differed from both me and Sluga, and, indeed, all other commentators, was in apparently placing a low estimation on the value of Frege's work, and regarding him as advancing unintelligible and confused doctrines and making elementary philosophical errors. In my opinion, some of the other interpretations of Frege that have been proposed would have this consequence; but none is intended to have it.

In this year (1979), many universities have had the idea of holding conferences in celebration of the centenary of the publication of Frege's *Begriffsschrift*; I know of six, and have participated in three, such conferences. The number of individual works of philosophy, or, indeed, of science, of whose publication it would be appropriate to celebrate the centenary is very small indeed. It might be an amusing parlour game to propose membership of this exclusive category; but it is certainly a mark of Frege's greatness that the *Begriffsschrift* is unquestionably one of them. My own interest in Frege dates from being bowled over by reading the *Grundlagen*, which seemed and continues to seem to me the most nearly perfect single work of philosophy ever written. It simply is not possible that the inventor of quantification theory or the author of those writings in which Wittgenstein found his most profound inspiration should have been a philosopher of mediocre merits; any interpretation which has that consequence can thereby be judged to be mistaken.

In the body of this book, I have not mentioned Baker or Hacker by name, since it is unfair to subject to criticism in print remarks made only in a lecture or seminar; a good deal of what I have written bears on things they had to say, but is not presented explicitly as doing so. I understand that they are planning a book on Frege; if so, they may, by the time of publication, have revised upwards their estimate of Frege's merits, and may have abandoned their first inclination to regard him as an epistemological atomist, in which case I must apologize for having here alluded to those preliminary and unpublished views. But I thought that, unfair as it would be to cite for criticism unpublished expressions of opinion, it would be equally unfair not to acknowledge the extent of the inspiration which I have derived, by reaction, from their work on Frege.

These three factors—my reading, in the course of writing my introduction, of writers like Angelelli and Kluge, whose work I had not previously studied closely, my controversy with Sluga, and the seminar given by Baker and Hacker—combined to make me more vividly aware than I had formerly been of the variety of interpretations of Frege currently in the field. It is inevitable that there should be differences of opinion concerning the truth and the value of the doctrines of so profound a thinker, and their relation to those of other philosophers. It is only to be expected that there should also be divergent interpretations on points of detail. But the diversity between existing interpretations goes far beyond points of detail: radically divergent constructions have been put upon the fundamental tenets of Frege's philosophy. Thus Angelelli, followed by Kluge, regards Frege as having a metaphysical system comparable to those in the classic tradition of European philosophy; among those disposed to think of him in this way, I, among many others, am viewed as being at fault for having failed to see Frege in this light. At the opposite end of the spectrum, Sluga has repeatedly attacked me personally for putting an inappropriately ontological interpretation on Frege's doctrines. Admittedly, these bare remarks need elucidation before we can be sure just what is being said: but, even without it, it is evident that these writers must disagree, not merely with me, but even more violently with each other, about the basic content of Frege's doctrines. To take a slightly more specific example, Max Black has dubbed Frege's context principle—the thesis that a word has meaning only in the context of a sentence—'barely intelligible', maintaining that he abandoned the principle in his later writings.[1] Ignacio Angelleli, even more decisively, regards the principle as one *expressly* rejected by Frege after *Grundlagen*, and as, in any case, of minor importance, not admitting the interpretation put on it by Wittgenstein, Quine and commentators on Frege such as Stegmüller and Patzig. I once said, in print, that the context principle was the most important statement Frege ever made; but I maintained in *FPL* that, after *Grundlagen*, Frege neither reiterated nor expressly repudiated it, but that he adopted a position inconsistent with it in its original form. Sluga has attacked me for 'not giving due weight' to the principle, and putting only a weak interpretation on it, and, further, for failing to observe that, in his later writings, Frege expressly reiterated it. Once more, it is apparent that these opposed criticisms of the view espoused by me imply an even

---

[1] *A Companion to Wittgenstein's Tractatus*, Cambridge, Mass., 1964, p. 117.

more radical disagreement on the part of these authors with one another. Once more, there is utter disagreement about what Frege meant, and even about what he said, and on a matter that cannot be called a point of detail, since it affects the interpretation of the very foundations of Frege's philosophy.

This divergence of interpretation is both regrettable and, in my view, unnecessary. It is regrettable since, when the experts disagree about the basic meaning of Frege's writings, the incentive for non-specialists and students to study those writings is much diminished: how are they likely to understand them correctly when it is apparently so difficult to be sure of doing so? It is unnecessary, because Frege is one of the clearest of all philosophical writers. He does not, as Wittgenstein often does, deliberately leave the reader to draw his own conclusions: he labours to state the conclusions as lucidly and explicitly as he can; and Frege's standard of lucidity is very high. I think, therefore, that there is no good reason for this divergence over fundamental questions concerning what Frege was about. Since the divergence exists, it is urgent to seek a rapprochement, and so arrive at a consensus about the fundamental import of Frege's doctrines. Some divergences may be revealed as only apparent, and due to misunderstandings by some exegetes of the writings of their colleagues; but the genuine and deep divergences that remain ought to be able to be resolved by careful discussion of the texts in Frege on which they are based. To that process, the present work is intended as a contribution.

I was compelled to pay attention to these matters if I was to reply to criticisms, especially those of Sluga, and to correct the misinterpretations of me on which some of them were based; but, of course, what concerned me much more deeply were what appeared to me as misinterpretations of Frege. When I first read Sluga's articles, and first replied to them, these misinterpretations struck me as merely wanton. My only surmise was that they were motivated by a desire to play down, not Frege's merits, but his originality. But, as I reflected on them in the course of writing my introduction to *FPL*₂, I came to gain more insight (so I believe) into what prompted such interpretations, how their authors could have arrived at what still appeared to me to be travesties of Frege's thought; and, in this process, reflection on the opinions advanced by Baker and Hacker in their seminar at Oxford played a major part. And so the objective of my introduction changed in the course of composition. Originally I had aimed only to discuss various isolated points, rebutting criticisms or, in certain cases, accepting them, explaining changes of mind, and correcting misunderstandings of what I had written. But, as I proceeded, the aim became more ambitious and more unified: to set my reading of Frege in position alongside divergent ones, to explain why I thought Frege should be interpreted as I believed he should and where I thought other interpretations went wrong, and, in so doing, to provide what was lacking from *FPL* (as well as textual references and a full index), a *justification* of my interpretation.

As the scope became more ambitious, so I found it impossible to keep to the assigned limit of space. When I had reached 250 pages, I realized that to include what I had written as an introduction to *FPL₂* was no longer practicable; and yet I did not want to throw it away, because I had attempted something different from what I had done before, and something in itself worth while. After discussion with my publisher, it was agreed to issue, as a separate volume, what had originally been planned as an extensive introduction: the result is the present book. The book serves a dual purpose. It is still intended to explain and comment on the few textual changes from *FPL₁* to *FPL₂*, all of which it lists. In some cases, however, the chapters have been greatly expanded beyond a simple mention and explanation of the emendation, to form a fresh discussion of the relevant topic, a discussion intended, in each case, to bear on rival interpretations in the field. The book also contains elucidations of points from *FPL* that seem to me to have been misunderstood, some expressions of changes of mind, and replies to criticisms; much of the discussion of competing interpretations has necessarily taken the latter form. In these ways, the book remains a companion volume to *FPL₂*. But it is also an independent work, as being a defence of one interpretation of Frege against conflicting ones. I have not, indeed, attempted to expound Frege's views *de novo*, for that would have involved repeating parts of *FPL* and rewriting it as a whole, just the task that limitations of time and considerations of cost rendered impossible. The book is therefore not intended to *replace FPL*, and I have been forced to presume some acquaintance, at first or second hand, or from my writings on Frege included in *Truth and Other Enigmas*,[1] with the way I interpreted Frege in *FPL*. I am not trying here to set out that interpretation, but to justify and defend it.

If my hope is realized, and a consensus over the main outlines of Frege's philosophy is attained, this will not put an end to discussion of his work; it will only make it more fruitful. Disputes over the interpretation of a philosopher are never an end in themselves: they are a preliminary to discussion of the truth of his doctrines, once it has been established what they are. Frege's ideas are of such profundity and importance that discussion

[1] London and Cambridge, Mass., 1978.

of this kind will continue to be fruitful for many decades, at least; disagreements about the substance of his ideas merely hamper such discussion, and are therefore to be resolved as quickly as possible. In *FPL* I attempted not only to expound Frege's views, as I understand them, but to engage in such discussion; and, as I remarked, to decide whether what Frege said was true, it is often necessary to consider questions not explicitly discussed by him. This results, of course, from the manifold connections that exist in philosophy between theses concerning distinct topics; Wittgenstein once said that no philosophical problem is solved until all philosophical problems are solved. Perhaps the least perceptive remark made by any reviewer was the objection by Gregory Currie[1] to what he called my 'startling claim' that, to judge whether Frege spoke the truth on certain matters, one may need to consider other topics of which he did not treat:[2] 'Surely', he protested, 'in order to decide whether or not somebody has spoken the truth we need not look further than what he said, and the logical consequences thereof.'[3] I find it hard to see how such an objection could be lodged by anyone with any experience in philosophy: it is a commonplace that it may be impossible to judge the truth about one matter until the truth about some related matter has been decided.

However this may be, I have kept discussion of the truth of Frege's views to a minimum in the present book, and hence have avoided as far as possible discussion of questions not explicitly considered by him: the main point of this book is to establish how Frege should be understood. As explained in Chapter 5, this has prevented me from engaging in an enquiry into the relation between the notions of meaning, understanding and knowledge. Since writing FPL_1, I have come to see that the relation of the meaning of a word in the language shared by a community of speakers and the understanding that an individual speaker has of it is far more problematic than I then supposed, as also is the question whether an understanding of a word or of a language is genuinely a case of knowledge. I further believe that these are prime examples of questions which need to be settled before we can accurately evaluate Frege's philosophy of language. But they are very difficult questions, demanding extensive discussion; and they are questions about which nothing explicit is said by Frege. For this reason, I have not here gone into them, despite my awareness that the lack of an adequate treatment of them is perhaps the principal lacuna in *FPL*.

On one matter I wish to express a certain disgruntlement. Sluga opens

---

[1] *British Journal for the Philosophy of Science*, vol. 27, 1976, pp. 79–92.
[2] *FPL*, p. xii.
[3] Op. cit., p. 81.

his 'Frege's Alleged Realism'[1] with the definition, 'I will call any interpretation that is based on such affirmations'—viz. that Frege was a platonist
or realist, and that he was concerned with advancing an ontological theory
—'a version of the *standard* interpretation', and goes on to label the interpretation presented in *FPL* such a version. In his earlier article, 'Frege and
the Rise of Analytical Philosophy',[2] he had written, without appeal to any
stipulative definition, 'Dummett rejects' Tugendhat's interpretation 'and
perseveres with the standard interpretation of Frege's doctrine of sense and
reference which ignores the contextual principle'.[3] In a similar way, Drs
Baker and Hacker inaugurated their seminar by announcing that they
wished to overturn the 'orthodox' interpretation of Frege by a more attentive
reading of the texts; under subsequent questioning, they named no other
proponent of this supposed orthodoxy than myself. 'Orthodox,' of course,
properly means 'right-believing'; but I do not think the term was employed
in this sense, and I wish to protest against the innuendo conveyed by this
term and Sluga's word 'standard'. The innuendo is, of course, that there was
in existence a received interpretation of Frege, which I uncritically picked
up and unthinkingly embodied in *FPL*, the content of which book could
therefore be reduced to the sentence 'The received interpretation is correct
in every detail'. I realize the possibility of construing it in a much more
complimentary way, namely, that by my writings on Frege, I have induced
others to treat my own interpretation of him as the received one. I am
perfectly certain that such a compliment would be undeserved. There
is no received interpretation, as a glance at the secondary literature will
show; it is precisely the absence of one that I have been bewailing in this
Preface. I am equally certain that no such compliment was intended by
the authors of these remarks; and I think their imputation unjustified.
There was not, any more than now, a generally received interpretation
of Frege during the years, from 1950 to 1964, when I was studying Frege,
and, towards the end of that period, composing the original version of my
book on him, some chapters of which, in duplicated form, circulated for
some years at Stanford University. As already remarked, this is evidenced
by the disagreement of the authors, myself among them, of the essays
included in Klemke's collection:[4] how could there have been a received
interpretation at a time when Grossmann could claim it as certain that Frege
drew no distinction between sense and reference for predicates and functional

[1] *Inquiry*, vol. 20, 1977, pp. 227–42.
[2] *Inquiry*, vol. 18, 1975, pp. 471–87.
[3] Ibid., p. 478.
[4] E. D. Klemke (ed.), *Essays on Frege*, Urbana, Chicago and London, 1968.

expressions? Not, indeed, that writers of that period could resist the temptation to accord to some view to which they were opposed the opprobrious epithet 'orthodox': William Marshall, for example, in his reply to me,[1] opened his article with the remark that 'Mr Michael Dummett . . . answers these questions in the orthodox way'. The questions to which he alluded were whether Frege admitted a notion of sense for predicates, and whether, if so, it was to be distinguished from their reference. Marshall's interpretation of Frege on these questions was to be confuted by the publication of Frege's *Nachgelassene Schriften*; there is no merit in being heterodox, that is, in disagreeing with everyone else (though, actually, Marshall by no means disagreed with everyone else), when it also involves being plain wrong.

Because I found enlightenment in only a few of the articles published concerning Frege, I made no effort to keep abreast of the secondary literature, preferring to read and reflect on Frege's own writings, and thus incurring Kluge's rebuke: it is hard also to be accused, by innuendo, of tramping along in the rear of some vast army. One debt, in my study of Frege, especially in the early years, is profound, that to Peter Geach, who was a student of Frege before I ever read him, and with whom I have discussed Frege, off and on, since our first meeting in 1951. From him I learned a great deal, and, without doubt, my interpretation of Frege has been coloured by my discussions with him and by reading his writings, though at no time were we ever in complete agreement on these topics, and certain of my differences with him were expressed in *FPL*. Other debts, of a more general character, were acknowledged in the Preface to *FPL*, namely to Elizabeth Anscombe and to Donald Davidson. Of the philosophers I have known personally, these three are those from discussion with whom I have learned most, although, of course, there are many others whose ideas have stimulated me; and doubtless these more general debts are often apparent in what I wrote about Frege, though in none of these cases do our overall views coincide; I hope that I may have contributed in some measure to their thinking also. I do not believe that any of these three has established an orthodoxy, in philosophy generally or in the interpretation of Frege. No doubt also the way I have come to understand Frege has been strongly influenced by a philosophical background in which Wittgenstein has been that figure of the modern era overshadowing all others. Whether this is harmful for the interpretation of Frege depends on whether Wittgenstein understood Frege correctly or incorrectly. It seems, on general grounds, overwhelmingly probable that he understood him aright; but, again, it

---

[1] 'Sense and Reference: a Reply', *Philosophical Review*, vol. LXV, 1956, pp. 342–61, reprinted in Klemke, op. cit., pp. 298–320.

is unlikely that Wittgenstein himself has been well enough understood, or his influence sufficiently widespread, among those who have written about Frege, for that influence to have created an 'orthodox' or 'standard' interpretation. To the extent—far too narrow an extent—that there has been an agreed interpretation of Frege's doctrines, I believe this to be due, not to the influence of any particular commentators, but to the clarity of his own exposition. It always looks grander to adopt the posture of one bravely defying an oppressive orthodoxy than simply that of someone advancing one among a multiplicity of views: but philosophical interchange is not facilitated by such posturing.

It is certainly my opinion, and one I tried to convey in certain passages of *FPL*, for instance on p. 9, that one cannot properly understand Frege if one does not place him in his epoch. But, for me, this means, primarily, that one needs to prescind from things that were not yet known when Frege was writing, and to take account of what, among the views then current, he was concerned to oppose. We must, for example, try to conceive of the impression made on him by his invention of quantification theory, for us a commonplace and uncontroversial tool, for him an overwhelming discovery which dominated all his subsequent thought. Again, we must read his criticisms of formalism as a philosophy of mathematics in the light of the formulations of that doctrine then available, formulations which appear crude to us because incapable of incorporating our conception of a formal system. Yet another example is this. If it be asked why Frege should bother with the notion of sense as well as that of reference, when mathematical reasoning need not invoke the senses of expressions, and when, in his own words, 'logical laws are in the first place in the realm of references, and relate to sense only mediately',[1] many answers can be given: Frege was not exclusively concerned with mathematics, nor, within the philosophy of mathematics or elsewhere, with the representation of deductive reasoning. But there is also a simple answer to the question on its own terms, one which turns on the ideas then prevalent which Frege had to combat. For us, it is obvious that the equals sign of mathematical equations expresses identity, but this was an opinion for which Frege had to contend: only a distinction between sense and reference could counter the intuitive objections to such an understanding of the sign '='.

These examples have all to do with the historical situation, with what was new and what controversial, that to us is familiar or undisputed. It has never seemed to me that much illumination is to be expected from a

---

[1] 'Ausführungen über Sinn und Bedeutung', 1892–5, *N.S.*, p. 133, *P.W.*, p. 122.

search for influences on Frege or for parallels to his ideas in the works of his predecessors. I confess to having made no thorough investigation, such as Sluga has carried out, of possible sources of Frege's ideas in the writings of German philosophers of the period immediately preceding him. It is certainly worth pursuing such researches; I am sceptical about the light they will throw on Frege's thought, but, until they have been carried out and proved not to throw any, my opinion is no more than a conjecture. The assessment of the results of such enquiries rests with those who have not made them more than with those who have; the latter will naturally be reluctant to conclude that so much labour has yielded no harvest. My scepticism is more than a hunch. It rests on the indubitable fact that Frege's formal logic has no predecessors: in the writings of nineteenth-century logicians before *Begriffsschrift*, not one hint can be found of the ideas underlying Frege's discovery of quantification theory. But Frege's formal logic is the principal factor determining the subsequent development of his philosophy, and certainly of his philosophy of language; it forms the backbone of that philosophy, which collapses if it is extracted. Frege came to philosophy from mathematics, and specifically from a mathematical discovery, the invention of modern mathematical logic, with profound philosophical consequences; and, from this starting-point, he constructed a philosophical system of his own, one which owed, I believe, not very much more to previous philosophical work than did his formal logic to previous work in that field. Sometimes, it is true, we can find analogies between things Frege said and what was being said by others; but since those others were not speaking from the standpoint of an analysis of logical structure similar to Frege's, the analogies are merely superficial. For instance, it was commonplace at the time to maintain, as Frege maintained, that logical analysis should take the judgment as prior to the concept rather than conversely, an opinion cited, though rejected, by Lotze. It is even conceivable that Frege was prompted to adopt his opinion, or at least to express it as he did, by similar-sounding theses advanced by other writers, though there is no indication of this in his writings; but, even if so, the analogy remains superficial. The reason is that what Frege meant by the thesis, as he propounded it, can be explained only in terms of his analysis of the structure of sentences and the thoughts expressed by them; no one who did not have such an analysis in mind could mean the same by any apparently similar form of words. My suspicion is that most other parallels between Frege and other philosophers will prove superficial in the same way. I have, in Chapter 19 of this book, given reasons for rejecting one comparison that has been made between Frege and Lotze, but I have not attempted to go systematically into claims concerning the sources of Frege's ideas and his affinities with other contemporary German philosophers; I content myself with the reason just stated for doubting that such claims will prove sustainable. Frege's philosophy looks forward, not backward: the fruitful comparisons are with later ideas, not with earlier ones—which is not to say that we shall interpret Frege aright if we fail to project ourselves imaginatively into the intellectual situation in which he stood when he was engaged on his philosophical work.

New College, Oxford, 1981   M.D.

CHAPTER 1

Apologies and Emendations

As EXPLAINED IN the Preface, this book grew out of a proposed introduction to the second edition of my *Frege: Philosophy of Language* (*FPL*), and remains, in part, a companion volume to it. Only a very few changes have been made, in the second edition of *FPL*, to the actual text; in the course of the present book, I will note and comment on all but the most trivial of these. Five, I regret to say, are in places where I had given a textual reference, and had done so inaccurately. For this I owe an even more earnest apology than for the general paucity of such references; I much regret the trouble that may have been caused to conscientious readers, vainly searching for the passages wrongly referred to. These four references are as follows. On p. 308 of *FPL* I referred to 'Die Verneinung' instead of to 'Der Gedanke'. On p. 543, I referred to *Function und Begriff*, and should have referred to Frege's review of Husserl. On p. 312, I referred to p. 234 of Wittgenstein's *Notes on Logic*; this was a reference to the publication of them in the *Journal of Philosophy*, vol. LIV, 1957, but since I listed, not this, but the volume *Notebooks 1914–1916*, in the bibliography of *FPL*, it could not have been easily traced. Finally, the reference to Chapter 11 on p. 450 of *FPL*, and that to Chapter 12 on p. 453, should both have been to Chapter 10: I thus achieved the dismal distinction of having given erroneous references to my own book.

Another small change relates to Frege's terminology. The problem of rendering into English the technical and quasi-technical vocabulary that Frege borrowed from everyday German usage presents many difficulties, of which the most notorious is the translation of the terms '*Bedeutung*' and '*bedeuten*'. As I indicated on p. 84 of *FPL*, it was with reluctance that I followed the established tradition in rendering '*Bedeutung*' as 'reference' and '*bedeuten*' as 'stand for'; but to use 'meaning' and 'mean', as I did in my encyclopaedia article,[1] would have been to debar myself from using these words in a non-Fregean sense, for instance to express what I meant by saying that 'reference is not an ingredient of meaning'.[2] I particularly regret my use of 'referent', which, as used of what is referred to, rather than of what refers, is a solecism offensive to anyone familiar with Latin grammar. But 'referee' was impossible, and 'referend' would have invited comedy; since I wanted a word cognate with 'reference', I acquiesced in the existing use of 'referent' in the required sense, but apologize for having done so. An anonymous reviewer in the *Times Literary Supplement*[3] denied with great vehemence my claim[4] that Frege used '*Bedeutung*' in different ways, urging that he used it only in the sense I expressed by 'referent'. In fact, the reviewer was mistaken; there is a handful of passages in which '*Bedeutung*' cannot be rendered 'referent'. For instance, in his letter to Peano published in the *Rivista di Matematica*,[5] Frege says that an expression ought to have a *Bedeutung* that is independent of the other parts of the sentence: what is required to be independent of the other parts of the sentence obviously cannot be the referent itself, but is, rather, the expression's having that reference. Frege goes on to object to conditional definitions on the ground that a concept-word so introduced would not have a *selbständige Bedeutung*. He cannot be complaining that the *referent* of the concept-word would not be *selbständig*, since he maintained the well-known thesis that a concept is not *selbständig*: he means to demand that the concept-word, considered in itself, should have whatever reference it has independently of the context.[6] Nevertheless, the reviewer's remark is so nearly true that I thought it better to excise the claim made on pp. 93–4 of *FPL₁* from the second edition. It would not have been an improvement, however, to have replaced 'referent' everywhere by 'reference'. The distinction needs making, and lack of it can create ambiguity, as in the phrase 'know the reference'. Without it, I could not have raised, at least in the way I did, the question whether lack of a referent need entail lack of a reference;[7] nor could Victor Dudman have argued that I had shown predicates to have a reference, but not to have referents.[8]

[1] Paul Edwards (ed.), *The Encyclopaedia of Philosophy*, New York, 1962, s.v. 'Frege', or *Truth and Other Enigmas*, no. 8.

[2] *FPL*, p. 91.

[3] 30 November, 1973.

[4] *FPL₁*, pp. 93–4.

[5] Vol. 6, 1896.

[6] Op. cit., p. 56.

[7] *FPL*, pp. 409–10.

[8] '*Bedeutung* for Predicates', M. Schirn (ed.), *Studien zu Frege*, vol. III, Stuttgart and Bad Canstatt, 1976, pp. 71–84.

Acutely conscious as I am that I ought, before publishing *FPL*, to have checked all the ascriptions of philosophical views to Frege, I am nevertheless relieved, now that I have done so, to find that I seldom attributed to him anything that he did not say; the defence of my *interpretation* of what he said will be the principal burden of the present book. There are, however, a few passages of *FPL* that, having made that check, I have modified in the second edition. In this first chapter, I shall deal only with the most minor of them.

The most trivial of these occurs on pp. 97 and 98 of *FPL*. When FPL_1 came out, Frege's *Briefwechsel* had not yet been published, and I was reporting the Afla/Ateb example from memory, and unintentionally slightly embroidered it. On p. 97, I have altered some of the details of the example, so as to accord with those given by Frege.[1] I have allowed some of the embroidery to remain: Frege does not say that the two names pass into common use, nor speak of the identification of Afla and Ateb as occurring only many years later, to the surprise of all, but merely says that 'It later emerges from a comparison that the two explorers saw the same mountain'; but I cannot suppose that anyone would think any philosophical point depended upon the rather starker description of the example given by Frege. I have, however, altered one detail which I misreported and which some people might think to be philosophically important, though I should not. I misremembered the explorers as having travelled in uninhabited regions, and as having simply invented the names 'Afla' and 'Ateb', and, on p. 98 of FPL_1, drew attention to this supposed feature of the example. Actually, Frege takes them both as having borrowed these names from the local inhabitants. Note that there is a brief allusion by Frege to the same example in his unpublished 'Logik in der Mathematik' of 1914.[2]

I remain puzzled about the unpublished article by Frege referred to at the bottom of p. 212 of *FPL*, and discussed in the footnote; but, as I said in that footnote, my memory may have played me false. However, the notation '$\grave{\epsilon}\Phi(\epsilon)$', which I mentioned on p. 215, will be found in a letter to Russell;[3] I have altered the last line of p. 214 accordingly.

I said, on p. 253 of FPL_1, that the three arguments (1) to (3) found on pp. 250–3 are Frege's; this was to overstate the case. The arguments are, I think, in the spirit of Frege, and argument (3) may reasonably be ascribed to him, but arguments (1) and (2) do not occur in his writings exactly as I stated them; I have reduced the claim to one that the arguments are essentially Frege's.

[1] On p. 128 of the *Briefwechsel*.
[2] *Nachgelassene Schriften*, p. 242, *P.W.*, pp. 224–5.
[3] *BW*, p. 218, *P.M.C.*, p. 136.

One such change I think it would have been wrong to make. On p. 314 of *FPL* I said that I knew no passage in Frege's published writings where he excludes the possibility of asserting what is in fact false; I also cited a passage in a letter where he in effect does say this. I said that I knew no such passage in the published writings because I might have overlooked one; but a reviewer from the London School of Economics, Gregory Currie, after remarking with ponderous sarcasm that 'as a statement about Dummett this may well be true', cites a sentence from 'Die Verneinung' in refutation.[1] After arguing that a false thought is not one without being, Frege has gone on to deny that negation dissolves a thought into its constituent parts, and remarks that the thought proposed to a jury for decision is true or false independently of whether their verdict is right or wrong. He then says that, if we insert 'not' into a sentence expressing a true thought, we obtain one whose content is not a non-thought, but which can with complete justification be used as antecedent or consequent in a conditional sentence. To this he adds, '*Weil er falsch ist, darf er nur nicht mit behauptender Kraft ausgesprochen werden*' ('It is only that, since it is false, it may not be uttered with assertoric force.')[2] The entire context makes it perfectly obvious that Frege intends to say that one may not justifiably utter the sentence assertorically, that one should not do so, which is why he uses 'darf' and not 'kann'; if he meant what Currie thinks, he would be committed to the view that the jury would be incapable of pronouncing an incorrect verdict. Currie's interpretation is especially odd in view of its being stated in a footnote to a passage where he is rebuking me for having discussed, on the preceding page, Frege's curious thesis that we can make inferences only from true premisses; according to Currie, such observations, 'when seen in their context, . . . can be seen as a careless shorthand for "only thoughts taken to be true (i.e. asserted) can be premisses of inferences" '. I thought it worth considering why, instead of saying something of this kind, Frege said what he did, partly because carelessness of this sort, though ubiquitous in the writings of most philosophers, is very rare in Frege's later writing, and partly because the statement is reiterated repeatedly, never in the form given by Currie's emendation.[3] Indeed, one

---

[1] *British Journal for the Philosophy of Science*, vol. 27, 1976, pp. 79–92; see p. 81, fn. 4.

[2] 'Die Verneinung', p. 148.

[3] 'Über Schoenflies', 1906, *N.S.*, p. 195, *P.W.*, p. 180; 'Über die Grundlagen der Geometrie', 1906, pt. III, p. 425; Frege's notes of 1910 to Jourdain's article in the *Quarterly Journal of Pure and Applied Mathematics*, vol. XLIII, 1912, p. 240, cf. *BW*, p. 118; 'Logik in der Mathematik', 1914, *N.S.*, p. 264, *P.W.*, p. 244; 'Gedankengefüge', 1923, p. 47.

such passage is in 'Die Verneinung' itself.[1] If Frege had meant by his remark on p. 148 what Currie takes him to mean, that false thoughts *cannot* be asserted, then no carelessness would be involved in his statement on p. 145 that nothing can be inferred from a false thought, since that statement, understood literally, would follow from Currie's emendation of it. I am driven to the conclusion that Currie was so eager to find me in error that he ceased to care what absurdities he ascribed to Frege.

[1] P. 145.

CHAPTER 2

Principles of Frege Exegesis

BEFORE DISCUSSING IN detail how Frege's ideas are to be understood, it is worth pausing to consider the general principles that should govern the interpretation of his writings. No one would be tempted, in discussing such a philosopher as Russell, to ask what he thought about such-and-such a topic; he changed his mind so frequently and so explicitly that one can sensibly ask only what he thought at a certain period. But Frege is different: he refined his ideas, but, except in the very last phase, jettisoned few of them; and it is therefore tempting to treat his work as a single whole, and to cull citations from works separated by two or even three decades to support an interpretation of this or that doctrine. And this has a certain justification. Of all philosophers, perhaps of all theorists of any kind, Frege pursued, in his work, the most extraordinarily single-minded course. He was not inhuman; he turned aside from that course occasionally to write a short piece, mathematical or philosophical, about some topic with which his life's work was not directly concerned. It is nevertheless remarkable how seldom he strayed, either as a mathematician or as a philosopher, from the course which, from the time of writing *Begriffsschrift*, he had set himself to pursue. He restricted his work, almost completely, to a certain area, one that overlapped the disciplines of philosophy and of mathematics. He hardly ever attempted anything outside that area; but he aimed, not just, like most scholars, to make some progress within that area, but to establish the complete and definitive truth concerning it. From 1879 until 1903, therefore, almost everything that he did was subordinated to the goal, conceived at the outset, of producing his *magnum opus*, *Die Grundgesetze der Arithmetik*, which was to present, once and for all, a definitive treatment of the foundations of what he called 'arithmetic', namely number theory and analysis, or, more accurately, the theories of cardinal numbers and of real numbers. *Grundgesetze* is, therefore, not just *a* book that Frege wrote: it was intended to be the definitive summation of his life's work.

In view of this, when people discuss 'Frege's theory' of this or that, without qualification as to the period of Frege's work to which they are referring, we may take their discussion to relate to his mature period, which, in FPL_1,[1] I reckoned as the third of six periods into which his career may be divided, and took as running from 1891 to 1904. There were, of course, substantial changes, both in his formal logic and in his philosophy, between the writings of his first two periods and those of this mature period. But, precisely because Frege worked so single-mindedly at the perfection of his theories, every change, whether he commented on it or not, must be regarded as fully deliberate; views expressed in the mature period must be taken as having more weight than earlier ones with which they conflict, and later formulations of old views as having more weight than the earlier formulations. *We*, of course, are at liberty to think that, in this or that case, Frege was wrong to change his mind. But what we should never do is to interpret what he said in his mature period in the light of his earlier writings; whenever he went back on what he had earlier said, or expressed it in a different way, he did so of set purpose and in the belief that he had arrived at the true account.

Of all philosophers, Frege took the greatest care to express himself with precision. Even so, in interpreting work extending over half a century, or, if one confines oneself to the mature period, over fourteen years, one must exercise some judgment: not even his writing will withstand exegesis by text-slinging, by tearing passing remarks from their contexts and pressing home the literal senses of the words. There are some obvious principles. One is that what is said repeatedly is thereby shown to be something which Frege took seriously and about which he had a settled opinion. This principle must be applied with the greatest care. We are not entitled to assert the converse, that what is said only once is not to be taken seriously, or was not so taken by Frege. For one thing, we do not have the data. We know, from the posthumous writings, that some theses of great importance are not formulated in the published work; so, if we are to count occurrences of individual theses at all, we must include the posthumous writings. But we do not have the whole of the posthumous writings. The writings themselves were destroyed during the bombing of Münster in the Second World War; with a very few exceptions, what we have are only typescripts made at the instance of Professor Heinrich Scholz, the

[1] Pp. 642–3.

custodian of the *Nachlass*, and these were made of less than half of the total material. What remains to us, therefore, is not even a random fraction of the whole: it represents a selection made by an individual according to his ideas of what was important and interesting, and therefore, in that sense, is already coloured by an interpretation. Furthermore, although in certain respects Frege's writing is exceptionally repetitive, he, no more than any other philosopher, repeated something just because he was pleased with it: he repeated that of which he was dissatisfied with the formulation, and was striving to perfect it. The fact, therefore, that something is not repeated may be explicable in either of two ways. It may be that Frege had never attached any importance to it, or that he had taken it as important but later came to think it mistaken. But it may equally be that he felt completely satisfied with it, and saw no need to say it again.

A more compelling principle is that we should consider a remark in relation to the point being argued. It may be a passing remark, that could be excised from the argument without loss, in which case no great weight need be attached to it. But, if it has a role in the argument, we need to consider carefully what its role is: we must not so interpret it that it can no longer play that part in the argument it is intended to play, but, on the other hand, need not pay too strict an attention to the manner of its formulation, in so far as that does not bear on the argument. I shall subsequently cite a good example of the neglect of this principle of interpretation.

What is of far more importance than how often something is said is *where* it is said. We now have some of Frege's philosophical correspondence to read, and some of it is of great interest. But it is obvious that what someone puts down in a letter may be his first thoughts, and we should never pit what Frege says in his correspondence against what he says in other writings: I do not know how many philosophers could stand to have their correspondence published and pored over. In a similar way, what Frege wrote in work he did not submit for publication bears less weight than what occurs in his published writings; and, above all, what is said in *Grundgesetze* carries more weight than anything else.

We can extend this conclusion about the greater weight to be attached to *Grundgesetze* than to other writings if we study the structure of *Grundgesetze* itself. As published, two volumes with an interval of a decade between them, it is an unfinished work, prematurely curtailed by the disaster of Russell's discovery of the contradiction. What was published is arbitrarily lopped into volume-length segments with little regard for its natural division into parts and sections. There are three Parts. Part I, 'Darlegung der Begriffsschrift' (Exposition of the Formal System), which is translated in full in M. Furth's *The Basic Laws of Arithmetic: Exposition of the System*,[1] explains the notation, states, informally but concisely, the intended interpretation of the system in terms of Frege's apparatus of objects and functions of various types, the sense/reference distinction, etc., sets out the axioms and rules of inference, states the general principles governing formal definitions, and lists the first nine of the definitions to be used. Part II, 'Beweise der Grundgesetze der Anzahl' (Proof of the Basic Laws of Cardinal Number), sets out formal proofs, within the system, of a succession of theorems relating to cardinal numbers and to the natural numbers considered as finite cardinals. Part III, 'Die reellen Zahlen' (The Real Numbers), which is incomplete, treats of Frege's theory of real numbers. Volume I contains Part I and the first eleven sections of Part II; Volume II contains the remaining four sections of Part II and what must have been intended to be about half of Part III, the final paragraph being headed 'Die nächste Aufgabe' ('The next task'), together, of course, with the Appendix attempting to deal with Russell's paradox.

Now, as remarked, since *Grundgesetze* was intended to be a definitive work, what it contains should be given more weight than anything Frege wrote elsewhere, whenever there is an overlap in subject-matter. The greater part of what he published before *Grundgesetze* is intended as a preliminary study for it; there is therefore a presumption in favour of interpreting earlier writings in the light of *Grundgesetze*, rather than the other way round. *Grundgesetze* may help us to see the intention behind an earlier, less exactly formulated, statement; and, in those cases in which Frege had an actual change of mind, what is to be found in *Grundgesetze* represents his fully considered mature opinion. *Begriffsschrift*, in particular, constituted a preliminary study for the logical system used in *Grundgesetze*; but, by the time that volume I of the latter was published, much had been changed, both in Frege's logic and, more especially, in his theory of logic, so that all this had to be presented anew in the later book. *Grundlagen*, however, is in a somewhat different position. When we compare Parts II and III of *Grundgesetze*, we see that they are divided differently. Part II, which is wholly formal, is divided into sections labelled with capital Greek letters. But Part III has a level of division higher than this: it falls into two sub-parts, numbered 1 and 2, of which (1) is headed 'Kritik der Lehren von den Irrationalzahlen' and (2) is headed 'Grössenlehre' ('Critique of Theories of Irrational Numbers' and 'Theory of Magnitudes'). (1) is entirely in prose, and consists of a destructive philosophical criticism of

[1] Berkeley and Los Angeles, 1964.

the theories of various other writers, Cantor, Heine, Thomae, Dedekind, Hankel, Stolz and Weierstrass; excerpts from it are to be found in the well-known volume of translations by Geach and Black. Of the two last sections of (1), section (*f*) draws some general morals, from the lengthy destructive criticisms preceding it, for the form that a correct treatment of the theory of real numbers should take, while (*g*) sets out in rough outline the actual procedure to be adopted. (2) then constitutes an unfinished formal construction of Frege's theory within the formal system of *Grundgesetze*, and thus corresponds to Part II of the book, being divided, like it, into sections to which capital Greek letters are assigned, volume II containing the first six of these sections.

This plan of exposition will be very familiar to readers of *Grundlagen*. The destructive sections (*a*) to (*e*) of Part III(1) correspond to the destructive part, §§ 5–44, of *Grundlagen*; the transitional sections (*f*) and (*g*) correspond, respectively, to §§ 45–54 and §§ 55–69 of *Grundlagen*; and Part III(2) corresponds to the construction in §§ 70–86 of *Grundlagen* of Frege's positive theory of cardinal numbers, save, of course, that *Grundlagen* eschews symbolism and is not set in the framework of an axiomatic system. The point is not that Frege must have been pleased with the plan he adopted in writing *Grundlagen*; it is, rather, that, when compared with Part III, Part II of *Grundgesetze* is seen to be defective. *Grundgesetze* was intended to be a definitive work, presumably in three volumes. When treating the theory of real numbers, Frege proceeds as he had done in *Grundlagen*, attempting to make his theory plausible by first exposing the defects of rival theories. It is not so much that *Grundgesetze* contains no direct criticism of rival theories of the natural numbers; it might be thought that he was weary of making such criticisms, although in fact he never seemed to tire of that. It is, rather, that it contains neither any informal exposition nor any justification or suasive argument in favour of his theory of natural numbers; it simply throws the theory at the reader, clothed only in his logical symbolism. As a definitive work, the book is defective in lacking a Part II(1) corresponding to the Part III(1). It has to be presumed, therefore, that Frege thought he had already done this work well enough in *Grundlagen* for it to be unnecessary to repeat it. The construction of the positive theory has, of course, to be repeated, since in *Grundlagen* the proofs were presented only informally and in outline, although, apart from the fact that in *Grundgesetze* numbers are defined as classes of classes, rather than as classes of concepts as in *Grundlagen*, the correspondence of the development of the theory in the two books is very exact. But the destructive criticisms, and, above all, the sections §§ 45–69 of *Grundlagen* in which Frege attempts to demonstrate the plausibility of and the necessity for his approach, are not reworked and presented anew in *Grundgesetze*. We must presume that, although they would have needed some rewriting to take account of the sense/reference distinction, he did not incorporate any revised version of them because he thought, not that they were dispensable, but that they were so nearly correct that it would be pointless to repeat them. These parts of *Grundlagen* should therefore be thought of as belonging with *Grundgesetze*, as essentially being a part of that definitive work on the philosophy of arithmetic to which so much of his effort was single-mindedly directed.

This conclusion is important, because *Grundlagen* contains many highly significant observations and arguments not elsewhere repeated: above all, the characterization of analytic and synthetic, a priori and a posteriori truths; the statement of the context principle; the thesis that with any proper name a criterion of identity must be associated; and the procedure misleadingly named (not by Frege) 'definition by abstraction'. If one thinks of *Grundlagen* as an early work *replaced* by *Grundgesetze*, one is liable to underestimate the significance of these ideas in Frege's philosophy. The correct principle is, I believe, to assume that whatever is stated in *Grundlagen*, and, in particular, in the crucial §§ 45–69, was retained by Frege, save for what is manifestly in conflict with his later ideas. Two, related, ideas that are in manifest conflict with his later thought are the tolerant attitude he displays in *Grundlagen*, §§ 60–5, towards contextual definitions and the context principle itself. The former attitude we know to have been replaced by hostility to any form of definition other than an explicit one. As for the context principle, it survived only in a modified form after Frege had assimilated sentences to proper names, since he could no longer regard the former as having a special role in language. The reason for saying this is not just an argument from silence: in § 10 of *Grundgesetze*, vol. I, there is an explicit appeal to a generalized context principle, namely that the reference of a term can be fixed by fixing the reference of the result of inserting it in an argument-place of any (primitive) functional expression; the generality lies in the fact that predicates and relational expressions are not singled out from other functional expressions. By contrast, although Frege never reiterated his thesis concerning criteria of identity, his subsequent practice is fully consonant with it. The chief complaint that could be made in this regard is that he never discusses the criterion of identity for truth-values; and the oddity of asking for such a criterion may be taken as yet one more indication that he was in error in taking truth-values to be objects. Without positive evidence that he abandoned the principle, it should be assumed that it was retained; if it had been rejected, we should not know how to reconstruct the justification, missing from Part II of *Grundgesetze*, of the approach there adopted to the foundations of the theory of cardinal numbers.

An excellent illustration both of a failure to give special weight to what Frege says in *Grundlagen*, and of the mistakes that can result from not observing the role of a remark in the argument in which it is embedded, is provided by the reviewer in the *British Journal for the Philosophy of Science*, Gregory Currie. He alludes[1] to my mention[2] of Frege's argument that we should define 'the direction of ξ' in terms of 'ξ is parallel to ζ', and not conversely, on the ground that we can acquire an understanding of the latter in advance of an understanding of the former, but could not come by them in the other order (*Grundlagen*, § 65). But he dismisses this as having no *general* significance, but as deriving 'from Frege's peculiar views on geometry, not from his views about meaning', these peculiar views consisting in his acceptance of the Kantian idea that geometrical notions are founded on our a priori intuition of space. Nothing could be more implausible if we consider the context. Frege is at an extremely important point in the book: the section (§§ 62–9) is that which leads up to, and explains the need for, the use of the notion of a class (extension of a concept) in defining cardinal numbers. Having already argued, in §§ 55–61, that numbers must be regarded as objects, Frege first proposes a contextual definition of the operator 'the number of Φ's'. He then considers in turn three objections to this: the first two he rejects, but the third he sustains, and concludes that an explicit definition must be given in terms of the notion of class. However, the second and third objections, and the resolution of the third objection by an explicit definition, are set out, not directly as relating to the operator 'the number of Φ's', but as relating to what Frege asserts to be an analogous operator, 'the direction of ξ'. In § 64 he gives examples of three other such operators, all geometrical ones; and in § 65 he mentions two more, 'the length of ξ' and 'the colour of ξ'. It is true that, when making the point which I cited concerning parallelism and direction, he appeals, in speaking of intuition, to the geometrical character of the example; but in a footnote to § 65 he observes that he has discussed the matter in terms of directions for convenience of expression only, saying that 'the argument can readily be transferred in essentials to the case of numerical identity'. Indeed, even had no such footnote been provided, we should have assumed that this was his intention: not only does the text

[1] Op. cit., pp. 85–6.
[2] *FPL*. pp. 240 and 678.

expressly compare the introduction of the concept of number to that of direction, but it is incomprehensible that, at a critical point in his argument, Frege should suddenly engage in an irrelevant digression concerning geometry. He therefore did not suppose that any step in the argument depended upon the geometrical character of the example chosen. In transposing to the numerical case, the reference to intuition has indeed to be dropped: but it is crucial that the point about priority should stand. Unless Frege means us to understand that, just as we should define 'direction' in terms of 'is parallel to', rather than defining 'parallel' as 'having the same direction', so we should define 'number' in terms of 'equinumerous with', rather than defining F and G to be equinumerous when the number of Fs and of Gs is the same, the entire argument collapses. If this were not so, the whole of §§ 64–8, save for the very last sentence of § 68, would indeed be an irrelevant digression, and the point of that last sentence, which contains the definition of the numerical operator which is the real topic of the whole passage, would be left unexplained. It would be wholly unwarranted for Frege to have made his argument turn on any special features of the direction example: the whole point was supposed to be to discuss the character of a very general type of transition, of which that from speaking of there being just as many things of one kind as of another to speaking of the number of things of a given kind is the instance under consideration, and that from speaking of lines as being parallel to speaking of the direction of a given line is another instance. In that context, the point which I cited could not possibly be meant to be just a glimpse into Frege's philosophy of geometry; and, from its placing in a crucial section of *Grundlagen*, we are entitled to infer, in the absence of any specific reason to suppose that he had changed his mind, that it was an idea by which he continued to stand.

Part I of *Grundgesetze* differs from Parts II and III in not presenting a construction of a mathematical theory out of the basic logical system, but in giving the intended interpretation—the semantics—of that system. This is done, informally but rigorously, by employing the whole apparatus of Frege's philosophical logic: sense and reference, thoughts, truth-values, judgments, assertions, objects as opposed to concepts, relations and functions of one or two arguments, of first, second or third level, value-ranges, classes, double value-ranges, extensions of relations. These notions are tersely explained, and then used: but there is no attempt to justify them, either as legitimate notions in themselves or as adequate for the purpose of imposing an interpretation on the formulas of the system. This stands in striking contrast to Frege's procedure in other writings in which he discusses these notions from his philosophy of language. We have in

Grundgesetze none of the arguments used elsewhere for the necessity of distinguishing sense from reference; none of the characterization of senses as objective but non-sensible, capable of being grasped but existing independently of being so; no discussion of the need to differentiate senses from ideas and from all other mental contents; no explanation of the distinction between sense and tone; no arguments against admitting thoughts with variable truth-value; no demonstration that truth-values are the proper choice for the referents of sentences. Likewise absent are the arguments to show that an analysis in Frege's terms is sufficient for the display of logical structure, for instance that the distinction of subject and predicate is irrelevant for this purpose.

All these are recurrent features of Frege's many other discussions of these topics. There are two possible explanations for their absence from Part I of *Grundgesetze*. The first is this. In other places, Frege was concerned to apply the technical notions of his theory of meaning to sentences of natural language, or to demonstrate that his logical formulas were apt for representing the logical structure of the thoughts expressed by such sentences. But, in *Grundgesetze*, he was not concerned with the representation of sentences of natural language or of the thoughts expressed by them: he was setting up a formal language, the senses of whose formulas were to depend solely on his stipulations in Part I. These formulas were therefore not responsible to anything. They were not meant to serve a pre-assigned purpose, and so did not need to be shown to achieve it: they meant whatever Frege's stipulations laid down that they were to mean. And, for that reason, there could be no question of *justifying* those stipulations, or the terms employed to express them; the formal language has just that interest which Frege's stipulations confer on it.

The other explanation is quite different. Throughout his life, Frege attempted to write a comprehensive treatise setting out his views on that branch of philosophy which he called simply 'logic', by which he meant something much wider than formal logic or the theory of deductive reasoning, and which covered all the notions listed above, with their elucidation and justification. He attempted this at least four times: once in the 1880s, once in his mature period, in 1897, once in 1906, and finally towards the end of his life. None of these attempts were completed; the only parts of them to be published were the first three chapters of the final attempt, which appeared as the *Logische Untersuchungen*, comprising 'Der Gedanke', 'Die Verneinung' and 'Gedankengefüge', the third coming out as long as five years after the second. Evidently, then, Frege thought it important to achieve a satisfactory account of these topics, and strove to compose a definitive treatment of them; but, equally evidently, he was never satisfied that he had succeeded. On this explanation, it was because *Grundgesetze* was intended to be definitive, and yet Frege felt unable to write about these matters in a definitive manner, that he omitted from Part I of *Grundgesetze* all justification, and all but the barest explanation, of the notions he there employed.

Our decision which of these two explanations is the right one has substantial importance for the interpretation of *Grundgesetze*. As will be seen in Chapter 19, there is some ground for saying that Frege regarded the formal language of *Grundgesetze*, not as an ancillary to or extension of natural language, an addition to the *one* language we already have, still less as a means of perspicuously representing the sentences of natural language, but as an independent language in its own right, or, perhaps more accurately, the beginning of one. To the extent that this is a correct expression of his intention, it tells in favour of the first explanation. Nevertheless, without being at all certain, I am strongly disposed to believe the second explanation to be the correct one. For, if the first explanation were correct, it would be hard to see with what right the formal system of *Grundgesetze* could be claimed to be a *logical* theory; and, if it is not, the construction of arithmetic from it in Parts II and III loses most of its interest. The avowed aim of the construction, as stated in *Grundlagen* and, less explicitly, in the 'Über formale Theorien der Arithmetik' of 1885, is to show the truths of arithmetic to be analytic, that is, to be derivable, by means of appropriate definitions, from purely logical principles. It is therefore not enough for Frege to show arithmetic to be constructible from some arbitrary formal theory: he has to show that theory to be logical in character, and to be a correct theory of logic.

Logic is that theory which is required for the analysis of deductive reasoning in general. Within particular regions of discourse, distinguished by subject-matter, there may be forms of inference peculiar to those regions, and they will not be the concern of logic as such: but logic must incorporate all principles of inference that may need to be invoked independently of the subject-matter. Of course, logic is not concerned merely to *state* the laws governing correct inference, but with whatever is required for the explanation of the terms in which they are stated and for their formal or informal justification. More generally, since the test for the validity of a form of inference is that it be truth-preserving, logic is concerned with the way in which a sentence, or the thought expressed thereby, is determined as true in accordance with its composition, or in accordance with the structure of the thought as perspicuously or imperspicuously displayed by the sentence expressing it; this is why Frege says of logic, in the broad sense in which he understood this term, that the word 'true' indicates its subject-matter. All this means that logic must be a theory applying to any language capable of expressing thought.

The difficulty of being certain of Frege's intentions in *Grundgesetze* arises precisely out of the absence from Part I of that work of those explanations for the lack of which we are seeking to account. We have, therefore, to look at his other writings to deduce in what relation he conceived his logical notation to stand towards natural language, and of both to thoughts. His strictures on 'language', by which he always meant 'natural language', are so frequent and so severe as to prompt the interpretation that he conceived himself capable of analysing the thoughts expressed by sentences without reference to their linguistic expression. 'A large part of the work of the philosopher,' he wrote in his 'Erkenntnisquellen der Mathematik' of 1924–5, 'consists . . . in a battle with language.'[1] It would, however, be as much of a mistake to conclude from this that, for him, language was merely an enemy, merely a means of obscuring the true structure of the thoughts expressed, and not equally an instrument of analysis, as it would be to draw the same conclusion from similar remarks made by Wittgenstein. In the very same essay he admits it as a necessity for human beings to associate a thought with a sentence expressing it:[2] we grasp thoughts as expressed by sentences. There does not exist in Frege any account of the structure of thoughts stated independently of some means of expressing them, whether in sentences of natural language or in formulas of his logical symbolism. There might therefore be proposed a less radical interpretation, namely that, although the analysis of a thought must be given in terms of an analysis of some means of expressing it, the relevant means of expression must be a purified logical notation such as Frege's own, and that sentences of natural language are quite useless for this purpose. This is, indeed, somewhere near the true account: for Frege, the symbolic expression of a thought displays its true structure, its verbal expression distorts it. He sometimes puts the point with great vehemence, as when he says, in a letter to Husserl of November, 1906, that 'someone who wishes to learn logic from language is like an adult who wishes to learn thinking from a child', and that 'the principal task of the logician consists in a liberation from language and in a simplification: logic ought to be a judge over languages'.[3]

[1] *N.S.*, p. 289, *P.W.*, p. 270.
[2] *N.S.*, p. 288, *P.W.*, p. 269.
[3] *BW*, pp. 102–3, *P.M.C.*, p. 68.

This, however, is not yet to the point that interests us. Our question is whether the logical theory embodied in the formal system of *Grundgesetze* is intended as a logic applicable to all languages capable of expressing thoughts, or merely as the logical basis of a language having no particular relation to the language we use in everyday life, in doing mathematics as well as for other purposes. If it is meant as a universal logic, there are two consequences: the formulas of the logical symbolism must express, no doubt more perspicuously, thoughts which we are capable of expressing in natural language or in ordinary mathematical notation; and the technical notions, of sense, reference, object, concept, etc., which Frege employs in specifying the intended interpretation of those formulas must be applicable to an account of sentences of natural language as well. But, if the logical symbolism can serve to express the very same thoughts as those we express, in however unsatisfactory a way, by means of natural language, then the structure of a symbolic formula must correspond at least to the hidden structure of the appropriate sentence; if it did not, it could not be said to express the same thought. It could not be, for Frege, that the structure of a thought corresponds not at all to the structure of a sentence of natural language expressing it: if the structure of a thought were in no way reflected in the structure of a sentence, then it could not be that thought which was expressed by that sentence, that is, which was the sense of that sentence; for the sense of the whole is compounded, in a manner corresponding to the composition of the linguistic expression, out of the senses of its parts. It follows that natural language cannot be quite useless for the analysis of thought, however much of a struggle is involved in basing such an analysis upon it. And, as was just argued, if a symbolic formula is able to express the same thought as that expressed by a sentence of natural language, then the manifest structure of the formula must correspond to some underlying structure that can be discovered in the sentence.

This, rather than the conceivable alternative, surely represents Frege's view of the relation of the logical symbolism of *Grundgesetze* to natural language and to thoughts in general. It could be held, of some presently existing logical notation, say the λ-calculus, that the structure of its formulas differed too widely from that of sentences of natural language for the thoughts, in Frege's sense, expressed by the former to be identified with those expressed by the latter. Perhaps we can give the semantics of such a symbolism in a rigorous manner, and thus determine the interpretation to be put on it; but we cannot, in more than an approximate manner, say in words what is said by a formula of the system. This would exactly correspond to the alternative conception of the logical symbolism of *Grundgesetze*, that which it would follow that Frege held if we adopted the first of the two explanations for the absence from that book of the elucidations and justifications of his philosophical logic found elsewhere. But, severe as is the contrast that Frege draws between his logical notation and natural language, he never once suggests that he takes such a view of the former. In *Begriffsschrift* he presents his notation as a means of exhibiting perspicuously the logical structure of the thoughts expressed by ordinary sentences, giving a wealth of examples of the latter; and the 'Anwendungen der Begriffsschrift' of 1879 is expressly devoted to showing how the notation can be used to express selected mathematical propositions and carry out mathematical proofs. In the very same letter to Husserl that was quoted above as instancing the vehemence of his hostility, on occasion, to natural language, he says that the purpose of a logical notation is to achieve a unique expression for what 'equipollent' sentences all have in common, namely the thought they express; there is no suggestion that it is meant to express more rarefied thoughts than can be put into the words of natural language. In general, whenever he contrasted the structure of his logical formulas with that of sentences of natural language, and argued for the superiority of the former, above all by calling attention to the absence from them of the grammatical distinctions between subject and predicate or subject and object, the reason he always gave for the divergence is that the formulas capture only the *senses* of our sentences, i.e. the thoughts we express by them; they leave unexpressed the other features of the meaning of ordinary sentences, features relating to psychological reactions. Probably the best guide to his intentions in *Grundgesetze* is the lecture 'Über die Begriffsschrift des Herrn Peano und meine eigene' given in 1896. Here he speaks in the familiar way of the advantages, in investigating the foundations of mathematics, of a logical symbolism, which can avoid the various defects of natural language, such as ambiguity, and for which we can formulate the rules of inference so as to allow an effective verification of the conformity of a proof to them, without the slightest suggestion that, by this means, we attain a grasp of thoughts previously quite unexpressible.

It is, of course, true that Frege did not attempt to explain his logical notation by giving rules of translation from his formulas into sentences of natural language. Rather, when you grasp the senses of the primitive symbols, you thereby grasp the thoughts expressed by the formulas, which thoughts you are then able to express in any language known to you and capable of expressing them. But it is plain that he did not think that, in the logical notation of *Grundgesetze*, he had devised a language in which thoughts could be expressed that could not be expressed in any other way; the logic of *Grundgesetze* was intended as a universal logic, not one peculiar to a special language unconnected with the thoughts we are ordinarily concerned to communicate to one another. The meaning-theoretical notions used in Part I of *Grundgesetze* are therefore not to be considered as applying exclusively to Frege's formal system. They are to be taken as applicable both to it and to natural language, and perhaps as required for any intelligible language; and the theory of meaning that embodies them accordingly serves both as a theory of sense for natural language and as a foundation for the formal logic, understood under the interpretation informally expounded in Part I, from which Parts II and III construct arithmetic. A full justification of these notions, as applying in the first instance to the expressions of natural language, would therefore be required if the logical system were to be established as the universal logic which it was intended to be. If we did not understand those notions as applicable to natural language, then possibly we should be unable to grasp the informal exposition of the logical system in terms of them, and certainly could not recognize that system as capable of expressing the very thoughts we ordinarily express in words. It is this justification that would have been contained in that comprehensive work on 'Logic' that Frege repeatedly tried, and repeatedly failed, to write.

If these conclusions are correct, there is a substantial body of Frege's theory—precisely that comprising his philosophy of language—of which no definitive exposition, comparable to *Grundgesetze*, or even carrying an authority equal to that of *Grundlagen*, exists. We have, therefore, to rely on the ample material available: the formulations in Part I of *Grundgesetze*, together with occasional remarks elsewhere in the book, can be taken as regarded by Frege as being as final a statement as everything else in that work; but those in the various published articles, and, still more, in the numerous posthumous papers, are no more than interim drafts of a work never written. But, by the same token, we have the greater warrant, when expounding this part of Frege's philosophy, for relying on the posthumous writings of his early and middle periods; these are likely to contain ideas which Frege would have expressed in print if he had ever composed to his satisfaction the treatise on the subject which he wanted to write. We can do no more than surmise the reason why he never achieved a formulation of his general theory of philosophical logic. When one reflects carefully on the theory as we know it, one comes across certain unresolved tensions: observations made by Frege in different connections, though hardly ever in flagrant contradiction with one another, pull in opposite directions, leaving crucial questions unanswered. He may have been aware of some or all of these tensions, but unable to find a way of resolving them. If we are conscious of this possibility, we shall not demand, of any interpretation of this part of Frege's philosophy, that it settle every question that arises: perhaps the right interpretation is, precisely, one that leaves some question unanswered or unanswerable.

Begriffsschrift was, of course, a work of genius; it is staggering how close Frege was able to come, in one enormous stride, to what we should now regard as a satisfactory formalization of higher-order classical predicate logic. But, in interpreting his philosophical ideas, we have to view it and the other works of his first period as a first draft. Frege achieved so much in *Begriffsschrift* that it is unsurprising that the accompanying prose exposition does not present a satisfactory philosophical logic. Frege worked hard at this subject in the intervening years, and attained a great clarification of his ideas on the subject, though, as we have seen, not one that appeared complete to him. The changes that he made in that theory were made deliberately and as the result of intense thought. The subject was not merely one that happened to interest him as well as the philosophy of mathematics: it underlay his philosophy of mathematics. It was possible to give a systematic treatment of that branch of philosophy he called 'logic' without mentioning mathematics; but, for him, it was impossible to discuss the philosophy of mathematics without appealing to general principles of 'logic', precisely because that part of mathematics he called 'arithmetic' rested on logic. We should therefore respect his changes of mind, and recognize that, when he wrote *Begriffsschrift*, he did not conceive of himself as yet having attained a satisfactory theory of logic, regarded as a branch of philosophy. This applies, of course, in particular, to the undifferentiated notion of 'content' employed in *Begriffsschrift*, within which, as Frege later said, he subsequently distinguished sense and reference. When that undifferentiated notion is pressed, it proves not properly coherent, and it was just this that Frege came to realize, and that prompted him to adopt the sense/reference distinction. It is a mistake for us to press the notion of 'content' without admitting that distinction, and father on Frege some misbegotten theory for which there is no warrant even in his early writings; and even more of a mistake to try to interpret the writings of his mature period in the light of such a theory.

Up to the end of his mature period, almost all of Frege's writing had been directed towards a single goal, the production of *Grundgesetze*. His career had, indeed, been one of repeated disappointments. The *Begriffsschrift* of 1879, that work which inaugurated the entire modern era in formal logic, was not understood by any of those, including John Venn and Ernst Schröder, who reviewed it.[1] Frege's most sustained attempt to explain his revolutionary system of formal logic, a full-length article entitled 'Booles rechnende Logik und die Begriffsschrift', was rejected in the course of the year 1881 by three editors of journals. At the very height of his powers, Frege wrote his *Grundlagen der Arithmetik* (1884) as a summary of his logical construction of the theory of natural numbers and of cardinal numbers generally, eschewing the use of symbols in order to render it accessible to a wide readership. It attracted almost no attention, and Georg Cantor, who ought, of all philosophers and mathematicians, to have been the most sympathetic, reviewed it with hostility and misunderstanding.[2] In the Preface to *Grundgesetze*, vol. I (1893), Frege complained of the neglect of his work by those, such as Richard Dedekind, whose own work lay closest to his.[3] Discouraged by the poor reception of vol. I, he did not publish vol. II until ten years later: and then, while the volume was in press, there came the shattering blow of Russell's discovery of the contradiction.

Frege's life's work was halted by this discovery. *Grundgesetze* was left unfinished, presumably because he came quickly to realize that crucial proofs, above all that of the infinity of the series of natural numbers, would no longer go through under the weakened Axiom V proposed in the Appendix to vol. II. It can have taken him only a short time to discover that such proofs could not easily be adapted. But it seems likely that he spent until mid-1906 attempting to give alternative proofs. Indeed, Frege's posthumous papers allow us with high probability to date almost exactly Frege's disillusionment over the attempt, to which he had devoted his life, to derive arithmetic from logic. Frege began, but did not complete, an article commenting on one by Schoenflies, published in January 1906, on the logical paradoxes of set theory, and mentioning also another article by Korselt published in April 1906.[4] The plan of Frege's article contains the phrase 'Concepts which coincide in their extension, although this extension falls under the one but not under the other': this shows that he was still

---

[1] G. Frege, *Conceptual Notation and Related Articles*, trans. and ed. T. W. Bynum, Oxford, 1972, reprints, pp. 209–35, all the contemporary reviews of *Begriffsschrift* in English translation.

[2] The statement made on p. 630 of *FPL₁*, that this review by Cantor was the only one that Frege's *Grundlagen* received, was in error. As recorded in the bibliography to Bynum's *Conceptual Notation*, there were two others, one by R. Hoppe in *Archiv der Mathematik und Physik* for 1885, and the other by K. Lasswitz in the *Zeitschrift für Philosophie und philosophische Kritik* for 1886. I have in *FPL* emended the remark accordingly.

[3] P. xi fn.

[4] *N.S.*, pp. 191–9, *P.W.*, pp. 176–83.

attempting to pursue the 'solution' of Russell's paradox which he had proposed in his Appendix to *Grundgesetze*, vol. II. Tantalizingly little of the article survives, or, more likely, was ever written; very probably it represents the very moment at which Frege came to realize that the attempt was hopeless. There is a tiny fragment, dated 5 August 1906, entitled 'What can I regard as the outcome of my work?'[1] This includes the apologetic remark, 'the extension of a concept or the class is not for me the first thing' —the first being the concept itself. Why was Frege moved at just that moment to ask himself what his work had achieved? It must have been because he had finally come to recognize that his ambition to set beyond doubt the derivation of arithmetic from logic had irrevocably failed. Instead of completing the project, he had to acknowledge that it could not be accomplished; and he wanted to take stock of what survived from the disaster, what truths he had nevertheless established.

My division, in Chapter 18 of *FPL*, of Frege's career into six periods can therefore be improved by letting the third, mature period run from 1891 not, as I said in FPL_1, until 1904, but until mid-1906, including in it his second series of articles on the foundations of geometry published in that year. I have, in FPL_2, amended the relevant passages on pp. 642 and 657 accordingly. Having surveyed, in the fragment just mentioned, what survived from the wreck of his life's work, Frege bravely began, on the very same day on which he composed that fragment, his third attempt to write a comprehensive treatise on the philosophy of logic, 'Einleitung in die Logik';[2] this was no longer just an attempt to set out in a definitive manner the philosophical doctrines underlying the formal logic of *Grundgesetze*, and the semantics of that logic as expounded in Part I of that work, but a statement of those truths which remained intact after the disaster of Russell's contradiction; and they were largely truths belonging to logic in general, rather than to the philosophy of mathematics, for, as the first sentence of the fragment 'What can I regard as the outcome of my work?' says, 'Almost everything is connected with the symbolic notation (*Begriffsschrift*)'. 'Einleitung in die Logik' was not finished; in the same year, 1906, Frege began a second draft, 'Kurze Übersicht meiner logischen Lehren',[3] but this was unfinished also. Over the next seven years he produced virtually nothing; his publications were restricted to a brief continuation of the polemic against the formalist Thomae and the comments on Jourdain's article about him, about which Frege expressed the hope,

---

[1] '*Was kann ich als Ergebnis meiner Arbeit ansehen?*', *N.S.*, p. 200, *P.W.*, p. 184.

[2] *N.S.*, pp. 201–12, *P.W.*, pp. 185–96.

[3] *N.S.*, pp. 213–18, *P.W.*, pp. 197–202.

in one letter to Jourdain, that it would gain many readers for his works.[1] Seven years is an exceedingly long time for any academic, let alone a fertile genius such as Frege, to produce next to nothing: but, in view of the setbacks which Frege had suffered, and the final collapse of the grand project to which he had devoted his life, it is surprising that he ever wrote again at all. We should know more of his thought during this period had the correspondence with Löwenheim of 1908–10 been preserved; but the letter to Russell of June 1912 indicates a state of great depression.

In 1914 Frege started writing again, on general logical topics; and, from 1919, he returned to the philosophy of mathematics. Coming finally to terms with the failure of his logicist programme, he decided that the very notion of a class was a delusion born of misleading forms of linguistic expression, and that there were therefore no logical objects and could be no reduction of arithmetic to logic; and, in his very last years, he courageously began an attempt to found arithmetic upon geometry. Obviously, his late writings on mathematics represent a viewpoint utterly distinct from that which he had formerly held.

His writings on logic from 1914 onwards do not present the same obvious discontinuity with his earlier work. The *Logische Untersuchungen* do, at first sight, give the appearance of a new approach; on nearer inspection, however, there is a close affinity between them and the uncompleted 'Logik' of 1897. Certainly there are some views expressed in these late writings which are not to be found in those from before 1914, and we have no warrant to read them back into his earlier philosophy. To my mind, however, there is no *conflict* between his late views on logic and those of his middle period from 1891 to 1906. This is a matter of *interpretation*: there can be no presumption either of continuity or of discontinuity. Frege had in June 1902 received a shattering blow. It had taken him until August 1906 to comprehend the full magnitude of it; and then he had ceased productive work altogether for seven years. What did he conceive of himself as doing in the logical writings from 1914 onwards? Was he trying, as in the writings on the philosophy of mathematics of 1924–5, to make an altogether fresh beginning? Or was he trying belatedly to do what he had begun but failed to carry through in 1906, to make a systematic review of that part of his earlier philosophy, the logical part, which had remained unaffected by the contradiction? Neither hypothesis has a greater a priori probability than the other: we have to look at his writings and judge from them.

[1] *BW*, p. 115, *P.M.C.*, p. 76.

It has been maintained that, in Frege's writings from 1914 onwards, there is an entirely new interest in the notion of understanding. Certainly, it is from the writings of this period that we find Frege raising the question how we are able to understand new sentences we have not heard before. The first mention of this question occurs in the draft of a letter to Jourdain from 1914, the same one as that in which he gives the Afla/Ateb example. In answer to Jourdain's question 'whether, in view of what seems to be a fact, namely, that Russell has shown that propositions can be analysed into a form which only assumes that a name has a "Bedeutung", and not a "Sinn", you would hold that "Sinn" was merely a psychological property of a name',[1] Frege replies, 'I do not believe that we can dispense with the sense of a name in logic; for a sentence must have a sense, if it is to be of use (*brauchbar*). But the sentence consists of parts which must in some way contribute to the expression of the sense of the sentence, and must therefore themselves in some way be endowed with sense (*sinnvoll*). Let us take the sentence "Etna is higher than Vesuvius". In it we have the name "Etna", which also occurs in other sentences, e.g. in the sentence "Etna is in Sicily". Our capacity to understand sentences that we have never heard before obviously rests on the fact that we build up the sense of a sentence out of parts which correspond to the words. When we find the same word, e.g. "Etna", in two sentences, we recognize something in common, that corresponds to this word, in the corresponding thoughts also. Without this a language in the proper sense would be impossible. We could indeed agree that certain signs were to express certain thoughts; like the signals on the railway (line clear); but in this way we should always be restricted to a very narrow domain and we could not construct a quite new sentence that is understood by another although no special agreement on this case has been previously made.'[2] He then goes on to argue, in a familiar way, that Etna itself, the mountain with its lava, cannot be part of the thought expressed by the sentence. In the unpublished 'Logik in der Mathematik' of 1914 he similarly says, 'It is remarkable what language achieves. By means of a few sounds and combinations of sounds it is in a position to express a vast number of thoughts, including ones which have never before been grasped and expressed by a human being. How are these achievements possible? By the fact that thoughts are built up out of building blocks (*Gedankenbausteinen*). And these building blocks correspond to groups of sounds, so that the construction of the sentence out of sentence-parts corresponds to the construction of the thought out of thought-parts.

[1] *BW*, p. 126, *P.M.C.*, p. 78.
[2] *BW*, p. 127, *P.M.C.*, p. 79.

And one may call the thought-part the sense of the corresponding sentence-part, just as one will regard the thought as the sense of the sentence.'[1] He then goes on to discuss the same example, of a sentence concerning Etna, as before. 'Gedankengefüge' (1923) begins, 'It is astonishing what language accomplishes, in that it expresses by means of a few syllables unsurveyably many thoughts, that it finds, for a thought that is now grasped for the first time by an inhabitant of the Earth, a clothing in which another, to whom it is quite new, can recognise it. This would not be possible if we could not distinguish within thoughts parts that correspond to the parts of sentences, so that the construction of the sentence can serve as a picture of the construction of the thought. Admittedly we are in fact speaking metaphorically when we transfer the relation of whole and part to thoughts. But the metaphor lies so close to hand, and proves so apt in general, that we hardly find any inconvenience in its occasionally going lame.'

In these passages, sense is evidently correlative to understanding. More exactly, when we bear in mind the distinction between sense and tone, sense is part of meaning, where meaning is considered as correlative to understanding: what a speaker knows when he understands an expression is what that expression means, and the most important ingredient in its meaning is its sense. Frege is, in these passages from his writings from 1914 onwards, putting to use the view that he had firmly held throughout his mature period, that the sense of a sentence-part is part of the thought expressed by the sentence, in order to explain the fact that we are capable of understanding quite new sentences. From my own standpoint, this represents no divergence from his earlier views: in *FPL*, I treated his notion of sense as being, from the start, an ingredient in meaning, where meaning is correlative to understanding. The warrant for so interpreting Frege's theory of sense, as it was in his mature period, is that sense is, for him, something that we *grasp*. It is connected, in 'Über Sinn und Bedeutung', with what it is that we know when we know a sentence to be true; in the 'Kurze Übersicht meiner logischen Lehren' of 1906, whether or not two sentences have the same sense depends on something that must be immediately recognized by one who knows their senses.[2] To grasp a thought, *tout court*, is simply to have that thought, without necessarily judging it to be true or false; and to grasp a sense other than a thought is to have a concept in a non-Fregean sense of 'concept'. But to grasp the thought expressed by a sentence is to understand that sentence, and to

---

[1] *N.S.*, p. 243, *P.W.*, p. 225—see also *N.S.*, p. 262, *P.W.*, p. 243.
[2] *N.S.*, p. 213, *P.W.*, p. 197.

grasp the sense of an expression is to understand that expression: speakers *attach* (*verbinden*) senses to expressions.[1] It is therefore wrong to say that, in his mature period, Frege was unconcerned with understanding: the notion of understanding words, expressions and sentences figures in the writings of that period under the guise of grasping their senses.

Whether or not we have here a change in Frege's conception of sense depends upon the interpretation of the writings of his mature period. On the view, contrary to mine, referred to above, the notion of sense, as he conceived it during the mature period, did not relate in any way to meaning, as we intuitively think of meaning: sense was not the object, or any part of the object, of a speaker's understanding. In the late writings, on the other hand, it did become the object of understanding, according to this interpretation: Frege converted a notion introduced for one purpose to an entirely different purpose. It is not the intention of the present chapter to argue for one interpretation of Frege against another, but to lay down principles for judging such interpretations; and, as remarked, there is no prior presumption that Frege's later writings on logic agree with his earlier ones or that they disagree. In general, citations from these later writings may provide useful summaries of his earlier views, when there is positive evidence that he really did hold those views in or before his middle period; without such evidence, they cannot be used to sustain an interpretation of his pre-1914 writings. Such a warning would be unnecessary apropos of most philosophers; but, as observed at the outset of this chapter, the exceptional continuity of Frege's thought provides a special temptation to treat his work as a seamless garment. Conversely, we cannot take it for granted that views expressed by Frege in the writings of his mature period carry over into the last phase. Especially is this so if it be held that his later writings embody a radically different point of view: there is then a presumption that earlier views which, on the interpretation adopted, would flagrantly conflict with his later ideas, and about which he says nothing explicit in his later writings, for or against, would have been repudiated by him in the later period had he been asked about them.

To my mind, there is no alteration in Frege's conception of sense from his mature to his late period. The principal difference in attitude that I can discern is that towards natural language and its defects. The *Logische Untersuchungen*, like the 'Einleitung in die Logik' of 1906, start from natural language. Frege still believes that the structure of the thoughts expressed by sentences of natural language is better displayed by a more

---

[1] See 'Über Sinn und Bedeutung', p. 27, fn.

perspicuous logical notation diverging from natural language in certain respects; this was evidently to be introduced, in the *Logische Untersuchungen*, in stages, as the need for it was made apparent. Thus in 'Logische Allgemeinheit' ('Logical Generality'), the fourth, unfinished and unpublished chapter of the *Logische Untersuchungen*,[1] he speaks of a *Hilfssprache* (auxiliary language), which uses the notation of bound variables to express generality, as opposed to the *Darlegungssprache* (expository language) or metalanguage, which is ordinary German. Frege also remains convinced of the misleading character of natural language, of the need for the philosopher or logician to engage in a struggle with it. After all, he regarded his earlier belief in classes—the extensions of concepts—as the result of his having been seduced by misleading forms of linguistic expression. As he said in the fragment 'Zahl' of 1924, 'my efforts to cast light on the questions which attach to the word "number" and to individual number-words and numerical symbols seem to have ended in complete failure';[2] and he saw this failure as principally due to his having been misled by language.[3] In such circumstances, he could hardly have been expected not to remain suspicious of natural language. Indeed, all the most vehement remarks about natural language come from his writings after mid-1906; the most vehement of all, that from the letter to Husserl of November 1906 quoted above, may reflect the bitterness of his disillusionment at the moment when, according to the hypothesis here advanced, he had recognized the inadequacy of his attempted solution of the Russell paradox and the consequent failure of his logicist programme.

For all that, his perception, during his late period, of what constitute the principal defects of natural language seems to have shifted. Thus, surprisingly, what is singled out in that footnote to 'Der Gedanke'[4] in which he says that his proper concern is with thoughts, but that he is forced to attend to language, is the use of figurative expressions, something of which Frege had seldom previously complained. The occurrence in natural language of empty proper names is still a great grievance;[5] understandably, since an expression like 'the extension of the concept *fixed star*' is an instance of such a proper name, and the source of the belief in those spurious objects, classes. But, so far as we can tell in view of the fact that we have, in the *Logische Untersuchungen*, only the first three and a half

---

[1] *N.S.*, pp. 278–81, *P.W.*, pp. 258–62.
[2] *N.S.*, p. 284, *P.W.*, p. 265.
[3] See *N.S.*, p. 289, *P.W.*, p. 269.
[4] P. 66.
[5] See *N.S.*, p. 288, *P.W.*, p. 269.

chapters of what must have been planned as a full-sized book, Frege laid far less stress, in this late period, on the demand that sentences be treated as of the same logical category as proper names. The initial discussion of the reference of sentences, in 'Logik in der Mathematik',[1] affirms that two true sentences have the same reference, as do two false ones, while avoiding any mention of truth-values as objects; a little later, a thought is said to stand to its truth-value as the sense of a sign to its reference, so that truth is not a property of a sentence or a thought,[2] but the truth-values are still not spoken of as objects. Although in the fragment 'What can I regard as the outcome of my work?' of 1906 Frege had listed the functional character of concepts and relations as one of his most important discoveries, the idea appears in 'Logik in der Mathematik' only as a kind of option: 'it seems to be appropriate to regard the concept as a function, namely one whose values are always truth-values.'[3] In general, though those doctrines which, in the mature period, led to the most paradoxical-seeming consequences, such as that each concept and function should be defined for every object, appear still to be maintained, their paradoxical character is very much played down. In view of the fragmentary nature of the later writings, it would be far too much to say that there was really any change of opinion in these respects; but there was certainly a change of emphasis.

There is a fundamental cleavage, among logicians and philosophers of language, between those who do and those who do not think it legitimate to demand a revision of established linguistic practice: revisionists or radicals as against conservatives. Since linguistic practice does change, even if there is no standpoint from which one has the right to demand a change, and since it seems absurd to claim for existing practice a privilege denied to that of former times, conservatives tend to be relativists; radicals are more likely to take an absolutist view. Wittgenstein, even more than Quine, was an archetypal conservative. For him, meaning is constituted by practice: there is therefore no external standard to which practice must conform, no pre-established principles determining in advance what it ought to be. One may say of an individual that he reasoned incorrectly: but it would be senseless to accuse a whole linguistic community of reasoning wrongly.[4] The meanings of our words are determined in part by generally

[1] *N.S.*, pp. 251–2, *P.W.*, pp. 232–3.

[2] *N.S.*, p. 252, *P.W.*, p. 233.

[3] *N.S.*, p. 254, *P.W.*, p. 235 cf. *N.S.*, p. 263, *P.W.*, p. 244.

[4] See *Lectures on the Foundations of Mathematics*, ed. Cora Diamond, Hassocks, 1976, p. 110.

accepted linguistic practice regarding what is and what is not treated as being a valid inference. We have the right to make our words mean whatever we choose that they shall mean, and we therefore have the right to treat as valid whatever inferences we choose so to regard: there is nothing beyond our practice to which that practice is responsible. To put the matter in non-Wittgensteinian terms, we might say that the task of a theory of meaning is to explain a phenomenon, namely the practice of speaking a language; or, rather, not so much to explain it as to render it surveyable by describing it in a systematic fashion. The first test for the correctness of such a theory is therefore that it should agree with the practice that it seeks to describe; if it fails to do so, it is *ipso facto* shown to be mistaken.

The intuitionists are the most obvious example of revisionists who seek to alter established practice. Their quarrel with classical logic is of quite a different nature from, say, the dispute over the existential import of categorical propositions in the traditional logic. In the latter case, the mistake was one made, or alleged to have been made, by the logicians: when a certain ambiguity in natural language was resolved, in one way or another, it would be seen that not all the logical laws propounded as valid by the traditional logic would in fact be accepted as valid. But the intuitionists do not treat classical logic as an incorrect codification of the way in which mathematicians reason: it is a correct codification, but, at certain points, it reflects mistakes that mathematicians have been accustomed to make in their reasoning, mistakes which they ought henceforward to refrain from making. An example of a different kind, more closely resembling Frege, is Tarski, who holds that the semantic paradoxes are not due to unnoticed deviation from the accepted norms of deductive reasoning, but to principles of inference entrenched in established practice. For him, natural language, as in fact employed, is 'semantically closed'; and any semantically closed language is necessarily inconsistent. The paradoxes can be resolved only by a change in linguistic practice.

If there is to be room for a legitimate demand for the revision of established linguistic practice, in the matter of deductive reasoning or in any other respect, the practice of using language must be seen as involving a variety of components, which may be required to exhibit a certain harmony. On such a view, the complexity of our linguistic practice may impede our recognition that the harmony does not in fact obtain; but it is nevertheless a presumption of our practice in speaking the language that there should be such harmony, and a revision in that practice may justifiably be demanded if it can be shown to be the minimum change necessary to restore harmony. We cannot rest content with saying that we do what we do: the use of language has a *point*, as, indeed, a game has a point, and, if the necessary harmony between the different components is lacking, that point is destroyed or impaired. To say that an activity has a point is not to say that it has a goal which can be stated without reference to that activity, that, in other words, it is a mere means to an independently statable end; but it is to say that there is a standard by which it may be judged as achieving or failing to achieve what it is intended to achieve.

Frege was firmly in the revisionist camp. For him, natural language has many defects which impair its effectiveness as an instrument for the expression of thought; these defects need to be eliminated whenever we use language as a means of arriving at the truth, and especially when we engage in deductive reasoning. In Frege's case, it is not wholly appropriate to use the metaphor of harmony, which suggests that, in our employment of natural language, we are playing a game with conflicting rules. Rather, it is as if we were playing one for which no clear rules could be given. The use of language, if it is to have the point it is intended to have, must be a practice capable of being codified; but natural language resists such codification at several places. We therefore need to revise our practice, at least when we are seriously concerned with the attainment of truth, so as to make such codification possible. To express the matter in terms of a theory of meaning, no systematic theory of meaning will fit our linguistic practice as it actually is: but so much the worse for our linguistic practice, which ought to be revised so as to accord with such a theory.

A particular source of error in the interpretation of Frege lies precisely in the failure to distinguish between his descriptions of the functioning of language and of what he took to be its malfunctioning. Such an error can be made in two ways. First, we may mistake Frege's descriptions of natural language as it actually is for accounts of language as it ought to be. The most obvious examples of misrepresentations of this sort are statements contrasting Russell's theory of descriptions with the view attributed to Frege that sentences containing singular terms without reference are neither true nor false. Such a contrast, drawn without suitable qualification, makes Frege look like a predecessor of Strawson. We do not grasp Frege's view, however, unless we understand it as characterizing a type of linguistic malfunction to which natural languages are liable: in a properly constructed language, there will be no expressions lacking reference or sentences devoid of truth-value, whereas, for Strawson, such phenomena are perfectly in order. Secondly, we may make the converse error, and mistake what Frege says about a properly constructed language for a description of language as it actually is. Notoriously, Frege believed that such expressions as 'the Sun + 1' should be regarded as well formed and as having both a sense and a reference.[1] But we should not imagine that he is affirming that such an expression already has a definite sense and therefore a determinate referent. That it does not have is a reproach to natural language: it has, therefore, to be *given* a sense, which will assign some referent to it, if we are to reconstruct language so as to be able to reason by means of it without error and in accordance with principles which systematically determine every sentence as having a definite truth-value.

When the distinction between Frege's descriptions of language as it is and as it should be has been firmly apprehended, yet a further mistake is liable to be made, namely by representing the distinction as one between what Frege says about two wholly disparate kinds of language, natural language on the one hand and, on the other, an ideal language as expressed by means of a logical symbolism such as his own. Frege of course sometimes makes statements intended to apply only to his symbolic notation. Where he is speaking about those linguistic features in respect of which, according to him, a properly constructed language must diverge from natural language, then a sharp distinction is needed according to whether he is speaking of the one or of the other. But it is quite wrong to think that all of his observations concerning language are to be classified either as relating solely to natural language or as relating solely to a purified logical symbolism. On the contrary, when he is not specifically concerned with the defects of natural language and the contrasted features of a properly constructed language, his general statements about language are intended to apply equally to his logical symbolism and to natural language, in so far as it does function properly, and in the same way, by implication, to every possible language. The distinction he draws is not between two utterly different modes of expressing thoughts, but between language as functioning properly and as misfunctioning, or, in some cases, between language as serving to express thoughts and language as fulfilling other, ancillary, purposes. We should observe when he is talking about the one thing and when about the other; but we should not suppose that a logical symbolism is intended to function in a manner quite different from language as we ordinarily conceive it. Rather, it is intended to do effectively what ordinary language accomplishes only imperfectly, by methods that refine, rather than replace, those which natural language uses.

On Frege's view, natural language differs from his logical symbolism

---

[1] *Function und Begriff*, p. 19.

in three connected respects. In the first place, it is imperspicuous. Secondly, it is not concerned solely to express thoughts and to convey our judgments as to their truth, but also to evoke a variety of psychological states of feeling, expectation, etc. And, finally, as an instrument for the expression of thought, it is in various ways defective. Frege was interested in these irrelevancies and imperfections of natural language chiefly in order to get them out of the way: he is concerned with the analysis of *thought*, as effected by the analysis of the sentences of a purified language, his logical notation, which is to be as nearly perfect an instrument for the expression of thoughts as it is possible to devise. In so far as a sentence of natural language succeeds in expressing a thought, it must have the same kind of structure, though this structure may be concealed rather than perspicuous, and may be overlaid by other structures related to the other ends of natural language; if the structure required for the expression of thought cannot be uncovered, this represents one of the defects of natural language as an instrument for the expression of thought. It is this pre-occupation of Frege's which explains, for example, the fact that I pointed out that his discussion of what I called 'tone', for which he uses various terms such as *Färbung* (colouring), is unconvincing and inaccurate:[1] the topic has no real interest for him, save as indicating something to be distinguished from sense that does not need to be expressed in the formulas of the logical notation. This applies even more strongly when Frege talks about the actual defects of natural language. Among such defects are: ambiguity of construction; ambiguity of words, whether or not resolved, even systematically, by context; vagueness; the use of predicates and functors not everywhere defined; and the occurrence of empty proper names. The last two of these defects result in sentences lacking truth-values; vagueness results in sentences with no *determinate* truth-value; and ambiguity, whether of construction or of individual words, makes deductive reasoning unreliable or impossible. Indeed, Frege thought that all these defects had the latter effect. His discussions of these features of natural language are governed, not merely by his desire to clear them out of the way, but by his perception of them as *defects*. Had he been sufficiently interested to do so, he could have given an accurate account of the phenomenon of tone. But a systematic account of, e.g., vagueness, or of the working of a language allowing truth-value gaps, would have called in question his stigmatization of these features as *defects* of natural language. They are defects because no fully coherent account of a language exhibiting such

---

[1] *FPL*, pp. 85–8.

features is possible; so any account of them that is attempted is necessarily in part incoherent; and, above all, any attempt to state rules of inference governing sentences displaying these features necessarily leads to uncertainty or inconsistency. I do not mean that Frege abstained from giving a coherent account in order to make such features appear as imperfections of language: rather, it is because he thought he saw that no coherent account is possible that he regarded them as imperfections which had to be remedied when we devised a language fully apt for the expression of thoughts and the unassailable execution of deductive argument.

For just this reason, little weight is to be attached to the remarks Frege makes when attempting to characterize those features of natural language he regarded as defects; the observations are not meant to be fully coherent, and, if they were, Frege would have shown such features not to be defects, but, at worst, inconveniences. We should not, for example, wrestle too hard with the thesis that there can be determinate thoughts that lack a truth-value: it is to be regarded as the closest we can come to a characterization of certain sentences of natural language, sentences which ought not to occur in a properly constructed language. If the thesis can be shown not to be fully coherent, all the better: that will be a demonstration of Frege's view that such sentences ought to be excised from the language, or at least from a logical notation that does not have to serve the manifold purposes of everyday communication. Just the same goes for vagueness. For Frege, it is useless to enquire at which step the reasoning goes wrong in the paradox of the heap, where one proves, by induction, that a single bean constitutes a heap: one just cannot reason using expressions such as 'heap'. In *Begriffsschrift*, § 27, Frege, alluding to this paradox, says that, owing to the vagueness of the concept 'heap', there are certain z's such that, where F is the property of being a heap of beans, $F(z)$ is not a judgeable content. The idea behind this passing remark is evidently that, if 'x is a heap of beans' is definitely true, and 'y is a heap of beans' definitely false, then both sentences have a content, whereas, if z is a borderline case, 'z is a heap of beans' lacks a content. This idea yields no coherent account of vague predicates. As remarked, that would not worry Frege. It is because no coherent account of vague predicates is possible that we cannot reason by means of them, and that their presence is a defect to be eliminated from a properly constructed language; what would worry Frege would be a coherent account of them. What we must not do is to infer that it was part of Frege's theory of language at the time of writing *Begriffsschrift* that we may form a sentence out of a name and a predicate both possessing a content, and yet have no guarantee that the sentence so formed itself has a content. It is just that that is the sort of thing we find ourselves forced to say when dealing with vague predicates; and it is not really coherent, which is why we cannot reason by means of them. Its incoherence implies precisely the opposite of the supposed thesis, namely that, in a properly constructed language, a sentence properly put together out of parts each of which possesses a content *must* itself have a content; it is just because the alternative is incoherent that the presence of vague expressions is a defect of natural language, a point at which it ceases to be an apt instrument for the expression of thought. In connection with the very same example, Frege made a later attempt, in his published letter to Peano of 1896, to describe the phenomenon, saying that, in natural language, a sentence may express a thought even though its parts lack a sense and a reference. The idea is similar. The predicate 'ξ is a heap' lacks a reference, since the condition for a predicate's having one is, according to Frege, that it should be everywhere defined and sharply bounded. If a predicate lacks a reference, it must also lack a sense; at least, Frege never tries citing such an expression as an instance of one possessing sense but not reference. On the other hand, a sentence of the form '*a* is a heap' may be definitely true; and if a sentence has a truth-value, it must express a thought: it follows that it does so despite having a part lacking either reference or sense. But, as before, it would be a grave mistake to try to deduce from this remark a coherent theory, according to which we grasp the sense of a sentence only as a whole, rather than as compounded out of the senses of its parts, and that only in special cases can the parts of the sentence be said to have a sense. No coherent theory can be constructed out of the remark, and that is just the point; if a coherent theory of vague expressions could be constructed, vagueness would not be a defect. On the contrary, it was Frege's consistent position that the sense of the whole is compounded out of the senses of the parts; and the observation about vague predicates occurs, by way of contrast with what should happen if we are to be able to carry out deductive reasoning, in a passage where Frege is arguing that each expression should have a reference of its own which remains the same in every context. If we announce as Fregean doctrines generalizations of his intentionally inarticulate accounts of the defects of natural language, we shall interpret him as holding the very opposite of what he really believed.

My contention is not that we should allow Frege to set the terms of the discussion by excluding from consideration whatever features of language he chooses to deem undesirable. On the contrary, it is a serious question for his philosophy of language whether he is right to deem them so. If we can show that a coherent semantic account *can* be given for a language containing, e.g., empty proper names or vague predicates, then Frege's theory of language is thereby proved mistaken. I am urging only that his descriptions of what he takes to be defective features of natural language should not be criticized for failing to be fully coherent, since they are not meant to be; still less should we extract from them general principles which we then represent as part of Frege's theory of how language functions.

CHAPTER 3

Was Frege a Philosopher of Language?

SOME CRITICS BELIEVE that I went wrong on the very title-page of *Frege: Philosophy of Language*: according to them, Frege was not concerned with the philosophy of language at all, or only in very small part, as an auxiliary to other enquiries. To others, however, it will seem absurd even to raise the question whether he contributed to this part of the subject: so much of the philosophy of language since him has been an elaboration of themes to be found in his writings, or a reaction against theses that he advanced. How, then, can it be denied that he occupied himself with the philosophy of language, and how can this denial be reconciled with the obvious bearing of his work on that part of philosophy?

One version of the denial is sketched by Sluga, when he calls Frege's account of sense and reference 'an appendix to a philosophy of mathematics' and not 'the center of a philosophy of language'.[1] Even if the diagnosis of Frege's motives were correct, this would necessarily be an underestimation of his work. A crucial tenet of his philosophy of mathematics was that number theory and analysis are reducible to and derivable from a logic that is not specific to mathematics. To make out such a thesis, what is required is not an appendix, but a very substantial prolegomenon: the logic appealed to must be plausibly made out to be of universal validity before the thesis can have any interest. But the assessment is palpably mistaken even as an account of Frege's motives. He was, indeed, a mathematician who turned into a philosopher. The *Begriffsschrift* was written in the service of mathematics, as an instrument for the attainment of that complete rigour to which the axiomatization of mathematical theories was only a half-way step. It is, however, plain that the researches into that part of philosophy which he called 'logic', which was, for him, a much

---

[1] 'Frege and the Rise of Analytical Philosophy', p. 475.

broader area than the study of inference, took on in his mind an interest of their own, as is evident from the series of attempts he made to write a comprehensive treatise on the subject, often with the sparsest use of mathematical examples: the 'Logik' of the 1880s, that of 1897, the 'Einleitung in die Logik' of 1906[1] and the *Logische Untersuchungen* of the late years. Sluga apparently believes that Frege overvalued this part of his work; I do not.

Granted that Frege occupied himself with a branch of philosophy, for which he used the name 'logic', not only as a preface to a philosophy of mathematics, but for its own sake, the question arises how that branch of philosophy ought to be labelled. Since I think that the term 'logic' is best reserved for the study of inference and what arises out of that study, I should prefer a different name for it. Frege says that, while all the sciences have truth as their goal, the predicate 'true' defines the subject-matter of what he calls 'logic'.[2] It thus becomes natural to use 'the theory of truth', understood in analogy with 'the theory of knowledge', as a name for this branch of philosophy. Now the notion of truth, as the object of philosophical enquiry, has always been recognized by philosophers as closely allied to that of meaning. The reason is that truth attaches to what people say, and to what they may say or might have said, but not, of course, in virtue of the sounds they utter, but of the meanings attached to them. It therefore seems that, in attempting to state the general condition under which something that is or may be said will be true, we have to take its meaning as given. The attempt to do this, an attempt embodied in classic philosophical theories of truth such as the correspondence theory and the coherence theory, fell at one time into disfavour, and, in consequence, it came to be thought impossible to give a general characterization of what it is for a proposition to be true. It is a mistake, however, to suppose that there is any a priori reason for ruling out such a characterization as impossible; it may be possible or it may not be. In the language-game semantics of Hintikka, for example, if the notion of truth for atomic sentences is taken as given, that for complex sentences may be defined as the existence of a winning strategy for a player who commences by uttering the given sentence; one cannot rule this semantics out a priori on the ground that it admits a general characterization of truth. The fault of theories like the correspondence theory did not lie in attempting a general characterization of truth, but in attempting to do this without setting the notion of truth against the background of an account of meaning. The use of the word 'proposition' by

[1] *N.S.*, pp. 1–8, 137–63, 201–12; *P.W.*, pp. 1–8, 126–51, 185–96.
[2] *N.S.*, p. 139, *P.W.*, p. 128.

the philosophers who argued the rival merits of the classic theories of truth reflected their taking the meaning of an actual or possible utterance as given in the sense of simply assuming it to have some definite meaning, without offering any account of how its meaning is given or of what it is for it to have a meaning. Now, indeed, if we take meaning as given in *this* sense, and proceed to formulate a general characterization of the condition for possessing the property of being true, the best we can achieve is utter vacuity; we are more likely to fall into vicious circularity or into actual error. The remedy is to link the account of truth with an account of what, in general, it is for a sentence to have a meaning. The account of meaning that is adopted may be one for which it is necessary to *employ* the notion of truth in giving that account. It may, on the other hand, be one for which this is not necessary; and, in this case, the notion of truth will be explicable in terms of the notions which are employed in the account of meaning, as in the language-game semantics. In the former case, a philosophical elucidation of the notion of truth will involve exhibiting its role in the account of meaning; but, in either case, an account of truth will depend upon an account of meaning. For this reason, I should prefer to label this branch of philosophy 'the theory of meaning', again understood in analogy with 'the theory of knowledge', rather than 'the theory of truth'.

This choice has a disadvantage, however, in that the phrase 'a theory of meaning' has, with great utility, come to be used, not even for a particular doctrinal position within a certain branch of philosophy, but for a hypothetical theory relating to some one language and embodying a specification of the meanings of all its expressions. It was for this reason that I felt driven to relinquish the term 'the theory of meaning' for the branch of philosophy to which I intended to refer, and adopt in its place the term 'the philosophy of language', which I like much less well.

It may well be objected that either term, 'the theory of meaning' or 'the philosophy of language', begs the question, since both embody a particular view of what Frege was at, or, more generally, of how a certain range of philosophical problems should be tackled. Frege was perfectly clear about that to which truth attaches, to which the predicate 'is true' is applied: it is a thought which is the primary bearer of truth or falsity, which is, in the first place, said to be true or false; a sentence can be said to be true or false only in a derivative sense, as expressing a true or false thought. Now Frege's notion of a thought looks both ways. On the one hand, a thought is the sense of a sentence, its sense being that part of its meaning which is relevant to its truth or falsity. If we concentrate on this aspect of the notion, it will appear quite faithful to Frege to subsume the theory of truth under the theory of meaning. On the other hand, however, a thought is for Frege something eternal and immutable, which does not depend for its existence upon our either expressing it or even grasping it, nor yet upon our ability to do either. It seems to follow that, just as, since a thought exists, and is true or false, independently of our grasping it or recognizing its truth-value, an account of thought and of truth and falsity ought to make no reference to our minds, so, since a thought exists, and is true or false, independently of our expressing it, such an account ought to make no reference to our language. So regarded, what Frege called 'logic' has nothing to do with language. And that seems to accord with the sort of thing Frege sometimes says, for instance in footnote 4 of 'Der Gedanke': 'I have to content myself with presenting to the reader the thought, which is not in itself an object of the senses, wrapped in its perceptible linguistic form. The figurative nature of language gives rise to difficulties in this connection. What belongs to the senses always intrudes and makes the expression figurative rather than literal. Thus there arises a struggle with language, and I am obliged still to concern myself with language, although that is not here my proper task.'

Perhaps, then, the agreement of all might be secured for the adoption, as a neutral designation for that branch of philosophy which Frege called simply 'logic', of the term 'the philosophy of thought', which, as he would have been the first to insist, is to be sharply distinguished from a philosophical account of *thinking*. Using this terminology, we can explain how it could be that, even if Frege had not the slightest concern with the philosophy of language, his work could still present itself to subsequent philosophers of language as being so fruitful. The term 'analytical philosophy' is imprecise; the term 'linguistic philosophy', though more descriptive, is, on the other hand, tied to that quite special version of analytical philosophy which flourished at Oxford in the 1950s and 60s, so I shall use the former. The basic tenet of analytical philosophy, common to such disparate philosophers as Schlick, early and late Wittgenstein, Carnap, Ryle, Ayer, Austin, Quine and Davidson, may be expressed as being that the philosophy of thought is to be equated with the philosophy of language: more exactly, (i) an account of language does not presuppose an account of thought, (ii) an account of language yields an account of thought, and (iii) there is no other adequate means by which an account of thought may be given. Suppose, now, that Frege did make a great contribution to the philosophy of thought, but that he did not hold the basic tenet of analytical philosophy, and therefore did not regard his work as more than tangential to a philosophical account of language. Now, if the basic tenet of analytical philosophy is true, then, given that Frege's work in the philosophy of thought had great merit, it must necessarily bear on many of the proper concerns of a philosopher of language: on these hypotheses, he contributed obliquely to the philosophy of language, even though he had no intention of doing so. If, on the other hand, the basic tenet of analytical philosophy is false, the philosophy of thought being independent of and prior to the philosophy of language, those who believe otherwise are likely to occupy themselves with matters that belong properly to the former, though categorized by them as belonging to the latter. It will, therefore, still remain unsurprising that philosophers of language of the analytical tradition should find Frege's work relevant to theirs, even though they mistakenly view it through linguistic spectacles.

However Frege is to be interpreted, there will *be* such a thing as the philosophy of language, whatever its relation is, or was conceived by him to be, to the philosophy of thought. Even if a philosophy of thought is possible without appeal to language, it remains a legitimate philosophical enquiry how we contrive to express thoughts by means of language, in what their expression consists. Now, as Frege repeatedly said, the expression of a thought is a sentence; and a sentence is essentially complex, as he also said from his early period. He continued to insist that 'I do not start from the concepts and put together the thought or the judgment out of them, but I attain to the parts of the thought by decomposing the thought'.[1] But what can be analysed or decomposed must already be complex; and he said precisely this in the essay 'Booles rechnende Logik und die Begriffsschrift' of 1880–1: 'The expression of the judgeable content must, indeed, already be articulated, in order to be able to be thus analysed.'[2] 'Complex', or, as Frege says, 'articulated', does not, of course, mean merely 'made up out of distinguishable and recurrent parts', as written words are made up out of letters, or a Chinese character from a radical and other recurrent elements: it means that an apprehension of its composition out of these parts plays an essential role in our identification of the thought expressed. A sentence must be complex in this sense if, as Wittgenstein, Chomsky and others are never tired of pointing out, and as Frege himself pointed out, we are able to understand new sentences. There are therefore two possibilities. Either the sentence is understood as expressing the thought it does in virtue of its mirroring the structure of the thought; or the complexity of the sentence corresponds to the structure of the totality of thoughts,

[1] 'Aufzeichnungen für L. Darmstaedter', 1919, *N.S.*, p. 273, *P.W.*, p. 253.
[2] *N.S.*, pp. 18–19, *P.W.*, p. 17.

of what may be called the system of thoughts, as map references identify places by appeal to their spatial disposition on the surface of the globe. If I pick out Burford by means of its latitude and longitude, you will not find anything in Burford corresponding to the structure of the designation I used; but I have picked it out by reference to its location with respect to Greenwich and to the North and South Poles.

The map-reference view of language is not very plausible; but, if it were adopted, it would be necessary to say on the basis of what relations between thoughts the map reference was given, that is, the sentence indicated the thought to which it corresponded; this might, for instance, be done by reference to logical relations, of entailment, incompatibility, and so on, between thoughts. Even on this view, therefore, the philosophy of language would have some bearing on the philosophy of thought, since the structure of a sentence would reflect, not indeed the inner structure of the thought it expressed, but its logical relations to other thoughts.

As remarked, Frege's notion of sense faces in two ways. Thoughts inhabit the realm of sense, a realm not accessible to sense-perception. They are, indeed, objects. An expression like 'the principle of double effect', 'Boyle's law', 'the Riemann hypothesis' or 'Desargues's theorem' is, in Frege's terminology, a proper name; in fact, it is a proper name in an unextended sense. It therefore stands for an object. But it also stands for, though it does not express, a thought, which can be expressed by a sentence: the realm of sense is not disjoint from, but included in, the realm of reference. Now when we concentrate upon Frege's conception of thoughts as eternal and immutable objects, it appears immensely plausible that his view of language should have been the map-reference one. We have the faculty of grasping thoughts. We also have the faculty of expressing them by means of sentences and thus communicating them to one another. But they do not depend for their existence upon our either grasping or expressing them; and there therefore seems no reason to assume that our means of expressing them will reflect their internal structure. This accords very well with Frege's saying that it is the thought that is primarily said to be true or false, and the sentence only in a derivative sense. He sometimes says that a sentence *expresses* a thought and *stands for* a truth-value. But it seems that we ought not to regard it as doing both things simultaneously, as it were, that is, as being said with equal right to do each of them. Rather, it stands for a particular truth-value *in virtue of* its expressing a true or a false thought. Thus it seems that we should say that what we primarily do by means of a sentence is to express a thought, to indicate a particular one of those eternal, immutable, imperceptible objects. One of the features of thoughts is that most of them possess one of the properties of being true and of being false; if the thought expressed by the sentence has one of those properties, that property may then, in a derivative manner, be ascribed to the sentence. Analogously, a complex proper name should not be regarded as, in its own right, doing two things, expressing a sense and standing for an object. Rather, what it primarily does is to express a sense. Senses of this kind have, for the most part, the property of being associated with a particular object; in a derivative sense, the proper name may then be said to stand for this object.

This conception leaves us weltering in philosophical perplexity. It will be the task of the philosophy of language only to explain how we contrive to indicate, by means of a sentence, the thought we wish to convey. The philosophy of thought, conceived of as independent of and anterior to the philosophy of language, will have the harder task. It will have to explain in what the properties of being true and being false, possessed by the bodiless denizens of the realm of sense, consist; and, if it merely declares them unanalysable, it will surely be judged to have abdicated its responsibilities. It will have, in the same way, to explain in what that association consists between those senses that are capable of being senses of proper names and objects of various kinds that confers on a proper name the derivative property of standing for an object. If Frege is claimed to have been concerned with the philosophy of thought, so conceived, he cannot be represented as having made a great contribution to it, since these explanations are wholly lacking from his work, as also is the recognition that such explanations are called for. It may be granted that Frege did not aim to contribute to the philosophy of thinking: but this part of the subject will, on the present conception, have an equally hard task, namely to explain how we come to be able to grasp thoughts, how we know enough about them to know that they have the property of being true or that of being false, and even to judge that a particular thought has the one property or the other. When we revert to the philosophy of language, we find that it has to grapple with a special difficulty. A map reference tells you where a certain feature is, but it does not tell you what it is: to discover that, you have to go there and see. But a sentence does not merely tell you where to locate the thought in the realm of sense; it conveys the thought to you directly. It would be stretching credulity too far to maintain that, having heard and understood the sentence, the hearer has to carry out a further operation in order to grasp the thought expressed, namely to make a mental journey within the realm of sense to the site of the indicated thought: rather, he grasps the thought immediately from the sentence. It follows that, even if the sentence does not indicate the thought by appeal to its internal structure, but by reference to its relations with other thoughts, these relations must be *internal* relations in the sense that, once you know in which such relations the thought stands to others, you thereby know what the thought is. This greatly reinforces our previous conclusion that, even on the map-reference view of language, a detailed account of the way in which thoughts are determined by the structure of the sentences expressing them will throw great light on the philosophy of thought itself.

Closer scrutiny of the map-reference view of language discloses, however, that it bears no resemblance to Frege's ideas. In the first place, just because, on the map-reference view, the structure of the sentence in no way reflects the inner structure of the thought, there can be no justification for speaking of the senses of expressions smaller than whole sentences, where such senses are taken as ingredients of thoughts expressed by sentences containing those expressions; there would, for example, be no such thing as the sense of a proper name. But, from the moment when he first introduced the notion of sense, Frege not only characterized a thought as the sense of a sentence, but spoke freely of the senses of constituent parts of sentences. It was in connection with proper names that he first argued for the necessity of distinguishing sense from reference; and he held that, to every expression to which it is proper to ascribe a reference, a sense may also be attributed. He held, not merely that a thought is complex and has parts, but that the sense of the whole is compounded out of the senses of its parts, that is, that the sense of the whole expression is compounded out of the senses of its constituent parts. He spoke of the senses of proper names, of predicates (concept-words) and of functional expressions of all kinds: one of his favourite arguments that a name like 'Mont Blanc' must have a sense and not just a referent is that a mountain is not the sort of thing that can be part of a thought, an argument that has no force unless it be assumed that the name must correspond to a constituent of the thought expressed by a sentence in which it occurs. All this would be nonsense on the map-reference view of language: it would be as senseless as asking which part of Burford corresponded to the '51°', which to the '44″' and which to the 'North'.

Secondly, the map-reference view demands the introduction of a third feature of sentences, one which stands to the sense of a sentence as sense stands to reference. In effect, the map-reference view interprets the relation of expression between sentence and thought as like the relation of reference, as Frege conceived it: in accordance with a certain systematic procedure, the sentence picks out that one among the totality of thoughts which it is to convey. We might, on this conception, call the thought expressed by a sentence its *immediate* referent, distinguishing its truth-value as the *ultimate* referent. There would be no reason to regard the particular way in which a sentence picks out a thought as integral to the thought. In different languages, immediate reference might be achieved in different ways and in accordance with different principles: there might be a way of picking out thoughts by appeal to different relations between them, or one appealing to the same relations but using different co-ordinates. Even if the system of thoughts has only one relevant kind of structure, there could be different ways of determining a position within this structure, just as the chessboard remains an 8 × 8 square even though there are alternative notations for the constituent squares. It is this possibility that would force us, on this view, to acknowledge a third feature of sentences, which we might call their *significance*: the significance of a sentence would consist in the particular manner in which it indicated a specific thought. It might, perhaps, be argued that, within any one language, significance corresponded one to one with sense; but sentences in different languages could express the same thought even though their significance, the way in which they indicated the thought, differed radically. The conclusion that the parts of a sentence would not have senses, regarded as ingredients of the thought, would not entail that they did not contribute in a regular manner to the indication of the thought. On the contrary, just because the sentence is complex, because it indicates the relevant thought in accordance with a system of representation, each constituent part of the sentence would contribute in its particular way to determining what thought was expressed, just as the constituent parts of an actual map reference contribute to the meaning of the whole. This contribution would, however, constitute the *significance*, not the *sense*, of the constituent expression: it would play a role in picking out the thought expressed, but not by mirroring any component of that thought.

It is now apparent, not only that the map-reference view of language is not Frege's, but where Frege would say that it had gone wrong, namely by misconceiving the relation between sense and reference: by misconstruing sense as immediate reference, and regarding what Frege called *Bedeutung*, the ultimate reference, as being achieved only by means of a relation borne by the immediate referent to the ultimate one, a place has been left for a conception of the particular manner in which a sentence picks out a thought. But the whole point of Frege's notion of sense is that there is no place for such a conception: one and the same sense cannot be expressed now in accordance with one system, now in accordance with another. A proper name, for example, stands for an object; and the particular manner in which it does this *is* its sense. The same object may be picked out in different ways, and the different possible ways of picking it out constitute different possible senses that can be borne by different proper names all of which stand for that object: there is no room for a further notion of the particular way in which the sense of the name is picked out, because everything that belongs to the manner in which the expression functions to determine a referent is part of its sense. And what goes for a complex proper name goes also for a sentence. The sentence stands for a truth-value; and the particular manner in which it determines one or other of the two truth-values as that which attaches to it *is* the thought it expresses. That is why the way a constituent part of a sentence contributes to the condition for the sentence to be true is, as being the sense of that constituent, *part* of the thought expressed.

It therefore seems that the correct way of putting the matter is that what the proper name primarily does is to designate an object: there are different possible routes from an expression to its referent, and the route taken is the sense of the expression. In fact, however, this is not quite the right way of putting it. Frege did indeed conceive of sense as related to referent as route to terminus, as when he wrote of 'different signs for the same thing, the difference between which indicates only the different routes (*Wege*) by which one can arrive at this same thing'.[1] He does not, however, say that what the name primarily does is to stand for an object. On the contrary, when he assigns priority at all, as between sense and reference, he assigns it to the sense: the clearest such statement is in 'Über Sinn und Bedeutung', where he says, 'The regular connection between the sign, its sense and its *Bedeutung* is of such a kind that to the sign there corresponds a determinate sense and to that in turn a determinate *Bedeutung*'.[2] The most immediate indication that the formulation proposed above is unsatisfactory is that it precludes the ascription of a sense to a name lacking a referent. As has been observed by Gareth Evans, if we say that what a name primarily does is to pick out an object, and characterize its sense as the way in which it does so, then an empty name lacks a sense: there *is* no 'way in which it picks out an object', since it fails to pick one out. *Before* he drew the distinction between sense and reference, Frege seems to have favoured just such a conclusion: no. 10 of the 'Siebzehn Kernsätze zur Logik' reads 'The sentence "Leo Sachse is a man" is an expression of a thought only when "Leo Sachse" designates something.

---

[1] 'Über den Begriff der Zahl', 1891–2, *N.S.*, p. 95, *P.W.*, p. 85.
[2] 'Über Sinn und Bedeutung', p. 27.

In the same way the sentence "This table is round" is the expression of a thought only when the words "this table" designate something definite for me, and are not empty words.'[1] But, as soon as he had the sense/reference distinction, Frege allowed that a name lacking reference might still possess a sense, and hence that a sentence containing such a name might express a thought; so we cannot explain the sense of a proper name by means of the metaphor of a route, if a 'route' is understood as the path by which a particular goal was reached. More generally, it is only in exceptional cases that we can represent the speaker as having a goal given in advance, an object to which he intends to refer, and as selecting a particular route which he believes will take him to that goal. There are some such cases, which have interested Donnellan. When, in such a case, the speaker's intention miscarries, we may distinguish between the object to which his *words* referred and that to which *he* referred or intended to refer; an example in which the intention did not miscarry occurs in *Grundlagen*, § 56, where Frege, speaking of Julius Caesar, uses, for rhetorical variation, the phrase 'that famous conqueror of Gaul'. But, in general, the speaker's intention is to be seen in the words he uses: he employs an expression designed to pick out an object in a certain way, with the intention of referring to whatever object is so picked out; his intention can miscarry only if, contrary to what he supposes, no object is in fact picked out. We may continue to use the metaphor of a route, but we must not think of the route as a route to a pre-assigned goal. We may then say that what the expression primarily does is to determine the route, and that the route of itself determines its terminus, which may then by transference be associated with the expression; and we may add, with no suspicion of inconsistency, that the route may sometimes be found to lead nowhere.

The case of a complete sentence is indeed somewhat different. When the sentence is uttered assertorically, there *is* a pre-assigned goal, truth. On the other hand, this is quite unlike the exceptional kind of case in which a speaker uses a name or description with the intention of referring

---

[1] *N.S.*, p. 189, *P.W.*, p. 174. This short unpublished work is vaguely dated by the editors of *N.S.* to '1906 or earlier'; but they themselves point out that the name 'Leo Sachse', which was that of an actual high-school teacher in Jena, was also used by Frege as an example in the unpublished 'Dialog mit Pünjer über Existenz', dated to before 1884. Terminologically, the 'Kernsätze' are hard to date, since, while they use *'Dinge'* instead of *'Gegenstände'*, suggesting a date before 1884, they also use *'Gedanke'* in place of *'beurtheilbarer Inhalt'*, suggesting one after 1884. But, in view of the complete absence of the *'Sinn'/'Bedeutung'* terminology, or of the idea underlying it, I concur with Christian Thiel in regarding the 'Kernsätze' as belonging to the 1880s. This conclusion is reinforced by their being comments on Lotze's *Logik* (1874, 1880); see pp. 523–5.

to an object which he has independently in mind, for, in such a case, we may say that the speaker's only purpose was to refer to that object, and that he was indifferent to the manner in which he did this. By contrast, someone making an assertion is not concerned solely to utter a true sentence, without particularly caring what makes it the case that he said something true. This has, of course, to do with the very special role that sentences play in language, which is the reason that they ought not to be assimilated to complex proper names; truth and falsity are not just two abstract objects with equal rights, so that there could be people who went in for denial as we go in for assertion. But this gives a special point to Frege's dictum that it is the thought to which truth and falsity are primarily ascribed, the truth-value attaching to the sentence only in a derivative sense. What we must not do is to misinterpret this dictum in a manner that falsifies the principle on which Frege insisted equally, that a thought is related to its truth-value as the sense of a name is related to its referent, or in one which obscures the principle that sense is related to reference as route to terminus. It is only in this way that we can avoid the intractable problems that we saw as arising from the map-reference view of language, concerning the remarkable powers of being associated with objects in the world possessed by the senses of names, or the mysterious properties of being true and of being false with which thoughts are endowed: if the sense is a route to the referent, such problems do not arise. The condition for avoiding such pseudo-problems is to adopt just that conception of sense; a thought is then a particular means by which a truth-value is determined, not an abstract object which has some special relation to a truth-value and which we might be able to pick out in various ways, which is why, although we can refer to a thought, e.g. as 'Fermat's last theorem', without expressing it, we cannot do so without alluding indirectly to its expression. In adopting such a conception of sense, we leave no place for any idea of a route from the sentence to the thought expressed, which is to say that we reject the map-reference view of language. It is precisely because he held a quite different view of language that Frege leaves these spurious problems unmentioned.

It is plain that Frege held the alternative view of language, according to which the structure of a sentence reflects the structure of the thought that it expresses, so that the senses of the constituent parts of the sentence are parts of the thought, which is the sense of the sentence. He says so, expressly and repeatedly: one of the most explicit such statements is to be found in the 'Aufzeichnungen für Ludwig Darmstaedter', where he says, 'The sentence can be regarded as representing the thought in such a manner that, to the part/whole relation obtaining between the thought and its constituents, there by and large corresponds the same relation obtaining between the sentence and its constituents.'[1] On such a view, the philosophy of language is far more closely allied to the philosophy of thought than on the map-reference view: the analysis of the structure of sentences will give a direct insight into the structure of thoughts.

It is true that there stand opposed to this the repeated complaints Frege makes about natural language. Natural language is unsatisfactory in two ways, which Frege does not sharply distinguish. First, it is an imperfect instrument for the expression of thought. An obvious example is the occurrence of ambiguous sentences, whose ambiguity may be due to the presence of ambiguous words or to ambiguities of construction. Another example is the use of vague expressions, resulting in sentences for which it is not provided whether they are true or false. To a sentence involving these or like defects, there will be no corresponding formula in Frege's symbolic notation, since that notation is free of the ambiguity, vagueness and other imperfections that disfigure natural language.

Secondly, natural language is not perspicuous: the surface form of the sentence does not reveal its true structure. This is, of course, a very familiar idea to us. Chomsky and other linguists hold that it must be adopted even for an account of syntax: the formation of sentences must be explained as taking place in two principal stages, at the first of which the 'deep structure' is formed, which is then converted into the surface form of the sentences we actually utter by various rules of transformation. Frege, however, does not propound any theory of the syntactical structure of the sentences of natural language, and so we must ask what it means to speak of that structure which corresponds to the structure of the thought expressed but is not perspicuously revealed by the superficial form of the sentence. In talking of structure in this sense, we are concerned with the *dependence* of the sense of one expression upon that of another. To know which thought a sentence expresses, we have to grasp how its sense depends upon the senses of its parts; but the grammatical form of the sentence does not reveal what, for this purpose, are to be taken as being the parts of the sentence. In a statement of Euclid's theorem, 'Every number is less than some prime', the expression 'Every number is less than . . .' is not, in this sense, a part of the sentence; the thought expressed by the whole does not depend on it, but does depend on the sense of '. . . is less than some prime'. The metaphor of the step-by-step construction of sentences, as employed in

[1] *N.S.*, p. 275, *P.W.*, p. 255.

Chapter 2 of *FPL*, was not intended as a contribution to a syntactical theory; it was meant to explain Frege's account of what is involved in grasping the thought expressed by a complex sentence. It is in terms of the notion of dependence of sense that the metaphor is to be cashed: the sense of the complex sentence depends in a certain manner on the senses of those atomic sentences from which we may metaphorically represent it as having been built up. The representation of these relations of dependence might be called the 'essential structure' of the sentence: it is only by reference to it that we can explain how the sentence is determined as true or as false in accordance with its composition. The precise means by which we discriminate the essential structure of a sentence of natural language from others that might seem possible from its surface appearance do not interest Frege, since he does not regard them as contributing to the sense; the syntactical form of a formula of his symbolic notation reveals its essential structure perspicuously. But, in so far as the sentence of natural language expresses a definite thought, the corresponding symbolic formula displays a structure already present in the sentence.

Some might want to propose that intuition is required to apprehend the essential structure of a sentence of natural language, and, thereby, to know how to represent it in Frege's symbolic notation. It is wrong for a philosopher to entertain a superstitious horror of the notion of intuition; but this is a case in which an appeal to it is useless. Either there are linguistic conventions which determine how the sentence is to be understood, or it is ambiguous; for instance, either it is impossible to understand 'Every number is smaller than some prime' and 'Some prime is larger than every number' as equivalent, in which case we must be capable of formulating the rules that render it impossible, or at least one of the sentences must be ambiguous. In the former case, no appeal to intuition is needed, unless such an appeal is taken as involved in tacit compliance with a statable rule; and, in the latter case, no appeal to intuition will be of any help, since there is no fact to be intuited.

None of this amounts to an equation between the philosophy of thought and the philosophy of language: it demonstrates only a close relation between them, since they analyse isomorphic structures. Presumably, if a philosophy of thought independent of the philosophy of language is possible, it will, when sufficiently developed, provide a means of indicating a specific thought and talking about its structure without reference to, that is, without citing, its linguistic expression. But Frege attempts no such thing. He alludes to particular thoughts only by citing their expression either in symbolic notation or in natural language. In the latter case, he complains of the imperfections of the expression, as in the footnote from 'Der Gedanke' cited above; but the burden of the complaint is that he cannot escape attending to these imperfections, since he can reach the thought only via its linguistic expression. In an essay of 1882, 'Über die wissenschaftliche Berechtigung einer Begriffsschrift', Frege gave it as his view that we can think only by means of words or symbols.[1] This remained his constant view: in the unpublished 'Logik' of 1897 he remarked that 'we think in some language or other',[2] and in the likewise unpublished 'Erkenntnisquellen der Mathematik' of 1924–5 he says expressly that it is a necessity for human beings, if they are to grasp a thought, to clothe it in the sensible form of a sentence that expresses it.[3] It thus appears that, for him, the philosophy of thought and of language are not merely closely related, but indissolubly entangled with one another: they can be pursued only simultaneously.

A thought may have a property that we do not recognize it as having: it may, for instance, be analytic, although we have discovered no proof of it. But Frege's conception of thoughts as existing independently of us prompts us to enquire what *sorts* of properties they can have; can they have properties of which we have no conception, or which we have no means of recognizing? May a thought have spin, for example, or possess a magnetic field, or some non-physical analogue of these physical properties? The suggestion is absurd; and it is only slightly less absurd to attribute to Frege a conception of thoughts that would make such a suggestion possible. The particular means by which we express a thought, the particular conditions necessary for us to grasp it, may be adventitious, may not reflect anything intrinsic to the thought. The notion of sense is nevertheless correlative to those of expressing a sense and of grasping it; a sense cannot have any features not discernible by reflection on or deduction from what is involved in expressing it or in grasping it. Only that belongs to the sense of an expression which is relevant to the determination of the truth-value of a sentence in which it occurs; if we fail to grasp some features of its contribution to the truth-conditions of certain sentences, then we fail fully to grasp its sense, while, on the other hand, any aspect of its meaning that does not bear on the truth-conditions of sentences containing it is no part of its sense. It cannot be, therefore, that the sense has all sorts of other features, not detectable by us. If those features bore on the truth-values of sentences containing the expression, then, since we could not

[1] Pp. 49–50 (*B.a.A.*, pp. 107–8); *C.N.*, p. 84.

[2] *N.S.*, p. 154, *P.W.*, p. 142.

[3] *N.S.*, p. 288, *P.W.*, p. 269.

detect them, the expression would have a sense which we could never fully grasp; if they did not, they could not be features of the *sense*. A thought is, for Frege, an eternal object, existing independently of us: but this does not annul our right to draw conclusions about its constitution from what is involved in grasping it. A thought is transparent in the sense that, if you grasp it, you thereby know everything to be known about it as it is in itself. You may not know whether it is true, for that depends on how the world is; nor whether it is believed, for that depends on its relation to thinkers; nor whether it is analytic, for that depends on its deductive relations to other thoughts: but it can have no further internal properties of which you lack all conception.

Can we go further and characterize Frege as an analytical philosopher in the sense explained? It is not essential to analytical philosophy to hold that a thought, or a constituent of a thought, can be grasped, even by us, only *as* the sense of a linguistic expression. Frege did hold that it can be grasped only so *by us*. It would, however, be at odds with his conception of sense as existing independently of us to ascribe to him the view that the sense of a word can no more be conceived otherwise than as the sense of some word than the power of a chess piece can be conceived otherwise than as the power of a piece in a game; and, in the passage already quoted from the late 'Erkenntnisquellen der Mathematik', he says explicitly that it is not a contradiction to assume the existence of beings who can grasp the same thought as we do, without needing to clothe it in sensible form.[1] But that does not put him at variance with the fundamental tenet of analytical philosophy. The crucial question is, rather, in what our attaching a sense to a word consists. Assume, for the sake of argument, that we can attribute a grasp of that sense—a grasp of the concept, in a non-Fregean sense of 'concept'—to an individual antecedently to his acquisition of language. When he acquires language, he comes to associate that sense with the word: and now we have to ask what it is to associate the sense with the word. We might think of it as an inner mental connection: when he hears the word, that sense comes into his mind. This, however, is opposed to all that Frege says about senses. A sense is not a mental content, like an idea (*Vorstellung*) or an image: there is no such process as a sense's coming into the mind, and, when we try to conceive of it, we fall back on the coming to mind of some representative of the concept, a mental picture or the word itself. Moreover, this account runs foul of Frege's attack on psychologism, which is wrong because it makes sense subjective.

---

[1] *N.S.*, p. 288, *P.W.*, p. 269.

If this associationist explanation were right, then I should have to take it on trust that you understand me as I intend to be understood, that you associate the same sense with the word as I do. You may, of course, in fact understand the word differently: but, since sense is objective, this is something in principle discoverable, whose falsity therefore does not *have* to be taken on trust.

The solution offered by analytical philosophy is that what constitutes the speaker's attaching a particular sense to the word is his *using* the word —more exactly, using sentences containing the word—in a particular way. In describing this use, we can take no advantage of a prior grasp of that sense by the speaker; even if we assume that he could be said to grasp it, and in fact did so, before he acquired language, we are unable to make any use of that assumption in giving an account of what constitutes his treating the word as bearing that sense. Furthermore, our account of his use of the word will, by itself, be a sufficient explanation of his grasp of its sense, that is, in non-Fregean terminology, of his grasp of the concept. A grasp of a concept may be manifested in different ways; and one such manifestation, adequate in itself to ground an attribution to someone of a grasp of the concept, is the use of a word which, in the language to which it belongs, expresses that concept. Hence an account of language will, by itself, be an account of thought: even if an account of thought, independent of language, is possible, it is unnecessary, since an account of language, the provision of which is a legitimate philosophical demand, can make no appeal to it. If, now, it be granted that there are *some* thoughts which we cannot grasp save as expressible in language, the fundamental tenet of analytical philosophy is established: the only way in which we can give a philosophical account of thought is by giving an account of language.

Now, it may be urged, Frege got as far as recognizing the inadequacy of the associationist explanation, but he did not take the next step. His recognition that senses are not inner mental contents was one of his principal motives for locating them outside the mind in a special compartment of reality independent of our apprehension of it: grasping a thought, or judging it to be true, was for him an act of the mind, but the thought itself was external to the mind. Only so did he think that he could safeguard the objectivity of sense: and that was precisely because he did not have the idea of identifying the sense of a word with its observable use.

Frege's view of senses as existing eternally and independently of us can seem bizarre until we recall our propensity to think in the same way of proofs of mathematical propositions. It is natural to think, of a given mathematical proposition, that either a proof of it exists or no such proof exists, where 'proof' here means any intuitively valid proof, not just one in some fixed formal system. The existence in question is a timeless existence, independent of whether we ever discover the proof or not; and so the proof itself, which is just an array of interrelated propositions or thoughts, is likewise conceived of as an eternal object whose *esse* is not *concipi*. Now no doubt part of Frege's motive for adopting this view of senses is to safeguard their objectivity, given his belief that mental images and other mental contents are subjective and not fully communicable. But that cannot be the end of the matter, because it leaves the original question unanswered, namely in what a speaker's attaching a given sense to a word consists. An associationism which connected the word with an act of adverting to something external to the mind, though apprehended by it, would be little improvement on the version which took the sense to be a mental content: even though the sense itself would be objective, the theory would be open to the same objection as before, that it rendered the attachment to the word of that particular sense subjective. It is no compliment to Frege to suggest that he overlooked this point; it is, more-over, an error, since he raised this precise point in 'Über Sinn und Bedeu-tung'.[1] There he considers the objection that, just as different people may connect different ideas with a word, so they may attach different senses to it; and his answer is that there is a 'difference in the mode of connection' in the two cases. It is sometimes possible to establish a difference in the ideas that two people have, but an exact comparison is impossible: the implication is that it is *always* possible to establish conclusively whether or not two people attach the same sense to a word, and what senses they attach to it when these are different. We might wish that Frege had said more on this matter; but we are debarred from interpreting him in a way that would make comparison between the senses attached to a word by different speakers impossible in principle. We know, moreover, what, in his mature period, Frege took the sense of an expression to consist in: it is, namely, the manner in which the referent of the expression is given. The sense of the expression constitutes its contribution to the thought expressed by a sentence in which it occurs.[2] The referents of the constituent parts of the sentence jointly fix its truth-value; and the thought expressed by the sentence is the thought that the condition for it to be true is fulfilled.[3] This condition depends upon the way in which

[1] Pp. 29–30.
[2] *Grundgesetze*, vol. I, § 32.
[3] Ibid.

the referents of the constituent parts of the sentence are given. Hence to grasp the sense of a word is to comprehend its contribution to fixing the condition for any sentence containing it to be true. This conception of sense makes it at least plausible that what sense a speaker attaches to a word is objectively ascertainable by other speakers; there is therefore no warrant for ascribing to Frege a view of senses that would make it a mystery how anyone could discover this about anyone else.

How close is the conception of sense as contributing to truth-conditions to the idea of meaning as exhibited by observable use? To obtain the latter from the former, we should have to say that what a speaker takes the truth-condition of a sentence to be is manifested by the use he makes of that sentence and of others containing words occurring in it. No statement of this thesis is to be found in Frege; but it is difficult to frame a consistent interpretation of him which conflicts with it. For him, thoughts are contrasted with mental images and the like in being wholly communicable. I do not, by means of my utterances, merely convey something of what my thoughts are like: I communicate those very thoughts themselves. At least, this is what Frege says most of the time. It is true that, in 'Der Gedanke', he entertains the notion of a private incommunicable sense; but even there he insists that the sense of a sentence addressed to another must be a communicable thought. A sentence has a communicable sense if speaker and hearer take it as expressing the very same thought: as Frege makes plain, it is not sufficient that each should attach to it his own private sense, with a presumption that the two private senses are suitably analogous. How is this communicability of thoughts secured? It is not enough that thoughts themselves should be objective: it must also be an objective, that is, an objectively ascertainable, matter that a given speaker attaches a certain sense to a sentence, that is, regards its truth-value as being determined in a particular way. But the thought is communicated by the mere utterance of the sentence, unaided by any other contact between mind and mind. It would therefore appear to follow that the sense which a speaker attaches to a sentence must be ascertainable from his observable behaviour, from what he says and does. Frege does not spell out this conclusion: but any alternative to it appears to run foul of his rejection of psychologism and his insistence on the objectivity and communicability of thoughts.

An explicit adherence to the fundamental tenet of analytical philosophy thus cannot be claimed for Frege; but what can be claimed is that his philosophy of thought and of language leads almost inexorably in that direction. However this may be, the attempt to construe him as altogether

unconcerned with language is quite wrong-headed. Thoughts exist independently of us: but, before this thesis can be stated, let alone evaluated,
we must know what a thought is. One explanation would be that a thought
is what is said to be true or false; but this would not rule out our counting
a coin, or a friend, as a thought. We have to say that a thought is what
is conveyed by a sentence if we wish to pick out the relevant applications
of 'true' and 'false'. Frege puts a particular interpretation upon this, identifying what a sentence conveys with a certain aspect of its meaning, an
identification that is plausible because what is conveyed by a sentence
depends upon, and only upon, its meaning. It is indeed difficult to answer
the question of how the notion of meaning is related to that of understanding,
and that in turn to the notion of knowledge. Is understanding a language
a case of knowledge properly so called? To explain what meaning is, do
we have to explain in what an individual speaker's understanding of a
language consists? Whatever the answers to these questions, it is plain
that an understanding of an expression is a grasp of its meaning; so an
account of what is grasped by one who understands it is an account of its
meaning. Our only access to the general notion of a thought, to that which
is in the relevant sense said to be true or false, is via that of the meaning
of a sentence; our only access to particular thoughts is via their linguistic
expression. Frege thought that there were good grounds for holding that
that which is grasped as the sense attached to an expression exists independently of its being the sense of any expression. We have no warrant to
infer from this that, for him, it may have properties irrelevant to the meaning
of an expression whose sense it is or to what is involved in our grasping
it; he did not even think that *we* could grasp it otherwise than as the sense
of some expression. Whether or not Frege is to be regarded as an analytical
philosopher, he was without question a philosopher of language; construing
him otherwise will make nonsense of his doctrines.

CHAPTER 4

Idealism

CHAPTER 19 OF *FPL* presents a particular assessment of the significance of Frege's work to philosophy in general, both for us at the present time and in the long term. On this view, its significance lies principally in a change of perspective, an altered conception of the starting-point of philosophy and of the relations of dependence between the different parts of the subject. This shift of perspective has now been effected, at least among philosophers of the analytical tradition, and governs our whole approach to philosophy; I argued that it was Frege who was the first to execute it. It may be suggested that phenomenology involves a similar shift of perspective. If so, Frege deserves a large share of the credit for that, too, since it was surely the power of his attack on the psychologism of Husserl's *Philosophie der Arithmetik* of 1891 that induced Husserl to reject psychologism and, in his *Logische Untersuchungen* of 1900–1, to make his rejection of it a fundamental thesis of his philosophy. But, in his later work, Husserl slipped back into something rather hard to distinguish from psychologism; and the reason for this is precisely that the study of essences is not grounded on a philosophy of language.

Husserl was a pupil of Brentano, and Brentano is celebrated for having insisted upon the directedness, or what he called the intentionality, of mental acts: one cannot simply be afraid, but, if afraid at all, must be afraid *of* something; one cannot simply be amused, but only amused *at* something; one does not just experience pleasure, but takes pleasure *in* something. The relation between object and act is, in these cases, an internal, not a causal, one. One who is amused must be able to say at what he is amused; if it merely happens that something, say being tickled, causes one to laugh, that does not constitute the cause of the laughter an object of amusement. One thing, say an injection, might cause one to be amused at something quite different, say the doctor's face; and, when there is no object of amusement, the laughter is not expressive of amusement, as with the laughter that results from being tickled, which may not be amusing at all, but only annoying. But, although the relation of object to act is in this sense internal, Brentano, as a realist, resisted the conclusion that the intentional object is in the mind; on the contrary, it is part of an objective external reality. If the doctor's face amuses me, it is really his face, something that exists independently of myself, at which I am amused, and not some mental representation of it. Indeed, anxious to avoid the conception which notoriously leads to sceptical problems or to idealism, that of mental contents—sense-impressions and the like—which are the *immediate* objects of our awareness, Brentano, in opposition to philosophers such as Lotze, refused to admit that a mental act, whether an act of perception or any other, had any inner object distinct from the external one, namely a mental representation (*Vorstellung*) by which the external object was presented to the mind: for him, there was, on the contrary, only the mental *act*, the direct object of which was the external one.[1] In this, he differed from Frege, who did recognize such entities as 'ideas' (*Vorstellungen*), distinct from acts of the mind and comprising an inner world, 'a world of sense-impressions, of creations of the imagination, of sensations, of feelings and moods, a world of inclinations, wishes and decisions', as he said in 'Der Gedanke',[2] adding that he understood the word '*Vorstellung*' as applying to all of these with the exception of decisions.

Brentano's position evidently creates a problem concerning those cases in which someone thinks he perceives, or, again, is (say) frightened of, something that is not really there, for instance when a child is frightened of the lion that he falsely imagines to be lurking under his bed. Brentano did not succeed in resolving this problem. Meinong admitted a distinction between content and object not allowed by Brentano, but not for the purpose of handling the present problem, which, instead, he dealt with by distinguishing between being and existence. For him, existence was a property that some objects have and others lack: there really is a lion under the bed, not merely in the child's mind, which is the object of the child's fear; it merely happens to lack the property of existence. Husserl resolved the problem differently, namely by generalizing Frege's distinction between sense and reference to all mental acts. What corresponds to sense he called the *noema*. Directedness is characteristic of the *noema*, as it is of sense. It is intrinsic to sense that it is related to a referent (of the

---

[1] See Franz Brentano, *Psychology from an Empirical Standpoint* (1874), ed. O. Kraus, trans. L. McAlister, London, 1973, p. 79.

[2] P. 66.

appropriate logical type), and it is because reference primarily attaches to the sense of an expression that the expression may derivatively be said to have a reference. Likewise, it is intrinsic to the *noema* that it be directed towards an object, and it is in virtue of its being so directed that the mental act is said to have an object. But, just as the sense of a proper name may purport to stand for an object, although there is in fact no object fulfilling the condition for being its referent, so the same can be true of the *noema*: a mental act must always be informed by a *noema*, which is not itself the object of the act, but that in virtue of which it has an object; but it need not always have an actual intentional object, though, when it does not, our consciousness will be exactly *as if* it did.[1]

In the second of the two essays just cited, Føllesdal quotes Husserl[2] as explicitly characterizing the notion of the *noema* as a 'generalization of the notion of meaning to the realm of all acts'. For Frege, to attempt such a generalization would have been completely wrong-headed. To be sure, any account either of perception or of mental acts possessing intentionality must admit a vague analogy if it is to avoid appealing to Meinong's distinction between being and existence and so countenance non-existent objects and yet to acknowledge any contrast between consciousness and the external world. But, taken as more than a vague analogy, the generalization destroys what Frege regarded as the unique characteristics of senses. For Husserl, a *noema* is a structure of our consciousness, whereas, for Frege, senses are *not* in any way mental contents, but objects independent of the mind to which the mind is related; they are not themselves the objects to which we refer, when we refer to objects, except when we employ *oratio obliqua* constructions or happen to talk directly about senses, but their existence is as objective and independent of our thinking as are those objects to which, by using expressions bearing the appropriate senses, we do refer. Senses inhabit what, in 'Der Gedanke', Frege called the 'third realm', as opposed both to 'ideas', i.e. mental contents, and to the things which belong to the realm of reference, those things we talk about. A sense differs from an idea precisely in having no bearer; an idea must be my idea or your idea or someone else's, but the senses of the words we use in communication are not mine or yours,

---

[1] For a clear account of all this, see Dagfinn Føllesdal, 'Brentano and Husserl on Intentional Objects and Perception', *Grazer philosophische Studien*, vol. 5, 1978, pp. 83–94, and 'Husserl and Heidegger on the Role of Actions in the Constitution of the World', in E. Saarinen, R. Hilpinen, I. Niiniluoto and M. Provence Hintikka (eds.), *Essays in Honour of Jaakko Hintikka*, Dordrecht, 1979, pp. 365–78.

[2] P. 366.

but something independent of us both. To attempt to generalize the notion of sense to all mental acts is to obliterate what was, to Frege, the crucial distinction between senses and ideas; and so, if Frege followed Husserl's later philosophical career, in particular if he read the *Ideen* of 1913, it can have been no surprise to him that Husserl relapsed into something indistinguishable from transcendental idealism, of which he claimed phenomenonology to be the first scientific version.

The relation between act and object is not, of course, the same for all the phenomena classified by philosophers as mental acts or mental states. When someone is surprised by or alarmed at something, he takes it for granted that the thing which surprises or alarms him is there and is as he supposes it to be, and his surprise or alarm would evaporate if he found that he was mistaken; but, while no one can simply expect or hope without expecting, or hoping for, something, even if he is merely hoping for the best, there is no presumption that expectations will be fulfilled or hopes satisfied. If, however, perception and memory are classed as mental acts, as they were by Husserl, as by Brentano, the relation between act and object ceases, in these cases, to be internal in the same straightforward sense. When someone is surprised by something, he of course assumes that what surprises him is really there, but he does not take his surprise as a ground for supposing it to be there. It is intrinsic to the notion of perception, on the other hand, that taking oneself to perceive something provides a reason, though not in all instances an overriding reason, for supposing it to be there and to be as one perceives it. It is not, indeed, part of the concept of perception that the object perceived actually be the cause of one's perceptions: as remarked by John Foster, someone who accepted the occasionalist theory of Malebranche, that God, rather than the objects perceived, is the immediate cause of our perceptions, but that He arranges those perceptions to conform to the objects which do as a matter of fact surround us, would not have overthrown the concept of perception, since perceiving something would still supply him with a reason for taking it to be there. This feature of the concept of perception thus does not require, but most certainly allows, the relation between perception and its object to be causal, although, of course, not everything that causes a genuine or spurious perception counts as an object of that perception; and something similar holds in the case of memory, which is why these 'mental acts', unlike the others so far mentioned, are channels of information.

This diversity among 'mental acts' makes it particularly unlikely that the relation between act and object is to be explained uniformly for all cases by a generalization of the notion of sense. For Frege, the analogy with sense could be fruitful only if it ceased to be an analogy, that is, if the mental act were taken to involve having a thought, and so to constitute or comprise a 'propositional attitude': in such a case, the intentional object would be the referent of a constituent of the thought, and the instances in which the object was not really there would be those in which the thought contained a part lacking a reference. On the face of it, such a thesis would be plausible in some cases, such as expectation and regret, and implausible in others, such as aversion, adoration, and, in particular, perception. In 'Der Gedanke', however, Frege makes some remarks which, though vague, suggest that he would have applied the thesis to *all* mental acts, including perception; or, at least, that he thought that every mental act, in so far as it has an intentional object, involves the grasping of a sense, if not in every case of a complete thought. He remarks[1] that to have visual impressions is not yet, by itself, to see things: what is needed, in addition, is something non-sensible, that is, something that belongs to the realm of thoughts and their constituent senses. He does not attempt to work this out into an actual theory of the epistemology of perception, to which branch of philosophy this late essay is his closest approach, so it is impossible to say whether he thought that every perception involved a judgment, or merely that perception is informed by concepts, in a non-Fregean sense of this word, that is, by the senses of concept-words in his sense and of relation-words.

However this may be, Frege's theory of sense admits of being *applied* to the explanation of certain 'mental acts', and possibly, on the view hinted at in 'Der Gedanke', to all of them; but it does not admit of being *generalized* to them in the way Husserl attempted to do. The relation of the sense of an expression to its referent is unique, because of the way in which that relation is to be explained, an explanation which must, in accordance with the context principle, display the sense of that expression as its contribution to the senses of sentences containing it. Nothing which was not capable of being the sense of a linguistic expression could bear even an analogous relation to an external object. The cases in which there is an intuitive analogy will be precisely those in which it is plausible to say that a thought, expressible by a sentence, is involved, and in which, therefore, no generalization is required and no analogy need be invoked, since the relation in such cases will just be that between sense and referent. For this reason, the analytical tradition of philosophy, of which Frege

---

[1] P. 75.

is the grandfather, took quite a different course from the phenomenologists in the study of philosophical psychology, and, in this, was loyal to Frege's ideas. For it, the correct approach was not to try to generalize notions proper to the philosophy of language so as to be capable of application to the whole heterogeneous range of what philosophers classify as mental acts, including perception, thereby diluting those notions and robbing them of explanatory power, but to give an account of such mental acts by giving an account of the associated parts of language: utterances by which mental acts and mental states are evinced, and those by which one speaker ascribes a mental act or state to someone else. For analytical philosophy, the philosophy of language is not an exemplar for other parts of philosophy, but their base.

My judgment regarding Frege's significance in the history of philosophy was that his principal achievement consisted in a shift of perspective which displaced epistemology from its position as the starting-point of all philosophy. Some have sought to confute this judgment by pointing out that he was directly concerned, in his philosophy of mathematics, with questions of justification. The impression that I thought otherwise would never have arisen if I had done what I originally intended, and published a book dealing simultaneously with Frege's philosophy of language and his philosophy of mathematics, or if I had not been hampered by other work in completing the companion volume, the end of which is now in sight, on the latter subject. But, even in *FPL*, I gave clear indications that I was not advocating the view that Frege was indifferent to questions of justification. On p. 117 of *FPL* I pointed out that, for Frege, the status of a truth, as analytic, synthetic a priori or a posteriori, depended on the kind of justification that could be given for it, and was therefore an epistemic notion; and, naturally, I am well aware that the declared aim of *Grundlagen* is to demonstrate that the truths of arithmetic are analytic. On p. 679 of *FPL* I recalled the repeated emphasis, in that book, on the cognitive character of Frege's notion of sense, and contrasted this with the excessive purge, in Wittgenstein's *Tractatus*, of all epistemic notions as belonging to the province of psychology. In *Tractatus* 4.1121, Wittgenstein criticizes psychologism in the same manner as Frege, saying that, in regarding the study of thought-processes as essential to the philosophy of logic, philosophers became entangled in inessential psychological investigations; and he couples this with the observation that 'epistemology is the philosophy of psychology'. This was not Frege's view of epistemology: on the contrary, he concluded his review in 1885 of Cohen's *Das Prinzip der Infinitesimalmethode* by agreeing with the author 'that knowledge as a mental process does not form the subject-matter of epistemology, and hence that psychology is to be sharply separated from epistemology'. To say, as I did, that Frege displaced epistemology from its position as the starting-point of philosophy is not at all to say that he took no interest in it. In the unpublished 'Logik' of the 1880s, written at about the same time as the Cohen review, Frege says that we can sometimes justify our recognition of a truth by appeal to other already recognized truths, but that, if we are to be able to recognize truth at all, this cannot be the only kind of justification; it is the task of logic to enquire into justifications of the former kind, that of epistemology to enquire into justifications of other sorts.[1] He himself was obviously concerned primarily with logical, that is, deductive, justifications, such as he believed could be provided for arithmetic. To take epistemology as the starting-point of philosophy, even construed as embracing all justifications of whatever type, is to assume that questions concerning what we know and what is the basis of that knowledge can be discussed in advance of an analysis of the meanings of the sentences that express that knowledge. Frege, on the contrary, did not think that we could profitably undertake to enquire into the justification for our acceptance of the basic laws of arithmetic, and of the theorems provable from them, without first achieving a thorough analysis of the meanings of the statements in which those laws and theorems are expressed. This was, for him, a deep investigation, not a mere preliminary clarification of terminology; moreover, it rested on the foundation of a general account of meaning. In everyday life, we should rightly be impatient if, on asking someone what he meant by a word he had used or a sentence he had uttered, we were to receive in reply a challenge first to say what meaning is. But, when a philosophical account of the meaning of some expression or form of sentence is called for, one cannot be sure of giving a correct answer, or even one that has the right form, unless one has a satisfactory general theory of meaning, unless one can say what it is for a word or sentence to have a meaning.

The task that Frege set himself, at least from the time when he wrote *Begriffsschrift*, was to uncover the foundations of number theory and analysis. From the outset, he saw, as required for this task, the construction of a logic in the narrow sense of the word, that is, a theory of deductive reasoning. This logic should be adequate at least for the inferences that occur in mathematics, and should be embodied in a symbolic language in which mathematical statements could actually be expressed, so that,

[1] *N.S.*, p. 3, *P.W.*, p. 3.

in this language, mathematical reasoning could be carried out in a manner that admitted no uncertainty as to the cogency of the proofs. But it was not logic in this narrower sense which Frege induced us to treat as the foundation of the rest of philosophy. We have seen that, in the 'Logik' of the 1880s, Frege treats logic in this sense as on the same level as epistemology. If there are to be truths known by us at all, there must be judgments whose justification, if indeed they need any, must rest on something other than previous judgments, since any chain of inference must begin with some premisses; and it is the task of epistemology to investigate such non-inferential grounds for the recognition of truth. Logic, on the other hand, he characterizes as concerned with justifications that invoke previously recognized truths. In the course of his investigations, however, Frege found himself driven into enquiries into the general theory of meaning, which he also called 'logic', in a much broader sense of the word. He was driven to conduct researches into this part of philosophy precisely because he perceived the necessity for a foundation in the theory of meaning for his studies in the foundations of arithmetic. It is this part of philosophy which Frege treated as fundamental to all the rest; and it is his work in this area that explains his enormous importance even for philosophers who are not, as I happen to be, particularly interested in the philosophy of mathematics.

There is a further difference between Frege's approach and that of most empiricist or idealist philosophers. When epistemology is treated as the starting-point of philosophy, this is usually because it is believed that no advance can be made until the answer has been found to sceptical arguments which purport to demonstrate that we cannot know certain general propositions for which common sense does not bother to seek a justification, such as that not only I am conscious, that the world has not only just come into being and that we can know something of its past, and, above all, that there is an objective reality external to us, about which we receive information through our senses and can make judgments. Frege's investigations into arithmetic are not of this character. He maintained, indeed, that no justification had been provided where one was called for, and set himself to remedy this lack; but he was not involved in trying first to overcome a sceptical argument that there could be no justification and that we did not know what we supposed ourselves to know. Frege displays very little interest in such scepticism; almost the only one of his writings that attempts to tackle it is 'Der Gedanke'. Most of the time, he simply ignores it, arguing, indeed, that what we say cannot, in general, be regarded as referring to our ideas, but must be taken as intended to refer to what is objective and external to us, but simply assuming, without argument, that this intention is capable of being fulfilled and, in the normal case, is fulfilled.

What Frege did repeatedly attack was psychologism, the explanation of logical laws as governing the process of thinking, and of the meanings of words and sentences as mental contents. He attacked it as destructive of objectivity, and hence as entailing idealism. Thus, in the Preface to *Grundgesetze*, vol. I, he takes Benno Erdmann's *Logik* of 1892 as representative of what he calls 'the dominant logic',[1] and remarks that it is 'infected through and through with psychology'; he argues that, under this psychologistic interpretation of logic, 'everything drifts into idealism',[2] and says, of Erdmann himself, that 'he is therefore an idealist'.[3] Likewise, in the unpublished 'Logik' of 1897, he says that 'Psychological treatments of logic have their basis in the mistake that a thought . . . is something psychological like an idea (*Vorstellung*)', and remarks that this mistake 'then necessarily leads to epistemological idealism'.[4] Psychologism cannot, on his view, account for the objective validity of arguments; if my thinking processes differ from yours, or human ones from Martian ones, then validity for me may fail to coincide with validity for you, validity for human beings with validity for Martians; there would be no standard by which one could be deemed right as opposed to the other. In the same way, psychologism destroys objective truth: the truth of a thought can no longer be distinguished from its being recognized as true, whereas, according to Frege, 'being true is something different from being taken to be true . . . and is in no way to be reduced to it'.[5] Psychologism destroys the objectivity of thought itself: sense ceases to be objective or even communicable; I can no more convey my thoughts to you than I can share with you my mental images or sensations. 'No one has another's idea (*Vorstellung*), but only his own,' he wrote in his review of Husserl,[6] 'and no one so much as knows how far his idea—of red, for example—agrees with that of another; for I cannot express the particularity of the idea which I associate with the word "red". . . . It is quite otherwise with thoughts: one and the same thought can be grasped by many people.' So, if a thought is an idea, and hence one of the contents of an individual consciousness, then the same sentence would express a different thought

---

[1] P. xiv.
[2] P. xix.
[3] P. xxi.
[4] *N.S.*, p. 155, *P.W.*, p. 143.
[5] *Grundgesetze*, vol. I, p. xv.
[6] P. 317.

to different people, each having his own thoughts which he could not share with others, and, as Frege remarks in 'Der Gedanke',[1] we ought not to speak of 'the theorem of Pythagoras', but only of 'my Pythagorean theorem', 'your Pythagorean theorem', and so on. Of course, if sense is not objective, there can be no objective truth: if the same sentence conveys different thoughts to different speakers, there is no possibility of asking whether 'the' thought expressed by it is true. There are, nevertheless, two distinct arguments against psychologism here, from the objectivity of truth and from the objectivity of sense, since the converse inference, from the latter to the former, requires strong assumptions if it is to go through. From the fact that a sentence expresses the very same thought to all who understand the language, it by no means immediately follows that we possess any notion of truth for it distinct from that of its being generally taken to be true: in order to arrive at that conclusion, we need some powerful pre-supposition about the kind of sense that a sentence can have, and how that is related to truth and falsity. Frege drew no careful distinction between these two arguments; for him, the objectivity of sense and the objectivity of truth were both threatened by psychologism, and were both vital to maintain. If we are to resist idealism, if we are to preserve the conviction that there is an objective reality about which we judge and which renders our judgments true or false independently of our recognition of their truth-values, and that we can communicate our judgments to one another, then, on his view, we must reject psychologism *in toto*.

The last paragraph of Chapter 19 of *FPL*, and of the book, set out the view that, although Frege was indeed a realist, and although he himself regarded this as an essential and important ingredient of his philosophy, as of course it was, it is not in it that his most significant contribution to philosophy lay, but, rather, in the shift of perspective mentioned above. The question then arises what is the relation between these two aspects of Frege's philosophy. It was argued, on the last page of *FPL*, that they are independent: the recognition of the theory of meaning as the foundation for the rest of philosophy in no way entails the adoption of a realist view. On the contrary, the issue between realism and idealism or other varieties of anti-realism remains, after such a recognition, as live as ever, but is transformed into an issue concerning the kind of meanings we succeed in conferring on our statements, that is, on the form which a correct theory of meaning should take; metaphysics is then itself seen to rest on logic, where the term 'logic' is used in the broad sense employed by Frege.

[1] P. 68.

But, in the same final paragraph, I also expressed the opinion that, in order to have effected the shift in perspective, it was probably at the time psychologically necessary for Frege to have been, as he was, a realist. The reason is that, not only was Frege right to have argued that psychologism leads to idealism, but the converse is also true: idealism gives an impetus towards psychologism.

This is very clearly seen in the work of the founder of intuitionism, L. E. J. Brouwer: as platonism is merely realism in respect of mathematical objects and structures, so constructivism, of which intuitionism is one variety, is merely idealism in respect of mathematics. So regarded, intuitionism is the most thoroughly thought-through presentation of idealism in modern philosophy. The gap on which Frege insisted between truth and the recognition of truth is precisely what Brouwer rejected, at least for mathematical statements: on his view, we have no conception of truth for such statements that transcends the means by which we are able to recognize them as true, namely mathematical proof; we have no notion of their being determined as true or as false by something which obtains independently of our having the means to recognize it as doing so. Our notion of truth for any range of statements of which an idealist view of this kind is to be taken will therefore not allow us to regard them as, in each case, being determinately either true or false. The assumption of bivalence for a given statement is legitimate only if we are capable of recognizing it either as true or as false, not in the mere sense that at least one of these two possibilities, that we should come to recognize it as true and that we should come to recognize it as false, remains open, but in the sense that we are assured of the existence of that by means of which we could recognize it as true or as false. In the mathematical case, we can be assured of this only if the statement is effectively decidable, so that we have an effective method of finding a proof or disproof.

The most obvious ground for denying that we have such a transcendent conception of truth, though not given by Brouwer in this form, appeals to the intimate connection between the notions of truth and meaning: in acquiring a grasp of the meanings of mathematical statements, what we learn is when to recognize their truth as being established; and there is no way to go from this to a conception of what it is for them to *be* true independently of that by means of which we recognize them as true. Brouwer's philosophy of mathematics is, however, presented in the most thoroughly psychologistic manner conceivable. Mathematical objects do not exist independently of us, but are products of human thought, whose being is to be conceived; and there is no attempt by Brouwer to distinguish reason or thought from thinking—mathematical objects are the products of our mental processes. Instead of presenting his philosophy of mathematics as a consequence of a correct theory of meaning for the language of mathematics, Brouwer regards language with scepticism, not because it is an imperfect instrument of communication, but because communication itself is possible at best in a very imperfect manner; the proofs whose existence supplies the only legitimate notion of mathematical truth are *mental* constructions, of which symbolic or verbal renderings provide a necessarily defective representation. His thought thus notoriously drives towards that most subjective form of idealism, solipsism.

On the last page of *FPL*, I said that, in view of the strength of Frege's arguments against psychologism, idealism can be tenable only if it is expressible in a non-psychologistic form. Currie maintains, in effect, that Frege's arguments all depend on the premiss that subjective idealism is false: 'his arguments in favour of his notion of sense . . . attempt to show that the view that sense is something essentially psychological leads to an intolerable relativism,' he says,[1] and goes on to deny that the attack on psychologism relates to a correct account of meaning or of what it is to grasp meaning. If this were correct, then the remark about stripping idealism of its psychologistic apparel would be a complete non-sequitur: whether or not he adhered to psychologism, an idealist would be untouched by the objection that it led to idealism. But the supposition is quite incorrect. Some, indeed, of Frege's arguments against psychologism proceed from the premiss that there exists an objective reality about which we speak, and which renders our thoughts true or false and our judgments correct or incorrect, independently of what we know or can know, in short, from the assumption of the objectivity of truth. Other arguments proceed from the assumption of the communicability of *thought*; and yet others, such as those contained in *Grundlagen*, §§ 58–60, turn on the inadequacy of any account in terms of mental processes or mental images to explain in what an expression's possession of a meaning consists. ('The impossibility of forming an image of the content of a word is no reason for denying it a meaning' is Frege's summation in § 60 of his argument.) Brouwer's solipsistic tendencies confer on his philosophy of mathematics a gross implausibility: one of the most evident features of mathematics is that it is a communal enterprise, that the results of one mathematician can be communicated to another mathematician. To strip intuitionism of its psychologistic character would not be to denature it: as remarked above,

---

[1] Currie, op. cit., pp. 84–5.

there is no immediate inference from the objectivity and communicability of thought to the objectivity and determinateness of truth. Nevertheless, although a non-psychologistic version of idealism is possible, and indeed the only version worth considering, it would have been psychologically difficult, in the atmosphere of late nineteenth-century philosophy, for anyone to wage war on psychologism in the name of the communicability of sense and the necessity for an adequate account of it who did not also fight under the banner of realism.

On p. 240 of *FPL* I wrote, 'When Frege engages in polemic against psychologism, what he is concerned to repudiate is the invasion of the theory of meaning by notions concerned with mental processes, mental images, and the like, and the confusion between the process by which we come to acquire a grasp of sense and what constitutes such a grasp.' The last part of this sentence, concerning the way in which a grasp of sense is acquired, was intended to relate to passages like *Grundlagen*, § 26, where Frege says, 'It looks as though the way in which number originates in us can give information about its nature. The matter would thus become one for a psychological investigation', and, after quoting a remark by Lipschitz along these lines, comments, 'This seems to describe much better how we acquire, say, the intuition of a constellation than how we construct numbers . . . No description of this kind of the mental processes which precede the delivery of a judgment of number . . . can ever take the place of a genuine determination of the concept.' He goes on to speak of the objectivity of number, and to make a comparison with physical space. 'We cannot even know whether (space) appears the same to one person as to another; for we cannot, in order to compare them, lay one person's intuition of space beside another's. There is, nevertheless, something objective contained in space. . . . What is objective in it is what is subject to laws, what can be conceived (*das Begriffliche*), what can be judged (*das Beurtheilbare*), what is capable of being expressed in words. What belongs to pure intuition (*das rein Anschauliche*) is not communicable.' He goes on to construct an example, based on the principle of duality in projective geometry, of two individuals whose spatial intuitions, restricted to projective properties and relations, differ systematically but undetectably. These two people, he says, 'could understand one another very well, and would never realize the difference between their intuitions. . . . Over all geometrical theorems they would be in complete harmony; they would only translate the words differently into their own intuitions. . . . One may therefore say that (the word "point") means something objective; only one must not understand by this meaning (*Bedeutung*) what is peculiar to their intuitions.'

As a final example, he takes the word 'white', of which he says that it makes us think of a certain sensation, 'which is of course, wholly subjective', but that, even in everyday speech, the word bears an objective sense, to express an objective quality which we recognize by means of a particular sensation, and that it signifies that objective quality rather than our subjective sensation.

Now the sentence quoted above from p. 240 of *FPL* did not occur in the course of an exposition of Frege's attack on psychologism. On the contrary, it served to counter an objection to what the paragraph containing it was principally concerned to argue, namely that Frege's notion of sense must be considered a *cognitive* notion. One might reject this claim as conflicting with Frege's opposition to psychologism. I argued that there is no such conflict, and concluded the paragraph by denying that 'Frege wanted to extrude everything epistemological from logic or from the theory of meaning' (the word 'epistemic' might have been better than 'epistemological'). In support of my contention that Frege's notion of sense was a cognitive one, I alluded, in the sentence immediately preceding that quoted above, to the fact that in 'Über Sinn und Bedeutung' the notion was introduced in connection with that of the cognitive value of a sentence. Yet Currie[1] quotes the very same sentence from *FPL* as an example of my supposedly mistaken conception that Frege took psychologism to have anything to do with meaning. He criticizes me, in this connection, for two things: first, for thinking that Frege had no interest in epistemic notions; and, secondly, for supposing the notion of sense to be related to that of understanding. Conceiving himself to be disagreeing with me, he urges that Frege's notion of sense relates to that of knowledge; his argument for this contention is: that in 'Über Sinn und Bedeutung' the notion was introduced in connection with that of the cognitive value of a sentence.[2] Evidently he had not troubled to read the rest of the page from which he took the sentence that he quoted from me; of course, to say, as he also quotes me as saying on p. 669 of *FPL*, that Frege displaced epistemology from its position as the foundation of all philosophy is not at all the same as to maintain the absurd thesis that he had no concern with any epistemological questions. Currie correctly remarks that Frege opposed psychologism as leading to subjectivism; but it is obscure what he considers psychologism to be a theory *of*. In claiming Frege's notion of sense to be a cognitive one, Currie is agreeing, not disagreeing, with me; but, in claiming that it is not related to the notions of meaning and

[1] Ibid., p. 85.
[2] Ibid., p. 83.

of understanding, he is genuinely and emphatically disagreeing. It is perplexing to think what Currie can suppose that Frege meant by 'grasping a sense'. As far as I can understand him, his proposal is simply to *equate* the sense of a sentence with its cognitive value. It would be hard to sustain this interpretation on the basis of the many passages of his writings, other than 'Über Sinn und Bedeutung', in which Frege discusses sense without mentioning cognitive value; but there is a more immediate objection, which indeed occurs to Currie.[1] This is that the cognitive value of a sentence evidently depends upon its meaning. This objection has two prongs. First, on the assumption that this connection was equally evident to Frege, his invocation in 'Über Sinn und Bedeutung' of the notion of cognitive value provides no demonstration whatever that he did not intend sense to be taken as an ingredient in meaning. Secondly, if Frege did not intend sense to be construed as an ingredient in meaning, but to be equated with cognitive value, we are left with a wholly unexplained, though intuitively very close, connection between sense (cognitive value) and meaning. Currie does not address himself to the second of these two difficulties: possibly he did not perceive it. He deals with the first difficulty by claiming that Frege's 'arguments in favour of his notion of sense', which he equates with Frege's arguments against psychologism, in no way relate to the notion of meaning. I do not see how anyone could reflect on *Grundlagen*, § 26, discussed above, without recognizing it to be all about the meanings of words, the objective senses which we convey by means of them when we use them in communication; nor do I think that an unprejudiced reading of *Grundlagen*, §§ 58–60, will fail to confirm my claim that some of Frege's arguments against psychologism do not directly relate to the subjectivism to which it leads, but simply to its inadequacy as an account of meaning.

Assuming that it conforms to the context principle, so that the meaning of a word consists in its contribution to the meanings of sentences in which it occurs, the general form of any theory of meaning is determined by the model it provides for the meaning of an arbitrary sentence. There are a number of general features of sentences, all of which are intuitively connected with their meanings; and theories of meaning differ from one another in selecting different such features as directly constitutive of meaning. For instance, one well-known theory, or proposal for a theory, is that the meaning of a sentence consists in the method of its verification. But, for a theory of meaning to vindicate itself as adequate to the task required of such a theory, it must show how everything that depends

[1] Ibid., p. 84.

upon the meaning of a sentence is derivable from that which it takes as constitutive of that meaning. That is, for any feature of sentences which intuitively depends on, and solely on, their meanings, the theory must be able, for each sentence, to display this feature as a consequence of its meaning, relative to the way the theory represents its meaning as being given. Now Frege takes the sense of a sentence as given by the condition for it to be true, that is, the way in which, on the basis of its composition, we understand what would determine it as true. One thing that depends solely upon meaning is the logical relation that a sentence bears to other sentences; given the meanings possessed by certain sentences, it must be determinate whether one of them is entailed by the rest. This is, of course, something that is very well explained by Frege's theory of reference. Another thing that depends solely upon its meaning is the cognitive value of a sentence. This, too, is perfectly explained on Frege's theory: there is virtually no gap between the sense of a sentence, conceived of as given by its truth-condition, and its cognitive value: what we learn, upon learning that a sentence whose sense we grasp is true, is, precisely, that the condition for it to be true is satisfied. The smoothness of the connection between cognitive value and meaning is one of the greatest advantages of a truth-conditional account of meaning, or, more generally, of one that takes understanding as a form of knowledge, the meaning of an expression being what you know about it when you understand it (or 'know its meaning'). Where a realistic theory of meaning, such as Frege's, has much greater difficulty is over the notion of evidence. What are to be counted as grounds for accepting a sentence as true is another thing that depends on the meaning of the sentence; and precisely because a realistic theory forces so large a gap between what makes a statement true and that on the basis of which we are able to recognize it as true, the theory has difficulty in explaining how we derive our grasp of the latter from a knowledge of the former. The difficulty becomes acute when the grounds for accepting the sentence as true are not deductive ones, and particularly when they fall short of being conclusive. Here, of course, is the meeting-point between epistemology and the theory of meaning; it is an area Frege left unexplored.

In setting out my view of the relation between Frege's realism and what I take to be his most important contribution to philosophy, the shift of perspective, I said in *FPL*, what I am sure is true, that it would have been impossible to see the matter in this light earlier in this century (say in 1920), but that, at that time, his realism would have been seen as the salient feature of his philosophy. I went on to say that his chief importance would then have been seen 'as lying in the part he played in bringing about the downfall of Hegelian idealism.'[1] This was in any case an ill-judged remark, since Frege's purely philosophical influence, before Geymonat's Italian translation of *Grundlagen* in 1948 and Austin's English one in 1950, was transmitted only through a very few philosophers who had read him, some of major importance: Husserl, Russell, Wittgenstein, Waismann, Carnap, Scholz, Church and Quine. Since this influence was principally felt, even though only at second hand, within the Austro-Anglo-American analytical tradition, it is obvious that Frege could not have had any *direct* part in the overthrow of Hegelian idealism. Hans Sluga, who in 'Frege as a Rationalist'[2] assembles much interesting historical material, has made a strong case that the demise of Hegelianism in Germany had occurred well before Frege's earliest writings. For both these reasons, I have in *FPL*₂ altered the beginning, on p. 683, of the last paragraph of the book.

Sluga also complained of two other passages of *FPL*,[3] in which I mentioned Frege's opposition to a prevalent idealism. I did not intend, in those passages, to refer particularly to Hegelian idealism, but to a very general orientation; and, though I am open to conviction, it remains my impression that a general idealist orientation did prevail, partly as an inheritance from Kant and the post-Kantians. Sluga argues that the dominant influence was a scientifically oriented empiricism, in reaction against Kantian and post-Kantian idealism; but, even if he is right, empiricism is far from being in itself inimical to certain forms of idealism, as the history of British philosophy shows. Psychologism is represented by Sluga as a product of this empiricism, but he does not conceal its origin in the work of the neo-Kantian J. F. Fries.[4] At any rate, Frege saw psychologism as informing 'the 'dominant logic'[5] and, as we have seen, argued that it led inevitably to idealism. In the late nineteenth and early twentieth centuries, there arose in Germany a small group of realist philosophers, principally Brentano, Meinong and Husserl in his *Logische Untersuchungen* period, roughly comparable to the Moore and Russell who led the attack on the absolute idealism which really was dominant in England; and I suppose that, in the early twentieth century, anyone who knew about Frege and thought of him as more than a logician would have been inclined to classify him with these realists. He

---

[1] *FPL*, p. 683.

[2] M. Schirn (ed.), op. cit., vol. I, pp. 27–47.

[3] On pp. 197 and 470.

[4] See J. Passmore, *A Hundred Years of Philosophy*, London, 1957, p. 188, fn. 2, and H. Sluga, 'Frege's Alleged Realism', *Inquiry*, vol. 20, 1977, p. 229.

[5] *Grundgesetze*, vol. I, p. xiv.

had indeed influenced one member of that school in the person of Husserl, by converting him from psychologism; but his realism was more sophisticated than that of Meinong, and very much more so than that of the early Moore and Russell. The mere existence of a small school of realists in Germany is enough to show that the general run of German philosophers, at the time Frege was writing, were at least strongly influenced by idealism of one variety or another. For these reasons I have left the allusions to idealism on pp. 197 and 479 unaltered in FPL_2.

CHAPTER 5

Meaning and Understanding

In *FPL*, I maintained that a theory of meaning is a theory of understanding This thesis is in line with the views of the later Wittgenstein, but the train of thought that led me to it was prompted by reading Quine. Quine says that we go astray if we ask what sort of things meanings are: the most we need or can hope to do is to interpret certain phrases containing the word 'meaning', such as 'has a meaning' and 'has the same meaning as', although he is sceptical about our chances of success in this more modest enterprise. My reaction to these remarks was that Quine omitted the most important context in which the word 'meaning' occurs, namely the phrase 'know the meaning'; and from this reflection it is only a short step to the thesis. I believe that thesis to be in line, not only with the thought of Wittgenstein, but also with that of Frege, in whose terminology one could express it by saying that an account of sense is an account of what it is to grasp a sense; and this is connected with the observation that I made repeatedly in *FPL*, that Frege's notion of sense is a cognitive one.

I nevertheless now regard the thesis as considerably more problematic than I did. What does it amount to to say that a theory of meaning is a theory of understanding? One reply might be as follows. If we want to explain what it is for something to be a language, that is, for the words and sentences of the language to have the sorts of meanings that they do, we have to sketch a theory of meaning for the language. Such a theory describes the practice of speaking the language; or, better, it serves to render intelligible the phenomenon of interchange in that language, as other theories serve to explain other phenomena. In doing so, it need not confine itself to actual description, but may, as other theories do, employ theoretical notions, those of reference and of truth, for example. Given such a theory, we may then explain an understanding of the language as consisting in the implicit knowledge of the theory of meaning. The notion of implicit knowledge may, however, be called in question: what does it mean to impute such knowledge to someone, and how is it explanatory? Does not the mastery of a language consist merely in the possession of a practical capacity, the capacity, namely, to participate in that practice which is described, or explained, by the theory of meaning? This raises the question whether an account of understanding requires an appeal to the notion of *knowledge*, whether knowledge of a language is genuinely a case of knowledge. If it be replied that it is a case of practical knowledge, we may then ask whether, and in what cases, practical knowledge (knowledge-how) rests on, or may be represented as, theoretical knowledge (knowledge-that). These questions arise quite independently of the relation that is taken to hold between the notions of understanding and of meaning; but the answer to them powerfully affects the account to be given of that relation.

How does the theory of meaning 'render intelligible' the practice of speaking the language? It is tempting to answer that it does so by appeal to the implicit knowledge that the speakers are supposed to have of the theory: assuming them to have this knowledge, their utterances and related actions then become intelligible as the acts of rational agents. More generally, we may be disposed to regard the notion of understanding as prior to that of meaning and as capable of yielding an explanation of it. If we contemplate some fragmentary linguistic exchange, say a question asked and answered, and then ask ourselves, 'What gives these sounds the meanings that they have?', we are liable to answer that it is the understanding which each speaker has of the language they are speaking. We are then likely to conclude that what must come *first* is an explanation of that in which an understanding of the language consists, one that can be given in advance of an account of the practice of speaking the language; once we have an explanation of what it is to understand the language, we can then easily explain the practice of speaking the language as the utterance of sentences by speakers who have that understanding. But have we not now relapsed into psychologism, or into something that is objectionable on the same grounds as psychologism? What gives meaning to the sounds that a speaker utters no longer lies open to view: the meaning he attaches to them depends upon something interior to him, his understanding of the language, perhaps conceived as his implicitly knowing a theory of meaning governing it, and his communication of that meaning to his hearer depends upon the hearer's being in the same interior state.

This objection prompts us to adopt a different view. Like a linguistic utterance, a move in a game of chess has a significance not apparent to casual observation. To grasp its significance one has to know the rules of chess, that is, to understand the conventions constitutive of the practice of playing the game; but, it seems, all that is required is a knowledge of this practice, a description of which does not appear to need to make any allusion to an individual player's mastery of it. It is, no doubt, a legitimate philosophical enquiry in what a player's knowledge of chess consists; but it does not seem, on the face of it, that an account of the game, which is what is required for an explanation of what it is for a move to have the significance that it has, depends upon the answer to that enquiry. In the same way, on the present view, all that is required, in order to explain what it is for a sentence of a language to bear the meaning that it does, is to describe the practice of speaking the language. What it is for an individual speaker to have a mastery of that practice—to know the language—is a legitimate topic of philosophical enquiry; but an account of the practice of speaking the language does not require us to undertake that enquiry, but may leave it on one side. What must come first is a *direct* description of the practice, that is, of what the speakers say and do, not mediated by an appeal to their understanding of it, thought of as something that could be explained in advance of an account of the practice; and, if all we are concerned to explain is what it is for the words and sentences of the language to have the meanings that they do, no appeal to the individual speakers' understanding of the language will be necessary at all.

In the criticism of the view that the notion of understanding is prior to that of meaning, there will be recognized something allied to the criticism of that conception made by the later Wittgenstein. It does not follow that the view just stated is Wittgenstein's. On the contrary, it implies that the thesis that an account of meaning is an account of understanding is unfounded, whereas that was a thesis to which Wittgenstein subscribed. His view must, rather, be taken to be that an account of the practice of speaking a language and an account of what it is to understand it must proceed together.

If this book were intended as a replacement for *FPL*, I should feel constrained to go into these enormously difficult questions, because an answer to them evidently bears on the correct estimation of Frege's philosophy, even though he returned no answer to them himself. I hope to go into them in a projected volume, *What is a Theory of Meaning?* As explained above in the Preface, this book is not a replacement for *FPL*: it is concerned neither to expound nor to evaluate Frege's philosophy, but to argue for a particular interpretation of it. Since the questions as to the relation of meaning to understanding and of understanding to knowledge would demand very extensive discussion to be adequately answered, I must here ask to be excused from investigating them further.

At any rate, the notions of meaning and understanding are very closely related, as is shown by the intuitive equivalence between 'to understand *A*' and 'to know what *A* means', whether or not, in the latter phrase, the verb 'to know' is to be taken seriously. Meaning is correlative to understanding: meaning is, we may say, the *object* (or, alternatively, the *content*) of the understanding. If the relation of understanding to knowledge were not problematic, we could express this by saying that the meaning of an expression is what someone knows when he understands the expression. To explain what it is to understand a particular expression involves explaining what that expression means; however uncertain the converse may be, this much is clear.

Frege does not use the term 'meaning'. That is to say, he uses the ordinary German word for 'meaning' as his word for 'reference', and he has no general word to cover all that is correlative to understanding. But in *FPL* I represented sense, as Frege conceived of it, as an ingredient in meaning: the sense of an expression—word, phrase or sentence—is part of what we understand when we understand the expression; it is part of the conventional significance of the expression within the language. Now, as remarked in Chapter 3, Frege's notion of sense faces two ways. On the one hand, thoughts are immutable objects existing independently of us, and the sense of an expression which forms part of a sentence is part of the thought which the sentence expresses: thoughts are what are true or false, and senses are that to which reference primarily attaches. On the other hand, thoughts are expressed by sentences, and the senses that are parts of thoughts are expressed by parts of sentences. The claim that sense is part of meaning, conceived as correlative to understanding, therefore needs substantiation.

This bears on the question, raised in Chapter 2, how continuous were Frege's ideas on logic, as opposed to the philosophy of mathematics, during his late period from 1914 to his death in 1925, with those of his mature period from 1891 to 1906. It is not disputable that, in his late period, Frege was concerned with our understanding of sentences, as dependent upon their composition, and that he used the notion of sense to explain this. In this connection, he seldom actually employs the verb 'to understand':[1] he prefers to use the expression 'to grasp (*fassen*) the

---

[1] He does so in his draft letter to Philip Jourdain of 1914, *BW*, p. 127, *P.M.C.*, p. 79.

thought expressed'; this is, of course, more accurate when we are concerned with *sense* rather than with those other ingredients of meaning classified as *Färbung* or tone. It is apparent that Frege identifies sense as *expressed* with sense as *grasped*. The problem stated in the letter to Jourdain, how we are able to *understand* new sentences, becomes, in the 'Logik in der Mathematik' of the same year, the problem how language is able, by means of new sentences, to *express* thoughts; and, in the opening paragraph of 'Gedankengefüge', the two problems are stated simultaneously. They are one and the same problem: in explaining what it is for a sentence to express a thought, we explain what it is that we grasp when we understand that sentence. This is not to say that there does not remain a residual problem about what, in general, grasping a thought is.

External indications strongly favour the view that, in his late writings on logic, Frege's conscious aim was not, as in his late writings on mathematics, to embark on some quite new approach, but, rather, to consolidate the work of his mature period by finally composing that treatise on the philosophy of logic which he had failed to complete in 1897 and had again failed to complete when, in 1906, facing the failure of his life's work as a whole, he had begun to set down in order what remained of his work after the calamity. The 'Einleitung in die Logik' of 1906 faithfully follows the list of the preliminary topics given in the fragment 'What can I regard as the result of my work?': the detachment of assertoric force from the predicate; hypothetical sentence-composition; generality; sense and reference. The unfinished 'Kurze Übersicht' of the same year had a more detailed division into sections: the thought; the detachment of assertoric force from the predicate; negation; hypothetical sentence-composition; generality. One cannot but be struck by the correspondence with the first four chapters of the equally unfinished *Logische Untersuchungen* of 1918–23: the thought; negation; thought-compounds; logical generality. Nor can one fail to be struck by the close resemblance in content and even in the examples used between the *Logische Untersuchungen* and the unfinished 'Logik' of 1897, itself divided into: the predicate *true*, thought, consequences for the treatment of logic; the separation of the thought from its wrappings (*Umhüllungen*); negation; combination of thoughts. There is every appearance of repeated attempts to do the very *same* thing, and to do it in accordance with the same essential plan. This is borne out by an examination of the contents of the late works, the *Logische Untersuchungen* and the unpublished 'Logik in der Mathematik' (1914), 'Meine grundlegenden logischen Einsichten' (1915) and the 'Aufzeichnungen für Ludwig Darmstaedter' (1919). There is certainly a redistribution of emphasis, and, especially in 'Der Gedanke', new questions are explored; but there is no single component doctrine from his earlier philosophy of logic for which there is evidence that it had been jettisoned.

The evidence of continuity, within Frege's philosophy of logic, though not in his philosophy of mathematics, from Frege's mature to his late period creates a certain presumption that sense, as he conceived it in his mature period, is part of the object of our understanding, as it certainly was for him during the late period. This presumption is confirmed by the writings of the mature period. Frege speaks more of a word's expressing a sense and of a sentence's expressing a thought than of our grasping the sense or thought expressed, because his interest lies in what sense is rather than in the process of apprehension, if it is rightly called a process: but he leaves us in no doubt that the sense is part of that conventional significance which we apprehend if we understand the expression. In a letter to Peano of 1896–7, Frege says that 'a speaker must attach a sense to a name (*einen Sinn . . . mit den Namen verbinden*)'.[1] In a similar way, he speaks in 'Über Sinn und Bedeutung',[2] of someone's attaching a sense to a proper name, and of a sense as what people associate with (*verknüpfen mit*) a word;[3] in the published letter to Peano of 1896,[4] he speaks of people's attaching a thought to a sentence, as also in the 'Logik' of 1897;[5] and in the 'Einleitung in die Logik' of 1906 he speaks again of a sense's being attached to a proper name.[6] The terminology of *grasping* a sense or a thought, prominent in the later writings, is used at all stages. In the 'Logik' of the 1880s, written before the sense/reference distinction had been made, he speaks of a judgeable content as being grasped.[7] In 'Über Sinn und Bedeutung', he says that 'the sense of a proper name is grasped (*erfasst*) by anybody who is sufficiently familiar with the language . . . to which it belongs',[8] and observes that two people may grasp (*auffassen*) the same sense.[9] Likewise, in his review of Husserl of 1894, he says that 'one and the same thought can be grasped by many people'.[10] In the Preface to *Grundgesetze*, vol. I, he says that 'if we want to emerge from the subjective

[1] *BW*, p. 196, *P.M.C.*, p. 127.
[2] P. 27, fn.
[3] P. 29.
[4] Pp. 55–6.
[5] *N.S.*, p. 145, *P.W.*, p. 133.
[6] *N.S.*, pp. 208, 209, *P.W.*, p. 191.
[7] *N.S.*, p. 7, *P.W.*, p. 7.
[8] P. 27.
[9] P. 29.
[10] Pp. 317–18.

at all, we must conceive of knowledge as an activity that does not create what is known, but grasps (*ergreift*) what is already there. . . . That which we grasp (*erfassen*) with the mind also exists independently of this activity'.[1] The 'Logik' of 1897 contains repeated references to the grasping of thoughts.[2] In the 'Einleitung in die Logik' of 1906 Frege says that 'to think is to grasp thoughts';[3] and in the 'Kurze Übersicht' of the same year he speaks of a grasp (*Auffassung*) of the content of a sentence,[4] and says that 'we grasp thoughts, but do not create them' and that 'we can grasp a thought without judging it to be true'.[5]

Since, on Frege's view, 'we think in some language'[6] to grasp a thought is, for us, to understand a sentence, although other beings may be able to grasp thoughts not clothed in words or symbols. At any rate, to grasp the thought expressed by a particular sentence is to understand that sentence, and similarly with senses of expressions that go to compose sentences. Frege tells us much about what senses are. In the terminology of *Begriffsschrift*, repeated in the draft letter to Jourdain,[7] the sense of an expression is a manner of determining its referent (*Bestimmungsweise*); in that of 'Über Sinn und Bedeutung', it is a way in which the referent is given to us (*Art des Gegebenseins*)—not *the* way it is given, but a particular way out of many possible ones.[8] The referents of the constituent parts of a sentence jointly determine its truth-value; so the senses of these parts determine the condition for it to be true, the sense of each being its contribution to the thought that that condition is fulfilled.[9] Since the thought expressed by a sentence thus corresponds to the condition for its truth, it follows that to grasp a thought is to grasp the condition under which it is true, and to grasp the sense of an expression is to grasp its contribution to determining the truth-condition of the thought expressed by a sentence in which it occurs, of which that sense is a constituent. That still leaves

---

[1] P. xxiv.

[2] *N.S.*, pp. 149 (twice), 150, 152 and 157 (twice), *P.W.*, pp. 137, 138 (twice), 140, 145 (twice).

[3] *N.S.*, p. 201, *P.W.*, p. 185.

[4] *N.S.*, p. 213, *P.W.*, p. 197.

[5] *N.S.*, p. 214, *P.W.*, p. 198.

[6] 'Logik', 1897, *N.S.*, p. 154, *P.W.*, p. 142.

[7] *BW*, p. 128, cf. p. 234; *P.M.C.*, p. 80, cf. p. 152.

[8] For an excellent discussion of Frege's notion of sense, with particular consideration of this way of explaining it, see David S. Shwayder, 'On the Determination of Reference by Sense', in M. Schirn (ed.), *Studien zu Frege*, vol. III, Stuttgart and Bad Canstatt, 1976, pp. 85–95.

[9] Cf. *Grundgesetze*, vol. I, § 32.

unanswered the question what it is to 'grasp' such a condition; and, if Frege talks more about what sense a word or sentence expresses than about what it is to grasp that sense, that is because he does not have an answer to the question in what grasping a condition for the truth of a thought consists.

It was stated above that Frege does not resolve the twin problems of the relation of meaning to understanding and of understanding to knowedge: but he was quite clear that grasping a thought, or grasping a sense in general, is a case of knowledge. If we accept too crude a characterization of understanding as possessing a practical ability, we shall see no reason to suppose that anyone should know whether he attaches any meaning, correct or incorrect, to an expression. If some people were like dogs, and swam instinctively as soon as they found themselves in the water, while others had to learn to swim, as in reality we all have to do, then someone might quite well not know whether or not he could swim. But understanding is *not* like this. It is easy to be unsure whether one understands a word correctly, or to believe that one does when one does not; and it is possible, sometimes, to have a false impression of understanding, that is, to think that one attaches a sense to some sentence composed of familiar words when in fact one attaches none. For all that, in the normal case one knows whether one understands or not. If, for example, I am listening to a speech in a language of which I have an imperfect knowledge, I am able to answer immediately if a friend asks me, 'Do you understand what he is saying?'; and the same goes if I am asked whether I understand a particular word of my own language. Any adequate account of understanding must do justice to this fact: Frege did so by directly connecting knowledge with grasp of sense, without going into questions about the character of this knowledge, as explicit or implicit, or about what constitutes the possession of such knowledge and how it is manifested. In *Function und Begriff*,[1] he deduces that 'the Morning Star' and 'the Evening Star' have different senses from the fact that one who did not know that the Morning Star is the Evening Star might regard a sentence containing the one name as true and the corresponding sentence containing the other name as false. In the personal letter to Peano quoted above he deduces the same consequence from the fact that a speaker does not need to know that the two names have the same reference;[2] and, in the same vein, he says that the fact that the coincidence of the reference of the two names is not self-evident implies that their senses are distinct.[3] In the 'Kurze Übersicht,'

---

[1] P. 14.
[2] *BW*, p. 196, *P.M.C.*, p. 127.
[3] *BW*, p. 234, *P.M.C.*, p. 152.

whether or not two sentences have the same sense is said to depend on whether one who recognizes either as true must immediately so recognize the other.[1] In 'Der Gedanke' Frege argues[2] that Herbert Garner and Leo Peter attach different senses to the name 'Dr Gustav Lauben' on the ground that, though they in fact use it to refer to the same man, they do not know that they do. Sense, unlike reference, is a matter of what the speaker *knows*: that is why, in 'Über Sinn und Bedeutung', the sense of a sentence is connected with its cognitive value, that is, with what comes to be known when one learns that it is true.[3] There is no room for any doubt that, for Frege, sense is the content of understanding, or, rather, the principal ingredient of that content: it is that which one who knows the language apprehends as objectively associated with the expression; and that apprehension is an instance of knowledge.

---

[1] *N.S.*, p. 213, *P.W.*, p. 197.
[2] P. 65.
[3] Cf. also *BW*, pp. 235, 247, *P.M.C.*, pp. 152, 164.

CHAPTER 6

Indexicality and Oratio Obliqua

FREGE'S OCCASIONAL OBSERVATIONS about token-reflexive or indexical indexicals expressions do not, at least at first sight, provide an adequate or convincing account of them. It is natural to connect this fact with the observation made at the end of Chapter 2 concerning Frege's treatment of the defects of natural language. Whether he regarded the use of indexical expressions as, strictly speaking, a defect of natural language is not fully clear: but he surely took it as a feature that must be eliminated from a purified logical notation, as having the gross disadvantage that the thought expressed is not fully determined by the words or symbols used. But, whether he viewed indexicality as an imperfection or as a mere inconvenience, his remarks about it are interesting for the light which they throw on his conception of thoughts.

On pp. 367 and 384 of *FPL*, I mentioned Frege's view that, by the use of correlative token-reflexive expressions, different sentences could be used, on different occasions, to express the same thought; the example I gave on p. 367 of *FPL*$_1$, involving 'yesterday' and 'today', is Frege's, from 'Der Gedanke',[1] where he also mentions 'here' and 'there'. The topic is also discussed in the unpublished 'Logik' of 1897, and I have inserted a reference to this on p. 367 of *FPL*$_2$. In 'Logik', Frege makes a more surprising claim, namely that the thought expressed by one speaker who uses the word 'I' may be expressed by another speaker who uses the name of the first speaker.[2] I have, in *FPL*$_2$, replaced the example on p. 384 of *FPL*$_1$ by that cited on p. 367 of *FPL*$_1$, and, on p. 367, reported the claim made in 'Logik'. The passages in 'Der Gedanke' and in 'Logik' (1897) are virtually the only ones in Frege's writings in which he expressly

[1] P. 64.
[2] *N.S.*, p. 146, *P.W.*, pp. 134–5.

considers token-reflexive expressions; and I shall in this chapter set out exactly what he says about them in these two passages.

The middle paragraph of *FPL*, p. 367, requires a gloss, although, in *FPL*₂, I have left it unaltered, as being accurate as far as it goes. In 'Logik'[1] Frege says, what is obvious, that the word 'I' designates different people according as it is uttered by different people; and he also says that a sentence containing that word expresses a different thought, according as it is uttered by one person and by another. I remarked, on p. 367 of *FPL*, that 'this feature of Frege's notion of a thought cannot be arrived at merely from the characterization of a thought as the sense of a complete sentence'. This is surely correct. If one appealed only to the conception of a thought as the sense of a sentence, one would naturally say that the thought expressed by a sentence containing the word 'I' was one whose truth-value could alter according to the identity of the speaker. To arrive at a different conclusion, one would have to appeal to Frege's principle that a thought is something that is true or false absolutely, whose truth-value cannot therefore shift from one utterance to another. But, even when this principle is regarded as remaining in force for thoughts expressed by sentences containing token-reflexive expressions, the natural conclusion would be that the thought expressed by such a sentence is not dependent solely upon the sense of the sentence; for one would naturally say that the word 'I' retained the same sense in the mouth of one speaker and of another, and that what determines its reference on each occasion is who utters it, not anything that expresses a sense: words carry sense, as perhaps also do intonations, facial expressions and gestures, but circumstances do not. But Frege does not draw this conclusion: he is unwilling to break the correlation between thought and sense. In 'Logik', he says that, when such a word as 'I' is used, 'the mere words do not contain the whole sense, but it is also a matter of who utters them', and, further, that 'words like "here" and "now" only obtain their full sense from the circumstances in which they are used'. He even wishes to maintain the formulation that a thought is the sense of a complete sentence: he says that, when someone says, 'It is raining', one has to supply the when and where, and that, when such a sentence is written, it often ceases to have a complete sense, because the indications are lacking when and where it was said.

Now do these slightly surprising remarks tally with Frege's general views on sense? John Perry has maintained that they do not.[2] He argues[3]

---

[1] *N.S.*, p. 146, *P.W.*, p. 134.

[2] 'Frege on Demonstratives', *Philosophical Review*, vol. LXXXVI, 1977, pp. 474–97.

[3] P. 485.

that we cannot 'extract from a demonstrative an appropriate completing sense', since 'such a sense . . . would have to be intimately related to the sense of a unique description of the value of the demonstrative in the context of utterance'. I should like, first, to register a mild protest at the assimilation of token-reflexive expressions, properly so called, to demonstratives: 'this' and 'that' differ from 'I', 'you', 'today', 'yesterday', etc., in demanding supplementation by a gesture if their reference is to be unambiguous. More importantly, Perry is here assuming that Frege held what Kripke has called the 'description theory' of the senses of singular terms, namely that any such sense can be conveyed by means of a definite description. In *FPL*, I denied that there is any ground to ascribe such a thesis to Frege.[1] The thesis is particularly absurd when it is applied, not merely to proper names in the restricted sense, but to singular terms consisting of or containing token-reflexive expressions, because it implicitly becomes a much stronger thesis than when viewed as merely one about proper names. It becomes, namely, the thesis that the sense of every singular term can be given by means of a definite description *not containing any token-reflexive expression*; and there is no possible reason for believing such a thesis. Who could devise a description, framed in purely general terms, applying uniquely to the Sun, out of all the stars there are or ever have been or will be in the universe? The Sun is the heavenly body which gives *us* light and heat, which, for *us*, is far the brightest in the sky: there is nothing in any of Frege's writings that warrants saddling him with the absurd theory that the sense we attach to the name 'the Sun' can be expressed by some definite description devoid of indexical expressions. The late Gareth Evans, whose early death in the summer of 1980 was so great a loss to British philosophy, read a paper on 'Understanding Demonstratives' to a conference at Cerisy-la-Salle in 1979. In that paper, he was entirely right to have taken issue with Perry on this point.

The fact that Perry's argument is unsound does not show that his conclusion is wrong; and Evans, in his paper, undertook to demonstrate this stronger thesis. He was, indeed, mistaken in citing *FPL*, p. 384, as showing me to be among 'many philosophers' who 'have concluded that Frege intended to abandon a notion of "what is said" or "the thought expressed" which was "psychologically real" in the sense of being the object of propositional attitudes, and was giving expression to the idea that two people would express the same thought provided that they refer to the same object (in whatever way) and say the same thing about it'. What is said

---

[1] Pp. 97–8, 110–11.

on p. 384 of *FPL* relates only to utterances involving correlative token-reflexive expressions, like 'It is cold today' said on one day and 'It was cold yesterday' said the next, or 'I am cold' said by Smith to Jones and 'You are cold' said by Jones to Smith. The broader interpretation suggested by Evans is expressly blocked by the remark that it is 'unnecessary to suppose that a thought expressible by the utterance on a particular occasion of a sentence containing token-reflexive expressions can also be expressed by some "eternal" sentence containing no such expressions'; though indeed this remark tallies badly with Frege's suggestion in the 1897 'Logik' that the thought conveyed by Smith to Jones could also be conveyed by Jones to Robinson by means of the sentence 'Smith is cold'. It remains, however, that some obscurity attends the notion of a thought as Frege is using it in this connection. How are we to conceive of the thought expressed by the utterance, on a definite occasion, of such a sentence as 'I am cold'? What are we to take the constituents of such a thought to be—those constituents that correspond to the pronoun 'I' and to the present tense, together with the circumstances that serve to determine their reference? In particular, the notion of sense seems here to have come apart from that of the significance of an expression, the principle governing its use in sentences. For there seems no doubt that such a word as 'I' has such a significance, which does not vary according to its utterance by different speakers, but is known by all speakers and governs their understanding of one another: as Evans observed, 'the expression type, "today", certainly has a meaning, which does not vary from occasion to occasion, which . . . Perry calls its role.'

independence from context

For Frege, truth and falsity attach, in the first place, to thoughts: sentences are called 'true' or 'false' in a derivative sense, as expressing true or false thoughts. Thoughts are eternal and immutable: there cannot be a thought which is true at one time, false at another, or true as expressed by one speaker, false as expressed by another. *We* grasp thoughts only as expressed in (verbal or symbolic) language: but thoughts exist independently of being so expressed, and the primary purpose of language is to provide us with an access to them. Senses are constituents of thoughts: so whatever contributes to determining the thought expressed, which is true or false absolutely, must be part of the sense. What is dominant here is the conception of senses as thought-constituents; in this connection, this notion of sense begins to pull apart from the intuitive notion of sense as (part of) the conventional significance of a means of communication. If we dwell on this latter, intuitive, notion, we shall of course be disposed to say that the sense of a sentence containing words like 'I', 'now', 'here', etc., is something that can be true in certain circumstances and false in others, and, likewise, that the senses of these words are such that their reference depends systematically upon the context. But Frege is debarred from taking either view. An utterance of a sentence has, for him, failed in its purpose unless it conveys to us a thought that is true or false absolutely. As for the individual token-reflexive expressions, he could not describe them as having a constant sense, but a reference varying according to the context, for sense alone determines reference. They are therefore one of two things; which, it is unclear. Either they are ambiguous, even though systematically so; or, contrary to surface appearance, they are functional in character. In the first case, their presence is a defect in natural language, namely an instance of a more general defect. In a properly constructed language, each expression has a reference independent of context, as laid down in the letter to Peano; if the reference of an expression varies, even systematically, a sense cannot be ascribed to it, since sense determines reference uniquely. We could avoid this conclusion by taking up the other option, and regarding token-reflexive expressions as requiring completion, namely as standing for fixed functions from circumstances to persons, places and times; and, indeed, this seems to be the account to which Frege was leaning when he made the remark quoted above, that a sentence containing a token-reflexive expression, when taken apart from the context of utterance, does not express a complete sense.

On p. 268 of *FPL*, I suggested that we should emend Frege's doctrines of indirect sense and indirect reference by holding that the *sense* of an expression in *oratio obliqua* remains unaltered: only its reference shifts. Under this emendation, we must still distinguish between the direct and the indirect reference of an expression, but there will be no such thing as its indirect sense: the unique sense which (if it is indeed univocal) it has in all contexts becomes one determining it as having one reference in one type of context, another in another. The point of the emendation was to save the theory from Russell's objection in 'On Denoting', and to eliminate the potentially infinite hierarchy of multiply indirect senses and references. Russell's point is that, as he expresses it, 'there is no backward road' from reference to sense: it follows that, from knowing the ordinary (direct) sense of an expression, and knowing that, in indirect speech, that ordinary sense becomes its referent, we cannot derive the indirect sense of the expression which is supposed to determine it as having that referent in such a context. If, however, its sense in that context remains the same as elsewhere, we face no such problem. Russell indeed thought that his argument refuted, not merely Frege's theory of indirect sense,

indirect sense

but his theory of sense in general. Simon Blackburn and Alan Code argue in favour of Russell's evaluation of his own argument.[1] They make the valid point that any adequate theory must be capable of explaining the possibility of inferring 'Jones believes something true' from 'Jones believes that Aristotle taught philosophy' and 'Aristotle taught philosophy'; that is to say, the fact that, on Frege's theory, a sentence stands, in ordinary contexts, for a truth-value, and, in *oratio obliqua*, for a thought, cannot be represented as a mere case of ambiguity. Of course, the inference presents no problem, provided that, from 'Aristotle taught philosophy', we may infer 'It is true that Aristotle taught philosophy', where the substantival clause is construed as being in *oratio obliqua*: so we may concentrate upon inferential steps of this type. Now the difficulty occasioned by an inference of this kind does not lie in formulating the general principle governing it: nothing could be more trivial. The difficulty lies only in our coming to terms with the fact that the validity of the inference does not depend solely upon the references of the expressions occurring in the premiss. On Frege's own theory, it does not depend solely upon their *senses*, either, but on references that the expressions would have if they occurred in such a context that they came to bear different senses, namely their indirect senses. On my proposed emendation of Frege's theory, the validity of the inference would depend solely upon the senses of the expressions contained in the premiss; it would not depend solely upon the references they had *in* that premiss, but on other references which they have, in accordance with their unaltered senses, in another type of context, exemplified by the conclusion. There is no intrinsic difficulty about this, even if there is such a difficulty for Frege's unamended theory, and nothing but prejudice stands in the way of accepting it.

For the rest, it does not seem that Blackburn and Code have any more to say in favour of Russell than to observe that, if Frege's theory, amended or unamended, is to be accepted, we are entitled to require a more substantial account of what the sense of an expression is than Frege offers us; and I, for one, should not dispute that. They justly observe that, on enquiring what, on Frege's theory, the indirect referent of 'Aristotle' may be, we cannot rest content with being told that it is the (ordinary) sense of 'Aristotle', since we are owed an explanation of what it is that the phrase 'the sense of "Aristotle"' stands for. Russell's argument purported, however, to be more than a complaint that an explanation had not been provided; it was meant to demonstrate that it was inherently

[1] 'The Power of Russell's Criticism of Frege: "On Denoting", pp. 48–50', *Analysis*, vol. 38, 1978, pp. 65–77.

impossible to provide one. It may succeed in showing this for Frege's indirect senses; but it does not do so for ordinary senses, and hence it leaves untouched the theory as emended in accordance with my suggestion.

In his review of *FPL*,[1] Herbert Heidelberger argues, correctly, that the phrases 'The Moon is round' and 'the thought that the Moon is round' cannot have the same *ordinary* senses, since their ordinary referents are different, the first standing for a truth-value and the second for a thought; if we allow that truth-values are objects, and hence that sentences may stand on either side of the sign of identity, we even have a single context in which the replacement of one phrase by the other will convert a true statement into a false one. Heidelberger therefore urges that we have, after all, a means of saying what the indirect sense of 'the Moon is round' is to be: it is the same as the ordinary sense of 'the thought that the Moon is round'. What could be more natural? In *oratio obliqua*, 'the Moon is round' is to bear a sense determining it as standing for the ordinary sense of the sentence 'The Moon is round': what could that *oratio obliqua* sense be but that of the most direct means we have, in a non-technical sense of 'direct', of referring, in ordinary contexts, to the sense of that sentence? Blackburn and Code might object that the stipulation would be unexplanatory, since we still have not been told what the sense of the sentence *is*; but this would be irrelevant. Heidelberger does not deny that, if Frege's theory is to be made out, a more substantial account of sense must be provided than he offered us. His point is, rather, that we must also take account of the fact that, within our language, we have the means of referring to the senses of expressions; we must therefore not only say what senses are, but also explain the senses of those expressions, such as 'the thought that . . . ', by means of which we refer to them. When we have done this, he thinks, we shall thereby have provided an account of the *indirect* senses of all expressions. Of course, this suggestion is intended as a competitor to my emendation of Frege's theory: the point hardly needs labouring, as it is laboured by Blackburn and Code, that if the sense of 'Aristotle' in *oratio obliqua* is the same as its sense in ordinary contexts, then its sense in contexts of the former kind cannot also be equated with the ordinary sense of the phrase 'the sense of "Aristotle" '.

As Heidelberger notes, on p. 267 of *FPL* I dismissed, as 'rather implausible', the suggestion that he favours, namely that the indirect sense of 'Socrates' is the ordinary sense of 'the sense of "Socrates" '. I am no longer quite sure why I said this with such confidence. A bad reason for

[1] *Metaphilosophy*, vol. 6, 1975, pp. 35–43.

doing so, though natural at first blush, would be that the phrase 'the sense of "Socrates" ' involves explicit reference to the *name* 'Socrates', whereas an occurrence of 'Socrates' in *oratio obliqua* does not appear to involve such reference. Frege held that 'the thought that the Moon is round' stands for the sense of the sentence 'The Moon is round'; and, on a non-Fregean use of the word 'concept', it might be held that 'the concept of citizenship' stood for the sense of the word 'citizen': but we cannot refer to the senses of most expressions save by explicit allusion to the expressions. The use of such an argument against the suggestion favoured by Heidelberger, and dismissed by me as implausible, assumes that, in *oratio obliqua*, we achieve a reference to the ordinary senses of expressions not mediated by any reference to those expressions themselves; not merely the indirect reference, but also the indirect sense, of an expression might survive its replacement by a distinct expression, perhaps in the course of translation into another language. Now Heidelberger does make this assumption, and so the argument may fairly be used against him, at least, as in the example used on p. 267 of *FPL*, with regard to expressions other than sentences. The assumption is, however, gratuitous.

Heidelberger makes easy work of defending Church's celebrated argument against construing belief as an attitude to sentences against my irreverent remark, on p. 372 of *FPL*, that it is difficult to treat it very seriously. He does so, however, only by assuming that the conventional German translation of an English sentence involving the construction '. . . believes that . . .' is strictly synonymous with its English original; he comments that I did not deny this synonymy. I certainly meant to; or, rather, I meant to deny that we had any right to *assume* a strict synonymy between the two sentences. That was precisely the point of my saying that 'there is no ground for presumption that the practical canons of apt translation always require strict synonymy'. In translating, say, a historical narrative, we are accustomed to render into the language of the translation even sentences occurring in *direct* quotation. Church's argument demonstrates, what is in any case obvious, that, in the case of *oratio recta*, such a translation does not preserve strict synonymy with the original text. Several critics have complained that, in this passage, I missed the point of Church's argument; but it appears to me that it is they who have missed the point of my observation. What force is there in an argument which requires as an axiom that strict synonymy is maintained when we translate, in our accustomed manner, a sentence involving indirect quotation? If belief is an attitude to sentences, then, indeed, we cannot wholly translate a sentence ascribing a belief to someone into another language while preserving strict synonymy: from where does the assumption come that we *must* be able to do so?

Since Heidelberger accepts Church's argument, he obviously believes that clauses in *oratio obliqua* involve no covert reference to the expressions they contain; he is therefore precluded from holding that, when the name 'Socrates' occurs in *oratio obliqua*, its sense becomes the same as that, in ordinary contexts, of the phrase 'the sense of "Socrates"', which involves an overt reference to the name 'Socrates'. Inconsistently, however, he appears to wish to defend just this identification. The inconsistency would vanish if Church's argument, and the assumption underlying it, were jettisoned. As remarked above, the assumption is gratuitous. There is nothing in what Frege says about direct and indirect sense and reference to rule out the possibility that, although distinct expressions, in the same or different languages, may have the same sense, no sense can be given to us save as the sense of some particular expression; such a thesis would fit very well what Frege sometimes says to the effect that *we* can grasp thoughts only via words or other symbols. But, if so, then, if an expression stands for a sense, and does so in virtue of *its* sense, that sense must involve a reference, overt or covert, to some expression—the same or different—whose sense its referent is. This would remove the present objection to taking the indirect sense of 'Socrates' to be the direct sense of 'the sense of "Socrates"'. Frege remarks that the replacement of an expression in *oratio obliqua* by another having the same ordinary reference may alter the truth-value of the whole, while its replacement by one having the same ordinary sense will not: this is the ground for saying that the expression cannot, in this context, have its ordinary reference, and for proposing that its referent, in this context, is its ordinary sense. But he advances no claim that the replacement of an expression in *oratio obliqua* by another having the same ordinary sense will leave the *sense* of the whole unaltered, i.e. that expressions having the same ordinary sense will necessarily have the same *indirect* sense: for all that he says, the indirect senses of any two distinct expressions may be distinct.

Though Frege's theory does not rule out that supposition, and though Heidelberger's interpretation entails it, it has a very implausible consequence for double *oratio obliqua*. Suppose that 'is similar to' has the same (ordinary) sense as 'resembles', and suppose that the sentence 'Barry thinks that Harvard resembles Oxford' is true. Then, on Frege's theory, 'Barry thinks that Harvard is similar to Oxford' must also be true; and this accords with intuition. It is worth noting that the validity of this transition does not depend upon Barry's knowing the sense of the word 'similar'; he might be unfamiliar with the word, or attach a mistaken sense to it, but his unwillingness, in these cases, to assent to the sentence, 'Harvard is similar to Oxford', will not vitiate the truth of the statement that he thinks that they are similar. But, now, if, in the quoted sentences, 'resembles' and 'is similar to' have their indirect senses, and if these coincide, respectively, with the direct senses of 'the sense of "resembles" ' and 'the sense of "is similar to" ', the *senses* of the quoted sentences, the thoughts expressed by them, will differ. Hence it will not follow, from the truth of 'Ayrton knows that Barry thinks that Harvard resembles Oxford', that 'Ayrton knows that Barry thinks that Harvard is similar to Oxford' is true. But this is contrary to intuition. The only case in which it might seem plausible to say that Ayrton knew that Barry thought that Harvard resembled Oxford, but did not know that he thought that they were similar, is that in which Ayrton is ignorant of, or mistaken about, the sense of the word 'similar': but, if we admit this as a legitimate counter-example, then we likewise ought to deny that it follows from Barry's thinking that Harvard resembles Oxford that he thinks they are similar; and, if we deny this, we reject Frege's whole theory of senses as indirect referents. Our intuitive inclination is to hold that whatever principles govern sub-stitution *salva veritate* within single *oratio obliqua* must also govern it within double *oratio obliqua*. It is this which makes it plausible that the reference of an expression in double *oratio obliqua* is the same as its reference in single *oratio obliqua*, and, therefore, by Frege's argument, that its referent in both cases is its ordinary sense. But, if the referent of an ex-pression occurring as part of a clause in *oratio obliqua* is the sense which that expression has when the clause stands alone, it follows that the referent of an expression in double *oratio obliqua* is the sense which that expression has in single *oratio obliqua*. From these two theses, taken together, it follows that the sense of an expression in *oratio obliqua* is simply its ordinary sense, in conformity with my suggested emendation.

Heidelberger might retort that his proposal does accord both with the thesis that the referent of an expression occurring within a clause in *oratio obliqua* is the sense which that expression has when the clause stands alone, and with the thesis that the same principles govern sub-stitution *salva veritate* within double as within single *oratio obliqua*. It is on the strength of the former thesis that we infer that an expression in single *oratio obliqua* must stand for its ordinary sense, one in double *oratio obliqua* for its (simply) indirect sense; and it is on the strength of the latter thesis that we conclude, indirect sense being what it is, that Barry's ignorance of the sense of 'similar' makes no difference to the truth of 'Barry thinks that Harvard is similar to Oxford', but that Ayrton's ignorance of it is fatal to the truth of 'Ayrton knows that Barry thinks that Harvard is similar to Oxford'. The analogy between single and double *oratio obliqua* would indeed fail if we made the invalidity of the inference from 'Ayrton knows that Barry thinks that Harvard resembles Oxford' to 'Ayrton knows that Barry thinks that Harvard is similar to Oxford' turn on Ayrton's ignorance of the sense of 'the sense of "is similar to" ', i.e. on the sense which 'is similar to' has in 'Barry thinks that Harvard is similar to Oxford'. But we must presumably say that, even though Ayrton does not know the sense of 'similar', he *does* know the sense of 'the sense of "is similar to" '; the failure of the inference is due, rather, to Ayrton's not knowing the *reference* of 'is similar to' in 'Barry thinks that Harvard is similar to Oxford'. Such a retort certainly vindicates the consistency of Heidelberger's interpretation: my complaint was not that it was internally inconsistent, but that it was intuitively implausible.

Our discussion so far has, however, left the contrast between Frege's theory, as emended by me, and as interpreted, in its unamended form, by Heidelberger, too stark. Let us go back to Church's argument. That argument proceeded from the premiss that, say, 'Jones believes that the Moon is round' and 'Jones glaubt, dass der Mond rund ist' have just the same sense; and its conclusion was that belief cannot be an attitude to sentences, but must be an attitude to propositions, thoughts or the like. Now on Frege's theory, amended or unamended, the substantival clause in a sentence ascribing a belief to someone stands for a thought, and therefore belief must be taken as an attitude, or at least a relation, to thoughts. But we saw that, on Heidelberger's interpretation, despite his defence of Church, the English and the German sentence cannot have the same sense. In the English sentence, the phrase 'the Moon' has the sense that 'the sense of "the Moon" ' ordinarily bears, whereas in the German sentence the phrase 'der Mond' has the sense that 'der Sinn von "der Mond" ' ordinarily bears; these senses cannot be the same, since one has a constituent standing for an English phrase where the other has one standing for a German phrase. Thus Church's postulate, that a sentence ascribing a belief to a subject is translatable with strict preservation of sense, is much stronger than the conclusion he derives from it, and shares with Frege as interpreted by Heidelberger, namely that the object of belief is a thought (or some like non-linguistic entity). The conclusion requires only that the substantival clause in a sentence ascribing belief stand for a thought, and hence that expressions within that clause may be replaced by others having the same ordinary sense without a change in the reference of the clause or the truth-value of the whole; but the postulate demands that such a replacement may be made without altering even the *sense* of the whole, and, as we saw, there seems no reason to believe this. It is perfectly consistent to combine the thesis that the object of belief is a thought with the thesis that we can apprehend a thought only as the sense of a sentence (in a verbal or symbolic language). It is therefore equally consistent to combine the thesis that a clause in *oratio obliqua*, or an expression within that clause, stands for its ordinary sense with the thesis that, in understanding it as referring to that sense, we apprehend that sense as being the sense of that clause or expression. It is presumably because Heidelberger, surely quite rightly, sees Frege as adhering to both these theses that he adopts his interpretation of Frege's theory of indirect reference; it thus appears that that interpretation is at least consistent with all that Frege says about his theory. It was for reasons connected with this that I also said that it is difficult to take seriously the entire issue of whether the object of belief is a thought or a sentence.[1]

But, given the basic principle of Frege's theory of indirect reference, namely that an expression within *oratio obliqua* stands for what is ordinarily its sense, does not Heidelberger's interpretation of indirect sense actually follow from the thesis that we can allude to a thought only as being that expressed by some one or other sentence, or, more generally, to a sense as being that carried by some expression? Is my emended version of Frege's theory, under which each expression has, in *oratio obliqua*, the same sense as it has in ordinary contexts, compatible with that thesis? My emendation implies that, if 'The Moon is round' can be translated into a given language with strict preservation of sense, then so can 'Jones believes that the Moon is round', in other words, that Church's postulate is true. So, if Heidelberger was inconsistent in advancing his interpretation of indirect sense while yet endorsing Church's argument, was I not equally inconsistent in proposing my emendation of Frege's theory while rejecting Church's argument? Well, at any rate, not quite equally. One cannot accept Church's arguments as cogent without accepting as true the postulate he uses as a premiss; but one can, as I did, reject his argument on the score that he was not entitled to *presume* the truth of his postulate, without necessarily denying the postulate. But the degree of inconsistency is unimportant: the material question is whether, if we accept the thesis that a sense can be presented to us only as the sense of some expression, we are not bound to accept Heidelberger's interpretation and reject my emendation.

---

[1] *FPL*, p. 372.

To say that a sense can be given to us only as the sense carried by some particular expression implies that the most direct means by which we can refer in English to the sense expressed by, say, 'the Moon' is by using the phrase 'the sense of "the Moon" '. Frege's theory is that, in an *oratio obliqua* context, the words 'the Moon' are understood as standing for their ordinary sense. It therefore appears to follow that, in so understanding them, we are taking them as standing for a sense given to us as being that either of the phrase 'the Moon' itself or of some other synonymous expression; and the only reasonable choice is the former, since no systematic rule for selecting a synonym can be conceived. And, since there is no reason not to suppose that the referent of 'the Moon', when it occurs in *oratio obliqua*, is not given to us in the most direct manner possible, it becomes natural to suppose that the sense which the phrase 'the Moon' bears, in such a context, coincides with the ordinary sense of the phrase 'the sense of "the Moon" '. This is to say that Heidelberger's interpretation does appear to follow from the two theses, taken together: the thesis that a sense can be given only as the sense of some expression, and the thesis that an expression in *oratio obliqua* stands for its ordinary sense. If so, then any denial that, in *oratio obliqua*, 'the Moon' has a sense distinct from its ordinary one, namely the ordinary sense of 'the sense of "the Moon" ', must involve the denial of one or other of the two theses. But is it really so?

In holding that an expression in *oratio obliqua* has an indirect sense as well as an indirect reference, Frege's idea was that it must have a sense which would, independently of context, determine it as having the reference which, in that context, it does have. How, then, do we grasp what sense it has in that context? Even if, once we grasp the indirect sense, that determines the indirect reference without our further adverting to the particular type of context, we must advert to that context in order to recognize the expression as bearing, in that occurrence, its indirect rather than its ordinary sense. Moreover, on *any* interpretation of Frege's unamended theory, knowing the ordinary sense of the expression, and knowing that it occurs in *oratio obliqua*, and therefore has its indirect sense, do not together suffice to yield a grasp of its indirect sense: for its ordinary sense is its indirect referent, and, as Russell insisted, there is no backward road from referent to sense. This is quite evident on Heidelberger's interpretation. From simply knowing that we have, in *oratio obliqua*, an expression whose ordinary sense is that of the word 'resembles', we cannot read off the indirect sense of the expression: it might, for instance, be the ordinary sense of the phrase 'the sense of "is similar to" ', which, though it has the same referent as 'the sense of "resembles" ', has a different sense, since the referent is given as the value of the same function for a different argument. In order to apprehend the indirect sense of 'resembles', we have therefore to take cognisance of the fact that it is that very word that occurs.

The fact that, on Heidelberger's interpretation of Frege's theory, and probably on any interpretation which retains Frege's notion of indirect senses, we are required to advert to the particular expression employed, and not just to its ordinary sense, is not, in itself, an objection to that interpretation. As Blackburn and Code insist, it is incumbent upon Frege's theory to explain the connection between the use of an expression in *oratio obliqua* and its use in ordinary contexts, both because they are inferentially connected and to make it unmysterious that we understand *oratio obliqua* as in fact we do. If we demand that this connection be exhibited as depending on the ordinary sense of the expression alone, we run against Russell's objection that there is no backward road from reference to sense: no convention can determine the indirect sense from the direct sense. This was one reason for my proposing that the notion of indirect sense be jettisoned. But Heidelberger has an alternative method of disposing of the problem of the backward road, one, in itself, quite legitimate. If hearing or reading a sentence were not a conscious process, but we were aware only of the thought which, by some mechanism unknown to us, was generated in our minds by the sentence's unconsciously impinging upon our sense-organs, then any special sense borne by an expression in a particular type of context would have to depend solely upon that context together with its ordinary or general sense, and would have therefore to be invariant under the replacement of that expression by another with the same ordinary sense. Since, however, this is obviously an incorrect picture of what happens, we have no need to explain the functioning of language in the manner we should have to adopt if it were correct. There is no paradox in the fact that the sense of our words sometimes embodies an allusion to those words themselves, as in the type of example cited by Quine, such as 'Little John was ironically so called'.

Nevertheless, the complexity of Frege's unamended theory is unjustified. Even on that theory, we have to take the context into account in order to recognize that the expression has its indirect, not its direct, reference. Since we do, there is no need to postulate that the immediate effect of the context is to endow the expression with an indirect sense which then determines the indirect reference independently of context; instead, the context should be taken as operating immediately upon the reference, rather than mediately, through the sense. That is to say, the convention which we tacitly understand as governing the occurrence of words in *oratio obliqua* may be taken as one relating to its reference. Given that we know the ordinary sense of the expression, and given that we know the convention governing *oratio obliqua*, we thereby know what the indirect referent of the expression is: there is no need to suppose that the immediate effect of the context is to induce us to attach a special sense to the expression, in accordance with which we then take it to stand for its ordinary sense. The ordinary sense of the expression, together with the principle that in *oratio obliqua* it stands for that sense, is sufficient to enable us to judge of the truth-value of the whole sentence; and that is all that sense is required to do. It is therefore superfluous to suppose that there is any further ingredient of the sense possessed by the expression in this context. To represent us as arriving at the indirect referent via some indirect sense is to make our route unnecessarily circuitous.

How, then, on this emended version of Frege's theory, is the indirect referent of the expression, that is, its ordinary sense, given to us? If we accept the thesis that a sense can be given only as the sense of some expression, then we must reply that it is given as the ordinary sense of that very expression. That is to say, just as, on Heidelberger's interpretation, our grasp of the indirect reference is mediated by an indirect sense which we identify only by adverting to the actual expression that occurs, so, under my emendation, we apprehend the indirect referent as being the sense of the expression which we perceive as occurring in the *oratio obliqua* clause. The point of the thesis which compels us to accept this way of regarding the matter—the thesis, namely, that a sense can be given to us only as the sense of some expression—is that the expression is neither a code for its sense nor an external cause, of which we might be unaware, of our grasping the sense. If it were either of those things, then we might apprehend the sense independently of its being the sense of any expression. But our grasp of the sense of the expression consists, on Frege's account, in our knowledge of how to determine the truth-conditions of sentences containing it. This leaves it open that the same sense might be apprehended by beings with different faculties from ours, independently of any means of expressing it: but it leaves us with no access to that sense save as the sense of some expression. We can easily understand what it is for two expressions to have the same sense; but our way of grasping what the sense of an expression is renders us incapable of detaching the sense from every actual or hypothetical means of expressing it.

To hold that, when we take the expression in *oratio obliqua* as standing for its own sense, we are conceiving of that sense as the sense of that very expression, is no more objectionable on the emended version of Frege's theory than on the account which Heidelberger's interpretation forces on us; and it does not compel us to adopt that interpretation. The difference between the two accounts is simply that, on Heidelberger's, we confer on the expression in *oratio obliqua* a new and special sense from which we then determine its (indirect) referent, whereas, on mine, knowing the (ordinary) sense of the expression, we go, guided by the convention governing *oratio obliqua*, straight to the indirect referent. There is no need to say that the convention in question is one in accordance with which, by adverting to the specific expression that occurs, we endow it with a special sense from which we then determine it as standing for its ordinary sense; we can simply say that, in accordance with that convention, we take the expression as standing for that sense which is given to us as being the sense of that expression.

The upshot, so far, is this. The merit of my emendation, as against the interpretation espoused by Heidelberger and so brusquely dismissed by me in *FPL*, is slighter than I claimed in that book, inasmuch as Heidelberger's interpretation offers an alternative escape from the problem of the backward road. Nevertheless, that interpretation leaves the problem concerning double *oratio obliqua* unresolved; and the theory of indirect sense is in any case a needless and unjustifiable complication. Heidelberger's interpretation has proved not, after all, to be entailed by the thesis that sense is given to us only as the sense of some expression; that thesis can be accommodated by the emended version of Frege's theory which dispenses with indirect sense.

In arguing this, however, I have made the contrast between Heidelberger's interpretation and my own emendation less stark than originally appeared, as I promised above to do; and, in doing so, I have provided further justification for saying that the issue whether the object of a belief is a sentence or a thought is less serious than it has been taken to be. What is, indeed, a serious issue is whether we can grasp a thought independently of any means of expressing it; Frege did not think that we could. It is also a serious issue whether, if we cannot do so, it makes sense to suppose the existence of beings who can, as Frege thought it did. But, if it is granted that we can grasp a thought only as expressed in some way, it makes comparatively little difference whether we hold that the object of belief is a sentence, considered as having a particular sense and thus expressing a particular thought, or that it is a thought, which we apprehend as expressed by a particular sentence.

What our discussion has uncovered, once more, is a tension between different constituents of Frege's notion of sense. One way in which Frege explains the sense of an expression is as the way in which its referent is given to us, that is, the manner in which we apprehend its referent as being the referent of that expression. If we construe the notion of sense in this way, then, notwithstanding the foregoing argument, Heidelberger's interpretation really does follow from the thesis that a sense can be given only as the sense of some expression, granted that the referent of an expression in *oratio obliqua* is to be its ordinary sense: it does so precisely because the indirect referent of the expression is given to us as being the ordinary sense of that expression. If, however, we regard sense as what was called above the conventional significance of an expression, or, more precisely, as that which a speaker must know about it in order to determine its referent, then the arguments used above in favour of my emendation in preference to Heidelberger's interpretation find their application. To know what an expression occurring in *oratio obliqua* stands for, according to Frege's theory, we need know no more than the ordinary sense of the expression and the principle that an expression stands, in such a context, for its own sense: since nothing further need be known, the postulation of an indirect sense is, on the conception of sense as conventional significance, entirely redundant. On the former conception of sense, as the mode of presentation of the referent, an expression which has different referents in different occurrences must also have different senses. On the conception of it as conventional significance, on the other hand, we shall want only sparingly to ascribe more than one sense to the same expression; if there is a connection between the uses of the expression in different contexts, especially one of inferential importance, we shall want to construe it as having different senses only if no systematic principle determines in which way it is to be taken as being used. The latter of the two conceptions of sense is the most natural when we have in mind the construction of a whole theory of meaning for a language. The former conception accords better with Frege's usual way of speaking about sense; but, as we shall see, some of the theses he held concerning it gain their plausibility from a tacit appeal to the conception of sense as an ingredient in significance.

The final upshot of our discussion is, therefore, that no definite preference can be given to my emendation or to Heidelberger's interpretation: it depends to which conception of sense we are appealing. If we appeal to the conception of sense as the mode of presentation, then we must adopt Heidelberger's interpretation. But, if we do, we must be aware of what we are doing. We shall be saying only that the indirect referent of an expression is given to us as being the ordinary sense of the expression used; we shall not be saying that, in grasping the sense of the sentence, we need know any more about the expression than its ordinary sense and the general principle concerning indirect reference. And, even so, we shall be in difficulties; we shall still be unable to handle the difficulty about multiple *oratio obliqua*. We might try denying the general principle that the referent of an expression in an *oratio obliqua* clause is the sense that it would have if that clause stood alone, so that its doubly indirect referent will be its simply indirect sense; we might lay down, instead, that its multiply indirect sense always coincides with its simply indirect sense. Such a stipulation would indeed allow us to pass from 'Ayrton knows that Barry thinks that Harvard resembles Oxford' to 'Ayrton knows that Barry thinks that Harvard is similar to Oxford'; but the trouble will only break out in a different place. For, if the indirect sense of 'resembles' differs from that of 'is similar to', as, on Heidelberger's interpretation, it must, and if the sense of a constituent expression is part of the thought expressed by the sentence, it follows ineluctably that 'Barry thinks that Harvard resembles Oxford' and 'Barry thinks that Harvard is similar to Oxford' express distinct thoughts, even though 'resembles' and 'is similar to' have the same ordinary sense; and then, if the inference cited above is valid, it will follow that knowledge, and likewise belief, cannot have thoughts as their objects. That thoughts, defined as the senses of complete sentences, are the objects of belief, of knowledge and of other propositional attitudes is a plausible thesis; but it becomes untenable if sense is strictly construed as the mode of presentation of the referent. That is not to say that the notion of the mode of presentation is irrelevant to an account of the object of belief; still less is it to say that, in this connection, it is to be replaced by the conception of sense as conventional significance. We shall come back to this topic later in the present chapter.

mode of
presentation

It should now be quite clear why I have chosen to discuss indexicality and *oratio obliqua* in a single chapter. They are both topics which tend to pull apart from one another the diverse ingredients in Frege's notion of sense, and to do so in much the same manner. In other connections, it is far less apparent that Frege's notion does indeed contain such diverse ingredients; on reflecting on either of these two topics, we become acutely conscious of them. If sense is taken as the mode of presentation of the referent, then we are debarred from adopting the apparently harmless and natural view that 'I', as used by different speakers, has a constant sense but varying reference. Either we must say that its sense alters, as it is used first by one speaker and then by another; or we must allow it a constant sense, but deny that, taken by itself, even on a specific occasion of utterance, it stands for a person, or for an object, at all, regarding it as a functional expression, whose argument is supplied by the circumstances of its utterance, with a misleadingly 'complete' or 'saturated' linguistic form. In the first case, we sever the notion of sense from that of conventional significance; in the second, we have to deny that the so-called pronoun 'I' is, as it appears to be, a singular term, even considered as part of a particular utterance. At the beginning of this chapter, I defended my remark, on p. 367 of *FPL*, that the view that the same sentence, containing the word 'I', expresses a different thought as it is uttered by different speakers cannot be derived merely from the characterization of a thought as the sense of a sentence. It then appeared that, to grasp Frege's conception of a thought, we had to treat his thesis that thoughts are true or false absolutely as a principle constitutive of the notion; and the two ingredients of his notion of sense which we then saw as pulling apart under the strain of its being applied to indexical expressions were the conception of sense as conventional significance and the conception of it as a thought-constituent, where thoughts are conceived of as having absolute and invariant truth-values. Our discussion of *oratio obliqua* has now yielded another way to view the matter; this time the second ingredient of the notion of sense, besides the conception of it as conventional significance, is to be taken to be the notion of the mode of presentation. If we regard sense exclusively in *this* light, then it becomes obvious that 'I' cannot have the same sense when it refers to different speakers; and from this it follows at once that the thoughts which those speakers express—defined as the senses of the sentences they utter—must likewise be distinct whenever they use that pronoun.

It was a mistake to say, as I did on p. 267 of FPL_1, that the emendation which I proposed to Frege's theory of indirect reference was in harmony with all his other views; and I have accordingly corrected the passage in which I made this claim. It is *not* consonant with his views that an expression with a constant sense should vary in reference according to context; as we have seen, this conflicts, not merely with the principle that sense determines reference, but with the conception of sense as the mode of presentation. The idea has, indeed, a certain natural harmony with Frege's principle that it is only in the context of a sentence that a word has a reference; but the point is certainly not to be pressed, since he never suggested any such application of his context principle. We can go further: even the theory of indirect reference as Frege himself presents it, according to which not only the reference, but the sense, of an expression shifts when it occurs in *oratio obliqua*, is out of harmony with his other views. To speak more exactly, the theory should be viewed as analogous with his thesis that there are proper names which have a sense but lack a reference, and that sentences containing them express thoughts devoid of truth-value. Such a theory applies only to natural language, not to a purified language; and it applies only because of one of the defects of natural language. It is not to be assessed as a coherent account of how language functions, but as the nearest possible approximation to a coherent description of a language that functions only imperfectly. The defect of natural language exemplified by the *oratio obliqua* construction is that of systematic ambiguity; in a properly constructed language, each expression ought to have an invariable sense, and therefore an invariable reference, independent of context. It is for this reason that, in one of his letters to Russell, Frege says that 'strictly one would indeed have to have special symbols in indirect speech, in order to avoid ambiguity, symbols whose connection with the corresponding ones in direct speech would nevertheless be easily recognizable'.[1]

It could be objected that Frege's remark about avoiding ambiguity begs the question: it assumes that variation in reference implies variation in sense, and thus ignores the possibility of emending the theory of indirect reference so as to dispense with indirect sense. Ambiguity of sense, it might be said, is incontestably a defect of language: but a shift of reference from one context to another, in accordance with a fixed sense, is unobjectionable and ought not to be called 'ambiguity'. We have seen, however, that the notion of a sense that serves to determine the reference systematically from the context goes with the conception of sense as the significance of an expression, as whatever is involved in the way the expression works. Such a notion would be unavailable to anyone who thought, instead, of the expression as a means of getting us to the sense, that sense being something existing independently of being expressed or grasped, and graspable independently of being expressed. As we have seen, *this* conception of sense is not Frege's. For him, the sense does indeed exist independently of its being expressed or grasped, but we cannot conceive of it or grasp it otherwise than as the sense of some expression, even if there are beings who can do so; moreover, although, when he is speaking of the timeless existence of senses, and of the mental operation of grasping them, he can make it sound as though a sense were a terminus of some mental route, that is not really his view: there is no route to the sense,

---

[1] *BW*, p. 236, *P.M.C.*, p. 153.

but the sense is itself a route, namely to the referent. Frege did, however, think of the sense as being that which is, in the first instance, the first term of the relation of reference, so that the expression is said to refer only in virtue of the sense's referring: to speak of the sense as the mode of presentation of the referent, the manner in which it is given to us, is a specific way of expressing the same conception; a specific way, also, of conveying that the sense is the route and not the terminus. But, once more, on such a conception of sense, the notion of context-dependent reference is still unavailable: if an unambiguous sense is expressed, it must, unaided, determine the reference uniquely.

Faced with such a reply, the objector must reformulate his point. If sense is mode of presentation, then there is nothing wrong with systematic variation in sense. It is only when the sense of an expression is conceived as its significance in the language that variation in sense is a fault to be corrected: so long as the significance remains unaltered, there is nothing amiss if the mode of presentation of the referent, or the referent itself, varies systematically according to the context. This objection is entirely just: if sense is construed *only* as mode of presentation, there is no warrant for describing systematic variation of sense pejoratively as 'ambiguity', and no ground for objection to it. But it is not that Frege adopted the conception of sense as the mode of presentation in preference to the conception of it as significance. Rather, he ran the two conceptions together: he made it plausible, and was himself convinced, that ambiguity, even if systematic, was a defect precisely because he tacitly assumed sense to be the major constituent of conventional significance. As already remarked, it is only in particular connections—ones with which Frege concerned himself only occasionally—that the different ingredients of Frege's notion of sense pull apart from one another; he himself seems to have remained unaware of this.

In our preliminary look at Frege's treatment of indexicality, the tension that we discovered within his notion of sense was that between sense conceived as conventional significance and senses as constituents of thoughts taken as independently existing, eternal objects. Frege's characterization of senses as eternal and existing independently of us is most naturally explained by his desire to safeguard the *objectivity* of sense. Given that the objectivity of sense had thus been secured, little further use is made in Frege's theory of the conception of senses as existing immutably and independently of our grasping or expressing them; almost everything he says in detail about senses can be interpreted in terms of the conception of sense as significance. We saw in Chapter 3 that the conception of the significance of an expression as a way of getting us to the sense cannot be made coherent: rather, the sense is a way of getting us to the referent. But, when Frege applies his notion of sense to indexical expressions, the conception of senses as existing eternally and independently of us appears to play a critical role in determining what he says about them. Given only the conception of sense as linguistic significance, we should say that a sentence containing 'I' expresses something that can be true in the mouth of one speaker, false in that of another: but thoughts, as eternal, immutable objects, must be true or false absolutely. Likewise, because sense alone must determine reference, independently of context or the mode of expression, a word in *oratio obliqua*, since it does not have its ordinary reference, cannot have its ordinary sense. Is there any way to render this more intelligible, or should we simply dismiss it as an unfortunate consequence of Frege's taking too literally an image he employed in order to insist that senses are objective?

objects of belief

In examining his views on *oratio obliqua*, we found it apter to explain them by appeal to the conception of sense as mode of presentation than to the idea of thoughts as eternal objects; and this worked equally well in explaining why, for Frege, a sentence containing 'I' expresses different thoughts when uttered by different speakers. In seeking a rationale for these views, therefore, we must find a means of connecting these various ingredients of his notion of sense: the conception of sense as mode of presentation; the thesis that sense determines reference without regard to context; and the idea of senses as constituents of thoughts that are true or false absolutely. Despite the fact that we observed a conflict, at one particular point, between the conception of sense as mode of presentation and the thesis that the object of a propositional attitude is a thought, it is this latter thesis that secures the connection between these ingredients. It was Gareth Evans's perception of the relation of this thesis to the conception of sense as mode of presentation that prompted him to speak, in the sentence already quoted at the beginning of this chapter, of 'Frege's notion of "what is said" or "the thought expressed" ' as being ' "psychologically real" in the sense of being the object of propositional attitudes'.

When Frege makes general remarks about thoughts, what he usually stresses is that they are the bearers of truth and falsity, and that we are capable of grasping them, although they exist independently of our doing so. But we can do more than grasp a thought: we can also judge it to be true; and knowledge, for Frege, is embodied in judgments. Hence thoughts may also be characterized as the objects of knowledge and belief; and, as already observed, the thesis that a sentence in *oratio obliqua* stands for the thought it ordinarily expresses has the same consequence. Thus the thought that I express when I say, 'I am cold', must be that which I know to be true and am bringing my hearer to know; likewise, the thought which I express when I say, 'I shall never have the chance to visit this place again', must be that which I believe to be true. But I do not know or believe something which is true now but may become false tomorrow, or which is true for me but false for you; my belief can only be correct or incorrect in an absolute sense, and what I know must likewise be true absolutely. Looked at in this way, Frege's insistence that a thought must be true or false absolutely can be seen as much more reasonable than appears when we concentrate on the definition of a thought as the sense of a sentence, and conceive of sense as linguistic significance; indeed, as more reasonable than I allowed on pp. 384–5 of *FPL*. Evans sought to unify Frege's conception of the senses borne by non-indexical and by indexical expressions precisely by appealing to the notion of the sense as a route to or mode of presentation of the referent; and he did so in a manner which firmly embeds the grasping of a thought in the process of *thinking*. 'Frege's idea,' he said, 'was that, to understand an expression, one must not merely think, of the reference, that it is the reference, but that one must, in so thinking, think of the reference *in a particular way*. The way in which one must think of the reference of an expression in order to understand it is that expression's *sense*. No substantial or positive theory of the notion of a way of thinking is presupposed by this conception of sense. If the intuitive notion needs to be supplemented, we can appeal to the general idea of an account of what makes it the case that a thought is about the object which it is about: two people will then be thinking of an object in the same way if and only if the account of what makes the one person's thought about that object is the same as the account of what makes the other person's thought about that object.' And the contribution of an indexical expression to the thought expressed by a particular utterance containing it is to be explained in the same general manner, for instance as what makes a man's thought to be a thought about a particular day when he thinks of it as the current day, i.e. as 'today'. 'To give an account of how a thought concerns an object is to explain how the subject knows which object is in question'; and this knowledge consists, at least in part, in his dispositions to judge the thought as true or false in various circumstances.

On one point I am in disagreement with Evans, namely over his contention that, in allowing that natural languages contain names having sense but no reference, Frege was being unfaithful to his conception of sense as a route to or mode of presentation of the referent. In general, however, his account of Frege's notion of thoughts appears to me illuminating; these considerations certainly provide a more powerful reason for Frege's having said what he did about indexical expressions than an appeal to a piece of mythology. Evans was quite right to say that, if we regard thoughts as the objects of propositional attitudes, we shall take them as true or false absolutely, not relatively to an occasion. He was also right to hold that, if we concentrate upon the conception of sense as the mode of presentation, we shall find it natural to allow that an indexical expression may bear different senses on different occasions, while preserving a constant significance. He was, of course, again right to insist that, in general, if the singular terms occurring in the expression of a thought are regarded as contributing to it only in virtue of their references, the resulting notion of a thought cannot be identified with that of the object of a propositional attitude. Suppose, to amplify an example of Heidelberger's, that Murray is lunching tête-à-tête with Orwell, whom he knows well; Murray has heard of Blair, and knows a little about him, but is unaware of ever having met him, and has no idea that Orwell *is* Blair. Then, evidently, Murray knows that Orwell is present, but does not know that Blair is present. Evans rightly remarked that one test of whether two sentences express the same thought, where a thought is the object of knowledge or belief, is whether it would be possible to judge either to be true without at the same time judging the other to be true; this, on the supposition that the speaker grasps the sense of each sentence, is a test proposed by Frege. Evans also rightly remarked that this test is not sufficient, by itself, to settle all relevant questions. Now suppose that, on Tuesday, Smith says to Jones, 'It will be fine on Wednesday'; on Wednesday it rains, and on Thursday, when it is fine, Jones meets Smith and says, 'You were wrong to say it would be fine yesterday'. Smith denies that he said any such thing, and, after some confusion, it turns out that, on Tuesday, Smith thought it was Monday, and has been making the same mistake ever since. The test shows that, if thoughts are to be the objects of belief, more than the references of the singular terms contained in sentences is required to determine the thoughts expressed by them: for on Thursday Smith judged the thought he had expressed by saying, 'It will be fine on Wednesday', to be true, and that which would then be expressed by saying, 'It was fine yesterday', to be false.

On p. 384 of *FPL* I did not envisage ascribing to Frege the general principle that singular terms occurring in the expression of a thought contribute to it only in virtue of their references: to explain his views on indexical expressions in this way would be to have him abandon the whole sense/reference distinction, at least for singular terms. I did envisage him as at least toying with the restriction of this principle to indexical expressions. It is far less clear than in the general case that Evans was right in thinking that such a restricted principle would likewise debar thoughts from being the objects of propositional attitudes. Let us modify the foregoing example by supposing that what Smith said on Tuesday was 'It will be fine tomorrow'. He can, of course, judge on Thursday that the thought then expressible by saying, 'It was fine yesterday', is false: but the above-mentioned test yields no conclusion from this, since he will not at the same time judge that the thought he expressed by saying, 'It will be fine tomorrow', was true. Or, rather, he can continue to think that what he said on Tuesday was true only if he has forgotten when he said it; and that renders it dubious whether he now knows *what* thought he expressed by means of those words. The thought expressed by a sentence containing an indexical expression depends, on Frege's account, on the circumstances in which it was uttered; and, if one mistakes the circumstances, one presumably also misidentifies the thought expressed. In the same way, if Smith says to Jones, 'I am cold', and Jones says a little later to Smith, 'You are cold', Smith can judge that the thought expressed by Jones is false only if he supposes him to be addressing someone else; and it is again plausible to say that Smith does not know what thought Jones expressed.

The suggestion made on p. 384 of *FPL* thus appears defensible even when the primary characteristic of a thought is taken to be that it can be an object of belief. My actual comment on the suggestion was that Frege had 'weakened his claim that thoughts are that to which truth and falsity are primarily ascribed'. It in no way weakens this claim to regard utterances of the same sentence as expressing different thoughts, when that sentence contains a token-reflexive expression: what weakened it, according to me, was allowing that utterances of different sentences might express the same thought. In the subsequent pages of *FPL*, pp. 385–400, I argued this particularly in relation to indications of time, which, as it seemed to me, have a rather different status from indications of place or person. The argument was to the effect that, even if we are entitled to admit a notion of a thought according to which 'It will be fine tomorrow' or 'It will be fine on Wednesday', said on Tuesday, and 'It was fine yesterday' or 'It was fine on Wednesday', said on Thursday, express the same thought as 'It is fine today', said on Wednesday, thoughts in this sense should not be regarded as the *primary* bearers of truth-values, which should rather be taken to be statements in a sense in which the utterances on the different days make distinct statements (and, equally, utterances of any one of these sentences on different days would also make distinct statements). This argument indeed turned on considerations bearing on our understanding of sentences, that is, on our grasp of their conventional significance in the language, rather than with them as expressions of belief or knowledge. It is, however, plausible to say, with Evans, that the assertion on Thursday of 'It was fine yesterday' may 'manifest the persistence of a belief', that belief, namely, which was manifested on Wednesday by the assertion of 'It is fine today' (though it would be less plausible to add 'and on Tuesday by the assertion of "It will be fine tomorrow" '). For this reason, when we regard thoughts as the objects of belief and knowledge, we may take both utterances (or even all three) as expressing the same thought, and still plausibly view thoughts as the primary bearers of truth-value. But, whether Frege's opinions about token-reflexive expressions be regarded as stemming from his conception of thoughts as eternal, immutable objects or from the need to treat them as the objects of knowledge and belief, they impose a distinction between a Fregean sense and the conventional significance of a linguistic expression. That does not entail that it is mistaken to interpret Frege as virtually identifying sense with conventional significance, or, rather, with a particular aspect of it, an interpretation argued for in Chapters 3 and 5, for he seems to have seen the relation between the two as closer than it actually is: as already remarked, it is only when we consider his views on token-reflexive expressions and on *oratio obliqua* that we become aware of the divergence, in his thought, between them.

public and private

The difference in fact comes out in ways unacknowledged by Frege. The significance of an expression, its meaning as an expression of the language, is a matter of a common practice, of what the speakers of the language will ultimately agree in recognizing as correct; but what belief a speaker expresses by means of a sentence he utters is a matter of his private understanding of that sentence. Despite his reiterated emphasis on the objectivity of sense, Frege in fact described language as governed by the private understanding of it possessed by each speaker: the sense that a given speaker attaches to a word is the manner in which he takes it as contributing to determining the truth-value of any sentence in which it occurs. What, on such a view, makes a language a possible instrument of communication is the ascertainability by one speaker of another speaker's private understanding of it; what makes it an efficient instrument of communication is the approximate coincidence of the private understandings of different speakers. Frege thus in effect assumes that an account of what confers on the expressions of a language the meanings that they have can be given by appeal only to the knowledge which each individual speaker has concerning the language. As far as sense is concerned, though not, perhaps, as regards force, he furthermore assumes that what each speaker knows involves no essential reference to the use of the language as constituting a common practice. In both respects, he is surely wrong. That he is wrong, and the full extent to which he is wrong, do not directly concern us in the present connection. What matters to us in the present context is that, on any account, a divergence has to be admitted to be possible, in any given instance, between the meaning of an expression in the common language and a speaker's private understanding of it; it is with the former that Frege is usually concerned when he speaks of the sense expressed by a word or phrase, and it is the latter that is relevant to the content of a speaker's beliefs.

The use or meaning of a word in a language is embodied in an accepted practice. Such a practice need not be fully known to all speakers of the language able to make use of the word; what is required is that the correct application of the word can be ascertained by appeal to sources which all speakers recognize, or can be brought to recognize, as authoritative. In uttering a sentence, a speaker holds himself responsible to the meanings that his words have in the common language; and it is because he is understood as doing so that he can transmit information without himself fully knowing those meanings. If Alice has been told that her uncle lives in Lima, she can pass on this information even though she herself knows no more about Lima than that it is the capital of Bolivia, Peru or Ecuador, and cannot remember which. In this way, she can use the name 'Lima'; but can she be said to believe that her uncle lives in Lima? Doubtless she would ordinarily be said to do so; but when we are concerned with the precise content of a belief expressed by means of an utterance, we must take that as depending, not upon the public meanings of the words composing it, but on the speaker's private understanding of them. If Alice had adopted a private name of her own for the city where her uncle lived, and had forgotten its real name, she could not be said to believe that he lived in any definite city if all she remembered about it was that it was the capital of one of the three South American countries. If she remembers that its true name is 'Lima', all that connects that name with a particular city is its use in the language; so the content of Alice's belief is more aptly expressed by saying that she believes that her uncle lives in the South American city that is called 'Lima' than by describing her outright as believing that he lives in Lima.

The point is forcefully illustrated by an excellent example given by Saul Kripke.[1] Pierre, a Frenchman, learns the use of the name 'Londres' in geography classes at school, and, from pictures that he is shown, forms a belief which he expresses by saying, 'Londres est jolie'. Later, he travels to England, and learns English by the direct method; he settles in London, but fails to grasp that 'Londres' is to be translated into English as 'London', the name he learns to use for the city in which he is living. From his experiences there, he forms a belief which he expresses by saying, 'London is ugly', without in any way modifying his former beliefs. Now we can, of course, truly say that Pierre believes both that the city called 'Londres' is pretty and that the city called 'London' is ugly, and there is no paradox here. But the subtlety of Kripke's example lies in Pierre's unlikeness to Alice. Alice was able to employ the name 'Lima' in communication with others; but we could not say of her that she had fully mastered the use of the name. Pierre, on the other hand, knows quite as much about the name 'Londres' as do many Frenchmen who would be acknowledged to have a mastery of its use, one quite sufficient for us to ascribe to them beliefs about London and not just about the city called 'Londres'. He also knows quite as much about the name 'London' as do many residents of the city to whom we should not hesitate to ascribe an understanding of the name and a variety of beliefs about London. Pierre is, indeed, ignorant that 'Londres' is the French equivalent of 'London'. 'Londres' is not merely the usual translation of 'London', but the *established* translation, a linguistic convention as much a matter of agreed common practice as any other. Hence what Pierre does not know is a fact of accepted linguistic usage. But it is a fact unknown to many speakers both of French and English, his ignorance of which ought not to disqualify him from being able to express, in either language, a belief about London. For many words of a language, including proper names, we do not demand, for a speaker to be said to have a mastery of them, that he know everything that pertains to their use. Pierre's knowledge concerning the names 'Londres' and 'London', unlike Alice's concerning 'Lima', is sufficient for him to be credited with a mastery of them; but what he knows about the two names is different, and it is this that enables him without inconsistency to express apparently contradictory beliefs.

It is somewhat unclear whether Kripke would accept this conclusion. He argues[2] that to explain Pierre's adherence to apparently contradictory

---

[1] 'A Puzzle about Belief', A. Margalit, *Meaning and Use*, Dordrecht, Boston and London, 1979, pp. 239–83.

[2] Ibid., pp. 260–3.

beliefs by representing him as attaching distinct senses to 'Londres' and to 'London' is not an adequate solution, if these senses are taken as expressible by identifying descriptions fixing the reference of the names. The argument consists in modifying the example; this time Pierre is imagined never to leave his native France, but again to learn English by the direct method; his instructor gives him, in English, an explanation of the name 'London', beginning, say, 'London is the largest city in England, . . .', which happens to be an exact translation of the explanation he was given at school of the name 'Londres'. He still does not realize that 'Londres' is the French equivalent of 'London'; acquiring beliefs which he expresses by 'Londres est jolie' and 'London is ugly', he infers that the names stand for different cities, and that therefore 'Angleterre' and 'England' denote different countries, etc. Because of this possibility, Kripke argues, the solution would be adequate only if we can reach an ultimate level where the defining properties are 'pure' properties not involving proper names; but it is implausible that any such ultimate level can be reached.

This argument is extremely weak, for two reasons. First, even on its own terms, it is unconvincing. There is no reason to debar indexical expressions from occurring in the descriptions used at the ultimate level: one such 'pure' description might be 'the planet we inhabit'. Given, by this means, the proper name 'the Earth', Pierre would need only quite an elementary knowledge of geography to frame, in terms of it, a uniquely identifying description of Great Britain. The regress argument therefore fails even if aimed only at Kripke's favourite target, the description theory of proper names.

Secondly, the argument embodies a failure to perceive where the burden of proof lies. Before anything can be inferred from an example, it must be made plausible that it illustrates a genuine possibility. Kripke's original example was plausible precisely because, in it, the connection made by Pierre between the name 'Londres' and its referent plainly differed from that which he made between 'London' and its referent. What made it paradoxical was that he knew enough about each name to be able, in principle, to identify its referent without relying on other speakers; it was this that ruled out a solution which represented him as merely having beliefs about the city called 'Londres' and that called 'London'. In the modified example, this second feature is retained; but the first one is not. No version of the example *could* be constructed in which there was no difference in Pierre's understanding of 'Londres' and of 'London', because the existence of such a difference is a condition of its plausibility. In giving his modified example, Kripke does not argue that there need be no such difference.

But he does argue that the difference need not be of a particular kind; and the argument is devoid of force unless the example is filled out to show what other difference there may be. In the modified example, Pierre's understanding of the names 'Londres' and 'London' is assumed to be mediated by descriptions that fix their references; and there is no difference in these descriptions, save that they are formulated in different languages. There must, therefore, be some difference in his understanding of the corresponding names occurring in them, such as 'Angleterre' and 'England'. If this is again mediated by definite descriptions, we may need to enquire into his understanding of further pairs of names, and so on. Now either, in the course of thus tracing back the source of his divergent understanding of 'Londres' and of 'London', we shall come upon a pair of names whose references he fixes by non-equivalent descriptions, or we shall come upon a pair his understanding of at least one member of which is not given by means of any such description. If it be assumed, as part of the example, that we shall never come upon any difference at all, then the example is deprived of all plausibility. It is not, of course, my intention here to defend the description theory; the propensity which Pierre has to identify the referent of some proper name may, for example, rest upon his capacity to recognize that object, even though he cannot, in its absence, describe it. I have been concerned merely to emphasize that Kripke supplies no ground for doubting the proposition that Pierre's situation arises because his personal understanding of the French word differs from that which he has of the English word of which it is the accepted translation; I remain uncertain whether it was his intention to do so.

A speaker does not in general know all that is involved in the public meanings of his words, even when he knows enough to be said to understand them perfectly well; and he will also often know things that for him determine the references of his words, even though what he knows is not part of their public meanings. If we are concerned with exactly what belief a speaker expresses by means of a sentence, it is his private understanding of the words that determine this. We shall usually not go far astray if we take the sentence, regarded as having the meaning that it does in the common language, as determining the belief that he expressed by means of it; but we may sometimes have to take account of the fact that we have thereby characterized his belief only imprecisely. If the objects of belief are said to be thoughts, and if thoughts are to be described as the senses of sentences, then sense should not be equated with any ingredient of meaning within the common language; it must, rather, be the content of private understanding. Precisely this is how Frege presents his notion of a thought in 'Der Gedanke'. In the example given there,[1] Leo Peter identifies Dr Gustav Lauben by his present occupation and residence, while Herbert Garner identifies him by his date and place of birth; Frege describes this state of affairs as entailing that each of them expresses a different thought when he says, 'Dr Gustav Lauben has been wounded'.

Frege even says, about this example, that the two men speak different languages; this could be expressed less tendentiously by saying that their idiolects do not wholly coincide. Though Frege himself says nothing of the kind, we might say that his picture of a language, in the ordinary sense in which German is a language, is as a range of largely overlapping idiolects: on such a view, the notion of an idiolect is the primary one, that of a language which is the common property of a community a notion derivative from it. It seems justifiable so to characterize at least Frege's account of *sense*. Frege does not tell us enough about force for us to be able to say whether or not he regarded it in the same light; it is, however, clear that it would be a mistake so to regard it. To understand a linguistic construction as indicating that, say, an interrogative force was to be taken as attaching to the sentence obviously involves knowing what interrogative force is, that is, what it is to ask a question. To ask a question is not, in general, to evince a propositional attitude, for instance to profess ignorance or to express a desire to know; if it were, barristers, interviewers and examiners would be in the same category as actors. One could therefore hardly be said to know what it is to ask a question unless one knew what it is to ask *someone else* a question; and from this it follows that one cannot, in general, grasp the force attached to an utterance, or the significance of a linguistic indication of that force, without understanding the role of such an utterance in converse. Although Frege does not advance any such argument, he does not give us any warrant for thinking that he wrongly regarded a question as related to some propositional attitude as assertion is related to belief. We should therefore not be justified in stating quite generally that he regarded public meaning as derivative from private understanding; but there is considerable reason to interpret him as holding just such a view of sense.

Frege often remarks that, in fiction and in poetry, we are concerned with the thoughts expressed by the sentences, but not with whether they are true; and in 'Über Sinn und Bedeutung' he observes[2] that the two objects, the True and the False, are recognized, even if only implicitly, by everyone who judges something to be true. But if, as Frege says in

[1] P. 65.
[2] P. 34.

Grundgesetze, vol. 1, § 32, the thought expressed by a sentence is the thought that the condition for it to be true is fulfilled, then, although a thought can be grasped without being judged to be true or to be false, it cannot be grasped by anyone who lacks the conception of its being true or false. A strong case is to be made for saying that the conception of a thought's being true or false is unattainable in the absence of the conception of its being expressed with some kind of force. If so, to attach a sense of any kind to a sentence would to some degree depend upon regarding it as capable of being used in communication. This is not an argument of Frege's. It serves merely to indicate the point at which a fully developed Fregean theory of meaning might make the link between the use of a language as an instrument of communication and the senses borne by the words and sentences of the language, even when the sense of an expression in the language was taken to be no more than that which accorded with the private understanding of it by most of the speakers.

In so far as Frege did tacitly take the notion of an idiolect as logically prior to that of a language in the ordinary sense, he was surely wrong. We do not have first to explain what it is for a single individual to attach a particular sense to a word, and then to state what it is for him to be correct in doing so, as far as the language spoken by the community is concerned. Rather, we have first to say what it is for a word to have a certain sense in the common language, and then to explain what it is for an individual speaker to understand it rightly or wrongly. If the notion of a language is in this way taken as prior to that of an idiolect, the distinction between public meaning and private understanding will be explained differently, and appear sharper, than in Frege's observations concerning sense. But, whether we regard the notion of a language or of an idiolect as the primary one, we are bound to admit some difference between a particular speaker's grasp of an expression and the meaning that it has in the language. Modalities such as necessity and possibility relate to the latter; but the content of a speaker's belief depends on his personal understanding of the words he uses to express it. When we use the notion of a thought as that of the object of a propositional attitude, we must construe the notion of the senses which compose the thought accordingly.

Before considering Frege's views on indexicality further, we may pause to consider the upshot, so far, of our discussion for the question what is the object of a belief. I am not meaning by this to revive the pseudo-question whether it is a sentence or something non-linguistic conveyed by the sentence; the problem is, rather: what serves to characterize the precise content of a belief, and what features of a sentence render it apt as the expression of that content? Frege's answer is, in effect, that, given a sentence that the subject would accept as expressing his belief, another sentence will express it equally provided that it expresses the same sense as the first sentence. Where the original sentence contains neither an indexical expression nor an *oratio obliqua* clause, we may equate sense with significance, or, more exactly, that ingredient in significance which is relevant to the truth-value of the thought expressed. There is no doubt that, in practice, we are disposed to apply just this criterion, except where indexicality is involved: we should normally allow, for instance, that the content of an assertion had been reported correctly, provided that the meaning of the sentence used to report it tallied with that of the utterance by which the assertion was made, modulo the appropriate changes in tenses, pronouns, etc. This is what makes Frege's doctrine of indirect reference prima facie plausible. We have, however, been looking at special cases for which this straightforward account of the matter requires modification.

(1) If the sentence by which the subject makes his assertion or expresses his belief contains an indexical term, preservation of linguistic significance is obviously not the right criterion. Frege still demands preservation of sense, and this must be interpreted to mean mode of presentation. Whether, provided that another indexical term is used, preservation of reference will guarantee the required preservation of mode of presentation, and whether Frege thought that it would, remain for the time being unclear.

(2) If the original sentence expressing the subject's belief itself contained an *oratio obliqua* clause, for instance if it was 'Barry thinks that Harvard resembles Oxford', then the criterion we should intuitively use is that of preservation of significance, not of mode of presentation. In the sentence 'Barry thinks that Harvard is similar to Oxford', the mode of presentation would differ, as we have seen; but the sentence would be accepted as a faithful expression of the speaker's belief.

(3) More generally, the content of a belief appears to depend, not on the mode of presentation as determined by commonly agreed linguistic convention, together with the relevant circumstances, but on the connection which the individual subject makes between the expression and its referent, a distinction hardly acknowledged by Frege.

The last point is, in cruder cases, quite obvious to us. If someone thinks that 'similar' means what 'superior' in fact means, we should not suppose the sentence 'Harvard is similar to Oxford' to be an apt expression of the belief which he expresses by uttering that very sentence. In Kripke's example, however, Pierre could not be said to misunderstand either 'Londres' or 'London'; and two contradictory sentences had equal claims to give the contents of beliefs of his, although those beliefs were not themselves contradictory. This brings out the fact that, not only in Pierre's case, but in others where no paradox arises, an accurate characterization of a speaker's belief requires an account of his personal understanding of the words by means of which he expresses it; in Pierre's case, of the connection which he makes between the names 'Londres' and 'London' and their common referent. At certain points in his essay,[1] Kripke seems to rule out any solution of his paradox that does not supply a single sentence as giving the content of Pierre's beliefs. It should be obvious in advance, however, that, unless the description theory is correct, the conditions of the case preclude our devising any such sentence. If the (private) sense attached by Pierre to the name 'Londres' could be expressed by some definite description, 'the city which is P', and that attached by him to the name 'London' by some non-synonymous description, 'the city which is Q', there would be no difficulty in stating his belief as being that the city which is P is pretty and the city which is Q is ugly. In default of such a pair of definite descriptions, no such statement is possible. It is therefore useless for anyone who does not espouse the description theory to cast around for a 'solution' such as Kripke demands. The correct conclusion is that, when we follow our usual procedure of characterizing someone's belief by means of a sentence considered as having the meaning that it does in the language to which it belongs, we are very often giving only an approximate statement of the content of that belief. Kripke's example shows how, in following that procedure, we may find ourselves involved, not merely in ascribing contradictory beliefs to one who is quite consistent, but in contradicting ourselves.

For obvious reasons, we seldom have occasion to characterize one another's beliefs with complete precision. We content ourselves, in reported speech, with preserving the significance which the subject's words have in the language, except where a change of reference would result, as when indexical expressions are involved or the subject's misunderstanding of some word affected its reference. This provides the explanation of the phenomenon noted under (2) above. In going from 'Barry thinks that Harvard resembles Oxford' to 'Barry thinks that Harvard is similar to Oxford', as an expression of what Ayrton knows, we are preserving the

---

[1] E.g. p. 259.

significance of the words, and we are also preserving the reference of the *oratio obliqua* clause: in both sentences, that clause denotes the thought judged true by Barry. What has changed is only the manner in which that thought is presented; and this, by itself, is too small a change to prompt us to disallow the transition, even when the question is as to the content of Ayrton's knowledge.

Kripke refers to an argument by Benson Mates[1] to show that such a transition would not be justified. The argument, if correct, would establish that, in Frege's terminology, the doubly indirect referents, and thus the simply indirect senses, of two expressions could differ even though their direct senses coincided, a thesis which we eventually concluded to be justified if sense is equated with mode of presentation, but not when it is construed as significance. Kripke[2] regards Mates's argument as directed against Frege's position. Actually, of course, it would, if sound, tell in favour of his unamended view that distinguishes indirect from direct sense, and against my emendation that identifies them: there is no ground, on Frege's unamended view, for expecting expressions having the same ordinary sense to be intersubstitutable *salva veritate* in double *oratio obliqua*. Mates's argument is designed to show that they are not. To adapt Mates's example, it may be true to say, 'No one doubts that all who believe that Harvard resembles Oxford believe that Harvard resembles Oxford', but also true to say, 'Some doubt that all who believe that Harvard resembles Oxford believe that Harvard is similar to Oxford'. I agree with Kripke's judgment[3] that examples of this type are not cogent. As he remarks, someone who doubts the truth of 'All who believe that Harvard resembles Oxford believe that Harvard is similar to Oxford' on the ground that some acquaintance accepts as true 'Harvard resembles Oxford', but not 'Harvard is similar to Oxford', either himself misunderstands 'resembles' or 'similar', or is in a condition of conceptual confusion in thinking himself entitled to ascribe to his acquaintance the belief that Harvard resembles Oxford but not the belief that they are similar; it is therefore at best dubious that he can be truly said to doubt that all who believe that Harvard resembles Oxford believe that they are similar.

If asked to justify the transition from 'Ayrton knows that Barry thinks that Harvard resembles Oxford' to 'Ayrton knows that Barry thinks that

---

[1] 'Synonymity', *University of California Publications in Philosophy*, no. 25, Berkeley, 1950, pp. 201–26, reprinted in L. Linsky (ed.), *Semantics and the Philosophy of Language*, Urbana, 1952.

[2] Op. cit., p. 275, fn. 15.

[3] Ibid., pp. 281–3, fn. 46.

Harvard is similar to Oxford', we might naturally appeal to Frege's test. The two sentences about Barry are so related that anyone who correctly understands both will immediately grant the truth of the other if he judges either to be true; hence, if one serves as an apt expression of what Ayrton knows, so does the other, whether or not Ayrton himself has a correct understanding of both sentences. Kripke's example shows, however, that this principle must be applied with the greatest care. On the face of it, anyone who understands the two sentences 'Londres est jolie' and 'London is pretty' must admit the truth of the other if he grants the truth of either; but, given what we are accustomed to allow as constituting an understanding of such sentences, this is not so.

There is thus no neat answer to the question what is the object of a belief. We have established conventions governing the characterization of the contents of beliefs; but these cannot in all cases be maintained. The best approximation to a brief answer is probably something like 'the subject's grasp of the content of a sentence expressing his belief'; but this is no more than an approximation.

'I'   This leaves unresolved the problem of the content of beliefs expressed by sentences containing indexical expressions, that is, of the thoughts expressed by such sentences, as Frege used the term 'thought' in this connection. Although, for him, the existence of a thought does not depend upon our grasping or expressing it, it remains essential to it that it is apt for linguistic expression: any thought must be able to be expressed by a sentence. This could be understood in a weaker or a stronger sense. In the weaker sense, the thought is claimed to be expressible by some utterance, which may involve indexical expressions; in the stronger sense, the claim is that the thought must be able to be *fully* expressed by words alone. From the stronger version of the claim it will follow that a thought expressed by means of an utterance containing an indexical expression must also be capable of being expressed by a sentence devoid of such expressions—just the consequence which, on p. 384 of *FPL*, I repudiated. It may be that it was some such train of thought that prompted Frege to say in the 'Logik' of 1897 that the thought which someone expresses by saying, 'I am cold', can also be expressed by someone else, who employs the first speaker's name. It is thus possible, he goes on to observe, for a thought to be clothed in a sentence which, by being independent of the thinker, is more apt for the purpose, since a thought, as such, is impersonal and exists independently of any thinker.[1] This thesis is in-

[1] *N.S.*, p. 146, *P.W.*, p. 135.

defensible on any interpretation of the notion of a thought save that which Evans mistakenly regarded me as ascribing to Frege, namely that a singular term contributes to a thought only in virtue of its reference. It cannot be reconciled with construing thoughts as the objects of knowledge and belief: the first speaker knows that he is cold, but might not know, if he were an amnesiac who had forgotten who he was, that what the second speaker said, using the first one's name, was true. In so far as the view propounded in 'Logik' was Frege's considered opinion at the time, it may have appeared to him a justification of his usual practice of ignoring the phenomenon of indexicality; but it is found only in this unpublished work, and he may have thought better of it, since what he wrote on the topic in 'Der Gedanke', though it does not flatly contradict it, tends in the opposite direction.

In that late essay, Frege treats of the topic at greater length, and in a somewhat different way. On p. 65, he raises the question just discussed. Dr Gustav Lauben says, 'I have been wounded'; Leo Peter hears this, and says, some days later, 'Dr Gustav Lauben has been wounded'. Does the sentence uttered by Leo Peter express the same thought as that voiced by Dr Lauben? Frege does not deny, though he also does not affirm, that it may do. What he does is to argue that the mere fact, implicit in the example, that Leo Peter recognized the man who spoke as Dr Gustav Lauben does not guarantee the identity of the thoughts expressed by Lauben's utterance and his own. It depends, he says, upon the sense attached to the proper name 'Dr Gustav Lauben'. Leo Peter may be speaking to someone who was also present when Lauben said, 'I have been wounded', say Rudolf Lingens. If Peter, in saying, 'Dr Gustav Lauben has been wounded', were expressing the same thought as that expressed by Lauben's own utterance, and if Lingens grasped this thought, then Lingens must know that Peter is speaking of the man whom he heard say, 'I have been wounded'. In fact, although Lingens may attach a sense to the name 'Dr Gustav Lauben', say as standing for the only physician living in a certain house known to him, he may not know Lauben personally and hence may not realize that the man being spoken of is the one he heard exclaim that he had been wounded. This proves only that the thought which Lingens grasps in consequence of hearing Peter's remark need not be the same as that voiced by Lauben. To arrive at the desired conclusion, Frege makes the assumption that Peter, although he does know Lauben personally, uses the name 'Dr Gustav Lauben' in the same sense as that which Lingens attaches to it. In communicating with someone else, Frege tacitly assumes, a speaker may invest his words only with a sense available to his hearer.

On p. 66 of 'Der Gedanke', Frege goes on to argue that everyone is presented (*gegeben*) to himself in a special way, one in which he can be presented to no one else. Hence, when, e.g., Dr Lauben thinks to himself, 'I have been wounded', the reference of the 'I' is probably mediated by this mode of presentation; if so, his thought will be one that he alone can grasp. Evans's comment is that this provides the clearest possible evidence that Frege did not hold that all ways of thinking about objects must be given by giving some individuating definite description. This is true; but, on the face of it, Frege here reveals himself as a believer in the possibility of a private language in just the sense denied by Wittgenstein in the *Investigations*. This disturbs Perry greatly; he remarks[1] that 'nothing could be more out of the spirit of Frege's account of sense and thought than an incommunicable, private thought'. Now it is true enough that the idea of an incommunicable thought does not sit naturally with Frege's general conception of thoughts. In 'Der Gedanke' itself, he contrasts thoughts with ideas, understanding the term 'ideas' (*Vorstellungen*) in a broad sense to embrace virtually all mental contents; an idea, he says, requires a bearer, that is, one whose idea it is, whereas a thought does not. It is part of the identity of a sensation or a mental image that it is a particular individual's sensation or image, and, for this reason, there cannot be a sensation or an image, nor, likewise, a mood or a wish, that is not someone's sensation, image, mood or wish. But the very same thought may be communicated by one person to another; since the identity of a thought does not depend upon its being any particular person's thought, it is not in the nature of a thought to require a bearer: a thought does not need a thinker. In many passages of his writings, he insists that thoughts do not depend for their existence on being thought, grasped, expressed or judged to be true or false, and he remarks on the suitability of the expression 'to grasp a thought', on the grounds that you can grasp only what is already there.[2] Likewise, he frequently affirms, as characteristic of thoughts, that they can be grasped by different people. Since a thought does not depend upon any particular thinker, it does not depend upon a thinker at all; it is not a condition of its existence, of there being such a thought, that anyone should think it. But, if a thought that I have is incommunicable, so that only I can grasp it, because it is expressed by means of the word 'I' used in a sense that only I can grasp, since it presents me in a way that I can be presented only to myself, it becomes obscure how the existence of that thought can be independent of my existence:

[1] Op. cit., p. 474.
[2] See *Grundgesetze*, vol. I, p. xxiv, and 'Logik', *N.S.*, p. 149, *P.W.*, p. 137.

if I had not existed, it would be a thought that no thinking being could have grasped.

Frege's example is nevertheless extremely natural. If I wake up in hospital suffering from amnesia, and ask myself in panic, 'Who am I?', this 'I' can certainly not be replaced by 'Dummett'; and it is the same 'I' as occurs when I think to myself, 'I have been wounded'. If we were to explain this 'I' as meaning 'the thinker of this thought', we should have committed ourselves to Frege's idea of the unique mode of presentation of oneself to oneself, since the explanation would be useless if, like most thoughts, this thought were one that others could think; 'the thinker of this thought' would not then pick out a unique thinker. It is natural to suppose that no one else can have the very same thought, relating to me, as I have when I think, 'I have been wounded', just as, in Prior's example, when I think, 'Thank God it's over', I think a thought which I could not have thought five minutes before.[1]

Evans labours to show that there is no inconsistency in Frege's admission, in this one passage, of incommunicable thoughts. He remarks that, while Frege observes that the same thought *can* be grasped by different people, he never says that this must be possible for all thoughts. The point seems somewhat legalistic. Though Frege speaks, ambiguously perhaps, of 'a thought' rather than of 'every thought', the natural construction is that he was citing characteristics of thoughts in general. Thus, after speaking, in his review of Husserl, of the incommunicability of ideas, Frege says: 'It is quite different for thoughts (lit. for the thought): one and the same thought can be grasped by many people.'[2] In 'Der Gedanke' itself, he makes great play with the thesis that a thought, unlike an idea, does not need a bearer. But Evans's reply is that this is true, too, for those thoughts which only one person can think: there may be many such thoughts which never occur to me, which, since no one else can have them, are never thought by anyone at all; the existence even of an incommunicable thought is independent of its being thought by anyone.

Now it is true that Frege usually says that thoughts are independent of *being thought* or of *being grasped*, rather than of the existence of a thinker; but he does sometimes say the latter.[3] In general, Evans's defence of Frege on this point has the ring of special pleading; Perry is surely right in detecting a tension here. Rather than watering down Frege's pervasive

---

[1] A discussion of this 'I' is to be found in G. E. M. Anscombe, 'The First Person', in S. Guttenplan (ed.), *Mind and Language*, Oxford, 1975, pp. 45–65.

[2] Pp. 317–18.

[3] *N.S.*, p. 146, *P.W.*, p. 134.

insistence on the independence and communicability of thoughts, it appears to me better to question his statement that the thought expressed by 'I have been wounded', as one might say that to oneself, cannot be communicated. For, on reflection, there is something wrong with saying that the thought in question is incommunicable. God reads all the thoughts of men; He can hardly be held incapable of grasping those thoughts concerning ourselves we have when we are soliloquizing. Suppose that, in telling you of my experience, I say, 'I thought to myself, "I have been wounded".' Frege would say that the first 'I' in that sentence is the 'I' of communication, which he considers different; but the second 'I' is certainly the 'I' of soliloquy. Do you not nevertheless know exactly what thought I had? Not only do you know what thought it was: you may also judge it to have been true. Rather than saying that I am presented to myself in a special way which you can never know, we should do better to say that we all know the special way in which each man is presented to himself. There does indeed appear to be a sense in which, although you, the hearer, know what thought I had when I thought to myself, 'I have been wounded', you cannot *think* that thought yourself. What this shows, however, is that Frege was wrong to say, as he did, that to think is to grasp thoughts,[1] at least if grasping a thought is the same as knowing what thought it is. Hence, even if there are thoughts which only one person can think, or which only a person in some given situation can think, there is no need to conclude that there are thoughts that cannot be communicated. Frege ought not to have committed himself to a belief in incommunicable thoughts, and did not in fact believe in them in the sense in which Wittgenstein denied them to be possible. Thus, without violating any essential principle of Frege's philosophy, or convicting him of heinous error, we may agree with Evans that 'there are thoughts which one can have only because one occupies a particular position in space or time, or because one is currently perceiving an object'; the thought that we should express by saying that the Earth goes round the Sun is probably one of them. And, by the same token, there are thoughts which only he can have, i.e. can think, who is the subject of them.

Having observed, in 'Der Gedanke', that, when someone thinks to himself, 'I have been wounded', his thought is one that only he can grasp, Frege goes on to say that, when the same person says to someone else, 'I have been wounded', he cannot then be communicating a thought that only he can grasp; no such thought could be communicated. He must,

---

[1] *N.S.*, pp. 201, 223, *P.W.*, pp. 185, 206.

therefore, now be using 'I' in a sense that the other can grasp; when the word 'I' is used by one person in converse with another, it must be being used in a sense accessible to the hearer. Frege's actual suggestion for what this sense may be, namely that of 'he who is this moment speaking to you', is not a happy one, as can be seen if we ask what the corresponding sense of 'you' may be; if we were to say, 'he to whom I am this moment speaking', we should go round in a circle. Evans appears to accept the general argument, though not the specific suggestion, since he quotes, apparently with approval, Frege's contention that successful communication requires a thought that can be grasped by different individuals, having previously accepted his idea of thoughts about myself which only I can grasp. But if we make the distinction between grasping a thought, in the sense of knowing what thought it is, and thinking that thought, it is not apparent that we need distinguish between the 'I' of soliloquy and the 'I' of communication. The price of denying this latter distinction will, however, be that we can no longer hold that, when the hearer says to himself, 'He has been wounded', or says out loud, 'You have been wounded', he is entertaining or expressing the very same thought that the speaker did by saying to him, 'I have been wounded'; for what the hearer says to himself or to the speaker must express a thought that he can think, and if the 'I' used by the speaker is the same as the 'I' of soliloquy, then he conveyed to the hearer a thought that the hearer could not himself think.

To obliterate the distinction between the 'I' of soliloquy and the 'I' of communication is to depart from Frege's views as stated in 'Der Gedanke'. In attempting to state the sense of the 'I' of communication, Frege appears to be taking the word as capable of being used, in common discourse, in the *same* sense by different speakers, in each of whose mouths it has a different reference. For, if it is correct to say of *any* speaker that he uses the 'I' of communication in the sense 'he who is at this moment speaking to you', it must be true to say of *every* speaker who uses the 'I' of communication that he is using it in that sense. If so, Frege must here have been using the term 'sense' to mean the conventional significance of the word in the language. To this, however, it may be objected that the question has been begged. The phrase 'he who is at this moment speaking to you' has itself a constant sense only if its constituent expressions 'this moment' and 'you' have a constant sense. We therefore have no reason to assume, contrary to what is apparently implied by Frege's general remarks about indexical expressions, that he wished to treat the 'I' of communication as having a constant sense, unless we have some prior reason for supposing him to be treating 'this' and 'you' as doing so.

However this may be, Frege's argument started from the premiss that a speaker can communicate to another only such thoughts as the other is capable of grasping. Since a thought cannot be true for one person and false for another, it follows that the thought communicated by means of a sentence containing the 'I' of communication cannot be equated with the sense of that sentence, taken by itself independently of the circumstances of utterance. So far as I know, there is no explicit warrant in any of Frege's writings for the assumption that, if someone can grasp a thought, there must exist the means for him to express it. The assumption is, however, a natural one; and, if we make it, it will follow that the hearer can express the very same thought as that conveyed to him by the speaker when he said, 'I have been wounded'. If we accept this conclusion, we shall find it irresistible to say that the hearer can express that thought by saying to the original speaker, 'You have been wounded'; and this precisely accords with what Frege in fact says about 'today' and 'yesterday', 'here' and 'there'. The general principle thus arrived at is that suggested in *FPL*: a thought expressed by means of a sentence containing one or more token-reflexive expressions can also be expressed, in different circumstances, by one containing correlative token-reflexive terms. There is less intuitive plausibility to an extension of the foregoing assumption, to the effect that, if someone can grasp a thought, there must exist the means for him to express it in any circumstances, for instance at any time or to whichever listener. When Lauben says to Peter, 'I have been wounded', can Peter express the thought thereby conveyed to him to some third person, perhaps by saying, 'He has been wounded'? 'He' is not a token-reflexive expression in the strict sense of Reichenbach's term of art; when it is used to refer to some definite person who has not previously been mentioned, it functions as a demonstrative. Frege does not tell us enough to make it certain what he would have thought about this case.

From all this there has not emerged a very coherent doctrine. If, as suggested above, we take Frege's tentative account of the sense of the 'I' of communication as giving the significance of that pronoun in the common language, we have further evidence that he failed to make a sharp enough distinction between sense as significance and sense as mode of presentation. It is, however, the latter conception that we need for the explanation of his notion of a thought expressed by a sentence containing an indexical expression. The significance in the language of such a sentence as 'I have been wounded' remains the same whoever utters it: what we need to arrive at is a sense expressed by a particular utterance of the sentence which would not be expressed if it were uttered by a different speaker, but which may perhaps be expressed by someone else's saying, 'You have been wounded', or even, 'He has been wounded'. We saw reason to doubt that Frege's account of the sense of the 'I' of communication need be understood as a rendering of its significance; let us therefore try interpreting it, instead, as stating the mode of presentation of the referent. Gustav Lauben says to Leo Peter, 'I have been wounded'. In using the word 'I', Lauben takes himself to be referring to a particular person, and Peter also takes him to be doing so. How does Lauben conceive of the person to whom he is referring? If Peter's command of the language is so erratic that he fails to comprehend the first-person singular pronoun, Lauben might say to him, ' "I" stands for the person who is at this moment speaking to you'; but he would hardly think to himself, 'By "I" I mean the person who is at this moment speaking to him', even if, in so thinking, he was able to avail himself of a different 'I', the 'I' of soliloquy. Of Peter, however, it might be said that, in understanding Lauben's utterance, he was applying a rule which he might formulate to himself by saying, 'The word "I", used in a sentence addressed to me, stands for the person who is speaking to me'; and, if there is an 'I' of soliloquy, then the 'me' that occurs here may reasonably be taken to be its accusative case. Of course, in Peter's statement of the rule, the reference to himself is super-fluous; he could formulate the more general rule, 'The word "I" stands for the person who is speaking'. When we are concerned with how Peter identifies the person referred to in that particular utterance, however, the reference to himself is not superfluous. Doubtless there are many people speaking at the time; but Peter, hearing Lauben's words, identifies the person referred to as 'I' as the man who is speaking to him: that is the 'mode of presentation' of Lauben to Peter by means of Lauben's use of the pronoun 'I'. It is thus apparent that, considered as a representation of the mode of presentation embodied in the 'I' of communication, Frege's formula 'he who is at this moment speaking to you' was misconceived. The occurrence of the second-person pronoun forces us to take it as representing the mode of presentation of the speaker to himself, which it cannot be; but what we need is the mode of presentation of the speaker to the hearer. Frege was misled by the desire to represent the sense in which the speaker is using the word, a sense that the hearer must be able to grasp if the thought expressed is to be communicable to him. But what the hearer must know, if he is to understand the speaker's utterance aright, and what the speaker must exploit, in order to convey what he wishes to the hearer, is the *significance* of the word: the thesis that the speaker, if he is to communicate with the hearer, must use words in accordance with the senses which the hearer attaches to them is one appropriate only to the conception of sense as significance. Once again, we have an illustration of Frege's failure to separate the different ingredients in his notion of sense. As soon as the conception of sense as significance has been clearly separated from the conception of it as mode of presentation, we cease to have a warrant for thinking in terms of 'the sense in which a word is used': that notion belongs to the conception of sense as significance. We may legitimately speak of the *significance* with which a word is used by a speaker, and of the hearer's taking it, or failing to take it, as having the same significance. But, as in the present case, the significance may be such that the referent cannot be presented to the hearer in the same manner as it (or he) is presented to the speaker.

'same thought'

This reinforces our previous conclusion, that there is no distinction such as Frege supposed between an 'I' of soliloquy and an 'I' of communication: Lauben is not presented to himself in any different way when he says to Peter, 'I have been wounded', from when he says it to himself. But, now, can we say that the thought which Peter grasps when he hears Lauben say, 'I have been wounded', is the very same as that which Lauben voices? Communication certainly occurs; Peter understands Lauben's utterance in accordance with the accepted significance of the words in the language, and Lauben uses those words with the intention that Peter will so understand them. But Peter's understanding of Lauben's words, in accordance with their established significance in the language, results in his conceiving of the person referred to in a manner different from that in which Lauben himself conceives of him. Peter, to identify that person, has to observe from whose mouth the words come. To be more exact, he has at least to be aware of that particular utterance: he might be able to do no more than this, for instance if he were in a cave and unable to see the speaker or to tell from which direction his cry came, or yet to recognize his voice. Lauben, however, does not need to be certain that he has succeeded in speaking audibly: in an abnormal condition, he might even be unsure whether or not he had spoken aloud, but he would still know to whom 'I' referred, in that sense in which he knows this even if he has forgotten who he is.

Since Peter understands the word 'I', that is, knows its significance, he knows the manner in which, in saying, 'I have been wounded', Lauben identified himself to himself. He thus knows what thought Lauben was voicing; but, if the mode of presentation is taken as constitutive of the thought, Peter cannot himself think that thought, since he cannot identify the individual referred to in the same manner. He may judge the thought voiced by Lauben to be true; but, in so judging, he still does not think that very thought, but, rather, some such thought as 'That man was speaking truthfully'. The thought that is conveyed to Peter by Lauben's utterance is a different one: it is the thought that Lauben meant to convey to him, but, in so far as it involves a reference to Peter, who identifies the subject as 'the man who addressed me' or 'the man whose cry I heard', it is a thought that Lauben, in turn, cannot himself think. If Peter now reiterates to Lauben, 'You have been wounded', the thought he then expresses is different again, for he is now identifying Lauben to himself as 'the person whom I am addressing'; and the thought thereby conveyed to Lauben is different yet, since Lauben must identify the person referred to as 'you' as 'the person to whom the statement was addressed'. Thus, so far from the same thought being able to be expressed by the use of suitably correlative token-reflexive expressions, it can happen that the thought conveyed to the hearer is not the same as that expressed by the speaker, although no misunderstanding is involved. Where Frege took a false step was in arguing that communication must involve the hearer's thinking the very same thought as that voiced by the speaker, whereas all that is necessary is that he should attach the same significance to the words as the speaker does.

These results may be felt to be preposterous; so much the worse, it may be said, for a strict application of the principle that the mode of presentation is constitutive of the thought. We have, in fact, already glanced at a means of tempering the severity of this principle. It is this. Let us say that someone knows what thought is expressed by an utterance if he both grasps the significance of the words used and knows at least the minimum necessary for him to identify the referents of any indexical expressions occurring in the utterance. This stipulation will be useless if we allow the minimum required for identification to shrink to what is guaranteed by a grasp of the words' significance together with a specification of the utterance in question. For example, we previously appealed to this principle as a ground for saying that, if I remember saying, 'It will be fine tomorrow', but have forgotten on which day I said it, I no longer know what thought I expressed; so we must not count my knowledge that I was referring to the day after that on which I made the prediction as amounting to the minimum necessary for the identification of the day referred to. In the same way, we must deny that someone reading an undated letter containing the sentence, 'We are going fishing today', knows precisely what thought is thereby expressed. This, admittedly, calls in question whether the man hearing the cry in the cave does know what thought is expressed by it. If, nevertheless, we admit this principle, with not too lax an application, we may then appeal to Frege's test of whether two utterances express the same thought, namely whether it is possible to judge either to be true without immediately granting the truth of the other. Frege's proviso for the application of this test was that the subject should grasp the thought expressed by each of the utterances; if we replace this by the proviso that he knows what thought they express, construing this in accordance with the above stipulation, we shall arrive at the conclusions which Frege draws. If Peter says to Lauben, 'You have been wounded', Lauben will know what thought Peter is expressing only if he knows that Peter is addressing him; and so he cannot but judge what Peter says to be true, if he believes his own statement, 'I have been wounded', to be true. Hence, on this criterion, Peter's utterance and Lauben's express the same thought, even though, strictly speaking, the mode of presentation is different for the two sentences, and, for each utterance, for speaker and hearer.

Frege's few remarks, in 'Der Gedanke' and in the 'Logik' of 1897, do not yield a fully coherent account of indexicality; partly because he was not deeply interested in it, and partly because he failed to attain a full awareness of the different ingredients in his notion of sense. His observations are, however, of great interest for the light they throw on his notion of a thought and, more generally, of sense. Evans was entirely justified in emphasizing the role of thoughts as the objects of propositional attitudes; this is quite as deeply embedded in Frege's observations concerning thoughts as is that more austere and at the same time more fanciful conception of thoughts as objective, non-sensible objects. Both play a role in his saying what he does about indexical expressions, as in his doctrine of indirect reference: but, in both cases, what he says forces us to distinguish the sense of an expression, as conceived by him, from its significance in the common language. It is just as important for the understanding of Frege that he himself was only dimly aware of the extent of the divergence. In effect, he treats sense as linguistic significance—more exactly, as the salient component of linguistic significance—except where other theses that he wishes to maintain render this impossible, as when he treats of the topics discussed in this chapter; and even then he is not fully conscious of the degree to which he has departed from that conception. Since most of what he has to say about sense relates neither to indexicality nor to indirect speech, we may usually equate Fregean sense with linguistic significance without doing violence to the notion.

We may usually equate Fregean sense with linguistic significance, it may be said, so long as we are concerned only with Frege's philosophy of language; but, when we attempt to derive anything resembling an epistemology from his work, the strains between the different components of his notion of sense start to tear that notion asunder. This comes out, above all, if we attend to the point of disagreement between myself and Evans so far skated over. Evans, following John McDowell,[1] deprecated Frege's willingness to regard proper names, both in the normal and in his extended sense, as capable of lacking a reference without thereby being deprived of sense. It was, for Frege, a defect of natural language that such names occur in it; but, in the view of Evans and McDowell, it was a defect in his notion of sense that such a possibility, however reprehensible, was even conceivable. If the sense of a proper name consists in the way in which an object is given to us as its referent, then, if there is no object, there is nothing to be given, and hence there can be no sense.

The motivation for this emendation of Frege's doctrines is twofold. One part of it is the idea that the sense of an expression cannot be *stated*. All we are able, and all we need, to state is the reference of the expression: by the particular means that we adopt for stating this, we *show* what its sense is; for an expression with the same reference but a different sense, we should state its reference in a different way. This conception of the matter was canvassed on p. 227 of *FPL*; and it is true that a great deal of what Frege says about senses is independent of whether we can either state them or refer to them. If, then, a name lacks reference, we cannot display it as having a determinate sense, because we could do so only by asserting it to have a particular reference, characterized in a suitable manner, and we cannot do this knowing it to have no reference.

Closely connected with this motive for thus emending Frege's view is the desire to safeguard the realism of his philosophy of language and of thought. If my thought purports to be about an object, then it really is *about that object*, provided that there is such an object: it reaches right out to it, one might say. As Frege insisted in 'Der Gedanke',[2] if I use the expression 'that lime-tree', it is the tree itself of which I mean to speak, not one of my ideas: if I intend to express a thought about a tree, that thought could not turn out, in spite of me, to have been about an idea. If there was no tree, then it would not have been about anything; and it seems only a short and harmless step to say that I expressed no thought at all.

It would be quite wrong to appeal to the fact that, once he had introduced the notion of sense, Frege felt no need to take refuge in such a

---

[1] J. McDowell, 'On the Sense and Reference of a Proper Name', *Mind*, vol. LXXXVI, 1977, pp. 159–85.
[2] P. 68.

empty names

doctrine, in order to call in question the strength of his realist convictions. On the contrary, it illustrates the robustness of that conviction that he felt no such need: provided that the name has a reference, the thought expressed by the sentence in which the name occurs is really about that object, not about some intermediary or representation: we succeed in speaking, and thinking, about that objective reality which exists independently of ourselves. McDowell and Evans, however, are convinced that this realism cannot be maintained unless Frege's doctrine of sense is amended to exclude senses with no corresponding reference; in making this emendation, they feel assured that they are remaining faithful to Frege's deepest concern: otherwise the sense itself becomes an intermediary, and the problem arises once more how we can reach beyond it to the object in the realm of reference.

For all that the thought is really about the object, the object is not, for Frege, itself a constituent of the thought: it is one of his favourite arguments for the necessity to ascribe senses to proper names that a mountain, for instance, is not the sort of thing that can be a constituent of a thought, although there must be such a constituent common to the thoughts expressed by different sentences containing the same proper name for some mountain. For Russell, on the other hand, an object, if it is the meaning of a genuine proper name, is a constituent of the proposition. If we have to say, we must assign Russell's propositions, unlike Frege's thoughts, to the realm of reference rather than to that of sense: but it is misleading to assign them to either, just because Russell rejected the very distinction between sense and reference. He rejected it because he thought it incompatible with a realistic theory of meaning, one that would leave it unproblematic that our statements relate to external reality.

Realism, consciously opposed to the absolute idealism that prevailed at the outset of Russell's philosophical career, was the original driving force of his philosophy, a realism learned in the first place from G. E. Moore. Although Frege was a realist, too, Russell felt compelled to reject Frege's distinction between sense and reference in order to safeguard realism from a danger to which Frege appeared blind. In 'On Denoting', Russell offered an argument against the distinction, an argument somewhat obscure in itself, and rendered more so, as Geach has pointed out,[1] by Russell's equating his own pair of terms, 'meaning' and 'denotation', with Frege's '*Sinn*' and '*Bedeutung*' respectively, even though Russell's 'meaning' was much more akin to Frege's '*Bedeutung*' than to his '*Sinn*'. John Searle has supplied

[1] P. T. Geach, 'Russell on Meaning and Denoting', *Analysis*, vol. XIX, 1959, pp. 69–72.

an image to represent Russell's argument, which is, essentially, that the notion of sense is incoherent because, whenever we attempt to refer to the sense of an expression, all that we succeed in referring to is its referent. Searle imagines tubes along which marbles pass to drop into holes below; in some cases, different tubes may lead to the same hole.[1] We cannot succeed, however hard we try, in lodging a marble in a tube: it always passes through the tube to the hole beneath. I shall not here attempt to examine the details of Russell's argument, or to decide whether he really makes out a case that any attempt to refer to the sense leads only to our speaking about the referent. At first sight, even if the argument is wholly successful, it cannot demonstrate that the entire distinction between sense and reference is spurious, for the reason already stated: that we can refer to senses is no part of the fundamental thesis that expressions have sense as well as reference. Frege indeed believed that we can and do refer to them, both directly, as when we speak of Pythagoras's Theorem, which is, for Frege, a thought, and indirectly, as when we use words in reported speech; Russell's argument does create a difficulty concerning such reference to senses. But, if we decided that the difficulty was insuperable, we might be able to jettison that part of Frege's theory, regarding senses as incapable of being referred to or stated, and able only to be shown or conveyed; on p. 227 of *FPL* I suggested that as a possible retort to Russell. Russell's concern becomes more intelligible, however, if we regard him as having aimed slightly off target. His true concern is not so much with whether senses can be objects of *reference*, as with the more fundamental question whether they can be objects of *apprehension*. He is responding to that strand in Frege's notion of sense according to which the primary operation of a linguistic expression is to direct the hearer towards the appropriate sense, which he grasps and which has, in favourable cases, the property of in turn pointing towards a referent: that strand in Frege's notion which, as we have seen, wars with the conception of the sense as the manner in which the referent is given, and which leads, when pressed, to the conception of language as a code. That conception, of which the map-reference view of language is one version, is in the end unintelligible, because it provides no explanation of what senses are or of how they come to have the property of referring to things in the external world. Russell's argument is best understood by turning it on its head. If we *could* refer to senses, then we could never succeed in referring to anything else (if the marbles could stay in the tubes, they would never reach the holes); we could then never get beyond senses to objects in the realm of

---

[1] J. R. Searle, 'Russell's Objections to Frege's Theory of Sense and Reference', *Analysis*, vol. XVIII, 1957, pp. 137–43; reprinted in *EF*, pp. 337–45.

reference, and the realist conception of language and of thought would once
again be shipwrecked.

For Frege, at least when we attend to the healthier of the divergent strands
within his notion of sense, the sense of a proper name is the way we arrive
at the object, but not conceived as a means to a separable end: the apprehension of the object is not an outcome that may be detached from the
process that led to it. From this standpoint, sense is better understood as the
manner in which we pick out the object than as the route we take to it. We are
never given an object, complete in itself; we can think about it, speak
of it or apprehend it only as presented to us in some particular way, just
as Evans says. Russell, with his theory of knowledge by acquaintance,
wanted to deny even this, and to reject Frege's notion of sense altogether;
but Evans is aware that, so far, the thesis does not threaten realism, any
more than to say that we can at any time see a building only from a particular angle casts doubt on the proposition that we can see buildings. But,
for Evans, as for McDowell, in admitting senses to which no reference
corresponds, Frege took a fatal step, that of construing the way in which an
object is presented to us as a mode of presentation capable of existing without the object presented. For them, the step is as absurd as to conclude that
our visual experience of architecture consists in apprehending entities of a
special kind, buildings-from-an-angle, not guaranteed to correspond to any
actual building. Here the mode of presentation has indeed been detached
from the object, by regarding it as itself a kind of object. For Frege, of
course, 'object' is equivalent to 'object of possible reference': to say that
something is an object is to say that we can refer to it by means of an expression that functions like a proper name. Since the phrases 'the sense of the
name "Mont Blanc",' 'the thought that the Earth is larger than the Moon'
and 'Pythagoras's Theorem' do appear to function as what Frege called
'proper names', there is, for Frege, no question that at least some senses are
objects. If we criticize that strand in Frege's notion of sense in accordance
with which senses are themselves objects, however, we are, once more,
concerned with whether they are rightly conceived as objects of *apprehension*,
rather than whether they can be objects of *reference*: it was precisely because
Frege failed to distinguish between these two senses of the word 'object', or
these two ingredients in our notion of an object, that Russell came to aim off
target, in his criticism of Frege, in the way already noted. For Evans and
McDowell, by treating the mode of presentation as if it were itself an object
of apprehension, we are detaching it from the object which is the referent,
not by making our identification of that object an independently intelligible
result of the means by which we achieved it, but by making it apparently

unattainable. The step was therefore fatal, as well as absurd, because, if it is only by the medium of senses, as thought-components, that we can apprehend objects, we appear to be threatened by the same danger as threatened the empiricists who saw us as enclosed in a world of mental images and sense-impressions, the inner world of ideas of which Frege spoke in 'Der Gedanke'. How can we know that we ever do reach the object, or that there really is any object, if a sense always interposes between us and it, a sense that carries no guarantee of any corresponding referent? Though Frege appeared oblivious of the danger, he thereby led us to the edge of a precipice from which we could tumble into an idealism differing from that of Berkeley only in assuming a more intellectual guise, substituting the senses of expressions for ideas in the sense common to Frege and the empiricists. In 'Der Gedanke', Frege attacked the idealists who would leave us shut up within our inner world of ideas; but, as Evans and McDowell appear to see the matter, his own doctrine, if unamended, risks leaving us as inescapably locked into the third realm inhabited by thoughts and their components, equally unable to reach the outer world of actual physical things.

It is in this context, that of the need to safeguard a realistic theory of meaning, that we should view the immense importance which Russell attached to his Theory of Descriptions. One important difference between Frege and Russell lies, in this connection, in their different attitudes to natural language. Russell believed that the Theory of Descriptions un-covered the mechanism governing the use of definite descriptions in natural language: the theory adopted in his formal logic therefore represented no more than an improvement on natural language in respect of a more perspicuous notation and a device, in the form of the scope-indicators, for removing ambiguities. At least, this is how it appears from 'On Denoting'; in 'Mr Strawson on Referring', published in 1957,[1] Russell evinces a more Fregean attitude, expressing himself as 'persuaded that common speech is full of vagueness and inaccuracy, and that any attempt to be precise and accurate requires modification of common speech both as regards vocabulary and as regards syntax'. At any rate, the stipulation which Frege laid down in the *Grundgesetze* as governing terms formed by means of his description operator was not intended to correspond to anything in the workings of natural language: the functioning of definite descriptions in natural language constituted one of its many defects, a feature that must therefore be replaced rather than merely rendered more explicit.

[1] B. Russell, 'Mr Strawson on Referring', *Mind*, n.s. vol. 66, 1957, pp. 385–9; reprinted in B. Russell, *Essays in Analysis*, ed. D. Lackey, London, 1973, pp. 120–6.

The major difference between Frege and Russell was, however, the following. It is obvious that a definite description may be significant although there is no unique object satisfying it, and although a speaker, without making any linguistic mistake, may be unaware that there is no such object. Hence, for one who, like Frege, is disposed to minimize the difference between definite descriptions and other singular terms, the necessity for a distinction between sense and reference is undeniable, and the possibility of a sense with no corresponding reference unproblematic. But, for Evans and McDowell, the very possibility of a realistic theory of meaning depends upon excluding senses to which no reference corresponds, and, for Russell, it depended upon rejecting the distinction between sense and reference altogether. It was for this reason that Russell had to find an account of definite descriptions which explained them away as not being singular terms at all, as they appear at first glance to be: without such an account, his entire philosophy must collapse.

In this connection, however, it is a delicate matter to distinguish a defence of Frege from a criticism of him. In describing natural language as containing names possessing sense but devoid of reference, Frege was coming as close as he could to giving a coherent account of what he regarded as a defect of natural language. To maintain, as do McDowell and Evans, that the account is not fully coherent is not, therefore, to criticize Frege, but to agree with him: if the account were coherent, the feature so explained would not be a *defect*. But to suggest, as they do, that the incoherence can be rectified by emending the account is to criticize him: it is to suggest that what is at fault is not natural language itself, but Frege's description of its working. According to Frege, what needs emendation is not the description, but what is described: we need, for scientific purposes, to work with a purified language in which expressions having sense but not reference cannot be formed. The mistake which, from Frege's standpoint, Evans and McDowell make, is to replace one necessarily incoherent account by one that is even more incoherent, instead of giving up the misguided attempt to find a fully coherent account of natural language at all. The account preferred by them, according to which the notion of sense is so construed that an expression without a reference cannot be regarded as having a sense, relies on a conception of sense lacking one of the essential features of the notion, as Frege understands it, namely that sense is transparent. The transparency of sense involves that anyone who knows the language must thereby know, of any expression considered as belonging to that language, whether or not it has a sense; under the McDowell/Evans 'emendation', this ceases to be so. The proposed emendation is therefore not a minor one:

it destroys a central feature of Frege's notion of sense. The problematic question, for Frege's doctrine, is whether there really could be a language having the characteristics of the purified language of which he conceived: one the expressions of which could all be recognized by anyone who knew the language to have a sense, and to have a sense of such a kind as to guarantee a reference for them.

Suppose that someone is devising a formalized language for geography. He introduces various individual constants (proper names) and various predicates, and stipulates their intended meanings. One such stipulation might take the form:

'Lon' is to denote London.

By this means he *states* the reference of his symbol 'Lon' and *shows* its sense. Because 'Lon' has been introduced by means of this stipulation, it has, in the formalized language, just the same sense as that of 'London' in English, at least provided that it functions in the formalized language more or less as does a proper name in English. Now suppose that we are engaged in setting out a theory of meaning for an existing language, say Italian. McDowell favours our doing so by means of similar specifications, for instance:

'Londra' denotes London.

What such a specification overtly does is to state the reference of the Italian word 'Londra'; what it is supposed to show is the sense of that word, namely that it has the same sense as the English word 'London'. The reference of 'Londra' might have been correctly stated in different ways; by choosing this particular way, we show what its sense is. Since this is not actually a stipulation, i.e. a means of introducing the word, some questions might be raised about what guarantees that this particular specification, rather than some equally correct one such as ' "Londra" denotes the city where William Blake was born', serves to show the sense of the word; but let us pass these by, assuming the answers given to them to be satisfactory. Now there is a dispute between McDowell and myself over whether such a specification sufficiently serves the purpose which, in philosophical discussions of meaning, we require a theory of meaning for a language to fulfil: he holds that it does, I that it does not, but that the theory ought to spell out what it is to use a proper name with the sense that the name 'London' has in English. This dispute is of relevance to the general question whether it is possible to *state* the sense of a word or only to show it. It would be possible to maintain that the sense of a word can only be shown, in the manner indicated above, and yet to hold that a theory of meaning must spell out what it is to use a word with the sense of the word 'London', only if one thought that this could be done by means of some complicated specification beginning ' "Londra" denotes the city which . . .'; that is, if one held the description theory of the senses of proper names, which I do not. I should say that it is not always possible to state the sense of a word, but that it is always possible to state what is involved in attaching a given sense to the word, and that this is what a theory of meaning must be required to do. All this, however, is quite irrelevant to the immediate question at issue, which is how we are supposed to explain the senses of names for which it is in doubt whether they have a reference. Let us therefore grant to McDowell, for the sake of argument, that the only way in which the sense of a name is to be conveyed, within a theory of meaning, is by a specification which uses an equivalent name in the language in which the theory of meaning is couched. Suppose now that McDowell, constructing a theory of meaning for Italian, and working through the letter O, comes upon the name 'Orlando'. His idea is that he must first investigate the historical question whether or not there really was such a person as Roland. If he decides that there was, he will add to his theory of meaning the specification:

'Orlando' denotes Roland.

If he decides that there was no such person, he will omit the name 'Orlando' from the vocabulary of Italian altogether. This is evidently absurd. What, according to him, a theory of meaning for a language is supposed to do is to encapsulate a body of knowledge such that anyone who has it would be able to speak that language; tacitly, it is not supposed to include anything irrelevant to the purpose. But if, as he intends, McDowell means to be so understood that, by using the name 'Roland' in the metalanguage (English), he conveys that he takes it as having a reference, he has certainly included more information than is possessed by every competent speaker of Italian if he does decide that he is right to include the above specification in his theory of meaning; and, if he decides to suppress the name 'Orlando' altogether, he is omitting something known to any competent Italian speaker. The only way in which such a name may be correctly handled, so as to include no more and no less than is known to competent speakers of the object-language, is to employ in the metalanguage such a predicate as 'is Roland', taken as true of a person only if he is the referent of the name 'Roland', and then to specify:

For any x, 'Orlando' denotes x iff x is Roland.

Other parts of the theory of meaning will have to lay down the truth-value, or semantic status, of sentences containing a name that lacks a reference; but that necessity is one that arises out of the way natural languages are. Frege indeed held that no coherent semantic theory can be given for such a language, and, if he was right, the enterprise is doomed: but nothing whatever is achieved by allotting to the one who frames the theory of meaning the burden of discovering, for each name, whether or not it has a reference. Rather, he should treat in the above manner every proper name for which it cannot be maintained that anyone who knows the language must know whether or not it has a reference, regardless of whether he himself has that knowledge. More exactly, the requirement should not be framed in terms of what any *one* competent speaker of the language must know, but in terms of the use the word has in the language. It would be possible to maintain that the name 'London' could not have the use which it has in English if there were not such a city as London, and if there were not many speakers who knew that there was such a city. In such a case, it would be legitimate to employ, in the theory of meaning, the simple form of specification ' "Londra" denotes London'; but, in any other case, the more complicated form illustrated above for the name 'Orlando' would have to be employed. There is thus no argument at all to the thesis that lack of reference entails lack of sense either from the premiss that sense cannot be stated but only shown, or from the premiss that a theory of meaning should be 'modest' or 'austere'.

To adopt a conception of sense which renders it impossible for a name lacking a referent to have a sense is to move very close to regarding objects as constituents of thoughts. The thesis is trifling if it embodies no more than a stipulative definition that a significant sentence of a language containing a name lacking a reference will not be said to express a thought: and neither McDowell nor Evans intends anything trifling. Though they concede that the name presents the object to us in a particular way, the manner in which it does so constituting its sense, they must regard it as constitutive of the thought itself that it is about that object. The sense of the name thus degenerates into something like an auxiliary device enabling us to reach the object; it becomes a serious question whether there is any stable position, such as they wish to occupy, intermediate between Frege and Russell, accepting the distinction between sense and reference but denying the possibility of a sense without a reference. For them, it must be an integral feature of thoughts that they are about something, the prototypical case being that of a thought expressed by a singular sentence, to which it is intrinsic that it not merely purports to be but actually is about an object. From this standpoint, it is an internal, not an external, feature of the thought that it is about an object; it must be for that reason that there cannot be a thought that purports, but fails, to be about one. We obviously may be unaware whether a particular *sentence* contains a name lacking a reference, and hence, on this view, whether it succeeds in expressing a thought: but, it must be held, the thought itself must reveal that it is about an object, or would do if, as it were, we could inspect it stripped of its linguistic clothing, since, if it were not about one, there would be no thought to inspect. Evidently, on this conception, to have a thought must be something of much greater substance than just to grasp the significance of a sentence.

It thus seems possible that, contrary to what Evans and McDowell hope, Russell may have been right in believing that to make it intrinsic to the proposition or thought expressed by a singular sentence that it is about an object entails abandoning the entire distinction between sense and reference. If so, it is plainly not a question of a minor emendation; Frege's entire mature philosophy of language is in jeopardy. And yet it seems that we have been given no direct reason to disbelieve in singular terms having sense but not reference; we have merely been threatened with dire consequences if we continue to believe in them. However much we dwell on the differences between definite descriptions and proper names in the restricted sense, differences emphasized by Geach and above all by Kripke, we cannot see it as mandatory to deny to the former the status of singular terms as the Theory of Descriptions would have us do. If we allow that definite descriptions can be construed as singular terms, we cannot maintain that there is any general obstacle to the possession of a sense to which no reference corresponds.

The crisis need not be presented so starkly. It was not the admission of some singular terms having sense but not reference that generated the danger of an intellectualized form of idealism. That danger arose, rather, from the combination of the following theses: that we apprehend an object only as presented in some particular way; that the mode of presentation is a sense; and that to *no* sense is it intrinsic that there is a corresponding reference. We shall therefore escape the danger if we deny the last of these three theses; we need hold only that there are some ways in which an object may be given to us for which there is no question whether or not there really is any object. This seems very satisfactory, since, as we have seen, the thesis that there is no sense for which a reference is guaranteed is not one to which Frege subscribed. In a purified language, such as the formal language of *Grundgesetze*, all expressions will have senses of such a kind as to guarantee a reference for them. And thus, it seems, the danger is over: granted that there are at least some such senses, we cannot be entrapped in the realm of sense, unable to break through into that of reference.

This explains why Frege was unworried, but does not itself solve the problem: we need to know how we can ensure a reference for an expression, what characteristics a sense must have if a referent is to be guaranteed. Frege's stipulation concerning the description operator provides the model: the expression must be understood in such a way as to stand for something in each possible circumstance out of some logically exhaustive range. But, equally, this stipulation yields no ultimate account of the matter, since, for the case in which a definite description would ordinarily lack a reference, Frege assigns it the same reference as another term (when '*a*' does not denote a unit class, '*a*' has the same reference as '*a*'). If every term is to be guaranteed a reference, there must be some terms known to have one independently of whether any other does; and it remains to be discovered how this is achieved. Frege's answer, in *Grundgesetze*, vol. I, §§ 10 and 31, is, in effect, to appeal to his context principle. As we shall see in Chapter 19, it is not a full-fledged version of the context principle of *Grundlagen* to which he appeals, but a generalized form which really may be stigmatized as barely coherent; but here we may ignore this complication, and state the argument in terms of the original context principle. The claim is then as follows. The reference of a singular term within a language may be considered fixed if determinate truth-conditions have been stipulated for every possible sentence containing that term. A simple-minded picture of the provision of a semantics for a formal language is this: we stipulate directly for which objects the primitive individual constants are to stand; we stipulate which function, described as defined over the domain, each primitive function-symbol is to denote; and finally we stipulate, for each primitive predicate, for which concept or relation, again described as defined over the domain, it shall stand. But Frege's idea is that we need not go about the matter in this way, so long as we really determine, not necessarily effectively, the truth-conditions of all sentences of the language. We do not, after all, display the objects for which the terms of the language stand: since an object can be given to us only in some particular way, we have, in the metalanguage, to characterize them in one or another manner. According to Frege's idea, not stated quite explicitly by him, we do not need to characterize them in any manner that is taken as already understood; we can characterize them merely as the referents of the formal terms, provided that there is no circularity in our assignment of truth-conditions to the sentences. The model for this is, of course, the stipulation of the truth-condition for a statement of identity between two value-ranges:

securing reference

'$\grave{\varepsilon}\, f(\varepsilon) = \grave{\alpha}\, g(\alpha)$' is to be true just in case, for every $\mathscr{a}$, $f(\mathscr{a})$ is the same as $g(\mathscr{a})$. This is not sufficient by itself to determine the references of value-range terms: for this, we must also fix the truth-conditions of every other sentence in which such a term may occur, including one of the form '$\grave{\varepsilon}\, f(\varepsilon) = q$', where '$q$' is not of the form '$\grave{\alpha}\, g(\alpha)$'. But if we can do this, we shall then have fixed the references of all value-range terms. In order to do it, there may be no necessity at any stage to characterize those objects for which in fact value-range terms are to stand otherwise than *as* the referents of such terms; and, if we have, by means of our stipulations, determined a truth-value for every sentence containing such a term, our failure to state the references of those terms directly, by means of some expression of the metalanguage taken as already understood, in no way vitiates our claim to have fixed the references of the terms.

The only objects referred to in the formal language of *Grundgesetze* are logical objects. Whether or not there are *logical* objects is not here to the point, which is, rather, whether there are what in Chapter 14 of *FPL* I called 'pure abstract objects'. Let us call a 'wholly abstract term' one that contains no terms for or predicates or functional expressions defined over concrete objects, and is not defined as equivalent to a term violating these conditions; 'the Equator', for example, is not a wholly abstract term. (A wholly abstract term can stand only for a pure abstract object; but a pure abstract object may be able to be referred to by means of an only partially abstract term.) Then only three attitudes to wholly abstract terms seem possible: (1) they are illegitimate; (2) they are to be assimilated to concrete terms; and (3) they are to be justified in some such manner as that proposed by Frege. To assimilate them to concrete terms is to postulate some faculty of intellectual apprehension, the analogue of perception for concrete objects, by which we are aware of their referents. The first attitude is unattractive and the second implausible: Frege's approach therefore demands serious consideration. But he certainly did not successfully carry out his own programme, as he himself came to recognize; Miss Eva Picardi has pointed out to me that, in his first letter to Russell, he conceded, in face of the contradiction, that his stipulations in *Grundgesetze*, vol. 1, § 31, did not suffice to ensure a reference in every case to the formal terms.[1]

However this may be, abstract objects form a special case, though an important one. It is natural to suppose that Frege's principle that a word has reference only in the context of a sentence applies only to abstract

---

[1] *BW*, p. 213, *P.M.C.*, p. 132.

terms. We have no need to justify the use of concrete terms in a similar way, since we do have faculties of perception enabling us to observe concrete objects. According to the context principle, there is no gap between using an abstract term in sentences for which a determinate sense has been provided and referring to an abstract object: we do not need to assure ourselves that, by doing the one, we achieve the other, since they are one and the same thing. More exactly, what ensures a reference for a term is not merely the possession of a definite sense by every sentence containing it, since the term, and hence the sentence, may have a sense even though the term lacks reference: what ensures it a reference is that every such sentence has a determinate value, true or false. Ordinarily we take it as being *because* a term occurring in it lacks a reference that a sentence is, according to Frege, deprived of truth-value; but, in the case of an abstract term, it might be the other way about—because the senses of sentences containing it did not serve to determine a truth-value for them, the term must be denied to have a reference. For a sentence to have a definite sense, it must be determinate under what conditions it would be true and under what conditions false; but what is required for every expression in it to have a reference is that it should be determinately one or the other. However plausible this may be, it would lose its plausibility if applied to concrete objects; and so it seems that the context principle can hardly be meant to cover terms for them.

Natural as this line of thought is, it is mistaken: in stating the context principle, Frege does not so much as hint at any such restriction. Still, he in fact invokes the principle only in order to justify ascribing a reference to abstract terms. The principle *allows* us to determine the truth-conditions of sentences containing certain terms otherwise than by appeal to a prior specification of the references of those terms; but it does not *compel* us to proceed in this manner. When the determination of the references of the terms of some range constitutes a step towards fixing the truth-conditions of sentences in which they occur, the principle does not, therefore, need to be denied: but its content then dwindles to that allotted to it by Professor Anscombe in her book on the *Tractatus*, namely that the determination of the references has significance only as a preparation for fixing the truth-conditions of the sentences.

We are, then, back with the question how a reference may be guaranteed to some terms purporting to denote concrete objects. An adequate answer would require a fully developed epistemology such as Frege did not offer us; but the key is obviously to be found by asking what difference it makes that concrete objects are (in general) perceptible, or, more generally, actual in Frege's sense, i.e. discernible by their effects. The immediate reply must be that the senses of sentences containing concrete terms are given in such a way that observation plays a part in determining their truth-values. Now the question we are seeking to answer is the following. Granted that, in general, the possession of a sense does not guarantee the existence of a referent, and granted that an object can be given to us only in some particular way, namely by our grasp of a suitable sense, how can we ever establish that, by means of an expression with a certain sense, we have in fact succeeded in referring to an object, that there really is an object for which that expression stands? Two types of solution, both compatible with Frege's general doctrines, are conceivable.

One would involve repudiating altogether the idea that the context principle provides a justification for the ascription of reference only to abstract terms. Given an account of how we determine, in part by observation, the truth-values of sentences containing names of concrete objects, it will be apparent that we can establish some such sentences as being true, and thereby establish those names as having reference: on this conception, there will, in this case, too, be no gap between the determination of the truth of the sentence and that of the referentiality of the name; in particular, the latter will not be a step on the way to the former. This would be a heroic line to adopt; it is not the line I took in *FPL*. It is not suggested by anything Frege says; it leaves us with no clue to *how* we can explain the senses of empirical statements, when we are not to appeal to the notion of reference in the course of doing so; and it deprives the notion of reference of any functional role in the theory of meaning. For all these reasons, it is unlikely to tally with Frege's intentions: but it is undeniably consistent with everything he actually affirms.

The alternative is to treat the identification of the referent of a concrete term as a discriminable ingredient in the canonical procedure for establishing the truth or falsity of a sentence containing it: and here we once more run against the apparent difficulty of breaking out of the third realm of senses into the external world of physical objects. At this stage, however, it is evident that our difficulty has arisen precisely from that ambiguity in Frege's notion of sense with which this chapter has been concerned. It is as a thesis in the philosophy of language that the proposition that a term may have sense but yet lack a reference seems unproblematic; and, on this level, the claim that we can often establish that it genuinely has a reference appears equally unproblematic. But the conception of the mode of presentation of an object, the way in which it is given to us, conflates two distinguishable things: our grasp of the linguistic significance of a term; and our apprehension of an object which we can presently perceive or discern. The most natural way to understand the conception of the sense of a non-indexical and non-demonstrative singular term is that which I adopted in *FPL*, namely as the grasp of whatever principle governs the correct identification of an object as the referent of the term. If, now, we add that we can never be given an object save under some mode of presentation, and identify the mode of presentation with a sense as thus conceived, an apparent paradox is created: we seem to be unable to break out of the circle of senses to the real object beyond. To speak of the identification of an object as the referent of a term presupposes a means of picking out the object for which no further question of identification arises: our problem then was how we could arrive at such a terminus. But the sense in which an object may be said to be given to us in a particular way when it is observed is altogether different from that in which it is said to be 'given' by our grasp of the sense of a name or description used to speak about it. It was certainly part of Frege's thought that we can pick out a particular object—either in the sense of indicating it to another or in that of discerning it as an individual object—only by grasping the appropriate criterion of identity, and hence by regarding it as falling under a suitable sortal concept. This may be regarded as an amplification of Kant's dictum that percepts without concepts are blind: we see the world as ordered by the concepts we employ just as ineluctably as one who can read sees a line of print as a sequence of letters; just as he cannot see the name of a railway station on the platform as an illiterate man would see it, so we cannot see the everyday world save as composed of objects falling under the concepts which we are accustomed to use; and we should not see it as composed of objects at all without our grasp of some system of concepts. It is for this reason that Frege says in 'Der Gedanke'[1] that it is what belongs to the 'third realm' of senses that leads us from the inner world of sense-impressions to the outer world of perceptible things. But it in no way follows that what determines which particular object it is that is perceived or picked out in ostension is in the least comparable with what determines for which particular object a name or description stands.

There is, indeed, no ground to claim even the process of ostension, considered as involving appeal to a sortal concept, as infallible: there is often room for a mistake over whether an object of a given sort is present at all, and, if so, only one. The point is only that, if, as I claimed in *FPL*

[1] P. 75.

and continue to think, ostension must play a role in any adequate account of the senses of terms for concrete objects, we are not trapped by an infinite regress within the bloodless realm of senses. At the level at which the question of verifying that a definite object has indeed been picked out by ostension arises, we are operating with perceptual procedures, which, as Frege rightly says, involve an interplay between sensation and conceptual thought. The verification does not require us to move from one sense or mode of presentation to another: we do not have, in the process, to identify in some different way the object which we have picked out, but only to check that we have succeeded in picking one out; and so the apparent regress is broken. That there should have been even the appearance of one is due solely to Frege's wavering use of 'sense' to mean both the significance of an expression and the manner in which we discriminate a particular object. Once this is appreciated, the temptation to make a mystery of senses without corresponding referents vanishes: it no longer appears to be constitutive of any thought that it is really about a particular object, though of course what makes a thought to be about a certain object, when it is so, varies greatly when the object is apprehended in perception or in memory and when it is grasped solely in thought, that is, by means of a sense expressible by a name or description not of a purely indexical or demonstrative character. Nor, once the ambiguity in Frege's notion of sense is clearly apprehended, and all temptation to force either component of the notion into the mould of the other forsworn, does any wish remain to convict Frege of a mistake, either in allowing expressions to bear senses which merely purport to determine a referent, or in envisaging a way in which it merely appears that an object is given to us in perception.

Note on quantification into mixed contexts

If the relevant notion of senses can be made clear, Frege's doctrine of indirect reference has the advantage that quantification into *oratio obliqua* becomes quite unproblematic, the range of quantification consisting of senses. Quantification into apparently mixed contents, in which one occurrence of the variable lies in a *prima facie* transparent context, and another in a *prima facie* opaque one, gives trouble on any account. At least within the framework of Frege's theory, there can be only two types of solution: the sentence must be transformed so that either both occurrences of the bound variable lie within an opaque context, or both occurrences lie within a transparent one. On pp. 276–7 of *FPL*, I opted for the former solution. Assume that we can justify the transition from 'Orwell is at Murray's table' to

'It is true that Orwell is at Murray's table', where in the latter sentence the substantival clause is taken to constitute an opaque context to be construed in accordance with Frege's theory of indirect reference. We may then interpret 'There is someone at Murray's table whom Murray knows to be there' as meaning 'For some u, it is true that u is at Murray's table and Murray knows that u is at his table', where the bound variable ranges over a suitably restricted class of senses. It will then be indisputable that (i) 'There is someone at Murray's table whom Murray knows to be there' is a logical consequence of 'Orwell is at Murray's table' and 'Murray knows that Orwell is at his table'.

In his review of *FPL*, Heidelberger objects to this analysis on the following ground. Suppose that 'Orwell is at Murray's table' and 'Murray knows that Orwell is at his table' are both true; and suppose that Murray has heard of Blair, but does not know that Orwell is Blair. Then 'Blair is at Murray's table' and 'Murray does not know that Blair is at his table' will also be true. But, on the proposed analysis, it will also hold that (ii) 'There is someone at Murray's table whom Murray does not know to be there' follows from 'Blair is at Murray's table' and 'Murray does not know that Blair is at his table'. Heidelberger objects that the statement 'There is someone at Murray's table whom Murray knows to be there, and there is someone at his table whom Murray does not know to be there' would normally be taken to imply that there are two people at Murray's table besides himself, which may very well be false.

It is obvious that this conclusion would indeed be drawn by anyone hearing the statement made without qualification. It is less evident that the inference depends upon a deductive implication, in the strict sense, rather than upon an implicature in the sense of Grice. If the former, then we cannot accept both (i) and (ii) as logical principles. We can avoid this by adopting the alternative solution. This is to interpret 'There is someone at Murray's table whom Murray knows to be there' as meaning 'For some x, x is at Murray's table and Murray knows, of x, that he is at his table'; the second, as well as the first, occurrence of the bound variable now lies within a transparent context, and the variable ranges accordingly over denizens of the realm of reference, specifically over human beings. The validity of principle (i) will now depend upon the validity of the step from 'Murray knows that Orwell is at his table' to 'Murray knows, of Orwell, that he is at his table'. If this step is taken to be valid, the step from 'Murray does not know that Blair is at his table' to 'Murray does not know, of Blair, that he is at his table' must be declared invalid. On the contrary, if 'Murray knows, of Orwell, that he is at his table' is true, then so is 'Murray knows, of Blair, that he is at his table', even though 'Murray knows that Blair is at his table' is false, just because, in the first of these three sentences, 'Orwell' occurs in a transparent context. Hence, on this interpretation, if (i) is valid, (ii) is invalid, and Heidelberger's difficulty is resolved.

If this solution is to work, the principle governing the transition from 'Murray knows that Orwell is at his table' to 'Murray knows, of Orwell, that he is at his table' must be of quite general application. For instance, from 'Orwell is at Murray's table and Murray knows that Orwell is there' we can evidently infer

'Murray knows Orwell's whereabouts'; and the natural way to interpret this latter sentence is as meaning 'Orwell is somewhere such that Murray knows that Orwell is there'. If this is, in turn, to be interpreted in the same manner as 'There is someone whom Murray knows to be at his table', it must be taken as having the form 'For some place *s*, Orwell is in *s*, and Murray knows, of *s*, that Orwell is in it'. That is to say, we cannot dispute that a real *transition* is involved. We cannot evade the question whether 'Murray knows, of Orwell, that he is at his table' follows from 'Murray knows that Orwell is at his table' by declaring that it is only the former of which we have a right to claim that it entails 'There is someone whom Murray knows to be at his table', blaming appearances to the contrary on the imprecision of natural language; for, if we said this, we should have either to deny that there was any one premiss from which both 'Murray knows Orwell's whereabouts' and 'There is someone whom Murray knows to be at his table' follow, or, heroically, to identify this single premiss as being 'Murray knows, of Orwell and of his table, that he is at it.'

What, then, is the principle governing a transition of this kind, say that from 'Orwell is Blair and Murray knows that Orwell is at his table' to 'Murray knows, of Blair, that he is at his table'? It is, evidently, that, from the former sentence, we may infer 'For some *s*, it is true that *s* is Blair, and Murray knows that *s* is at his table'; indeed, this may be taken as the analysis of 'Murray knows, of Blair, that he is at his table'. To justify the transition, we therefore have to admit the step from 'Orwell is Blair' to 'It is true that Orwell is Blair', where, again, the substantival clause forms an opaque context. The sentence by means of which we now analyse 'Murray knows, of Blair, that he is at his table' is of precisely that form which, on the former, rejected, interpretation, we should have assigned to 'There is someone who is Blair and whom Murray knows to be at his table'. Thus the interpretation of sentences involving quantification into an apparently mixed context which Heidelberger's objection, if taken as cogent, compels us to adopt in place of that previously favoured by me has no advantage of economy. To validate it, we have still to appeal to that transition on which the rejected interpretation depended.

The rationale of Heidelberger's objection is that being known to be present, being expected to come, etc., are properties of a person or thing, i.e. of an object, so that if Orwell has any such property, so does Blair. Suppose that the Vice-Chancellor has asked the Dean of some college to call on him at a certain hour. The Dean, on arrival, quite properly answers 'Yes' to the secretary's question, 'Is the Vice-Chancellor expecting you?'; but, when he enters the room, the Vice-Chancellor may, without making him a liar, exclaim, 'Good Heavens! I wasn't expecting *you*', not having known that someone very well known to him had recently been appointed Dean. There are many occasions when, to interpret what we naturally say, the direct object of a verb such as 'expect' must be treated as standing in an opaque context, contrary to that Heidelberger assumes. It is, however, useless to press the question whether it is always to be so treated, as it is useless to press the question whether Heidelberger's inference depends on an implication or an implicature: our language has not been fashioned by speakers keenly alert to these distinctions. This is a paradigmatic instance of an area of discourse which requires regimentation before a systematic theory can be given; linguistic intuition alone will not yield one. Frege's theory of indirect reference forces us to make sharper distinctions than are allowed by common speech, which avoids ambiguity by periphrasis or pleonasm. It forces us to explain quantification which apparently governs a transparent and an opaque context simultaneously by transforming the opaque context into a transparent one or conversely. So far as I can see, there can be no basis for preferring either strategy to the other, and certainly none for claiming either as more faithful to the practice of ordinary speakers; it suffices if Frege's theory can be made the framework of a workable account of sentences ascribing propositional attitudes. Certainly he would neither have claimed that, nor cared whether, it accorded at all points with the usage of natural language.

CHAPTER 7

Frege's Notion of Reference

ANYONE WHO READS Frege for the first time will be struck by two facts concerning his use of the term '*Bedeutung*'. As applied to proper names, it appears to be used for the bearer of the name, or, by a natural extension to definite descriptions and other complex singular terms, for the object which we use the name to speak about. On the other hand, the term is also applied to incomplete expressions of all kinds and to whole sentences; and, although Frege devotes much discussion to what the referents of expressions of these other categories are, he seldom stops to justify his extending the notion of reference to them at all. In the 'Einleitung in die Logik' of 1906, he does offer a justification, of a rather unconvincing kind:[1] but usually he simply takes it for granted that every significant unit of a sentence, including the sentence as a whole, has a reference, and is concerned only with what that reference is. Now if we assume that the notion of *Bedeutung* is to be explained solely as being that relation which a proper name has to its bearer, or that which an expression has to what we use the expression to talk about, we shall see Frege's extension of it to expressions other than proper names as quite unwarrantable: as resting on the so-called 'Fido'-Fido fallacy ascribed by Ryle to Carnap, the delusion, namely, that every expression is a kind of name. (This impression will be reinforced by the fact that in *Grundgesetze*, Part I, Frege does apply the term 'name' to every logically unitary expression.)

I suggested in *FPL* that the way to avoid this misunderstanding was to see the notion of *Bedeutung* as having from the outset two distinct ingredients: the name/bearer relation; and what I called 'semantic role'. Within a complete theory of meaning for a language, we must distinguish, if we follow Frege, between the theory of reference and the theory of sense;

---

[1] *N.S.*, pp. 209–10, *P.W.*, p. 193.

the theory of reference is the semantic component of the theory, in the strict sense of the term 'semantic'. The notion of semantic role of course belongs to a semantic theory. Within formal logic, the need for a semantic theory arises out of the necessity for having some means of surveying all possible interpretations of a formula containing schematic letters, and so arriving at a means to demonstrate the validity of a formula or of an argument-schema, or the soundness or completeness of some formalization of logic. Validity is defined in terms of the notion of an interpretation and that of truth under an interpretation. The primitive notion of an interpretation is that of an interpretation by replacement, that is, by converting a formula into an actual sentence by replacing its schematic letters by actual expressions of the appropriate kinds. In order, therefore, to arrive at a notion of interpretation suitable for use in mathematical demonstrations, we have to ask the question: what properties must we ascribe to constituent expressions of each given type in order to determine each sentence as being true or otherwise? The properties so ascribed may then be said to constitute the *semantic roles* of the expressions. If, as Frege did, and as is normally done in the semantic theories used by logicians, we assume that the semantic role of each expression can be stated as its having something of an appropriate type associated with it, we may call that which is so associated with an expression its *semantic value*. An interpretation of a formula will now no longer be thought of as a replacement of the schematic letters by actual expressions of the appropriate type, but as a direct assignment to them of possible semantic values of such expressions.

Without any prior assumption, the formulation just given is insufficiently general. To achieve full generality, we should rephrase our question as: what is it necessary to associate with constituent expressions of each given type in order to determine that feature of each sentence on which its being true or otherwise depends? The simpler formulation is possible only if it be assumed, as Frege assumed, and as is assumed in any classical semantic theory, that each sentence of a logically correct language is determinately either true or not true. For instance, on the intuitionistic theory it is not assumed that every sentence is determined either as being true or as not being true; that feature of a mathematical sentence on which its being true depends, and which is determined when the meanings of its constituent expressions have been fixed, is what counts as a proof of the sentence, and it is to be recognized as true just in case we have such a proof. Hence, in an intuitionistic context, the question which prompts the construction of a semantic theory reduces to: what is it necessary to associate with constituent expressions of each given type in order to determine, for each sentence, what is to count as a proof of it? But, when we make the assumption which Frege made, and which underlies any realistic theory of meaning, that every sentence is, determinately, either true or not true, we can frame our question as: what is it necessary to associate with constituent expressions of each given type in order to determine each sentence as being true or otherwise? That which, in answer to this question, is associated with any one expression is its semantic value.

The semantic value of an expression will not be its *meaning*, in the sense in which meaning is correlative with understanding, since a sentence will not be directly determined as true or otherwise solely by the meanings of its constituents; its truth-value will, in general, be determined, given those meanings, by how the world is. The semantic value will therefore be something that, in view of how the world is, is determined by the meaning of the expression. Furthermore, so long as two expressions are interchangeable in sentences without affecting their truth-values, those two expressions will have the same semantic value, even though their meanings differ. What is asked for is something that is sufficient, given the semantic values of other expressions, to determine any sentence in which the expression occurs as true or otherwise, and must, therefore, in general depend, not only on the meaning of the expression, but on how the world is. But, also, what is asked for is no more than is required to determine every sentence in which the expression occurs as true or otherwise, given the semantic values of the other expressions, and therefore may be associated with other expressions differing in meaning.

What Frege identifies as being the referent of an expression of each logical type is, precisely, what has here been called its 'semantic value', according to a certain particular semantic theory. Moreover, that is precisely how he conceived of reference. It is an essential feature of his notion of reference that the references of the parts of a sentence suffice to determine it as true or false; moreover, the reference of an expression never involves anything not so bearing on the truth-value of some sentence in which it occurs, since, if two expressions differ in reference, there will be some sentence whose truth-value will be altered by the substitution of the one expression for the other. The determination of the truth-values of the symbolic formulas is effected in *Grundgesetze* by stipulations determining the references of the component symbols. It is because he conceives of reference as semantic value that it seems so evident to Frege that every expression which can be a constituent of a sentence must have a reference;

it must by some means contribute to the determination of the truth-value of the sentences in which it occurs. It would be misleading to say that Frege anticipated model theory. On the contrary, he cannot concern himself with a variety of interpretations of a formula or set of formulas, since he does not officially recognize any such thing as a schematic letter. In *Begriffsschrift*, the italic letters do, for all practical purposes, function like schematic letters, but officially they are bound variables governed by an initial universal quantifier. This way of looking at things impeded Frege from framing any semantic notion of the validity of a formula, or, therefore, of the completeness of a formal system for logic. But his theory of reference anticipates later formal semantics in the sense that it provides precisely the framework within which the notion of a semantic interpretation can be defined; and, within that framework, his specification of the references of the primitive expressions of his system constitutes, in precisely the sense of classical two-valued semantics, a stipulation of the one intended interpretation of the system.

In discussing Frege's philosophy of language, it is essential to bear in mind that what served as the foundation for all the rest was his syntactic analysis. This analysis displays the workings of the sentences of natural language, which is not obvious from inspection of their surface structure; it may therefore be said to uncover the hidden structure of those sentences. The syntactic analysis is embodied in Frege's symbolic notation, the formulas of which make manifest their structure as so analysed. The syntactic analysis expresses Frege's conception of the way in which sentences are to be viewed as having been constructed out of their components; and its point lies in the fact that it serves as a base for the semantic theory embodied in his theory of reference. It is not just a syntactic analysis adequate for the purposes of syntax alone: it is one that is apt for the purpose of constructing a semantic theory. The symbolic notation, taken over, in essentials, into the quantificational languages studied by modern logic, of course departs at various points from the mode of sentence-formation employed in natural language; but it remains the case that we can apply Frege's doctrines to natural language only in so far as we view its sentences as constructed in the same way as those of Frege's formal language, even though the end-product does not reveal the mode of construction in the same perspicuous manner. For example, in asking which expressions have reference, and what kind of referents they have, we can answer only in terms of Frege's categorization of the different possible types of constituent of the sentences of his formal language, and of expressions of natural language regarded as falling into corresponding categories in virtue of a parallel account of the underlying structures of its sentences. This is certainly true when the interpretation of Frege's semantic doctrines are in question; but it is also true that we are hardly in a position to provide a semantic theory for a language that does not have a quantificational syntax, and cannot readily be exhibited as transformable into one that does. We shall almost certainly misread Frege if we allow ourselves ever to lose sight of the magnitude of his achievement in providing a syntactic base adequate for the construction of a semantic theory, or to forget that, throughout his career, this achievement, taken for granted by us, remained controversial.

One might think it obvious that Frege connects his notion of reference with that of name to bearer, or, more generally, with that of a word to what one uses the word to talk about: 'when one uses words in the ordinary way,' he says in 'Über Sinn und Bedeutung',[1] 'that of which one means to talk is their reference.' What needs explaining, rather, is Frege's identification of reference with semantic value; this both uncovers the reason for his extending the notion to incomplete expressions and to whole sentences, and displays the importance of the notion in his theory of meaning. But there are now those who deny that the notion of *Bedeutung* has anything to do with the relation of name to bearer. One of these is Hans Sluga. He calls my description of Frege as a realist an 'unsubstantiated claim',[2] a claim that he rejects. And he regards the view that the name/bearer relation was one of the ingredients of Frege's notion of reference as part of this erroneous interpretation of Frege as a realist, and rejects it also. One would think that the natural conclusion from this surprising view is that I was right in only half of what I said, namely in giving the notion of the semantic role of an expression as another ingredient in Frege's notion of reference; but not at all. Sluga pays no attention to my repeated observation[3] that the conception of reference as semantic role is a distinguishable ingredient of the notion, which usually complements the other but is sometimes in tension with it; on the contrary, he actually assimilates the two, and attacks both together as part of my allegedly mistaken realistic interpretation of Frege. His position is rendered confusing, however, by his commendation of Ernst Tugendhat's account of Frege's notion of reference as 'truth-value potential' (t.v.p.). While Sluga regards what I cited as two distinct ingredients of Frege's notion of reference as virtually identical, and reproaches me for failing to adopt Tugendhat's

[1] P. 28.

[2] 'Frege and the Rise of Analytical Philosophy', pp. 471–87.

[3] E.g. *FPL*, pp. 199–200, 223, 401.

new interpretation, Tugendhat himself equates his notion of t.v.p. with my notion of 'semantic role'.[1] Tugendhat, in his Postscript of 1975, acknowledges, what was not apparent from his article of 1970, that there is another ingredient in Frege's notion of reference, saying that 'in Frege the interpretation of reference as truth-value potential is bound up with an ontological (*gegenstandstheoretische*) conception'[2] and identifies such an 'ontological conception' with that under which the name/bearer relation serves as prototype for the relation of reference:[3] his view is thus not, like Sluga's, that Frege's notion of reference did not have this component, but that it would be improved by extruding it. Since, as Tugendhat remarks, I had, in *FPL*, p. 199, already suggested, though with the qualification 'in effect', the equation of his notion of t.v.p. with my notion of semantic role, it appears that, as far as our *interpretations* of Frege go, the gap between them is narrower than originally appeared, unlike that between mine and Sluga's: the issue between Tugendhat and myself is mainly one of evaluation. Nevertheless, it is interesting to consider the result of trying, as Tugendhat does, to strip Frege's notion of reference of its so-called 'ontological' component; by so doing, we become clearer about the function of that component in Frege's thought. Especially is this so because the equation of t.v.p. with semantic role, suggested by me and accepted by Tugendhat, is rather loose.

Tugendhat defines 't.v.p.' by laying down that two expressions have the same t.v.p. if, when each is expanded into a sentence by means of the same expression, the two resulting sentences have the same truth-value. How are we to understand this ambiguous stipulation? Hardly as meaning that if there is any *one* addition that converts both expressions into sentences with the same truth-value, they have the same t.v.p., for then we should infer, from the possibility of prefacing both by 'Brutus respected every man other than', that 'Brutus' and 'himself' had the same t.v.p., and even, from the possibility of supplementing both by 'killed Caesar', that 'Brutus' and 'Cassius' did. Obviously, we must interpret the stipulation by reading 'when' as 'whenever'.

Now is this really the same notion as that which in *FPL* I called 'semantic role', or as that which I called above 'semantic value'? Not exactly: it

---

[1] See his 'Postskript 1975' to the German version 'Die Bedeutung des Ausdrucks "Bedeutung" bei Frege' of his article in *Analysis*, vol. 30, 1970, 'The Meaning of "Bedeutung" in Frege'; the German version and the Postscript are to be found in M. Schirn (ed.), op. cit., vol. III, pp. 51–65, 65–9. See especially pp. 67–8.

[2] P. 68.

[3] P. 67.

is the definition of a relation between two expressions which is a necessary condition, and, under certain assumptions, also a sufficient one, for them to have the same semantic value. Given the assumption that every sentence is determinately either true or not true, the semantic value of an expression was defined to be that which must be associated with it if we are to explain how every sentence in which it occurs is determined as true or otherwise. It is, therefore, the starting-point of an enquiry, an invitation to construct a semantic theory, which will lay down, for each specific expression and each type of expression considered, what, or what kind of thing, its semantic value is. Tugendhat does not provide for the question what a t.v.p. is: he has merely defined an equivalence relation expressed by 'has the same t.v.p. as', and therefore, as he now acknowledges for sentences and predicates, but inconsistently denies for names, the most we can take a t.v.p. to be is an equivalence class of expressions. This does not lead to the construction of a semantic theory, or even urge us in that direction: it merely draws attention to an interesting relation between expressions, that of interchangeability *salva veritate*.

This notion naturally recalls Leibniz's law, of which Tugendhat claims his definition, for the case of names, of the relation of having the same t.v.p., to be a more detailed formulation.[1] Of course, it is not, at least when the law is expressed, as he expresses it, as a definition of identity ('a = b = *Def.* (P) Pa ≡ Pb'): Tugendhat's relation is between expressions, whereas identity is a relation between *objects*.

But can we not infer that '*a*' and '*b*' will have the same t.v.p. just in case '*a* = *b*' is true? No doubt we can, if we have adopted the theory that the semantic value of a proper name is the object for which it stands, that is, in Tugendhat's terminology, that two names have the same t.v.p. iff they stand for the same object, and if we have explained what it is for a proper name to stand for an object; or if, instead of giving such an explanation, we have assumed, as part of our theory, that there is an association of names to objects, which we call 'standing for', such that '*a*' and '*b*' stand for the same object just in case '*a* = *b*' is true. But this is to bring the name/bearer relation into our semantic theory; and not only has Tugendhat given no indication that any semantic theory is needed, but he has claimed that Frege's account of language would be better off without any appeal to the name/bearer relation. If, then, we are exploring a reconstruction of Frege's views which forswears appeal to the name/bearer relation, we cannot arrive at the desired connection between

---

[1] Ibid., p. 55.

Leibniz's law and Tugendhat's definition of 't.v.p.' in either of the ways suggested.

Before we attempt to find another route for the inference we want to make, let us ask what the symbol '=' means here. Presumably it represents whatever expression functions, in the language with which we are concerned, as the sign of identity. But when is an expression to be identified as the sign of identity? It is no use answering, 'When it stands for that relation in which every object stands to, and only to, itself.' If we are exploring the consequences of the definition of 't.v.p.', without appeal to the name/bearer relation, then, at this stage, there has been no talk of objects: we have not the right to help ourselves to the notion of a *relation* defined over *objects*. Even if we did know what it was to define such a relation, we may not assume that it has anything to do with an expression which, when placed between two names, yields a sentence. We may, perhaps, presume ourselves already to have successfully picked out the category of proper names: but we cannot assume that we know any connection between a name and an object; and, for just this reason, we also may not assume a knowledge of what it is for an expression to stand for a relation, or that there is any connection between relations and expressions which, together with two names, make up a sentence; to establish such a connection, we must first establish one between names and objects.

Cannot we appeal to Leibniz's law itself, in order to identify the sign of identity in the language? We can do so, provided that we can explain the range of the predicate-variables in the definiens. But, as Tugendhat observes, to get identity, or to arrive at anything resembling Frege's conception of the condition for two names to have the same reference, we must restrict the range to (the referents of) *extensional* predicates. The parenthesis may be dropped if, as is natural here, we understand the quantification as substitutional: but how are we to characterize *extensional* predicates? We had better not say that '$F(\xi)$' is an extensional predicate if, for any names 'a' and 'b', if '$F(a)$' and '$a = b$' are true, so is '$F(b)$', or we shall go round in a circle. But the only other possibility is to say that it is extensional if, for any two names 'a' and 'b' that stand for the same object, if '$F(a)$' is true, '$F(b)$' is true: and this appeals to the proscribed notion of a name's standing for an object.

Thus, at every turn, the attempt to give substance to the empty notion of t.v.p. proves to involve an illicit appeal to the very notion, that of the name/bearer relation, which we were supposed to be getting on so much better without; each such attempt is thwarted when the appeal is disallowed. But suppose that we permit an appeal to the name/bearer relation simply in order to define 'extensional predicate': can we then say that '*a*' and '*b*' have the same t.v.p. just in case '*a* = *b*' is true? Only if the language is extensional, i.e. there are *only* extensional predicates. Otherwise we must say that '*a* = *b*' may be true even though '*a*' and '*b*' do *not* have the same t.v.p.: for in the definition of 't.v.p.' there was no mention of *extensional* expressions. If, to rectify this, we now incorporate a require-ment of extensionality into the definition of 't.v.p.', then, since we can explain the notion of extensionality only by appeal, ultimately, to the relation of name to bearer, we have built an appeal to this relation into the notion of t.v.p. itself.

As I pointed out in *FPL*,[1] Tugendhat's attempt to derive Frege's thesis that the *Bedeutung* of a sentence is its truth-value suffers, not this time from an improper appeal to the notion supposed to be being eschewed, but from a misinterpretation of his own definition, or a simple fallacy. Tugendhat's attempted proof of Frege's thesis runs as follows:

> When [in the definition of 't.v.p.'] we put sentences in place of Φ and Ψ, we obtain the following statement: two sentences 'p' and 'q' have the same t.v.p. just in case, when each is expanded into a sentence by means of the same expression, the two resulting sentences have the same truth-value. But since 'p' and 'q' are already sentences, no additional expression is needed in order to expand them into sentences. Hence the clause, 'when each is expanded . . .', is in this case superfluous, and the definition is reduced to the simple form: two sentences 'p' and 'q' have the same t.v.p. just in case they have the same truth-value.

But if we read Tugendhat's original definition of 't.v.p.' in the only way that makes reasonable sense, namely by taking 'when' in the sense of 'whenever', we see the fallacy of the proof. We must consider the null supplementation, among others, and so it is *necessary* for the two sentences to have the same truth-value; but it is not *sufficient*, since we must consider all other possible supplementations as well, that is, all pairs of complex sentences, of one of which the one sentence is a constituent and of the other of which the other is, and which are otherwise alike. Only if the members of all such pairs have the same truth-value can we conclude that the two original sentences have the same t.v.p. Needless to say, if we apply this test without first adding to the definition of 't.v.p.' provisos allowing us to ignore a whole range of cases in which one sentence is

[1] P. 200.

an intensional constituent of another, we shall arrive at the result that many sentences which agree in truth-value have different t.v.p.s.

Before we proceed further, let us ask what we want the notion of reference (or semantic value) *for*. If we do not keep asking that question, we are liable to fall victims to scholasticism, in the pejorative sense, at least in interpreting Frege. In logic, we need the notion of reference or of semantic value in order to characterize validity; but, more generally, we need it as the basis for a theory of sense: it has a point if, and *only* if, it plays a role in our account of sense. What, then, do we need a theory of sense for? We need it as forming a large part of a theory of meaning, that is, of a theory that will explain in virtue of what features of our use of them our sentences bear the meanings that they do. Frege's idea was, of course, that the sense of a sentence is to be explained in terms of the condition that has to be satisfied for it to be true, i.e. of what we take as making it true if it is true. Sense determines reference; the specification of the references of the constituent parts of a sentence therefore provides a basis for an account of how we see the sentence as being determined as true or otherwise in accordance with its composition. Provided only with an assignment of truth-values to sentences, however, we cannot work back to an account of what makes them true or false; even given a syntactic analysis of them, we cannot deduce how their parts contribute to determining their truth-values. In particular, the conception of a name as standing for an object is not attainable by comparing the truth-values of sentences formed by replacing one name by another, although, without that conception, we have no account of how the name contributes to the determination of a sentence as true or false: the conception must therefore come from outside. It is useless for Tugendhat to object to me, as he does,[1] that the necessary relation to something extra-linguistic is already provided by starting from the truth-values of sentences, on the ground that it is extra-linguistic reality which determines them as true or false. The point is that his definition of 't.v.p.' appeals only to the *results* of that determination, and says nothing about how it is effected; and there is no way of working back from those results, together with the internal structures of the sentences, to an account of *how* they are determined as true or false, in accordance with that structure, of the specific contributions made to that determination by their constituent parts.

If we do construct a theory of how the language works, more exactly, of the semantic values that its various expressions have, it is likely to

[1] Postskript, p. 67.

employ some notion of a name's standing for an object. Two questions now arise: one concerning our ability to construct and understand the theory, the other concerning its explanatory power. In constructing the theory, from where did we get the notion of an object, so as to explain the semantic role of a name as consisting in its standing for one? The notion of an *object* is, in itself, vacuous: to have any substantial conception of proper names as having bearers, we must be able to specify particular names as standing for particular types of objects, e.g. personal names as standing for human beings. We must therefore ask: from where do we get the conception of a human being? It is no use to reply, 'From our use of proper names of human beings and of predicates applying to them': unless it is explained in what our construing a given personal name as standing for a human being consists, the answer is circular. And this leads us to the second question, which no longer concerns how we are able to frame the semantic theory, but with the substance of that theory. The semantic theory, the theory of reference, postulates an association between names and objects: but in what is that association supposed to consist? What makes it the case that a given proper name stands for a certain object? Well, to say that a name stands for an object is to say that we use it as standing for that object; but then we must ask: what is it so to use it? What gives substance to the semantic theory or theory of reference is the theory of sense; it is this which must supply the answer to the question what constitutes the association between a given expression and its semantic value. Since Frege's whole strategy was to interpret sense as relating to truth-conditions, our question must now take this form: what feature of our treating certain conditions as those required for the truth of sentences containing the name 'a' constitutes our taking 'a' to stand for the object u?

A natural answer would be that it is our taking any sentence '$F(a)$' containing 'a' to be true just in case the predicate '$F(\xi)$' is true of u. But now it must be asked what it is for a predicate to be true of an object; and, if we were to answer that it is true of an object if the sentence resulting from inserting a name of the object in the argument-place of the predicate is true, we should once more go round in a circle. It is not enough to concede that we must appeal to the name/bearer relation in constructing a semantic theory, or that such an appeal is implicit in Frege's use of the notion of *Bedeutung* as applied to proper names. We must ask what makes the notion of the bearer of a name so transparent to us, and why we accept Frege's speaking of 'Jupiter' as standing for a heavenly body and of 'Aristotle' as standing for a man as unproblematic. My answer in *FPL* was that the notion of a bearer is embedded in very basic linguistic practices above all in the use of what I called 'recognition statements', sentences of the form 'This is *a*', where an object picked out by ostension is identified as the bearer of a name.[1] This appeal to ostension was not put forward as reproducing anything in Frege, but as a possible answer to the legitimate question how the notion of the bearer of a name is itself to be explained.

The notion of semantic role or of semantic value remains purely programmatic until a specific semantic theory be propounded. Frege did not, of course, first explain what a semantic theory would be, and then supply a particular such theory; that is why his notion of reference cannot be identified with the general notion of semantic value. The purpose of alluding to this notion in this connection is twofold: to show the point of Frege's notion of reference, the role that it was intended to play; and to explain why he took it as relatively unproblematic that expressions other than proper names have a reference. What Frege did was to explain his notion of reference in such a way as thereby to provide a semantic theory; he did not clearly separate out what he wanted the notion for and what he took the references of different types of expression to be, and, just for that reason, his notion of reference cannot be understood unless it is viewed as having more than one ingredient. If we forget to enquire what the notion was intended to do, we may lose ourselves in a network of stipulations the point of which has been lost; if we overlook the very specific content of Frege's semantic theory, we shall be left with an entirely barren notion such as that of t.v.p. It is unthinkable that Frege could have proceeded in any other way than he did: there was not available the general notion of a semantic theory, or even any example of one from which it would have been possible to generalize. Frege had both to explain why a semantic theory was needed, and to create a specific such theory, and it was inevitable that he should have done both simultaneously. He did it by generalizing a notion that has its immediate natural application to singular terms in such a way as to apply to expressions of all logical types; and it is a measure of his genius that he did this with so sure a touch, finding, in every case, precisely the right analogue.

A fundamental principle of Frege's semantic theory is that a proper name (singular term) stands for an object, and, moreover, precisely the sort of object that we intuitively take to be its bearer. If we started from a purely programmatic notion of semantic role or semantic value, two names would have the same semantic value just in case they had the same t.v.p., and there would therefore be a presumption, in view of the existence of

[1] *FPL*, p. 406.

intensional contexts, against their always having the same semantic value when they had the same bearer. We might, nevertheless, find some reason to reserve intensional contexts for special treatment. But that is not at all the way in which Frege argues: he simply *starts* from the assumption that the *Bedeutung* of a name is its bearer, and concludes that, in an intensional context, it cannot have its ordinary *Bedeutung*, because it was from the name/bearer relation that he derived the notion of *Bedeutung* in the first place. The fact that Frege takes the semantic role of a proper name to consist in its having a certain relation to an object comes out in the mere fact that he uses the transitive verb '*bedeuten*'. That he takes this object to be what would ordinarily be taken to be the bearer of the name comes out in many things. Among them are the connection he makes in *Grundgesetze* between standing for (*bedeuten*) and designating (*bezeichnen*), summarized by the statement 'by means of the name I *designate* that which it stands for';[1] his occasional use of '*bezeichnen*' or of '*benennen*' ('to name') as synonyms for '*bedeuten*' as applied to proper names, as in 'both designations have the same reference, they designate or stand for or name the same thing'[2] and 'the reference of a proper name is the object which it designates or names';[3] and, above all, the fact that he takes it for granted that the *Bedeutung* of 'Jupiter' is a planet, that of 'Aristotle' a man, and so on. How, after all, could we have any conception of what a man was, independently of having some means of referring to particular men? But the most decisive sign is his assumption that, where 'X' is a proper name, it will have the same *Bedeutung* as, and may therefore be replaced by, the phrase '*die Bedeutung von* "X"' or '*was* "X" *bedeutet*'. If proper names have bearers, and may be said to stand for them, then, of course, the bearer of the name 'X' is what the name 'X' stands for. If, further, a definite description may be said to stand for the object that uniquely satisfies it, then the name 'X' stands for the same object as does the phrase 'what the name "X" stands for'. All this is obvious, however, only in so far as the relation of reference (of standing for something) is connected with that of proper name to bearer, and extended in a natural way to definite descriptions. If we start with the notion of semantic value, we can make no assumption that the phrase 'the semantic value of "X"' is able to replace the name 'X', or, as I remarked in *FPL*,[4] that 'Ernst Tugendhat' is

---

[1] *Grundgesetze*, vol. 1, § 2.

[2] 'Über die Begriffsschrift des Herrn Peano und meine eigene', 1896, p. 369.

[3] 'Ausführungen über Sinn und Bedeutung', 1892–5, *N.S.*, p. 128, *P.W.*, p. 118; cf. also *N.S.*, p. 133, *P.W.*, p. 122.

[4] P. 202.

replaceable by 'the truth-value potential of "Ernst Tugendhat" '. The assumption that what 'Rome' stands for is the same as that for which the phrase 'what "Rome" stands for' or 'the object which "Rome" stands for' stands is tantamount to assuming that the semantic role of a name consists in its association with an object, and just that object we take to be its bearer; at least, it is when reference is equated with semantic role, i.e. when it is by means of its reference that the name is thought to contribute to the determination of the truth-values of sentences containing it.

This is not to say that the straightforward equation of the semantic value of a name with its bearer, implicit in Frege's employment of the notion of reference, creates no problems. A second fundamental principle of Frege's semantic theory, the most important of all, is that which Tugendhat falsely believes that he can derive from his definition of 't.v.p.': that the semantic role of a sentence consists simply in its being true or being false, that the *Bedeutung* of a sentence is its truth-value. A third fundamental principle is that, if a constituent of a complex expression lacks *Bedeutung*, the whole lacks *Bedeutung*. When the *Bedeutung* of a singular term is identified with the object for which it stands, that which it is used to talk about, this last principle is evident for complex singular terms, but less so for expressions of other kinds. It leads Frege to regard a sentence containing a proper name that lacks a bearer as devoid of truth-value; but, as I explained in Chapter 12 of *FPL*, the thesis that such a sentence *must* be so regarded cannot be sustained. What is at fault here is not the analogy between names and sentences, but the starting-point. There is no intuitive justification for denying to a sentence containing an empty name a semantic value; but, by the same token, there is no justification for denying a semantic value to a name without a bearer, either. That is simply to say that there is no demonstration that a workable semantic theory could not be constructed for a language admitting such names and such sentences; and, in such a theory, the semantic value of a name could not be straightforwardly identified with its bearer, but only with its having such-and-such a bearer, or with its having none. That it never occurred to Frege that a name lacking a referent might yet be said to have a reference, or even to employ a terminology allowing for this distinction, is further evidence that the name/bearer relation was an integral ingredient of his notion of reference, as well as a demonstration that the association he made between this relation and the semantic role of names was too tight.

There is no doubt that the name/bearer relation was, for Frege, the *prototype* of the relation of *Bedeutung* as borne by expressions of other logical types. This is already evident from the fact that he also admitted terms referring to such expressions as subjects for the transitive verb '*bedeuten*'; and it is confirmed by his extended use in *Grundgesetze* of '*Name*' (name), as opposed to '*Eigenname*' (proper name), to apply to any expression having *Bedeutung*, and thus to incomplete expressions of all kinds. But suppose it acknowledged that Frege's notion of *Bedeutung* did have, as an essential component, that of the relation of name to bearer. Suppose it acknowledged, further, that, in constructing a semantic theory agreeing in essentials with Frege's theory of *Bedeutung*, we should need to appeal to that relation, that the first fundamental principle would of necessity appear in such a reconstructed theory. Suppose it acknowledged, in addition, that the second and third fundamental principles would also so appear; and suppose it acknowledged, finally, that the essential question for such a semantic theory is *what* contribution an expression makes to determining the truth-value of sentences containing it, not whether it makes the same contribution as some other expression (has the same t.v.p. as it). Then what remains of Tugendhat's contention is just the following restricted thesis: that the name/bearer relation is not a prototype for the relation of *Bedeutung* as borne by expressions of other types, and that, in so far as Frege took it to be, this part of his theory is better dropped; there is no true analogy between the relation of a proper name to its bearer and that of an expression of any other type to its semantic value. Is there not some merit in this restricted thesis?

Given the first two fundamental principles, concerning the semantic values of singular terms and of sentences, a great deal of the rest of the semantic theory is already determined, although our realization of this owes much to Frege. If the semantic value of a name is an object, and that of a sentence a truth-value, then the semantic role of a first-level predicate can only be to map objects on to truth-values, that of an expression for a first-level relation to map pairs of objects on to truth-values, and so through the whole hierarchy of logical types. Now even before we have any conception of a fully fledged semantic theory, it is intuitively natural for us to extend the conception of a name's standing for or denoting a particular object to incomplete expressions, to say, for example, that a certain such expression stands for a certain relation. It makes no sense to say of an expression that it stands for a relation between objects except by appeal to the conception of singular terms as standing for objects; given that conception, it is virtually irresistible, because we inevitably come by the idea of the relational expression as holding between two objects. It was surely this intuitive analogy that prompted Frege to adopt a notion of *Bedeutung* considered as applicable to expressions of all logical types, which is not to say that, in constructing such a theory, there were not numerous pitfalls which he surefootedly avoided. The greatest of such pitfalls, one into which virtually every philosopher before Frege had fallen and many after him were to fall, was to allow that a relation, for example, could be referred to by means of a non-relational expression, one having the form of a singular term; that the *Bedeutung* of an incomplete expression of a given type can be the *Bedeutung* only of an expression of that type is part of the content of Frege's doctrine that the *Bedeutung* of an incomplete expression is itself incomplete, which may be taken as the fourth fundamental principle of his theory of *Bedeutung*.

It may be objected, with Dudman,[1] that, without reliance on the analogy between the *Bedeutungen* of names and of other expressions, expressions other than proper names would have been taken to have a *reference*, that is, a semantic role, in the sense of making a particular contribution to the determination of the truth-value of a sentence, but not a *referent*, that is, a semantic value, in the sense of a particular thing, of the appropriate logical type, in terms of their association with which that contribution could be explained. For instance, if we were simply starting out to construct a semantic theory along Fregean lines, we should naturally say that the semantic role of a predicate consisted in its being true or false of each object, but not that it consisted in its standing for a concept. That is true enough, as regards the first step; when we came to consider quantification over concepts, however, we should be unable to dispense with an expression for that whose being is to map each object on to a truth-value, and, since just that *is* the being of a Fregean concept, it is not apparent that there is any genuine contrast here. Now if Frege had introduced words like 'relation' and 'function' for the first time, he would probably have succeeded in getting his meaning across, but it might nevertheless have seemed a questionable linguistic device. In fact, although he used 'concept' ('*Begriff*') where most people would have used 'property' ('*Eigenschaft*'), these words were already well entrenched, even in everyday discourse. He came, however, to recognize them, even though they suited his purpose so exactly, as constituting a questionable linguistic device, as I explained in *FPL*, Chapter 7. In attempting to correct this defect, he fastened on precisely the feature which we have seen as embodying the assumption that the semantic role of a proper name is to enable us to talk about its bearer, namely that 'X' and '*was "X" bedeutet*' ('what "X" stands for') have the same *Bedeutung*, and he extended it to concept-words, as in his example

---

[1] V. H. Dudman, '*Bedeutung* for Predicates', in M. Schirn (ed.), *Studien zu Frege*, 1976, vol. III, pp. 71–84.

'Jesus is what the concept-word "man" stands for' (*'Jesus ist, was das Begriffswort "Mensch" bedeutet'*), understood as equivalent to 'Jesus is a man'.[1] Just as, in speaking of what a name stands for, we refer to its bearer, so, in speaking of what a concept-word stands for, we say of the bearer just what the concept-word itself says: what could be a clearer proof of the correctness of the analogy than that? We need to add the proviso that the reconstructed terminology can be made to work; I argued in Chapter 7 of *FPL* that it can.

There was not supposed by Frege to be more than an analogy between *Bedeutung* as borne by proper names and as borne by predicates and functional expressions; rather than rejecting the analogy, it seems better to enquire where it holds, and where it fails, which is what I attempted to do. I observed in *FPL*[2] that an important disanalogy lies in the fact that there appears to be no use for the notion of identifying a concept as the referent of a predicate. I even concluded from this that, although, in accordance with Chapter 7 of *FPL*, the application to incomplete expressions of the '*Bedeutung*'/'*bedeuten*' terminology could be made coherent, still 'Frege's attribution of reference' to them 'appears in the end unjustified', because the notion cannot be made to do the same kind of work in their case as in the case of names in an account of sense.[3] This conclusion now seems to be too strong: it would have been better to locate the disanalogy and pass on. I have let it stand in FPL_2, however, because it does not seem to me to be definitely wrong: where an analogy is claimed, who is to say how great the analogy must be for the claim to be justified? It is, in any case, qualified by the remark on p. 245 of *FPL* that I did not mean that we are entitled to deny that there are concepts, or, more properly, that there is something for which 'horse' or 'agile' stands; the intelligibility and truth of the statement has been shown to stand or fall with that of higher-level quantification.

In Sluga's rejoinder, 'Frege's Alleged Realism', to my reply to him, 'Frege as a Realist', his original objection to making an appeal to the name/bearer relation in explaining Frege's notion of *Bedeutung* has dwindled to a complaint[4] that I have not yet shown 'that such diverse ingredients can constitute one coherent concept', and an admission[5] that he had given an oversimplified account of my view. I hope that the present explanation

---

[1] 'Ausführungen über Sinn und Bedeutung', *N.S.*, p. 133, *P.W.*, p. 122.
[2] Pp. 241–4.
[3] *FPL*, p. 243.
[4] P. 239.
[5] Fn. 18.

clarifies the matter. The conception of *Bedeutung* as semantic role explains what the notion is to be used for, while the appeal to the name/bearer relation is needed in order to specify what the semantic value of a proper name is taken by Frege to be; this, together with the principle that the semantic value of a sentence is its truth-value, determines what the semantic value of every other type of expression must be. This running together into one notion of two ingredients, one relating to the use that is to be made of it, the other to how it is to be applied, is a very familiar phenomenon; it is just in such cases that we can say that the notion embodies a theory, which may be sharp or may be fuzzy, and Frege's notion of *Bedeutung* certainly embodies a theory. An example might be the intuitive notion of the validity of inferences. Logicians separate out the proof-theoretic notion of validity, which has to do with how we recognize inferences as valid, from the semantic or model-theoretic notion, which has to do with the purpose for which we need the notion. But, in everyday speech, the distinction is not drawn; we could say that the ordinary notion of validity incorporates both ingredients, though of course in a very imprecise form. Reflection on such examples, which are as numerous in natural science as in common discourse, may help to dispel any unintended appearance of mystery in my account of Frege's notion of *Bedeutung*.

CHAPTER 8

The Functional Character of Concepts

THERE IS ONE leading idea of Frege's mature philosophy of language which I now think that, in *FPL*, I seriously undervalued. This is the conception of concepts and relations as functional in character. It is, in fact, the very first thing that it occurred to him to mention when drawing up a balance-sheet in the fragment 'Was kann ich als Ergebnis meiner Arbeit ansehen?' of 1906. It is not that I think that anything I said in *FPL* on this subject was actually wrong, which is why I have made no alterations in this regard in FPL_2; it is rather that there is missing from that book any due recognition of the profundity of the idea. On p. 184 of *FPL*, I allowed that the incompleteness of a function is an easier conception to grasp than that of the incompleteness of a concept, for reasons which I stated on p. 255 of the book; hence Frege's assimilation of concepts to functions, namely as functions (of one argument) whose value is always a truth-value, and the corresponding assimilation of relations to functions of two arguments, had the advantage of providing a clear rationale for regarding concepts and relations as incomplete. But, on p. 644 of *FPL*, I dismissed this advantage as not very great; and, in general, I tended to dismiss Frege's later subsumption of concepts under functions as a mere consequence of his mistaken assimilation of sentences to complex proper names. It is precisely because sentences are, rightly, felt to be quite different from proper names that to call functions incomplete seems, at first glance, more natural than to call concepts incomplete. A function, we naturally think, of its nature calls to be completed by an argument, and then provides a way of arriving at the corresponding value; but, while it is of the nature of a concept that some objects fall under it and others do not, it is hardly to be said to be completed by an object that falls under it, and still less by one that does not. This reaction is, indeed, quite superficial; but it is prompted by the fact that when a term is inserted into the argument-place of a functional expression, what we obtain, in the typical case, is a complex term for an object of the same sort as that which served as argument, a number, for example; whereas, when we insert a term into the argument-place of a predicate, what we obtain is a sentence, and this does not appear to stand for an object of any sort.

It now seems to me quite incorrect to set aside Frege's later view of concepts as functional in character as unimportant; on the contrary, it embodies a genuine insight. Suppose that we are engaged in defining a semantic notion of interpretation for the formulas of an arbitrary first-order language of the standard kind, that is, a language with the same syntactic structure as Frege's formalized language, save that sentences are not treated as of the same type as singular terms. The notion of interpretation at which we wish to arrive is one suited to some non-classical logic, so that we cannot make use of the classical two-valued semantics. We first specify that an interpretation must assign some domain of objects to the individual variables, to each individual constant an object in that domain, and to each function-letter a function from and into that domain; admissible domains and admissible functions over them may or may not be circumscribed in some way. Next, we have to decide what, in general, the possible semantic values of sentences are. Our choice must enable us to give a semantic account of the occurrence of any sentence as a sub-sentence of a more complex one. Many different possibilities are open to us here, according to the particular logic which we want to capture. It is on our solution to this problem that the character of our semantic theory will depend, and hence the main outlines of any theory of meaning that can be constructed on it as basis. Once we have arrived at the solution to this problem, our task is very nearly completed. We have, indeed, to make specific stipulations governing the particular logical constants we wish to consider; but there remains no further choice about what the semantic value, under a given interpretation, of a predicate is to be taken to be. It can be nothing else but a function from the domain to the set of possible semantic values of sentences; for just what a predicate is required to do is to yield a sentence, having some one such semantic value, for each term, denoting an element of the domain, that is inserted into its argument-place. Suppose, to take a concrete example, that what we are aiming at is a semantic theory adapted to intuitionistic logic. We have, then, in any case, to have a representation of the possible semantic values of complete sentences, because any sentence can occur as a constituent of some more complex one. There is then no further problem about what is to constitute a possible semantic value for a predicate; it is simply a function from elements of the domain to the possible semantic values of sentences. Conversely, we cannot arrive at a specification of semantic values for predicates, say as species in the intuitionistic sense, by any other route; if we have a suitably precise notion of a species, that will have to be understood as something which, for any given object in the domain, determines a possible semantic value for a sentence. Thus the conception of the semantic value of a predicate as a function from the domain of objects to the semantic values of sentences is of quite general validity for any possible semantic theory, and gives the only way in which we may arrive at the correct notion for a given theory. In the classical case, it is easy to overlook this, just because the set of possible semantic values of sentences is so tiny, consisting only of the two truth-values, *true* and *false*: if we say that the semantic value of a predicate is a concept, under which each object in the domain either falls or does not fall, or a set, of which each such object is or is not a member, we easily overlook the relation to the two truth-values. But when we have any other semantic theory, in which the possible semantic values of sentences form a larger and more complex totality, the only way to obtain the relevant analogue of the classical notions of concept or set is precisely by adopting a functional conception of the semantic values of predicates. It is a remarkable instance of Frege's insight that, although he was concerned only with a two-valued semantics, he nevertheless perceived the right way of setting out the relation between the semantic values of sentences and those of predicates.

To say this is not to retract my rejection of Frege's subsumption of concepts under functions. That did not turn on denying the functional character of concepts and relations, but on refusing to recognize truth-values as objects, or, equivalently, sentences as proper names. As I remarked on p. 249 of *FPL*, if truth-values are not objects, then truth-functions are not functions, but of a different logical type. But, evidently, this provides no ground for denying the analogy between truth-functions and, say, arithmetical functions, or the legitimacy of, indeed necessity for, interpreting sentential operators, within a two-valued or many-valued semantics, as standing for truth-functions. We can perfectly well admit the functional character of concepts, that is to say, the *analogy* between concepts and functions, precisely as I envisaged on pp. 184–5 of *FPL*, without taking the former as a special case of the latter. On this view, functions proper map objects on to objects, truth-functions map truth-values on to truth-values, and concepts and relations map objects on to truth-values, the logical type being different in all three cases; to acknowledge the analogy is to recognize that the notion of mapping plays an essential role in grasping the character of all these logical types. This is obvious for truth-functions, although the fact has no tendency to make us regard sentences as proper names, nor, therefore, truth-values as objects. It is less obvious for concepts and relations; all the more credit to Frege for having perceived their functional character, that is, the analogy, even though he made the mistake of taking it to be more than an analogy.

As I observed in *FPL*,[1] Frege's ontology of objects, concepts, relations and functions is not a contribution to the traditional debate over particulars and universals, but clears it away and supersedes it. It is utterly misleading to write, as did Ignacio Angelelli: 'Entities in Frege as well as in traditional ontology are supposed to be exhaustively classified into singulars and universals. One of Frege's contributions to philosophy is precisely the fact of having stressed very much such a distinction. . . . Given any entity, Frege . . . would ask: Is it a singular or a universal?'[2] Frege's distinction between objects, concepts and relations falls in a different place: the colour red, the species *panthera tigris*, the extension of the concept *horse* are all *objects* for Frege.[3]

Equally, Frege's ontology is remote from traditional dilemmas concerning the relation of universals to particulars, or of accidents to substances, and the mode of existence of universals and of accidents. The only notion of properties admitted by Frege is that under which they are equated with concepts: 'I call the concepts under which an object falls its properties', he says in 'Über Begriff und Gegenstand'.[4] It would therefore be for him nonsense to say that an object is compounded out of its properties, that is, the concepts under which it falls, or that it is merely the sum of those properties; and just as much nonsense to deny this and maintain that the object was a featureless *suppositum* in which its properties inhered. E.-H. W. Kluge[5] cites[6] polemics of Frege's against abstractionism to show that he rejected the idea of objects lacking all properties;[7] the fact

---

[1] Pp. 174–8, 471–3.

[2] *Studies on Gottlob Frege and Traditional Philosophy*, Dordrecht, 1967, p. 47.

[3] Contrary to what I wrote on p. 72 of *FPL₁*, Frege does mention colours as, by implication, objects, namely in *Grundlagen*, § 65, where 'the colour of the surface' is instanced as logically analogous to 'the direction of the line'; this passage has therefore been changed in *FPL₂*. In 'Über die wissenschaftliche Berechtigung einer Begriffsschrift' (1882), he says that in 'The horse is a herbivorous animal', 'the horse' denotes the species; see p. 50 (*B.a.A.*, p. 108), *C.N.*, p. 84.

[4] P. 201.

[5] 'Freges Begriff des Logischeinfachen', in M. Schirn (ed.), op. cit., vol. II, pp. 51–66.

[6] P. 60.

[7] A good example is Frege's ridicule of 'natureless things' in *Über die Zahlen des Herrn H. Schubert*, 1899, pp. 10–11.

that there could not be an object falling under no concept could in any case be established by the *reductio* argument that, if there were, it would fall under the concept *falling under no concept*. But, although there cannot be a featureless object, no object is made up out of the concepts under which it falls: the relation of falling under a concept is just not to be identified with that of containing as a part. In the same article, Kluge misguidedly attempts to argue that, for Frege, there can be no simple objects by means of the following reasoning. If there were a simple object, it would have either to have no properties or to have just one. The former possibility is ruled out by Frege's view that there are no property-less objects. But if there were a logically simple object having just one property, it would have to be identical with that property: for the alternative is that it would consist of a substratum in which that one property inhered, and this would contradict its logical simplicity. But the possibility of an object identical with its own sole property is ruled out by Frege's denial that a property (concept) can ever be identified with an object.[1] A more thoroughly un-Fregean argument could hardly be devised. The only notion of logical simplicity considered by Frege is that of unanalysability or indefinability, which is a matter of the *sense* of an expression, not of its reference. For instance, 'true' is said by Frege to be indefinable: but the True can be picked out from other objects by means of any true sentence. Or, again, the notion of an object is said to be simple and unanalysable: but the extension of the predicate 'ξ is an object' coincides with that of 'ξ is the same as ξ', so that it would be easy to introduce the former by defining it to be equivalent to the latter, if preservation of reference were all that concerned us. But, even if Frege were concerned with simplicity in the sense of absence of intrinsic structure, an argument such as that advanced by Kluge would be quite contrary to the spirit of his philosophy. Of course there cannot be an object having only one property, since every object must have the property of being identical with itself, and must, besides, have properties that distinguish it from other objects. But, in any case, the properties an object has, the concepts under which it falls, are not components of it, and the possession of any number of them—say being blue, not being red, being either blue or red, etc., etc.—would not violate its intrinsic simplicity if it were intrinsically simple. The argument derives from trying, like Angelelli, to fit Frege into place within a traditional framework which it was a large part of the point of his logical doctrines to jettison as worthless or misconceived.

[1] Op. cit., pp. 59–61.

If we try to place Frege within the realist/nominalist controversy over whether universals exist on their own or only *in* the particulars that exemplify them, then, in so far as we misleadingly assimilate Frege's concepts to the universals of the traditional debates, we shall have to classify him as a realist or platonist, since he unequivocally held that, for a predicate to stand for a concept, it was not necessary that it should be true of anything, or even that it should be logically possible for it to be. But this is not open to the objections of nominalists or of moderate realists, who demand to know how a universal can exist apart from the particulars in which it inheres, on the grounds that a universal needs support from a particular. What is confusedly expressed by this notion of support is the perception that the notion of a universal derives, in the first place, from the linguistic practice of predication: and this perception is made fully explicit by Frege's doctrine that a concept is unsaturated and in need of completion. But this does not mean that the concept is in any sense *in*, or a constituent of, the objects falling under it: to make reference to a concept, it is enough to have something that can be predicated of objects, whether or not it can be truly predicated of any.

The very adoption of the term 'concept' ('*Begriff*'), rather than the more natural 'property' ('*Eigenschaft*'), as Frege's regular word for the referent of a one-place predicate, which was probably due to the gradual refinement of Frege's terminology from *Begriffsschrift* onwards, helped to safeguard Frege from becoming entangled in these traditional pseudo-problems: even when we have grasped that, for Frege, a concept is something objective and belonging to the realm of reference, not to that of sense, so that to predicate something of a concept, such as that there are three objects falling under it, may be to make an a posteriori judgment, there is less temptation to think of an object as compounded out of the concepts under which it falls than as so compounded out of the properties which it possesses or which attach to it. But what finally places an impassable barrier between Frege's ontology and the traditional confusions is the recognition of the functional character of concepts and relations; this provides Frege with an explanation of the unsaturated or incomplete nature of concepts alternative to the conception of properties as requiring support from or as inhering in their objects. Kluge says that, for Frege, every object is a completed function.[1] This is true, so long as we remember that the completion of a function is no longer a function: every object is the value of some function for some suitable argument. In the mode of

---

[1] 'Frege et les termes sans référence', *Dialogue*, vol. XIV, 1975, pp. 254–80; see p. 275.

speaking adopted by Frege in 'Über Sinn und Bedeutung', p. 36, according to which the referents of the parts of a complex expression are parts of the referent of the whole, this would mean that every object has a function as a part, together with the relevant argument as another part. But Frege came to recognize this way of speaking as a false analogy with the correct principle that the sense of the part is part of the sense of the whole, and repudiated it,[1] as I noted on p. 160 of *FPL*. In any case, this has nothing to do, as Kluge seems to suppose, with any thesis that an object has as a part a concept under which it falls. Xanthippe was the wife of Socrates, and thus the value, for the argument Socrates, of the function denoted by 'the wife of ξ': so, on the doctrine that the referent of the part is part of the referent of the whole, Socrates and the function for which 'the wife of ξ' stands would be parts of Xanthippe, just as Socrates in turn could be decomposed into Xanthippe and the function denoted by 'the husband of ξ'. But, even on that misbegotten doctrine, there is no reason to say that the concept for which 'ξ is a woman' stands is any part of Xanthippe. On the contrary, that predicate stands for a function that maps Xanthippe on to the True and Socrates on to the False. Given the mistaken conception of the argument and the function as parts of the value, this compels Frege, in 'Über Sinn und Bedeutung', to the misguided conclusion that, in judging a thought to be true or false, we are 'distinguishing parts within a truth-value'. But we do not thereby distinguish parts within the *argument*, i.e. within the subject of the judgment, within Xanthippe or Socrates: the concept for which 'ξ is a woman' stands has no more intimate connection with Xanthippe than with Socrates, but merely maps the former on to one truth-value and the latter on to the other.

The notion of a function is, as Frege frequently remarks, a primitive one, in the sense of being incapable of definition. We should certainly not identify it with a class of ordered pairs, since it is not an object, as a class is. We should not even identify the value-range of a function with a class of ordered pairs.[2] If the notion of class (or set) is taken as primitive, then we may dispense with a separate notion of (the value-range or extension of) a function, since a class of ordered pairs will, in such a framework, serve as an adequate surrogate for the extension of a relation, and a function can be conceived as a special kind of relation. But such a class of ordered pairs is not the same thing as the extension of a function, i.e. a value-range, as Frege conceives of value-ranges, namely taking the notion as primitive;

[1] See 'Aufzeichnungen für L. Darmstaedter', *N.S.*, p. 275, *P.W.*, p. 255.
[2] As does Rulon S. Wells in his 'Frege's Ontology', in E. D. Klemke (ed.), op. cit., pp. 3–41; see p. 16.

it is only a surrogate for it. Conversely, a class, as conceived by Frege in the *Grundgesetze*, is the value-range of a concept, in turn a special kind of function, one whose value is always a truth-value; such a class is not to be identified with one in a theory in which the notion of class is primitive: it merely serves the same purpose. Likewise, in Frege's system, a function is not a special kind of relation: rather, a relation (*Beziehung*) is a special kind of function of two arguments, namely, again, one whose value is always a truth-value. Frege does not, strictly speaking, admit the notion of the extension of a function of two arguments, since he can provide an adequate surrogate for one in the form of what he calls a *double value-range*: for the function of two arguments denoted by '$\xi + \zeta$', its double value-range is the value-range of the function which, for each n, maps n on to $\dot{\varepsilon} \, (\varepsilon + n)$, i.e. on to the value-range of the function of one argument denoted by '$\xi + n$'.[1] What serves as a surrogate for the extension of a relation, namely as what Frege calls a *Relation*, is then the double value-range of that relation considered as a function of two arguments, mapping any two objects on to a truth-value. Thus Frege does not need to make use of the notion of an ordered pair; and, if that notion were introduced into his system, as it could be, a class of ordered pairs would differ both from the extension of a function (value-range) in general and from a *Relation*, the double value-range which serves in place of the extension of a relation (*Beziehung*).

Thus neither a function, in Frege's sense, nor even its value-range is to be taken to be a class of ordered pairs. A function is a mapping: to arrive at the general notion of a function, one who is more familiar with the notion of a class, taken as primitive, may find it helpful to think of a class of ordered pairs, provided that he bears in mind that a function requires completion, and is not a *selbständiger* object like a class. To allow for this, he might simply think of the function as a binary relation, a functor being formed with the help of the description operator; and he might think of a relation, in turn, as a concept under which fall ordered pairs of objects. All these, however, are not definitions or explanations of the Fregean notions, but stepping-stones to facilitate the transition from a different point of view to that of Frege. The general notion of a value-range can, according to Frege, be arrived at only via that of a function: we can think of a value-range only as the extension of a function. The second-level function for which the abstraction operator '$\dot{\varepsilon} \, \varphi(\varepsilon)$' stands is again primitive: we have no more general way of explaining the operation which carries each function into an abstract object which represents it

---

[1] *Grundgesetze*, vol. I, § 36.

in the sense that its (first-level) properties, and its very identity, depend solely on the extensional (second-level) properties of the function, and thus, ultimately, on which values the function has for different objects as argument. To gain the notion of a value-range, we have to come by the conception of a domain of objects the criterion of whose identity is the extensional equivalence of functions, that is, the conception whereby a universally quantified identity-statement '$\forall x\ f(x) = g(x)$' may be transformed into a singular statement of identity '$\grave{\varepsilon}\ f(\varepsilon) = \grave{\alpha}\ g(\alpha)$'. We cannot conceive of a value-range *except* as arrived at by the application of this operation to a function. More exactly, since Frege insists that no one individual object need ever be given in a unique manner, it is better to say that we cannot attain the *general* notion of a value-range save as what is arrived at in this way; we may be able to refer to particular objects that are in fact taken by Frege to be value-ranges, e.g. cardinal numbers, real numbers and truth-values, otherwise than *as* value-ranges. In the same way, if we were to take the notion of class as primitive, that of a concept would be prior: even though the class-abstraction operator was primitive, we could think of a class only as the extension of a concept; or, at least, we could think of classes generally only as the extensions of concepts. This may seem to be contradicted by formalized theories in which, not class-abstraction, but class-membership is primitive, '$\{x \mid F(x)\}$' being definable as '$\imath y\ \forall x\ (x \epsilon y \leftrightarrow F(x))$'. But Frege would insist, surely correctly, that we could not come by the correct intuitive interpretation of the class-membership symbol 'ϵ' save via the notions of falling under a concept and being the extension of a concept: to gain the notion of a class, we have to arrive at that of an abstract object serving as the representative of a concept, and uniquely determined by its extensional properties. However, for the reasons explained, we do not need both the notion of a function and those of a concept and a relation as primitive, nor, therefore, those of the operation yielding value-ranges (extensions of functions) and of that yielding classes (extensions of concepts). And for one to whom the notion of a class is the more familiar, the conception of a class of ordered pairs may be a helpful stepping-stone to Frege's notion of a value-range.

On p. 184 of *FPL*, I spoke of the sense in which a function stands in need of completion as a mere analogy for that in which a concept does so. If truth-values are not regarded as objects, then indeed it is an analogy, not a more general case: predicates and functors will not be interchangeable in the notation, and the class-abstraction operator must be notationally distinct from the value-range operator. For all that, the analogy is *exact*, as exact as that between truth-functions and arithmetical functions. There can be no objection to the functional conception of concepts; their predicative nature is fully catered for under this conception. It would, for example, be absurd to object to the conception that it would make every concept equinumerous to every other, on the ground that every object would be an argument of each concept: obviously, one concept is equinumerous to another only if it maps just as many objects as does the other on to the value True. What, in *FPL*, I failed to recognize is that, when due allowance is made for the distinction Frege ought to have drawn between objects and truth-values, the functional conception of concepts is, when rightly considered, inescapable, and provides *the* correct account of their incompleteness. As was observed above, the semantic role of a predicate cannot but be regarded as carrying us from the denotation of a proper name that might occupy its argument-place to whatever is taken as the semantic value of the resulting sentence; expressed in Fregean terminology, the referent of a predicate can only be a mapping from the referents of proper names to the referents of sentences. If the referent of a sentence is taken to be a truth-value, then that of a predicate must be a mapping from objects to truth-values. Only such an account reflects faithfully what it is that constitutes the basic mode of employment of predicates in the language, namely to form sentences by inserting proper names into their argument-places. Moreover, only such an account leaves an unproblematic place for the notion of a relation, allowing us smoothly to explain the semantic role of relational expressions. On the traditional explanation of the predicative nature of qualities or properties, namely that they inhere in or are supported by substances, no sense could be made of relations: it appeared perplexing how there could be a kind of universal that simultaneously inhered in, or was supported by, *two* substances, except in so far as it inhered in, or was supported by, each of them separately. This, of course, is the source of the persistent philosophical tradition according to which relations are 'merely ideal' or are in some way reducible to or founded upon properties attaching to the terms of the relation, taken separately, a misconception to which even Leibniz fell victim. We are no longer subject to this temptation. The reason why we are not lies in the success of modern mathematical logic, that logic, namely, originally invented by Frege. But what made possible that advance was a viewpoint from which relations could be seen as no more problematic than properties, as functions of two arguments are no more problematic than functions of one argument: and that viewpoint was attainable only by acknowledging the exactness of the analogy between the two pairs, that is, by recognizing the functional character of concepts and relations. If we do not at least tacitly acknowledge the functional character of concepts, we can give no account of them that does not make relations unintelligible. It was Frege who first attained this fundamental insight, without the help of any hints from previous or contemporary logicians or philosophers. In doing so, he went too far, and wholly assimilated concepts and relations to functions from objects to objects by treating sentences as proper names of two special objects, the True and the False. It is ungrateful to dwell too heavily upon this mistake without recognizing the enormous liberation from the confused metaphysics of centuries which his basic insight effected.

Kluge[1] takes issue with Grossmann over Frege's attitude to facts and states of affairs. Grossmann[2] had maintained that manifold defects in Frege's philosophy stemmed from his failure to admit states of affairs into his ontology. Kluge argues that Frege *did* admit facts into his ontology, and goes so far as to say that it is a fact ontology.[3] He does so on three grounds. First, he quite rightly objects to Grossmann's psychologistic interpretation of the content stroke, according to which, while '*A*' represents 'a complex idea', '——*A*' represents 'the mental act of having the idea, of thinking or considering the idea *A*'.[4] Rather, Kluge says, '——*A*' denotes a state of affairs (obtaining or not obtaining). Secondly, since judging is 'distinguishing parts within a truth-value', the True and the False must themselves be states of affairs, dispositions of objects in certain relations and the like.[5] Thirdly, Frege's objects are not, as Grossmann says,[6] 'simples' or 'bare particulars', merely externally related to the concepts under which they fall. Rather, as Kluge says again,[7] objects are completed functions, no longer needing completion, and are incapable of being simple; since a name of an object is always capable of definition, the object must be 'ontologically complex'.[8] Such ontological complexes just are states of affairs.

Kluge's first argument is sound, so far as it goes: to the extent that we can give a clear answer to the question how Frege conceived of judgeable contents at the time of *Begriffsschrift*, it was as states of affairs. Put

---

[1] 'Reflections on Frege', *Dialogue*, vol. IX, 1970, pp. 401–9.
[2] *Reflections on Frege's Philosophy*, Evanston, 1969.
[3] Kluge, op. cit., p. 405.
[4] Grossmann, op. cit., p. 5.
[5] Kluge, op. cit., p. 404.
[6] Grossmann, op. cit., pp. 98–9.
[7] 'Frege et les termes sans référence', p. 275.
[8] 'Reflections on Frege', p. 405.

that way, the point is really independent of the content-stroke: for, in *Begriffsschrift*, it is only if the content of '*A*' is already 'judgeable', i.e. capable of being meaningfully asserted, that '——*A*' is well formed. This seems to leave the content-stroke superfluous; and, indeed, in the system of *Begriffsschrift*, it really seems to be superfluous. However that may be, the dispute between Kluge and Grossmann, as exhibited in Kluge's second and third arguments, is a beautiful example of the misconstructions of Frege that result from trying to fit him into the framework of traditional ontology. Questions such as whether, for Frege, an object is a 'bare particular', externally related to the concepts it falls under, or is a complex of which those concepts are ingredients, are simply misconceived: the point of Frege's ontological categories is to extricate us from this quagmire, not to adopt a particular position at which to sink into it.

The views expressed in *Begriffsschrift* and other writings of the same period were not Frege's mature opinions. Until he had made the fundamental distinction between sense and reference, it was virtually inevitable that he should have taken the content of a sentence to be a state of affairs, that which someone may, by an assertoric utterance of the sentence, assert to obtain. But, when once he had drawn the distinction, he discriminated, within a judgeable content, between the thought expressed and its truth-value. Since the reference of any true sentence coincides with that of any other true sentence, and likewise that of any false sentence with that of any other false one, neither distinct facts, as ordinarily conceived, nor distinct states of affairs, thought of as capable of obtaining or not obtaining, can belong to the realm of reference. All that can correspond to distinct false sentences, reflecting the differences between them, must therefore belong to the realm of sense; they are, namely, false thoughts. These are not, of course, states of affairs as these are ordinarily conceived, that is, as constituents of external reality and as complexes of which physical objects such as Mont Blanc may, among others, be themselves constituents; they are, rather, entities of the same kind as the senses of words. As for facts, Frege does not repudiate them, but, in 'Der Gedanke',[1] assigns them likewise to the realm of sense, identifying them with true thoughts. Facts, for Frege, do not belong together with objects, concepts, relations, functions and truth-values, as inhabitants of the realm of reference, but, as the senses of true sentences, with the senses of expressions.

If there are candidates for being states of affairs within the ontological system of Frege's mature period, they are truth-values, as suggested by

---

[1] P. 74.

Kluge's second argument, and not objects, as suggested by his third one. Kluge's thesis that all Fregean objects are complex is not one stated by Frege. But it is plausible if interpreted to mean that, for every object, there is some complex proper name, e.g. a definite description, that stands for it; it is certainly true that Frege never entertains the idea of logically simple objects in the sense of those which can be referred to only by simple proper names. Kluge[1] rightly distinguishes two types of simplicity recognized by Frege: the simplicity of an expression, namely as consisting of only a single word or symbol, whether primitive or introduced by definition; and its unanalysability or indefinability. Actually, it is better to admit three types of simplicity, distinguishing between expressions that are simple in the first sense according as they were introduced by definition, or were not in fact so introduced but could have been, or possess the stronger property of being incapable of being defined, that is, insusceptible of logical analysis. In constructing a theory, we may pick one set of primitives, where we might have picked another set, so that some of the terms we treat as primitive might have been defined, if we had chosen differently; such terms are undefined but not indefinable. Likewise, a word of natural language may not in fact be explained by definition, although logical analysis may uncover a way in which it might have been defined. In *FPL*, I spoke of a proper name as being simple only in the weakest of the three senses, namely as not being compounded out of several words whose senses jointly determine the sense of the name. As I remarked on p. 25 of *FPL*, Frege has no conception corresponding to Russell's 'logically proper names'; and, of the terms explicitly claimed by Frege as indefinable or unanalysable, none is a name of an object. It is indeed unlikely that there could be a proper name which had the strongest type of simplicity, in that it not only had not been introduced by definition, but was absolutely indefinable and resistant to logical analysis. There are, indeed, some problems concerning Frege's attitude to definitions, which affect the distinction just made between the undefined and the indefinable and bear on the content of calling an expression 'indefinable'; these will be explored in more detail in Chapter 14. But, for the time being, let us assume that Kluge is probably right in holding that Frege would not have allowed that there could be indefinable proper names.

He errs, however, in thinking that, if there were such an unanalysable proper name, the object for which it stood would be featureless—a bare

[1] 'Freges Begriff des Logischeinfachen', p. 52.

particular. The error is embedded in the manner in which he first introduces the distinction between the weaker and the stronger sense of 'logically simple', namely as one between the simplicity of the sign and the simplicity of its referent.[1] He quotes Frege[2] as saying that the reference of the definiendum is determined by the references of the signs used in the definiens;[3] but, unless we hold Frege to the mistaken conception, briefly advanced in 'Über Sinn und Bedeutung', but later repudiated, that the referent of the part is part of the referent of the whole, it does not follow, as Kluge wishes to make it appear, that the referent of a proper name introduced by definition is itself a complex object. Kluge gives this impression by alluding to the case of the definition of a concept-word, citing from 'Der Gedanke'[4] a passing remark to the effect that such a definition cites characteristics (*Merkmale*) of the concept, where characteristics of a concept are explained by Frege as being properties that an object must have if it is to fall under the concept, and a remark by Frege that 'the characteristics of a concept are concepts which are logical parts of it.'[5] This latter remark, very natural in the context, is not one to be pressed: it is probably to be explained as a case in which Frege is thinking of concepts as more like the senses than the referents of predicates, and so adverting to a more ordinary use of the word 'concept' than that which he normally makes; if not, it is defensible only by appeal to the thesis that the referent of the part is part of the referent of the whole. Kluge argues that, if Frege had 'recognized logical simplicity in the domain of signs, but not in the realm of references', the indefinability of a sign would imply that the referent of the sign was either a function or concept devoid of characteristics, or an object devoid of properties, and thus would itself be logically simple, contradicting the hypothesis. Even on the assumption that the definability of a sign would imply the complexity of its referent, as having parts that were the referents of the parts of the definiens, this would not follow: it would have to be proved that the simplicity of its referent was the *only* conceivable obstacle to defining an expression.

In fact, however, it is a mistake to suppose that Frege was committed to regarding an object denoted by a complex proper name as having, as parts or constituents of it, the referents of the parts of the proper name; still less did he think that an object has as a constituent each concept under

[1] Ibid., p. 52.
[2] Ibid., p. 56.
[3] 'Über die Grundlagen der Geometrie', 1906, I, p. 302.
[4] P. 60.
[5] 'Über die Grundlagen der Geometrie', 1903, II, p. 271.

which it falls.[1] Since a concept under which an object falls is not a constituent or ingredient of it, a logically simple object, if there were one, might still fall under many concepts, and would not need to be featureless as Kluge supposes.

The complexity of that which has, or would admit of, a complex designation is a complexity of *designation*, not of *constitution*. A good example would be the centre of mass of the Solar System, which has a complex designation but, as a point, is not internally complex. There is thus absolutely no warrant for considering Frege's objects, in general, to be anything resembling states of affairs. Somewhat more plausible is the interpretation in this manner of the two truth-values. If we take seriously Frege's manner of speaking in 'Über Sinn und Bedeutung', the True must contain within itself the referents of the parts of all true sentences, and will admit a decomposition corresponding to each true sentence. It thus becomes, in effect, an immensely complex structure, as it were the single all-inclusive Fact, which is how Kluge conceives of it, making it virtually indistinguishable from the world. But it would be hard to conceive of the False, analogously, as the single all-inclusive Non-fact. How can one state of affairs, however all-embracing, comprise *every* falsehood, e.g. the Sun's having no planets and its having a hundred and ten? It is more natural to allow that there is only one actual world, but to propose many different maximal states of affairs which fail to obtain, as in possible-worlds theories: even so, to accord with Frege's views, we should have to admit logically or a priori impossible states of affairs, which would render doubtful what maximality would be. These difficulties arise from taking seriously the talk of truth-values as having parts. This is an application of the thesis that the referent of the part is part of the referent of the whole, a thesis perhaps rendered more plausible in the first place by the lack of a verbal distinction between reference and referent. The thesis was never stressed by Frege, and, as already observed, was later withdrawn by him. It is much to be doubted whether Frege ever regarded the True as being the one great fact. If he ever did, such a conception played the most minimal role in his thought; and there would be no place in his system for ordinary little facts. At least, they could not be considered as

[1] If it did, we should be embarrassed to say whether a relation was a joint constituent of two objects between which it held. Being larger than Mars would be a constituent of Jupiter, and being smaller than Jupiter would be a constituent of Mars. It would seem unnecessary in addition to regard the relation of being larger as a constituent of both; but, if we did not, relations would appear to be mysteriously free-floating in a way in which properties or concepts were not.

constituents of the one great Fact: rather, each would have to be regarded as an aspect of that great Fact, taken as a whole, a particular way, out of many, of decomposing it. It throws no light on Frege's thought to squeeze it into yielding bizarre metaphysical conceptions of this kind. At the end of his review of *FPL*,[1] Kluge accused me of imitating William of Ockham, who, in his commentary on Porphyry, mounted a critique of his subject's views, so Kluge tells us, under the guise of explaining away some 'unfortunate' turns of phrase. I am unrepentant: 'distinguishing parts within a truth-value' *was* an unfortunate turn of phrase, which Frege later came to regret. If, instead of setting it aside, we press it, we come up with a piece of fantastic metaphysics which illuminates our understanding neither of reality nor of Frege's work.

[1] *Dialogue*, vol. XVI, 1977, pp. 519–33.

CHAPTER 9

Kripke on Proper Names as Rigid Designators

I HAVE IN *FPL*$_2$ made some alterations on pp. 111, 132–3 and, above all, 127 in order to remove the attribution to Saul Kripke of the definition of the meaning of a singular term as a partial function from possible worlds to objects in those worlds, an error already acknowledged on pp. xlv–xlvii of *Truth and Other Enigmas*. Kripke has no business to accuse Frege of having confused the meaning of a term with the way in which its reference is fixed, since he offers no explanation at all of what he takes meaning to be. My misattribution occurred as follows. 'The length of the standard metre rod is 1 metre' is supposed to be true a priori, but not necessary. It is true a priori because the reference of 'the length of the standard metre rod' and of '1 metre' are fixed in the same way. But it is contingent because, while '1 metre' is a rigid designator, 'the length of the standard metre rod' is not, at least if the designator 'the standard metre rod' is construed as rigid: they therefore do not denote the same lengths in all possible worlds. What implies that 'the length of the standard metre rod' has a different meaning from '1 metre' is the fact that the former is a flexible designator, while the latter is rigid. It is therefore tempting to conclude that that on which the status of the statement, as necessary or contingent, depends, namely the denotations of those terms in all possible worlds, is to be identified with their meanings; to this temptation I succumbed.

Kripke argues that proper names and definite descriptions behave differently in modal contexts. As I had already remarked in *FPL*[1] before reading Kripke's essay, Geach had earlier maintained that they behave

---

[1] P. 168; cf. p. 111.

differently after the verb 'to be'; and, as I pointed out on pp. 131–2 of *FPL*, they certainly behave differently after the verb 'to become'. Since, in these contexts, they contribute in diverse manners to the determination of the truth-conditions of the sentences in which they occur, they must certainly have different senses, as Frege uses 'sense'. Many of the differences of behaviour after 'to be' and 'to become' are due, like those in modal contexts, to conventions of scope, where tense is regarded as an operator governing the clause. As subject, a definite description has wide scope, i.e. behaves as rigid in Kripke's sense: 'The world chess champion was once a tiny baby' does not mean that it once was true to say, 'The world chess champion is a tiny baby', but that it once was true to say of the man who is (now) the world chess champion, 'He is a tiny baby'. As complement, however, a definite description assumes a narrow scope; 'Karpov was not then world chess champion' means that it was not then true to say of Karpov, 'He is the world chess champion'. But even if I stipulate that I am introducing the name 'Krishnaram' to denote the inventor of chess, I cannot say of the man so designated that, as a child, he was not yet Krishnaram, as I can say of him that he was not yet the inventor of chess; proper names are temporally as well as modally rigid.

These and like conventions tacitly govern our understanding of proper names and of definite descriptions; and a full account of the senses of expressions of both types must make such conventions explicit. It follows that, when a proper name is introduced by means of a definite description, it cannot be intended to be taken as strictly synonymous with it; it will be subject to the general conventions governing proper names, as the definite description is subject to those governing definite descriptions. Is the charge, then, that Frege overlooked these conventions and the resulting divergences in the behaviour of different types of singular term? If it is, there is some justice in it; the oversight was due to Frege's near indifference to the phenomena of tense and of modality; he was interested in necessity, but not in the necessity-operator. We could say that, in this respect, Frege wrongly assimilated definite descriptions to proper names, rather than the other way round, as he is accused of doing. Whenever he considered tense in connection with definite descriptions, he wanted to build it into the definite description itself, so as to obviate the need for any conventions of scope; he wanted to be able to regard definite descriptions as in effect proper names, which is after all what he called them, in the sense that each denoted one and the same object in every context.

Suppose, then, that the general conventions governing the use of proper names and of definite descriptions in the presence of tenses, modal operators and copulative verbs have been laid bare: these must be regarded as going to characterize the senses of all expressions of these two types, and also as tacitly understood whenever a proper name is introduced by means of a definite description, the latter not being taken as transmitting its character as a definite description to the proper name so introduced. In the same way, the indexical character of a definite description used to introduce a proper name is not understood as being transmitted to the proper name: if I say, 'Melvin is my son's dog', I shall not be construed as stipulating the synonymy of 'Melvin' with the phrase 'my son's dog'.[1] But, when these conventions governing the use of proper names and definite descriptions, and the introduction of proper names by means of definite descriptions, have been acknowledged, what else remains of the alleged distinction between the meaning of a term and the way in which its reference is fixed? Nothing. Given the general conventions, all that is needed in order to arrive at the sense of a particular proper name or definite description is to know how its reference is fixed, that is, what is required of an object for it to be the referent of the term: the conventions concerning scope determine whether, for each given occurrence of the term, the method of fixing the reference shall be taken relative to the present time or to that referred to, to the actual world or to a possible one. We can, of course, consider some other notion which is labelled 'meaning', e.g. that called 'connotation' in FPL_2,[2] namely the function from each possible world to the denotation of the term in that world; but such a notion does not fulfil the role which Frege intended his notion of sense to play, and has no intuitive claim to be entitled 'meaning'.

For the assessment of the bearing of Kripke's theses concerning modality on Frege's account of proper names, that is all that needs to be said. The observation, not of course made in those terms, that proper names are usually temporally rigid designators, in contrast to definite descriptions, which sometimes behave as rigid and sometimes as flexible, is not infrequent in the literature on the subject prior to the publication of Kripke's essay. The parallel observation that they are usually modally rigid, again in contrast to definite descriptions, is to be reckoned a genuine discovery. It cannot, however, bear the weight of an assault on Frege's whole notion

---

[1] An exception is a case in which the indexical feature relates to the position of the human race as a whole. It is unlikely that we could frame, in purely general terms, a description picking out the Sun from among all the stars in the universe; the Sun is the star near *us*, which gives light and heat to *our* planet, and something of this kind must be taken as involved in a grasp of the sense of the proper name 'the Sun'.

[2] Pp. 127, 132–3.

of sense, as applied to singular terms, namely as resulting from a confused amalgamation of two quite different features: there are no two such features to be distinguished. As to Kripke's views on modality in general, as expressed in 'Naming and Necessity', I remain convinced that what I wrote about it in *FPL* is essentially on the right lines; but I shall not take the space to argue that here, or to go into the matter more thoroughly, since it remains my intention to engage in a detailed discussion of the topic of necessary truth in my volume on Frege's philosophy of mathematics.

CHAPTER 10

The Causal Theory of Reference

As I POINTED out on pp. 135–6 of *FPL*, Kripke's arguments concerning what determines reference in the actual world are wholly distinct from those relating to modality. The latter are indifferent to how reference is determined in the actual world. As far as they are concerned, what Kripke calls the 'description theory' of proper names, viz. that, for each proper name, there is a definite description whose reference in the actual world is determined in the same way as that of the proper name, could be true. The divergence occurs only when we are concerned with the reference in other possible worlds: the referent of the definite description is that object which, in the given possible world, satisfies a certain condition, while the referent of the proper name is that object which, in the *actual* world, satisfies the corresponding condition. The other battery of arguments is designed to show that the 'description theory' is *not* true, that it misrepresents the manner in which, in the actual world, the reference of a proper name is determined.

Before encountering Kripke's essay, I had already repudiated the attribution to Frege of the 'description theory'.[1] As admitted on p. 97 of *FPL*, it is true enough that, in giving instances of the senses carried by proper names, Frege cites definite descriptions as embodying those senses; but there is no passage in his writings in which he advances any thesis to the effect that the sense of a proper name can always be so expressed. It would be particularly absurd to attribute to him the view that the sense of a proper name can always be framed in purely descriptive terms, not involving any indexical element in the extended sense illustrated by the above example of the name 'the Sun'. But, more generally, it is sufficient, for a proper name to have an objective sense, that there be a shared ability to

[1] *FPL*, pp. 97–8; cf. pp. 110–11.

recognize an object, in certain circumstances, as the referent of the name; there need be no available analysis of the way in which this recognition is effected, just as most of us are able to recognize people by their features, although we should make a very bad shot at giving a verbal description of them. For the name to have a determinate sense, it is necessary that there should be an agreed method of resolving a clash in immediate judgments, which may consist in a simple appeal to a majority verdict, or may invoke criteria not otherwise brought into play: but it is not necessary that there be any known method of stating, in general terms, the basis of recognition, nor even that there exist a vocabulary capable of framing such a statement. In FPL_1,[1] I ascribed the view that a proper name is in this sense replaceable by a definite description to Quine; but this was inaccurate, and I have in FPL_2 removed the reference to him. Quine is interested in eliminating the entire category of proper names from the language, but not necessarily without a compensatory addition to the stock of predicates; it is precisely because we cannot assume that the language permits the formation of a predicate uniquely true of the referent of the name that Quine allows that, in eliminating a proper name in favour of a definite description, we may need to add a predicate to the language, replacing, say, 'Margaret Thatcher' by 'the thatcherizer'; for, if the name had a sense, then we may endow a predicate, intended to be true of and only of its referent, with a corresponding sense.

An ability to recognize an object must be capable of further specification, namely as to the distance and angle from which it must be seen, the conditions under which it must be heard, etc., for the ability to be exercised. Moreover, it is impossible that the use of a name for an object that cannot have more than one location, like a town, or of one that cannot have more than one location at a time, like a horse, should rest solely on a shared ability to recognize it, since it is part of the sense of the name that it is a name of an object of the sort in question; we do not use a name like 'Luton' in such a way that, if there should turn out to be another town looking exactly the same, we should accord it an equal right to be called 'Luton', and accordingly declare the name void of reference for ambiguity. While an ability to recognize an object as the referent of a name, either upon inspection or after applying some test, is, when supplemented by a due method of resolving conflicts, sufficient to endow the name with a sense, it is not, on Frege's view, necessary. All that is necessary is that there be some condition, which we are capable of grasping, that an object

[1] P. 98.

must satisfy for it to be the referent of the name; the name then has a reference if that condition is satisfied by one and only one object.

As I remarked in *FPL*,[1] the acknowledgment that Frege held a far less specific conception of the possible senses of proper names than that admitted by the 'description theory' robs Kripke's account of its appearance of a head-on clash with the Fregean notion of sense. It would nevertheless be a mistake to set it aside as no more than a theory concerning the form that the sense of any proper name must take, and as therefore in no kind of conflict with Frege's views, because it raises certain issues which Frege overlooked. Kripke commits the mistake, common amongst those who discuss proper names, of concentrating almost exclusively on one particular variety, personal proper names; these, together with names of animals, ships and the like, have certain peculiarities which, while rendering them extremely interesting, also make them atypical of proper names as a class. There are a great many types of proper name for which even the description theory seems unproblematically correct. We should hardly allow that someone could be said to know what 'the Ka'aba' or 'the scirocco' meant who could not *say* what they stood for, in a more or less standard manner. No one would be said to know the meaning of the word 'July' who could not explain that it denotes the seventh month of the Western calendar, or else the month after June or before August. The term 'the Sicilian defence' is properly understood only by those who can state the moves involved, while an understanding of the name 'chess' itself demands at least a vague account of the game, and, possibly, an actual knowledge of the rules. All these are unquestionably proper names; yet we have no temptation to regard them as not really belonging to the language, or to deny them to bear senses capable of transmission by explicit verbal definitions. But personal proper names differ from most others in two ways. First, most of them have bearers with whom only speakers belonging to a limited circle are acquainted, unlike, say, names of constellations. Secondly, they include names whose bearers, though once objects of acquaintance, no longer exist. Both features make them problematic.

Personal proper names share the first feature, but not, on the whole, the second, with place-names. Now suppose that Mary Reid has never heard of Milan, but is told, concerning Tom Evans, who is well known to her, 'He is living in Milan now'. We cannot say that she learns from this that Evans is living in Milan, any more than, if she had never heard of chiropody, she would have learned that Evans had become a chiropodist

---

[1] Pp. 143, 146–51.

by being told, 'He has become a chiropodist'; she has learned only that Evans is living in some place called 'Milan'. What shows that Kripke's account cannot be correct as it stands is that it leaves no sufficient room for a distinction between knowing that someone lives in Milan and knowing that he lives in a place called 'Milan'. Nevertheless, without discovering where Milan is, or even whether it is a city or a country, Mary Reid can pass on the fact that Evans is living in Milan to someone else; asked if she knows where he is now living, for example, she may quite properly say, 'I was told that he is living in Milan'. In doing this, she exploits the fact that 'Milan' is part of the common language, English, which she is speaking, and holds herself responsible to its established use in that language, even though that use is unknown to her. This capacity which a speaker has to use words that he does not fully understand, holding himself responsible to the senses that they bear in the common language, is a very pervasive feature of ordinary linguistic communication, by no means confined to proper names; and it is to this feature that Kripke's account of proper names implicitly, though not explicitly, draws attention. The fact that, in speaking a given language, speakers hold themselves responsible to the ascertainably correct uses of their words in that language is what vitiates Frege's observation in 'Der Gedanke' that two speakers whose means of identification of the bearer of a proper name used by both of them differ are speaking different languages.[1] We should come nearer the truth if we said that two people are speaking the same language if they conceive themselves to be doing so; more accurately, they are speaking the same language if they would acknowledge the same authorities as decisive for determining the correct use of a word. As I remarked on p. 142 of *FPL*, authority concerning linguistic usage is diffuse, and includes standard reference works, experts on various subjects (for technical terms and words like 'temperature' that straddle the boundary between a technical vocabulary and the general one) and an ill-defined class of educated speakers; but there can be no language without standards of correctness, and, unless there is universal agreement, there can be no correctness without some authority, however diffuse. For place-names, there is a well established network of authorities, including atlases, bilingual dictionaries and local inhabitants, which determine their reference in a publicly ascertainable and generally accepted manner; it is this background which makes it possible for a speaker to use a place-name with a definite referent, even though having only a hazy idea what it is, or no idea at all.

---

[1] See *FPL*, p. 584.

Frege's neglect of this feature of language is a serious defect in his treatment of it. Despite his insistence on the objectivity and communicability of sense, his account of language makes the notion of an idiolect central: he conceives of the sense of an expression as something which is grasped by an individual speaker, and, in so far as it can be stated, as capable of being stated without reference to the existence of other speakers, that is, to the fact that it belongs to a common language. Speakers then succeed in communicating in so far as they happen to attach the same senses to their words, or as near as makes no practical difference: the basic notion is thus that of an idiolect, and a language, such as German or English, would have to be explained as a range of closely overlapping idiolects. The objectivity of sense would then reside only in the fact that it is possible for two speakers to discover that, and how, their idiolects diverge. Such a conception of language falsifies its character at many points: in particular, it obscures the phenomenon to which Hilary Putnam first drew attention, called by him 'the division of linguistic labour'. Certain words—Putnam's example is 'gold'—belong both to the general vocabulary and to a technical one, without being ambiguous; a knowledge of the technical use is not taken as required for a full understanding of the term as part of the general vocabulary, and yet speakers will hold themselves responsible to the judgment of experts in disputed cases. But probably the gravest defect of the conception according to which the notion of an idiolect is the primary one lies in the account to which it gives rise of the senses of words for perceptual qualities and for inner sensations: it leads naturally to the idea of the private ostensive definition and of the incommunicable private sense, an idea which Frege seems, towards the end of his life, to have admitted, as was noted above. The whole point of Wittgenstein's attack on this idea is that words of this kind can exist, can bear the senses, or have the uses, that they do, only as words of a public language: any account of their senses, or their uses, must therefore involve essential reference to the linguistic community. It would take us too far afield to pursue this further here; but it is plain that, having started from the principle that sense is essentially something communicable, Frege must have gone astray in developing this idea if he arrived at a view according to which there can be incommunicable senses.

If we consider a place-name like 'Milan' as a word of the common language, and ask what establishes the connection of that name to a particular city, we shall arrive at a fairly rich answer, that network of connections mentioned above that underlies, among much else, the functioning of the postal and travel services. This rich background falls away if we concentrate upon an individual speaker, in the extreme case Mary Reid in the example, and ask what in that speaker's use of the name determines its reference. In telling someone else that Evans was living in Milan, Mary Reid was certainly referring to Milan, even though she knew nothing whatever about it save that Evans was living there; and now the only fact that establishes a connection between the city and her use of the name appears to be that she had picked up the name from someone else who used it to refer to that city. Now, Kripke argues, we cannot represent her as using 'Milan' to mean 'the place referred to by Bill Smith when he used the name "Milan" ', since she may very well have forgotten from whom she first heard it; and, if our contention is that it is the sense of a name that establishes the connection between it and its referent, we cannot without circularity maintain that the generally understood sense of the name 'Milan' is 'the city called "Milan" ', since 'called', in this context, simply means 'referred to as'. But even if Bill Smith, who first told Mary Reid that Evans was living in Milan, knows a bit more about Milan than she does, he may well not know enough to distinguish Milan from all other cities, say from Bergamo or even from Turin, save of course by the fact that it is called 'Milan'; and so the question what makes the connection between the city and the name as *he* uses it is therefore apparently to be answered in the same way as before. The chain thus initiated cannot, of course, go on for ever. We shall, or should, if we could actually trace it, come upon the person who first introduced the name 'Milan' into the language. Perhaps he introduced it to be the English equivalent of the Italian 'Milano', and, if so, we must pursue another chain, reaching back to what Kripke calls an 'initial baptism' by whoever it was who first proposed that the city should be called 'Milano'.

This theory is arrived at by asking the wrong question at the outset. What makes it the case that, by using the name 'Milan', Mary Reid was referring to Milan is that she meant to be understood as using the name in conformity with its established use in the common language: the proper question is therefore what establishes the connection between the city and the use of the name in English. Someone who insists on asking about the knowledge possessed by an individual speaker will do better to fasten on the fact that Mary Reid, having no idea where Milan was, could not be said to know that Evans was living in Milan, and to ask how much someone must know about Milan to be said to know such a thing. There is, of course, no sharp line between one who knows perfectly well what the name 'Milan' stands for, and one who has merely heard it, but knows no more than that it is a place-name; there is only a gradation of intermediate cases. In practice, a knowledge that Milan is a city in Italy, and a rough idea of its location, will suffice for someone to be reckoned as knowing the use of the name, and one who has been there for any appreciable time may be allowed an even vaguer grasp of its geographical position; it is not required of a speaker that he should, by appeal only to his existing knowledge, be able to identify the city. What makes this unnecessary, however, is the existence of the background of recognized means of identification; if this background is removed, the connection between name and referent crumbles.

For someone to be said to have a *belief* that can be expressed by means of a name, almost any piece of personal knowledge concerning its referent, however idiosyncratic, will suffice. Suppose that Mary Reid sees a headline, 'Street Battle in Milan'; inferring that it is a town or city, but still otherwise knowing no more about it than that it is where Tom Evans is living, she may be said to believe that there has been a street battle in Milan. But for someone to be said to understand the name as a word of the language, he must at least know that Milan is a city in northern Italy; he must, that is, have a minimal grasp of the *typical* explanation of what it stands for. Let us now consider personal names of celebrated individuals, say 'William Blake'; and let us suppose that Bill Smith is quite ignorant of painting and of poetry, but is very interested in genealogy, and has come upon William Blake as a cousin by marriage of one of his wife's ancestors. In using the name, he is of course referring to the man; but, even though his William Blake really is the famous one, he cannot be said to understand the name 'William Blake' as an expression of the common language unless he has the minimal knowledge that its bearer was a painter or a poet. This is genuinely a case of a use of a name with different senses but the same referent; Smith must undertake research if he is to establish that he is referring to the same man as other speakers who use the name.

Personal names like 'Gandhi', 'Confucius', 'Mahommed', 'Tolstoy', 'Rembrandt', etc., belong, as do names of continents and names like 'Tokyo', 'Delhi' and 'Rome', to the general vocabulary; but most personal names do not. Place-names may be compared to technical terms and to ones belonging both to the general vocabulary and to a technical one, in that their use is backed by expert authority and official sources. To the extent that a society recognizes a system of legal nomenclature, underpinned by some procedure of registration, this is partly true of personal names also; so let us assume that we are dealing only with nick-names, assumed names or other unofficial ones. The name of a living but not famous individual is obviously used principally by his acquaintances, and its use by them rests on their capacity to recognize him, governed by the fact that it is a personal name, and therefore subject to the criteria for personal identity. Its use will not, of course, be confined to his acquaintances; it will radiate out to a still restricted circle of those who do not know him but have heard of him and know something about him. These other speakers cannot be said to hold themselves responsible to the use of the name in the language, for it has no use in the language as a whole; their use of it, as having the reference that it does, depends on the use made by those who are capable of identifying its bearer. The acquaintances of the bearer play something of the role played by experts where the meaning of a technical term is in question; the other speakers do not need to remember precisely from whom they first learned the name, but they do have to be able, if need be, to locate the circle of speakers who know the individual in question and upon whose use of the name theirs is parasitic.

For cases of this kind, Kripke's account is approximately correct, but not exactly so, because it is the current use of the name by those best qualified to pronounce on it, and not its original bestowal, that is decisive for its reference. As is remarked on pp. 149–51 of *FPL*, Kripke's account leaves no room for an unintended shift of reference. It is unproblematic how such a shift may occur in the case of place-names, as in Gareth Evans's excellent example of 'Madagascar', originally used for part of the mainland: what makes this possible is that the present use of the name overrides its historical origin in determining its referent, and that use rests on accepted means of identification. But the same is true of names of people, at least when, as here, we are prescinding from any considerations concerning someone's 'true' or legal name. If (after baptism) one baby is substituted for another in the cradle, and the exchange goes undetected, there might later be a point, if an inheritance were in question, in revealing the substitution with the words, 'This is not Henry Fanshawe!'. But, in most contexts, we should have the right to turn Kripke's argument against the description theory back on to his own theory: someone told that, in using the name 'Henry Fanshawe', he had actually been referring, unknown to himself, to the true son of Mrs Fanshawe, of whom he had never heard, could reasonably object that he had been referring to the person everyone knew as Henry Fanshawe. When someone's *true* name is not in question, the only criterion for his being the referent of a personal name is that it is the name by which he is known, which means the name used by those who know him, with the added requirement, absent in the case of dogs, horses and ships, that it be a name that he acknowledges as his.

What makes personal names so different from place-names is that we use a great range of them after their bearers are no more. Not knowing where Ophir and the land of Uz were, we do not use these names, except in poetry or quotation; but, although our information about Uriah the Hittite is sparse, the parallel difficulty does not arise in his case. For this reason a shift of reference can hardly occur for personal names of the dead; and the causal theory has therefore its most plausible application here. The question for whom a personal name stands is the question for whom we should take it to stand, if we knew the full facts. It is a merit of Kripke's account to have drawn attention to the fact that, in case of dispute concerning the referent of a name for someone no longer known at any time to any living person, we should give weight to the way the name had come down to us. There is a range of dissimilar cases even here, according, in part, to whether there are many written sources, or only a few, or, the name having been handed down by oral tradition alone, none. In the last case, a name never comes down to us save as part of some tradition concerning its bearer, round which our interest centres. It is quite as much of a mistake to concentrate exclusively on the historical line through which the name itself reached us as on what we believe to be true of its bearer. There are, again, different types of case according as we are disposed to believe much or little of the tradition: someone who believes very little of the tradition may reasonably say that he believes that there was such a man as King Arthur, whereas someone may deny that there was any such person as Socrates on the ground that two distinct traditions have been conflated. In many cases, it matters little to us whether the name has been handed down correctly, or whether some mistake has occurred in its transmission, provided that the substance of the tradition is correct. This is not to say that the historical transmission is unimportant: if we thought that the tradition was due to later invention or confusion, we should have no reason to believe it to be true; but, if we improbably discovered that, by an extraordinary fluke, it was, we should not in most cases want to insist that the name, as we had used it, referred to the man of whom the tradition, though unfounded, was by a coincidence true. But what is usually of importance is the transmission of the tradition, not of the name itself. Kripke's examples to show the falsity of the description theory lack the necessary generality: they concern the composition of literary works and the making of scientific discoveries, which are exceptional as acts which can confer fame and yet the credit for which may be stolen. There is no possibility that Alexander the Great or the Prophet Mohammed owed their fame to acts which other men had performed. In cases like those of Kripke's examples, it is therefore possible that the tradition has been faithfully transmitted, although it was in origin a false tradition; we can therefore make sense of the supposition that the *Iliad* was written, not by Homer, but by another man (even one of the same name), since 'Homer' may be taken to stand for the man believed by his contemporaries to have written the *Iliad*, and we do not need to presume anything about the name by which they knew him to describe someone as the object of a belief on the part of his contemporaries. But there is no possibility of a correctly transmitted but mistaken tradition in the case, say, of Jinghiz Khan: either the substance of the tradition is true, or there was no such person; and, if some error has occurred in the transmission of his (conferred) name, that is not of crucial importance.

The appearance that we have here a complete alternative picture of the way in which reference is bestowed on proper names is, therefore, illusory. The emphasis, for a very special class of proper names, though one very important to us, on the historical dimension is a just corrective to any picture too close to the description theory, though even here the point is not correctly stated; of much greater importance to the philosophy of language in general are the considerations leading to a recognition of the distinction between an individual speaker's understanding of an expression and its sense in the common language. This genuinely represents an aspect of language inadequately handled by Frege; but what we do not have is any argument that calls in question Frege's idea that proper names have sense, and that it is their senses that determine their references. Since the publication of FPL_1, I have written further on this topic in 'Frege's Distinction between Sense and Reference' and in 'The Social Character of Meaning',[1] to which the reader is referred for further discussion.

---

[1] *Truth and Other Enigmas*, nos 9 and 23.

CHAPTER 11

Geach on Identity

THE OPINION HAS been expressed to me that, in preparing a second edition of *FPL*, I ought to omit Chapter 16, 'Identity'. Since FPL_2 does not represent a complete re-setting, but admitted only a limited number of changes, I did not have that option; but I should not have wished to take it even if I had. Whether the advice sprang from a failure to see what I was trying to do in that chapter, or from a judgment that I had done it so badly that it were better not attempted at all, I am unsure; as far as the quality is concerned, I confess that I had been quite proud of the chapter. On this, of course, I am especially liable to error; but on what my intention was, I am an authority. The bulk of the chapter is taken up with a close critical examination of certain theses advanced in Peter Geach's book, *Reference and Generality*; but this, like other similar sections of the book,[1] was not meant to be seen as a digression. *FPL* does not purport to contain discussions of or replies to all important criticisms of Frege's doctrines; if it did, it would be much longer. I proceeded in this manner only in those cases in which it seemed to me to provide the best way in to an examination of some point left obscure by Frege or of some objection unforeseen by him, when a failure to have examined that point or that objection would have rendered the book seriously incomplete as a discussion of Frege. In the present instance, the earlier passages in *FPL* dealing with Frege's crucially important notion of a criterion of identity did not give an adequate treatment of the subject, since they evaded the question for the truth of what kind of statement a criterion of identity is a criterion. It appeared to me that the best way of going more deeply into this question was by examining certain views on the matter advanced by Geach. I did, indeed, disagree with his views. But this does not mean that I did not have a high

---

[1] Chapter 17 and the appendix to Chapter 5.

regard for the writings in which Geach had advocated those views. It is a commonplace to everyone who engages in philosophy that one can learn quite as much from what one finds oneself disagreeing with as from what one is convinced by. Though I did not agree with Geach's conclusions, I believe that the process of reflecting on his arguments and trying to formulate my disagreement with them left me clearer about the issues than I had been before; indeed, it is precisely for that reason that I thought it would be useful for the readers, as it had been for myself, to approach the question through a consideration of Geach's views.

To the best of my recollection, the bulk of the chapter was written in 1964, and originally formed a chapter called 'The Number of Red Things', placed after one on Frege's definition of (cardinal) number, and thus in the section on philosophy of mathematics; when I came to divide the book into two, it seemed to me much better placed in the volume on the philosophy of language. As I have indicated, I reject the criticism that I should have approached the matter solely in terms of what Frege said, rather than in terms of what Geach had said; when a single writer has said things that demand discussion, it is less, not more, fair to him to refer to his remarks impersonally by means of phrases like, 'It has been argued that . . . '. Where I can be criticized, no doubt, is in not having revised the chapter to take account of what Geach had subsequently written on the subject. I have attempted to emend some passages in which I may have given a misleading impression of Geach's views. Thus in FPL_2 I have altered lines 10–12 on p. 551, where I originally wrote that ' "the same" operates in the same way on a general term "X" to yield the relational expression "the same X" as it operates on another general term "Y" to yield the (non-synonymous) relational expression "the same Y" '. This remark does not accurately express Geach's view, or what has emerged as being Geach's view. Since the publication of *Reference and Generality*, he has more and more stressed the contention advanced in the last paragraph of that book, and alluded to by me on p. 564 of *FPL*, that, for any substantival general term 'X', what has first to be explained is the relational expression '. . . is the same X as . . .', the predicate '. . . is an X' then being explicable in terms of it as meaning '. . . is the same X as something'; and he has made an explicit comparison with the explanation by 'derelativization' of such a term as 'parent'. We cannot first explain the predicate '. . . is a parent', and then, by appeal to this predicate, explain the relational expression '. . . is a parent of . . .'; instead, we have to take the latter as primary, and explain '. . . is a parent' as meaning '. . . is a parent of someone'.

I doubt whether my original inaccurate formulation on p. 551 of FPL_1 would have been seriously misleading, because the very next paragraph explains that, on Geach's view, the sense of 'the same X' is not derivable from the sense of 'X' in the way that it is plausible to suppose that the sense of 'a good X' or of 'a real X' is derivable from that of 'X'. That paragraph is, I think, correct as it stands, and so I have let it stand; but it requires a gloss. In speaking of the sense of the general term 'X', I meant to allude to the sense of the *word* 'X', which of course involves the meanings of all expressions containing this word. In this sense, it is a correct representation of Geach's view to say, as I do, that 'the sense of "the same X" . . . is given with [the sense of "X"] and is in part constitutive of it'; it is not, of course, *wholly* constitutive of it, since otherwise 'X' would have no significant occurrence outside the phrase 'the same X'. It would, however, be plausible to say something stronger about 'real' and 'good' than what I did say, understood in this manner. I actually said that, 'if the sense of "X" is given, . . . we can determine the sense of "a real X" or of "a good X"'; but in fact one can say more. It is not merely that, if one knows the sense of the *word* 'X', one can determine from it the sense of 'a real X' and, if it has one, of 'a good X'; it is that one can determine the senses of these latter expressions from knowing that of the *predicate* '. . . is an X'. This fact might tempt a reader to understand the expression 'the sense of "X"' in a way I did not intend, namely as referring to the sense of the predicate '. . . is an X'. It would *not* be an accurate account of Geach's view to say that the sense of 'the same X' is given with the sense of '. . . is an X' and is in part constitutive of it; on the contrary, the sense of 'the same X' is, for him, given in advance of that of '. . . is an X', and is wholly constitutive of it in the sense that '. . . is an X' is to be explained in terms of 'the same X'.

I have also, in FPL_2, altered lines 16–24 of p. 564 and lines 2–6 of p. 565, in order to avoid the impression, which I formerly gave, that Geach acknowledged a sense in which a criterion of application is prior to a criterion of identity; in view of the doctrine mentioned above (and in FPL, p. 564), which has become very central to Geach's later discussions of 'relative identity' and of substantival general terms, such an impression is seriously misleading. On p. 564 of FPL, I explained the sense, which is not Geach's, in which the two criteria may be said to be independent of one another, as contrasted with that in which we might express the doctrine in question by saying that the criterion of identity is prior; and on p. 565 I mentioned a sense, again not acknowledged by Geach, in which the criterion of application is prior, even on Geach's own views, namely that, while a general term may have a criterion of application but lack a criterion of identity, the reverse is not possible. Of course, this is a matter of terminology; the question which criterion is prior is not univocal. When I originally wrote the chapter, I was unaware how important the doctrine stated in the last paragraph of *Reference and Generality* was to become; in view of the stress subsequently placed by Geach upon it, it is dangerously misleading to ascribe to him any view concerning priority other than that the criterion of identity is prior to the criterion of application.

It is only a matter of terminology, however: the point that I was aiming to bring out still stands. To say that '*Z*', whether it is grammatically an adjective or a noun, is an adjectival general term is to say that the predicate '. . . is (a) *Z*' has a sense, but that the relational expression '. . . is the same *Z* (thing) as . . .' has none, or at least no unequivocal sense independent of context. The existence of such terms is acknowledged by Geach, whereas the existence of ones for which the converse holds good is not; and this, I argued, created a certain difficulty for the interpretation of Geach's view, the amorphous-lump interpretation, which I was considering.

In 'Existential or Particular Quantifier?'[1] Geach remarks that 'those who read me as rejecting unrestricted quantification in earlier works mistook my meaning'.[2] He may have me in mind as one of these, and I will try here to set the record absolutely straight. In *Reference and Generality*,[3] Geach accepts the equation of 'Anything that is *F* is *G*' with 'Anything is, if *F*, then *G*', and of 'Something that is *F* is *G*' with 'Something is both *F* and *G*': but these transformations do not for him provide models for the transformation of 'Any *A* is *G*' into 'Anything is, if an *A*, then *G*', and of 'Some *A* is *G*' into 'Something is both an *A* and *G*', where '*A*' is a substantival term. I shall understand the phrase 'restricted quantification' as relating to sentences of these latter forms, 'Any *A* is *G*' and 'Some *A* is *G*', rather than to forms such as 'Anything that is *F* is *G*' and 'Something that is *F* is *G*'; Frege, of course, would not distinguish between them.

In *Reference and Generality*,[4] Geach first says that 'it is commonly held that restricted quantifiers can be got rid of by reducing them to the unrestricted "for any *x*" and "for some *y*" ', namely by the transformation indicated above, replacing 'for any boy *x*' by 'for any *x*, if *x* is a boy, then . . .'.

---

[1] Paul Weingartner and Edgar Morscher (eds.), *Ontology and Logic*, Berlin, 1979, pp. 137–51.
[2] P. 141.
[3] P. 149.
[4] P. 106.

He announces, at this stage, that he will 'use restricted quantifiers without prejudging the legitimacy of this reduction'. On p. 149, he says that many logicians have thought that it is possible to explain 'any' and 'some' in terms of 'anything' and 'something'; 'it is a standard procedure in modern textbooks of formal logic to reduce "any A" and "some A" to "anything that is A" and "something that is A", and then eliminate the relative pronoun "that" in the way just explained', viz. as in the preceding paragraph. 'This view is perhaps most clearly stated in Quine's writings', he continues,[1] 'but is in no way peculiar to Quine; as regards the working-around of restricted into unrestricted quantification, Quine is orthodox'. He goes on to say that he takes issue with Quine 'about the . . . generally accepted treatment of referring phrases like "some A" '. This does not constitute a topic on which Geach has since changed his mind; in 'Existential or Particular Quantifier?' he is of the same opinion about restricted quantification, as exemplified by the use of noun-phrases of the form 'any A' and 'some A', as in *Reference and Generality*.

On p. 552 of *FPL*, I said that 'Geach uses his doctrine about identity to call Frege's treatment of quantifiers in question'; and, in the circumstances, this does not seem incorrect. On pp. 552–3, I said that Geach held Frege to have been mistaken in regarding 'y is the same X as z' as meaning 'y is an X and y is the same (absolutely) as z', the unqualified 'y is the same as z' being, for Geach, meaningless. This is also certainly correct, but leaves it unclear whether the fault lies only with the unqualified identity-relation or also with the unrestricted quantifier. But I went on, on p. 553 of FPL_1, to say that 'a totally unrestricted quantifier . . . is also meaningless' for Geach; the greatest range that, on his view, a bound variable can have is over a category in my, not his, sense of 'category', namely a maximal range of objects in connection with which the same criterion of identity is applicable. Now this remark was certainly misleading, and required qualification. But, on p. 557 of FPL_1, I acknowledged as much, and gave the necessary qualification. I wrote, 'Earlier I described Geach as rejecting unrestricted quantification as meaningless, but this was misleading; he rejects it only in so far as it is explained in the classical fashion. He is not opposed to unrestricted quantification as such, but only to taking it as fundamental and explaining restricted quantification in terms of it. For him the direction of explanation should be the reverse: unrestricted quantifiers are to be explained in terms of restricted ones'.

It may be objected that this emendation of the view I was ascribing

---

[1] P. 150.

to Geach comes too late. For, on p. 553 of *FPL*, I had asked, 'How does Geach pass from his doctrine about identity and about substantival general terms to his view about quantification?', and had gone on to refer to Geach's use of the Heraclitean paradox about the same river; and on p. 554 I had said that 'this paradox is announced' by Geach 'as a refutation of what' he had called 'the "orthodox" view that restricted quantification is to be interpreted in terms of unrestricted quantification'. Geach, I added, was 'simultaneously arguing for his thesis about identity and his thesis about quantification'; and I urged that, if we took the grounds for his thesis about identity as given, the Heraclitean paradox was 'less than compelling' as a way of passing from that thesis to the one about quantification. My reason for saying this was that the thesis about identity already supplied a resolution of the paradox. If 'x is the same water as y' does not mean 'x is water and x is the same as y', then the rendering of 'Heraclitus bathed in some water yesterday and bathed in the same water today' as 'For some *w*, *w* is water, and Heraclitus bathed in *w* yesterday, and Heraclitus bathed in *w* today' is already incorrect, without the need to invoke any particular thesis concerning the quantifier.

But was this not unfair, in view of my coming retractation of the assertion that Geach regarded unrestricted quantification as meaningless? I do not think so. On p. 150 of *Reference and Generality*, Geach introduces the Heraclitean paradox as telling against what he has described as the 'accepted view' that restricted quantification may be reduced to unrestricted; and I was seeking, on p. 554 of *FPL*, to understand in what way it did so, not to derive from it the stronger claim that unrestricted quantification is altogether meaningless. However, the suggestion on p. 553 of FPL_1, that Geach regarded unrestricted quantification as meaningless, withdrawn as misleading on p. 557, was productive of confusion; and I have, in FPL_2, emended both accordingly.

What, then, is, for Geach, the relation between 'Some A is G' and 'For some x, x is an A and x is G'? If the latter is a legitimate form of expression, wherein does it differ from the former? Rather than giving the answer at this stage, it is better to consider Geach's general doctrine of substantival general terms, for which 'A' is here schematic. In his later writing, Geach has preferred to use the term 'count-noun' for substantival general terms; the word is somewhat unfortunate, since it threatens to obliterate the distinction, still acknowledged, though never satisfactorily accounted for, by Geach, between substantival terms in general—roughly speaking, nouns that both have a plural and admit the prefix 'the same'—and the subclass consisting of countable ones—roughly, those for which it makes sense to ask 'How many *A*'s?'.[1] So expressed, the doctrine mentioned above and on p. 564 of *FPL*, which, since *Reference and Generality*, has acquired such prominence in Geach's discussions of this subject is that, for *every* count-noun '*X*', the proper, and only correct, order of explanation is first to introduce the relational expression '. . . is the same *X* as . . .', and then to explain '. . . is an *X*' as meaning '. . . is the same *X* as something'. The grounds for this doctrine are essentially as follows. We must recognize a connection between these two forms of expression, since the term '*X*' does not occur ambiguously in the two contexts; and the simplest way of explaining the connection is to exhibit one as definable in terms of the other. We cannot, however, according to Geach, explain '. . . is the same *X* as . . .' in terms of '. . . is an *X*' by defining it to mean '. . . is an *X* and is (absolutely) the same as . . .', there being no absolute relation of identity; we must therefore adopt the opposite order of explanation. It is no objection to this doctrine that there occur adjectival terms '*Z*', for which '. . . is (a) *Z*' cannot be explained in this way; since there is no expression of the form '. . . is the same *Z* (thing) as . . .' to be considered, the impossibility of explaining it in terms of '. . . is (a) *Z*' creates no problem. Indeed, it could be claimed as a merit of the doctrine that it accounts for the fact that there are no general terms with which is associated a criterion of identity but not a criterion of application: given any expression of the form '. . . is the same *W* as . . .', it lies to hand to introduce '. . . is a *W*' as meaning '. . . is the same *W* as something'.

Even when its premises are conceded, the argument just sketched is full of gaps, above all because there may be ways of explaining '. . . is the same *X* as . . .' in terms of '. . . is an *X*' without invoking the proscribed absolute identity-relation. It is, not surprisingly therefore, apparent that the doctrine is, at best, exaggerated; there are many count-nouns to which it does not apply. As observed on p. 564 of *FPL*, it is implausible, as a piece of conceptual analysis, to say that we learn most count-nouns '*X*' by learning, as a unitary expression, the use of '. . . is the same *X* as . . .', that we cannot discriminate, within what we learn about the use of the count-noun, that which belongs to the criterion of its application and that which belongs to the associated criterion of identity. In acquiring such terms as 'spaniel' and 'collie', for example, we do not first learn the uses, as units, of the expressions 'is the same spaniel as' and 'is the same collie as', subsequently coming, by analysis, to discern a common element in these; we learn what differentiates spaniels and collies from dogs of

[1] See *FPL*, pp. 548–9.

other kinds. This reflects the fact that, if we know what '. . . is a spaniel' means, we can perfectly well explain '. . . is the same spaniel as . . .' as meaning '. . . is a spaniel and is the same dog (animal) as . .   '. In general, if '. . . is an X' implies '. . . is a Y', and '. . . is the same X as . . .' is equivalent to '. . . is an X and is the same Y as . . .', then it is always untrue that it is necessary to explain '. . . is an X' as meaning '. . . is the same X as something', and frequently implausible that this is a natural form of explanation. If, for instance, 'X' is 'postman', the natural explanation of '. . . is a postman' is as meaning '. . . is a man who earns his living by delivering the mail', and the natural explanation of '. . . is the same postman as . . .' is as meaning '. . . is a postman and is the same man as . . .'. We may call count-nouns of this class 'derivative count-nouns': they form a large class of exceptions to Geach's doctrine.

Geach is not in a position to deny the existence of derivative count-nouns, since he himself acknowledges the existence of a certain sub-class of them when he compares his preferred explanation of '. . . is an X' in terms of '. . . is the same X as . . .' to the explanation of a term such as 'parent' by derelativization. It is impossible that it should both hold good that the only legitimate explanation of '. . . is a parent' is as meaning '. . . is a parent of someone' and that the only legitimate explanation of it is as meaning '. . . is the same parent as someone'; and, since the first is evidently correct, the second is wrong. That leaves '. . . is the same parent as . . .' to be explained; and the obvious explanation is as meaning '. . . is a parent and is the same person as . . .'. Since Geach must admit such terms as 'parent', 'president', etc., which may be called 'derelativized count-nouns', to be derivative ones, he can hardly resist admitting 'postman' and 'spaniel' to be derivative count-nouns as well, although they are not derelativized terms.

There are also count-nouns 'X' of which it is natural to say that the relation expressed by '. . . is the same X as . . .' is defined over X's, i.e. that we have provided no sense for saying of anything other than an X that it is, or that it is not, the same X as anything. For example, the relation expressed by '. . . is the same direction as . . .' is defined over *directions*; it has no sense to say of something other than a direction that it is, or that it is not, the same direction as something. (I am here prescinding from that use of 'is the same direction as' in which, when in London, one may say that High Wycombe is the same direction as Oxford. Whether or not this mode of expression is condemned as an ungrammatical variant on saying that the one is *in* the same direction as the other, it is here irrelevant, since 'is a direction' could not then be even truly equated with 'is the same direction as something', High Wycombe, for instance, not being a direction.) Now, in a case like this, one could as well explain '. . . is a direction' as meaning '. . . is *not* the same direction as something' as explain it in Geach's manner; but either form of explanation is implausible, since it appears that one must know what directions are before one can understand '. . . is the same direction as . . .'. For at least a large range of count-nouns of this kind, Frege provided, in *Grundlagen* §§ 63–6, a convincing alternative pattern of explanation. According to this, the expression which has first to be introduced is the term-forming operator 'the direction of . . .'. This has to be explained for all the contexts in which we want it to occur, and, in the first place, for identity-statements of the form 'The direction of a is the same as the direction of b', which will be explained as equivalent to some statement '$R(a,b)$', where '$R(\xi,\zeta)$' denotes an equivalence relation. Having similarly provided explanations for every other type of context in which terms of the form 'the direction of a' are to occur, we may then explain '. . . is a direction' as meaning '. . . is the direction of something', and 'For any direction x, . . . x . . .' as meaning, 'For any a, . . . the direction of a . . .'. For cases of this kind, Frege's pattern of explanation is highly convincing in itself, and evidently preferable to Geach's; Geach's would leave it obscure how '. . . is the same direction as . . .' was to be explained in the first place, and provide no means for introducing the operator 'the direction of . . .'. Without implying that all abstract substantival general terms fit this Fregean pattern of explanation, we may call those that do 'abstract count-nouns'.

Geach holds that there is not, and could not possibly be, any absolute relation of identity, but that, for each count-noun 'X', '. . . is the same X as . . .' stands for an equivalence relation. An equivalence relation so expressed he calls a relation of relative identity, and holds that two objects may stand to one another in one such relative identity-relation, but fail to stand to each other in another such relation. (The expression 'two objects' is awkward here, since Geach holds that a count has sense only taken in respect of some specific count-noun, and 'object' does not qualify as such; so it might be better to say that, for certain count-nouns 'X' and 'Y', there may be two distinct Y's which are nevertheless the same X as each other.) A relative identity-relation must, presumably, be defined over objects of a kind we already know how to refer to, since we can have no conception of objects of a kind we do not know how to refer to, and we can hardly grasp the criterion for a relation to obtain between objects of which we have no conception.

Geach's pattern of explanation thus bears a certain resemblance to

Frege's, in that both begin with an equivalence relation E defined over a certain domain D which we already grasp. It is therefore instructive to compare the two patterns. For Frege, we adopt, as a means of expressing that E holds between objects a and b in D the form, 'The X of a is the same as the X of b', while, for Geach, we employ the form 'a is the same X as b'. For Frege, we explain '. . . is an X' as meaning, 'For some u, . . . is the X of u', whereas, for Geach, we explain it as meaning, 'For some u, . . . is the same X as u', which, since we are dealing with an equivalence relation, is equivalent to '. . . is the same X as itself'. Now how, on each account, can we pick out a particular X? For Geach, this means picking out something of which '. . . is an X' is true: and so we pick out an X in exactly the same way as we pick out an object in D, namely any such object that happens to be in the field of E; such an object simply *is* an X. For Frege, on the other hand, nothing requires that '. . . is an X' should be true of any element of D. It remains true, for him, that, to pick out an X, we must pick out an element a of D; we then indicate that it is an X that we are picking out by means of the expression 'the X of a'.

Frege's pattern is obviously intended to have only a restricted application, since not every substantival general term 'X' admits of a use in the context 'the X of a'. It is characteristic of substantival general terms, however, that they can significantly occur in a variety of contexts other than those of the form 'a is the same X as b', 'a is an X' and 'There are just n X's': among them, contexts of the forms, 'a is an X which is F', 'the X which is F' and 'Some X is F'. Though the definite description form is mentioned on p. 572 of *FPL*, Chapter 16 of that book suffers from a virtual absence of discussion how the occurrence of a substantival term 'X' in these other contexts is to be explained; Geach's later expositions of his relative identity thesis suffer, however, from precisely the same defect. A little reflection shows that what needs to be determined, in order to provide an interpretation for all these other contexts, is what can be predicated of an X, and under what conditions such a predication is true. Frege, indeed, says little enough about this question in his exposition in *Grundlagen* of his pattern of explanation of what we called abstract count-nouns; but he does say just enough to show what the answer should be. The passage is worth quoting in full:

In universal substitutivity all the laws of identity are . . . contained. In order, therefore, to justify our proposed definition of the direction of a line, we should have to show that it is possible, if line a is parallel to line *b*, to substitute 'the direction of *b*' everywhere for 'the direction of *a*'. This task is made simpler by the fact that we are being taken initially to know of nothing that can be predicated of the direction of a line other than its coinciding with the direction of some other line. We should thus have to demonstrate substitutivity only in such an identity-statement or in the contents of judgments which contained such identity-statements as constituents. Anything else to be predicated of directions would have first to be defined; and for these definitions we may lay down the rule that the substitutivity of the direction of a line by that of a line parallel to it must be safeguarded.[1]

The talk of substitutivity here refers to Leibniz's law, which Frege has just cited. Expressed in more modern terminology, and rendered more explicit, the argument is that the legitimacy of this manner of introducing the term 'direction' depends on the preservation of the general laws of identity, namely the substitutivity without change of truth-value of 'the direction of *b*' for 'the direction of *a*' whenever 'the direction of *a* is the same as the direction of *b*' is true. The truth-value of a sentence of this form has been explained as coinciding with that of '*a* is parallel to *b*'; and the substitutivity of 'the direction of *b*' for 'the direction of *a*' in any sentence 'The direction of *u* is the same as the direction of *v*', also of this form, is guaranteed by the fact that parallelism is an equivalence relation. If we wish terms of the form 'the direction of *a*' to figure in other types of context, we must provide express explanations for such other contexts. The aptest way to do so is, for each predicate '*F*' which we wish to introduce as applying to directions, to explain 'The direction of *a* is *F*' as equivalent to some sentence '*A(a)*', not involving reference to or quantification over directions, expressing that the line *a* falls under a certain concept A*, and, for each expression '*R*' which we wish to introduce as standing for a relation between directions, to explain 'The direction of *a* is *R* to the direction of *b*' as equivalent to a sentence '*B(a,b)*', not involving reference to or quantification over directions, expressing that the line *a* stands to the line *b* in a certain relation B*. In order to guarantee that the laws of identity are not violated, we lay down, as a general requirement on any such explanation, that parallelism must be a congruence relation with respect to A* and B*.

At this stage, Frege has not yet proposed his device of construing 'the direction of *a*' as standing for an equivalence class of lines under the

---

[1] *Grundlagen*, § 65.

relation of parallelism.[1] There is therefore no requirement, as yet, that directions be identified with any objects referred to otherwise than by means of the operator 'the direction of ξ'; and it is precisely for this reason that we are not already provided with a range of predicates applicable to directions, and a knowledge of the conditions for their application, but must introduce such predicates as we require and explain under what conditions they apply. In effect, in introducing the general term 'direction', we are simultaneously introducing a new type of object. It would, for Frege, be heresy to say that we were *creating* those objects; but it would surely be correct, from his standpoint, to say that we were introducing a means of referring to objects to which, previously, we had no means of referring.

For Geach, the matter stands differently, in two respects. First, we are in *no* sense introducing new objects by introducing the new count-noun 'X'; X's, that is to say, objects of which the predicate 'ξ is an X' is true, belong to the domain D which we were presumed already to grasp and to whose elements we already had other means of referring. Hence we are already provided with a range of predicates applicable to X's, namely all those which we are already accustomed to apply to elements of D. This comes out very clearly in Geach's discussion of his artificial example of 'X' as 'surman', where 'a is the same surman as b' is explained as equivalent to 'a is a man having the same surname as b'; '. . . is a surman' then comes out as true of just those men who have surnames. Geach insists that he does *not* have specially to stipulate the conditions under which various predicates are to apply to surmen: we can say of a surman that he lives in Leeds, has guts in his belly, etc., just because we can say those things of men with surnames (as of other men).

Secondly, Geach does not have to ensure the satisfaction of the laws of identity. He does, indeed, require of a relative identity-relation that it be an equivalence relation, i.e. that certain of the laws of identity hold good of it: but the more general requirement of substitutivity *salva veritate* in all contexts can be imposed only on the (spurious) relation of absolute identity. This already follows from the fact that, for suitable a, b, X and Y, a may be the same X but not the same Y as b: if Leibniz's law held for the relation expressed by '. . . is the same X as . . .', a would have to be the same Y as b.

It thus appears that the questions what may be predicated of an X, and under what conditions such a predication is true, do not arise for

[1] *Grundlagen*, § 68.

Geach. However, Geach both accepts and advocates Frege's thesis that with each proper name is associated a criterion of identity; and it can be true that no problem arises about what can be predicated of X's only if there is no proper name 'a' the criterion of identity associated with which is that expressed by '. . . is the same X as . . .'. If such a criterion of identity were associated with the proper names 'a' and 'b', then 'b is F' would follow from 'a is F' and 'a is the same X as b'; hence it would be required, of any predicate 'F' that could intelligibly be attached to a proper name 'a' of this kind that it satisfy the condition of applying to anything that was the same X as something to which it applied.

There are two possible conclusions to be drawn from this. (i) An account of the way in which meaning is conferred on a substantival general term 'X', including its use in the context '. . . is the same X as . . .', does not, in general, provide for the possibility of introducing proper names the criterion of identity associated with which is the relation expressed by '. . . is the same X as . . .': for this, new stipulations are required. Alternatively, it might, on the contrary, be maintained that: (ii) An adequate account of the use of a substantival general term 'X' *does* always provide for the introduction of such proper names, and hence Geach's pattern of explanation is, at best, seriously incomplete.

It is evident, on reflection, that (ii) is the correct conclusion to draw. Geach's account determines the use of the general term 'X' only in three restricted types of context: '. . . is the same X as . . .', '. . . is an X' and 'There are just n X's'. If we want to give an account of other contexts, such as those mentioned above, in which we should normally expect 'X' to be able to occur, we must solve the problem what can be predicated of an X. Consider, for example, the truth-conditions of a sentence of the form, 'Some X is both F and G'. Suppose that we know that '. . . is F' is true of an object u, that '. . . is G' is true of an object v, and that '. . . is the same X as . . .' holds between u and v: may we conclude that 'Some X is both F and G' is true? We should, normally, assume just this, for that is how expressions of the form 'Some X . . .' ordinarily work. However, unless 'F' and 'G' satisfy the requirement of being true of anything standing in the relation expressed by '. . . is the same X as . . .' to anything of which they are true, the principle will yield bizarre results: if they do not satisfy the requirement, 'G' might be 'not F'. The requirement is therefore to be imposed on any predicate 'F' if it is to be admitted to the context 'Some X is F'. But the predicates which we use as applying to the domain D will not, for the most part, satisfy the requirement, when used in their original senses; for instance, when 'X' is 'surman' and D consists of men, the predicate 'lives in Leeds' will be true of a man who is the same surman as a man of whom it is false.

It thus becomes apparent that Geach is mistaken in believing that, once he has specified the uses of '. . . is the same X as . . .', of '. . . is an X' and of 'There are just n X's', no further stipulation is needed for 'X' to play the role ordinarily played in the language by a count-noun. On the contrary, just as on Frege's pattern of explanation, there is a need for stipulations as to what predicates are to be applied to X's and what their satisfaction-conditions will be. At this point, the gap between Geach's and Frege's patterns of explanation has narrowed very considerably. The main difference between them lay in the fact that, for Frege, X's were not taken to be members of the domain D; for instance, directions of lines were not taken to be lines. One could say, indeed, that while, for Frege, there was no requirement that a direction be a line, there was equally no requirement that it not be. It is precisely because Frege takes it that there is no bar on identifying directions with objects referred to otherwise than *as* directions that he thinks it legitimate to go on to identify a direction with a class of parallel lines. Indeed, more could be said: Frege advances it as a reason for identifying directions with some objects referred to by other means that, if we do not do so, we shall have provided nothing to settle the truth-values of identity-statements on one side of which stands a term of the form 'the direction of a' and on the other a term of a different form. Frege did believe, therefore, that some such identification was required: it is just that no *particular* such identification could be demanded in advance. Just as we are entitled, if we find it convenient, to identify the complex number i with the Moon (*Grundlagen*, § 100), so, in introducing the term 'direction', we are free to identify directions with anything we please, so long as we find some reference for terms of the form 'the direction of a' that allows us to determine truth-conditions for all sentences in which it occurs. For, as Frege remarks in the footnote to § 100, the meaning of such a term was not unalterably fixed before we made that identification, but is decided by the identification that we elect to make. Since we can thus identify directions with whichever objects we please, we may, in particular, identify them with lines. But here the contrast is not merely that, on Geach's pattern of explanation, X's *must* be taken as in the domain D: it is that, though we may take all directions to be lines, there can be no more lines that are directions than there are directions of lines, even when we start with finitely many lines, some of them parallel to others. Thus we might, e.g., identify the direction of the line a with that line through some fixed point O which is parallel to *a*; but we cannot in this way, or in any natural manner, secure that every line is a direction, since we require that, when the direction of *a* is the same as that of *b*, a line with which the direction of *a* is identified shall be the same *line* as that with which the direction of *b* is identified, because the identity is conceived as absolute.

For Geach, on the other hand, every element of D which is in the field of the equivalence relation is an *X*, and distinct elements of D may be the same *X*; for instance, every man who has a surname is a surman, and distinct men may be the same surman. But, for just this reason, though '. . . is an *X*' may be predicated of an element of D, to say of an *X* that it is a particular element of D is not to predicate something of an *X* in that sense which is required for interpreting sentences of the form 'Some *X* is *F*'; it must, rather, be construed as predicating something of an element of D, an element of which '. . . is an *X*' happens to be true. Harold Wilson is a surman; but it cannot be said of any surman that he (it) is Harold Wilson—not in that sense which would license the assertion 'Some surman is Harold Wilson'; that can be said only of a certain man of whom '. . . is a surman' is true. Thus the phrase 'a surman' quickly comes apart from the phrase 'a man who is a surman'; the explanation of the satisfaction-conditions of '. . . is an *X*' proves to have little to do with most ordinary occurrences of the expression 'an *X*'.

It is now clear that, as soon as it has been admitted, as it must be, that, in order to interpret phrases of forms such as 'an *X* which is *F*', 'the *X* which is *F*' and 'some *X*', we need, as Frege does, stipulations as to what predicates may be applied to *X*'s and under what conditions they are true of them, the identification of *X*'s with elements of D is seen to play at least as small a role in a rectified Geachian pattern of explanation as in a Fregean one. For virtually every purpose for which the count-noun '*X*' will be used, *X*'s may be considered as constituting a type of object distinct from every other.

I have avoided applying Geach's pattern of explanation to Frege's example of the general term 'direction', because it would involve admitting sentences of the form 'The line *a* is the same direction as the line *b*', understood as equivalent to '*a* is parallel to *b*', whereas Geach takes the view that such a sentence is ungrammatical. My own inclination is to agree that it is; but it is surprising to find Geach taking a stand on a mere fact of usage—'mere' because it can easily be imagined otherwise. Grammarians might unanimously admit, as a fact of idiom, that such a sentence was well-formed. If they did so, they might nevertheless favour a theory that it was elliptical for '*a* is in the same direction as *b*', as 'It happened the very day I arrived' is elliptical for 'It happened on the very day on which I arrived'. Even so, that would only be a *theory*, which we should not be bound to accept; and Geach's pattern for the explanation of count-nouns would provide a rationale for not accepting it, since it would be entirely consonant with that pattern of explanation that '. . . is the same direction as . . .' should be used, without ellipsis, as standing for an equivalence relation between lines, as '. . . is the same surman as . . .' was introduced as standing for such a relation between men. Geach would hold that '. . . is the same species as . . .' is grammatical and non-elliptical, and that it stands for an equivalence relation between individual animals; and he also thinks that '. . . is the same type-word as . . .' stands for various equivalence relations between token words, according as the types are taken as orthographic, phonetic, semantic or lexicographical. In each case, we merely consider the domain D (of individual animals or of token words) in the light of different relative identity-relations and hence of different principles of counting; but each token word *is* a type word of each kind, since it stands in the field of the relevant equivalence relation. But to each of these various cases, the considerations urged above apply: to learn to use the word 'species' or the phrase 'type-word', we have to come to know what can be predicated of a species, or of a type-word, and when such a predication is true; and, when we have learned this, there remains only the most tenuous sense in which we can say, conversely, that a type-word just *is* a token word, since the sort of predication admissible for the latter, e.g. 'is in Jones's handwriting', is not admissible for the former.

When we see how close a rectified Geachian explanation would come to a supplemented Fregean one, we see also that the Fregean one is not as restricted in application as we at first supposed. 'Species' and 'type-word' may both be subjected to Frege's treatment, provided that we allow a certain latitude in the construction of the basic term-forming operator: to 'the direction of . . .' will correspond 'the species to which . . . belongs' and 'the type of which . . . is a token'. Geach's 'official personage' example is more complex. First, as I remarked parenthetically on p. 571 of *FPL*, it is not really a genuine example; 'official personage' does not function in our language as a fully-fledged count-noun. We should never, for example, express the fact that one Prime Minister reversed the policy of his or her predecessor by saying that the Prime Minister first supported and then opposed devolution, or that some official personage did so. Secondly, as H. W. Noonan has pointed out in his Cambridge Ph.D. thesis, *Objects and Identity*, what Geach requires here is not a straightforward binary equivalence relation, but a four-termed relation with arguments for times, expressed by '*a* is (was) at *t* the same official personage as *b* is (was) at *t'*'. For the Fregean pattern we should similarly have a binary term-forming operator 'the official personage that *a* is at *t*'.

Geach's pattern required rectification in a manner he expressly denied, while Frege's required supplementation in a way he expressly acknowledged. Further, to deal with terms like 'species' and 'type', Frege's needed a relaxation of the form laid down for the term-forming operator; and both require extension to cover cases where there should be arguments for times. But, once all these changes have been made, there appears little more than an idiomatic difference between them, though one that tells in favour of Frege, since it shows up principally in the use of the phrase '. . . is an *X*', whose use according to Geach's pattern is seen to be irrelevant to the important features of the use of the count-noun '*X*', and for that reason confusing. But the really crucial question is that which arises concerning those count-nouns which cannot be explained in accordance with either pattern. We start with an equivalence relation defined over a domain D: but how did we form the conception of the domain D in the first place? If we say that '. . . is the same species as . . .' or '. . . belongs to the same species as . . .' expresses an equivalence relation defined over individual animals, and that '. . . is the same type-word as . . .' or '. . . is a token word of the same type as . . .' one defined over token words, we can surely not explain '. . . is the same individual animal as . . .' and '. . . is the same token word as . . .' as expressing equivalence relations defined over the same domains: for, in order to introduce such equivalence relations, we should already have to grasp the relevant domain, to know what an individual animal or a token word was. We here come upon a new class of count-nouns, which we may call 'basic count-nouns', of more funda-mental importance than the others: those that are neither derivative count-nouns nor explicable in accordance either with Frege's or with Geach's pattern. Just as, unless we admit its grammatically suspect use, '. . . is the same direction as . . .' expresses a relation whose domain of definition we can explain only as consisting of *directions*, and which therefore constitutes absolute identity over that domain, so the domains of definition of the relations expressed by '. . . is the same individual animal as . . .' and by '. . . is the same token word as . . .' can be explained only as con-sisting of individual animals and of token words respectively, so that the two relations again constitute absolute identity-relations over those domains.

The most serious defect of Chapter 16 of *FPL* was that it raised a question which it did not clearly answer, the question, namely, whether an interpretation of a formalized first-order language *without* identity presupposes an identity-relation over the domain of the variables. Consideration of Geach's discussion in *Reference and Generality* of the Heraclitean paradox makes this question inescapable, since, as we have seen, Geach derives from his thesis that there are many relative identity-relations, but no absolute one, the conclusion that a fundamental mistake is involved in the standard treatment of quantification. As already noted, I remarked on p. 554 of *FPL* that, if Geach is right that '. . . is the same water as . . .' is not to be equated to '. . . is water and is the same as . . .', this would resolve the paradox without the need for invoking any supposed mistake in the standard treatment of quantification. If, however, the interpretation of quantified sentences without identity *does* involve a surreptitious appeal to an identity-relation, Geach would have a ground for thinking that a conclusion about the interpretation of such sentences would follow from his thesis about identity. On pp. 554-5 of *FPL* I sketched an argument for saying that the interpretation of quantified sentences presupposes an identity-relation, turning on an appeal to existential quantifications of conjunctive sentences similar to that made in this chapter. But, on p. 555 of *FPL*, I pointed out that Geach himself repudiated just such an argument; we are therefore left, as I observed, unclear about what Geach supposes to be the connection between his thesis about identity and his remarks concerning quantification. The question arose again on p. 561, where I quoted Quine's review of *Reference and Generality*, in which Quine vehemently endorsed the claim that the interpretation of quantified sentences presupposes identity: 'grant quantification, and there remains no choice about identity'. On p. 562 of *FPL* I hedged on the issue, saying that, in explaining what constitutes an interpretation of a first-order formula without identity, no appeal is made to identity, and that there is therefore no formal entailment between Geach's rejection of absolute identity and his opposition to the classical treatment of quantification, but adding that our picture of a domain of objects such as is invoked in interpreting a first-order language is that of one on which is defined, or at least definable, an absolute relation of identity.

These remarks are true so far as they go, but they leave the matter obscure. The corresponding question for natural language is: does the understanding of an expression of generality involve appeal to a criterion of identity? We have seen, in effect, that the answer to this question is 'Yes'. A tacit appeal to a criterion of identity is involved in understanding any sentence of the form 'Some X is F', since 'F' is required to be true of whatever is the same X as anything of which it is true; and frequently, when 'some X' is followed by a conjunctive predicate, the appeal will be explicit. It is just this that shows that 'official personage' is not, as Geach supposes, a count-noun subject to his pattern of explanation, but, rather, a derivative count-noun meaning 'person who holds an official post', since the criterion of identity to which we must appeal in interpreting 'some official personage' is that given by '. . . is the same person as . . .', and not that given by '. . . is the same official personage as . . .', as Geach understands it. The only exception in natural language is the use of expressions of unrestricted generality, as in 'There is something sticky on the table-cloth', which I discussed on pp. 576–7 of *FPL*.

We can go rather further. In so far as any predicate or relational expression of natural language is considered as having been introduced as applying to or holding between *objects*, it, too, must be thought of as associated with some criterion of identity, or, perhaps, with a range of different ones, if the predicate is introduced as applying to objects of different categories. This is nearly a tautology: for the basic principle underlying Frege's introduction of the notion of a criterion of identity is that, in order to have a conception of any particular object, we have to know what constitutes the correct recognition of that object as the same again; so, if a predicate is introduced as applying to objects of one or more kinds, a grasp of the appropriate criterion of identity forms the basis of our apprehension of what objects of each of those kinds are. It was this idea which supported the assumption that was made in the preceding discussion that, if we grasp an equivalence relation, we must conceive of it as defined over some already understood domain of objects. The interesting question is which predicates and relational expressions it is correct to regard as having been introduced as defined over one or more domains of objects. One such, 'narrow-minded', was cited on p. 573 of *FPL*, and contrasted with adjectives for sensory qualities like 'red' and 'smooth'; but much more discussion is required before the line can be more exactly drawn. What concerns us at the moment is that it seems hard to construe Geach's notion of an equivalence relation, the starting-point for his pattern of explanation of a count-noun, otherwise than as being defined over a domain of objects, while Frege is quite explicit that this is what he intends.

Exactly the same, however, is to be said about the standard conception of an interpretation of a first-order language. The first step in setting up such an interpretation is to specify a domain for the variables. The normal method of doing so would be by the use of a count-noun: we might take the domain to consist of all the men from Adam to the present day, or of the universities in Western Europe. If we specify the domain in this way, we supply the criterion of identity for objects in the domain by the mere use of the count-noun, with which a specific criterion of identity is associated. The same applies if we specify the domain by giving a list of the members of the domain: a list is a string of proper names, and a criterion of identity is associated with each proper name, so that the list itself would supply a criterion of identity associated with the domain. It is evident that any means of specifying the domain which did not supply a criterion of identity, for instance by saying that it was to consist of things that were in London at a specific time, would be inadequate: it would fail precisely because it would not tell us what would count as a determinate interpretation of any one-place predicate over this domain. As against this, Geach argues that, in specifying a domain by means of a list, we have no warrant to concern ourselves with whether the list contains repetitions. This is untrue: if the list contains distinct entries referring to the same object, this will impose a restriction on what we are entitled to admit as an interpretation of a predicate over that domain effected by specifying, for each entry on the list, whether or not the predicate was to be true of the object referred to. But, even if this were not so, such a list would determine a finest possible identity relation over the domain, namely that holding between each entry on the list and itself, and between no entry and any other entry. To escape this conclusion, Geach argues that we may come to recognize some of the entries on the list as not being proper names after all, but only common names, shared by objects between which we can now discriminate; there is no limit to the fineness of the discriminations we may come to be able to make, and hence to the fineness of the equivalence relations we can define over a given domain. In the same way, we have no warrant to assume that the relation expressed by '. . . is the same token word as . . .' is the finest possible equivalence relation over the relevant domain. If we do assume that, then that relation is, in effect, an absolute identity-relation over that domain; and Geach has set his face against the possibility of any relation of absolute identity. At the moment, 'token word' represents the finest discrimination we are able to make: but we may later be able, for any given token word, say the first word on the (token) page you are currently reading, to discern many different objects (let us call them nekot words), all of which are the same token word as one another.

Though I shall not argue the point at length here, I do not think that this conception can be made coherent. A proper name, just because it has a criterion of identity associated with it, cannot turn out after all to be a common name; if there are found to be two or more objects with equally good claims to be its bearer, then it has no reference at all, but we cannot turn it into a common name by appealing to a different criterion of identity. Even without any great powers of discernment, we could easily introduce some notion of nekot words, if we wished; for instance, for printed words, we could divide their life-history into stages, taking each boundary between stages to mark the replacement of one nekot word by another. Having done so, we could, if we wished, substitute a domain of nekot words for one of token words. But we should then have a new domain; there would be no sense in which it remained the same as the old one. In particular, we could not, as Geach appears to suppose, motivate the change from token words to nekot words by citing some predicate, defined over the old domain, which was true of one nekot word and false of another that was nevertheless the same token word, on Geach's way of speaking, i.e. a different stage in the history of the same token word; no such predicate could have been defined over the old domain. But, however this may be, it in no way calls in question the distinction, within the language as it is at any one time, between basic count-nouns and others. We might have a notion of nekot words, on the basis of which we could introduce the count-noun 'token-word' in Geach's, or in Frege's, way; but we do not have such a notion, and we therefore do not introduce the term in either way. If there are to be substantival general terms introduced after the manner of Geach or of Frege, then there must be some which were not so introduced; it is not necessary to maintain that there are any which, the language being different, could not have been so introduced.

How, then, are basic count-nouns introduced? If the criterion of identity associated with them does not coincide with the criterion for the obtaining of some equivalence relation over a previously understood domain, what is it the criterion *for*? I see no reason to modify the answer I gave in Chapter 16 of *FPL*. We cannot give a correct representation of our language if we do not recognize, as underlying that level at which we may be said to refer to objects and to predicate things of them, a more fundamental level at which there is as yet no reference to or discernment of objects; formalized languages serve to regiment only the higher, less primitive level. At the primitive level, what takes the place of the use, at the higher level, of proper names and other singular terms is the use of demonstratives, accompanied by the appropriate kind of pointing gesture. Demonstratives, attached to count-nouns, continue to be used at the higher level, as when someone, pointing or using some substitute gesture, begins a sentence with 'That man . . .'; but what marks off the use of demonstratives that occurs at the most primitive level from the use of proper names and other singular terms is not, primarily, the ostensive component, but the fact that no criterion of identity is invoked or appealed to. At this level, we employ what on p. 232 of *FPL* I called 'crude predications', sentences of the form 'That is *P*', where, since no criterion of identity is presupposed, we cannot be said to be predicating anything of an *object*; '*P*' must be a predicate of such a kind that the truth of what is said can be judged on the basis of the pointing gesture alone, without our having any conception of what would count as pointing to the same thing again. '*P*' must therefore be a predicate like 'smooth', 'red' or 'sticky', or a term like 'fog', expressing what Strawson, in *Individuals*, called a 'feature concept', and not one like 'narrow-minded' or 'widely travelled'.

The transition to the next level, at which we refer to objects and apply predicates to them, takes place in several stages. As Strawson points out in the same work, 'That is a cat' or 'There is a cat' cannot be regarded as a crude predication, or as what he calls a 'feature placing statement', because one of the characteristic properties of cats is their shape; a cat is not a lump of feline material. But, as Strawson remarks, one can learn to recognize the presence of a cat without yet knowing that there is any place for distinguishing between the reappearance of the same cat and the appearance of a different one, any more than there is with rainbows.[1] The transition, in all its stages, may be represented as mediated by a progressive acquisition of the use of an expression of the form '. . . is the same *X* as . . .', where '*X*' is a basic count-noun. The simplest use of such an expression is in a sentence of the form, 'This is the same *X* as that', accompanied by two pointing gestures, a form of sentence which on p. 573 of *FPL* I labelled a 'statement of identification'. This is, of course, a schematization of what actually occurs: a child does not in fact acquire the use of the word 'cat' in the first place by learning to point simultaneously to, say, the head and the tail of a cat and to say, 'This is the same cat as that'. Nevertheless, this schematic account correctly represents what is involved in advancing from crude predications to the use of basic count-nouns, namely the acquisition of what Frege called a criterion of identity. A statement of identification, of the form 'This is the same *X* as that', does not, of itself, take us beyond the primitive level of language, since it is itself merely a crude relational statement, like 'This is darker than that': statements of identification are important as providing a *basis* for an advance to the next level of language, at which there is reference to ostensible objects (objects that can be pointed to). And in this respect, too, the schematic

[1] See *Individuals*, London, 1960, pp. 202–7.

account is faithful to what is involved in making such an advance. Since identity is a relation between objects, any criterion of identity must be a criterion for the identity of objects of a certain sort: but it is a mistake to suppose that the criterion must consist in the recognition that a certain equivalence relation obtains between objects of the same, or another, sort; this seems to be the fundamental mistake underlying Geach's views, and leading him to deny the existence of any absolute relation of identity. '. . . is the same X as . . .', as used in statements of identification, is *like* an expression for an equivalence relation, in that, in an obvious sense, it must be symmetric and transitive; but it does not stand for such a relation, since it is not at this stage used to express a relation between *objects* at all. To grasp the criterion of the identity associated with a basic count-noun, it is not necessary to have any prior conception of objects of any sort.

The first advance into the higher level of language is effected by the use of a count-noun in referential position, together with a predicate of the kind that has previously occurred in crude predications, as in 'The cat is wet' or 'The cat is black'; in such cases, however, modifications will be introduced in accordance with the fact that something is now being predicated of an *object*, for instance the possibility of qualifications like 'The cat is mostly black' or 'The cat is partly black'. The next step is the introduction of predications that can be made only of objects (of certain sorts), as in 'The cat is asleep'. The really important step of course occurs when the criterion of identity is extended over time. In practice, this is principally mediated by the introduction of proper names of objects of the appropriate sorts; it may be schematically represented by statements of identification of an extended type, involving a relative clause and the past tense, namely those of the form 'This is the same X as the one which . . .'. Obviously, the acquisition of a criterion of identity over time is a long process; a child has not yet a full comprehension of the changes an object may undergo while retaining its identity, nor, therefore, of those which it *cannot* undergo.

I thus remain essentially of the same opinion as when I originally wrote *FPL*, Chapter 16: as stated in that chapter, on p. 577, the picture of reality as an amorphous lump, not at the outset articulated into objects, is a correct one; but Geach's presentation of it misses coherence, because it fails to make the crucial distinction between the most primitive level of language, at which we have not yet effected any such articulation, and the higher levels, at which we have. Any reference to objects, properly so called, and any predication of objects, involves the tacit or explicit invocation of a criterion of identity, as does quantification over objects, in an interpreted formalized language, or generalization about them, in natural language. There is therefore no place, at this level, for competing relative identity-relations. That is not to say that we have any right to rule out of order the use of an expression of the form '. . . is the same X as . . .' to stand for an equivalence relation broader than identity; it is to say that Geach's pattern for the introduction of count-nouns *cannot*, without supplementation, serve as a mode of explanation for any substantival general terms, and *does not*, even when supplemented, represent a true account of how any such terms are in practice used. To convert Frege's notion of criteria of identity into the doctrine of relative identity-relations is to distort it. For a large range of count-nouns, those I called above 'abstract count-nouns', the associated criterion of identity is indeed related to an equivalence relation defined over objects of a sort already grasped; but, when this equivalence relation holds between two distinct objects of that sort, the abstract count-noun so introduced can apply to at most one of them. For basic count-nouns, however, the criterion of identity does not rest upon an equivalence relation: it can be represented, rather, as resting on the use, at the primitive level, of an expression resembling one for an equivalence relation, but whose two argument-places do not require to be filled by terms denoting objects at all.

I have not yet fully redeemed the promise given early on in this chapter, to set the record completely straight concerning restricted and unrestricted quantification. Let us begin by asking what is the difference that Geach sees between the forms 'Some X is F' and 'For some y, y is an X and y is F'. Suppose that 'X' is 'surman'. Then 'For some y, y is a surman and y is F' is true just in case there is something of which we can truly predicate both '. . . is a surman' and '. . . is F'; for instance, if 'F' is 'fat', it will be true if there exists a fat man with a surname. One way of putting this is that 'For some y, y is an X and y is F' is true just in case there is some proper name 'a', either already in the language or introducible into it, such that 'a is a surman and a is F' is a true sentence; with this Geach makes it clear that he would agree. But this is not enough for the truth of 'Some X is F', which presumably depends upon its being possible truly to predicate '. . . is F' of a surman, in just the sense of 'predicating something of a surman' explained above in connection with sentences of this form: '. . . is F' must be a predicate such that, if it is true of y, and y is the same surman as z, it must be true of z. Geach would, I think, accept as a condition of the truth of 'Some surman is F' that there be a proper name 'a' *for* a surman, either already in the language or introducible into it, such that 'a is F' is a true sentence; here a proper name is a name *for* a surman if the criterion of identity associated with it is that expressed by 'the same surman'.[1] We might, though Geach does not, introduce the predicate '. . . is A SURMAN', as applicable, not to everything of which '. . . is a surman' is true, but only to such objects as have associated with them the criterion of identity given by 'same surman'. Possibly Geach might object to this, holding that, while a criterion of identity is always associated with a proper name, it is incorrect to speak of such a criterion as being associated with an object; but, at any rate, the truth-value of every sentence formed by putting a proper name into the argument-place of the predicate has been fixed. Using this predicate, we could say that 'Some surman is *F*' is equivalent to 'For some *y*, *y* is A SURMAN and *y* is *F*', which is much stronger than 'For some *y*, *y* is a surman and *y* is *F*'. I do not think that Geach would like this way of putting the matter; but it serves to bring out the difference that he sees as obtaining between the two forms.

This explanation does not turn on any peculiarity of the 'surman' example; we could similarly distinguish between 'Some man is *F*', taken as equivalent to 'For some *y*, *y* is A MAN and *y* is *F*', and 'For some *y*, *y* is a man and *y* is *F*'. For this to be more than a merely notional distinction, there must be a genuine possibility of something's being a man but not A MAN. In 'Existential or Particular Quantifier?', Geach indicates what this might be. Acknowledging that, as urged on p. 556 of *FPL*, his Heraclitean example suffered from the use of a mass term, 'water', alongside a count-noun, 'river', without reference to the logical difference between them, he provides a new version of the argument. 'In England the members of the Heralds' College have a range of special names, such as "Garter", "Rouge Dragon", "Portcullis". These are grammatically, and I think also logically, proper names. Each of these is a name *for* a herald; by repeated use of it we have in mind not one and the same man, but one and the same herald—the filler (whoever he may be) of one and the same heraldic office'.[2] If, between successive visits of Brown to the Heralds' College, Witherspoon, who had been Portcullis, dies and is succeeded by Murgatroyd, then Brown saw a herald one week and saw the same herald the next, but did not see the same man on the two occasions, although every herald is a man; the paradox is thus reconstructed. Now, we may say, Portcullis is a man, all right, but he is not A MAN. Hence, if on Brown's second visit, Portcullis rescinds the decision made by Portcullis on Brown's first visit, the sentence 'Some herald rescinded his previous decision' is true,

[1] 'Existential or Particular Quantifier?', p. 145.
[2] P. 146.

as is the sentence 'For some y, y is a man and y rescinded his previous decision'; but 'Some man rescinded his previous decision' is not (or, rather, not on that score). I think that this accords with the account Geach now wishes to give of the form 'Some X is F', though, as he is not quite explicit, I am not completely sure.

We may agree that, with this example, Geach has shown how a distinction may be drawn between restricted quantification and the form of sentence, involving unrestricted quantification, to which he claimed that it was incorrect to say that it could be reduced. We may, indeed, doubt whether we have much need for the distinction, since, as we have seen, count-nouns do not, in general, behave as Geach supposes. Heralds are a particular kind of official personage, and I have already expressed scepticism over whether we really talk—or whether those who are accustomed to discussing heralds really talk—about Portcullis as a continuing individual, persisting through changes of office-holder, any more than we speak of the Monarch of England as a single individual whose head was once cut off and who is now female. Even if we did, then, as observed by Noonan, this terminology would not exactly exemplify Geach's pattern, because of the temporal aspect. We could hardly say that a particular herald is, as such, a man, since no herald is the same man as once he was; we can say only that, at any given time, each herald is the same man as himself, and so that every herald is, at every moment of his existence, a man (heralds may, of course, enjoy a discontinuous existence). But none of this is very much to the point. The fact is that, in this matter, we have a sharp illustration of how tangled the entire discussion of identity, relative and absolute, has become. Geach's distinction between 'Some X is F' and 'For some y, y is an X and y is F' reflects an acknowledgment of precisely that feature of the use of an expression of the form 'some X', where 'X' is a count-noun, which is *not* provided for in his pattern for the introduction of count-nouns, and ignored in his declaration that this pattern needs no supplementation he had failed to provide; on this interpretation of 'some X', it cannot be true to say, 'Some surman lives in Leeds'. The defence of the unreducibility of restricted to unrestricted quantification requires a recognition of the need for such a supplementation.

But even this is of less importance than the fact that, by this means, Geach has shown that, under certain conditions, restricted quantification is *not*, indeed, reducible to the unrestricted variety. The condition is that, if '. . . is an X' corresponds to '. . . is a man', and '. . . is an X^*' to '. . . is A MAN', there should be objects of which '. . . is an X' is true but '. . . is an X^*' is false. And this does show a link between Geach's thesis about identity and his criticism of Frege's conception, inherited by Quine, of restricted quantification as reducible to unrestricted: just that link which, on pp. 553–4 of *FPL*, I asked after but failed to locate.

Was I then wrong to argue, on p. 554 of *FPL*, that Geach's thesis about identity already resolved the Heraclitean paradox without the need for any further thesis about quantification? The argument was that, if Geach was right to say that 'x is the same water as y' does not mean 'x is water and x is the same as y', then the rendering of 'Heraclitus bathed in some water yesterday, and bathed in the same water today' as 'For some y, y is water and Heraclitus bathed in y yesterday, and Heraclitus bathed in y today' collapsed, and with it, the paradox: so no further problem then arose about quantification as such. Let us transpose this to Geach's revised example about heralds. Suppose that we render:

(1*) Brown called on some herald last week, and called on the same herald this week

as:

(3*) For some y, y is a herald, and Brown called on y last week, and Brown called on y this week.

And suppose that we also render:

(4*) Brown called on some man last week, and called on the same man this week

as:

(6*) For some y, y is a man, and Brown called on y last week, and Brown called on y this week.

And suppose that we represent:

(i*) Whatever is a herald is a man

as:

(ii*) For any y, if y is a herald, y is a man.

Then, as before, (6*) follows from (3*) and (ii*); but (4*) does not follow from (1*) and (i*) (cf. *FPL*, pp. 553–4). My observation, transposed to this example, was that Geach already holds that 'x is the same man as y' does not mean 'x is a man and x is the same as y', and that this of itself implies that (4*) is not to be rendered by (6*). How, then, should (4*) be rendered? Presumably by:

(6**) For some *x*, for some *y*, Brown called on *x* last week, and Brown called on *y* this week, and *x* is the same man as *y*.

Likewise, (1*) should be rendered:

(3**) For some *x*, for some *y*, Brown called on *x* last week, and Brown called on *y* this week, and *x* is the same herald as *y*.

And now, given Geach's doctrine that '*x* is the same herald as *y* and *x* is a man and *y* is a man' can be true without implying the truth of '*x* is the same man as *y*', the paradox has disappeared: for (6**) gives no appearance of following from (3**) and (ii*). So it appears that I was right to say that Geach's doctrine about identity was sufficient to resolve the paradox without appeal to any special doctrine about quantification.

My claim was correct: but only on a technicality, as people say of acquittals. Identity, relative or absolute, is brought explicitly into the matter by Geach's choice of a mode of expression, '. . . bathed in the same river', or, in the amended example, 'Brown called on some herald last week, and called on *the same herald* this week'. By using this form of words, Geach expressly made the matter one relating to identity; and then, of course, his doctrine of relative rather than absolute identity was enough to resolve the paradox. But identity need not have been made to appear explicitly in question. (1*) could have been expressed as 'Brown called on some herald both last week and this week', and (4*) as 'Brown called on some man both last week and this week'; and then it would have had to be *argued* that an appropriate criterion of identity is being appealed to in each case—that expressed by 'same herald' in (1*) and that expressed by 'same man' in (4*). Such an argument would have shown precisely what has been maintained in the present chapter, namely that the use of a phrase of the form 'some *X*' tacitly involves an identity-relation, normally that expressed by '. . . is the same *X* as . . .': *that* is the link between Geach's doctrine about identity and his doctrine about quantification.

I cannot, however, be blamed too severely for not having represented the matter in this way in *FPL*. On pp. 554-5, I actually suggested this as an interpretation of Geach, one that would explain the 'connection between his rejection of the one absolute relation of identity in favour of many relativized identity-relations and his opposition to the "orthodox" conception of unrestricted quantification'.[1] The interpretation I suggested

---

[1] P. 554. I have altered this wording slightly in FPL_2, so as to avoid any suggestion that Geach is opposed to unrestricted quantification as such.

was that 'the classical semantics of first-order predicate calculus even without identity presupposes the spurious notion of the single absolute relation of identity'; the understanding of formulas containing more than one occurrence of a variable bound by any one quantifier, such as 'For some x, $F(x)$ and $G(x)$', would tacitly appeal to an absolute identity-relation. And, likewise, I observed on p. 555 of *FPL* that the same would go, *mutatis mutandis*, for restricted quantification: a sentence of the form 'For some man y, $F(y)$ and $G(y)$' would contain a tacit appeal to the identity-relation expressed by '. . . is the same man as . . .', and similarly for other count-nouns 'A' in place of 'man'. This, at least as applied to restricted quantification, was surely the view that Geach ought to have taken, and would indeed, as I observed, have explained the connection between his views on identity and on quantification. I even remarked that we might take Geach's preference for phrases such as 'that same A' over repeated bound variables as subliminal propaganda for such a view. But, as I also remarked in *FPL*, p. 555, Geach had, in *Reference and Generality*, p. 190, expressly rejected the view, saying that 'subject-uses of "the same A" signify only that a number of predicates are supposed to be true all together of a certain individual for which the common name "A" stands; and our understanding of "true all together" depends not on the difficult notion of a criterion of identity, but on the much clearer notion of a predicable's being formed out of predicables by a truth-functional connective (viz. by "and")'. Since Geach himself had so explicitly rejected the very interpretation that would have explained how the different parts of his theory hung together, I naturally had some difficulty in seeing what the explanation was. If Geach had been fully explicit about his present interpretation of the form 'Some A is F', I should have felt obliged, in *FPL₂*, to qualify this quotation from *Reference and Generality* by a remark to the effect that Geach now accepted the interpretation he there rejected; but, in the circumstances, I have felt that the risk of misrepresenting him prohibited me from attributing to him something which, so far as I know, he has not expressly said.

Why should Geach have rejected this natural—and surely correct—interpretation of his argument? Possibly just because he wished to defend unrestricted quantification. If restricted quantification involves a tacit appeal to a relative identity-relation, then unrestricted quantification presumably involves a tacit appeal to an absolute relation of identity, as I said on p. 554 of *FPL* in introducing the suggested interpretation: since Geach wanted to defend unrestricted quantification, but to reject an absolute relation of identity, it would have been dangerous for him to argue that restricted quantification involves an appeal to a (relativized) identity-relation.

On pp. 557-8 of *FPL*, I stated how, in *Reference and Generality*,[1] Geach did explain unrestricted quantification: namely for any predicate '*F*', the sentence 'For some *x*, *x* is *F*', where the quantifier is unrestricted, is to be understood as being true provided that, for *some* count-noun '*A*', the sentence 'Some *A* is *F*' is true. This is equivalent, Geach thinks, to saying that 'For some *x*, *x* is *F*' is true just in case there is *some* proper name '*a*', already in or introducible into the language, such that '*a* is *F*' is true, since for any such proper name there will be a count-noun '*A*' (already in or introducible into the language) such that 'the same *A*' gives the criterion of identity associated with '*a*'. At least, the equivalence holds whenever '. . . is *F*' is what Geach calls a 'Shakespearean' predicate (p. 165), i.e. an extensional one. On this, I made, on p. 560 of *FPL₁*, the following comment. 'First, it seemed that Geach wanted to reject unrestricted quantification altogether. Then, that, while he allowed it, he wanted to explain it in terms of restricted quantification, rather than the other way round. Next, it appeared that a direct explanation of unrestricted quantification could after all be given, though one which Geach claimed as being, on analysis, essentially equivalent to the explanation in terms of restricted quantification; so the emphasis now was on a substitutional explanation of the quantifier in contrast to the classical explanation. But now, finally, it turns out that, apart from the irrelevant case of non-Shakespearean predicates, the substitutional and the classical explanations of unrestricted quantification coincide: after all, if we may legitimately consider the totality of proper names which either belong to the language or could coherently be added to it, we may equally consider the totality of objects (which are or could be named). Thus Geach's polemic against the "orthodox" (i.e. wrong) conception of unrestricted first-level quantification ends by completely evaporating'.

This comment, though it may be judged unfair, arose out of a genuine puzzlement as to what it was that Geach was maintaining about unrestricted quantification. The initial remark, that it seemed at first that Geach wanted to reject unrestricted quantification, was, no doubt, unjustified. But, in explaining 'For some *x*, *x* is *F*' as meaning that, for some count-noun '*A*', 'Some *A* is *F*' is true, Geach was undoubtedly explaining unrestricted in terms of restricted quantification; and, in explaining it as meaning that, for some proper name '*a*', '*a* is *F*' is true, he was undoubtedly

---

[1] Pp. 154-5.

explaining it directly. Moreover, on pp. 155–8 of *Reference and Generality*, Geach does lay very considerable stress on substitutional quantification, remarking against Quine that 'on my specification as to the use of "for some x", the question "For which entity x?" will not arise at all. For unrestricted quantifiers construed as I suggest, there will be no question which entities they "refer to" or "range over"; such questions seem appropriate only because we wrongly assimilate the use of quantifiers now under discussion to the use of quantifiers when they are tacitly restricted to some "universe", which will be delimited by some substantival term'.[1] And yet, as I remark, the restriction to 'Shakespearean' predicates undoes the effect of insisting on substitutional quantification. We could just as well have interpreted the unrestricted quantifiers classically, that is to say, ontically or objectually (to offer a choice between two unlovely words); the 'assimilation' complained of by Geach would do no harm at all. Thus I think that I was right, on the strength of *Reference and Generality*, to say that the polemic against the 'orthodox' view appeared in the end to evaporate.

We nevertheless now know that this appearance was illusory. We have seen in the present chapter that Geach does have a genuine distinction to draw between restricted and unrestricted quantification, at least one that is genuine if we grant his premiss that something can be the same man as itself without being A MAN. This was the very distinction to which the interpretation that I suggested on pp. 554–5 of *FPL* would immediately have led: an interpretation which, as I have here explained, I expressed myself in *FPL* as tempted to put on Geach's doctrine, but as compelled to reject because Geach had expressly rejected it on p. 190 of *Reference and Generality*; hence my impression that the thesis had evaporated. In the circumstances, I have tried to put the matter right, on p. 560 of FPL_2, by various emendations. First, I have removed the suggestion that Geach seemed at the outset to want to disallow unrestricted quantification entirely. Secondly, I have softened the suggestion that the thesis evaporates by saying instead that it appears to do so. Finally, I have replaced the entire short paragraph at the bottom of p. 560, in which I said, in FPL_1, that Geach's position 'ultimately dissolves in confusion', by one encapsulating the position adopted by Geach in 'Existential or Particular Quantifier?' and expounded in the present chapter.

Frege rejected the traditional logic of terms. There were several motives for his doing so. One was his perception, on which he insisted so frequently,

[1] Pp. 157–8.

that the distinction of subject and predicate had no place in logic. Another was his clear perception of the radical distinction between a singular and a general term, a distinction on which Geach, in company with Leśniewski, wants to go back. I regard this as a retrograde step, but shall not argue that here. It would, nevertheless, have been possible, and even natural, for Frege to have taken the universal and existential quantifiers as *binary* operators, that is to say, as acting simultaneously on *two* predicates as arguments. It would have been natural, first because the traditional logic treated the basic forms of categorical proposition as all involving *two* terms, and secondly because the notion of a binary quantifier is more general: the quantifiers occurring in 'Most F's are G', 'There are more F's than G's' and 'There are just as many F's as G's', with the last of which Frege was especially concerned, are all irreducibly binary. Nevertheless, Frege had the great insight to perceive that, within a given context, that is, when operating with a fixed domain or universe of discourse, restrictions of the universal or existential quantifier could be handled by means of sentential operations: 'for any positive x, ... x ...' could be represented as 'for any (number) x, if x is positive, then ... x ...', and 'for some positive x, ... x ...' as 'for some (number) x, x is positive and ... x ...', the quantifiers being treated as unary, i.e. as taking only a single predicate as argument. On my view, it was a false step to generalize this insight by throwing away a second traditional notion, the conception of the universe of discourse, whereby, in any given context, we restrict the range of generality to some specifiable domain. Indeed, I think it to be the step, above all, which led Frege to set up a logical theory containing Russell's contradiction: *the* false step which was responsible for the disaster which overtook Frege in mid-career. But it is very readily intelligible that it should have happened. Rejecting the distinction between subject and predicate, and insisting on that between singular terms and general ones, were manifest successes; treating universal and existential generalization as unary operations was equally so, and doubtless a yet more surprising one. Who, then, could have suspected that so great a danger lurked in the simple extension of a successful idea that led from taking 'for every positive number x' to mean 'for every number x, if x is positive' to taking 'for every number x' to mean 'for every (object) x, if x is a number'?

The difference between, e.g., 'all' and 'most' is sharp: given a domain D for the variables, and a quantifier meaning 'For all x's in D, ... x ...', we can, by the use of sentential operators, express 'All F's in D are G'; whereas, given only a quantifier meaning 'For most x's in D, ... x ...', we cannot so express 'Most F's in D are G'. It is for this reason that Frege could take the universal quantifier to be unary, whereas 'most' is irreducibly binary. We might express this difference between 'all' and 'most' by saying that, if we start with 'all' considered as a binary quantifier, but with a *fixed* first argument, we can express in terms of it the general binary universal quantifier, for any predicate as first argument whose extension is contained in that of the fixed one, but that we cannot do the same thing for 'most': hence, relative to a domain representing the extension of the fixed first argument, 'all' may be taken as unary, though 'most' may not. Frege's mistake was to conclude erroneously from this that 'all' may be taken as absolutely unary, or, equivalently, that its first argument may be taken to be an all-embracing predicate applying to all objects whatsoever, a conclusion that does not follow from the premiss. One reason why absolutely unrestricted quantification is not intelligible emerges from the present discussion. To provide an interpretation for bound variables, we require an identity-relation defined over the domain; but the formal concept 'object' does not supply such an identity-relation.

It was at this point that I appear seriously to have misinterpreted Geach. As he has now made clearer, he attacked the 'orthodox' doctrine, not for treating unrestricted quantification as intelligible, which Geach himself believes it to be, but for taking restricted quantification to be reducible to it. It is far from obvious that such a position is open to anyone. On the face of it, if unrestricted quantification is intelligible, then quantification restricted to A's can be expressed by 'For every x, if x is an A, then . . . x . . .'. That, for Geach, this does *not* follow is due to his surprising view, previously explained in the present chapter, that, where 'A' is a count-noun, '. . . is an A' can be true of objects other than A's, i.e., in our previous notation, of objects of which '. . . is an A^*' is not true. *This* thesis was not stated in *Reference and Generality*, and so I think that, in so far as I was to blame, it was for failing to study Geach's writings subsequent to *Reference and Generality*; reliance on that book alone could hardly give the key to what made it possible for him to hold that restricted quantification could not be reduced to unrestricted quantification without also holding the latter to be unintelligible. Nevertheless, almost all the discussion in *FPL* up to p. 567 was concerned with the former point, the explicability of restricted quantification in terms of unrestricted. But on pp. 567–8 of FPL_1, I criticized Geach for attacking modern formal logicians for treating quantification as unrestricted, assuming that he was opposed to such an interpretation. I did so on the ground that modern logicians do *not* treat quantification as unrestricted, but demand, of an interpretation, that it specify a domain for the variables. Now, indeed, for some, among them Quine, this is no more than a matter of convenience. Most logics, including classical logic, have what in *Elements of Intuitionism*[1] I called the *relativization property*. Let C be any closed formula, and let $Q(x)$ be any formula with one free variable x. The relativization C_Q of C to $Q(x)$ is obtained by replacing every subformula $\forall y \ D(y)$ of C by $\forall y \ (Q(y) \rightarrow D(y))$ (with suitable changes of bound variables), and every subformula $\exists z \ E(z)$ by $\exists z \ (Q(z) \ \& \ E(z))$. Then a logic has the relativization property if, whenever a closed formula B is derivable in it from closed formulas $A^1, \ldots, A^n$, then also B_Q is derivable from $\exists x \ Q(x)$ and $A_Q^1, \ldots, A_Q^n$. The property is not trivial: a logic that does not have it is the logic IC^+ obtained by adding as axioms to intuitionistic logic all instances of the schema $\forall x \ (P \vee R(x)) \rightarrow (P \vee \forall x \ R(x))$, as pointed out in *Elements of Intuitionism*.[2] But the relativization property is a desirable one, and most logics that are studied possess it. If a logic has this property, it is valid over any non-empty (inhabited) subdomain of any domain over which it is valid: hence, for such a logic, it will be convenient not to assume a single fixed domain for all interpretations, but to allow the domain to vary from one interpretation to another, so that restriction to the domain in which we are interested does not require explicit expression in the formulas. But, for the overwhelming majority of logicians, this is, as I said on p. 568 of *FPL*, not a convenience, but a necessity. They do not think it possible intelligibly to quantify over all objects whatever, that is, over a domain which includes every domain over which it is possible intelligibly to quantify; hence, to interpret any formula, we have explicitly to specify the intended domain.

Thinking that Geach shared this latter view, I criticized him for insinuating that logicians generally rejected it. I got him exactly wrong: he does *not* share it, but believes, as Frege did, in the possibility of absolutely unrestricted quantification over an all-embracing domain; and he now feels critical of contemporary logicians (other than Quine) for rejecting this view. This was difficult to tell from *Reference and Generality*, where the 'orthodox' and 'generally accepted' view, attributed to Quine, was said to be that restricted quantification is reducible to unrestricted; obviously, Geach did not then believe that the generality of modern logicians reject unrestricted quantification altogether. Fortunately, on p. 567 of *FPL* I mentioned only Geach's criticism of modern logicians for accepting the reduction of restricted to unrestricted quantification, not for believing in the latter; so, apart from softening 'no modern logician' in Gilbertian

[1] Oxford, 1977, p. 205.
[2] Pp. 206–7.

style to 'hardly any', I have felt no change to be demanded on that page. But, on p. 568, I have, in *FPL*₂, altered two sentences which implied that Geach saw acceptance of unrestricted quantification as an error. The amended sentences still ascribe to him the view that most modern logicians accept unrestricted quantification. So he must have thought when writing *Reference and Generality*, or he would not have spoken of 'orthodoxy' as he did. He appears to have changed his view of what is orthodox since then; he was orthodox where he thought himself heretical and heretical where he thought himself orthodox. But I could not work in a reference to this change of perspective without recasting two whole pages, which I had no licence to do.

I shall not here argue further against the Fregean view espoused by Geach, that we may quantify unrestrictedly over a single superdomain of all objects; I reserve further discussion for *Frege: Philosophy of Mathematics*. But I hope that I now really have set the record straight in the matter of unrestricted quantification; and, in the process, it has emerged into just how intricate a tangle the whole topic of relative and absolute identity had been twisted. I regret that unpicking it has been so laborious a process for the reader to follow; I regret also any part I had in creating the tangle. I think that the tangle has been partly due to Geach's not realizing to how great an extent his later reflections on the subject represented changes of mind, or at least additions to the doctrine as set out in *Reference and Generality* of theses which could not possibly have been guessed from that text and which crucially altered the interpretation of it: I do not think that very much of what I wrote in Chapter 16 of *FPL* could be convicted of being a misinterpretation of the text of *Reference and Generality* taken on its own. But I am seriously at fault for having published a critique of that work, written some years before, without revising it in the light of Geach's subsequent contributions to the subject. I hope at least that I have now helped to disentangle the confusion I may have had some part in bringing about.

The topic bears on Frege's philosophy of logic in three ways. The most obvious, already discussed, is how, in general, his notion of a criterion of identity is to be understood. The second, also already canvassed, is whether he was right to believe in a fixed all-encompassing domain of objects. The third concerns his view of count-nouns as predicative in character. One of the features of what Frege calls a 'concept' is that some determinate number belongs to it: the copula followed by a count-noun, with or without some further qualification by means of adjectives or relative clauses, is thus a pre-eminent example of an expression which Frege would regard as standing for a concept. Thus, in a footnote to § 65 of *Grundlagen*, he says, 'A concept is for me a possible predicate of a singular judgeable content'. In 'Über Begriff und Gegenstand', p. 193, he says, 'The concept —as I understand the word—is predicative', and in a footnote he adds, 'It is, namely, the referent (*Bedeutung*) of a grammatical predicate'; and on p. 198, referring to the passage just cited from *Grundlagen*, he remarks that he had not at that time made the distinction between sense and reference, and therefore then combined the two distinct notions of a thought and a truth-value in the single expression 'judgeable content'. For this reason, he says, he no longer wholly approves of the explanation he gave in *Grundlagen*, but remains essentially of the same opinion; he then goes on to repeat the same formulation as before, 'a concept is the referent of a predicate'. Again, § 56 of *Grundgesetze*, vol. II, opens with the words, 'A definition of a concept (possible predicate) must be complete, it must determine unambiguously for every object whether it falls under the concept (whether the predicate can be truly asserted of it) or not'. In the posthumous 'Logik in der Mathematik' of 1914 he says. 'The concept has a predicative character.'[1]

Now was Wittgenstein right to criticize Frege for this, saying, in the *Remarks on the Foundations of Mathematics*,[2] 'A concept is not essentially a predicate. We do indeed sometimes say: "This thing is not a bottle" but it is certainly not essential to the language-game with the concept "bottle" that such judgments occur in it'? The question is not easy to answer, precisely because Frege's analysis of language applies only at a level higher than the most fundamental one. Regarded as part of a formal language, the semantic role of a proper name, for instance, is completely fixed when it has been specified to stand for an object. We might say that, on Frege's own principles, this leaves out one of the most important features of the sense of the proper name, namely its having associated with it a particular criterion of identity; but we might prefer to say, instead, that, when it was spelled out in detail what it was for it to stand for that object which is its referent, the relevant criterion of identity would have to be invoked, implicitly or explicitly, to explain what an object of that sort is and what it is for a proper name to stand for such an object. It would be more illuminating to say neither of these things, but to say that the criterion of identity associated with the name had been swallowed up in the characterization of the domain. To grasp the intended domain over which the individual variables are to range, we have to know what

[1] *N.S.*, p. 246, *P.W.*, p. 228, cf. *N.S.*, p. 231, *P.W.*, p. 214.
[2] Revised edition, Cambridge. Mass., and London, 1978, v–47.

objects belong to it, and this involves knowing the criterion or criteria of identity to apply to them. It has been one of the principal themes of the present chapter that an interpretation of a formal language with a syntactic structure such as that introduced into formal logic by Frege does indeed assume a determinate relation of identity defined over the domain, even if the language does not itself contain a sign of identity: such an identity-relation will be absolute under that interpretation. If the domain is so given, we do not need to associate a specific criterion of identity with the proper names of the formal language: that has already been taken care of, and it is sufficient simply to specify the referent of the proper name as an element of the domain.

The same might be said of a substantival general term. Considered as an expression of natural language, the sense of such a word comprises not only a criterion of application but a criterion of identity; but, when the domain of a formal language is given, the identity-relation defined over it is thereby also given, and hence there is no need to make any specific association of a criterion of identity with a term of the language capable of being true or false of the elements of the domain. Looked at from this point of view, what are missing from such a formal language are not expressions corresponding to the substantival general terms of natural language, but those corresponding to adjectival ones which lack an associated criterion of identity: we cannot introduce a predicate into the formal language without guaranteeing that, under the intended interpretation, there will be a determinate number of objects to which it applies, a principle which will be expressible in the formal language, if it is rich enough, and will then be provable in any reasonable logical theory governing that language.

To put matters in this way, however, is not to reproduce any recognizable ingredient of Frege's thinking. That a proper name should have associated with it a criterion of identity is a principle he expressly enunciates; that the same applies to substantival general terms is a fairly evident corollary which he does not explicitly state. Indeed, he does not clearly draw any distinction between substantival and adjectival general terms, and comes close to doing so only in the somewhat confused § 54 of *Grundlagen* in which he says that the concept *red* does not delimit what falls under it in a definite manner, and that therefore no finite number belongs to it. Nor does Frege speak of the need for fixing a criterion of identity for the domain of the individual variables of a formalized language. Rather, as already mentioned, his general attitude is that we may take the domain to be, in all cases, the totality of all objects; and there is no criterion of identity associated with the term 'object'. But when, in Part I of *Grund-gesetze*, he gives the intended interpretation of the specific formal system employed in that work, he manifests a rather different attitude. Here, however we may assess the outcome, he does consider it necessary to specify what objects belong to the domain. Moreover, although he does not use the terminology of criteria of identity, he does treat a specification of the condition for the relation of identity to hold between objects in the domain as one requirement for the determination of the references of the formal terms. We shall study more closely what he says in this connection in the chapter on the context principle.

CHAPTER 12

The Notions of 'Object' and 'Function'

ON ONE POINT it now appears to me that in *FPL* I seriously misrepresented what is to be found in Frege's writings. On p. 194 of *FPL*, I spoke of Frege's saying that a relation can only be understood as being the referent of some relational expression; and on pp. 539–40 I asserted that 'Frege is even more explicit about the notion of "concept"—or . . . , more generally, that of "function"—than about that of "object", that we can attain to it only via the notion of the corresponding type of linguistic expression: there can be no general characterization of concepts save that they are things of the kind for which one-place first-level predicates stand'. These passages attribute to Frege a thesis that I have been unable to find that he ever states. Given his conception of truth-values as objects, the terms 'concept' and 'relation' do admit of definition: a concept is a function of one argument all of whose values are truth-values, and a relation is a similar function of two arguments.[1] The suggestion embodied in the remarks on pp. 194 and 539–40 of *FPL*, is that one can, without circularity, explain what it is for an expression to be a proper name, something I attempted in Chapter 4 of *FPL*; armed with this, one can then explain the notion of a predicate and that of a functional expression. An object can then be specified as something for which a proper name could stand, a concept as something for which a predicate could stand, and a function as something for which a functional expression could stand. These will not, indeed, be definitions, since, in accordance with the discussion on pp. 211–20 of *FPL*, a phrase such as 'what the functional expression "ξ^2" stands for' must be seen as involving quantification over functions, and one cannot understand quantification over functions unless one knows what, in general, a function is. Nevertheless, the suggestion is that there is a

---

[1] *Grundgesetze*, vol. I, §§ 3 and 4.

determinate order of explanation: one can attain to the general notion of a proper name in advance of having the general notion of an object, and to the general notion of a functional expression in advance of having the general notion of a function; but one cannot acquire the general notion of an object without first acquiring that of a proper name, or the general notion of a function without first acquiring that of a functional expression.

This suggestion cannot be substantiated, as I implied that it could, by direct quotation from Frege. On the contrary, in discussing the general notion of 'object' or 'function', Frege almost invariably says merely that we are dealing with something too simple to admit of definition, so that he can only give hints.[1] Frege does not, indeed, maintain that the corresponding linguistic notions, e.g. that of a proper name, are too simple to admit of definition; on the other hand, he does not propound the contrary view, that they do admit of precise definition, and I did not attribute it to him. What is more important is that I have been unable to find a passage in which he says expressly that the route to an understanding of what is comprised by any of the fundamental types of entity lies through a prior grasp of the corresponding type of linguistic expression. I think that I was in error in asserting that he maintained this, and have in FPL_2 altered the passages on pp. 194 and 539–40 accordingly.

I still believe, however, that my suggestion was in accord with the spirit of Frege's thought. The reason for saying this can be seen from the passage on pp. 56–7 of *FPL* where I discussed the question whether, from a Fregean standpoint, it is because we are compelled to regard numbers as objects that we accord the status of proper names to numerical terms, or whether, conversely, it is because we are compelled to regard numerical terms as being, in Frege's sense, proper names that we take numbers to be objects. I there argued, as against the view expressed by Geach on p. 136 of *Three Philosophers*, and now retracted by him, that the second alternative is not only correct in itself, but is the only one consistent with Frege's general views; the argument in no way involves attributing to Frege anything that he did not say.

The argument is essentially this. There is no intelligible enquiry whether a given thing is an object, a concept or a function. It is fundamental to Frege's philosophy that we cannot entertain any thought about a thing

---

[1] In *Function und Begriff*, p. 18, and in *Grundgesetze*, vol. 1, § 2, he says that an object is whatever is not a function; the main purpose of the remark is to induce the reader to accept that truth-values are objects, but it is otherwise of minimal help, since one evidently cannot understand what, in general, a function is without first understanding what, in general, an object is.

unless that thing is given or presented to us in some particular manner. The mode of presentation or manner in which it is given to us corresponds to the sense of a possible expression which stands for that thing. If we have such an expression, we must know whether it is complete, 'saturated', or incomplete, 'unsaturated', and, if it is incomplete, how many argument-places it has and which logical types of expression are required to fill them. We must know this, because it is an essential part of the characterization of the expression in question. But, if we know the logical type of the expression, we thereby know the logical type of its referent; whether or not that for which the expression stands is an object cannot be in question for us.

To the argument, as thus stated, it would be possible to object in either of two ways. First, it might be said that it holds only when the expression belongs to a language employing a logically correct notation. In natural language, the logical type of an expression is often not apparent from its form; as Frege remarks in *Grundlagen*, § 52, in 'four thoroughbred horses', 'four' and 'thoroughbred' play identical grammatical roles, namely as adjectives. Hence, the objection runs, we may be perfectly familiar with an expression, and grasp its sense, without knowing of what logical type it is, nor, therefore, to which logical type its referent belongs.

We cannot dispense with the notion of a purely implicit understanding. Someone who has never noticed that 'four' and 'black' function semantically in quite different ways may still fully grasp the sense of the word 'four'; he has mastered the 'tacit conventions'[1] governing the working of our language, though for him they remain merely tacit. We can, however, ascribe to him such a grasp of the sense of the word only so long as he continues to use it correctly; an implicit understanding is liable to be seduced by misleading grammatical analogies into improper uses of the word, and, at this stage, the understanding has been impaired. Such mishaps do not occur only to those engaged in doing philosophy, not only when the engine is idling.[2] A good example is provided whenever, during the past eighteen years, immigration has been raised as a political issue in Britain; politicians have then been eager to proclaim that what they object to 'is not the colour, it is the number', without ever noticing that what they are talking about is the number of *black people in the country*, and that they are therefore making a false antithesis, colour being, in the terminology of *Grundlagen*, a property of objects and number a property of concepts.[3] Are we to say of such a politician, assuming him not to be

[1] *Tractatus* 4.002.
[2] *Investigations*, § 132.
[3] See §§ 22 and 29.

engaged in deliberate sophistry, that he retains a grasp on the sense of the words he uses? Plainly not, or else he would be aware that the sentence which he takes to express a thought actually expresses no intelligible thought at all; we cannot allow that he any longer properly grasps the sense of the word 'number', even implicitly.

Nevertheless, to the argument as stated above, the objection is well taken. It is perfectly true that a sentence of natural language does not bear its true mode of composition upon its face; the speakers of the language grasp this mode of composition—in so far as they do grasp it—only implicitly, and it may require profound insight, and will often require hard work, to lay it bare. In no case is this more evident than with Frege's successful analysis of expressions of generality, expressions of which we all do have an implicit understanding, but the working of which it took a genius to uncover. But the objection does not prove the point at issue. I believe that Duns Scotus remarked that we may be uncertain whether or not something is a substance, and gave light as an example. Very well; if that is so, it shows that the distinction between those things which are and those which are not substances is not a distinction of logical type, like those which Frege drew between objects and concepts, and between first- and second-level concepts. In order to grasp the difference between, say, 'green' and 'four', when the latter is used adjectively, we cannot proceed by examining their referents, that is, by scrutinizing the first-level concept for which 'ξ is green' stands and the second-level one for which 'There are four Φ's' stands, as, by experiments with light, we might discover whether it was a substance or not. What, instead, we have to do is to attain an analysis of sentences in which 'green' and 'four' occur; that is, to arrive at an account of the construction of such sentences out of their components which is suited for a description of the way in which the truth-conditions of those sentences are determined in accordance with their composition. What we need, therefore, is a syntactic analysis apt for a semantic account; and, when we have attained such an analysis, no further doubt will remain concerning the logical types of the expressions in question. The investigations which pierce the veil of natural language still lie on the side of *language*; we cannot replace them by a scrutiny of the referents of the expressions.

The second objection fastens upon the notion of sense. Granted that we could not ask, of a given thing, whether it was an object or a concept unless that thing were given to us in a particular way, that is, as mediated by a sense that we could grasp, it may be denied that this sense needs to be conceived as the sense of even a possible expression; might we not grasp a sense without adverting in any way to a possible means of expressing it linguistically? For instance, when, in the passage already cited from 'Der Gedanke', Frege says that each one of us is given to himself in a quite special way, is it likely that he thinks that this special mode of presentation depends upon each individual's having, or having at least the conception of, a special use of 'I' to be employed in soliloquy? Is it not, rather, that, already being presented to himself in this special way before he learns any means of referring to himself, he can then use this mode of presentation as a way of mediating his reference to himself when he thinks to himself about himself? Did not Frege complain, in just this connection, that, since a thought is immaterial, he was forced to present it to his readers wrapped in linguistic form, although language was not his proper concern?[1]

It is possible that this objection represents a faithful interpretation of Frege's notion of sense; that one cannot demonstrate this to be otherwise is acknowledged on p. 157 of *FPL*. But, even so, the point is not greatly affected. If one grasps a sense, one must thereby know whether the sense is 'saturated', i.e. complete, or 'unsaturated', i.e. in need of completion: its logical type is as characteristic of the sense as it is of the expression or of its referent. Could not the two objections be combined, so that someone is imagined as having a grasp of some sense, not conceived as the sense of any actual or possible expression, which is nevertheless like the grasp which an unreflective user of a language may have of the sense of the word for 'four', allowing him to be unaware of its logical type? If we find it difficult to get hold of such a possibility, that reflects the obscurity we find in the conception of a grasp of the sense of an expression not embodied in a mastery of the employment of the expression in sentences; we can easily understand the conception of someone's having an idea of how an expression might be so employed, without his having any particular such expression in mind, but find it hard to see what it would be for someone to grasp the very same sense without so much as considering it as the possible sense of an expression. Nevertheless, if this is possible, the same reply must be valid in this case as to the first objection. For Frege, to grasp the sense of a sentence is to grasp the condition for it to be true. Hence to grasp a thought, otherwise than as the sense of a sentence, must be, likewise, to have the conception of something's being the case, that is, of the very same condition as one that may or may not obtain, though not, of course, any longer as the condition for a sentence to be true or for an assertion to be correct. The thought thus grasped must, to be the same

[1] 'Der Gedanke', p. 66n.

thought as that expressed by the sentence, have the same complexity; it, too, must be compounded out of constituent senses corresponding to the senses of the words which compose the sentence, which senses are components of the thought expressed by the sentence as a whole. If it is to be possible for the subject who thus grasps a thought not mediated by language to be unaware of the logical types of the component senses, the mode of composition must, like that of a sentence of natural language, be one that presents a misleading surface appearance. This means that, in the case of such thoughts also, there will be something corresponding to a syntactic and semantic analysis of the sentences of a language; there will be a way of describing how the whole thought is determined from the way in which it is put together out of its parts, and this will depend upon first arriving at a suitable account of how in fact it is put together out of its parts. By modulating out of the linguistic mode into the mode of pure thought, we achieve nothing; the recognition of the logical type of a sense will still depend upon an investigation into how that sense combines with others to form thoughts, and not upon an examination of its referent.

There cannot, therefore, be any such enquiry as one into whether a given thing is an object or a function, or a concept of first or second level. Apropos of a logically correct notation, there cannot be any enquiry as to the logical type of an expression, either; each expression will bear its logical type upon its face. But, when we are concerned with expressions of natural language, there may well be such an enquiry; and it is to be answered by an investigation into how we can give a systematic description of the way in which the truth-conditions of sentences containing such expressions are determined in accordance with their composition. Such a description falls into two parts, a syntactic part which states how the sentences are to be regarded as formed out of their constituents, and a semantic part which, by reference to the syntactic analysis, states how their truth-conditions are determined. In practice, the two parts of the investigation cannot be separated: it is possible that a language may admit of distinct syntactic analyses, which are equally good if all we wish to do is to characterize the well-formed sentences, but only one of which will serve as a basis for a semantic account; so, in arriving at the syntactic analysis, we must keep an eye on the semantic account we wish to frame on its basis. Nevertheless, the two are in principle separable: the syntactic analysis can be stated, if not justified, without invoking any semantic notions. Indeed, it is possible to be satisfied with a given syntactic analysis while questioning the semantic account which it was intended to subserve. For instance, the intuitionistic account of the meanings of mathematical statements involves a repudiation of the two-valued classical semantics to which Frege adhered; but it in no way calls in question Frege's syntactic analysis of the language of mathematical theories, his categorization of the types of primitive expressions or his account of the formation of complex sentences from atomic ones by means of sentential operators and quantification. It follows that there is a clear sense in which the notion of the logical type of an expression is prior to that of the logical type of the referent of an expression. One can, that is, state what one takes a proper name, a first- or second-level predicate or functional expression to be, for a formalized language in terms of surface appearance, for a natural language by appeal to a proposed syntactic analysis, without invoking the notion of reference or any semantic notion.

Syntactic analysis is not a uniform process. Frege's brilliant contribution was to lay the foundations for such an analysis by giving the outlines of an account of the types of expression of which atomic sentences are composed, and of the manner in which complex sentences are formed from them; indeed, the conception of such a distinction between atomic and complex sentences is his. But, when this is done, many problems remain; and one of them is when to accept that an expression which passes the most immediate tests for being of a given logical type is really to be acknowledged as such. The most immediate tests serve to uncover the purely superficial resemblances between logically disparate expressions, to show, for example, that 'nobody' is not a proper name, or to distinguish between 'four' and 'green'. An expression which passes these tests for being of a given logical type cannot be in fact of some other type; it is either genuine or wholly misbegotten. An example is the word 'function', already mentioned. On the most immediate tests, it is a concept-word, part of the predicate 'ξ is a function' standing for a concept of first level. But, if we understand it so, we cannot use it as we intended. It is therefore to be rejected as misbegotten; it must be extruded from the language, at least from a logically correct language, and what we meant to express by it must be expressed by a different expression of another logical type. At the end of his life, Frege came to believe the same to be true of class-names, that is, expressions of the form 'the extension of the concept F'. If such an expression is properly formed, it must be a proper name, since it passes the immediate tests for belonging to that type. Either, therefore, it is properly formed, and stands for an object, or it is not properly formed, but one of the illusions generated by natural language, in which case it has no correct use and does not stand for anything, but should be banished from our speech. Frege came to believe that this second alternative was the true one.[1] Language allows us to transform the statement 'A thing is F if and only if it is G' into the form 'The extension of the concept F is the same as the extension of the concept G'; but this transformation, so far from being the fundamental law of logic which he had presented it as being in *Grundgesetze*, was a mere linguistic phantasm, generating sham proper names for non-existent objects. There can be no question of declaring that class-names do not stand for objects, but for entities of some other type; they purport to be proper names, and, if they are not proper names, they are nothing, and have no business in the language. Needless to say, whatever be the principles by which such imposters are to be detected, their detection must depend upon linguistic considerations, and not upon an examination of their referents to discover whether they are genuine or spurious.

It still may be objected that, even if we can say what the various types of expression are without appealing to the notion of reference, it does not follow that we can, by appealing to that notion, explain what we understand by 'object', 'concept', 'function' and so on. Frege's idea is that, when we leave syntax and come on to semantics, we can explain the different semantic roles which expressions of different logical types play by associating with them entities of different types as their referents. In order to do this, we must have a conception of what objects, concepts, relations and functions are that is independent of the differences in logical type between the expressions that stand for them; if our only way of grasping what a concept is is to take it as the sort of thing for which a predicate stands, we shall learn nothing about the semantic role of predicates in the language to be told that they stand for concepts.

This objection appears to reduce to a trivial circularity the suggestion which I originally attributed to Frege, and am even now claiming to accord with his ideas. The thesis that we can attain to the general notion of a function via, and only via, that of a functional expression, namely as the sort of thing for which such an expression stands, was not, however, intended to relate to a context in which all that was yet known about functional expressions was their syntactic characterization. It was assumed, rather, that the explanation was given to one who was already familiar with complex proper names containing other proper names as constituents, and understood such terms; understood them implicitly, that is, in the sense of having a mastery of their use, not of being able to give a semantic account of their meanings. And that is just how Frege does go about the process of giving 'hints' to enable a reader to attain the notion of a function.[1] He exhibits a number of complex numerical terms resulting from putting different numerals in the argument-place of a relatively complicated functional expression.[2] From such examples, he explains the notion of a functional expression, that is, a common pattern displayed by all these complex terms, a pattern which yields a particular one of them when a specific term is selected to fill the gaps in it. A function is then to be understood to be the objective correlate, that is, the referent, of a functional expression.[3] The notion of the reference of a term (proper name) is here taken for granted, as involved in the understanding which the reader is assumed to have of such terms: as the functional expression systematically transforms a term standing for one number, the argument of the function, into a complex term for another number, so the function constitutes a systematic connection between every number considered as argument and some other number, the corresponding value. In the same way, when, in *Grundlagen* § 57, Frege wishes to argue that numbers must be taken to be objects, what he actually argues is that numerical terms behave as proper names; and when he wants to explain the sense in which, in saying this, he is using the word 'object', what he actually says is:

> The self-subsistence (*Selbständigkeit*) which I am claiming for numbers is not to be taken to mean that a number-word signifies something outside the context of a sentence, but only to preclude its use as a predicate or attribute, which appreciably alters its meaning (*Bedeutung*).[4]

That is to say, rather than characterizing objects directly, what he does is to characterize what he takes as being expressions standing for objects, that is, constituents of sentences, not themselves sentences, which are, in contrast to predicates or functional expressions, *selbständig* or complete. It is because we tacitly understand how singular terms (proper names) are used that we are able to attain the general notion of an object; it is because we tacitly understand how the reference of a complex term depends upon the reference of a constituent term that we can attain that of a function.

---

[1] *Function und Begriff*, 'Was ist eine Function?', *Grundgesetze*, vol. I, §§ 1 and 4 and 'Logik in der Mathematik', *N.S.*, pp. 254–61, *P.W.*, pp. 235–42.

[2] *Function und Begriff*, p. 6, *Grundgesetze*, vol. I, §1.

[3] 'Was ist eine Function?', p. 663, *Grundgesetze*, vol. I, § 1.

[4] *Grundlagen*, § 60.

It is plain that the notion of reference is required if we are to explain what is meant by 'object' by appeal to the notion of a proper name; and this seems legitimate, since we have a pre-systematic notion of the bearer of a proper name, of that which a proper name is used to refer to or to talk about. We already have such a notion long before we attempt to construct a systematic semantics. But we do not have such a corresponding notion for predicates and functional expressions; why, then, is it of any use to invoke the notion of reference when explaining what a function is by appeal to the notion of a functional expression? We have to convey that a function belongs to a different order from the functional expression which stands for it, and does not depend, for its existence, upon the existence of that expression. But that is not enough to distinguish it from the sense of the functional expression; as I remarked on p. 182 of *FPL*, we cannot properly understand Frege's use of the term 'concept' save by appeal to the sense/reference distinction, taking the term as applying, not to the sense, but to the referent of a predicate. What, at this stage, is conveyed by stipulating that a function is to be taken as the referent of a functional expression, or, more exactly, since we cannot expect to have an expression for every function, the sort of thing for which a functional expression can stand, is that a function does not belong to the realm of sense. More positively, that the function remains unaltered by any change in the expression for it which leaves unchanged the references of its constituent terms, and hence so long as it continues, for each argument, to have the same value as before. Thus the function is not dependent, as is the sense of the functional expression, on the particular means we have, in virtue of our understanding of the expression, to determine its value for each given argument, but is constituted solely by the relevant association of arguments to values. Furthermore, the function is something that we might, by the use of a suitable sentence, be said to be talking about; and, in such a sentence, the expression for the function would appear in its ordinary role, not in the special way that is required when we wish to talk about the sense of that expression. All this follows from the fact that, in stipulating that the function is the referent of the functional expression, we are laying down that it stands to the expression in a relation analogous to that of the bearer of a proper name to the name; if it were not so, the analogy would fail. Of course, it would then be quite legitimate to raise the question whether there is anything which stands to a functional expression in a relation analogous to that of bearer to name. This is the question to which I addressed myself in Chapter 7 of *FPL*, and it is to be answered by exploring the analogy further. The fact that the explanation may be called in question does not affect the present thesis, which is that the only possible route to an explanation of Frege's notions of 'object' and 'function' is via that of the corresponding types of linguistic expression, by appeal to the notion of reference.

The thesis relates to the first, informal introduction of the terms 'object' and 'function', not, as the objection that it is circular took it to do, to that part of a systematic theory of meaning for a language in which the semantic roles of its expressions are specified. A doubt may nevertheless remain. The informal explanation relied on the tacit understanding which we already have of the meanings of singular terms (proper names) generally and, in particular, of complex singular terms. But is not a theory of meaning supposed to make explicit what is merely implicitly involved in our every-day understanding of our language? With what right, then, may we make use, within that theory of meaning, of terms of art which were explained by appeal to our implicit understanding? Is that not to leave as still tacit what the theory of meaning is committed to rendering explicit?

Frege's inclination would probably have been not to treat such an objection very seriously. In the first place, the informal explanation does much more than merely label the referent of a functional expression a 'function', the referent of a predicate a 'concept', leaving it to our tacit understanding of such expressions to see what kinds of things their referents must be: it makes explicit what, as it were, constitutes the being of a function or of a concept. The whole being of a function consists in a correlation of arguments to values; the whole being of a concept consists in its cor-relating each object to a truth-value. Because we already know this about functions and concepts from the informal explanation, the stipulation that a certain expression is to stand for a function and another for a con-cept does not rely on our tacit understanding of functional expressions and predicates to give it substance, but makes highly explicit just what the semantic role of those expressions is to be. In the second place, it may be said that there is nothing wrong with the procedure objected to. We do in fact start with a tacit understanding of our language. If certain expressions are so basic that no actual definition of them is possible, there is nothing wrong in using a means of introducing them and conveying the meanings that they are to bear that works only because we do have that tacit understanding; and, once those expressions have been understood, there is then no harm in using them in giving a systematic account of the language which we tacitly understand.

It is more proper, however, to treat the objection more seriously. We saw in Chapter 7 what, in general, a semantic theory is, that component of a theory of meaning which, for Frege, assumed the form of his theory of reference. A theory of meaning must, however, comprise more than just such a semantic theory, in the strict sense. As well as the theory of reference it must comprise also a theory of sense, that is, a theory explaining what it is that confers on the expressions of our language the significance that they have. If meaning is to be explained in terms of understanding, we may say that a theory of sense must explain in what our understanding of those expressions, our mastery of their use, consists: in any case, it must give the *content* of our understanding of the words of our language, whether or not it needs to go into the question what it is for us to possess such an understanding. The theory of reference merely ascribes to each word and expression a particular semantic value: the theory of sense must explain in virtue of what each word and expression has the semantic value that it has; and that in virtue of which it has that semantic value must be something in terms of which a speaker's understanding of it may be explained. This, of course, is merely to state what the theory of sense is required to do: how it does it will vary greatly according to the underlying philosophy of language. If understanding is thought of as a practical ability, the capacity to engage in a common practice, then the sense of a word will be characterized directly in terms of its use. But, as we saw in Chapter 5, for Frege to grasp a sense is a cognitive act, that is to say, to understand an expression is to know something: so, for him, sense is to be characterized as a piece of knowledge that a speaker has concerning an expression.

Since different senses may correspond to the same reference, the reference of an expression does not determine its sense. But we may say something much stronger than that: the theory of reference does not even determine uniquely the *form* that the theory of sense will assume, the sort of thing that is to be said to constitute the sense of an expression of a given logical type. This is evident from the fact that we cannot tell, from the theory of reference, whether the sense of an expression is to consist in a set of principles governing the employment of sentences containing it, or in a piece of implicit knowledge, or in something else again; and, even when the general conception of sense has been settled, there is still room for much variation. Nevertheless, the theory of reference greatly circumscribes the character of a theory of sense: for it imposes severe conditions on what the sense of an expression of each logical type may be taken to be. That is because we know in advance what the theory of sense is required to do. In the first place, the sense of an expression must determine its reference: that is to say, it must be something which, in view of how the world is, determines whatever we have taken to be the semantic value of the expression. It is precisely for this reason that the theory of reference serves as a foundation for the theory of sense, and determines within strict limits the form that it can take. Secondly, because sense is distinguished from tone, only that may be assigned to the sense of an expression which, among the things that go to make up a speaker's mastery of its use, is relevant to determining its referent. And, finally, sense must be something that relates to the use of an expression by the speakers of the language. Since, for Frege, sense is something that is grasped by a speaker, his grasp of it constituting his understanding of the expression, and since that grasp of the sense is for him a piece of knowledge, this means that the sense of an expression must be something that a speaker may be said to know, at least implicitly, and that each speaker must know implicitly if he is to be said to understand the expression. It follows that a characterization of the sense of an expression must amount to a complete characterization of the piece of knowledge which a speaker may have, and in which his understanding of it consists. Thus, for instance, the sense of a proper name cannot consist merely in its having a certain object as its bearer, since it could never be a complete characterization of what, in virtue of his understanding of the name, a speaker knew concerning it to say that he knew, of some object, that it was the bearer of the name. Likewise, the sense of a predicate could not consist merely in its being true of certain objects and false of others, since, in general, one who understood the predicate could not be said to know, of each object, whether or not the predicate was true of it, and, if he did, that could not be a complete characterization of the piece of knowledge that he had. But, equally, nothing that a speaker may be said to know about a proper name can be regarded as part of its sense which is not relevant to determining which object is the bearer of the name, and nothing that he may be said to know about a predicate can be regarded as part of its sense if it is not relevant to determining, for some object, whether the predicate is true of it.

The theory of sense must do more than show what, in our understanding of an expression, determines it as having the referent that it has; it must also show in what the association between the expression and its referent consists. In the theory of reference, we merely postulate that such an association exists, because that is all we need to do in explaining how each sentence is determined as true or otherwise in accordance with its composition; we can then go ahead and introduce the notion of a semantic interpretation as consisting simply in an appropriate association of schematic letters with suitable semantic values. The theory of sense, however, must

justify the assumption that there is such an association for actual expressions of the language; it therefore cannot take as given the general notion
of an object, nor even the notions of each of the various sorts or categories
of objects.[1] For Frege, an important ingredient of the sense of a proper
name is the criterion of identity associated with that name;[2] but if the
theory of sense were to content itself with specifying, e.g., that 'chess'
is understood as the name of a board game, it would be relying on our grasp
of the criterion of identity for board games, and so leaving implicit what
it ought to render explicit. A full account of the sense of a proper name
will therefore comprise an explicit account of the procedure of identifying
an object of the appropriate kind as the bearer of the name, and hence
of the use of what on p. 232 of *FPL* are called 'recognition statements',
and, as underlying this, of what on p. 577 of *FPL* are called 'statements
of identification'; it must therefore pay attention to that fundamental
level of language of which Frege took so little account, in which the use
of demonstratives plays a crucial role. Only by such a means can it be made
explicit what it is to use an expression as the proper name of an object
of a given sort; and, in the process, the general notion of 'object' will
thereby be made fully explicit also, without the need for mere hints or
any appeal to a prior understanding of the object-language.

Thus, as it seems to me, when we have attained a fully adequate theory
of sense, that theory will itself explain the highly general notions of 'object',
'concept' and 'function' which are employed in the theory of reference;
no appeal will be made, in this explanation, to the notion of reference,
as in any degree already understood, because the theory will itself make
manifest what reference is. We are not in that situation; we have only
sketchy conceptions of how a theory of sense is to be constructed. Since
the theory of reference circumscribes the form that the theory of sense
may take, and since much can be stated in terms of the theory of reference
alone, for instance the characterization of the validity of a logical law,
we have good reason to follow Frege's example in constructing a theory
of reference in advance of tackling the harder and more elaborate task
of devising a theory of sense. For this purpose, we need to invoke such
notions as 'object' and 'function', and must have some provisional means of
explaining them. It is to this interim form of explanation that the thesis
which I mistakenly attributed to Frege, and still maintain is in accord
with his ideas, was intended to apply.

I am not claiming the support of Frege for these last remarks about

[1] See p. 76 of *FPL* for the use here made of 'category' and 'sort'.
[2] See *FPL*, pp. 179–80.

what, when we have it, a theory of sense will accomplish. On the contrary, I said above that Frege would probably have been disinclined to treat seriously the objection to which they were meant as a reply. It is a matter of common complaint, with which, on p. 227 of *FPL*, I partly associated myself, that Frege failed to spell out what he took the senses of expressions of the various logical types to be. But, as I said on the page of *FPL* referred to, and as I have argued in greater detail here, a great deal already follows concerning sense from Frege's theory of reference, given that we know both that sense is required to determine reference and that to grasp the sense of an expression is to have a piece of knowledge. It is possible that Frege thought that everything that could, in general, be said about sense followed from these two principles, together with his particular theory of reference, although, naturally, there may be much to be said about the specific sense that a particular expression bears; that, for the rest, in the terminology of the *Tractatus*, the sense of an expression is shown but cannot be stated, as I also suggested on the same page of *FPL*. On this interpretation of Frege, he did not believe in the possibility of a systematic theory of sense, such as I have just been canvassing. I confess that, on this point, I find myself in darkness about how Frege saw the matter; he certainly gave no hint that there remained some large task that he had not undertaken. What I have attempted to do in this chapter has been to make clear the content of the thesis which, on pp. 194 and 539–40 of *FPL*, I originally ascribed to Frege, and to defend it against objections, hoping that, in the process, I have at least made out that to reject it would necessitate a very grave departure from Frege's views.

CHAPTER 13

The Senses of Incomplete Expressions

A SPECIFICATION OF the references of the expressions of a language forms a base for an account of their senses; it does not uniquely determine what such an account shall be, but it greatly circumscribes it by specifying what the sense of each expression is required to do. But how does it do this? It does it in virtue of the fact that sense determines reference; but this thesis admits of two interpretations, a weak one and a strong one. On the weak interpretation, to say that sense determines reference involves only that two expressions with the same sense cannot have different references. If this were the correct interpretation, a specification of the references of a range of expressions would not very severely circumscribe the account to be given of their senses. On the strong interpretation, the sense of an expression constitutes the manner in which something is determined as being its referent, or, to put it in terms of our understanding of the expression, that is, of what is involved in grasping its sense, to grasp the sense is to apprehend the condition for something to be its referent. It is clear that we must adopt the strong interpretation at least for sentences: to grasp a thought, that is, the sense of a sentence, is to apprehend the condition which must hold for it to be true. It is, moreover, apparent that we need the strong interpretation for proper names also. The sense of a proper name is the manner in which some object is determined as being its referent: to grasp its sense is to apprehend the condition which an object must satisfy for it to be the referent of the name. This strong interpretation yields a much stronger conception of the way in which the theory of reference circumscribes the theory of sense. It has the great advantage of giving us a general idea of what the sense of a sentence or of a proper name is: on the weak interpretation, we know only that it is something that cannot be held in common by expressions with different referents; but, although the strong interpretation does not allow us to deduce, from a knowledge of the reference of an expression, what its sense is—which we can never do, given that expressions with different senses may have the same reference —it does tell us what sort of thing the sense of a sentence or of a proper name must be. The strong interpretation has the further advantage of according with what Frege says. In *Grundgesetze*, vol. 1, § 32, he wrote, of the formulas of his symbolic language: 'Every such name of a truth-value *expresses* a sense, a *thought*. That is to say, by means of our stipulations it is determined under what conditions it stands for the true. The sense of this name, the *thought*, is the thought that these conditions are fulfilled'. On p. 26 of 'Über Sinn und Bedeutung', in introducing the notion of sense, in the first place for proper names, he speaks of the sense of a name as the way in which the object is given to us ('die Art des Gegebenseins', translated by Black as 'the mode of presentation'); on p. 30, he expresses the same conception metaphorically in terms of the observation of the Moon through a telescope, the Moon corresponding to the referent and the real image projected into the interior of the telescope to the sense.

It is easy enough to acknowledge the necessity for the strong interpretation for sentences and proper names, but harder to hold on to it for incomplete expressions. But the strong interpretation of the thesis that sense determines reference entails the strong interpretation of that thesis for predicates and relational expressions in the presence of any one of the following: the strong interpretation of the thesis for sentences; the doctrine that the sense of the part is part of the sense of the whole;[1] and the principle that the reference of an expression constitutes its semantic role. There is an intrinsic connection between the doctrine that the sense of the part is part of the sense of the whole and the conception of reference as semantic role or semantic value. To quote once more the section of *Grundgesetze* already twice quoted, 'The names, whether simple or themselves already composite, of which the name of a truth-value consists, contribute to the expression of the thought, and this contribution of the individual constituent name is its *sense*.' In interpreting this remark, as indeed also that quoted in footnote 1, it must be borne in mind that in *Grundgesetze* Frege calls every logically unitary expression, every expression, that is, to which a reference or a sense can significantly be ascribed, a 'name'. Now if the sense of a proper name is the manner in which an object is determined as being its referent; and if the sense of the proper name contributes to, or is part of, the thought expressed by a sentence containing it; and if the thought expressed by a sentence consists in the

[1] 'If a name is part of the name of a truth-value, then the sense of the former name is part of the thought expressed by the latter', *Grundgesetze*, vol. 1, § 32.

way in which it is determined as being true or false: then it must be in virtue of its referent that the proper name contributes to the determination of the sentence, or, more accurately, the thought it expresses, as true or false, which is precisely what is meant by taking the reference of the proper name to be its semantic role. We may express this by saying that the determination of the truth-value of the sentence goes via the referent of the proper name. If it were not so, we could form no conception of *how* the sense of the proper name contributed to the thought expressed by the sentence. Let us consider an atomic sentence, consisting of a proper name and a simple predicate, say 'The Earth spins'. The sense of the proper name 'the Earth' consists in the manner in which its referent is given to us, and also contributes to the thought expressed by the sentence. The thought expressed by the sentence is the thought that the condition for it to be true is fulfilled. But what is this condition? It is the condition that a certain thing should hold good of the object given to us in a certain way, that way which is embodied in the sense of the name 'the Earth'. Once the proper name has specified the way in which the object is given, then it has made its contribution to the sense of the sentence; if it had not, then it would be impossible to see how its sense could *both* contribute to the sense of the sentence *and* consist in the way in which the object is given.

In his review of *FPL*[1], Geach defended the equation of the sense of a predicate with the function which carries the sense of a proper name into the thought expressed by the sentence that results from putting that proper name in the argument-place of the predicate from the criticism that I made of it on pp. 293–4 of *FPL*. On this conception, the sense of the predicate 'ξ spins' is itself a function, one which yields, for the sense of the name 'the Earth' as argument, the thought that the Earth spins as value. Of course, no one can deny that, once the sense of 'ξ spins' is fixed, such a function is determined: the question is whether the sense of the predicate just *is* that function. Geach approves of Frege's retractation of the thesis that the referent of the part is part of the referent of the whole. The denial of that thesis implies a more general negative thesis: neither the argument nor the function is *part* of the value of the function for that argument. But Frege did not retract his thesis that the sense of the part is part of the sense of the whole; yet, on Geach's interpretation of the notion of the sense of a predicate, to say that the sense of the proper name and that of the predicate were parts of the thought expressed by the whole

[1] *Mind*, vol. 85, 1975, pp. 436–49.

sentence would be to say that, in this case, both the argument and the function were parts of the value. Suppose that the sense of 'ξ spins' were given to us as a function from the senses of proper names to thoughts. Then the sense of the predicate would carry us from the sense of 'the Earth' to the thought expressed by 'The Earth spins', that is, to the condition for that sentence to be true. But what is that condition? What does determine the sentence as true or as false? On this conception of the sense of the predicate, we are left unable to say: or, if we can say, then it must be the satisfaction of some condition, given by the predicate, by the *sense* of the name 'the Earth'. The sense of the predicate is not, on this conception, a concept; we cannot say that the condition for the truth of the sentence is that the sense of 'the Earth' should fall under the concept which is the sense of the predicate. Rather, the sense of the predicate is a function whose values are thoughts. But it will be of no help to say that the condition for the truth of the sentence (more exactly, of the thought) is that the function should map the sense of 'the Earth' on to a *true* thought: for the thought on to which it should map it is the thought expressed by the sentence, and, in asking what is the condition for the truth of the sentence, we are asking what thought it does express. On this conception of the sense of the predicate, it is given to us as relating, in the first place, to the *sense* of the proper name, not to its referent; the referent of the name comes in only when we are engaged in explaining what the sense of the name is. But, on this supposition, we can form no conception of the condition that the sense of the name must satisfy for the sentence to be true; we therefore cannot explain what, specifically, the sense of the predicate is, or move a step beyond the generic explanation that it is a function from the senses of proper names to thoughts. But this is absurd: an explanation of the sense of the proper name and of the sense of the predicate ought to yield an explanation of the sense of the sentence, that is, of the condition for the thought it expresses to be true, just as Frege's stipulations in *Grundgesetze* determine the conditions for the truth of his formulas.

The trouble has been caused by taking the notion of the referent of the proper name as having played its full part once we have used it to explain the sense of the name, whereas, in fact, the reverse is the case: once the referent of the name has been determined, via its sense, the sense of the name falls away as not further relevant to the determination of the thought as true or false. The condition for the truth of the thought has to be viewed as the satisfaction by a particular object, given in a certain way, of a certain condition on it. The condition to be satisfied by the object is itself given in a particular manner, corresponding to the sense of the predicate: but it is a condition on the object, that is, on the referent of the proper name. In more Fregean language, the sense of the proper name determines an object as its referent; and the sense of the predicate determines a mapping from objects to truth-values, that is to say, a concept; the sentence is true or false according as the object does or does not fall under the concept, that is, according as it is mapped by it on to the value *true* or the value *false*. The mapping of objects on to truth-values is not the *sense* of the predicate, but its referent: the sense is, rather, some particular way, which we can grasp, of determining such a mapping. But the sense of the predicate is to be thought of, not as being given directly in terms of a mapping from the *senses* of proper names on to anything, but, rather, in terms of a mapping of *objects* on to truth-values. It is because the determination of the truth-value of a sentence containing a proper name goes via the referent of the name, and, in consequence, via the referents of the other constituents of the sentence, that we need to adopt, for incomplete expressions also, the strong interpretation of the thesis that sense determines reference: if there were any type of expression for which this were not so, then, although the notion of reference for expressions of that type might be defensible, it would play no part in the account of the senses of such expressions, nor even of their semantic roles.

CHAPTER 14

Definability

ON P. 25 OF *FPL* I remarked that 'Frege several times emphasized that it is impossible that every word of a language should be introduced by definition'; he did, indeed, repeatedly stress the undeniable truth that, in any system of definitions, some terms must be primitive. That, of course, does not imply that, for each language, or each given set of interrelated terms, there exists a unique maximal system of definitions satisfying those conditions that may reasonably be imposed, such as that no term be defined by means of others to which it is epistemologically prior. In *FPL* I observed that Frege was conscious of this fact: on p. 584 I said that 'he was very well aware that it is frequently possible to define an expression in different ways', and on p. 228 I alluded to his 'observation that, of a given circle of interdefinable expressions, it is indifferent which, in constructing an axiomatised theory, we select as primitive'. In *FPL₁*, however, I described this observation as 'repeated', an epithet that was unjustified: I have been able to find only two enunciations of the stated thesis in Frege's writings, one on p. 320 of his review of Husserl, where he applies it to the term 'conic section', expressly remarking that the alternative definitions confer different senses on it, and the other in *Begriffsschrift*, § 7, where he says that he might have taken 'and' as primitive in place of 'if', which can be defined in terms of 'not' and 'and'. As I remarked on p. 228 of *FPL*, the repudiation in 'Die Verneinung'[1] of an intrinsic distinction between affirmative and negative thoughts tells in the same direction. There is also a parallel with the statement in the unpublished 'Logik in der Mathematik'[2] that, in axiomatizing a theory, we may have a choice over which propositions to select as axioms, and which as theorems.

Granted, then, that there is no unique system of definitions, and that

[1] P. 150.
[2] *N.S.*, p. 222, *P.W.*, pp. 205–6.

there may therefore be some choice over which terms are taken as primitive and which as defined, it may still be that there are some terms which are inherently primitive, that is, which will be primitive in any acceptable system of definitions, and may therefore be said to be indefinable. On pp. 25–6 of *FPL*, I pointed out that this was also Frege's opinion. In FPL_1, I gave, as examples, only the terms 'same' and 'true'; to these I have in FPL_2 added the terms 'object' and 'function'. As expressing what Wittgenstein called 'formal concepts'[1] and as therefore not required in a satisfactory notation, these last two differ significantly from 'same' and 'true'.[2] Moreover, as Frege came to realize, the expression 'function' is misbegotten; it masquerades as part of a first-level predicate, 'ξ is a function', which is of the wrong logical type to be applied to those things to which we want to apply it.[3] Nevertheless, Frege's observations about the existence of indefinable expressions so frequently occur in a context in which the specific example is a term such as 'object' or 'function' that it seemed misleading to omit mention of them in this connection.

In FPL_2 I have altered the top few lines of p. 26. As framed in FPL_1, they were not exactly wrong; but they suffered from vagueness. Although I acknowledged that Frege recognized the existence of indefinable expressions, I wanted to play this down, remarking, correctly, that there were very few terms for which he advanced such a thesis, and going on to say, rather uninformatively, that he 'was not under the spell of the mystique of unanalysability'. It would be possible to quarrel with this. Certainly the notion of indefinability played no large part in Frege's thinking, and certainly, as I remarked, he had no conception in any way corresponding to Russell's 'logically proper names'. On the other hand, the observation that there are indefinable expressions occurs much more frequently in his writings than that to the effect that alternative definitions are possible for a given term. Moreover, my original remark that Frege did not associate indefinability with logical simplicity was definitely objectionable. There is, in Frege, a sharp distinction to be made between the simplicity of an *expression* and the simplicity of its *sense*. Thus, in *Grundgesetze*, vol. 1, § 33 (3), he lays it down as one of the requirements on a correct definition

[1] See *FPL*, p. 221, and *Tractatus* 4.126–4.1274.

[2] Wittgenstein, however, would have disagreed about 'same'—see *Tractatus* 5.53; possibly he would have disagreed about 'true' also. Indeed, Warren Goldfarb has argued that this ought to have been Frege's own conclusion, on the ground that his regress argument, given in 'Der Gedanke' and discussed on pp. 442–5 of *FPL*, really shows, not the indefinability, but the inexpressibility, of truth.

[3] See *FPL*, p. 213; *N.S.*, p. 210, *P.W.*, p. 193; *BW*, p. 218, *P.M.C.*, 136.

that the defined expression should be simple, that is, not composed of parts which themselves have a sense and contribute to the sense of the whole. It is nevertheless natural to think of the sense of an expression that has been introduced by definition as complex; and natural, further, to extend this to expressions capable of definition, even though they were not introduced in that way. By contrast, an expression which is absolutely indefinable may be regarded as having a pre-eminently simple, that is, unanalysable, sense. Frege did have such a conception: an example occurs on p. 193 of 'Über Begriff und Gegenstand', apropos of the term 'concept', where he wrote:

> Kerry contests what he calls my definition of 'concept'. I would remark, in the first place, that my explanation is not meant as a proper definition. One cannot require that everything be defined, any more than one can require that a chemist decompose every substance. What is simple cannot be decomposed, and what is logically simple cannot have a proper definition.

What I was driving at, in my original vague remarks about the mystique of unanalysability, was as follows. The fundamental theorem of arithmetic states that every natural number has a unique decomposition into prime factors. Likewise Moore, Russell and, above all, the Wittgenstein of the *Tractatus* adhered to what may be called the fundamental theorem of logical analysis: that every proposition admits of a unique ultimate analysis into unanalysable components. If 'unanalysable' means 'indefinable', in the sense in which Frege claimed 'same' and 'true' to be indefinable, or if the definitions of arithmetical notions given by Frege in his *Grundlagen* are examples of analysis, then there is hardly any trace of this fundamental theorem in Frege's thinking. For Russell, Moore and Wittgenstein, unanalysable expressions had an overwhelming importance because they represented the ultimate terms of logical analysis. There is just one passage in Frege's writings, known to me, where he comes close to expressing such a conception, namely in his second series of articles 'Über die Grundlagen der Geometrie' (1906), where he says that 'we must recognize basic logical elements (*logische Urelemente*), which are not definable',[1] adding that, once we have agreed about these basic elements and their symbolization, we can easily arrive at agreement, by means of definitions, about what is logically complex. Frege did indeed repeatedly admit the existence of

---

[1] Part I, p. 301.

absolutely indefinable expressions, and sometimes made a point of insisting on the indefinability of some particular expression. But, with the sole exception of the remark just quoted from 'Über die Grundlagen der Geometrie', he does not suggest the existence of a system of definitions each primitive term of which is absolutely indefinable. It will follow that we should not, on Frege's view, regard the work of logical analysis as remaining incomplete until we have reached a definition framed wholly in terms of expressions that may be claimed as indefinable in an absolute sense. The passages cited above, that from the review of Husserl admitting alternative definitions of 'conic section', that from *Begriffsschrift* admitting a choice over the sentential connectives selected as primitive, and that from 'Die Verneinung' denying the existence of an intrinsic distinction between affirmative and negative thoughts,[1] all strongly suggest that Frege's view of logical analysis differed in just this way from that of Russell and Wittgenstein. For this reason, the notion of unanalysability did not have for him the same importance as it had for those philosophers.

We cannot merely say this and leave the matter there, however, for a denial of the fundamental theorem of logical analysis appears to conflict with Frege's conception of a thought as complex and as compounded out of its constituent senses. If an expression *can* be defined, must we not give its definition if we are to analyse its sense? If we continue to do this, then, unless the fundamental theorem is true, we shall, in general, arrive at expressions that cannot be defined without creating a circularity in our system of definitions, i.e. can be defined only in terms of expressions that we have already defined in terms, ultimately, of them, but which are not absolutely indefinable. This seems to imply that even a maximal non-circular system of definitions of the terms involved in the expression of a thought, together with those that occur in the definitions, will not suffice to reveal how the thought is constructed out of its constituents; we shall need, rather, to survey all possible such systems of definitions before we have a full awareness of the structure of the thought. For instance, 'if' is not absolutely definable, since it may be defined in terms of 'not' and 'and', and 'and' is not absolutely indefinable, since we may define it in terms of 'not' and 'if'. Likewise, we might say that neither 'smooth' nor 'rough' is absolutely indefinable, since we may define 'smooth' as 'not rough' and 'rough' as 'not smooth'; but, in neither case can we admit both definitions in the pair into one system. Now one may explain this by saying that, if one understands 'rough', 'smooth' and 'not', then

[1] An observation also made at length in the 'Logik' of 1897, *N.S.*, pp. 161-2, *P.W.*, pp. 149-50.

one will see that 'rough' has the same sense as 'not smooth' and 'smooth' the same sense as 'not rough'. But if I say, 'The surface of the table is not rough', the sense of 'rough' must be a constituent of the thought I express, while, if 'smooth' has just the same sense as 'not rough', I must express the very same thought by saying, 'The surface of the table is smooth'. We have here two senses which are constituents of one another; being a proper constituent of a sense cannot be an asymmetric relation, and hence no non-circular system of definitions can reveal all the cases in which this relation holds. Now none of this is incoherent, and does not even contradict the idea that there is a *unique* analysis of a thought into its constituents. But, though it seems to follow from what Frege says, it does not look like anything to be found in him. For instance, it implies that neither the *Grundlagen* nor the *Grundgesetze* can give a complete analysis of the arithmetical notions of which they treat, since they present only *one* possible system of definitions, whereas it would be necessary to present all possible systems and to demonstrate that there were no others, if we were to attain a complete such analysis.

When we look at what he actually does say, a quite different impression emerges. It was noted above that, in saying that 'conic section' admits of alternative definitions, he adds that these different definitions would confer different senses on it. It thus does not appear that he demands, of a definition of a term already in use, that it exactly preserve the sense of the term; when a term is said to be indefinable, therefore, more is being claimed than that no sense-preserving definition can be given. This impression is confirmed by his discussion of definitions in the unpublished essay 'Logik in der Mathematik' of 1914. There he distinguishes sharply between a definition of a newly introduced term and an analytical definition, which purports to give the sense of a term that has long been in use; and he says that only the first of these ought properly to be called a 'definition', since a definition is, strictly speaking, a matter of arbitrary stipulation.[1] When we arrive, by means of logical analysis, at an analytical definition of a term already in use, we are, he says, entitled to claim that the definiens gives the sense that the term already had only when this equivalence is immediately obvious; and, in this case, we should do better to avoid the word 'definition' and present our statement of the equivalence as an axiom. If the equivalence is *not* immediately obvious, then the better course is to avoid the use of the old term altogether and to use our definition, which can now properly be called such, to introduce a new term

[1] *N.S.*, pp. 226–8, *P.W.*, pp. 209–11.

to replace the old one. It is plain why Frege says all this: he thinks that, if two expressions have the same sense, anyone who grasps their senses must know that they are the same. Without rejecting this principle, one could still claim that the recognition need not be absolutely immediate, but may wait upon reflection; but then the question would arise how much reflection may be allowed, and what, in the course of such reflection, are the deciding considerations. In any case, Frege's position is clear: logical analysis does not require that the definitions given strictly preserve the senses of the defined expressions.

This conclusion resolves the foregoing perplexities about the constituents of a thought. Presumably what, in 'Logik in der Mathematik', Frege refers to as 'logical analysis' is just the sort of investigation he conducts in the *Grundlagen* into the (analytical) definitions possible for arithmetical notions. An investigation of that kind was what Russell and Wittgenstein took to be necessary for the analysis of propositions; but, on Frege's considered view, it was not required for the discernment of the constituents of a thought. For the latter purpose, we require an analysis of the composition of a sentence expressing the thought, and an explanation of the senses of the expressions revealed as genuine constituents of it. Where one of these expressions has in fact been introduced by definition, an account of its sense will require an appeal to that definition; but, in enquiring into the manner in which a thought is compounded out of its constituent senses, we do not need to ask how any expression *might* be defined, since an analytical definition of it is unlikely to be faithful to its sense.

This conclusion is intuitively plausible; it is more reasonable to view Frege's account in *Grundlagen* as a reconstruction of arithmetic than as an exposition of precisely what we have always taken arithmetical statements to mean. Nevertheless, it creates further problems. For one thing, it entails that Frege could not claim to have shown arithmetical theorems, as they are ordinarily understood, to be analytic, but only certain statements expressing closely related thoughts. In *Grundlagen*, he does not moderate his claim in this manner; it is unlikely that he had yet thought through the question whether the definitions he was propounding preserved the pre-existent senses of the terms defined, especially since he had not drawn the distinction between *Sinn* and *Bedeutung*. But, given his mature view of the matter, the question arises what constraints are to be imposed on analytical definitions, what are the conditions for their admissibility. An attitude that has long been common to foundational theories in mathematics is that the most that can be required is to characterize up to isomorphism the relevant mathematical structure, e.g. the system of natural numbers or the field of real numbers, as it is ordinarily conceived, and then to construct or specify any one particular structure that may be proved to be of that isomorphism type; that structure, having, as it were, the right internal character, can then serve the same purpose as the intuitively conceived one. No one can read Frege's *Grundlagen* and suppose that this represents his conception of the enterprise which he there undertook; and the same holds good, I believe, of his construction of the real numbers, initiated, but not completed, in vol. II of *Grundgesetze*. On the contrary, he evidently conceived himself to be carrying out conceptual analysis of some kind, a process which, in the 1914 essay, he is prepared to call 'logical analysis'. The impression given is that the definitions of arithmetical terms given in *Grundlagen*, and, more formally, in *Grundgesetze*, are intended to be taken as in some sense canonical; they display the essence of the natural numbers, the essential meanings of the terms we use for them. To make this impression into a precise thesis, however, we should have to make explicit the conditions which must be met by a successful system of analytical definitions of this kind; and this Frege never attempted to do.

CHAPTER 15

Alternative Analyses

FREGE HELD THE following theses:

A1. A thought may be analysed in distinct ways.
A2. A thought is not built up out of its component concepts; rather, the
    constituents of the thought are arrived at by analysis of it.

But he also held the following two:

B1. The senses of the parts of a sentence are parts of the thought expressed
    by the whole.
B2. A thought is built up out of its constituents, which correspond, by
    and large, to the parts of the sentence expressing it.

On the face of it, thesis A1 and A2 are in conflict with B1 and B2; A2 and B2,
in particular appear to be flatly contradictory. It thus seems that there is a
radical inconsistency at the heart of his philosophy. The difficulty is not to
be circumvented by denying that he held any of these theses; there are
numerous expressions of all four of them. A1, for example, was stated thus
in 1892: 'a thought can be analysed (*zerlegt*) in different ways.'[1] It had
earlier been stated, in terms of judgeable content, in a letter to Marty of
1882: 'I do not believe that for every judgeable content there is only one way
in which it can be decomposed (*zerfallen*).'[2] A2 is also stated in the letter
to Marty: 'I think of a concept as having arisen by decomposition from a
judgeable content.' It is likewise stated in 'Booles rechnende Logik', of
1880–1: 'instead of putting together the judgment out of an individual thing
as subject and an already constructed concept as predicate, we, conversely,

---

[1] 'Über Begriff und Gegenstand', p. 199.
[2] *BW*, p. 164, *P.M.C.*, p. 101.

decompose (*zerfallen*) the judgeable content and so attain the concept.'[1] Its latest expression is in the 'Aufzeichnungen für L. Darmstaedter' of 1919: 'I do not start from concepts and put together the thought or the judgment out of them, but I attain to the parts of the thought by decomposition (*Zerfällung*) of the thought.'[2] B1 receives a very explicit expression in *Grundgesetze*: 'If a name is part of a name of a truth-value, the sense of the first name is a part of the thought expressed by the second name',[3] where, of course, a 'name of a truth-value' is a sentence, and a 'name', in general, is any significant expression. In the unpublished 'Logik in der Mathematik' of 1914, Frege expressed B2 by means of the metaphor of building blocks (*Gedankenbausteine*). 'It is marvellous what language achieves. By means of a few sounds and combinations of sounds it is able to express a vast number of thoughts, including ones which have never before been grasped or expressed by a human being. What makes these achievements possible? The fact that thoughts are constructed out of building-blocks. And these building-blocks correspond to groups of sounds out of which the sentence which expresses the thought is built, so that the construction of the sentence out of its parts corresponds to the construction of the thought out of its parts.'[4] It is also stated in the 'Aufzeichnungen für L. Darmstaedter', in the words, 'The sentence can be regarded as a representation of the thought in such a manner that to the part-whole relation between the thought and its parts there by and large corresponds the same relation between the sentence and its parts.'[5]

The B theses could be enunciated only when Frege had introduced his notion of sense and, with it, his notion of a thought, that is, from 1891 onwards. The A theses, on the other hand, could just as well be expressed in terms of the undifferentiated notion of a judgeable content; indeed, the term 'concept', as it appears in A2, is being used as Frege used it in his early period, to mean, in effect, a thought-constituent. The A theses thus appear in his very earliest writings, in which they are very prominent; the B theses do not appear until the mature period, and B2, in particular, is characteristic of the late writings. We cannot, however, resolve the conflict between them by appeal to a change of mind, taking Frege to have discarded the A theses in favour of the B theses: the overlap is far too great for that. Of particular importance, in this connection, is the occurrence of both A2

[1] *N.S.*, p. 18, *P.W.*, p. 17.
[2] *N.S.*, p. 273, *P.W.*, p. 253.
[3] *Grundgesetze*, vol. I, 1893, § 32.
[4] *N.S.*, p. 243, *P.W.*, p. 225.
[5] *N.S.*, p. 275, *P.W.*, p. 255.

and B2, within two pages of one another, in the 'Aufzeichnungen für L. Darmstaedter', a set of notes in which Frege summarized his doctrines. It therefore becomes critical to decide whether they can be reconciled, or whether the contradiction between them is genuine. If it is genuine, then there is a fundamental inconsistency, not merely in Frege's logical system, but in his whole philosophy of logic, a glaring inconsistency to which he was oblivious. The conception, embodied in the B theses, of a thought as having constituents, which are the senses of constituent expressions in the sentence that expresses the thought, suggests that the thought is capable of a *unique* analysis into its ultimate constituents. This seems hard to reconcile with thesis A1, that a thought can be analysed in distinct ways; and the difficulty is reinforced by Frege's saying, on the same page of 'Über Begriff und Gegenstand' as that on which he stated A1, that 'different sentences may express the same thought', especially since the sentences he gives as examples do not appear to have the same structure.

The A and B theses all concern the relation of a thought to its parts. We may consider two possible models for the relation of whole to parts. One is that of a molecule to its component atoms; the other that of a country to its component regions. The composition of a molecule out of atoms is a matter of its intrinsic structure. One can characterize the molecule without knowing anything about its internal structure, namely as a molecule of such-and-such a substance, and one may then be able to say something about its properties; but, in order to discover anything about the molecule in itself, for instance to explain its properties in terms of its constitution, it is necessary to uncover its structure as composed of atoms of various elements connected in a certain way. We may say that the molecule is *built up* put of the component atoms; and the analysis of the molecule into those atoms is unique. Contrasted with this is the relation between a country and its regions. The regions are to be considered, not in a political sense, as provinces with some degree of autonomy, but as a geographer might choose to differentiate them. One and the same country might be subdivided into regions in different ways for different purposes—in terms of geological structure, the kind of terrain, types of vegetation or climate, the languages, religions or culture of the inhabitants, etc. Indeed, two different subdivisions into regions, neither preferable to the other, might be proposed for the *same* purpose. The dissection of the country into regions is not part of its intrinsic structure. There is no unique correct way of so dissecting it, and one might know a great deal about the country without considering any such dissection: the dissection is not an essential part of every account of the internal character of the country, but merely a convenient means of systematizing a particular such account. It is therefore preferable to say that the country may be *divided* or *broken down* into those regions, rather than describing it as *built up* out of them.

Frege's A theses correspond to using the model of a country and its regions for our conception of the relation of a thought to its parts. His B theses similarly correspond to using a molecule and its component atoms as the model. The question before us is whether it is possible that, for nearly thirty years, Frege used these two different models without ever noticing their incompatibility.

Theses which it would be correct to advance if the model of a country and its regions were the right one will cause perplexity if they are interpreted in terms of the model of a molecule and its component atoms. The expression of such perplexity is very well conveyed in a passage from F. P. Ramsey,[1] appositely quoted by Geach in connection with Frege in his Wolfson Lecture of 1975.[2] We regard the proposition '*aRb*', Ramsey says, as being an 'incomprehensible trinity' of propositions, of which 'one asserts that the relation *R* holds between *a* and *b*, the second asserts the possession by *a* of the complex property of "having *R* to *b*", while the third asserts that *b* has the complex property that *a* has *R* to it. These,' he continues, 'must be three different propositions because they have three different sets of constituents, and yet they are not three propositions but one proposition, for they all say the same thing, namely that *a* has *R* to *b*.' The problem is: how *can* there be distinct possible analyses of the *same* proposition? Ramsey asks this question because, although he perceives that the same proposition can be analysed in different ways, he thinks of the analysis as revealing the constituents out of which the proposition is built up. He thinks of the analysis as like the analysis of a molecule: it is as if he were asking, 'How can the *same* molecule be made up out of distinct sets of atoms put together in different ways?'. The difficulty ought to dissolve soon as it is realized that the analysis of a proposition is not like the analysis of a molecule, but like the analysis of a country into regions.

This is essentially Geach's solution; but he presents it in a quite particular, and satisfactorily Fregean, way. According to him, the difficulty is to be resolved by appeal to the notions of function and argument. 3 is the positive square root of 9: but neither the number 9 nor the function *positive square root of* is a *part* of the number 3, and there is therefore no difficulty about the fact that 3 is not only the value of this function for this argument, but also the value of the function *cube root of* for the argument 27. All this relates to

---

[1] *Foundations of Mathematics*, London, 1931, p. 118.

[2] 'Names and Identity', in S. Guttenplan (ed.), op. cit., p. 146.

the realm of reference. The expression 'positive square root of 9' can be split into a complete part, '9', which stands for an object, namely a number, and an incomplete part, 'positive square root of ξ', which stands for a function, namely one from numbers to numbers: the whole expression is itself complete, and again stands for a number. To say that the reference of a part of an expression was part of the reference of the whole would involve that the value of a function for a given argument had, as parts, both the argument and the function itself; and this is manifestly absurd. Frege did indeed commit this mistake, when he said that a judgment is a distinction of parts within a truth-value, and went on explicitly to say that the reference of a word is part of the reference of the sentence.[1] It plainly is a mistake, however, and Frege later retracted it; as he observed,[2] one cannot say that Sweden is part of the capital of Sweden.

Geach proposes to transfer these considerations from the realm of reference to the realm of sense. A sentence must contain at least one incomplete expression; and Frege applies the same principle to the thought expressed by a sentence, regarding the sense of an incomplete expression as itself incomplete. Geach is quite right to observe that, for Frege, this explains 'what makes the senses of names and . . . predicates stick together to form a thought';[3] it is Frege's solution of what is sometimes called 'the problem of the unity of the proposition'. As he wrote in 1892, 'not all the parts of a thought can be complete; at least one must be unsaturated or predicative, or otherwise they would not stick to one another'.[4] Likewise, speaking in 1923 of the thought expressed by a negated sentence, he said that it 'appears as put together out of a part that needs completion or . . . is unsaturated, to which the negation-word corresponds linguistically, and a thought. We cannot negate without something to negate, and this is a thought. What brings it about that the whole holds together is that this thought saturates the unsaturated part or . . . completes the part that needs completion. And the conjecture lies to hand that, in logic generally, the construction of a whole always takes place through the saturation of what is unsaturated.'[5]

Geach's solution depends, however, upon his construing Frege's notion of the incompleteness of the sense of an incomplete expression in a quite particular way, namely in what is, perhaps, the most immediately natural way; he takes the sense of such an expression to be incomplete in exactly

---

[1] 'Über Sinn und Bedeutung', 1892, pp. 35–6.
[2] 'Aufzeichnungen für L. Darmstaedter', *N.S.*, p. 275, *P.W.*, p. 255.
[3] Op. cit., p. 150.
[4] 'Über Begriff und Gegenstand', p. 205.
[5] 'Gedankengefüge', p. 37.

the same way that its reference is, that is, by being a function. The sense of a predicate will not be a concept, since it will not have truth-values as values; but it will, on this interpretation, be a function, which, for the sense of a proper name as argument, yields a thought as value. Thus, as we saw in Chapter 13, on Geach's interpretation the sense of the predicate 'ξ spins', as it occurs in the sentence 'The Earth spins', will be a function which, for the sense of the proper name 'the Earth' as argument, has as value the thought that the Earth spins. The analysis of a thought will then constitute a representation of it as the value of some such function for some particular argument: not necessarily, of course, a function of one argument, and not necessarily a function of first level, but always a function whose arguments are senses and whose values are thoughts. On this interpretation, there will be no difficulty whatever in the same thought's being capable of distinct analyses; for the same thought can be the value, for different arguments, or perhaps even sometimes for the same arguments, of different functions, just as one and the same number can. No one would say that 16 must be two numbers which are yet one number on the ground that it is *both* the value of the function ξ^2 for the argument 4 *and* the value of the function 4^ξ for the argument 2.

This appears a satisfactory resolution of Ramsey's difficulty; but it is no resolution of *our* difficulty as exegetes of Frege. Our difficulty was to answer the question, 'Was Frege so confused as to fail to recognize a plain contradiction when it stared him in the face?'. If Geach's solution is correct, the answer to this question must surely be 'Yes'; for Geach's solution involves jettisoning the B theses, those which represent the relation of a thought to its parts on the model of a molecule and its component atoms. On Geach's interpretation, to think that the sense of a part is part of the sense of the whole would be a special case of thinking that a function and its argument were parts of the value of the function for that argument. Geach is, indeed, consistent in drawing just that conclusion; referring to the doctrine that the sense of a sentence is compounded out of the senses of its parts, he comments that 'it is quite true that Frege did use . . . this way of speaking', but that it 'should to my mind be charitably expounded, not imitated'.[1] Unfortunately, the doctrine is one that Frege constantly and emphatically reiterated. It is not at all like the thesis that the reference of the part is a part of the reference of the whole, which he stated once, never repeated, and in the end expressly repudiated, without mentioning that he had ever held it; it is a theme that runs through all his work, once the notion of sense had been introduced,

[1] Op. cit., p. 149.

with progressively greater attention given to it with the passage of time. We saw it stated in what he intended to be the definitive formulations of Part I of *Grundgesetze* in 1893. We find it in a letter to Russell of 1902, where he says that the sense of the sign '3 + 5' is part of the thought expressed by '3 + 5 > 7', and that 'likewise, the sense of "3", the sense of "+" and the sense of "5" are parts of the sense of "3 + 5" '.[1] And we have seen it elaborated in the late works. If Frege understood the senses of incomplete expressions as Geach believes that he did, and if he thought of the analysis of a thought into its components, as Geach supposes, as the representation of it as the value of some function for some argument or arguments, he would have had no more reason to say that the senses of '3', '+' and '5' are parts of the sense of '3 + 5' than to say that addition and the numbers 3 and 5 are parts of the number 8.

Fortunately for our estimate of Frege, we have already seen, in Chapter 13, that Geach's solution is not, in itself, defensible. On Geach's account, the sense of the predicate 'ξ spins' is given to us as a function from the senses of names to thoughts, one which carries us from the sense of 'the Earth' to the thought expressed by 'The Earth spins'. How, in such a case, should we grasp that thought? One can understand this question in two ways, namely as 'How should we ever come to apprehend the thought that the Earth spins?' and 'How should we recognize the sentence "The Earth spins" as expressing that thought?'; in whichever way it is interpreted, the question is baffling. Whether we conceived of the function as being the sense of the predicate 'ξ spins' or in some other way, how should we, on this conception, know *what* thought it was that constituted the value of that function for that particular argument? What, indeed, would it be to grasp a thought at all? It is apparent that Geach's account will not, of itself, supply any answer to these questions: it yields no conception of what is involved in grasping a thought or in recognizing which thought a particular sentence expresses. Before we can form any conception of numerical functions, we must already know what numbers are; and, likewise, before grasping the conception of functions whose values are thoughts, we must already know what thoughts are, and how to identify particular thoughts. Having first learned to speak of numbers, we may indeed then acquire the use of complex expressions for numbers, involving the use of specific functional operators like '+' or '.', without having the *general* idea of an arithmetical function or functional expression. It remains that, in order to grasp the use of any particular numerical functor, we must first have some conception of the objects for

---

[1] *BW*, p. 231, *P.M.C.*, p. 149.

which terms containing it are to stand. In the same way, in order to grasp the sense of 'ξ spins', as Geach conceives of it, we should already have to know what thoughts were. As Geach himself recognizes, the sense of the predicate would not be a part of, nor even a contribution to, the sense of 'The Earth spins'; rather, we should have already to grasp the thought expressed by that sentence in advance of understanding the sentence as expressing it.

There are two distinct difficulties here. The first is that Geach's account provides no access to the notion of a thought or to that of grasping a thought. The whole advantage of the account was that it removed the mystery from the conception of a thought as being capable of distinct analyses: we can think of 8 as the cube of 2 or as half of 16 because we do not need to think of it as either. But a heavy price is paid for invoking this analogy. It is natural to think that we might explain what it is to grasp the thought that the Earth spins in terms of what is involved in understanding the sentence, 'The Earth spins', and equally involved in understanding any sentence, of the same or another language, which has the same structure and whose component parts are used in the same way as the corresponding ones in 'The Earth spins'. But the price of adopting Geach's account is precisely to render it impossible to explain a grasp of the thought in that manner; for, if we did so, we should throw away the supposed advantages of the account. To explain a grasp of the thought in terms of understanding a particular sentence that expresses it, or any intensionally isomorphic sentence, would, on Geach's account, make a specific representation of that thought, namely as the value of the function that constitutes the sense of 'ξ spins' for the sense of 'the Earth' as argument, integral to the thought. The whole point of the account was, however, to deny that its being the value of that particular function for that particular argument is integral to or constitutive of the thought; once it is allowed that it is, it may as well be admitted that the senses of the parts are parts of the sense of the whole.

The first difficulty is, therefore, that Geach's account yields no philosophical explanation of what thoughts are. The second difficulty, allied to the first, but distinct from it, is that the account appears to entail that we are capable, in every case, of grasping a thought in advance of understanding any sentence expressing it: we must already be able to pick out a given thought before we can conceive of any function that has that thought as value for some argument. This difficulty does not relate to the needs of philosophers of language or of thought, but to the capacities of human beings as language-users and as thinkers.

It might be objected that, in the foregoing exposition, the second difficulty was exaggerated. The thesis that we cannot understand a functional expression unless we know in advance what it is to refer to those objects of which the functional expression will be used to construct complex names cannot be asserted without reservations. Numbers themselves provide a counter-example: it is incoherent to suppose that we *could* have a name, not involving a functional operator, for *every* natural number. Another kind of counter-example is a functor such as 'the direction of ξ', discussed by Frege in *Grundlagen*.[1] Unless one proposes, as in the end Frege appears to do, to introduce this functor by identifying directions with objects of some already known kind, it is natural to treat that functor as forming complex singular terms standing for objects of a sort with which we were not familiar before it was introduced. But neither of these counter-examples is of any help in extricating Geach's account from the difficulty. In fact, the counter-examples are in principle the same. If it be held that we can conceive of a totality containing all the natural numbers only by coming to understand some notation in which they can all be represented, for instance the notation that uses only 'o' and the successor-operator, this is just to hold that an awareness of the natural numbers depends upon a mastery of that or some similar notation. In that case, the representation of the natural numbers in the given notation assumes a canonical status: all other numerical terms are ultimately to be explained by reference to it. We may think of 27 as the cube of 3; but we could not think of it at all save as the successor of 26, and explaining what it is for it to be the cube of 3 would, if traced back, bring us once more to its representation as the successor of 26. The same would go for directions if 'the direction of ξ' were conceived in the proposed manner: we could not then think of a direction save as the referent of a term formed by means of that functor, and any other way of referring to one would have ultimately to be explained in terms of it. Thus, in these cases, there is a distinguished way of identifying natural numbers or directions, namely as the value of a particular function for a suitable argument. Natural numbers and directions, conceived in this way, do not seem to provide a good analogy with thoughts, since there is no *one* function such that grasping any thought involves taking it as a value of that function. But, once it is allowed that, for any particular thought, there may be some function for which it is integral to grasping that thought to take it as the value of the function, the original advantages of Geach's account have, once again, been lost.

The first difficulty seemed to involve divorcing our capacity to think from our capacity to use language, since an explanation of the former could not

[1] §§ 64–8.

be given in terms of the latter. It would, therefore, involve the repudiation of the whole analytic tradition in philosophy, that tradition which stems in large part from Frege; it would involve treating the philosophy of language as irrelevant to the philosophy of thought, and Frege as having gone astray in devoting so much attention to language when his avowed interest was with thought. Geach, of course, intends no such large consequences; but they follow from his view, for all that. Now, if we are attempting to interpret Frege, and if we have adopted Geach's view concerning the senses of predicates, what account are we to give of the senses of sentences, that is, of thoughts? Geach's view yields no account of what thoughts are; and so we shall have no recourse but to fall back on that given by Frege himself, namely that to grasp the sense of a sentence is to know the way in which its truth-value is determined. If the sentence is 'The Earth spins', how *is* its truth-value determined? The sentence is true provided that the referent of the name 'the Earth' satisfies a certain condition, the condition given by the predicate; as remarked in Chapter 13, the determination of the truth-value of the sentence goes via the referent of the name. As we saw there, once the referent of the name has been determined, its sense falls out of account, that sense having already made its contribution to the determination of the truth-value of the whole. The sense of the predicate therefore determines a function from objects to truth-values, just as Frege says; that sense must accordingly be given to us as a particular means of determining such a function. A function from the senses of names to thoughts plays no part in this: if we had such a function, it would not enable us to arrive at a concept, a function from objects to truth-values, unless we already knew the conditions under which the thoughts in question were true. By appealing to the only explanation of what it is to grasp a thought that is available to us, we have thus been compelled to abandon Geach's account of the senses of predicates and the analysis of thoughts.

In abandoning it, we have no need to deny that the senses of incomplete expressions are themselves incomplete, and we should be unfaithful to Frege if we did so. We have, rather, to recognize that they are incomplete not after the mode of referents, but after the mode of senses. To grasp the sense of an expression is no more than to grasp a means of determining its referent: so to grasp the sense of a predicate is to grasp a means of determining a function from objects to truth-values. It is integral to the understanding of the predicate that we recognize it *as* a predicate, that is, as an incomplete expression standing for such a function. It is in this that the incompleteness of its sense consists; there is no role to be played by an assumption that it is itself a function.

We have now arrived at a form of explanation of what it is to grasp a thought or to understand a sentence as expressing a particular thought that accords with Frege's own account of the relation of sense to reference. This explanation presents the senses of the component parts of a sentence as integral to the sense of the whole. It thus validates the B theses, those corresponding with the model of a molecule and its component atoms for the relation of a thought to its components. It therefore, so far, leaves the conflict between them and the A theses no more resolved than it was by Geach's account. How can it be resolved?

It can be resolved only by distinguishing two distinct types of analysis to which thoughts, and the sentences that express them, may be subjected. The distinction is not new; it was made in *FPL*,[1] and, as was there said, analyses of the two types serve quite different purposes. But the distinction was not heavily stressed in *FPL*, and discussion of it was intertwined with that of the difference between simple and complex predicates, with which almost everyone has disagreed, quite wrongly. Once the distinction between the two types of analysis is firmly established, the point about simple and complex predicates follows with little more ado; so, in this chapter, only the former will be discussed, the contentious matter of simple and complex predicates being reserved for the next chapter.

Frege himself never introduced any distinct terminology to differentiate the two types of analysis; hence the apparent contradiction between what he says when he has one type in mind and what he says when he has in mind the other. It is even possible that he did not remain as vividly aware of the distinction as he certainly was when he wrote *Begriffsschrift*. Nevertheless, I believe that it is clearly apparent from his writings, and embodies the only interpretation that will make clear sense of them. I shall, henceforward, reserve the word 'analysis' for the first of the two types, and use the word 'decomposition' for the second.

Analysis, as opposed to decomposition, is concerned to reveal the manner in which the sense of a sentence depends upon the senses of its parts. Thus the sense of the sentence 'Every number is smaller than some prime' is dependent upon the sense of 'ξ is smaller than some prime', but not on that of 'Every number is smaller than ξ'; the first step in the analysis of the sentence is to represent it as formed by attaching the expression of generality 'every number' to the predicate 'ξ is smaller than some prime', taking its sense as being immediately dependent upon the senses of those two expressions. Analysis takes place in several stages: if the parts into which the sentence is split by the first step of the analysis are themselves complex, we may ask in turn how they are to be analysed, until we arrive at simple constituents. I shall speak of the parts of the sentence, ultimate or intermediate, arrived at by analysis, pursued to any stage, as its *constituents*, reserving the word *components* for the parts revealed by the other process, that of decomposition; likewise for the parts of the corresponding thought.

Analysis, as just explained, is concerned with relations of dependence between the *sense* of a sentence and those of its parts, which is why we may with equal right speak of the analysis of a *sentence* and of a *thought*. It is to be compared with the analysis of a molecule into its constituent atoms; it displays what was called in an earlier chapter the 'essential structure' of the sentence, and may be said to uncover the internal structure of the thought it expresses. But in fact it can be explained at the level of reference, without invoking the notion of sense. A theory of reference, or semantic theory in the strict sense, seeks to characterize the manner in which the truth-value of every sentence of a given language is determined. It does this by assigning a reference or semantic value to every simple expression of the language, and specifying the way in which the reference of any complex expression depends upon the references of its immediate constituents. In bringing the theory to bear upon a given sentence, we have, therefore, first to proceed in the reverse direction, so as to exhibit the sentence as having been constructed, in stages, out of simple expressions in accordance with the principles of phrase- and sentence-formation embodied in the semantic theory (theory of reference). It is because the theory of reference necessarily proceeds by specifying the dependence of the references of complex expressions upon those, less complex, that occur within it that the metaphor of construction is so compelling, leading Frege, in his late period, to speak of building-blocks. The analysis of a sentence does not, of course, provide an analysis of its referent, as Frege was momentarily tempted to think; it merely displays the manner in which the referent of the sentence, which is its truth-value, and does not itself have parts, depends upon the referents of its constituent expressions. But it is rightly said to provide an analysis of the thought the sentence expresses, for the following reason. The sense of an expression is the manner in which its referent is given to us, that is, the way in which, from our knowledge of the language, we regard its referent as determined. If the expression is complex, our understanding of how its referent is determined is dependent upon our implicit grasp of the principles made explicit by the semantic theory; the referent of the whole expression is grasped as depending upon the referents of its ultimate constituents in accordance with the full analysis of the expression, the referents of those constituents being determined in ways corresponding to their senses. A grasp of the sense of a sentence or other complex expression involves grasping the senses of its constituent words and understanding how they have been put together; because the sense is the way in which the referent is given, an analysis which shows how the referent is determined in accordance with the structure of the expression also shows how its sense depends upon the senses of its parts.

Frege's logical symbolism was intended to be one the analysis of whose sentences is perspicuous. It is also unique: for every formula of the symbolic language, there is one and only one way to represent it as having been built up from primitive signs. For an unambiguous sentence of any language, analysis will be unique, modulo the stage to which it is carried: at any stage except the last, there is a unique next step.

The other process, decomposition, is undertaken for either of two purposes, quite distinct from that of analysis. One such purpose is to explain the validity of an inference in which the given sentence figures, or to exhibit such an inference as exemplifying some general pattern. The fact that analysis is not sufficient for this purpose comes about in the following way. The analysis of a quantified sentence, or of one involving some equivalent expression of generality, requires, as its first step, that we split the sentence into the expression of generality and a complex predicate: this complex predicate is therefore a genuine constituent of the sentence, and its sense is part of the thought expressed. But, in order to recognize the validity of inferences involving that sentence, we must be able to recognize the complex predicate as occurring in a simpler type of sentence, one resulting from the insertion of a proper name into the argument-place of the complex predicate. For instance, in order to recognize that, from the sentence 'If anyone killed Brutus, he was an honourable man', there follows 'If Brutus killed Brutus, Brutus was an honourable man', we must regard the latter sentence as containing an occurrence of the complex predicate 'If ξ killed Brutus, ξ was an honourable man'. This corresponds to a possible decomposition of the simpler sentence, namely into that complex predicate and the proper name 'Brutus'. If we could not recognize that simpler sentence as capable of being so decomposed, we should not, indeed, have the conception of that complex predicate at all; if we lacked that conception, we could neither frame nor understand the quantified sentence. The important fact is that no awareness, however implicit, of the possibility of that decomposition, and hence of the presence of that complex predicate within it, is required for an understanding of the unquantified sentence. The complex predicate 'If ξ killed Brutus, ξ was an honourable man' is a genuine constituent of the sentence 'If anyone killed Brutus, he was an honourable man'; but it is only a component, not a constituent, of the sentence 'If Brutus killed Brutus, Brutus was an honourable man'. The first step in analysing the latter sentence will be to exhibit it as formed by means of the connective 'If . . ., . . .' from its two constituent sub-sentences: an explanation of the sense of the sentence would therefore make no allusion to the occurrence in it of the complex predicate, and a grasp of that sense requires no recognition of its occurrence.

From 'If anyone killed Brutus, he was an honourable man' and 'Brutus killed Brutus', we may infer 'Brutus was an honourable man'. If we represent this inference as proceeding by first inferring 'If Brutus killed Brutus, Brutus was an honourable man' by universal instantiation, and then applying modus ponens, we shall not need to appeal to the occurrence in the first premiss of the predicate 'ξ killed Brutus', but only of the more complex predicate cited above. More exactly, if all inference were carried out by appeal only to simple elimination and introduction rules, then, in order to explain it, we should need to recognize the occurrence of a complex predicate only in sentences of two kinds: ones formed by attaching a quantifier to that complex predicate; and ones resulting from the insertion of a name into the argument-place of that predicate. In this case, not every constituent of a sentence would be a component of it. But, in actual practice, we reason in accordance with more complicated rules: from the two premisses, anyone could immediately infer the conclusion 'Brutus was an honourable man' without going through the intermediate step. Even if we were not so clever as to be able to do this by mere insight, it would be useful to us to establish general patterns of inference to which we could thereafter appeal. A pattern exemplified by the inference in question is from premisses of the forms 'For every α, if $F\alpha$, $G\alpha$' and 'Fb' to 'Gb'; but to see this pattern so exemplified, we have to recognize the predicate 'ξ killed Brutus' as occurring, not only in the second premiss 'Brutus killed Brutus', but also in the quantified first premiss. For this purpose, therefore, we need a more general conception of decomposition.

An exact account of the general notion of decomposition is arrived at as follows. We begin with a sentence, or, likewise, a complex singular term ('proper name'). The simplest type of decomposition is into a proper name and a (one-place) predicate or functor. This is effected by the removal from the sentence or complex term of one or more (not necessarily all) occurrences of a proper name: what is left is a predicate or functional expression, that is, an incomplete expression with one or more gaps, all considered as required to be filled by the same proper name, and hence jointly constituting a single argument-place. The most immediate generalization is to the case when the incomplete expression that is left has two or more argument-places, and so forms an n-ary relational expression or functor. When $n = 2$, there are two cases. The first is that in which we remove one or more occurrences of each of two distinct proper names; for determinacy, the argument-places of the resulting incomplete expression must be tagged as first and second. Thus 'Cane died and Visconti married Cane's widow' may be decomposed into 'Visconti', 'Cane' and 'ζ died and ξ married ζ's widow'; a distinct decomposition yields 'Cane', 'Visconti' and 'ξ died and ζ married ξ's widow' as components. The second case is that in which we remove, say, m occurrences of some one proper name, regarding k of them as to be filled by a proper name, the same for each of them, and the remaining $m - k$ by another proper name, perhaps a distinct one. If we overlook this case, we shall have disallowed the legitimate decomposition of 'Brutus killed Brutus' into 'Brutus', 'Brutus' and 'ξ killed ζ'.

Any decomposition is achieved in the same general way, namely by removing from a sentence or complex term one or more occurrences of each of one or more expressions, leaving an incomplete expression. In the more general case, the expression removed does not have to be a proper name, but may be a predicate or functor, indeed one of any level. In order to make the idea precise, we have to be clear what is meant by saying that a predicate or functor occurs in a sentence or term. This has to be explained inductively. In the first place, a predicate or functor (of any level) occurs in a sentence or term formed by filling its argument-place or places. Secondly, it occurs in a sentence or term if it occurs in a complete constituent of that sentence or term. And, finally, it occurs in a sentence or term if it occurs in a complete expression from which an incomplete constituent of that sentence or term could be formed, provided that, in the process of formation, no part of that predicate or functor was removed (but a bound variable inserted in its argument-place or places). Thus, by the first stipulation, 'ξ killed Brutus' occurs in 'Cassius killed Brutus'. By the second stipulation, therefore, it also occurs in 'If Cassius killed Brutus, Cassius was an honourable man', since 'Cassius killed Brutus' is a complete constituent of the longer sentence. From that longer sentence, we can form the predicate 'If ξ killed Brutus, ξ was an honourable man'; and that complex predicate is an (incomplete) constituent of the sentence 'For every α, if α killed Brutus, α was an honourable man'. In the process of forming the complex predicate, no part of the predicate 'ξ killed Brutus' was removed; so, by the third stipulation, that predicate occurs in the quantified sentence. By similar considerations, so does the predicate 'ξ was an honourable man'. We may therefore remove both predicates from the sentence, leaving the second-level relational expression 'For every α, if $\Phi(\alpha)$, $\Psi(\alpha)$'.

This explanation is still not fully explicit, but there is no need to make it so; enough has been said to indicate that, while the process of decomposition itself takes place in a single stage, the determination of when an incomplete expression is to be seen as occurring in a complete one, and hence as a candidate for being removed in a possible decomposition of it, depends on its analysis. As observed, the decomposition of a sentence is essential for the recognition of the validity of inferences in which it figures; but to give this as the only purpose which decomposition serves would be to understate its importance for Frege. It also plays an essential part in the formation of sentences and other complex terms, such as definite descriptions or names of classes; for, as explained in *Grundgesetze*, it is by decomposition that we arrive at complex predicates and other complex incomplete expressions in the first place. It is essential for us to be able to form complex predicates if we are to be able to form those sentences and terms of which they are genuine constituents, that is, in the first instance, those formed by attaching a quantifier or description operator to them. Although analysis and decomposition are distinct processes, they are therefore intimately linked. The analysis of a quantified sentence requires us to see a predicate, in general complex, as a constituent of it, and the conception of the complex predicate is attained by decomposition of a simpler sentence. Conversely, in order to decompose a sentence by the removal of one or more incomplete expressions, we must recognize those incomplete expressions as occurring in it, and this involves knowing the constituents, and hence the analysis, of the sentence.

Analysis is unique, and in general requires several stages. Decomposition is never unique; it is to the different decompositions that are always possible that thesis A1 relates. Decomposition occurs in a single step. Analysis proceeds by identifying the principal operator in the sentence, if it is a complex one, and the expression or expressions upon which it operates. Decomposition, as we have seen, is effected by selecting any one or more component expressions, which may be complete or incomplete, regardless of where they may occur in the sentence, and removing one or more occurrences of each of them to form a simply or multiply incomplete expression which can be viewed as a component, whose argument-places were filled by the components that have been removed. Analysis is essential to an account of the sense of the sentence; a grasp of that sense involves an implicit apprehension of the essential structure which analysis reveals. 'It is astonishing what language achieves, in that by means of a few syllables it expresses unsurveyably many thoughts, so that, for a thought which an inhabitant of the Earth has just grasped for the first time, it finds a clothing in which another, to whom it is quite new, can recognize it. This would not be possible if we could not distinguish parts in the thought which corresponded to the parts of the sentence, so that the structure of the sentence could serve as a picture of the structure of the thought.'[1] Decomposition, on the other hand, does not aim to explain in what our grasp of the sense of the sentence consists; rather, it takes that as already given. It is thus to be compared to dividing a country into regions; and there is no problem about its being able to be applied to the same sentence in several different ways. The decomposition of a sentence is the choice of a particular way in which to view it: it represents the discernment in it of one particular common pattern which it shares with other sentences.

To regard a complex predicate or functional expression as arrived at by decomposition is to supply an irrefutable ground for calling it incomplete; it is, and can be thought of only as, something obtained from a sentence or complex term by removing bits of it. Moreover, it is only in the light of its having been so obtained that we can conceive of its sense. We can understand a quantified sentence, formed by attaching a quantifier to a complex predicate, only if we grasp the sense of that predicate; and we can grasp its sense only by seeing it as a component of simpler sentences in which a proper name stands in its argument-place. It was a constant principle with Frege, from *Begriffsschrift* onwards, that we understand the complex predicate by understanding the sentence from which it was formed by decomposition, not conversely. More exactly, we grasp its sense as the common feature of the thoughts expressed by the various distinct sentences from any one of which it could have been obtained by decomposition; just as the predicate constitutes a common feature of the sentences themselves, so the thoughts which they express are uniformly related to the senses of the various expressions (proper names, if the predicate is of first level) which stand, in the different sentences, in the argument-place of the predicate. That is possible because the contribution of any expression to the manner in which the truth-value of a sentence containing it always goes via its referent. Hence, if the predicate is a first-level one, we can explain what it is for it to be true of any object as the condition for the truth of a sentence in which a name of that object is inserted into its argument-place; if, for any proper name, we have determined its referent, the manner in which we then determine the truth-value of the sentence so formed will be uniform. We grasp this, and hence grasp the sense of the complex predicate, precisely because we already

---

[1] 'Gedankengefüge', 1923, p. 36.

grasp the sense of any such sentence, provided that we understand the given proper name. But this is possible only because decomposition is *not* the same as analysis. Analysis lays bare what is involved in a grasp of the sense of the sentence; an understanding of the sentence as built up in that way from its ultimate constituents therefore demands an antecedent understanding of the constituents. But decomposition, in any non-trivial case, presupposes a prior grasp of the sense of the sentence; the components arrived at by its means are not, in general, genuine constituents of it, and our understanding of the sentence is therefore independent of our recognition of the complex predicate as occurring in it. It is this principle which is expressed by thesis A2, which relates to decomposition, and which accordingly in no way contradicts B2, which relates to analysis.

Frege considered the process of decomposition as applicable, not merely to the thought, but to the sentence expressing the thought. In the passage from 'Über Begriff und Gegenstand' already cited, he speaks of conceiving the same *sentence*, now as predicating something of a concept, now as predicating something of an object;[1] and in *Grundgesezte*, vol I, § 30, he speaks of forming the name of a first-level function from a name of an object by omitting certain constituent occurrences of some proper name. But he also thought that the sentences of natural language are framed in such a way as to indicate one or another preferred decomposition, in particular by bringing one or another part of the sentence into subject-position, one device for doing this being the distinction between the active and passive voices. From *Begriffsschrift* onwards, he was clear that the grammatical notion of the subject has no logical significance: and the possibility of so transforming a sentence as to bring a different part of it into subject-position is one reason why, in natural language, the same thought can be expressed by sentences of different grammatical forms. Thus, in the passage already quoted from 'Über Begriff und Gegenstand', he says that the sentence 'There is at least one square root of 4' predicates something of the concept *square root of 4*, but that the same thought could be presented as predicating something of the number 4, as in the sentence 'The number 4 has the property that there is something of which it is the square'. We should not here pay attention to the presumed connection between 'square root of' and 'square of', which Frege is not speaking about, but appealing to only for facility of expression; nor to the occurrence of the word 'property', which he puts in only to emphasize the fact that the thought is now being seen as saying something about the number 4: the point would be adequately

---

[1] P. 200.

made by citing the sentence 'The number 4 is such that there is something which is a square root of it'. Differences in grammatical structure of this kind leave the sense unaffected, and are hence irrelevant to the representation of the sentence in symbolic notation, and, equally, to the analysis that displays its essential structure. An ideal symbolic notation would have a unique form of expression for each thought. Frege says just this in a letter to Husserl of 1906: having explained that by 'equipollent sentences' he means ones that express the same thought, he remarks, 'One would need to have for every system of equipollent sentences only a single sentence in normal form (*Normalsatz*), and could communicate every thought by means of these sentences in normal form.'[1] Frege did not think he had attained this ideal, and suspected it to be unattainable; but his notation had suppressed much of the redundancy of natural language which permits the same thought to be expressed in different ways.

The reason why it is possible to suppress the devices present in natural language for indicating a preferred decomposition is that, once we have understood the principles according to which such decomposition may be carried out, the possible decompositions of a given sentence are apparent from its symbolic expression. Indeed, they are already apparent from the sentence of natural language: its taking a form that points towards one preferred decomposition does not make the others impossible. Now the idea that something may be complex and yet be exhibited as complex in different, equally good, ways is not in itself absurd. A mathematical tree is a complex structure: yet we can represent it both as consisting of nodes, subject to a partial order of a certain kind, or as consisting of paths, having certain relations of overlap. A thought might have a complexity of this type, allowing it to be analysed in either of two equally good ways; and, in that case, two possibilities would be open regarding sentences that expressed it. The complexity of such a sentence might reflect that of the thought only imperfectly, namely by being capable of being analysed in only one way, corresponding to one of the two possible analyses of the thought; the thought might then also be expressible by another sentence, admitting an analysis corresponding to the other possible analysis of the thought, and in this way there could be sentences of differing structures expressing the same thought. Alternatively, the thought might be expressible by a sentence that perfectly reflected its complexity, namely by admitting two equally good analyses, corresponding to the two possible analyses of the thought. Under either alternative hypothesis concerning the relation

---

[1] *BW*, p. 102, *P.M.C.*, p. 67.

of sentence to thought expressed, there is no intrinsic difficulty in the idea that a thought may admit of different possible analyses; no difficulty impelling us to say that there must be many thoughts that are yet only one thought, having constituents that are nevertheless not constituents. But, granted that there is no intrinsic difficulty in the idea, it does not appear to have been Frege's. On the restricted sense of 'analysis' here adopted, Frege does not seem to have envisaged the possibility of alternative analyses, but to have regarded each thought, and each sentence, as admitting only *one* analysis.

Still less is there any problem about the distinct decompositions of a thought, or of the sentence expressing it, which Frege does hold to be possible. A complete expression—sentence or proper name, simple or complex—can be a component of a sentence only by being an actual constituent of it. But an incomplete expression can be a component without being a constituent; and, in such a case, it is more aptly regarded as a *pattern* discerned in the sentence, which it shares with other sentences, than as a *part* of the sentence. Frege is inclined metaphorically to describe the constituents into which the sentence is to be analysed as that out of which it has been built up. Decomposition, on the other hand, starts with the sentence, and does not reveal how it was formed; on the contrary, it may itself involve a process of formation, since, as Frege states in *Grundgesetze*, vol. 1, § 30, it is one of the ways in which a name of a concept, relation or function is formed in the first instance. No inconsistency is involved in saying that the sentence, or the thought expressed, must be regarded as having been formed out of its constituents in one unique way, but that, once it is formed, it is possible to see it as exemplifying each of several different patterns.

As Frege stressed in 'Booles rechnende Logik und die Begriffsschrift', an expression for a concept, what in *Begriffsschrift*, § 9, he had called a 'function', must be regarded as extracted from a sentence by omission of one or more occurrences of a proper name, rather than as having been built up out of its constituents. 'In contrast to Boole I start from judgments and their contents rather than from concepts . . . The formation of concepts I treat as arising out of judgments in the first instance (*lasse ich erst aus den Urteilen hervorgehen*). Thus if in the judgeable content

$$2^4 = 16$$

one thinks of the 2 as replaceable by something else, say by (—2) or even by 3, as may be indicated by substituting x for the 2:

$$x^4 = 16,$$

then the judgeable content falls apart (*zerfällt*) into a constant and a variable part. The former, considered in itself, but with the place for the latter held open, yields the concept "4th root of 16".[1] This principle, which is thesis A2, applies to incomplete expressions of all kinds, and may be stated in terms of the expressions themselves, or, as in the passage just quoted, in terms of their contents (in the later terminology, of their senses). It may therefore conveniently be labelled the principle of the extraction of functions, using 'function' in its *Begriffsschrift* sense. An alternative label would be 'the priority thesis', that is, the thesis of the priority of judgments over concepts, since, in his early period, Frege sometimes expressed it in these terms, in accordance with the traditional division of logic into the theory of concepts, judgments and inferences. Such a label would not be entirely accurate. He said, in the letter to Marty already quoted, that he did not think 'that the formation of concepts can precede the making of judgments',[2] but he is careful to avoid saying conversely that concept-formation is always *subsequent* to judgment. The reason Frege gives to Marty for denying that it can precede it is that this would 'presuppose the independent existence (*selbständiges Bestehen*) of the concept', whereas he had already explained that 'the concept is unsaturated, in that it demands something that falls under it; hence it cannot exist (*bestehen*) on its own'. Here, therefore, the incomplete nature of concepts is cited as a ground for denying that we can form them in advance of the judgments involving them. The term 'concept' is, of course, here used in the manner proper to the period before the introduction of the distinction between sense and reference, and corresponds, rather, to the *sense* of a concept-word; likewise, he is using the term 'judgment' where, later, he would have preferred 'thought'. But the principle itself was one he never abandoned: we have seen it reiterated in 1919.

Some readers of Frege have regarded the two doctrines, that of the extraction of functions (A2) and that of the constituents of a thought (B2), as in flat opposition to one another. But the fact, which we noted at the outset, that both are stated, clearly and emphatically, within a few pages of one another in the summary of his doctrines which Frege wrote for Darmstaedter in 1919 implies either that, so far from being an exact thinker, he was incapable of recognizing a plain contradiction, or that these exegetes have misunderstood him. In fact, the distinction between analysis and decomposition, which resolves the apparent inconsistency, was already clearly implicit in *Begriffsschrift*, although there expressed in terminology primitive in comparison with that which Frege later developed. He first

[1] *N.S.*, p. 17, *P.W.*, p. 16.
[2] *BW*, p. 164, *P.M.C.*, p. 101.

states that the distinction between function and argument 'has nothing to do with the conceptual content, but is only a matter of our way of looking at it'.[1] This amounts to saying that decomposition does not reveal the inner structure of the thought expressed, nor, therefore, its intrinsic constituents, but is only the imposition by us of a pattern which we can recognize other thoughts as also exhibiting. He goes on to state the matter more exactly: 'The different ways in which the same conceptual content can be regarded as a function of this or of that argument have no importance for us so long as function and argument are fully determinate. When, however, the argument becomes *indeterminate*, as in the judgment "You can take an arbitrary positive integer as argument for 'being representable as the sum of four squares': the proposition always remains correct", then the distinction between function and argument acquires a significance in respect of the content . . . Through the opposition of the *determinate* and the *indeterminate* . . . the whole splits up (*zerlegt*) into *function* and *argument* in respect of its content, and not just according to our way of looking at it.'[2] In other words, the sense of a complex predicate is not a constituent of the thought expressed by a sentence resulting from the insertion of a proper name into the argument-place of that predicate: the recognition of that complex predicate as occurring in the sentence is a matter of 'our way of looking at it', a decomposition to which we can subject the sentence. If, for example, the predicate is 'If ξ is a positive integer, then, for some $n_1, n_2, n_3, n_4, \xi = n_1{}^2 + n_2{}^2 + n_3{}^2 + n_4{}^2$', its sense is not a constituent of the thought expressed by 'If 26 is a positive integer, then, for some $n_1, n_2, n_3, n_4, 26 = n_1{}^2 + n_2{}^2 + n_3{}^2 + n_4{}^2$'. But if we consider a sentence formed by attaching to that same complex predicate a quantifier, the sense of the predicate *is* a constituent of the thought expressed by the resulting sentence; for example, the sense of the above-mentioned predicate is a genuine constituent of the thought expressed by 'For every m, if m is a positive integer, then, for some $n_1, n_2, n_3, n_4, m = n_1{}^2 + n_2{}^2 + n_3{}^2 + n_4{}^2$'. It is no longer a matter of the way we choose to look at it; the recognition of the predicate as occurring in the quantified sentence is integral to a grasp of the thought which it expresses.

We have seen that a detailed account of the process of decomposition involves some complication. A complex predicate 'A(ξ)' needs to be seen as occurring in, and hence as removable from, sentences not only of the forms 'A(a)' and 'For every α, A(α)', but also of such forms as 'For every α, if A(α) and B(α), then C(α)'. This was necessary in order even to formulate rules of inference of greater complexity than the basic introduction

[1] *Begriffsschrift*, § 9.
[2] Ibid.

and elimination rules of a natural deduction system; but it was equally necessary for a statement of the rules governing second-level quantification. A quantifier binding a variable ranging over first-level concepts or relations forms a sentence when attached to a second-level predicate of suitable type; so if a predicate of second level is to be thought of as arrived at, like one of first level, by decomposition, we must have an appropriately general conception of when a first-level predicate or relational expression is to be said to occur in a complex sentence. But a detailed account of the process of analysis also involves certain complications, which Frege did not successfully resolve.

The process of constructing a complex sentence is, of course, the inverse of that of analysing it. The point of regarding it as having been constructed in a particular manner, and hence of analysing it in a particular manner, is to be able to give an account of how its sense depends upon its structure; this account is embodied in a semantic theory which gives a recursive specification of the truth-conditions of sentences in terms of the devices recognized as serving for the construction of a complex sentence from atomic ones. Now consider such a sentence as 'For every x, for some w, x is smaller than w and w is prime', which, when the variables are taken as ranging over numbers, expresses the thought that every number is smaller than some prime. This sentence may be regarded as having been constructed by means of the following steps. First we conjoin the atomic sentences '26 is smaller than 29' and '29 is prime' to form '26 is smaller than 29 and 29 is prime'. We then decompose that sentence into the proper name '29' and the complex predicate '26 is smaller than ξ and ξ is prime'. Attaching the existential quantifier to this predicate, we obtain the sentence 'For some w, 26 is smaller than w and w is prime', the condition for whose truth is that the predicate is true of some number. This sentence is now decomposed into '26' and 'For some w, ξ is smaller than w and w is prime', and finally the universal quantifier is attached to that predicate to obtain our sentence, the condition for whose truth is that the second complex predicate is true of every number.

This is all quite straightforward, provided that we accept that the process of decomposition yields a predicate of which we grasp the condition for it to be true of any arbitrary given object (in the domain). But when we reverse the process, seeking by analysis to uncover the constructional history of the sentence, we experience some difficulty in saying what are its constituents. In terms of the foregoing example, this is because we do not wish to admit the senses of the names '26' and '29' as constituents of the thought expressed by the final doubly quantified sentence. The condition for the truth of that sentence is given as being that for the predicate 'For some w, ξ is smaller than w and w is prime' to be true of every number. The condition for that predicate to be true of the number 26 is given, in turn, as the condition for the truth of a sentence formed by inserting a name for that number in its argument-place, for instance the sentence 'For some w, 26 is smaller than w and w is prime'. But we do not wish to regard the sense of the latter sentence as a constituent of the thought expressed by the universally quantified one; for that would make the *sense* of the name '26' a constituent of that thought, whereas, evidently, the thought can be grasped by one who knows nothing of Arabic (decimal) notation. That the sense of an instance of a quantified sentence is not a constituent of the sense of the quantified sentence is just a consequence of the principle that the determination of the truth-value of a sentence containing a proper name goes via the referent of the name: to grasp the sense of the predicate 'ξ is smaller than some prime' is to know what will determine a sentence of the form 'n is smaller than some prime' as true when the reference of 'n' is given.

The first step in the analysis of our sentence is unproblematic: it has as immediate constituents the quantifier (second-level predicate) 'For every α, $\Phi(\alpha)$' and the complex first-level predicate 'for some w, ξ is smaller than w and w is prime'. Now this predicate, being complex, must itself have constituents; but what are they? One, obviously, is the existential quantifier 'For some w, $\Phi(w)$'; but to what is that to be regarded as having been attached? If we say 'To the predicate "26 is smaller than ξ and ξ is prime"', we appear to have committed the error of making the sense of '26' a constituent of the sense of the original doubly quantified sentence. If, on the other hand, we say 'To the relational expression "ζ is smaller than ξ and ξ is prime"', we have adopted the conception of a quantifier as capable of being attached to an $(n + 1)$-place predicate to form an n-place predicate, rather than merely to a one-place predicate to form a sentence. We must then explain, not only the truth-conditions of a quantified sentence, but, more generally, the satisfaction-conditions of a predicate, of any number of places, formed by attaching a quantifier to a predicate with one more place. This is, indeed, a feasible manner of proceeding; it is that which was adopted by Tarski. It involves, however, a considerable cost. At the syntactic level, we must explain the construction of a quantified sentence as starting, not with atomic sentences, but with atomic open sentences, for instance, in our case, with the open sentences 'x is smaller than y' and 'y is prime'. (To begin with a primitive relational expression and a primitive predicate would not do, since we could not then make the required distinction between 'x is smaller than y and y is prime' and 'x is smaller than y and x is prime'.) At the semantic level, we shall have to introduce infinite sequences of objects, since we have no bound on the degree of the predicates we may need to consider.

Now whether or not I was right to say[1] that such a Tarskian explanation is only superficially different from Frege's, it is certainly different; and to adopt it is to throw away the advantages of Frege's approach. Frege appealed to the principle that a grasp of the sense of a predicate consists in a grasp of the sense of an arbitrary sentence resulting from filling its argument-place. If this is so, then we do not need especially to explain how the sense of the predicate depends upon the senses of its constituent expressions: we need explain only how the sense of a *sentence* formed by filling its argument-place depends on the constituents of that sentence. Thus, to explain 'some prime', as it occurs in the predicate 'ξ is smaller than some prime', and hence as it occurs in the sentence 'Every number is smaller than some prime', we need only to explain how it goes to determine the truth-condition of a sentence such as '26 is smaller than some prime': even though a quantifier or expression of generality may not be the principal operator in a given sentence, it is sufficient explanation of its sense as it there occurs to explain the contribution it makes to the senses of simpler sentences of which it is the principal operator. In the same way, although the sentential operators do not always attach to complete sentences, it is sufficient explanation of their senses in any complex sentence to explain their contribution to the truth-conditions of sentences of which they are the principal operators, and therefore do attach to complete sub-sentences. All this involves a quasi-substitutional account of quantification: the condition for the truth of 'Every number is smaller than some prime', is given as the truth of all sentences 'o is smaller than some prime', '1 is smaller than some prime', . . .; and the condition for the truth of any one such sentence, say '26 is smaller than some prime', written as 'For some w, 26 is smaller than w and w is prime', is given as the truth of at least one of the sentences '26 is smaller than o and o is prime', '26 is smaller than 1 and 1 is prime', . . . This makes the truth of each complex sentence depend, in a particular manner, on the truth-values of atomic sentences. Of course, this is not substitutional quantification conceived as obviating the need for names to have referents, since an appeal to the references of the names will be needed for an account of the truth-conditions of the atomic sentences; and we need due caveats about empty names, non-denumerable domains and the fact that the senses of the names do not enter the sense of the quantified sentence. Given such caveats, it is not seriously

---

[1] *FPL*, pp. 16–18.

misleading to say that Frege in effect gives a substitutional account of the quantifiers.

Frege's account yields a perfectly coherent doctrine. Moreover, in so far as we regard the symbolic formula as representing the essential underlying structure of the corresponding sentence of natural language, a Fregean account is more plausible than a Tarskian one, which involves the artificial devices of open sentences and infinite sequences. The difficulty arises only when we try to explain in terms of Frege's account his own notion of thought-constituents. The principle of the extraction of functions has two consequences: first, that the sense of a predicate arrived at by decomposition of a complex sentence is not, in general, a constituent of the sense of that sentence; and, secondly, that the sense of such a predicate is not to be explained in terms of the senses of its constituents, but, rather, in terms of the common feature of the senses of all sentences formed by inserting a name in its argument-place. For a predicate obtained by decomposition of a sentence, we need no notion of *its* constituents. Dispensing with this notion, however, lands us in difficulties how to explain what are the *ultimate* constituents of a quantified sentence. These difficulties may not be acute. Perhaps we might give such an explanation in terms of the constructional history of a sentence as presented above by appeal simply to the stipulation we used in explaining decomposition, namely that an expression that is removed in the course of the construction, or containing any part that is so removed, is not a constituent of the final sentence. Whether or not this would be an adequate solution, Frege did not address himself to the difficulty. For the most part, he wrote about senses as constituents of thoughts without concerning himself how exactly this notion was to be explained. In *Grundgesetze*, he was compelled to give more precise formulations; and the difficulty we have been examining explains a slightly surprising feature of these. In accordance with the principle of the extraction of functions, we should expect Frege there to admit only one method of forming a name of a function, namely by decomposition from a complex proper name (i.e. term or sentence). Instead, in a section entitled 'Two Ways to form a Name',[1] he gives this as only the second of two possible ways, the first consisting of the formation of a name for a function of one argument by inserting a proper name in one of the argument-places of a name of a function of two arguments. The admission of this first method of formation goes against Frege's own principles; it is, moreover, quite redundant in his stipulations, since, in laying down the semantic principles governing the quantifier,[2] he concerns himself only with

---

[1] *Grundgesetze*, vol. I, § 30 (title in Contents, p. xxviii).
[2] *Grundgesetze*, vol. I, § 8.

the truth-conditions of a quantified sentence, and not with the satisfaction-conditions of a predicate formed by attaching a quantifier to a relational expression. It is nevertheless probable that his admission of the first method of forming a functional expression is due to an imprecise recognition of the difficulty created by the principle of the extraction of functions for an accurate account of the constituents of a thought.

The sentence '26 is smaller than 29 and 29 is prime' may be decomposed into '29' and '26 is smaller than ξ and ξ is prime'. The condition for the truth of the sentence was not grasped as the satisfaction by the referent of '29' of the condition for the predicate to be true of it; rather, the condition for the predicate to be true of an object is, conversely, given as the condition for the truth of the sentence resulting from inserting a name of the object in the argument-place of the predicate. That condition is grasped in a manner corresponding to the unique analysis of the sentence. But whatever the direction of explanation, the equivalence remains: '26 is smaller than 29 and 29 is prime' is true just in case the predicate '26 is smaller than ξ and ξ is prime' is true of 29. Precisely this is what makes it legitimate to see the sentence as composed of '29' and that predicate: the condition for the sentence to be true is satisfied just in case the predicate is true of the referent of the name '29'. It is because we can state the condition for the truth of a sentence in terms of any one legitimate decomposition of it that decomposition is relevant to the validity of inferences, which depends upon the preservation of truth from premisses to conclusion. Analysis, on the other hand, is concerned with how the sense of the sentence is given to us, that is, with what it is to understand that sentence as expressing the thought it does. On Frege's account, if an expression is a component, but not a constituent, of a sentence, it would be a mistake to take the sense of the sentence as dependent on that of the component and to explain the former in terms of the latter, precisely because the sense of the component has to be explained in terms of the sense of that and other like sentences.

If one concentrates only on the A theses, one may come to think, contrary to what Frege repeatedly says, that, for him, thoughts are not intrinsically complex, or at least are not in the first place apprehended by us as complex, and that whatever complexity we ascribe to them is imposed on them by us. There would then be *no* explanation of the sense of a sentence in terms of its structure. Frege's entire semantic theory—his theory of reference, explaining the determination of the truth-value of a sentence in accordance with its structure, and his conception of sense as the manner in which the reference is given—is thus obliterated at a single blow. The fact is, however, that we can properly understand the principle of the extraction of functions only by contrast: we understand what Frege means by saying that the senses of certain expressions occurring in a sentence are not constituents of the thought expressed by it, and so not among the blocks out of which it was constructed, only by grasping what he *does* consider to be among those constituents or building-blocks.

Some people find especial difficulty in what we might call 'degenerate decompositions'. Consider first the sentence 'For every α, if 6 divides α, then α is even'. One possible decomposition of this is into the proper name '6' and the predicate 'For every α, if ξ divides α, then α is even': this would, for example, be required for the recognition of 'For some w, for every α, if w divides α, then α is even' as following from it. Another possible decomposition is into the first-level predicate 'ξ is even' and the expression 'For every α, if 6 divides α, then $\Phi(\alpha)$' for a concept of second level, where, as always, Greek letters indicate argument-places; this would be required for a recognition that 'For some f, for every α, if 6 divides α, then $f(\alpha)$' followed from the original sentence. In the same way, '6 is even' is to be analysed, and may therefore be decomposed, into the proper name '6' and the predicate 'ξ is even'; but it may also be decomposed into the first-level predicate 'ξ is even' and the second-level predicate '$\Phi(6)$', which stands, as Frege says in *Grundgesetze*, vol I, § 22, for the second-level concept *property of the number* 6. This, though an admissible decomposition, may be called a degenerate one, in that it involves the most trivial kind of second-level concept, represented by a specific completion of the first-level one that forms the argument. I have heard it argued that this decomposition really requires a different sentence, one that exhibits an expression for a second-level concept, to express the thought, conceived as so decomposed; and, further, that the possibility of such decomposition proves that the thought is ultimately unanalysable, containing within itself senses of expressions of indefinitely high level. But the original sentence *does* contain an expression for a concept of second level, in just that sense in which any sentence contains such an expression, namely the expression '$\Phi(6)$', which, as Frege remarks in *Grundgesetze*, vol. I, § 22, stands for a concept or function distinct from the number 6 itself, 'since, like all functions, it is unsaturated'; it may be called a degenerate case, but it is not an illegitimate one. 'For every α, if 6 divides α, then α is even' can be seen as saying something about the number 6, viz. that it divides only even numbers, or that it falls under the concept *dividing only even numbers*. It can also be seen as saying something about being even, viz. that every number divisible by 6 is it; or, to speak in a logically less accurate but less slangy way, it can be seen as saying of the concept *being even* that everything divisible by 6 falls under it. Likewise, '6 is even' is naturally seen as saying of the number 6 that it is even; but it may also be seen as saying of being even that 6 is it ('Being even is one the things 6 is'), or as saying of the concept *being even* that 6 falls under it. If there was any point in doing so, we could go further yet, and decompose '6 is even' into the second-level predicate '$\Phi(6)$' and the expression '$\Xi_\alpha \ \alpha$ is even' for a concept of third level, the concept *property of the concept 'being even'*: so viewed, it would say of the second-level concept *property of the number 6* that the concept *being even* fell under it. But there is no mystery about any of this: as observed, the possibility of every legitimate decomposition is already provided for in the original sentence, although every decomposition of a given sentence involving functions beyond a certain level will be a degenerate one in the sense explained. But this poses no problem for the conception of the thought as having determinate constituents, since decomposition is not analysis and does not in general reveal the constituents of the thought: as Frege already remarked in *Begriffsschrift*, the process does not concern the conceptual content, but only our way of looking at it. The component of the sentence is formed from it, and not, unless it is also a constituent, the other way about.

Rather than fastening on the abstract possibility of decompositions of arbitrarily high level, and trying to make it look like mumbo-jumbo, we shall do better to ask for what purpose we may need to recognize expressions for functions of higher level as constituents or components of a sentence. Since analysis and decomposition have different aims, we obtain different answers in the two cases. At any stage in the analysis of a sentence, at least one of the constituents will be a simple one, and the ultimate constituents will all be simple. We therefore need to recognize constituents of a given level just in case there are simple expressions of this level, that is, expressions which admit an argument of the next level below. For example, quantifiers binding an individual variable are applied to predicates of first level, and must therefore be regarded as standing for concepts of second level; since there are also quantifiers which bind function-letters, these have to be regarded as applied to expressions for concepts of second level, and therefore as standing for concepts of third level. For Frege's own symbolic notation, this is as high as we ever need to go for the purposes of analysis. For the purpose of decomposition, we must be prepared to recognize an incomplete expression of a given level as a component of a sentence if, in order to explain the validity of some inference involving that sentence, it is necessary to view it as a completion or that incomplete expression. If the language contains quantification over first-level concepts, then any sentence containing as a component an expression for a first-level concept may need to be viewed as resulting from a completion by that expression, and thus as having, as a component, an expression for a second-level concept; that is why we may need to invoke the decomposition of '6 is even' into 'ξ is even' and '$\Phi(6)$'. But the difference in this respect between analysis and decomposition lies in the fact that, in order to represent the general form of an inference, we need schematic letters for the *arguments* but not for the *operators* (the functors of which they are the arguments); for instance, in sentential logic we need schematic letters for sentences but not for sentential operators, which is why protothetic is so useless. In *analysing* a sentence involving quantification over first-level concepts, we must make explicit recognition of the level of the quantifier, namely as standing for a concept of third level; but, in representing the form of an inference involving such quantification, we use the specific operator, without having to represent it schematically, and therefore without the need to appeal to the general conception of an expression of that logical type. Hence, if the language contains quantification over functions only of the first level, we shall make no inferences for the sake of representing the general form of which we need to appeal to a decomposition yielding a component of level higher than the second: for that reason, the decomposition of '6 is even' into '$\Phi(6)$' and '$\Xi_\alpha\ \alpha$ is even' would be of no conceivable use in such a language. There is no limit to the complexity of the patterns we may impose upon even quite a simple structure; but there is a limit to the utility of this procedure.

The principle of the extraction of functions was, for Frege, the key to the understanding of the fruitfulness of deductive argument, and hence to the informativeness of analytic judgments and, in particular, of the theorems of number theory and analysis. If we think of predicates as always being formed out of their constituents, we shall admit only very simple methods of concept-formation, such as the conjunctive and disjunctive combination of predicates representable by means of Venn diagrams. When we recognize that, in general, a predicate is arrived at by means of the decomposition of a complex sentence, we see that, in forming new concepts, we do not merely make 'use of the boundary lines of already existing concepts to form the boundaries of the new ones', but draw 'quite new boundary lines'.[1] His favourite example for this is the concept of the continuity of a function of real numbers.[2] Any account of deductive inference faces the problem of having to account simultaneously for its justifiability and its fruitfulness. If it is to be displayed as

---

[1] 'Booles rechnende Logik', 1880–1, *N.S.*, p. 39, *P.W.*, p. 34.

[2] Ibid. and *Grundlagen*, § 88.

fruitful, a sense must be acknowledged in which the conclusion represents new knowledge; if it is to be justified, the conclusion must in some different sense have been contained in, or already given with, the premisses. Frege did better at explaining its fruitfulness than its justification, saying, not very helpfully, that the 'consequences extend our knowledge' and were contained in the premisses 'as plants are contained in their seeds, not as rafters in a house'.[1] But his account of the fruitfulness of deductive reasoning is clear. It depends on the fact that we can impose a pattern on a complex sentence no appeal to which was involved in grasping the sense of that sentence; we can therefore notice relations between sentences and between the thoughts which they express of which we had in no way to be aware in grasping those thoughts. The principle of the extraction of functions was thus not, for him, a mere device for a smooth syntactic or semantic theory: it was essential for an understanding of concept-formation in general, and, in particular, for an appreciation of the value of analytic judgments so underestimated by Kant.

[1] *Grundlagen*, § 88.

CHAPTER 16

Simple and Complex Predicates

THE DISTINCTION BETWEEN simple and complex predicates, discussed on pp. 27–33 of *FPL*, which I regarded as uncontroversial and thought had been clearly drawn, has prompted several objections. Sluga, for instance, wrote that 'This distinction, contrary to what Dummett says, has no basis in Frege's text'.[1] A glance will show that what I actually said was that 'Frege himself did not draw attention to' the distinction,[2] and that he 'was at no great pains to draw it'.[3] In fact, Frege does sometimes explicitly acknowledge the existence of simple predicates and relational expressions, as when he follows the remark, previously quoted from 'Booles rechnende Logik', to the effect that, in order to be capable of analysis, the expression of a judgeable content must already be articulated, by the observation that 'one can infer from this that at least the properties and relations which are not further analysable must have their own simple designations'.[4] Geach also criticizes my distinction, both in his review and in 'Names and Identity'; but he takes me, not, like Sluga, as purporting to report Frege, but as 'consciously diverging from' him.[5] Geach certainly looked with greater care than Sluga at what I wrote; but I did not really mean to correct Frege, but only to emphasize something which he glosses over, but which is not merely consonant with his views but important for the avoidance of a misunderstanding of them.

Under the interpretation of Frege's account of complex predicates expounded in the preceding chapter, in order to understand the sentence 'For every x, for some w, x is smaller than w and w is prime', we need,

[1] 'Frege and the Rise of Analytical Philosophy', p. 480.
[2] *FPL*, p. 30.
[3] *FPL*, p. 27.
[4] *N.S.*, p. 19, *P.W.*, p. 17.
[5] 'Names and Identity', p. 147.

in the first place, to understand the quantifier 'For every α, $\Phi(\alpha)$' and the predicate 'For some w, ξ is smaller than w and w is prime'. Just as this predicate represents a pattern in common to sentences such as 'For some w, 28 is smaller than w and w is prime', 'For some w, 100 is smaller than w and w is prime', etc., so the sense of the predicate is given as a common feature of the way the truth-value of each sentence exhibiting this pattern is determined: to grasp the sense of the predicate may be described as understanding an arbitrary sentence of the form 'For some w, n is smaller than w and w is prime'. Likewise, the understanding of a sentence of that form involves understanding the quantifier 'For some w, $\Phi(w)$' and understanding an arbitrary sentence of the form 'n is smaller than p and p is prime'. To understand, say, '4 is smaller than 11 and 11 is prime' requires an understanding of the connective 'ξ and ζ' and of the two sub-sentences; let us take '4 is smaller than 11' and '11 is prime' as being atomic sentences. What, then, is it to grasp the thoughts expressed by them?

It is natural to say that to understand '11 is prime' involves grasping the sense of the name '11' and of the predicate 'ξ is prime'. If we regarded this predicate as having been introduced by definition, we could explain its sense in terms of the sense of the definiens: but, in taking '11 is prime' to be atomic, I intended to treat the predicate as primitive (for the sake of example). Can we at this stage appeal as before to the same principle of the extraction of functions? To do so would be to say that to grasp the sense of 'ξ is prime' is to know the condition for it to be true of a number, and that this condition is given as the condition for the truth of a sentence formed by putting a name of that number in its argument-place. When the predicate in question was a complex one, this explanation got us somewhere, precisely because any sentence so formed would have the predicate as a component but not as a constituent; the condition for the truth of the sentence could then be taken as given in accordance with the analysis of the sentence into its constituents. But, when the predicate is simple, we shall go round in a circle. 'ξ is prime' will be true of 11 just in case '11 is prime' is true: but this takes us back to where we started. We cannot explain what it is to grasp the condition for '11 is prime' to be true in terms of grasping the conditions for 'ξ is prime' to be true of an arbitrary number, and then explain what it is to grasp *that* condition in terms of grasping the condition for '3 is prime', '6 is prime' ,'11 is prime', etc., to be true. Here the notion of extracting the predicate from the sentence is no longer of use to us: it seems inapplicable to this case.

We are now faced with a choice. One option is to say that the sense of the atomic sentence is grasped from those of the name or names and of the predicate or relational expression of which it is composed. The other option is to say that the sense of the sentence is grasped as a whole, and owes nothing to the complexity of the sentence. Some feel constrained to ascribe this view to Frege, because of the apparent generality of the principle of the extraction of functions. As this principle was explained in the preceding section, it applies both to the very discernment of the predicate as occurring in a sentence, and to the way its sense is apprehended. We recognize the predicate as a common component or common feature of certain sentences; and we grasp its sense in virtue of our already grasping the senses of those sentences (or a representative sample of them). When those sentences are complex, there is no conflict with the principle in holding that we grasp their senses in a manner related to their complexity; but, when the sentences in question are atomic, no conclusion seems possible but that we grasp their senses as a whole, in advance of any grasp of the sense of the predicates we may later discern as occurring in them. This reasoning is not fallacious, but the conclusion is not tolerable. I shall argue that it is a mistake to attribute it to Frege, and that he did not intend the principle of the extraction of functions to apply to simple predicates or relational or functional expressions.

Some exegetes, indeed, have gone further yet, and have ascribed to Frege the view that the thought expressed, not merely by an atomic sentence, but by *any* sentence, is grasped as a whole. Sluga is one of these. 'From a logical point of view, Frege argued, a proposition was, to begin with, a unity. For many logical purposes it was . . . necessary to distinguish parts in the sentence and the judgment expressed by it. . . In logic we must first speak of a judgment in which a whole thought is grasped. When we account for the logical relations that hold between judgments or the thoughts expressed by them, we may be forced to conceive of the judgment as falling apart into constituents.'[1] The terminology here is confusing: we have a sentence expressing a judgment and a judgment expressing a thought, and we also have a proposition, whose place in the scheme is obscure. The terminology is not, of course, Frege's. From the *Begriffsschrift* onwards, he objected to the traditional use of 'judgment', since it obscured the difference between what is said by a sentence, its *content*, and the judgment that what is said is true. Though, in the early period, he sometimes allowed himself to use 'judgment' in the traditional manner, he for the most part spoke of 'judgeable contents', as opposed to unjudgeable contents

---

[1] 'Frege and the Rise of Analytical Philosophy', p. 483.

to be ascribed to mere parts of sentences. Once he had, as he said, made the distinction between sense and reference within his previous undifferentiated notion of content, a judgeable content, the content of a sentence, is split up into its sense, the thought expressed, and its truth-value.[1] We therefore need no intermediary between a sentence and the thought it expresses, and, if we did, it would not be a judgment; the sentence may be uttered without assertoric force, the thought may neither be asserted nor judged to be true, and, if it is, the judgment will relate to the thought which the *sentence* expresses.

Sluga's intention is nevertheless plain. For Frege, he says, 'thoughts are first grasped as wholes': if there is any complexity in them, awareness of this complexity is inessential for a grasp of them. The attribution of complexity to a thought is warranted only as a means of representing its logical relations to other thoughts: 'what constituents we distinguish in a thought in logic does not depend on the words out of which a sentence expressing it is composed, but entirely on the logical consequences that are derivable from the thought.'[2] We first grasp the thought as a whole; 'later we come to understand the relations between thoughts, and this process leads us to divide the thought into constituents. to which objects and functions correspond'. That is to say that, on this interpretation of Frege, we may represent the logical relations between thoughts by ascribing to them a certain structure; but this has nothing to do with our grasping them in the first place. In attributing this remarkable thesis to Frege, Sluga does not restrict it to thoughts expressed by atomic sentences; it is quite general. He derives his interpretation, not only from the principle of the extraction of functions, but also from the 'context principle' that a word has meaning only on the context of a sentence; indeed, he conflates the two. Arguing against my assertion that Frege never explicitly stated the context principle after *Grundlagen*, and that this is to be explained by his later assimilation of sentences to complex proper names, which would present a grave obstacle to a view that accorded a distinguished role to sentences in an account of sense and reference, Sluga first cites the formulation in the 'Aufzeichnungen für L. Darmstaedter' of the principle of the extraction of functions as 'seeming to suggest' that Frege did not abandon the context principle, and, a few pages later, converts the citation into 'explicit textual evidence' that he 'reaffirmed' that principle. Actually, the two principles are quite distinct. The context principle applies to all words equally, and Frege is particularly concerned to apply

[1] E.g. *Grundgesetze*, vol. I, p. x.
[2] Op. cit., p. 484.

it to proper names; by contrast, Frege never speaks of extracting a proper name, simple or complex, from a sentence by any process of omitting parts of the sentence, a conception which would contradict his view of proper names as saturated or complete, unlike the unsaturated expressions which stand for concepts or functions. Not only does Sluga generalize his thesis to apply to *all* thoughts, but he goes further yet, and attributes to Frege the view that even *sentences* are 'primarily simple'.[1] This view, besides being intrinsically absurd, was expressly rejected by Frege, in his remark in 'Booles rechnende Logik', already quoted, that the expression of the judgeable content, in order to be able to be decomposed, must already be articulated.[2] Sluga quotes this same unpublished essay in his own support, saying that 'Frege relates his own conception . . . to the linguistic doctrine that the "sentence word" is the primary form of speech', and that he 'refers, in this connection, to a book by . . . A. H. Sayce'. This is quite true: the relevant part of Frege's footnote reads 'In this connection it is remarkable to me that some linguists of recent times regard the "sentence word" as the primary form of speech, a word in which a whole judgment is expressed, and assign to the root, as a mere abstraction, no independent existence. I see this from . . . the review by A. Fick of A. H. Sayce, *Introduction to the Science of Language*.' This footnote is attached to a sentence stating the principle of the extraction of functions: 'instead of compounding the judgment out of an individual thing as subject together with a previously formed concept as predicate, we conversely decompose (*lassen . . . zerfallen*) the judgeable content and so obtain the concept.'[3] But, since the very next sentence is that in which Frege says that, for such a decomposition to be possible, the sentence must already be articulated or composite, thus repudiating the bizarre doctrine of the 'sentence word', the footnote can hardly be cited as an endorsement of that doctrine; more likely, what Frege found remarkable was Sayce's unwarrantable exaggeration.

Setting aside the contention that *sentences* are not complex, the view thus ascribed to Frege amounts to denying that thoughts have any inner structure, and, a fortiori, that their structure corresponds in any way to that of the sentences expressing them. On such an account, our recognition of the thought expressed by the sentence must be explained by some version of the map-reference view; since Frege made no contribution to the further elucidation of this, it follows that he was unconcerned with the

---

[1] Ibid., p. 480.

[2] *N.S.*, pp. 18–19, *P.W.*, p. 17.

[3] *N.S.*, p. 18, *P.W.*, p. 17.

philosophy of language. In particular, a formula of Frege's symbolic notation *cannot* be intended to display the essential structure of the corresponding sentence of natural language. Nor can it be intended to reflect the structure of the thought expressed, since that thought *has* no inner structure. What, then, is such a formula intended to do? Sluga's answer is that it displays the logical relations of the thought to other thoughts. We grasp a variety of thoughts; we recognize particular thoughts as expressed by particular sentences—on what basis we do so is not Frege's concern; and, in addition, we recognize thoughts as standing to one another in various logical relations of entailment, incompatibility, etc. The symbolic notation was devised to represent such logical relations. Given two or more formulas, we can tell, or at least work out, the logical relations between the associated thoughts just from the forms of the formulas.

Sluga's interpretation should be sharply distinguished from another, superficially similar to it, that I have heard advanced. Frege's thesis, according to Sluga, is that a thought is grasped, as a whole, *in advance of* apprehending its logical relations to other thoughts. The thought has no intrinsic complexity: but we may ascribe a structure to it as a means of representing its logical relations. To deny that thoughts have an inner structure, or even, while admitting them to have one, to deny that it bears any relation to their mode of expression, in language or in symbolic notation, requires some explanation of what is taken to be intrinsic to the thought; and this is most naturally explained in terms of what grasping the thought consists in, which is why it is both natural and consistent for Sluga to say, as he does, that it is only *after* the thought is grasped that we come to perceive its relation to other thoughts. On this interpretation, therefore, we are owed an account, not given by Sluga, of how a thought is given to us, i.e. of what grasping it consists in: it may, perhaps, consist in apprehending the condition for it to be true; the one thing it *cannot* consist in is perceiving its entailment-relations to other thoughts.

A quite different view is that Frege took the content of a sentence to be *given* in terms of logical relations such as entailment. On this interpretation, the inner structure of the thought would have to be *identified* with its entailment-relations to other thoughts: the contrast between the inner structure of thoughts and their logical relations to one another would disappear. We should thus, in effect, be ascribing to Frege the conception of a theory of meaning taking entailment rather than truth as its fundamental notion. In Part I of *Grundgesetze*,[1] Frege provides a stipulation

---

[1] Vol. I, §§ 1–36.

of the reference of every expression of his symbolic language (and hence of the truth-value of every formula or 'name of a truth-value'); the reference of each primitive expression is directly stipulated, and, when it is a functional expression, this is done by stipulating the principle for determining the reference of any completion of it, so that the reference of every complex expression and every defined expression is thereby indirectly stipulated. A modest version of the interpretation in question would be to claim that Frege's original view, as stated in *Begriffsschrift*, was that content is given in terms of logical relations, and that he later replaced this by the quite different view that it is given in terms of truth-conditions; a more heroic version would involve reinterpreting the stipulations of *Grundgesetze* as relating to the logical powers of the formulas.

The ground for ascribing to Frege either the view just considered or that advanced by Sluga is exceedingly thin. It consists largely of Frege's attempt to make clear in *Begriffsschrift*, § 3, the distinction he wants to draw between what he calls the *conceptual content* of an expression and any other ingredients of its content. This distinction corresponds very closely with that which Frege later drew between sense and what in *FPL* I called 'tone' and for which Frege used terms like *Färbung* (colouring), with the important difference that, in *Begriffsschrift*, Frege did not have the distinction between sense and reference. Frege uses the word 'content', at the outset of *Begriffsschrift*, in quite a vague way, as he does throughout the *Grundlagen*, to signify what is conveyed by an expression; but, in *Begriffsschrift*, having singled out conceptual content as the logically important ingredient in the content of an expression, he for the most part thereafter uses the unqualified term 'content' to refer to this ingredient. The thesis which, after the distinction between sense and reference had been drawn, Frege maintained concerning senses, namely that they are timeless entities existing independently of our grasping or expressing them, is not applied, in *Begriffsschrift* or in the other writings of the same period, to contents in general or to judgeable contents in particular; Frege does not appear, at that stage, to have had any doctrine about what sort of thing a content was. The first appearance of the thesis, though in the more restricted form that contents are objective, is in the unpublished and unfinished 'Logik' which Frege wrote before making the sense/reference distinction; though it is only a fragment, I should judge it to be later than *Grundlagen*. 'A judgeable content . . . is . . . not the result of an inner process or the product of human mental activity, but something objective, which is to say, something which is exactly the same for all rational beings, for all who are capable of grasping it, just as, say, the Sun is something objective.'[1] It is of little use to enquire just what Frege's conception of a judgeable content was at the time when he wrote those words: the fragment breaks off a paragraph later, and subsequently Frege developed his mature theory which involved distinguishing sense and reference within the content. Still less is there any point in trying to elicit from *Begriffsschrift* a precise doctrine of the nature of judgeable and unjudgeable contents; it was plainly a matter which Frege had not at that stage thought through. Lacking the distinction between sense and reference, Frege identifies the content of a proper name with the thing for which it stands, and thus finds himself forced to say, in *Begriffsschrift*, § 8, that the sign of identity signifies a relation between the names, which therefore in this context stand for themselves rather than for their contents; he does, however, explain the necessity for such a symbol in terms of a notion of the mode of determination (*Bestimmungsweise*) of the content which bears a close kinship to his later conception of the sense of a name. A judgeable content, on the other hand, is certainly not taken to be a truth-value, and is not treated exactly like a thought, on Frege's later conception, either. It appears to be thought of as something like a state of affairs, being said (e.g. in § 7) to 'obtain' (*stattfinden*) or not to obtain.

The formulas of Frege's symbolic notation are to represent only that part of the content of sentences which Frege calls their *conceptual content*; they will not, for instance, express the distinction between 'and' and 'but' (§ 7). Frege attempts in § 3 to explain what belongs to the conceptual content and what does not, and is particularly concerned to point out that a sentence and its transform with the verb in the passive voice agree in conceptual content, and that therefore the notion of the grammatical subject has no logical significance. To do this, he distinguishes two ways in which the contents of two judgments may differ. 'The two sentences, "At Plataea the Greeks defeated the Persians" and "At Plataea the Persians were defeated by the Greeks", differ in the first way. Even if one can perceive a slight difference of sense, the agreement predominates. Now I call the part of the content which is the *same* in both the *conceptual content*. Since *this alone* is of significance for the symbolic notation (*Begriffsschrift*), we need not distinguish between sentences which have the same conceptual content. . . In (natural) language, the subject-position has the significance in the word-order of a *special* place where one puts what one wishes the hearer to notice particularly. . . This can serve, for instance, to indicate a relation of this judgment to others, thus facilitating for the hearer an

---

[1] *N.S.*, p. 7, *P.W.*, p. 7.

understanding of the whole context. Now all linguistic phenomena which result only from the interaction of speaker and hearer—for example, when the speaker takes account of the hearer's expectations and tries to put them on the right track even before uttering a sentence—have nothing corresponding to them in my symbolic notation, because here the only thing considered in a judgment is what influences its *possible consequences*. Everything necessary for correct inference is fully expressed; but what is not necessary is usually not indicated; *nothing is left to be guessed.*' All this is said in justification of the opening statement of the section that 'a distinction between *subject* and *predicate* has no place in my way of representing a judgment'. It is quite misguided to fasten on the remark that what belongs to the conceptual content is what bears on the possible consequences of the judgment as if it were the key to some theory Frege held at the time about the way in which the content is given. He was writing a logic book, a book that not only embodied for the first time what proved to be a treatment of the subject that made possible the whole vast advance within it that has taken place in this century, but carried that treatment to a remarkable stage of development. It was natural for him to fasten on the fact that his formulas represented all, and only, that part of the content of a sentence that is relevant to the validity of inferences involving it; but that does not mean that he had a theory, worked out or embryonic, to the effect that that part of the content is given in terms of the inferential powers of the sentence. And the same goes for his formulation of the two ways in which content can differ: 'first, it may be the case that the consequences that can be derived from the first judgment combined with certain others can always be derived also from the second judgment combined with the same others; secondly, this may not be the case'; from this, he goes on to say, in the passage already quoted, that the two sentences about Plataea differ in the first way. If we interpret 'can be derived' as meaning 'can be derived by some valid chain of inferences', Frege's formulation would have the consequence that any two analytically equivalent sentences will have the same conceptual content, a thesis completely out of accord with Frege's ideas even before he distinguished between sense and reference, as is evident from the statement in *Grundlagen*, § 91, that 'sentences which extend our knowledge may have analytic judgments as their contents'. To arrive at any more restricted interpretation of Frege's *Begriffsschrift* formulation, however, it would be necessary to specify some circumscription of the processes of derivation to which appeal could be made; and any indication of such a circumscription is quite lacking. If, nevertheless, we could supply it, there is no reason to assume that the result would conflict with the conception of the content as given by the determination of the condition for the truth of the sentence. As already observed, the whole point of a semantic characterization of logical validity lies in the fact that a valid inference is one which preserves truth from premises to conclusion, and that therefore an inference is determined as valid or otherwise once we know how the truth-values of the sentences are determined in accordance with their composition. Frege's remark that only the conceptual content is relevant to the possible consequences of a judgment is therefore wholly consonant with the idea that it is given by the condition of its truth. It is unnecessary to suppose that Frege had, when writing *Begriffsschrift*, any theory about the connection between the content of a sentence and the determination of it as true of false, even though, in discussing the sentential connectives in §§ 5 and 7, he comes very close to giving truth-tables for them, as he actually did in the 'Einleitung in die Logik' of 1906.[1] But it is even more superfluous to credit him with some rival theory, at which he occasionally hints; he had quite enough to think about in composing that astonishing work, without concerning himself very closely with such matters. At any rate, in his later period, he had a far simpler way of characterizing identity of sense than the manner attempted in *Begriffsschrift*: 'Two sentences *A* and *B* may stand', he says in the 'Kurze Übersicht meiner logischen Lehren' of 1906,[2] 'in such a relation to one another that anyone who recognizes the content of *A* as true must also immediately recognize that of *B* as true, and . . . conversely, where it is assumed that there is no difficulty in grasping the content of *A* and of *B*. The sentences do not need to be equivalent in every respect', and he goes on to speak of a 'poetic scent' (*Duft*) which may belong to one but not the other. He concludes that a part is to be severed from the content of a sentence 'which alone can be recognized as true or rejected as false'; 'this I call the thought expressed in the sentence'. This test is more direct; no consideration of additional premises and derivations is required: but it would have been quite sufficient to show the identity of the conceptual content of the active and passive versions of the sentence about Plataea.

Weak as is the ground for ascribing either of them to Frege, the thesis that content is given in terms of logical relations and Sluga's thesis that a thought is grasped as whole, while a symbolic formula represents its logical relations to other thoughts, share a common conception of the character of Frege's logical notation. At first sight, this conception involves denying that notation to be itself a *language* for the expressions of thoughts; and

---

[1] *N.S.*, p. 202, *P.W.*, p. 186.
[2] *N.S.*, p. 213, *P.W.*, p. 197.

this goes against what Frege himself says of it, since one of the main advantages he claimed for it as against the calculi of Boole and Schröder was precisely that one could use it to convey specific contents, and hence carry out mathematical or other reasoning within it. 'I did not wish to present an abstract logic in formulas, but to express a content through written symbols in a more precise and perspicuous way than is possible with words. In fact, I wished to produce, not a mere *calculus ratiocinator*, but a *lingua characterica* in Leibniz's sense.'[1] Indeed, on the title page of *Begriffsschrift*, he even *calls* it a 'formula language of pure thought' (*Formelsprache des reinen Denkens*). But, on reflection, it does not follow from either of the two interpretations that the notation is not a language. To say that we can, from the form of the formulas, tell what logical relations obtain between the associated thoughts presupposes that we have a way of associating thoughts with formulas: though he does, in *Begriffsschrift*, give examples, Frege does not stipulate, for each formula, which thought is to be associated with it, by citing a sentence of natural language expressing that thought; he takes it for granted that you can tell from the formula which thought is to be associated with it. It therefore follows that the symbolic notation *is* a language; and, if what the formula directly represents is the logical relations of the thought to other thoughts, it follows that, given those relations, you can identify the thought which stands in those relations. In other words, in the terminology of Chapter 3, the formulas indicate the associated thoughts precisely on the map-reference model, by appeal to the position of a thought in the system of thoughts considered under the logical relations.

For this to be possible, a large assumption must be made about this system: it must resemble the ordering of the ordinal numbers rather than that of the rationals. A rational number is identifiable by its position in the ordering of the rationals only in a weak sense, namely that no two rationals can occupy the same position with respect to other rationals: if, for every r, $p < r$ iff $q < r$, then $p = q$. But a rational number cannot be identified by its abstract position in the ordered set, i.e. its position described without the use of other means of identifying other rational numbers: for any two positive rationals p and q, there exists an order-preserving permutation of the positive rationals that maps p on to q. An ordinal, on the other hand, can be identified by reference to its abstract position: e.g. ω is the unique ordinal having infinitely many ordinals α smaller than it and such that, for each such α, there are only finitely many ordinals smaller than α. That is to say, there is no order-preserving permuta-

[1] 'Über den Zweck der Begriffsschrift', 1882, pp. 1–2 (*B.a.A.*, pp. 97–8); see T. W. Bynum (ed. and trans.), *Conceptual Notation*, Oxford, 1972, pp. 90–1.

tion of (any initial segment of) the ordinals save the identity. For it to be possible to indicate thoughts unambiguously by appeal only to their logical relations, there would have likewise to be no non-trivial permutation of the system of thoughts preserving those logical relations; this proposition is very far from being evident.

In any case, the proposed interpretation of Frege's symbolic notation would involve its recognition as a language. At this point, no ground survives for assuming that the symbolic formulas do *not* systematically correspond to the sentences of natural language. The formula identifies the thought associated with it by means of a map-reference system based on logical relations. On Sluga's interpretation, the thought is, in the first place, grasped as a whole; given that the sentence expressing it *is* complex, it must identify the thought by means of some unspecified map-reference system. The possibility is thus wide open that sentences of natural language function according to a map-reference system based on the same relations between thoughts as do the symbolic formulas, even though the mode of representation used in natural language is less perspicuous. The possibility is therefore also open that a formula exhibits perspicuously the mechanism of representation of the thought by the sentence. This is even more likely on the alternative interpretation, according to which the thought is from the outset given in terms of its logical relations; for, if it be supposed that its expression by a sentence of natural language mirrors the way it is itself given to us, it follows that natural language, like Frege's symbolic one, functions according to a map-reference system.

We have considered in Chapter 3 the difficulties of the map-reference view in general, and, in particular, the reasons for not ascribing it to Frege. These reasons apply even more strongly to symbolic formulas than to sentences of natural language, since Frege gives a more systematic account of the sense and reference of the parts of such a formula than he does of the parts of an ordinary sentence. In any case, it becomes difficult to assess the thesis, because it has simply not been worked out: we have nothing but a vague programme, and lack any detailed interpretation of Frege's symbolic language purely in terms of logical relations.

It is particularly absurd to maintain that, for Frege, the thoughts expressed by complex sentences are themselves simple, since he so consistently reiterated his view that they are complex. In his unpublished 'Logik' of 1897, he headed a section 'Verbindung von Gedanken' ('Combination of Thoughts');[1] he likewise spoke of a combination of thoughts as being

---

[1] *N.S.*, p. 163, *P.W.*, p. 150.

expressed by a conditional sentence, formed by combining two sentences hypothetically, in the 'Kurze Übersicht meiner logischen Lehren' of 1906;[1] the last essay he ever published was entitled 'Gedankengefüge' ('Thought-Compounds'). The only position worth considering, at least as an interpretation of Frege, is therefore a restriction of the thesis that thoughts are not complex, have no inner structure, and are grasped only as unarticulated wholes, to the thoughts expressed by atomic sentences.

Unfortunately, this thesis hangs together particularly badly with the conception that content or meaning can either be explained or represented purely in terms of logical relations. It is not implausible to consider the meanings of the logical constants as being given in this way. One might take their meanings, as Gentzen suggested, as being given by the introduction rules governing them: the whole meaning of 'and' is, on this view, contained in the stipulation that 'A and B' may be inferred from 'A' and from 'B', the whole meaning of 'or' from the stipulation that 'A or B' may be inferred from 'A' and also from 'B'. Even this is far from straightforward. That 'A or B' follows from the sole premiss 'A' and also from the sole premiss 'B' does not, by itself, distinguish it from 'A or B or C': we need to add that these are the *only* two ways in which we can arrive at the conclusion 'A or B'. But, of course, they are not: 'A or B' might be of the form 'Fa or Ga', and have been arrived at from 'For every α, $F\alpha$ or $G\alpha$'. So we need some principle of the form: whenever we can assert 'A or B', we *could have* arrived at it by means of an argument whose last step was an inference either from 'A' or from 'B'; and the explanation of this 'could have' occasions great difficulty. That such a principle is needed can be seen from the case of the modal operator 'possibly'. The ordinary introduction rule is that which allows us to infer 'Possibly A' from 'A': but the assumption that, whenever we could assert 'Possibly A', we could have arrived at it by inference from 'A', would entitle us to make the converse inference from 'Possibly A' to 'A', on the ground that an entitlement to assert the former would presuppose an entitlement to assert the latter.

Conversely, we might suppose the meanings of the logical constants to be given by the elimination rules, as Wittgenstein suggested[2] that the whole meaning of 'all' is contained in the rule of universal instantiation. On this conception, the meaning of a complex sentence is given, not by what we take as entitling us to assert it, but by what we can *do* with it or by what is involved in accepting it, this being essentially explained

---

[1] *N.S.*, p. 216, *P.W.*, p. 200.

[2] *Remarks on the Foundations of Mathematics*, Oxford, 1978, pp. 41-3.

by the rules governing the deduction of simpler sentences from it. Again, we need some principle, even harder to formulate, to the effect that any consequence of accepting a complex sentence *could* be mediated by an application to it, as major premiss, of one of the elimination rules. Again, the necessity for such a principle is evident from a modal counter-example, this time the operator 'necessarily'. The ordinary elimination rule for this operator is to infer '*A*' from 'Necessarily *A*': but if every consequence of accepting 'Necessarily *A*' could be mediated by this rule, we should be entitled to infer 'Necessarily *A*' from '*A*', on the ground that whatever could be inferred from the former could already be inferred from the latter.

The path to an explanation even of a logical constant in terms of the logical powers of a sentence in which it is the principal operator is thus not altogether smooth. It is of interest only if it does not make an appeal, at any point, to the notion of the truth of a sentence, since otherwise we might just as well fall back on the explanations of the sentential operators by means of truth-tables. That means that we have to frame a purely proof-theoretic definition of the validity of an inference; and that cannot be done simply in terms of the derivability of the inference from the given rules, since, in the one case, we have, as Gentzen said, to justify the elimination rules from the introduction rules, and, in the other, we have to do the converse. Moreover, it seems probable that the logic yielded by such an approach will be intuitionistic logic, and that classical logic cannot be handled in this way, which makes it unpromising as an interpretation of Frege; this is already evident from the fact that, in the context of classical logic, the principle that, whenever '*A* or *B*' can be asserted, it could have been arrived at either from '*A*' or from '*B*', could not possibly be justified without an appeal to the notion of truth. Nevertheless, the idea has great plausibility, and we may hope that it proves possible to work it out in detail, as Dag Prawitz has been engaged in doing in a series of articles, and as I also have been trying to do in lectures in Oxford and London. For present purposes, the difficulty is that it is precisely the atomic sentences for which the treatment seems implausible. To take the meanings of the logical constants as given by the introduction rules is, in effect, to treat the meaning of a complex sentence as given by the canonical, that is, the most direct, way of arriving at a position to assert it, where that way is taken to consist in the construction of a canonical argument, whose initial premisses are all atomic sentences and which as far as possible uses only the introduction rules, to the given sentence as final conclusion. Conversely, to take the meanings of the logical constants as given by the elimination rules is to treat the meaning of a complex sentence as given by the canonical way of drawing a consequence from it, of acting in accordance with what is involved in accepting it; and this is taken to consist in the construction of a canonical argument, using as far as possible only the elimination rules, from the given sentence as an initial premiss to some atomic sentence as final conclusion. Either enterprise is a particular realization of the general project of exhibiting the meaning of a complex sentence in terms of the meanings of its atomic sub-sentences (where an instance of a quantified sentence counts as a sub-sentence of it). For the explanation to work, the meanings of atomic sentences must be considered as already given. We might have some account of their meanings in terms of the general idea of what entitles us to assert them, or of what consequences flow from accepting them: but it is precisely for them that it is implausible that we could explain these notions in terms of their deduction from other sentences or the derivation of other sentences from them. To explain the logical constants by means of the introduction rules is to explain the more complex in terms of the less complex from which it is derived; to explain them by means of the elimination rules is to explain the more complex in terms of the less complex which is derivable from it: and both presuppose a termination with maximally simple sentences whose meaning is given in some other way.

Suppose that someone were to ask why the question how we grasp the sense of an atomic sentence is the business of a philosopher at all; or why, if it is, it should be thought to have been any concern of Frege's. Understanding is a mental act: and Frege professed himself unconcerned with psychology. Certainly, this was a difficulty that troubled Frege and that he failed to resolve. He struggled to remove sense from the domain of the psychological by declaring it independent of our grasping it; but he could not deny that the act of grasping it is an act of the mind. 'But the act of grasping (a thought) is still a mental (*seelischer*) process! Yes: but a process which lies at the limit of the mental, and which therefore cannot be completely understood from the purely psychological standpoint, because it is essential to pay regard to what is no longer mental in the proper sense, namely the thought; perhaps this process is the most mysterious of all. But just because it is of a mental character, we do not need to concern ourselves with it in logic. It is enough for us that we can grasp thoughts and recognize them as true; how that takes place, is a question on its own.'[1] Here, in this unpublished work, we see Frege

---

[1] 'Logik', 1897, *N.S.*, p. 157, *P.W.*, p. 145.

grappling with a difficulty he could not solve: his best answer was that he was not concerned to describe or explain the act of grasping a sense, but only to characterize the sense itself, which is not a mental content. This is unsatisfactory, because we need some access to the notion of sense, which is most readily provided by that of understanding. Unless we know what is the test for an adequate account of the sense of an expression, we have lost our grip on the notion of sense; we no longer have any idea what senses are. The most obvious test of an account of sense is that it gives a plausible explanation of our understanding of expressions. An alternative would be that it yielded a good description of our practice in using language, one that explained what made it *language*. Although we have seen that Frege's ideas drove in that direction, such an answer was not available to him: what, in his philosophy of language, connects the sense of a sentence with the practice of using it is the *force* attached to it. Frege not only attempted no account of the various types of force in terms of our practice in using sentences to which a force of each type is attached, but left it wholly unclear whether he believed such an account possible. He therefore tacitly relied on our perceiving his ideas about sense as embodying a plausible account of what is involved in our grasping the senses of expressions, that is, in our understanding them: and this leaves him open to the objection that he was concerning himself with the psychological, in violation of his own prohibition. The solution was provided by Wittgenstein, when he said that 'understanding is not a mental process'.[1] This solution Frege did not have. It does not follow either that he was *not* concerned with understanding or that he had no right to be: only that he could not satisfactorily explain why he had a right to be.

But *what* concern is it of a philosopher *how* we understand? Frege's account of himself is that he does not explain *how* we understand but only *what* we understand, that is, what we grasp when we understand. But is this an accurate account? When he asks what makes it possible for men to express new thoughts that no one has previously grasped, and answers that it is the fact that thoughts are built up out of building-blocks,[2] is he not trying to explain *how* the phenomenon occurs? It is a fact that someone who has had a certain training, which we call 'learning a language', understands sentences in that language, which someone who has not received that training does not. It is also a fact that someone who has been vaccinated does not usually contract smallpox, while someone who has not may do so. The latter fact can be explained; but the explanation is an

---

[1] *Philosophical Investigations*, I, § 154.
[2] *N.S.*, p. 243, *P.W.*, p. 225.

empirical one. What reason is there to suppose that the explanation of the first fact is not equally an empirical one, which the philosopher is neither equipped nor licensed to provide?

The answer is simple. We are not concerned with a phenomenon we can perfectly well characterize, but whose causal antecedents are mysterious to us. The difference between understanding a sentence and not understanding it, or, rather, between understanding it and the various different kinds of failure to understand it, is very familiar to us in everyday life: but to say what understanding is, what it is to understand a sentence, an expression or a word, remains beyond us; and that is a task for a philosopher. When I wrote FPL_1, I thought it clear that to say what understanding is is the same task as to say what meaning is; I still believe that this is true, but, as previously remarked, I think it far less clear. At least it is clear that, for a full account of understanding, an account of meaning is required, whether or not more is needed in addition and whether or not the converse holds. Frege's statement of the matter fails to resolve the problem: the sense expressed is that which we grasp when we understand, but, as for what grasping a sense is, that remains a mystery.

How are we able to understand a sentence we have never heard before? The obvious answer is: because we already understand the words in it and the mode of construction of the sentence out of them. But why is the question a philosophical one, and why does the answer claim to be a philosophical thesis? We are supposed to be saying *what* it is to understand a sentence: but the question *how* we are able to do so sounds more as though it called for an empirical answer; and with what right does a philosopher attempt such an answer, before he has even answered his proper question, what understanding is? He does so because he has a strong hunch that the answer to the subsidiary question will prove to be an essential part of the answer to the main question; a hunch that an account of what it is to understand the sentence, or of what it is for it to have the sense it does, must allude to its composition.

Why should this be? Is it not possible to state what it is to understand a given sentence without alluding to its structure? One can certainly know what a sentence means without grasping its grammatical structure or even its articulation into words; hearing a sentence of Basque, I may simply be told what it means. I should not be said to understand the sentence: this is a case where the notion of understanding an expression comes apart from that of knowing what it means. Suppose, now, that, in a way I cannot account for, I find that, whenever I hear a sentence of Basque, it comes to me what it means as a whole, without my gaining any insight into how it splits up into words or how they go together; and, equally, that when I am prompted to say something to a Basque speaker, it comes to me what sounds to utter, again without any idea of the structure of the sentence. Viewed from the outside, I manifest an ability to speak the language; but it is natural to say that I do not really understand or know Basque. Suppose that someone finds that, when he sits down to a game of chess, it just comes to him which move to make whenever it is his turn, without his having any idea of the point of the move; perhaps he cannot even state the rules. Externally viewed, he can play chess, and might even become a grand master; but he would not rightly be said to know how to play, nor, perhaps, actually to play.

The chess example may be said to illustrate the fact that playing a game is a highly conscious activity: where the consciousness is absent, that is, where the agent is unable to explain, when asked, the purpose of each step, we are reluctant to recognize the activity as occurring; the same would hold good for many other activities, say cooking. The chess example is therefore not a true analogue of the fantasy about speaking Basque: to make the latter more like the former, we should have to imagine that it came to me what sounds to utter without my having, in any sense, any idea of their meaning. Speech, like playing games, is also a highly conscious activity. The fact that, in this more fantastic case, I was unaware what I was saying would come out in my being unable to explain, in English, why I uttered the sounds I did, although, if I were to pass, to outward appearance, as a competent Basque speaker, I should have to be able, when asked, to explain in Basque why I said what I did; we should then have something like a split personality. But, in the original, more restrained, fantasy, I should be said to know both what I said and why I said it: so do we not here have an example of understanding without grasp of structure?

It might be objected that, in saying that I knew that a certain Basque sentence meant that the pigeons had returned to the dovecote, we should be saying only that I knew that it meant the same as 'The pigeons have returned to the dovecote', so that my 'understanding' of the Basque sentence was parasitic on my understanding of the English one. Davidson, on the other hand, would explain my understanding of the Basque sentence as my knowing it to be true if and only if the pigeons had returned to the dovecote. Suppose that we explain my knowing this as simply consisting in my *treating* the Basque sentence as true just in the stated case, and that we explain this in turn in terms of my use of the sentence and my responses to its utterance by others. So understood, I do have this knowledge, since, as far as Basque speakers can tell, I speak Basque perfectly. It thus appears that an understanding of a sentence is explicable without mention of its structure.

The appearance is illusory. I could not be said to treat a given sentence as being true just in case the pigeons had returned to the dovecote unless I displayed an ability to speak at least a considerable fragment of the language. To explain an understanding of a *language*—even to characterize the ability to make a correct use of sentences as viewed externally—does require an appeal to the composition of sentences, since, as Davidson has repeatedly insisted, we must provide a finite base for the capacity to employ correctly each of infinitely (or, at least, unsurveyably) many sentences. In the fantasy, one could have the feeling that my magical ability to express myself in Basque and to understand utterances in that language might desert me at any moment, and so not be willing to ascribe to me a knowledge of the language. But if one felt assured that I should retain the capacity, a description of my capacity would make essential appeal to the structure of Basque sentences, even though I could give no account of their structure. It is natural to feel uncomfortable about ascribing to me a knowledge of Basque, even though assured that my powers would not desert me, just because knowledge of a language is normally accompanied by explicit, though partial, knowledge of the articulation of the complex capacity corresponding to the articulation of the sentences; this is, of course, something appealed to in ordinary discourse, as when the hearer asks the speaker to explain some word he has used. But, even if we brush this discomfort aside, it remains that there is no such thing as understanding a sentence as a whole, without reference to its structure, since understanding a sentence requires an understanding of at least part of the language to which it belongs, and the understanding of a language cannot be described without reference to structure. In the fantasy, my understanding of Basque *issues in* my understanding of whole sentences, without my having any conscious grasp of their articulation into words or conscious knowledge of the meanings of the words: but my understanding of the language cannot itself be characterized without appeal to that articulation.

The Basque example degenerated into automatism or divided personality when we removed the feature that guaranteed that I knew what I was saying; and the description of the original example as possessing that feature traded on my already knowing, from my mastery of English, what it was for a sentence to mean that such-and-such a state of affairs obtained, even though the willingness of Basque speakers to acknowledge me as understanding the language depended only on my performance in it. The reason why we are impelled to speak of *knowledge* here is that speech must be a conscious activity, since it is *the* rational activity par excellence. Unless motive and purpose can be assigned to a speaker in saying what he does, he cannot properly be said to be using language, and the estimation of intention plays an important role in our linguistic communication with each other; but, to have an intention in speaking, a speaker must know what he is saying. We here tread closely on the range of problems concerning the relation between the notions of meaning, understanding and knowledge which I have asked to be excused from here going into. But, when we are considering a speaker's understanding of his mother tongue, so that we can ascribe to him, as in the Basque example, a prior knowledge of what it is for a sentence to mean that such-and-such is the case, these considerations make it dubious that we can, as suggested above, construe his knowledge of the meaning of what he says as amounting to no more than a practical capacity which might leave him unconscious of the structure of the sentences he employs.

Let us suppose, however, that it may be so regarded; and let us take, as a more plausible example of an atomic sentence whose constituents are not introduced by definition, 'Watling Street is straight'. An understanding of this sentence requires a grasp of the senses of the proper name 'Watling Street' and of the predicate 'ξ is straight'. When this understanding is held to reside in a grasp of the truth-condition of the sentence, this will be manifested by the ability to identify the road which is the bearer of the name and to judge, at least of such objects, whether they are straight, and the preparedness to accept that object's falling under that concept as determining the sentence as true. The ascription to a single speaker, or, equally, to an entire community of speakers, of those abilities and that preparedness cannot be grounded just on his or their response to or utterances of that sentence, considered in isolation. Given that we already know what the sentence means, and given an individual speaker who went to the trouble of actually verifying it, we might be able to recognize, from the way he went about it, that he grasped its sense correctly. That is not the point, however: we are concerned with what it is for a particular speaker, or a whole linguistic community, to attach that sense to the sentence; and that could not, even in the most favourable circumstances, be determined from behaviour relating to that sentence alone, because there would be no way of separating the essential from the inessential. Now if the speakers are conscious of the articulation of the sentence, the ascription to them of the practical capacities in which their grasp of the truth-condition of the sentence is being taken to consist might be grounded on the explanations they gave of its two components, the way they introduced those expressions to their children or to foreigners; this will, of course, be the normal state of affairs. But if, as we saw to be dubious, it be allowed that such a state of affairs is not *necessary* for the sentence to bear the sense it does, then the speakers may have no awareness of the structure of the sentence. In that case, their grasp of its sense will be manifested by the common feature in what prompts them to recognize as true other sentences containing the same name, together with the common feature in what prompts them to recognize as true other sentences containing the same predicate.

Now this talk of a common feature may appear to suggest that the senses of both the name and the predicate are to be extracted from the senses of the sentences containing them, grasped as a whole, even though they could not be extracted from the *one* sentence made up of both expressions, taken on its own. But if the language is like actual natural languages, it will contain sentences involving demonstratives, including recognition statements and crude predications.[1] A mastery of such sentences as 'This is Watling Street', 'This is the same road as before' and 'This road is straight' will of itself display that grasp of the senses of the name and the predicate which together yield an understanding of the sentence 'Watling Street is straight', given a due recognition of the relationship of that sentence to the others. The supposition that the senses of sentences are grasped by the speakers without an awareness of their articulation now shrinks almost to vanishing point, even without any appeal to the conscious nature of speech; if any such appeal is allowed, it vanishes altogether. But is it to be maintained that it is necessary, for the name and the predicate as they occur in 'Watling Street is straight' to bear the senses that they do, that the language should also contain sentences in which they occur together with demonstratives? I am disposed to believe this to be so, but am not prepared to assert it outright. What must hold good, for them to bear those senses, is that the recognition of the truth-condition of 'Watling Street is straight' as being fulfilled should involve two distinguishable elements, the identification of the object and the recognition that it satisfies the predicate. There is no process here which can be described as the extraction of the predicate, or of the name, from sentences, or of the sense of either from the thoughts expressed. To whatever extent the speakers' grasp of the senses of the sentences is held to presuppose a conscious awareness of their structure, there is nothing to be extracted; to the extent that they may be held to grasp them without such an awareness, no extraction takes place.

---

[1] See *FPL*, p. 232.

In 'Frege's Alleged Realism',[1] Sluga cites in support of his own interpretation the sentence in 'Booles rechnende Logik' immediately following that in which Frege speaks of the necessity that there be simple expressions for unanalysable properties and relations; this sentence, and the three succeeding ones, run as follows:

> From this it does not, however, follow that the ideas (*Vorstellungen*) of these properties and relations are formed without connection with (*losgelöst von*) things; rather they come into existence simultaneously with the first judgments, by which they are ascribed to things. Hence their designations never appear in isolation in the symbolic notation, but always in combinations which express judgeable contents. I should like to compare this with the behaviour of atoms, of which one assumes that none ever occurs on its own, but only in combination with others, from which it departs only in order at once to enter another combination. A sign for a property never appears unless a thing to which the property belongs is at least indicated, a sign for a relation never without indication of things which stand in that relation.

In the later part of this passage, Frege is making the evidently true observation that a predicate or relational expression is significant only as occurring in a sentence, and then only in combination with certain other expressions, namely one or two proper names or bound individual variables (for Frege, a letter used as an individual variable indefinitely indicates an object, but does not stand for one). In the first sentence quoted, he says that we form ideas of simple properties and relations at the same time as we make the first judgments involving them. This is an early application of the context principle, applied to simple predicates and relational expressions. It would be absurd to maintain that we gain an understanding of any expression in advance of acquiring an ability to use sentences containing it. If the expression is introduced by definition, we acquire such an understanding in advance of actually so using it, though the definition has succeeded in its purpose only if it renders us able to use such sentences. But, if the expression is simple and primitive, that is, not introduced by definition, we can only say that an understanding of it is acquired simultaneously with an understanding of some sentences containing it; anything else would be in conflict with the context principle, of which I remarked that 'Frege's views on sense and reference cannot be made coherent without

[1] P. 239.

it'.[1] But to say, as I also did,[2] that we come by an understanding of simple predicates 'otherwise than by extracting them from some previously understood sentence' is not to go back on the context principle, but to deny that the quite different principle of the extraction of functions applies to them. It is, namely, to deny that we attain an understanding of such a predicate by appeal to a grasp of the senses of sentences which we now view as containing it, those senses being given to us in another manner which does not demand a grasp of the sense of the predicate nor even our recognition of its presence as a component of those sentences. That is Frege's doctrine concerning complex predicates, which I regard as sound and defensible. It cannot be made to apply to simple predicates, and, though Frege was not at pains to point this out, I do not think he intended to be so understood; the passage quoted above will seem to imply that he did only if we overlook the crucial distinction between 'at the same time as' and 'in advance of'. That this should have escaped Sluga is due to his identifying the context principle with that of the extraction of functions; but they are not at all the same.

Sluga quotes another passage from Frege in support of his view.[3] This occurs in a letter from Frege to Peano printed in Peano's journal *Rivista di Matematica*.[4] The passage runs as follows:

> The task of our natural languages is essentially fulfilled if the people who communicate with one another connect the same thought with the same sentence, or at least approximately the same. For that it is not absolutely necessary that the individual words should by themselves have a sense and a reference, as long as the whole sentence has a sense. The matter stands differently when inferences are to be drawn; then it is essential that the same expression should occur in two sentences and that it should have exactly the same reference (*Bedeutung*) in both. It must therefore by itself have a reference that is independent of the other parts of the sentence.

He goes on to say that concept-words (predicates) that are not defined for every case fail to satisfy this condition, since the question whether the case is one for which the predicate is defined is to be answered by consideration of the rest of the sentence; they therefore cannot be accorded

---

[1] 'Frege as a Realist', p. 457.
[2] Ibid., p. 467.
[3] Op. cit., p. 240.
[4] Vol. 6, 1896, pp. 53–9; see *K.S.*, p. 236.

an independent (*selbständige*) reference, and it is for that reason that Frege rejects conditional definitions.

The observation contained in the first two sentences of the quoted passage certainly seems surprising; but Sluga's gloss on the passage perverts the plain sense of Frege's words. Sluga distinguishes three stages: that of ordinary language, at which 'senses of sentences can be apprehended without prior apprehension of the senses and references of the parts'; that at which a symbolic notation is constructed, when, by means of analysis, the senses and references of the parts must be distinguished 'in order to account for the inference relations'; and that *after* the symbolic notation has been constructed, 'when we can conceive of new combinations of the elements that we have reached by analysis'. But Frege does not say that an expression occurring in different sentences must have the same reference in all of them, independent of the other parts of the sentences, only when we come to *analyse* inferences: he says that this is essential for us to be able to *draw* them. It is not a matter of the symbolic representation, but of the occurrence, or at least the validity, of inference. Likewise, the discernment of 'new combinations' just *is* the process of extracting complex functional components from sentences, of which Frege's favourite example is the concept of continuity of a function of real numbers.[1] This is Frege's explanation for the fruitfulness of deductive reasoning; the consequences 'are contained in the definitions, but like the plant in the seed, not like the rafter in the house'.[2] But Frege did not think that the process waited upon the construction of such a notation as that of *Begriffsschrift*, that, e.g., the attainment of the concept of continuity had had to wait for his provision of the necessary tools in 1879; the symbolic notation renders the process perspicuous and makes possible a clear account of it, but it is not itself a precondition for the process.

What explains the oddity of the first two sentences in the passage quoted above is that Frege is referring to the occurrence in natural language of vague expressions like 'heap'. In the immediately preceding passage, he speaks of the demand that a concept be sharply delimited, and continues:

The fallacy known under the name 'Acervus' rests on words such as 'heap' being treated as if they designated a sharply delimited concept, whereas this is not the case. . . Logic must demand sharp delimitation of what it can recognise as a concept. . . Hence a symbol for a concept whose content does not satisfy this requirement is from the logical

---

[1] *Grundlagen*, § 88; 'Booles rechnende Logik', *N.S.*, pp. 38–9, *P.W.*, p. 34.
[2] *Grundlagen*, § 88.

standpoint to be regarded as devoid of reference (*bedeutungslos*). It may be objected that such words are used a thousand times over in the language of everyday life. Indeed: but our natural languages are not designed for the carrying out of inferences. And the defects arising out of this have been for me precisely the principal motive for devising a logical notation (*Begriffsschrift*).

There then follow the remarks already quoted. It may seem that the abuse of natural language is on this occasion really too severe: but perhaps it is to be expected from one symbolic logician to another. Vagueness was, for Frege, an unmitigated defect of natural language, like the occurrence of empty names; and, from the time of *Begriffsschrift*, he held that no reasoning can be carried out with vague expressions. The paradox of the heap was not, for him, to be solved, but simply dismissed: it was pointless to ask at which step the reasoning went wrong—it was wrong from start to finish. In the case of empty names, however, he at least had a clear description of the objectionable phenomenon: a sentence containing such a name expressed a sense but lacked a truth-value. Of vagueness he never achieved even a plausible description. In *Begriffsschrift*, § 27, he says that some sentences in which the predicate 'ξ is a heap' is applied to an object have a content, while others lack one. In terms of the sense/reference distinction, this would be hard to spell out. If we view a vague predicate as mapping some objects on to the value *true*, others on to the value *false*, and as undefined for yet other objects, it seems reasonable to say that some sentences of the form '*a* is a heap' will have a truth-value, while others will not. If, on the other hand, we regard a thought as something expressible by means of a sentence lacking all vagueness, it will not appear reasonable to regard any such sentence as expressing a thought, i.e. as having a determinate sense. We shall thus arrive at the intolerable conclusion that there are sentences lacking a sense yet having a reference, viz. a truth-value. Accordingly, in his mature period, Frege was disposed to say that a predicate which was not sharply defined for every object did not stand for a concept at all: there are no concepts with fuzzy boundaries. It should follow that no sentence containing any vague expression has a truth-value. It might, consistently, be held to express a thought; since an empty name may have a sense, though lacking a reference, the same might be held to be possible for a predicate, for which its having a reference just is, for Frege, its being defined for each object. But that, as already noted, is difficult to maintain: *what* thought does a vague sentence express? In the quoted passage, Frege is attempting to do justice to the undeniable fact that we do manage to communicate by means of vague sentences; and he does so by suggesting that different speakers connect approximately the same thought with such a sentence, even though its constituent words do not have senses or referents. The suggestion, which, so far as I am aware, is an isolated one, cannot be taken very seriously as an account of vagueness. In any case, it is directed specifically at that phenomenon, which in turn is mentioned only to bring out, by contrast, what is required for rigorous argument to be carried on, in order to attack Peano's practice of giving conditional definitions. It is therefore a mistake to elicit from the suggestion a general thesis that thoughts are normally conveyed by sentences whose constituents are devoid of sense: a remark about a feature of language that Frege regarded as a defect is not to be set against the doctrine concerning the constituents of thoughts that he stressed so often and so insistently; it contrasts with it, but does not contradict it, because it relates to a misfunction, while the doctrine relates to language as functioning correctly.

Granted, then, that there are simple predicates and relational expressions, and that they are not to be viewed as being extracted from sentences whose senses have been given independently of any recognition of those predicates as occurring in them, in what sense are they to be called 'incomplete' or 'unsaturated'? We must distinguish two questions: whether the expressions themselves are incomplete, and whether their referents are incomplete. The observation that I made on p. 28 of *FPL*, which prompted Geach to protest, was to the effect that such an *expression* cannot be said to be incomplete for the same strong reason that this can be said of complex predicates. Just because it is extracted from a sentence by omission of a proper name, a complex predicate of first level cannot be regarded as a part of, but only as a pattern within, the sentences in which it occurs; especially is this so in view of the fact that it may be essential to it that, in completing it, we put the same name in two or more places. The same holds good a fortiori for a higher-level predicate. The complex predicate is *unselbständig*: it cannot stand up on its own. But, by the nature of the case, this is not true of a simple predicate or relational expression; even if it be disconnected, like '. . . and . . . are cousins' or '. . . lets . . . alone', it is a unitary part of the sentence. We need to show how many proper names are needed to convert it into a sentence, and where they are to go; but we need no Greek letters to show which gaps must be filled by the same name, since any such restriction would violate the simplicity of the expression. Geach has, however, a powerful linguistic argument against this.[1]

---

[1] 'Names and Identity', p. 148.

In Latin, the distinction between the first and second argument of a relation expressed by a transitive verb is shown, not by the word-order, but by the case-endings of the nouns; and in Polish, apparently, it is even worse, since the verb must agree in gender with the subject. We cannot take the case-endings as literally *parts* of the relational expression, since what they are depends on the declensions and genders of the nouns; so there is no denying that, in such a language, even a simple relational expression is itself incomplete, a feature of a sentence, not a detachable part of it. My original thesis therefore requires modification. I ought not to claim that a simple predicate or relational expression must, in any language, be identifiable with a literal part of the sentence; only that, in some languages, it may be so identifiable: it is not of its very nature incomplete, as is a complex predicate.

Is the *sense* of a simple predicate or relational expression incomplete? Geach seems to think that I am committed to saying that it is not: he complains that I give no account of what makes the senses of names and simple predicates stick together to form a thought, and may suspect me of being unable to explain the difference between 'John killed Mary' and 'Mary killed John'.[1] But to recognize an expression as a genuine part of a sentence does not commit anyone to taking it as a kind of name, so that we should be left with the problem how a string of two or three names, of Herbert and of snoring, or of George, of love and of Margaret, can combine to form a sentence. Since I commended Frege for making a break with the tradition whereby, e.g., the word 'love', whether used as a verb or as a noun, is seen as denoting a universal, in favour of one which distinguished the kind of thing referred to—object, concept or relation—according to the logical role of the expression, I was hardly likely to be advocating a doctrine that accorded with the older tradition. To call an expression a predicate is just to say that it will, together with a name, form a sentence; and similarly for a relational expression. Our conception of the sense of a predicate or relational expression must be governed by Frege's thesis of the central role of sentences, so that our grasp of the sense of a predicate must issue in an apprehension of what it is for the predicate to be true of an object, our grasp of the sense of a relational expression in an apprehension of what it is for the relation to hold between two objects: our knowledge of the senses of simple predicates and relational expressions will directly supply us with a grasp of the truth-conditions of atomic sentences. The point that I was making holds also

---

[1] Ibid., p. 150.

for functional expressions. If we had no notation, like the signs for addition and multiplication, for arithmetical functions, we could form no complex numerical terms. Given such a notation, we can extract complex expressions for arithmetical functions from numerical terms; but, to be able to do so, we had to have available, at the outset, some primitive functional expressions that were not arrived at in this way. That does not imply that such primitive functors had to be introduced as if they were on all fours with numerals; their being functors depends upon their being introduced as such, viz. as combining with numerical terms to form further numerical terms. There is no call to treat it as mysterious what, on my view, a simple predicate stands for: it stands, like a complex one, for a concept.

What, then, is the point of distinguishing between simple and complex predicates? Surely what is of importance is the incompleteness of the *referent* of a predicate, and, thereby, of its sense: the functional character of the semantic explanation of its contribution to determining the truth or falsity of a sentence, and the fact that its sense must be given as determining a mapping from objects to truth-values; whether the expression itself has the character of a function is of secondary importance. Part of the point was to emphasize that it is not integral to Frege's doctrines that *every* predicate is to be thought of as arrived at only by being extracted from a sentence considered as already understood. Confusion arises if it is taken to be so; and I think that Sluga's interpretation of Frege is an instance of the type of confusion that so results.

There was, however, another point. It is, no doubt, not too difficult to explain why the senses of even simple predicates must be taken to be incomplete; but it is not so easy to explain why they are incomplete in a sense in which those of proper names are not. As I said in *FPL*,[1] in explaining the formation of atomic sentences, we should need some notion analogous to that of valency; this was a metaphor to which Frege himself appealed in the passage cited earlier from 'Booles rechnende Logik'. But this does not in itself provide us with a ground for regarding proper names as complete in a sense in which simple predicates are not. Even considered merely as *expressions*, that is, on the purely syntactic level, proper names might be considered, in some languages, to be incomplete, mere patterns in sentences. Consider once more Geach's example of Polish sentences. He rightly connects the case-endings with the relational expression: if the latter were not a transitive verb, but a verb taking a complement like 'is' as the sign of identity, then, I presume, the case of the noun for the

---

[1] P. 32.

second argument would be different. But why does he also rate the gender-inflection of the verb as part of the relational expression? Only because he already thinks that the relational expression is incomplete and the proper names complete. This would not convince one, like Ramsey, who was seriously exercised over whether there was a genuine ground for so distinguishing them. The case into which the noun filling the second argument-place goes depends on the verb, and so must be linked with it; but the gender-inflection of the verb depends upon the subject, and so, by parity, should be linked with it. Here a proper name is itself incomplete, considered as an expression: what stands for an object is a noun together with the termination of the verb in so far as that depends on it.

So far as I can see, if we concentrate wholly upon the simplest forms of sentences, atomic sentences formed from simple proper names and simple predicates or relational expressions, we shall find no reason to distinguish the former as complete or 'saturated' from the latter as 'unsaturated' or 'needing completion'. Suppose that we had a language with just atomic sentences and the results of applying the sentential operators to them. We should then have no need to recognize complex predicates as occurring in our sentences. We should also be most unlikely to have the notion of a function. But suppose, all the same, that we did conceive the idea of a mapping on to truth-values as part of an explanation how our language functioned. Why should we take predicates as standing for such a mapping rather than proper names? Perhaps because of the occurrence of relational sentences: proper names would otherwise have to stand, not only for a mapping of the referents of simple predicates on to truth-values, but for a mapping of the referents of simple relational expressions on to something like the referents of predicates (and so, in effect, a restricted class of complex predicates would be recognized). But this would not be an insuperable obstacle. The suggestion seems at first absurd; but only because it goes against the grain of so much that we are familiar with, and should not be familiar with if we had so restricted a language.

Sluga has criticized me for saying in *FPL* at the beginning of my chapter on abstract objects,[1] that 'the notion of an "object" itself, that is, the notion as used in philosophical contexts, is a modern notion, one first introduced by Frege': where, he asks, does this leave Leibniz and Kant? My remark was intended for shock effect, as should have been obvious; but, in the sense in which it was plainly meant, it continues to appear to me quite correct. I did not intend to deny the obvious fact that philo-

[1] P. 471.

sophers before Frege had employed the word 'object', '*Gegenstand*', or the like. I meant that that sense in which the word is now commonly employed by philosophers stemmed from Frege: that sense, namely, in which a distinction is drawn, among objects, between concrete and abstract ones, or in which the problem of ontology is taken to be that of saying what kinds of objects there are, or ought to be posited, and whether, for example, these include numbers or not; the alternative being, in the latter case, not to deny that numbers are objects, but to dispense with them altogether. Since the context evidently did not, as I had expected, make my intention obvious, I have slightly reworded the sentence in FPL_2 to make explicit that I was referring to current philosophical terminology. The very general notion of an object whose introduction I was attributing to Frege is one taken as applying to the referent of any expression behaving as a singular term. As I immediately went on to say, Frege's approach to ontology involved a clean break with tradition. His notion of an object did not correspond to the traditional notion of a particular; but it also did not correspond to particulars and universals, as traditionally conceived, taken together, because, for him, an object could not be referred to except by means of a singular term. If Sluga was meaning to maintain that Leibniz and Kant already had this conception of objects, his claim is open to the gravest doubt. At least with regard to Kant, Frege shared this doubt: he surmises, in *Grundlagen*, § 89, that Kant used the word '*Gegenstand*' ('object') in a sense different from his own, and remarks that, if so, he left no place for numbers, since they certainly are not concepts. In *Three Philosophers*, Geach argued that Frege's thesis that numbers are objects did not reflect any special feature of his use of the word 'object', but only a peculiarity in his view of numbers; later he retracted this opinion. Someone who took a view similar to that originally propounded by Geach would not agree with Frege that his complaint that Kant failed to allow for numbers, even if justified, entailed that Kant used the term 'object' in any different sense; but, as I argued in Chapter 12 and in FPL,[1] such a view is mistaken. Frege's use of the word 'object' has, I was contending, become standard in philosophical writing, at least within the analytical tradition; but it differed from the use of it made by his philosophical predecessors, and was based on very definite principles, principles sufficient by themselves to justify calling numbers 'objects' without appeal to any special philosophical thesis concerning numbers.

In introducing his notion of objects, however, Frege tacitly appealed

[1] Pp. 55-7.

to a great deal that he left inexplicit, a great deal that goes to make up our everyday idea of ordinary concrete objects; this appeal is made whenever he first explains the conception that the *Bedeutung* of a proper name is an object in connection with names of people, mountains, planets and the like. It has an air of paradox to suggest that, possessing a language containing names of such things and simple predicates applying to them, it might yet seem natural to us to think, as it were, of the predicates as standing for *things* and the names for properties of those things (or, say, locations of them). But Chapter 4 of *FPL*, though billed as providing criteria for discriminating proper names from other expressions, also, I think, serves to uncover some of the very familiar features of our linguistic practice that go to make up our intuitive conception of proper names as standing for objects; it is just those features of the way we talk that give us the feeling that one cannot but view a proper name as standing for *a single thing*, a thing that we make statements *about*. And the features in question are all related to the formation of complex predicates and to very elementary forms of inference involving generality; from a language lacking generality and the mechanism for the definition of new predicates as equivalent to complex ones, those features would be missing. The incompleteness of concepts, and the completeness of objects, are essentially bound up with the incompleteness of complex predicates, which then necessarily gets imputed likewise to simple ones. It is dubious whether, in a language for which it would be unnecessary to recognize complex predicates, there would be any clear sense in which the simple predicates could be described as incomplete in contrast to proper names.

CHAPTER 17

Synonymy

FREGE SELDOM TROUBLES to lay down conditions for two expressions to have the same sense. This may seem strange in view of his thesis, which he states quite generally, that, if we are to use a sign as designating an object, we must associate with it a criterion of identity (*Grundlagen*, § 62); it almost suggests that he did not, in his inmost heart, take the conception of senses as self-subsistent objects as seriously as he professed to do, but that the truly important notions for him were those of a word's or a sentence's, expressing a sense and of someone's grasping the sense of an expression. We have also seen, however, that he does propose a criterion for two sentences to have the same sense, viz. that, if one recognizes either as true, one must immediately so recognize the other, provided that one has no difficulty in grasping their senses.[1] This test allows no pause for reflection, such as might enable one to recognize the deducibility of one thought from another which, though closely related, was yet distinct. The criterion may seem an excessively psychological one: but it shows how intimate Frege took the connection to be between the sense of a sentence and what is involved in grasping it and in recognizing it as true. It would remain essentially the same, yet appear less psychological in character, if we said that *A* and *B* express the same sense if, from the fact that someone recognizes either as true, but does not so recognize the other, it follows that he has failed to grasp the sense of at least one of them. Frege adopts an effective criterion of this kind because he believes that, if one knows the senses of two expressions, one thereby knows whether they are the same (another respect in which sense is transparent): at least this principle holds good where the expressions are whole sentences. His view, previously cited, that, if a definition exactly reproduced the sense of a

[1] *N.S.*, p. 213, *P.W.*, p. 197.

term of any type already in general use, it must be immediately recognizable as correct, plainly rests on an extension of the principle to all expressions.[1] On the other hand, the context principle would allow us to infer, from the stated criterion for the synonymy of sentences, a criterion for that of other expressions; but it would not be an *effective* one. The criterion, so derived, for two expressions u and v to have the same sense would be, namely, that both members of *every* pair of sentences differing only in that v occurred in one where u occurred in the other were synonymous by the original criterion. This criterion is non-effective, since, of course, one cannot survey all such pairs of sentences; one might, therefore, fail to notice that u and v differed in sense, even though one understood both perfectly well, through failing to think of a pair of non-synonymous sentences that would reveal the difference between them. For instance, someone might say offhand that 'inefficient' and 'incompetent' were synonyms, forgetting that one can speak of being incompetent to take charge but not of being inefficient to take charge. It might be objected that a word is not to be considered as having the same sense, but only a related sense, in different constructions. On this view, we should compare two *predicates*, or two *relational expressions*, such as 'resembles' and 'is similar to', rather than two *words* in the lexicographic sense; and, when we do, the principle that synonymy is effectively decidable will be restored to full generality by applying Frege's test for the synonymy of sentences to schematic sentences like 'a is inefficient' and 'a is incompetent', or 'a resembles b' and 'a is similar to b'; to restrict the principle to sentences would be to deny that an unambiguous constituent of different sentences makes a uniform contribution to their senses, or to deny our capacity to grasp that contribution. But, to do this, we need first to decide when an expression is to be said to have two or more senses, and how they are to be discriminated; 'is fast' and 'is quick' are synonymous predicates, but not as they appear in 'The door is fast' and in the archaic 'He is not dead, but quick'. We cannot with confidence present any theory of the synonymy of expressions other than sentences as Frege's: there is too much work needed that he left undone.

It is just worth noticing, with surprise, that, in a letter to Husserl of 1906, written just four months after the fragment in which Frege offered the criterion for the synonymy of sentences just cited, he proposed a quite different, and incomplete, one, namely that, provided that 'there is not in the content of either sentence a logically evident sense-constituent',

---

[1] See *N.S.*, p. 227, *P.W.*, p. 210.

two sentences A and B express the same thought just in case, by appeal to purely logical laws, a contradiction can be derived from the supposition that A is false and B true or that A is true and B false.[1] For the restricted class of sentences which this is supposed to cover, the criterion involves that two analytically equivalent sentences express the same thought, a view irreconcilable with Frege's ideas about sense as stated in other writings; one should, I think, set the suggestion aside as an aberration. It is hard when a philosopher is held to account for remarks made in purely private correspondence.

The transparency of sense is in contrast to the opacity of reference. Can one know the reference of two expressions without knowing whether their referents are the same? To know the reference of, say, a proper name 'a' is, presumably, to know, of some object w, that 'a' stands for w. Suppose that 'a' and 'b' have the same referent: can one know, of some object w, that 'a' stands for it, and also know, of w, that 'b' stands for it, without knowing that 'a' and 'b' have the same reference? Let us say that a sentence of the form 'X knows, of c, that it is F' ascribes *predicative knowledge* to the subject, in contrast to one of the form 'X knows that A', which ascribes *propositional knowledge* (here 'A' schematically represents a sentence, 'X' the name of a rational subject, 'F' a predicative expression, and 'c' any proper name). Then, if there is irreducibly predicative knowledge, our question is to be answered negatively, at least when the knowledge of the references of the names 'a' and 'b' *is* irreducibly predicative. But, as explained in more detail in 'Frege's Distinction between Sense and Reference',[2] Frege's arguments for the sense/reference distinction should be understood as depending upon a rejection of the idea that there can be irreducibly predicative knowledge. If to say of X that he knows, of z, that it is F is to give a complete characterization of the piece of knowledge being ascribed to X, then that piece of knowledge may be said to be irreducibly predicative; if, on the other hand, a complete characterization of that piece of knowledge requires a sentence of the form 'X knows that A', ascribing propositional knowledge to X, then the predicative knowledge ascribed to him may be said to *rest on* that piece of propositional knowledge. To say that there is no irreducibly predicative knowledge is to say that each piece of predicative knowledge rests on some suitable piece of propositional knowledge, or, less precisely expressed, that all theoretical knowledge (knowledge-that) is propositional knowledge. This is probably what Frege intends to say when, in the unpublished and uncompleted 'Logik' of 1897,

[1] *BW*, p. 105, *P.M.C.*, p. 70.
[2] *Truth and Other Enigmas*, no. 9.

he remarks in passing that all knowledge is realized (*sich vollzieht*) in judgments.[1] An advocate of irreducibly predicative knowledge might reply that such knowledge is embodied in judgments expressed by the use of demonstratives. But this was not Frege's view: for him, a sentence containing a demonstrative expresses a complete thought, capable of being true or false, only because the object is still presented in a particular way, determined by the context. It follows from the thesis that all theoretical knowledge is propositional knowledge that there can be no such thing as a *bare* knowledge of the reference of a name, where this means a piece of knowledge the complete characterization of which is that it consists in knowing, of some specified object, that it is the referent of the name. Hence, if someone knows, of w, that 'a' stands for it, this knowledge will rest on his having a piece of knowledge to be expressed by saying something of the form, 'He knows that "a" stands for u' where 'u' is some simple or complex singular term. Likewise, his knowing, of w, that 'b' stands for it, will rest on a piece of propositional knowledge which is ascribed to him by saying, 'He knows that "b" stands for v', where 'v' need not be the same as, or have the same sense as, 'u': it will then not in the least follow that he knows that 'a' and 'b' have the same referent.

Why should Frege have supposed sense to be transparent, or synonymy to be a decidable relation? Understanding is surely a practical ability, the ability to use the expression correctly; and one who has a practical capacity may well be unable to give a correct description of what he does in exercising it. This brings us once more face to face with the question whether understanding is a case of knowledge, more exactly, of theoretical knowledge. What we call knowing a language is certainly to be classed as practical knowledge: to know the language is to know how to speak it, or, more accurately, how to converse in it. We must now ask whether practical knowledge (knowledge-how) is a special case of, or contains as a component, or rests on, theoretical knowledge, or whether it is quite independent of it. In one of P. G. Wodehouse's novels, X asks Y, 'Can you speak Spanish?', and Y replies, 'I don't know: I've never tried.' What makes this absurd? There would have been some absurdity if X's question had been, 'Can you swim?'. The absurdity here rests on the empirical fact that no one can swim unless he has undergone a certain training; if you know this fact, you can infer that you cannot swim from the fact that you have never been in the water. And, if you do not know the fact in question, you will see no absurdity in Y's answer. There is, after all, none in saying

[1] *N.S.*, p. 155, *P.W.*, p. 144.

that the empirical generalization admits of exceptions, e.g. that tiny infants will swim if placed in water.

Now is the absurdity of *Y*'s answer to the original question of the same kind? Does it rest on the merely empirical fact that no one can speak Spanish who has not undergone a certain training? It does not. The difference lies in the fact that someone who has not learned to swim may know perfectly well what swimming is: he can, for example, tell whether or not someone else is swimming; what he does not know is *how* to do it. Moreover, to become able to do it, he does not have to acquire theoretical knowledge of how he does it; he might even find that he had been doing it without realizing that he was. But, if *Y* has not learned Spanish, she does not know what speaking Spanish is: she cannot tell, for sure, whether someone is speaking it or not, except from the testimony of one who does know the language. She would therefore not know what it would be to *try* to speak Spanish, whereas someone who has not learned to swim can perfectly well try to do so.

All this suggests that practical abilities, and pieces of practical knowledge, are of two kinds: ones that have a component of theoretical knowledge, like knowing a language, and ones that do not, like knowing how to swim. The latter are spoken of as 'knowledge' *solely* because they are acquired by learning, by undergoing a certain training. But the former are more properly called 'knowledge'. Although we have several times been induced to trespass over the boundary that marks off this cluster of problems, I have had, as explained in Chapter 5, regretfully to exclude a full treatment of them from this book, because of their complexity; and so I shall take the matter no further here. It is enough to have indicated why Frege's intuitively plausible conviction of the transparency of sense is not to be dismissed as springing from a failure to make the identification of meaning with use.

I maintained in Chapter 15, and in *FPL*,[1] that, while there are many decompositions of a sentence, there is only one analysis of it; and it is the analysis which is relevant to its sense. For this to be faithful to Frege's intentions, there cannot be two sentences differing in essential structure but expressing the same sense; and so we must scrutinize carefully the comparatively rare cases in which Frege positively asserts that distinct sentences express the same thought. It does not matter that the grammatical form of such sentences should differ: the essential structure is what is displayed by the representation of the sentence in symbolic notation, and

[1] P. 65.

this will often suppress grammatical variation. One may have two models for translation. On one model, we apply quasi-mechanical rules of transformation, rules which could, in principle, be stated without appeal to the senses of the sentences. On the other model, we as it were first divest the thought expressed by a sentence of the one language of its linguistic clothing, and contemplate it in its nakedness: we then, turning our attention to the second language, intuitively apprehend how we should express the thought in that language. Frege certainly did not present the process of transforming sentences of natural language into symbolic formulas in accordance with the first model: he does not bother to give a detailed analysis of the way expressions of natural language function. It would be incoherent to suggest that there *are* no rules governing the combination of words to form the sentences of natural language and the semantic significance of different ways of combining them; it would therefore also be incoherent to suggest that it would be in principle impossible to state rules for transforming them into symbolic formulas. If a sentence of natural language is unambiguous, and if it can be represented at all in Frege's symbolism, then there must be some features of the sentence which determine it as representable in one way rather than another. The representation may be arbitrary in allowing a choice between evidently equivalent representations, as when we choose between representing 'Neither A nor B' as 'Not (either A or B)' and as 'Not A and not B', or 'If anyone gets to know of the report, there will be a scandal' as 'If, for some α, $F\alpha$, then C' and as 'For every α, if $F\alpha$, then C'; and Frege's practice of using only the conditional, the negation sign and the universal quantifier maximizes the number of such arbitrary choices. But, given a small number of such decisions, the representation is unique whenever it is possible at all, unless there is genuine ambiguity: and it must be on the basis of the form of expression used that we are able to tell what the correct representation is, even when we are not conscious of what exactly we are relying on.

It remains that, though it may be in principle possible to state the relevant transformation rules, for any given natural language, this is not what Frege does. We should not fall into the trap of adopting the second model for the process of rendering sentences of ordinary language symbolically. Of course, in many respects Frege's symbolism functions in accordance with different principles from natural language. But we may distinguish the essential structure from the form of representation: a formula of Frege's two-dimensional notation, in which the sub-sentences appear on different lines, one in the usual kind of modern notation, linear but using brackets, and one in Polish notation, where the connectives precede both subformulas instead of separating them, have their essential structure in common. As I remarked earlier, the structure perspicuously displayed by a formula of Frege's notation is already present in the sentence of natural language which it represents. As already observed, this essential structure is to be explained in terms of the way in which the sense of the sentence depends upon the senses of its constituents. What Frege leaves tacit and unanalysed is the mechanism of the forms of expression used in natural language which determine that we understand these dependence-relations as running in one way rather than another.

Now natural language leaves a good deal of slack: under certain grammatical transformations, the dependence-relations will be invariant, so that sentences of different grammatical forms will have the same essential structure and so will be representable by the same symbolic formula. Frege in effect regards only the essential structure as relevant to the sense, together of course with the senses of the ultimate constituents: that is to say, he does not regard the form of representation, in the sense of the devices of grammatical construction which tacitly indicate what the dependence-relations are to be taken to be, as contributing to the sense. It was argued in Chapter 3 that the sense of an expression is to be identified with the manner in which its referent is to be determined in accordance with its composition, so that the same sense cannot be expressed in accordance with two quite different systems. But we can now see that this requires a slight modification: different forms of representation, which leave the dependence-relations unchanged, are not to be regarded as affecting the sense, and so, to this extent, it can be said that the same sense can be expressed in two different ways. It is intuitively natural to adopt this attitude, at least where the thought expressed by a sentence is being identified with its sense, since Frege made the intuitively natural assumption that the same thought can be expressed in different languages.[1] Any two natural languages differ somewhat in form of representation, and some differ to a very marked degree: to count form of representation as contributing to sense would be to deem translation impossible.

The distinction here drawn between essential structure and form of representation is not Frege's. We have seen that Frege thought that many of the linguistic transformations of a sentence that leave its sense invariant are intended to indicate different preferred decompositions; these serve, as he says in *Begriffsschrift*, § 3, to help the hearer or reader to understand

[1] See *N.S.*, pp. 6, 143, 153, 222, *P.W.*, pp. 6, 131, 141, 206.

the connection with what precedes or what follows, often, we may add, by
making it easier to recognize the validity of the inferences being made. But
Frege is inclined to cite no other reason for the divergence between his
symbolism and the forms of representation used in natural language; its
grammatical constructions take the form they do because of an admixture of
logical and psychological purposes, and he even says in the 'Logik' of 1897
that, if this were not so, all languages would have the same grammar.[1] That
he should feel impelled to say this is good evidence that the account of his
notion of sense given in Chapter 3 is a correct one; but his claim cannot
be sustained. Not only did I cite above differences in form of representation between formalized languages, but Frege himself was perfectly well
aware that his own notation had arbitrary general features. Moreover,
even if it is correct, as a matter of causation, that the reason why natural
languages employ a form of representation, e.g. a means of expressing
generality, diverging so widely from that employed in Frege's symbolism
is that it subserves other purposes than the perspicuous expression of
thoughts, it remains that the form of expression serves both purposes at
once; the representation of the logical structure of the thought is effected
by means that simultaneously serve these other purposes. For this reason,
one cannot explain the matter without appeal to a notion of the form of
representation that does not contribute to the sense expressed, unless one
is prepared to categorize as bearing different senses sentences which Frege
would have regarded, or did regard, as expressing the same thought. In
any case, it is evidently no objection to ascribing to Frege the view that
each unambiguous sentence has a unique essential structure that he cites
distinct sentences of natural language as expressing the same thought,
where these are sentences that would be identically represented in his
symbolic language.

It is at first sight harder to account for the instances in which he asserts,
of two sentences that would have a different representation in his symbolism, that they express the same thought; for example, in 'Gedankengefüge', p. 39, he says this of any two sentences of the forms '*A* and *B*' and
'*B* and *A*', and, in the attached footnote 17, he says the same of the pair
'*A*' and '*A* and *A*'. The explanation is, I think, that he takes this to be
essentially the same phenomenon as the divergence between the syntactic
structure of a sentence of natural language and the corresponding symbolic
formula. Frege stressed the advantage which his symbolism gained by
exploiting the two-dimensional character of the printed page. A good

[1] *N.S.*, p. 154, *P.W.*, p. 142.

example of such exploitation would be something that never occurred to Frege, branched quantifiers as in '$\left.\begin{array}{c}\forall x \exists y \\ \forall z \exists w\end{array}\right\} A(x, y, z, w)$'. As Frege remarks,[1] in reply to Schröder's thoughtless observation, in his obtuse review of *Begriffsschrift*, that Frege's notation 'indulges in the Japanese practice of writing vertically', ordinary mathematical symbolism already does this, to the extent that each equation or inequality is written on a separate line. In this respect, that is, in the presentation of a deductive proof, Frege made no essential advance over a symbolism in which the successive steps of the proof are arranged linearly downwards, and the individual formulas written linearly from left to right: a more substantial exploitation of two-dimensionality was made by Gentzen in setting out proofs in tree form, with all the premisses of any constituent inference standing, on the same level, above its conclusion. Frege's most significant use of the available two-dimensional space lay in his setting out the subformulas of each asserted formula on separate lines, each subformula being written horizontally. What he thus perspicuously displays is not so much the logical relations between the asserted formulas constituting steps in the proof, as the inner relations between the subformulas of a complex formula. Frege observed[2] that the purely linear arrangement of natural language, spoken or written, fails to correspond with the logical relations through which thoughts are interconnected, presumably meaning the modes of combination of constituent thoughts in a complex one. But he also acknowledges, in the Preface to *Begriffsschrift*,[3] that even his notation fails to achieve the ideal of 'reproducing ideas in a pure form', and expresses the suspicion that this is probably inevitable for any external means of representation; and in 'Gedankengefüge'[4] he explains the existence of distinct means of expressing the same thought by saying that 'this divergence of the sign that expresses the thought from the thought expressed is an unavoidable consequence of the difference between the world of thoughts and that which presents a spatial and temporal appearance'. A perfect notation would be one in which the same thought could be expressed in only *one* way; in a letter to Husserl written about a month before that already quoted, Frege says that, after carrying out a proper logical analysis, one would need for each system of equipollent sentences

---

[1] 'Über den Zweck der Begriffsschrift', 1882, p. 8 (*B.a.A.*, p. 104), *C.N.*, p. 98.

[2] 'Über die wissenschaftliche Berechtigung einer Begriffsschrift', 1882, p. 53 (*B.a.A.*, p. 111), *C.N.*, p. 87.

[3] P. vii; *C.N.*, p. 106.

[4] P. 39.

only a single sentence in normal form (*Normalsatz*), equipollent sentences being ones that express the same sense.[1] But he regarded this ideal as unattainable. He evidently thought that the recognition that conjunction is commutative and idempotent is integral to a grasp of the sense of the connective 'and'; he had likewise referred, in *Grundlagen*, § 70, to forms of linguistic expression that acknowledge the symmetry of a relation, as in 'Peleus and Thetis were the parents of Achilles' (or 'Smith and Jones are neighbours'). Presumably, then, an ideal representation of the connective 'and' would involve writing the sub-sentences on top of one another, as in a monogram, but each only half as bold as their unconjoined counterparts. In such a notation, '*A* and *B*' would really be indistinguishable from '*B* and *A*', as would '*A*' from '*A* and *A*'.

An example of a quite different kind, to which my attention was drawn by Dr Gordon Baker, occurs in *Grundlagen*, § 64. Frege says:

> The judgment, 'The straight line *a* is parallel to the straight line *b*', or, in symbols, '*a//b*', can be interpreted (*aufgefasst*) as an identity. When we do this, we obtain the concept of direction, and say, 'The direction of the straight line *a* is identical with the direction of the straight line *b*'. We thus replace the symbol // by the more general symbol =, by distributing the particular content of the former between *a* and *b*. We split up the content in a manner different from the original one, and, by so doing, attain to a new concept.

Being from *Grundlagen*, this passage uses 'content', with a less precise significance, where Frege would later have used 'sense' or (on the second occurrence) 'thought'; the word 'concept' is also used, not in Frege's technical manner, but as applying to a thought-component, to something belonging to the realm of sense. The passage is nevertheless difficult to reconcile with Frege's ideas as expressed elsewhere. It plainly implies that the two sentences, 'The straight line *a* is parallel to the straight line *b*' and 'The direction of the straight line *a* is the same as the direction of the straight line *b*', have the same content, or, in the later terminology, express the same thought, whereas they plainly have different essential structures and would be represented by distinct symbolic formulas: the latter contains the two proper names 'the direction of the straight line *a*' and 'the direction of the straight line *b*' which do not appear, openly or in disguise, in the former. Moreover, the language used is reminiscent of the discussion in *Begriffsschrift*, § 9, of the different ways of regarding a

---

[1] *BW*, p. 102, *P.M.C.*, p. 67.

constituent of an expression as replaceable by another, and so decomposing it, and its conceptual content, into function and argument, and, in 'Booles rechnende Logik und die Begriffsschrift', of forming, obtaining or attaining the concept by just this process of thinking of one part as variable or replaceable and thus decomposing the judgeable content.[1] 'Booles rechnende Logik' had not, of course, appeared in print, and *Grundlagen* does not presuppose an acquaintance with *Begriffsschrift*; but whether or not Frege intended readers of both works to recall the *Begriffsschrift* passage when reading § 64 of *Grundlagen*, and, more importantly, whether or not he himself supposed the processes alluded to in the two works to be the same, or even akin, I do not know. What is clear is that the thesis that they are akin is totally indefensible. In making the transition from 'The straight line *a* is parallel to the straight line *b*' to 'The direction of the straight line *a* is the same as the direction of the straight line *b*', we are not merely attaining to a grasp of the sense of a new predicate, 'ξ is a direction', but to that of a new operator, 'the direction of ξ', by means of which names of objects are to be formed: one could say, in an imprecise fashion, that we recognize the existence of objects of a new kind, directions. As already noted, Frege maintains, in *Begriffsschrift* and the related writings, that we first obtain or form concepts by the process of regarding a sentence, or its conceptual content, as decomposing into argument and function; 'concept' here includes the concept of a relation.[2] But, although Frege says that 'instead of putting together the judgment out of an individual thing as subject and an already formed concept as predicate, we conversely decompose the judgeable content and so attain the concept',[3] he never speaks of arriving at the individual thing, i.e. the object, through decomposition of the judgeable content. The process of decomposition is, so to speak, applied in parallel to the sentence and to the judgeable content; and it proceeds by regarding the name, and likewise the individual thing for which it stands or which is its content, as variable. By doing this, we arrive, perhaps for the first time, at the functional expression, and, likewise, at the concept. But to be able to do it at all, we had first to be able to pick out the name, and understand it as standing for the individual thing. The process so described has no analogy with that involved in passing from speaking of straight lines as being parallel or not being parallel to one another to speaking of them as having directions which are the same or different.

[1] *N.S.*, pp. 17–18, *P.W.*, pp. 16–17.
[2] *Begriff einer Relation*, *N.S.*, p. 18, *P.W.*, p. 17.
[3] Ibid.

§ 64 occurs as part of a passage of *Grundlagen* of immense importance, in which, for the first time, Frege is discussing a certain transition in mode of expression which is, at the same time, a process of concept-formation (not in Frege's later sense of 'concept'). Frege makes plain that he regards this process as being of great importance, as indeed it is, and as having a very great many instances, of which that concerning directions is picked as being a representative example. He wants to explain the process and, moreover, to justify it. If we were to take the turns of phrase by which Frege characterizes the transition at the beginning of § 64 quite literally, then no justification would be needed: the two different forms of sentence would express one and the same judgeable content (thought), and would correspond merely to two different ways of viewing it, which would leave the conceptual content itself unaffected, as Frege says in *Begriffsschrift*, § 9, concerning the different possible decompositions into function and argument. One would therefore have to devise a single symbolic representation for this conceptual content, as he explains in *Begriffsschrift*, § 3: the different possible ways of viewing it, corresponding to the two forms of sentence in natural language, would relate to different kinds of inference in which it could figure, just as do the different decompositions into function and argument. In the latter case, the symbolic notation does not require us to distinguish the different alternative decompositions, because, given just *one* formula expressing the single judgeable content, the formalization of the principles of logical inference permit us to carry out, or to recognize as valid, all the inferences in which it can figure, those requiring one possible decomposition and those requiring a different one. If this were really an analogous case, the same would hold true here. It would then be possible to devise a notation in which both forms of sentence would be simultaneously represented by a single formula. By reference to this formula, one could explain in what the two ways of decomposing the content actually consisted, in some style corresponding to Frege's explanations of the process of carrying out alternative decompositions into function and argument; one could, in particular, explain how one and the same formula could be viewed both as containing certain complex proper names and as not containing them. And, most important of all, one could formalize the rules of inference that allowed, as equally valid, inferences appropriate to viewing the judgment as being to the effect that two lines are parallel and ones appropriate to viewing it as constituting a judgment of identity between objects of a particular kind.

Frege does nothing of the kind. He does not fill out his original characterization of the transition in any of these ways; nor does he treat it as being already a justification of the transition. Rather, he proceeds to discuss at length how it should be effected and justified. He considers the possibility of simply *defining* 'The direction of the straight line *a* is the same as the direction of the straight line *b*' as to be taken to mean the same as 'The straight line *a* is parallel to the straight line *b*'. If these were no more than two verbal expressions for the very same judgeable content or thought, such a definition could not be called into question, any more than one could call in question a stipulation that '*Y* is loved by *X*' is to mean the same as '*X* loves *Y*'. But, after a detailed discussion of the proposed definition, Frege decides that it is not admissible. It is evident that the form of words used at the outset to characterize the transition is simply not to be taken *au pied de la lettre*. *Grundlagen* is a highly argumentative book, one in which Frege is striving to convince his readers of the truth of his views; and the passage quoted is intended to soften up the reader so that he will be disposed to accept the type of transition under discussion as legitimate. It embodies an exaggerated claim; if we attribute this claim, literally interpreted, to Frege, we shall gravely distort his views.

The real topic of *Grundlagen*, §§ 63–9, is how to effect the transition from saying that there are just as many *F*'s as *G*'s to saying that the number of *F*'s is the same as the number of *G*'s; the direction example is discussed merely as a representative of the same general type of transition. What shows that the attitude just advocated to Frege's remarks in introducing that example is correct is that the transition which is the actual topic of discussion is formally entirely analogous to one which played a very important role in Frege's construction of arithmetic in *Grundgesetze*, and which led to the appearance of the contradiction in his logical system, namely that from saying that everything is an *F* iff it is a *G* to saying that the extension of the concept *F* (the class of *F*'s) is the same as the extension of the concept *G* (the class of *G*'s); or, in the more general form in which it appears in *Grundgesetze*, from saying that, for every α, $f(\alpha)$ is the same as $g(\alpha)$ to saying that the value-range of the function *f* is the same as that of the function *g*. In *Function und Begriff*, Frege's first report on the alterations in the logical system to be used in *Grundgesetze* from that presented in *Begriffsschrift*, he first introduces value-ranges (pp. 9–10) by saying that 'it is not provable, as it seems to me, that it is possible to regard the generalization of an equation between the values of functions as an equation, namely between value-ranges, but must be taken as a basic logical law', adding in a footnote that the notion of a function is logically prior to that of a value-range. On p. 11, he permits himself an expression suggesting that he viewed this transition in the same way as he had hinted, in *Grundlagen* § 64, that we should view that from saying that two lines are parallel to saying that their directions are the same, by saying that the universal quantification of an equation between the values of the functions 'expresses the same sense' as the equation between their value-ranges, 'but in a different way'. But, in subsequent writings, he never speaks of the transition as going from one method of expressing a thought to another method of expressing the very same thought: he always speaks of it, for instance in *Grundgesetze*, vol. I, § 9, as a *transformation*, with which we cannot dispense and which rests on a principle that must be regarded as a logical law.[1] In the Appendix to vol. II of *Grundgesetze*, concerning Russell's paradox, he confessed that he had not concealed from himself the lack of self-evidence attaching to his Axiom V, which embodies the supposed law of logic, a self-evidence that he claimed for the other axioms and acknowledged as required for a logical law,[2] and he referred to p. vii of the Preface to vol. I, on which he had admitted that Axiom V might be called in question. A transition from one way of expressing a thought to another way of expressing the same thought does not leave room for dispute; moreover, it cannot be said even to appeal to a logical law, which, though it must be self-evident, governs a passage from one or more thoughts to another. It was a disaster for Frege that he ever came to regard Axiom V as true, let alone as a fundamental law of logic. It is, to my mind, dubious in the extreme that he ever intended a literal construction to be put upon the words from *Grundlagen* quoted above. But, if he did, he very soon came to see the view so expressed to be untenable; if he had not, he would have claimed for Axiom V a status like that possessed, on his view, by the principle '*A* and *B* if and only if *B* and *A*'. The Russell paradox would then have been even more shattering to his philosophy than it was: it would have brought into question, not only the analytic character of arithmetical truth and the legitimacy of the notion of a class, but Frege's whole conception of the identification and differentiation of thoughts and of the processes of analysing and decomposing them.

Frege made the obvious distinction between constructive definitions and analytical ones, the former being of terms newly introduced and the latter of ones already in general use. We have seen in Chapter 14 that he gave it as his view that an analytical definition is unlikely to embody the exact sense that attaches to the word, as generally used, and that, if it does, this must be immediately evident. It ought to be equally evident,

[1] Cf. also *Grundgesetze*, vol. II, §§ 146–7.
[2] P. 253.

in other cases, that it does *not*; and Frege explains that, when a doubt arises, this must be because the sense of the word, as used before the analytical definition was given, was not clearly grasped, but appeared to us only in hazy outline as if through a fog.[1] It is to be hoped that this remark will not prompt anyone to try to reconstruct Frege's theory of the weather conditions in the space intervening between our minds and the realm of sense. But, for a word or symbol being introduced, say by himself, by means of a legitimate definition, as for one in general use which Frege took to have been introduced by definition, he had no doubt that definiens and definiendum had the very same sense. In *Grundgesetze*, vol. I, § 27, he characterizes definitions by saying, 'We introduce a new name by means of a *definition*, whereby we stipulate that it is to have the same sense and the same reference as one compounded out of already known symbols'; it should be recalled that in *Grundgesetze* the word 'name' applies alike to proper names and function-signs, i.e. to everything that can be said to have a sense or a reference. He says the same in 'Logik in der Mathematik': by means of the definition, the simple symbol, the definiendum, obtains a sense, the same sense, namely, as that which the group of symbols, the definiens, has.[2] For this reason, he says, like Russell, that definitions are not essential for the system; they have to do only with the symbolism, and add nothing to the content. The defined symbol has a sense that is built up out of the senses of the parts of the defining expression. We already noted, in passing, that he tacitly appeals to the identity of sense between an expression and that to which it was presumably introduced by definition as equivalent in giving examples. In the passage from 'Über Begriff und Gegenstand' discussed in the Chapter 15, the point was to illustrate how natural language, by casting a sentence into different forms, can highlight different preferred decompositions; but, in giving his examples of distinct sentences of natural language expressing the same thought, Frege presumes on the manner in which familiar mathematical expressions have been defined and so introduced. We have seen that he cites the sentences, 'There is at least one square root of 4' and 'The number 4 has the property that there is something of which it is the square' as expressing the same thought, which assumes that '*m* is a square root of *n*' was defined to mean '*n* is the square of *m*'. Subsequently, he remarks that 'There is at least one square root of 4' predicates something of a concept, but adds that this in no way effaces the distinction between object and concept; for in the sentence 'There is at least one square root of 4',

[1] 'Logik in der Mathematik', *N.S.*, p. 228, *P.W.*, p. 211.
[2] *N.S.*, p. 224, *P.W.*, p. 208.

the predicative nature of the concept is not belied. To bring this out, he adds that one can say, 'There is something that has the property of yielding 4 when multiplied by itself'. The whole point is, of course, to emphasize that the predicative character of the concept-expression, its use to ascribe a property to an object, is as essential to the understanding of the existential statement as to that of one in which a particular object is presented as falling under the concept, and Frege could simply have used, for this purpose, the form 'There is something that has the property of being a square root of 4': but the particular sentence he cites presumes, when 'square root' is taken as defined in terms of 'square', that 'n is the square of m' was defined to mean 'n is the number equal to $m.m$'.[1]

If the sense of a defined expression is identical with that of the expression by means of which it was defined, then, in order to arrive at the ultimate analysis of a thought into its constituents, we must, in a sentence expressing it, first replace any defined expressions by their definientia, and continue the process until we have nothing but primitive expressions, that is, ones that were not introduced by definition, and expose the essential structure of the sentence so obtained. Without doubt, if we really do want to give a complete account of the sense of any sentence, we must in this way work back to expressions that are in this sense primitive. To the extent that the sense of an expression, once introduced, does not shift, then, if it was introduced by definition, its being so defined is an enduring trait; an awareness of its definition remains essential to a correct understanding of it, or, otherwise expressed, a grasp of its sense consists in taking it to be replaceable, in any sentence, by its definiens. But the conclusion at which Frege finally arrived, that constructive definitions are really inessential and affect only the form of expression by allowing a terser sentence or symbolic formula—that they are, in the celebrated phrase, 'mere abbreviations'—is just that which Wittgenstein attacked in his criticism of Russell in the *Remarks on the Foundations of Mathematics*. Wittgenstein's criticism, though far from showing, as he seems to have supposed, that a successful reduction of arithmetic to logic is impossible, or would be circular or at least devoid of interest, is in principle just; and Frege, in adopting the view of definitions held by Russell and, indeed, by most mathematical logicians, was betraying earlier insights. In *Grundlagen* and in 'Booles rechnende Logik' he had insisted on the fruitfulness of good definitions, on the crucial role played by them in the advance of mathematical knowledge; this is, after all, hardly surprising in one who had devoted much

---

[1] 'Über Begriff und Gegenstand', pp. 199–200.

labour to framing exact definitions of fundamental notions, beginning with the definition in *Begriffsschrift* of the notion of following in a sequence (of the ancestral of a relation). Of course, it may be said that these are analytical definitions; but this is largely irrelevant. It does not matter a great deal for the fruitfulness of a definition whether the notion being made precise by it is being introduced for the first time or has long been hazily familiar; and, in any case, Frege has no explanation for any supposedly greater enlightenment resulting from analytical definitions, but can only suggest that it might be better if they were converted into constructive ones by employing a new symbol for the definiendum. As was remarked earlier, it is by reference to the fruitfulness of definitions that Frege, in his writings up to and including *Grundlagen*, explained why deductive reasoning, and in particular, analytic judgments, can advance our knowledge. The reason is that, on the account given by him in his earlier period, a definition is *not*, in general, a mere convenience of notation, but represents a process of concept-formation, in his earlier non-technical use of the word 'concept'; and the logical aspect of this process is to be explained precisely in terms of the conception, discussed above, of the decomposition of sentences and of their contents.

Consider a sentence containing an expression, say a predicate, introduced by some complicated and perhaps surprising definition, and consider the transformation of that sentence by means of the definition, i.e. by replacing the defined expression by its definiens. Certainly, the definition may have represented a great conceptual advance. If it was an analytical definition, it may have uncovered the principles, of which we had been unable to give an account, tacitly underlying our use of the predicate; or perhaps it replaced a hazy notion by a precise one. Or, if it was a constructive definition, it may have introduced us to a wholly unfamiliar but illuminating principle of classification. But the question before us is whether the sentence containing the defined expression and that containing its definiens ought to be regarded as having the same sense, or, more exactly, whether, consistently with his general philosophy of language, Frege ought to have said that they did. It appears, on reflection, evident that he should not have said so. It is a presupposition of the definition that we do already understand the sentence containing the definiens. But the whole point of Frege's account of the formation of incomplete expressions is that such an expression may occur in a sentence for the understanding of which we do not need to discern its presence; we arrive at it by decomposition of the sentence. By contrast, granted that an account of the sense of the defined expression must be given in terms of its replaceability by the definiens, a sentence containing it obviously requires, for a grasp of the thought expressed by it, an apprehension of the occurrence in that sentence of that expression. The sense of the defined expression cannot but be a constituent of the thought expressed by a sentence in which it occurs, whereas the definiens may well be only a component, not a constituent, of the sentence resulting from a replacement of the defined expression by it, and, in that case, its sense will not be part of the sense of the thought expressed by that sentence. In such a case, therefore, the first sentence and the second one cannot possibly express the very same thought, since the thought expressed by the first has a constituent to which no constituent of the thought expressed by the second corresponds. All we can say is that the senses of the two sentences are related in a special way: the sense of the defined expression is given to us as requiring that the sentence containing it be determined as true by whatever will determine the sentence containing its definiens as true. The term 'truth-condition', often immensely convenient, but incapable, I think, of exact definition, and frequently an impediment to clear thought, is liable to be one here. One may think: the definition embodies a stipulation that the condition for the truth of the first sentence is to be the same as that for the truth of the second sentence; so, if the sense of a sentence is determined by its truth-condition, their senses must be the same. But a more accurate form of expression is: the sense of a sentence is given by the way in which its truth-value is determined in accordance with its composition. If we grasp the sense of the defined expression by knowing its definition, then we shall recognize a sentence containing it as true by first replacing it by a sentence containing the definiens and then recognizing the latter sentence as true. The first step is an essential one, and is not to be described as merely operating with symbols: it is a step in thought, a transition from a thought having one essential structure to one having quite a different structure. The dependence of the sense of the defined expression on those occurring in the definiens is not in doubt: but, when we are concerned with the essential structure of a sentence or of a thought, the analysis ought to terminate with simple expressions and their senses, not, in general, with primitive ones.

It was pointed out to me by Warren Goldfarb that an extension of the principle that was applied in the preceding argument will threaten the possibility that there are any two sentences expressing exactly the same thought, except when one is obtainable from the other by successively replacing a single word by a synonymous word. If so, the distinction indicated above between form of representation and essential structure is likewise threatened, as is the idea that one can translate from one language to another with strict preservation of sense, if not of other ingredients in meaning. For example, it is a plausible account of the third-person singular reflexive pronouns, at least in some of their occurrences, that an understanding of them consists in a grasp of the equivalence of a sentence containing one of them with a sentence in which there is a second occurrence of the relevant proper name; after all, as I pointed out,[1] it is essential to an understanding of 'Brutus killed himself' that we recognize it as at least equivalent to a sentence from which the predicate 'ξ killed Brutus' can be extracted. But one could argue, in the same vein as the above argument that a defined expression does not have the same sense as its definiens, that 'Brutus killed himself' does not express the very same sense as 'Brutus killed Brutus'. In the determination of the truth of the first sentence, there is an additional first step, namely precisely its transformation into the second sentence. A grasp of the sense of the first sentence requires an explicit recognition of the presence in it, as a constituent, of the predicate 'ξ killed ξ', or, rather, of the natural-language surrogate, 'ξ killed himself', for it, whereas a grasp of the sense of the second sentence does not strictly demand an awareness that the same proper name occurs twice (however unlikely it be that, in so simple an example, anyone could overlook this). The thought expressed by the first sentence thus contains, as a constituent, the sense of 'ξ killed ξ' ('ξ killed himself'), which the thought expressed by the second sentence does not contain. Much as one might want to resist such a conclusion, it is not evident that it is possible to do so without retracting what was said above about definitions.

Adherence to the principle that the sense of an expression involves everything belonging to the way in which its reference is determined in accordance with its composition seems thus to lead to the conclusion that there probably is no sharp criterion for sameness of sense short of the rather boring notion of intensional isomorphism. And this reinforces the suggestion with which I began this chapter; namely, that synonymy is simply not the interesting question to pursue in discussing the notion of sense. If the conception of senses as objects, which Frege undoubtedly had, were really an important ingredient of the notion, the criterion for the synonymy of two expressions would necessarily be crucial, since it would be the criterion of identity for those objects; and, if we do not know what it is to speak of 'the same X', we do not know what it is to speak of such objects as X's. The present considerations appear to show that the relation of synonymy is not, in fact, very interesting, and that, to have a

---

[1] *FPL*, pp. 13–14.

good understanding or even philosophical analysis of the notion of sense, one does not really need a sharp criterion for that relation to hold. (It would of course follow, on Frege's account of sentences involving indirect discourse, that they have only imprecise truth-conditions; but, actually, that is in itself rather plausible.) The interesting notions, in connection with sense, are those of grasping a sense and of expressing sense, and a great deal may be said about these without the need for a sharp criterion of identity of sense. This conclusion, though it would have been unwelcome to Frege, accords very well with the thrust of the discussion in this book of his notion of sense, namely that his representation of thoughts and other senses as eternal objects existing independently of us was not so much an intrinsic ingredient of his notion as something that he felt forced to say by his desire to preserve the objectivity of sense and to keep it uncontaminated by the psychological, in the absence of an adequate philosophy of mind that would have enabled him to do so without resorting to mythology.

CHAPTER 18

Epistemological Atomism

IT WAS NOTED in Chapter 4 that Sluga may well be right in maintaining that in *FPL* I placed the downfall of Hegelian idealism in Germany too late by some decades.[1] If so, then obviously Frege's realism was not a reaction to Hegelianism. It was nevertheless argued, in that chapter, that Frege was a realist, and that he did see himself as in opposition to a predominantly idealist philosophical climate of opinion. This raises two questions. Was Frege a realist at all? And is there sufficient in common to the very different philosophies to which the general label 'idealist' has been attached to make that label a significant one? If Frege was not a realist, then certainly my interpretation of his work is seriously in error. If, on the other hand, he was a realist, but the word 'idealist' has too vague a meaning to be a useful tool for philosophical classification, then only the rare passages of *FPL* in which I used it demand revision.[2]

In 'Frege as a Rationalist', Sluga says that my 'interpretation of Frege as a "realist" in opposition to a prevailing idealism' is mistaken, and that, on the contrary, there was a 'close relationship between Frege and the philosophical tradition, specifically Leibniz and Kant, whose views appear closer to idealism than to realism'.[3] In 'Frege and the Rise of Analytical Philosophy', he terms my characterization of Frege as a realist an 'unsubstantiated (though widely accepted) claim'.[4] In neither of these essays does he come right out and say flatly that Frege was not a realist, though he stigmatizes a number of what he considers to be errors in interpreting Frege as springing from the view that he was one; but, in 'Frege's Alleged Realism', written in reply to my 'Frege as a Realist,'

[1] *FPL*, p. 683.
[2] On pp. 197, 470 and 683–4.
[3] P. 28.
[4] P. 478.

he not only speaks of 'Frege's supposed realism',[1] but says, with regard to mathematics, that 'Frege's position seems closer to Kantian idealism than it is to realism'[2] and, with regard to empirical objects, that Frege's position must be akin to the transcendental idealism of Kant.[3] We may thus finally take it that, for Sluga, Frege was *not* a realist, but a species of idealist. Ernst Tugendhat says, more cautiously, that Frege's 'so-called "realism" seems to be over-emphasized in the literature'.[4] Sluga thinks that it is my historical error in believing Hegelianism to have continued to be influential in Germany up to the early part of Frege's career that prompted my diagnosis of him as a realist: expose the historical mistake, and the alleged mistake of interpretation collapses. This is not so: I did not deduce that Frege must have been a realist from the supposition that Hegelianism was influential in his day, together with some presumption that he would be bound to have been against it, or even from the evident fact that he was not a Hegelian; I found a realistic philosophy advocated in his writings.

Sluga's denial that Frege was a realist springs partly from his denial that, for Frege, the referent of a proper name is its bearer; that has already been discussed in Chapter 7. It would go very well with Sluga's general view of Frege if he could claim, as Marshall and Grossmann once did, that Frege admitted no distinction between sense and reference for incomplete expressions: but since the publication of Frege's posthumous writings, that has been impossible. From these, which I already referred to in 'Note: Frege on Functions',[5] it is manifest that not only did Frege admit such a distinction, but he saw the referent of, e.g., a relational expression as being as much a constituent of external, objective reality as that of a proper name. 'It is unthinkable,' Frege wrote in his unpublished 'Einleitung in die Logik' of 1906, 'that there can be a question of a reference only for proper names, not for the remaining sentence-parts that connect them. When we say, "Jupiter is larger than Mars", of what are we speaking? Of the heavenly bodies themselves, of the references (*Bedeutungen*) of the proper names "Jupiter" and "Mars". We are saying that they stand in a certain relation to one another, and we do this by means of the words "is larger than". This relation obtains between the references of the proper

---

[1] P. 228.

[2] P. 236.

[3] P. 237.

[4] *Studien zu Frege*, vol. III, p. 61.

[5] *Philosophical Review*, vol. LXV, 1956, pp. 229–30, reprinted in *Truth and Other Enigmas*, London, 1978, pp. 85–6.

names, and must therefore itself belong to the realm of references. One must accordingly recognize the sentence-part "is greater than" as also having a reference, not merely as having a sense.'[1]

Sluga connects my saying that, for Frege, the referent of a proper name is its bearer with what he calls 'epistemological atomism', which he accuses me of ascribing to Frege.[2] He explains 'epistemological atomism' as the doctrine that 'knowledge is . . . in the first instance knowledge of objects and their properties', as opposed to the view that 'knowing is in the first instance always knowing that' and 'is always judgmental in character'.[3] This is ironic, in view of the fact that, before I had ever seen any of Sluga's publications, I had, in 'Frege's Distinction between Sense and Reference',[4] explained Frege's arguments for the necessity of the sense/reference distinction as resting on the principle that all theoretical knowledge is propositional, in the sense explained in Chapter 17. I absolutely agree with Sluga that Frege was not an epistemological atomist in the sense explained. As I remarked in *FPL*,[5] Mill's view of proper names involved that 'the world already came to us sliced up into objects', whereas, on the basis of Frege's view, we see that 'the proper names which we use . . . determine principles whereby the slicing up of the world is to be effected, principles which are acquired with the acquisition of the uses of these words';[6] and I based this on the principle, which Frege states quite generally (*Grundlagen*, § 62), that 'if we are to use the sign a to designate an object, we must have a criterion which decides in all cases whether b is the same as a'. Sluga would not like this derivation, since he sees the principle as restricted in application to logical objects.[7] But, although Frege is, in that passage, discussing numbers, and although he introduces the discussion by considering someone's asking, 'How, then, is a number to be given to us, if we can have no idea or intuition of it?', the text supplies no ground for restricting the principle to those objects which we cannot perceive or intuit. Some, indeed, would appeal to Frege's question how numbers are given to us[8] as showing that he conceived of non-logical objects as being given in sense or in intuition and hence that he *was* an

---

[1] *N.S.*, pp. 209–10, *P.W.*, p. 193.

[2] 'Frege and the Rise of Analytical Philosophy', p. 485.

[3] Ibid., p. 479.

[4] Originally published in Spanish in *Teorema*, vol. v, 1975, pp. 149–88, and reprinted in *Truth and Other Enigmas*, pp. 116–44.

[5] P. 179.

[6] Cf. also *FPL*, pp. 406, 504–5 and 577.

[7] 'Frege and the Rise of Analytical Philosophy', p. 486.

[8] See also *Grundlagen*, § 104.

epistemological atomist in precisely Sluga's sense. In fact, he does not use that terminology. He would agree that we derive our knowledge about such objects through our sense-experiences or through intuition: but it would be quite out of harmony with his other views to suppose that he thought that it is through sense-experience or through intuition alone that we are provided with the means to discriminate particular objects within what we sense or intuit. In this connection, Sluga rightly quotes from 'Der Gedanke',[1] 'Having visual impressions is indeed necessary for seeing things, but not sufficient. What has to be added is not anything sensible. And yet this is precisely what opens the external world for us; for without this non-sensible thing everyone would remain enclosed in his inner world.' What needs to be added, though not itself sensible, is thought, with the senses that are constituents of thoughts. This accords very well with what I said in *FPL*,[2] that 'the objects which serve as referents cannot be recognized quite independently of language: it is only because we employ a language for the understanding of which we need to grasp various criteria of identity . . . that we learn to slice the world up, conceptually, into discrete objects'. A language would not be necessary if we could have thoughts without language; as we have seen, Frege considered that a possibility in principle, but an impossibility for us. The point being made in 'Der Gedanke' is not precisely the same: there Frege was concerned, not with the discrimination of individual objects within the external world, but with awareness of the external world at all, since 'to have visual impressions is not yet to see things'; but the two ideas fit very harmoniously together into a single philosophy. If one has to say which of these two ideas of Frege's is that which makes that philosophy irreconcilable with epistemological atomism, it is the one expounded by me rather than that expressed in the passage quoted by Sluga.

Sluga thinks that to identify the referent of a proper name with its bearer is to adopt the following picture. We *first* have knowledge of objects: that is to say, before we have language, and, therefore, thought, we have, through sense-experience and perhaps also through intuition, an immediate direct awareness of various discriminable objects; we discern such objects, as given to us, in sense or in intuition, in advance of our having any thoughts, or making any judgments, about those objects. Not only *can* we do so, but we *must* do so: it is only because we have first discerned the object that we can start using a proper name as standing for it, and so express, and grasp, thoughts about the object. Having first become acquainted with the object, we then attach the name to it as a label: this association

[1] P. 75.
[2] P. 406.

of name with object is what confers upon the name its reference. Sluga does not, indeed, spell out this conception: but unless he is accusing me of attributing such a conception to Frege, I can make no sense of his charge that I ascribe an atomistic theory of knowledge to Frege.

To attribute that conception to Frege, as some would do, is only slightly more ridiculous than to attribute such an interpretation of Frege to me, although of course a far graver error. It would be a good account of Mill's view of proper names; but it is absurd as an interpretation of Frege, since it would leave no room for proper names to have sense as well as reference. Yet, if Sluga were right that the doctrine about criteria of identity were intended to apply only to proper names of abstract objects, and not to those of objects given to us in sense or in intuition, this conception would have to be Frege's, for names of the latter kind. At least, it would have to be Frege's conception *if* the referent of a proper name is its bearer, indeed if it is an *object* at all: that is at least one of the reasons why Sluga is driven to the desperate expedient of denying that the referent of a proper name is its bearer.

In any case, it should be evident, from a great many passages in *FPL*, that this is *not* my interpretation of Frege. Thinking, as I do, that Frege intended the principle concerning criteria of identity to be of general application, I am not in Sluga's dilemma. In *FPL*[1] I contrasted Mill's view of proper names unfavourably with Frege's. To regard the referent of a proper name as its bearer, the object which we use it to talk about, does *not* entail that we discriminate the object in advance of learning to use the name (or at least of having a language which, by containing proper names of objects of the same sort, or containing a suitable sortal noun, already provides for the introduction of a name with that sense); it does not entail that we have any knowledge of the object in advance of knowledge *about* it and in advance of being able to say things about it by using the name in sentences. On the contrary, as I understand him, Frege's view was that we have no conception of the object until we grasp the criterion of identity associated with it: we might come by this by learning to use the corresponding sortal noun, but we might, and no doubt often do, attain it in the first place by learning to use that name and the names of other objects of the same sort. The context principle expressly denies that there can be any grasp of the reference of a name antecedently to an ability to understand or use sentences containing it: it is only in the context of a sentence that the name even *has* a reference.

[1] Pp. 96–7, 179–80, 545 and 577.

Concrete objects differ from abstract ones in that they can be the targets of ostension. One use of a proper name of a concrete object in a sentence is therefore its use in what in *FPL* I called 'recognition statements'.[1] This should not be conceived as the expression of a primordial, prelinguistic and intrinsically simple capacity to recognize the object on perceiving it. On the contrary, it is already a fairly complex use of language, which has to be acquired; and its acquisition depends upon coming to grasp the relevant criterion of identity. Below it lies a more primitive layer of language, which involves as yet no reference to objects, exemplified in what I called 'crude predications';[2] the transition to the higher level can be schematically represented as mediated by the use of 'statements of identification'.[3] All this was discussed in Chapter 11. Frege did not himself go into these matters: but we have to go into them if we are to achieve a satisfactory explanation of what is meant by speaking of a criterion of identity for concrete objects. In *FPL* I accordingly tried to go into them, without, of course, attributing the resulting account to Frege: I aimed only to show that a plausible explanation of Frege's conception of the senses of proper names, construed as comprising associated criteria of identity, could be constructed.

Sluga and I are agreed that Frege was not an epistemological atomist; we are disagreed about the precise connection of this fact with his other doctrines. The disagreement has unfortunately become exceedingly difficult to disentangle, owing to Sluga's bizarre controversial methods, amounting at times to mere knockabout; I will nevertheless attempt the task. Sluga does not believe that Frege intended his notion of a criterion of identity to apply to concrete objects; but I made it very plain in *FPL* that I did, and praised Frege for rejecting a Millian account of proper names in consequence. This already makes it very odd that Sluga should have stated, without qualification,[4] that I made Frege an epistemological atomist, evidently assuming that I attributed to him the Millian view of proper names. His ground was my appeal to the notion of ostension, on which he commented that he knew no place in Frege's writings where it plays such a role. To this I replied,[5] 'If it is true, as I think, that Frege's notion of reference for proper names implicitly appeals to the name/bearer relation, we are entitled to ask in what this relation consists and with what right

[1] P. 232.
[2] P. 233.
[3] P. 573.
[4] 'Frege and the Rise of Analytical Philosophy', p. 479.
[5] 'Frege as a Realist', p. 459.

Frege appealed to it. I attempted [in *FPL*] to explain the relation as embedded in very basic linguistic practices, including the use of ostension to identify an object as the referent of a name. . . I did not purport . . . to be reproducing anything in Frege in this discussion, only to bring to light something I believe must underlie his use of the notion of reference.' I expressly disclaimed the attribution of epistemological atomism to Frege, saying that 'I wholly agree that Frege was not an atomist in this sense';[1] and I cited passages, from *FPL* and from 'Frege's Distinction between Sense and Reference', to show that this was no change of mind. Yet in his reply to me, 'Frege's Alleged Realism', Sluga simply serves up the same misinterpretation of me, not even reheated, without taking the slightest notice of my disclaimer or my explanations: 'The explanation for Dummett's peculiar misrepresentation of Frege's doctrine lies probably in his theory of reference according to which the name/bearer relationship is semantically fundamental. Dummett thinks that the notion of ostension underlies Frege's use of the notion of reference. . . That seems to commit Dummett to an "epistemological atomism" according to which there is a direct acquaintance with objects and knowledge is, in the first instance, knowledge of objects and their properties.'[2] He condescendingly adds, 'He seems to realise that this does not completely square with Frege's account'; this is his only acknowledgment of my express repudiation of such an interpretation.

Among the passages I cited to show that I had never thought Frege an epistemological atomist was a remark from 'Frege's Distinction between Sense and Reference' that, for Frege, all theoretical knowledge is propositional knowledge; and, in opposition to Sluga's assertion that 'knowledge is always judgmental in character', I commented, mildly enough, that 'I should not regard knowledge-how as always reducible to knowledge-that'.[3] This question is, indeed, a serious and important one, bearing on the problem of the character of the knowledge of a language; in my view, there are different varieties of practical knowledge, of which some have a theoretical component, and others do not, knowledge of a language, including one's mother tongue, being of the former kind. One might suppose that, in repeating that I regarded Frege as an epistemological atomist, Sluga had overlooked my statement that, for Frege, all theoretical knowledge is propositional; on the contrary, after quoting Frege's remark that 'all knowledge is embodied in judgments',[4] which he translates as

[1] Ibid., p. 462.
[2] 'Frege's Alleged Realism', p. 239.
[3] 'Frege as a Realist', p. 463.
[4] *N.S.*, p. 155, *P.W.*, p. 144.

'all knowledge is judgmental', he comments that 'Dummett takes exception to my claim that, according to Frege, all knowledge is judgmental. As is clear from the quotation I was merely repeating something asserted by Frege himself.'[1] This evidently alludes to my further denial that all knowledge-how is knowledge-that. Not only does this comment make it likely that he did not miss, but merely ignored, my preceding statement about theoretical knowledge, but it is in itself absurd. Frege's remark about knowledge, cited by Sluga, is a passing one, and obviously intended to bear only on theoretical knowledge, not on practical knowledge at all: it is ridiculous to claim it as committing Frege to thinking that knowledge-how can always be reduced to knowledge-that, and thus to disputing the only exception to Sluga's dictum that I had claimed.

To what does Frege's brief remark about knowledge commit him? Can it be read as an expression of his repudiation of epistemological atomism? It may reasonably be understood as telling in favour of knowledge-that, whether propositional or predicative, as against knowledge of objects, that is, acquaintance: we cannot know an object save in knowing something about it. Certainly Frege believed that; it follows from the context principle. It might well be an important point to make against some versions of epistemological atomism, for instance against Russell's view of the priority of knowledge by acquaintance over knowledge by description. I take it that Sluga, in speaking of 'knowledge of objects and their properties', means to separate the two; the atomist he has in mind claims to know objects, without knowing what properties they have, and to know properties, without knowing any objects that have them. But would Frege's remark necessarily tell against an account of proper names in the style of Mill, that account which Sluga believes I attribute to Frege and thinks commits me to regarding him as an epistemological atomist? It appears to me that it would not. One who subscribes to a Millian account of proper names is committed to the view that we can *discriminate* objects independently of and in advance of language; he is not, however, committed to any view that we have *knowledge of* objects independently of language, but could consistently hold that one can know an object only by knowing something about it. A Millian account of proper names therefore does *not* entail epistemological atomism, as characterized by Sluga. So, even if Sluga were right, instead of ludicrously wrong, in supposing that I ascribed such an account of proper names to Frege, he would still be mistaken in thinking that that committed me to taking Frege to be an epistemological

---

[1] 'Frege's Alleged Realism', fn. 6.

atomist; it would, indeed, commit me to denying that Frege believed that proper names have sense as well as reference. It is important, in this connection, to notice that the brief remark of Frege's concerning knowledge, taken on its own, in no way resolves the question of the relative priority of propositional and of predicative knowledge, that is, the question whether all predicative knowledge rests on propositional knowledge in the sense explained. It does not do so, for the simple reason that predicative knowledge may also be regarded as embodied in judgments, namely judgments about objects. One could, indeed, try to argue against this on the basis of other things that Frege said: one could say, for example, that a predicative judgment would have to be expressed by a sentence containing a demonstrative, and could then appeal to Frege's view that what is expressed by a sentence containing an indexical term can also be expressed by one containing no such term. But this would be very special pleading: the view about indexical terms was not, as we saw in Chapter 6, very well thought out by Frege, and was probably later abandoned; in any case, a demonstrative and an indexical expression are not quite the same thing. To argue in this way would therefore be to place far too heavy a weight on a brief passing observation in an unpublished and unfinished work. The question whether an assertion made by means of a sentence containing a demonstrative conveys a predicative or a propositional judgment is not to be equated with the question whether the same judgment could be conveyed by means of a sentence not containing one. One may say, 'That is blue', without being ready with any sortal noun whereby to answer the question, 'That *what*?', or to supply a criterion of identity; but in such a case, as Frege's principles imply, no reference to an *object* is made, as it would be if one said, 'That tie is blue'. Frege believed, further, that, in the latter case, a specific way of picking out the particular object is involved. But none of this can possibly be read into the single remark that knowledge is embodied in judgments.

Since Frege's remark about knowledge does not bear on the priority of propositional over predicative knowledge, it can have no relevance whatever to any interpretation of Frege's notion of reference. That is to say, it cannot be used as evidence that Frege held, what I nevertheless believe to have been his implicit view, that all predicative knowledge rests on propositional knowledge, nor, therefore, to deduce that there can be no such thing as the bare knowledge of the reference of a proper name and hence that Mill's account of proper names is false since it requires such bare knowledge of reference. To know the reference of a name, it is obviously insufficient to be acquainted with its referent; one would have to know, of the referent, that the name stood for it, and this would be predicative knowledge. Thus Sluga's quotation from Frege does not do a single one of the things he wanted it to do: it does not show, against me, that he held that all knowledge-how is knowledge-that; it does not imply that all predicative knowledge rests on propositional knowledge; and, in so far as it implies that epistemological atomism is false, it does not imply that a Millian account of proper names, from which Sluga seems to think that epistemological atomism follows, is incorrect. Of course, a reader of Sluga's reply to me who did not have the opportunity to consult the article replied to would be unable to judge of all this. He would know that I had denied that 'all knowledge is judgmental', but not that I had done so only with respect to practical knowledge; he would be unaware that, in the preceding sentence, I had reaffirmed that, for Frege, all theoretical knowledge is propositional; he would not know that I had recorded my agreement with Sluga's denial that Frege held the view that 'knowledge is, in the first instance, knowledge of objects and their properties'. He would know only that I advanced a thesis which, in Sluga's opinion, seemed to commit me to ascribing the latter view to Frege, although I manifested some dim awareness that this did not square with what Frege said. Polemic in this style can hardly be designed for the attainment of mutual understanding; its only effect is to obfuscate the issues.

As we saw, a defence of Frege against the attribution to him of epistemological atomism by appeal to the doctrine concerning criteria of identity is not available to Sluga. Much more to his taste is the invocation of the context principle, to which I briefly appealed earlier in this chapter: it is on this principle, rather than on the doctrine about criteria of identity, that Sluga bases his quite correct denial that Frege was an epistemological atomist. In 'The Philosophical Basis of Intuitionistic Logic', I cited Frege's context principle in order to argue that 'we cannot refer to an object save in the course of saying something about it. Hence, any thesis concerning the ontological status of objects of a given kind must be, at the same time, a thesis about what makes a statement involving reference to such objects true, in other words, a thesis about what properties an object of that kind can have. . . We cannot separate the question of the ontological status of a class of objects from the question of the correct notion of truth for statements about those objects.'[1] This is one version of a rejection of epistemological atomism on the basis of the context principle. Sluga accuses me, however, of failing to give due weight to the context

[1] H. E. Rose and J. D. Shepherdson (eds.), *Logic Colloquium '73*, Amsterdam, 1975, pp. 5–40, reprinted in *Truth and Other Enigmas*; see p. 230.

principle, of which I wrote that it 'is probably the most important philosophical statement Frege ever made';[1] in 'Frege's Alleged Realism', he says[2] that I put a weak interpretation on it. It is not really a question of strong or weak, however, but of right or wrong. We have already looked at the confusion which results from Sluga's quite erroneous conflation of the context principle with that of the extraction of functions. The crucial difference is this. We can come by a new (complex) predicate, one of which we have previously had no conception, and, with it, its sense, by decomposition of a sentence whose sense we had *already* grasped. We cannot, as Sluga supposes, come by a proper name, or the sense of that name, in a similar way: we do not arrive at the object (or the sense of a name of the object) by decomposition of a thought previously grasped only as a unity, or of one that did not contain the sense of that name as a constituent. The context principle implies that our grasp of the sense of the name is *simultaneous* with our grasp of the senses of sentences containing it: we grasp the sense of the name only *as* a contribution to the senses of such sentences, which from the start we grasp as complex.

In a certain respect, therefore, we could say that Sluga's interpretation of the context principle is too strong. But, in another respect, it is too weak. In 'Frege as a Rationalist', he makes a comparison between the doctrines of Frege and those of Lotze. He makes great play with the word 'ontological', remarking that, 'in calling Frege a realist, Dummett has laid much stress on the supposed ontological implications of Frege's doctrines';[3] likewise, in 'Frege and the Rise of Analytical Philosophy', he expresses himself as feeling 'acutely uncomfortable about the fact that Dummett puts ontological considerations at the heart of Frege's thought'.[4] On the contrary, he tells us in 'Frege as a Rationalist', 'Frege's theory of the objectivity of numbers, value-ranges, functions, etc., was never intended as an ontological theory.' 'It must rather be compared,' he continues, 'with Lotze's theory of validity, from which it may be historically derived. According to Lotze, ideal objects are not real, but merely possess validity. Lotze thought that drawing this distinction (which is paralleled by Frege's distinction between reality and objectivity as he makes it in the Preface to the *Grundgesetze*) preserves what is true in Plato's theory of ideas while being beyond both realism and nominalism. The

---

[1] 'Nominalism', *Philosophical Review*, vol. LXV, 1956, pp. 491–505, reprinted in *Truth and Other Enigmas*; see p. 38.

[2] P. 238.

[3] P. 29.

[4] P. 477.

latter are, according to Lotze, predominantly concerned with metaphysical issues, that is, with something that has "other than purely logical importance", whereas presumably the notion of validity is not a metaphysical but a logical one. That is not to say that Frege's and Lotze's doctrines are at all clear, but it is obviously a mistake to regard them as ontological theories, at least according to the intentions of their authors'.

To understand Sluga's thinking, as expressed in this remarkable passage, one needs to fathom the profound significance that the word 'ontological' evidently has for him; I shall attempt this later. What, then, is the doctrine here being ascribed to both Frege and Lotze? It appears, at least as regards Frege, to be a doctrine about 'numbers, value-ranges, functions, etc.'; that is to say, one about abstract or logical objects, and also about the referents of incomplete expressions, functions, relations and concepts. This is a bad start, because these are two completely different topics: there is no reason whatever to suppose that there is anything useful that can be said about both simultaneously. Frege indeed held that functions, concepts and relations are objective;[1] but he neither asserted nor denied that they were 'real' (*wirklich*), an adjective he used only to classify *objects*. Functions, relations and concepts are not, in general, abstract. 'When we say, "Jupiter is larger than Mars", what are we there speaking of? Of the heavenly bodies themselves, of the references of the proper names "Jupiter" and "Mars". We are saying that they stand in a certain relation to one another, and we do this by means of the words "is larger than". This relation holds between the references of the proper names, and must therefore itself belong to the realm of references'.[2] Since the relation denoted by 'ξ is larger than ζ' obtains between the physical objects, Jupiter and Mars, and can only hold between physical objects, or at least between ones that occupy space, it must belong, after the manner of relations indeed, to the physical world. Likewise, if we are to assign it to a particular segment of reality, the function denoted by 'the capital of ξ' belongs to the geographical realm. This is not to suggest that Frege was given to segmenting reality in this manner: the only segmentation that he ever does is the classification in 'Der Gedanke' into the inner world, comprising the contents of consciousness, ideas, images and sensations, the outer world of material, perceptible things and the 'third realm' of senses, including thoughts. That leaves no place for abstract objects, to which, in 'Der Gedanke', he makes no allusion; he may already have ceased to believe in logical objects by 1918, though it is unclear which, among objects, such as

[1] *Grundlagen*, § 47.
[2] 'Einleitung in die Logik', 1906, *N.S.*, pp. 209–10, *P.W.*, p. 193.

directions, identified in *Grundlagen* with extensions of concepts, were in consequence to be rejected as spurious. In any case, just as he says, in *Grundgesetze*,[1] that the division into physical and logical objects is not exhaustive, the classification in the late essay need not be taken as intended to be exhaustive, either. But, in so far as we may legitimately segment reality, there is no reason to lump physical properties and physical relations together with abstract objects; they belong, with physical objects, to physical reality. To classify the referents of incomplete expressions together with those of abstract proper names is a style of thought alien to Frege; it is a relic of the traditional ontology of particulars and universals which he discarded.

Against this may be cited what Frege says in a finely written passage of *Grundlagen*, § 87, namely that 'in the external world, the totality of what is spatial, there are no concepts, no properties of concepts, no numbers'. But, first, this was said before the sense/reference distinction had been drawn; and, secondly, Frege's chief concern, in § 87, is with the *laws* of number. He wishes to deny that the laws of number are applicable to external things: physical phenomena may be said to obey physical laws, but they cannot properly be said to obey arithmetical laws any more than logical ones. Arithmetical laws 'are applicable to judgments that hold of the things of the external world: they are laws of the laws of nature. They do not assert a connection between natural phenomena, but between judgments.' Frege's saying here that there are no concepts in the external world is doubtless due to the fact that, in *Grundlagen*, the word 'concept' is not yet consistently used for what belongs to the realm of reference; in many passages, it is employed with strong overtones of its more everyday use, namely for what belongs to the realm of sense. Frege had not yet attained to a clear equation between concepts, as he understands them, and what are ordinarily called 'properties', as expressed by his statement in 'Über Begriff und Gegenstand',[2] 'I call the concepts under which an object falls its properties; thus "to be Φ is a property of Γ" is just another way of saying "Γ falls under the concept of a Φ".' There is no reason to think that, once he had drawn the distinction between sense and reference, he would have had any ground to deny that the *referent* of a concept-word could belong to physical reality, although, indeed, its *sense* does not. Of the things said in § 87 of *Grundlagen* not to belong to the external world, concepts, properties of concepts and numbers, we know what Frege, in his mature period, considered numbers to be, namely logical objects.[3]

[1] Vol. II, § 74.

[2] P. 201.

[3] *Grundgesetze*, vol. II, §§ 74, 147, Appendix, p. 265.

However, though the laws of number may not properly be said to be applicable to natural phenomena, in *Grundlagen*, § 47, the objectivity of concepts is invoked to explain how assertions about concepts, in particular statements of number, may state facts concerning the external world. Statements of number—statements answering the question 'How many objects of a certain kind are there?'[1]—may be taken as involving, not numbers considered as objects, but only the corresponding properties of concepts, i.e. concepts of second level. A well-known argument, found in Wittgenstein and Russell, though not in Frege, might be used to block any inference from the factuality of statements of number to an assignment of second-level concepts to the external world: namely that, when the truth-values of all atomic statements are given, those of all complex statements are thereby determined; hence the world is fully describable by means of atomic statements alone; and therefore we have no reason to consider as belonging to the world the referent of any expression occurring only in complex statements. Even if that argument be appealed to, there would be no ground for excluding from physical reality the concepts denoted by the predicates occurring in atomic statements. At least as far as first-level concepts are concerned, Frege's remark in *Grundlagen*, § 87, is to be considered as springing from a lingering confusion between sense and reference, soon to be dispelled: we cannot credit him with the view that the physical world contains physical objects, but is devoid of physical properties and physical relations.

Let us therefore restrict the doctrine to abstract objects, of which Frege does indeed say that they are objective but not *wirklich*: what does it then amount to? According to Sluga, Lotze's ideal objects, and presumably likewise the logical objects of Frege, 'possess validity'; and this is something that the logician is competent to determine. At the very least, we should take this as meaning that expressions apparently denoting such objects and behaving like proper names, that is to say, as singular terms, are perfectly in order: we do not need to view sentences containing them as having a hidden structure distinct from their apparent form, a structure within which there are no longer any such names of these objects. We should take it, too, that such sentences have a determinate sense and are, objectively, either true or false. But, now, he says, such objects 'are not real'. The question whether they are real or not does not, indeed, fall within the logician's province, but is a metaphysical one; but the outcome of the metaphysical enquiry is a negative verdict. On the face of it, this appears to mean that a term for an ideal or abstract object, say 'the number one', does not really stand for an object,

_____

[1] *Grundgesetze*, vol. II, § 157.

though it is only the metaphysician who can determine that this is so; the logician has no concern with whether it is so or not, and can cheerfully allow the use of 'the number one' as a proper name, and regard sentences containing it as having an objective sense and an objective truth-value, without knowing whether or not it is so.

To propound such an interpretation of Frege certainly seems to be to repudiate any understanding of him as a realist in respect of abstract objects. But is it recognizable as the view put forward by Frege himself? It most certainly is not. It rests on a complete failure to understand the force of the context principle, as Frege employs it in *Grundlagen*, to justify the use of abstract terms and the ascription of a reference to them. As I said in 'Frege as a Realist', 'Frege would strenuously have denied that there is any place for a further philosophical enquiry, say a metaphysical one, which could have shown that, while from a merely logical point of view "the number one" is a proper name standing for an object, there is no real object for which it stands',[1] adding that to suppose that he would have allowed for such a possibility is to miss the entire point of his use, in *Grundlagen*, of the principle that a word has meaning only in the context of a sentence, to justify regarding abstract terms as standing for genuine, objective objects. Sluga's blindness, in this crucial connection, to the significance of the context principle is very surprising, not only in view of his general attack on me for failing to give due weight to that principle, but of his praise for my article 'Nominalism' of 1956, referred to above, in which I was almost exclusively (and, as I now think, complacently) concerned with this application of the principle. It thus becomes necessary to go into the question what the context principle means.

There is, however, a further surprise that Sluga has in store for us. In 'Frege's Alleged Realism', he quotes the sentence of mine from 'Frege as a Realist' quoted immediately above, and says that he completely agrees with it.[2] What can he mean? The passage from his 'Frege as a Rationalist', on which I was commenting, says expressly that, for Lotze, ideal objects, and, for Frege, numbers, value-ranges, etc., are not real, and that the notion of reality is a metaphysical one, having more than purely logical importance. Is it, then, that he thinks that Frege would have denied that 'the number one' is a proper name standing for an object? How could he think so, when Frege says just that, as clearly as can be conceived? If even that were denied, what would be the content of saying that the number one 'possessed validity' or was objective? Or is it that he thinks that what

[1] P. 457.
[2] P. 236.

Frege would have denied was that this was so from a merely logical point of view? If so, he would be right: but what then becomes of the thesis that the notion of validity, to which he assimilates Frege's notion of objectivity, is a logical one? The only possibility that immediately comes to mind is that Sluga distinguishes between 'There is no real object for which "the number one" stands' and 'The object for which "the number one" stands is not real', endorsing the latter but taking the former to mean 'There is not really any object for which "the number one" stands'.

If so, we are worse off than ever. Interpreting 'Numbers are not real objects' or 'Numerical terms do not stand for real objects' so as not to be equivalent to 'There are not really any such objects as numbers' or 'Numerical terms do not really stand for objects', but as meaning 'Numbers are objects, but not real ones' or 'Numerical terms stand for objects, but not for real ones', involves a *further* mistake beyond that of ignoring the context principle and asking after the meaning of a word in isolation: it involves, namely, misconstruing the word 'real'. The point is an elementary one, known to any beginner in philosophy. To say that a slow-worm is not a real snake is not like saying that a grass snake is a snake, but not a poisonous one. Snakes may be divided into poisonous and non-poisonous ones, and a grass snake is of the latter kind: but they cannot be divided into real and unreal ones. To say that a slow-worm is not a real snake is to say that it is not really a snake at all, where 'really' means 'in the strict sense of the word'. We therefore cannot say that a slow-worm is a snake, but not a real one; nor can we infer from the fact that a slow-worm is not a real snake that it is not real; it is, of course, a real lizard. Likewise, to say that a number is not a real object cannot be interpreted to mean that it is an object, but not a real one: it can be understood only as meaning that it is not really an object of any kind.

What this shows, of course, is that 'real' is not a real predicate: 'is a real snake' does not mean 'is real and is a snake'. 'Real', as ordinarily used, is what is often nowadays called a predicate modifier, acting in a uniform way on any predicate to yield a further predicate; moreover, the predicate so obtained does not differ in sense from the original one, save in being incapable of being used loosely though still correctly. To this it may well be objected that Frege did use the word *wirklich*, which Sluga renders 'real', as a genuine predicate, to discriminate between objects to which it applied and those to which it did not. He did indeed; and this very fact shows that it is tendentious to translate it, as it occurs in his writings, as 'real', although that it is a perfectly ordinary meaning for it in German.

So here we have something else that we shall have to go into: what did Frege mean by *wirklich*?

It may be that we are still far away from a correct interpretation of Sluga; he says that Frege's doctrines are not at all clear, whereas I should say that Frege was the clearest of all philosophical writers, with the probable exception of Berkeley. At any rate, I find understanding Sluga harder work than understanding Frege, though, admittedly, I have put less effort into it. The clue seems to be the word 'ontological'. He prefaces his profession of agreement with the sentence he quotes from me by saying that 'the doctrine of the objectivity of numbers, concepts and thoughts is not an ontological one for Frege', again coupling abstract objects and the referents of incomplete expressions; and he adds, after the quotation, 'But that does not show that Frege's claim of the objectivity of numbers is an ontological one, as Dummett seems to think.' As if these remarks were not sufficient of a puzzle in themselves, he explains that 'I certainly did not argue (as Dummett seems to think) that Frege was not a realist because he did not consider that which is objective as real'.[1] It is difficult to see how this squares with his observation, already quoted, in 'Frege as a Rationalist', that 'in calling Frege a realist, Dummett has laid much stress on the supposed ontological implications of Frege's doctrines'. But we may postpone these problems in Sluga exegesis until we have considered the meanings of Frege's theses that a word has meaning only in the context of a sentence and that numbers are objective but not *wirklich*.

---

[1] 'Frege's Alleged Realism', p. 232.

CHAPTER 19

The Context Principle

THE ONLY EXPLICIT statement of the context principle, namely that it is only in the context of a sentence that a word has a meaning, occurs in *Grundlagen*. There it is cited in the Introduction (p. x) as one of three fundamental principles observed by Frege in writing the book. It then makes its appearance in the main text in § 60, towards the end of the crucial passage, §§ 55–61, in which Frege argues for the necessity of regarding numbers as objects, and as an important part of the justification for so regarding them. It is then reiterated in § 62, at the beginning of the equally crucial passage, §§ 62–9, in which Frege sets out his reasons for defining cardinal numbers in the way he does, namely as classes of concepts. Finally, in § 106, in the course of recapitulating the principal results of the book, Frege again states the context principle, referring to it once more as a fundamental principle. The fact that it plays an important role in both of the two successive critical sections of the book, and that, both in the Introduction and the recapitulation, it is so heavily underlined, shows that, whatever Frege may have thought in the period before *Grundlagen* and in that which followed it, at the time of writing that book he was convinced that it was of the first importance. It is therefore certainly a mistake to attempt to play it down, as does Ignacio Angelelli.[1]

Angelelli agrees that the context principle is stated only in *Grundlagen*, and urges that, in his controversy with Hilbert, Frege maintained just the opposite of the context principle, namely that words must have a meaning independent of their contexts.[2] But, he argues, the principle cannot have either the meaning or the importance usually ascribed to it,

---

[1] Op. cit., pp. 73–5.

[2] Citing 'Über die Grundlagen der Geometrie', 1906, Part I, pp. 307–8, 'Über die Grundlagen der Geometrie', 1903, Part I, pp. 319–20 and 322, *Grundgesetze*, vol. II, § 66 and Appendix, p. 255, and 'Über Sinn und Bedeutung', p. 41, to this effect.

even when Frege did adhere to it; he instances Wittgenstein, Quine, Geach, Stegmüller and Patzig as overvaluing the principle in accordance with this incorrect interpretation of it, which, unfortunately, he does not attempt to characterize.

The value of the principle is a matter of philosophical opinion, and Frege's later attitude to it is indeed a controversial question. In fact, no explicit repudiation of it occurs in any of Frege's writings after *Grundlagen*. The most telling quotation Angelelli could have used for his purpose is one that he does not give, but which is cited by Michael D. Resnik as an 'explicit contradiction of the context principle':[1] this is the passage from Frege's published letter to Peano of 1896 in which he claims that, for reasoning to be possible, each word must have a reference, the same in all occurrences, independent of the rest of the sentence, that is, of the context; the passages to which Angelelli does refer are all cited by him as advancing this claim. The claim made by Frege in his letter to Peano is unwarranted. It would be reasonable to claim that, if we are to be able to give rigorous rules of inference that prohibit sophistries, each word must, in all contexts, have one and the same *sense*; but it would still be allowable that, in accordance with this unvarying sense, the *reference* should vary systematically from one context to another. I argued in *FPL*[2] that a recognition of this would have saved Frege from lumbering his plausible theory of indirect reference with the inchoherent addition of a notion of indirect sense, Russell's objection to which, in 'On Denoting', I conceded to be conclusive. We have seen, in Chapter 6, what feature it was of Frege's notion of sense that impelled him to make this addition; that does not alter the fact that, when sense is construed as significance, it is indefensible. Donald Davidson has argued[3] that Frege's theory of indirect reference is not workable, on the ground that it would render impossible a finitely axiomatized theory of truth for the language. This is a legitimate objection to the theory as Frege stated it, namely as involving an infinite hierarchy of multiply indirect senses and therefore of multiply indirect referents; but it is not evident that the objection holds good against the theory as emended according to my suggestion, under which the sense of an expression remains the same when it occurs in *oratio obliqua*, and the indirect referent, even in double *oratio obliqua*, is still just this invariant sense. Of course, if the axioms of the theory of truth state only the ordinary

[1] 'Frege's Context Principle Revisited', in M. Schirn (ed.), op. cit., vol. III, 1976, p. 46.
[2] Pp. 267-8.
[3] 'The Method of Truth in Metaphysics', *Mid-West Studies in Philosophy*, vol. II, Chicago, 1977, p. 250.

references of expressions, we shall be unable to derive from these axioms what their indirect referents, i.e. their senses, are; but it is unclear why there should not be axioms giving both the ordinary and the indirect references, and others laying down in which type of context a word has the one or the other reference. There is, indeed, a problem how the indirect reference of a word can be stated; but this problem is quite distinct.

Davidson's view is a corollary of the demand expressed by Frege in the letter to Peano for uniqueness of reference in all contexts. Indeed, it is a corollary of that demand that one and the same expression cannot have different references, a direct and an indirect one, in different contexts, which is why, in one of his letters to Russell, Frege says that, in order to avoid ambiguity, one strictly speaking ought to use special signs for words in indirect speech.[1] It thus seems impossible to acquit Frege of inconsistency on this point. In fact, however, the inconsistency is resolved if we take the theory of indirect reference as intended to resemble that of the theory of truth-value gaps arising from the occurrence of proper names having sense but not reference: namely, as the closest we can get to a coherent account of a feature of natural language that is ultimately incoherent. The accusation of inconsistency, and, with it, Davidson's objection, would, on this interpretation, appear as examples of the mistake against which a warning was given in Chapter 2, of confusing what Frege says about one of the defects of natural language with what he says, by contrast, about a properly constructed one. However this may be, it is plain how Frege came to overlook the possibility that sense determines reference only relative to context, since, as explained in Chapters 3 and 6, for him it is primarily to the *sense* that the reference attaches, and only secondarily to the *expression*, via its sense. One could attempt to transpose the idea of the relativity of reference to context to the mode of sense: to the sense attaches one reference when it enters into a certain kind of combination with other senses to constitute a thought, another reference when it enters into another type of combination with other senses. But this certainly sounds less natural than when expressed in the linguistic mode, and it is therefore a matter of no surprise that Frege overlooked the possibility, if indeed it is one.

Nevertheless, even the thesis that a word must have a unique reference, independent of context, does not, as Angelelli and Resnik suppose, clash directly with the context principle. In *Grundlagen* Frege evidently takes

[1] *BW*, p. 236, *P.M.C.* p. 153.

the context principle as licensing contextual definition, since in §§ 63–4 he expressly defends the principle of contextual definition: he rejects the objection that, in the proposed contextual definition, we shall be giving 'a special definition' of numerical identity, whereas, since identity holds not only between numbers, we ought not to define it specially for that case; on the contrary, he says, it is not proposed to define identity separately for a special case, but, 'by means of the already known concept of identity, to arrive at that which is to be regarded as being identical'. Now the admission of such a contextual definition does not, in itself, violate the principle that each expression must have the same reference in all contexts. Frege did later object to piecemeal definition on the ground that it failed to secure a unique sense and reference to the defined expression in all contexts; and, for instance in the letter to Peano, he objected to conditional definition on the ground that it made the reference of the defined expression dependent on the context, that is, on the satisfaction of the condition given in the definition. But his later objection to contextual definition was not on such grounds. It is, rather, that a contextual definition presents, as it were, an equation to be solved, not the solution to that equation.[1] This leaves it yet to be proved that the equation has a solution, and a unique one, i.e. that the definition does determine one and only one reference for the defined expression; and this is objectionable because a definition ought never to rest upon any presupposition that then requires justification, but must bear its legitimacy upon its face. It is true that, in *Grundlagen*, the particular contextual definitions proposed in §§ 63–5 are rejected, in §§ 66–7, as inadequate, and replaced, in § 68, by explicit ones: but the rejection is on a specific ground, namely that the proposed definitions do not supply a sense for all sentences, nor, in particular, for all identity-statements, in which we shall want the defined expression to occur. No argument is given to show that a parallel difficulty would arise for *every* contextual definition, and it is difficult to see how it could do so for definitions of expressions other than proper names.

Frege's later hostility to contextual definition might itself be urged as a proof of his abandonment of the context principle in his mature and later periods. But this, too, would be inconclusive, since, even in *Grundlagen*, the admissibility of contextual definitions is presented as a consequence of the context principle, not as its substance: the principle would not have been re-emphasized in § 106 as a crucial step in the argument of the book, which is there being summarized, if, in view of the explicit

---

[1] See *Grundgesetze*, vol. II, § 66.

definition of number eventually adopted, it had proved to be superfluous to the construction. In *Grundlagen*, the context principle is taken to render contextual definitions legitimate, but, even in cases where it is relevant to invoke it, not to require them in favour of explicit ones: we may need to invoke it in order to arrive at the right form for an explicit definition, or to recognize such a definition as correct. That we should not ask for the meaning of 'the number one' in isolation does not entail that we necessarily go astray in giving an explicit definition of 'the number one'.

Not only is the context principle consistent with giving explicit definitions, but it is equally consistent with the requirement that a word should have the same meaning—the same sense and the same reference—in all contexts. The context principle does not say that a word may have one meaning in one context and a different meaning in another; it says that it may be said to have a meaning at all only as occurring in *some* context. So stated, it may appear obscure, even, as Max Black has remarked, 'barely intelligible': but it is plain that it is a principle concerning what it is for a word to have a meaning, and does not imply that its meaning may legitimately vary from one occurrence to another. The proof offered by Angelelli that Frege abandoned the context principle in his later work is therefore fallacious.

Angelelli claims that he has an interpretation of the context principle differing from, and better than, the usual one. This interpretation is twofold: first, the principle is a piece of *ad hominem* common-sense advice for mathematicians incapable of conceiving objects that are neither subjective nor perceptible by the senses; and, secondly, it is a manoeuvre designed to extricate Frege from the embarrassment of proclaiming numbers to be immaterial substances, like angels, by declaring that 'numerals no longer have a meaning to be looked for'.[1] This 'interpretation' explains Frege's text, not as advancing a definite doctrine, but as a piece of dishonest evasiveness. The *ad hominem* advice appears to be that, *if* you cannot avoid taking number-words as standing for mental pictures when you ask for their meaning in isolation, then you should restrict yourself to assigning a meaning to sentences containing such words, taken as a whole. If this procedure were adequate, it is obscure why it should not be adopted by everyone, rather than only by those who suffer from the stated defect; and, if it is not adequate, the 'advice' would be dishonest. As for the manoeuvre, it is presented as palpably dishonest: Frege is represented as concealing an opinion that 'would hardly have been well received',[2]

---

[1] Angelelli, op. cit., p. 75.

[2] Ibid., p. 74.

namely that numbers are self-subsistent but non-sensible objects, by pretending to believe that number-words do not stand for anything at all. Whatever vices Frege may be charged with, they do not include lack of courage in maintaining unpopular opinions. In any case, the context principle is *not* explained as dispensing us from assigning a meaning (*Bedeutung*) to number-words, but as stating what is involved in assigning one to them; and Frege says, in so many words, that numbers are self-subsistent, objective but non-sensible objects.[1] Angelelli does not have an interpretation of the context principle, better or worse than that of other writers; he merely wants to brush the principle aside, because his account of Frege cannot accommodate it.

The avowed aim of *Grundlagen* as a whole is to make it plausible that the truths of arithmetic are analytic; and, given Frege's definition of 'analytic', this demands the deductive derivation of basic arithmetical laws from logical principles with the help of suitable definitions. It thus obviously also demands some analysis of fundamental arithmetical notions and of the content of arithmetical truths. In particular, it requires an answer to the question, 'What are the natural numbers?'; and it is at the crucial point of the book at which Frege is trying to arrive at his answer to that question that the context principle is invoked. Its immediate application, as cited in § 62, is to determine the character of the ensuing investigation as a linguistic one, in the sense of an enquiry into how the meanings of numerical terms are to be fixed. The question, 'What is the number 1?', is obviously equivalent to, 'What does "the number 1" stand for?': but this observation, by itself, tells us nothing about how the question is to be answered, since it could be said, with equal right, that the question 'What is the Crab Nebula?' is equivalent to 'What does "the Crab Nebula" stand for?'. Of course, there is an evident difference between the two cases. To discover what the Crab Nebula is, one must observe and analyse the radiation, light, X-rays and radio waves, emitted by it, whereas only reflection is needed to find the answer to 'What is the number 1?': as Frege remarks in *Grundlagen*, § 105, 'in arithmetic we are concerned with objects with are not known by means of the senses as something alien from without, but with ones which are immediately given to the reason, and which are, as reason's nearest kin, utterly transparent to it'. This shows a signal difference between the kinds of objects, celestial and mathematical, to which the two questions relate; but it tells us nothing about the character of the reflection required for arriving at a position

heuristic force

---

[1] *Grundlagen*, §§ 57–61.

to say what the natural numbers are. It may seem natural to those nurtured in the tradition of analytical philosophy to assume that reflection, when it does not result in a deductive proof, must take the form of an enquiry into the senses of words: no such conclusion would have occurred to Frege's readers. All that immediately follows from the fact that the Crab Nebula is accessible to our (assisted) senses, while the natural numbers are accessible to our reason, is that, to discover what the natural numbers are, we must train our intellectual telescopes upon them. But when, in § 62, Frege asks how numbers are given to us, since we have neither any idea (*Vorstellung*) nor any intuition of them, he replies, not by saying that they are given to our reason, but by invoking the context principle already enunciated in § 60.

According to this principle, it is only as occurring in the context of a sentence that a name can so much as be said to stand for an object. It follows that to determine what the proper name 'the number 1' stands for, and hence what the number 1 is, involves fixing the senses of sentences in which that proper name occurs, and does not involve anything beyond this. 'Determining what "the number 1" stands for' admits conversion back into the material mode as 'determining what the number 1 is', which is why adopting the former formulation of the task to be accomplished does not characterize the enquiry as a linguistic one. But 'fixing the senses of sentences in which "the number 1" occurs' resists any corresponding translation into the material mode: we could of course replace 'in which "the number 1" occurs' by 'about the number 1', but we should still have the reference to sentences. Hence this formulation, and the context principle which entailed that it pointed to the path to be taken to the desired goal, inescapably characterize the enquiry as a linguistic one, that is, as an enquiry into how the senses of a certain range of sentences are to be taken as given. In post-*Grundlagen* terminology, we are to enquire into the references of numerical terms by enquiring into their senses; and, in accordance with the context principle, we are to do this by enquiring into the senses of sentences containing them. The enquiry concerns senses, not ideas or any other psychological entities; but, as Frege claims both on p. x and in § 106, were it not for an acknowledgment of the context principle, words in general, and number-words in particular, would be liable to be thought to have as their meaning (*Bedeutung*) mental images or mental acts.

In the heading to §§ 62–9, Frege speaks of 'fixing the sense' (*den Sinn feststellen*) of a numerical equation, as I have done here. In § 62 itself, he uses the verb '*erklären*', which can mean 'to explain' or, more definitely, 'to define'. But to speak of 'explaining' the senses of certain sentences leaves the same ambiguity as to speak of 'fixing' them: namely, between 'determining what sense those sentences already have' and 'laying down what senses they are to have'. We saw in Chapter 14 that it was not for another thirty years, and then only in an unpublished paper, that Frege clarified this ambiguity; and even then the clarification was somewhat equivocal. The process, according to 'Logik in der Mathematik', was to be described as 'logical analysis'; but this was not to be thought of as a way of rendering just those senses which had all along been attached to numerical terms, but as supplying determinate senses which could replace the existing ones. This conception of the procedure exemplified by the definitions given in *Grundlagen* appears to resemble that described by Carnap under the label 'explication': precisely defined concepts are offered in exchange for the old, somewhat imprecise, ones, backed by some assurance that they will serve every purpose that the old, discarded ones served, but, in addition, will enable us to give unchallengeable derivations of statements involving them.

As already noted, § 62 of *Grundlagen* opens with the question how numbers are given to us, seeing that we have neither ideas nor intuitions of them. It would, as we have seen, be a mistake to infer from his asking this question that his principle concerning criteria of identity, stated later in the paragraph, was intended to apply only to objects which we can neither perceive nor intuit; there is no reason to take the quite general formulation of the principle otherwise than at face value. It would therefore also be a mistake to ascribe to Frege the view that some objects are 'given' to us in sense or in intuition, i.e. that sense-perception or intuition suffices for the awareness of them as discriminable objects with a persisting identity, without the need to appeal to our grasp of the senses of expressions that could be used to refer to them. That would be epistemological atomism, which we have already seen to be incompatible both with the context principle and with the principle concerning criteria of identity; as we also noted in Chapter 18, in 'Der Gedanke' Frege propounds the view that sense-perception itself, the perception of objects, is to be distinguished from the mere having of sense-impressions by the fact that it involves the grasp of thoughts and, presumably, judging them to be true. It would be an equally grave error to take the context principle, likewise stated in § 62 of *Grundlagen*, to be restricted to names of objects that we neither perceive nor intuit. Although it is, in this passage, applied to names of logical objects, it is not stated only for them, or even only for proper names, but for words quite generally. Frege is not endorsing the view that some objects are given in sense or in intuition, and producing a special thesis to explain how logical objects are given to us; if he had been, the natural thing for him to have said was that 'they are given directly to our reason', as he did say in *Grundlagen*, § 105. He would not consider that an explanation, since he does not himself rely on the idea of objects being *given* to us by means of this or that faculty. It is true that he does not, in *Grundlagen*, launch a general assault on that idea: he limits his repudiation, in § 89, of Kant's thesis that without sensibility no object would be given to us to its complete generality, adducing only numbers as counter-examples and leaving it open whether the dictum is true of some objects. But in § 26, he had stated his own view, namely that what is objective is independent of our sensation, intuition and imagination; that makes it at least improbable that he thought that *any* objective object can be 'given' in sense or in intuition, though indeed some can be perceived or intuited. In § 62, the question with which the paragraph starts poses a problem, in the manner that would be natural to a contemporary philosopher, the problem, namely, how we are able to think about or refer to numbers, since, as has appeared from the previous discussion in the course of the book, no appeal to sense-perception or to intuition can explain this. The answer is to be given in accordance with two quite general principles, one, the context principle, relating to all words, the other, the principle concerning criteria of identity, relating to all proper names in Frege's extended sense. Frege is not called on, in the *Grundlagen*, to work out the application of these principles to names of objects that we can perceive by our senses or that we can intuit. If it was worked out, it would plainly call in question the idea that such objects are 'given' in sense or in intuition;[1] but, since Frege does not attempt this, he can leave those who embrace this idea undisturbed, so far as his immediate purpose is concerned, namely to explore the foundations of arithmetic. This gives no warrant, however, to interpret Frege as intending a severe restriction on the application of either principle, a restriction which he carelessly omitted to state.

There is thus no reason to ascribe to Frege a belief that, for an object which we can intuit or perceive by sense, a name of that object could be grasped antecedently to an understanding of how to use it in sentences, nor a belief that a grasp of such a name would involve apprehending anything irrelevant to its use in sentences. On the contrary, we have seen that,

---

[1] Austin's translation, 'For surely everything geometrical must be given originally in intuition', of a sentence in § 64, is misleading: the text actually says 'must originally be intuitable'; to say that we are capable of intuiting something is not to say that it was *given* to us in intuition. Frege goes on to deny that directions are intuitable.

in 'Booles rechnende Logik', Frege expressly denied this for predicates and relational expressions, when he observed that 'it does not follow . . . that the ideas of these properties and relations are formed without connection with things; rather, they arise simultaneously with the first judgment, by means of which they are ascribed to things'.[1] The denial is very naturally extended to names of things, i.e. of objects, also, though there is, as far as I know, no passage in Frege's early writings in which this extension is made. As for Frege's mature period, after he developed the sense/reference distinction, the application of that distinction to proper names would square badly with any thesis to the effect that their referents could be 'given' in sense or in intuition, although it might be reconciled by means of some claim that the same object might be given in sense or in intuition in different ways. The very most that we are entitled to infer from what Frege says in *Grundlagen*, § 62, is that the sense of a sentence containing a name of an object of which we can have an idea or an intuition is to be fixed in some manner essentially different from that of a sentence containing a name of an abstract object, or, alternatively or in addition, that a name of the former kind may occur in sentences of a different form—say ones involving ostension—from those containing a name of the latter kind.

Given that the immediate consequence of the context principle, as invoked in § 62 of *Grundlagen*, is to determine the subsequent investigation into what numbers are as one into how the senses of certain sentences are fixed, what is the meaning of the principle itself? As I observed on pp. 495–6 of *FPL*, since in *Grundlagen* the distinction between sense and reference had not yet been drawn, we have to ask whether it is a principle concerning sense or concerning reference. The answer is that it is both, and has a somewhat different content under the two interpretations: but, in *Grundlagen* itself, it figures chiefly as a principle concerning reference.

As a principle concerning sense, the context principle singles out sentences as having a unique role in any account of the senses of expressions. The sense of any expression is its contribution to determining the condition for the truth of any sentence in which it occurs. More exactly, taking due account of the relation of sense to reference, the matter stands thus: the reference of an expression is, as we have seen, its semantic value, that feature of it which goes to determine the truth or falsity of any sentence containing it; and the sense of the expression consists in the manner in which the speakers of the language apprehend its reference as being

a thesis about sense

---

[1] *N.S.*, p. 19, *P.W.*, p. 17.

determined. This very general principle does not, of course, tell us what the sense, or the reference, of any expression is, or even what form it takes. But it is a principle by which to evaluate any proposed account of sense. We cannot evaluate, by appeal to this principle, any constituent part of such an account taken by itself, for instance an account of the sense of a particular expression or even of the kind of sense possessed by all expressions of a particular logical type. We have, rather, to enquire whether the accounts of the senses of expressions of all logical types provide us, when taken together, with a plausible explanation of how the truth-conditions of sentences are determined, and provide us with nothing more than is needed for this. An account of sense in terms of the associated mental imagery, for example, is shown by the principle to be both inadequate and superfluous: inadequate in that it does not yield a workable account of the resulting truth-conditions of sentences; and superfluous in that it invokes features irrelevant to such an account.

I argued, on pp. 192–6 of *FPL*, that the context principle, interpreted as relating to sense, is wholly acceptable; and I called Frege's apparent later abandonment of it a disaster,[1] because his theory of meaning cannot be made coherent without it. Can Frege be thought to have discovered the principle before he wrote *Grundlagen*? We have noted that the passage in 'Booles rechnende Logik' in effect embodies the context principle for simple predicates and relational expressions, though without expressing it in anything like the terminology employed in *Grundlagen*, but that we cannot find, in his early writings, a comparable statement concerning names of objects. It therefore seems reasonable to say that Frege had the essential idea from an early date, but not, as yet, clearly distinguished from the principle of the incompleteness of concepts and relations; he disentangled the two principles, and so achieved an explicit, and quite general, formulation of the context principle only when he wrote *Grundlagen*. This is in complete accord with the distinction drawn in *Begriffsschrift* between 'judgeable' and 'unjudgeable' contents, that is, between the contents of sentences (whether standing alone or as parts of more complex sentences) and those of sentence-constituents not amounting to complete sentences. The context principle, as enunciated in *Grundlagen*, embodies more than just the general relation of the meaning of a word to the contexts in which it occurs: it singles out the relevant segment of the total context as the *sentence*, and so gives sentences a special, distinguished role in language and hence in any theory of meaning. To a first

---

[1] *FPL*, pp. 196, 644–5.

approximation, at least, to understand a speech is to understand, in succession, the sentences composing the speech. But we cannot view a grasp of the thought expressed by a sentence as consisting, in a similar way, of a successive grasp of the senses of the words composing it, since we can grasp the senses of those words only as a contribution to the thoughts expressed by sentences containing them. Frege was the first to apprehend this clearly; but the logical doctrines which he developed in his mature period obscured it once more. One of the differences between the formal system of *Begriffsschrift* and that of *Grundgesetze* is precisely that, in the former, there is a restriction, embodied in the formation rules, on the placing of the 'content-stroke', which may precede only an expression with a *judgeable* content, i.e. one which is already a sentence; in *Grundgesetze*, there is no such restriction on the placing of what is now called merely the 'horizontal', which is expressly allowed to stand in front of any proper name, yielding a name of a truth-value, of the True if the original expression named the True and of the False in all other cases.

I did not say in *FPL*, as Sluga alleges,[1] that it was Frege's realism that led him to abandon the context principle; we shall see below what force there would be in such a suggestion. Still less did I say, as he also alleges,[2] that it was the distinction between sense and reference that had this effect. On the contrary, I said that that distinction 'is entirely consonant with the doctines of *Grundlagen*, and supplies the necessary complementation of them'.[3] Rather, I emphasized on many different pages[4] that what stood in the way of his reiterating the context principle was his assimilation, in his later doctrine, of sentences to proper names, or, otherwise expressed, the thesis that truth-values are objects; and I stressed that this thesis was a dispensable part of Frege's later philosophy.[5] Once Frege had assimilated sentences to complex proper names, he had debarred himself from a direct statement of the context principle, since this would have involved acknowledging a difference in logical role, of the utmost importance, between sentences and proper names of objects other than truth-values; I was suggesting this as the reason why Frege did not reiterate the context principle after *Grundlagen*. Such an acknowledgment would have been against the whole thrust of his logical doctrines, which was to recognize no difference between the kind of logical powers that different expressions

---

[1] 'Frege and the Rise of Analytical Philosophy', p. 478.
[2] Ibid., p. 485.
[3] *FPL*, pp. 643–4.
[4] Pp. 7, 196, 644–5.
[5] Pp. 411–12.

have save such as were explicable by a difference in logical type. After I had explained this once more in 'Frege as a Realist', Sluga commented that 'this argument is, of course, Dummett's and cannot be found explicitly stated in Frege's writings'.[1] This is true, in the sense that Frege gave no argument for rejecting the context principle. He could not do so, since he never explicitly rejected that principle: I had never claimed that he rejected it, but only that he did not reiterate it, and I added, as an explanation for this, that it would not easily fit with the assimilation of sentences to proper names. It could be pleaded that there is a stronger sense in which the argument is not Frege's, namely that he never enunciated the general thesis that any difference in the logical behaviour of two expressions must be accounted for by their belonging to different logical types. This is true. But the thesis is implicit in his whole procedure; nothing could illustrate it more aptly than the fact that, in the logical system of *Grundgesetze*, no distinction exists between sentential and individual variables, a sentence being able to stand in any place in which a singular term can stand and conversely. It is important that what creates the disharmony with the context principle is not the introduction of the sense/reference distinction as such, nor even the doctrine that sentences have referents, namely their truth-values: it is the doctrine that truth-values are objects and that therefore a sentence is merely a particular kind of complex proper name. And it is precisely our awareness of the fact that sentences play a quite special role in language, a role quite different from that of proper names of (other) objects, that prompts us, rightly as I argued, to reject the assimilation of sentences to proper names, and, with it, the view that truth-values are objects. The context principle gives the strongest possible endorsement of this intuition. It therefore hardly seems tendentious, or an imputation to Frege of what is not to be found in him, to claim that the assimilation of sentences to proper names is inconsistent, or at least in tension, with the context principle, and to suggest that this explains, partly or wholly, Frege's later silence concerning that principle.

Did Frege continue to adhere to the context principle, considered as a principle concerning sense, after *Grundlagen*? Concerning his late period, our data are insufficient. Certainly there was no explicit reaffirmation of it; we have already seen that Sluga's citation, in 'Frege and the Rise of Analytical Philosophy', of Frege's remark, in the 'Aufzeichnungen für Darmstaedter' of 1919, that 'I do not begin with the concepts and put the thought or the judgment together out of them, but I arrive at the parts of

---

[1] 'Frege's Alleged Realism', p. 238.

the thought by decomposition of the thought'[1] as 'explicit textual evidence' of such a reaffirmation is due to confusion on Sluga's part between the context principle and that of the extraction of functions. But we have also seen that the assimilation of concepts and relations to functions makes a reappearance, albeit tentative, in the 'Logik in der Mathematik' of 1914.[2] It could reasonably be claimed that Frege's thought, in his late period, was still implicitly governed by fidelity to the context principle. His interest in our ability to understand new sentences, to express thoughts that have never before been grasped, and his explanation of this ability by appeal to the construction of thoughts out of constituent 'building-blocks', are instances of this. The explanation is, indeed, in head-on conflict with Sluga's interpretation of the conflated principle of the extraction of functions and context principle, namely that thoughts are grasped, in the first instance, as unarticulated wholes; but that reflects no change of mind on Frege's part, but only the incorrectness of the interpretation. It strikes no one as in need of explanation how we are able to understand new speeches, or new paragraphs, that we have never heard before; if, for example, someone should hear a political speech entirely composed of familiar sentences, it would not seem to call for explanation that he could understand this speech, even though he had never heard those sentences arranged in just that order. This simply illustrates the fact, already remarked on, that, to a first approximation, the understanding of a speech just is the understanding, in succession, of the sentences composing it.[3] Someone who thought that words are related to the sentence they compose as the sentences are related to the speech they make up would find no need for any explanation of our understanding new sentences, either; if words are the primary vehicles of sense, it is unproblematic that, in order to understand an utterance of any length, it is necessary and sufficient to know the words. It is because we cannot give an account of the sense of a word taken in isolation that our ability to understand new sentences calls for explanation; it is because the true account of the sense of a word is in terms of its contribution to the senses of sentences containing it that such an explanation is forthcoming. Words—understood as comprising various inflections, prefixes and suffixes—are the smallest linguistic units that carry sense; if someone, upon mastering all the phonemes of a language,

---

[1] *N.S.*, p. 273, *P.W.*, p. 253.

[2] *N.S.*, pp. 254, 263, *P.W.*, pp. 235, 244.

[3] A second approximation would have to take account of one inessential feature, the back-reference of demonstratives and pronouns, and one essential one, the genuine or purported logical connections between the assertions made.

were thereupon able to understand all the words in it, we could not explain this ability by reference to the contribution of each phoneme to the sense of any word in which it occurred. And it is because the sense of a word must be conceived as a contribution to the sense of a *sentence* that Frege represents it as a building-block of *thoughts*.

Taken as a thesis concerning sense, the context principle, embodying, as it does, the principle of the primacy of sentences in the order of explanation,[1] can thus be recognized to have remained in the background of Frege's thinking in his late period, even though it is no longer explicitly asserted. How do matters stand as regards the mature period from 1891 to 1906? Here again, we can find no explicit statement of the context principle. Just as the efforts of Angelelli and Resnik to prove that Frege expressly repudiated the principle are in vain, so the most determined efforts of those, such as Sluga and Kluge, who believe that he reaffirmed it have failed to yield a single passage affording genuine evidence to that effect. In both cases, the passages cited prove, on examination, to concern a different point. Perhaps the most remarkable example is provided by Kluge, in his review of *FPL*[2] when he cites the unpublished 'Begründung meiner strengeren Grundsätze des Definierens' of 1897–8. Frege says, 'Inference from two premisses often, if not always, rests on there being a concept in common to both. If a fallacy is not to occur, not only must the sign for the concept be the same, but it must also have the same reference. It must have a reference independent of the context, and not first obtain one in the context, something that is, however, very often the case with words of (everyday) language.'[3] Kluge reports this as Frege's having 'stated an analogous view'—that is, one analogous to the context principle —'concerning words of ordinary language'.[4] What makes this citation so tendentious is that, in this passage, Frege is making precisely the same point as that made in the passage cited by Resnik from the letter to Peano of 1896 as an 'explicit contradiction of the context principle'. Resnik, as we saw, was in error, since the claim that an expression should have a reference that does not vary with the context is not incompatible with the context principle. But Kluge's error is greater, since, even if the context principle did entail a denial of that claim, it is perfectly plain that Frege is here criticizing natural language for what he takes to be a glaring defect; especially is this evident from his having just previously alluded to the

---

[1] Cf. *FPL*, p. 4.
[2] *Dialogue*, vol. XVI, 1977, pp. 519–33.
[3] *N.S.*, p. 168, *P.W.*, p. 155.
[4] Op. cit., fn. 36.

Acervus paradox, as he does also in the letter to Peano, and having commented that the paradox depends on our erroneously treating *heap* as a concept.

Another passage that some have cited to prove that Frege maintained the context principle occurs in 'Über die Grundlagen der Geometrie' of 1906. Speaking of variable letters, Frege says, 'Only in the context of a sentence do they have a definite role to fulfil, do they have a contribution to make to the expression of the thought. Outside this context, however, they say nothing.'[1] This, however, is not an observation about words and symbols in general: it is a quite specific remark about bound variables. The fact that Frege frames his remark in a manner which, by its phraseology, recalls the formulation of the context principle in *Grundlagen* is itself excellent evidence that he would no longer have used the same terminology to express a thesis holding good generally of words and symbols of all kinds. Towards the end of his mature period, Frege often used the notion of a contribution to the expression of a thought as contrasting with sense, properly so called, as the appropriate terminology for bound variables and similar improper constituents of sentences; for instance, in a letter to Hilbert of 1899 he says, speaking of mathematical sentences other than definitions, that they 'ought to contain no word (symbol) whose sense and reference, or (in the case of form-words, letters in formulas) whose contribution to the expression of the thought, has not already been completely specified'.[2] Kluge[3] cites this very letter, together with one by Frege to Hugo Dingler of 6 February 1917[4] and a passage from the 'Einleitung in die Logik' of 1906[5] to prove that 'the contextual element of the *Grundlagen*-thesis seems to be present at all stages of his development',[6] but philosophical topics cannot profitably be discussed in so impressionistic a manner. The latter two passages concern what Frege called 'improper sentences', viz. clauses of a complex sentence that contain a bound variable but do not form the whole scope of that variable; the same phenomenon occurs in natural language, with pronouns representing the later occurrences of the bound variable. Such improper sentences do not serve to express thoughts that may be judged true or false and are components of the thought expressed by the whole complex sentence; an example in

[1] Part I, p. 307.
[2] I. Angelelli (ed.), *Kleine Schriften*, Hildesheim, 1967, p. 408; cf. *BW*, p. 62.
[3] Op. cit., p. 525.
[4] *BW*, pp. 33–6, *P.M.C.*, pp. 19–23.
[5] *N.S.*, pp. 206–7, *P.W.*, p. 190.
[6] Ibid., p. 526.

natural language would be the antecedent and consequent of 'If anyone examines the proof, he will discover the mistake', which grammatically is a conditional but logically a generalized conditional. An example, using variables, given by Frege is '$a > b \rightarrow a + 1 > b + 1$', where this is tacitly understood as a universally quantified sentence. By the standards of *Grundgesetze* such improper sentences are not genuine components of the complex sentence at all, since they are not logical units; they are therefore not in the running for possessing a sense or a reference. Frege says of them, in the passages cited by Kluge, that they do not by themselves express a sense, but contribute to the expression of the sense of the whole complex sentence. This is a perfectly natural thing to say; but it is absurd to cite Frege's remarks about such merely apparent sentence-components as evidence for his retention of the context principle. The context principle states that no expression can have a meaning (*Bedeutung*) save in the context of a sentence. A later formulation would either substitute 'sense' for 'meaning', or retain the word '*Bedeutung*', to be understood in the new, more precise, manner. But what Frege says about the very special cases of bound variables and of improper sentences is entirely different: it is, namely, that these expressions, even in context, do not have a sense or a reference at all.

Another type of passage that may erroneously be cited as evidence for Frege's continued adherence to the context principle is that in which he is labouring to convey the old doctrine of the incompleteness of functional expressions and of their senses and their referents. Sometimes, indeed, he alludes, in explaining this, to the occurrence of an incomplete expression in combination with those that complete it; for example, in a footnote about Russell to the 1903 'Über die Grundlagen der Geometrie' he says, 'It is clear that we cannot represent a concept as self-subsistent (*selbständig*) like an object, but it can occur only in combination. One may say that it can be distinguished within this, but not separated from it.'[1] Frege is not here saying that a meaning can be ascribed to a predicate only when it occurs in combination with other expressions; he is saying that it cannot occur at all except in such a combination. We saw, in Chapter 16, that this claim is dubious for *simple* predicates; and, in the 'Gedankengefüge' of 1923, Frege acknowledged as much for the case of sentential connectives such as 'and'. Discussing the notion of an expression whose sense is 'unsaturated', he there said that 'as a mere thing, the group of letters "and" is indeed no more unsaturated than anything else. One may call it unsaturated

[1] Part II, p. 372.

in respect of its mode of employment as a sign that is meant to express a sense, in that it can have the intended sense only as placed between two sentences.'[1] Kluge cites this passage and claims it as 'an unequivocal statement of the *Grundlagen* thesis—thirty-one years after its alleged rejection'.[2] It is nothing of the kind, but, rather, an attempt to convey, for the case of a sentential connective, the notion of an expression's 'being unsaturated' or 'requiring completion' by virtue of the sense which it has. One cannot grasp the sense of an 'unsaturated' or 'incomplete' expression unless one knows that it is incomplete, and knows how many argument-places it has and how they are to be filled: that is fundamental to Frege's entire logical doctrine. In particular, a sentential connective is to be completed by sentences, the result being another sentence; if, as in the sentence 'Tom and Harry are brothers', the word 'and' occurs in a sentence that does not admit of an analysis under which 'and' was originally introduced as conjoining two sentences, then it cannot there bear the sense that it does when functioning as a sentential connective. The context principle, as stated in *Grundlagen*, does not embody the principle of the incompleteness of concepts and relations; if it did, it would be applicable only to predicates and relational expressions, whereas it is stated as holding uniformly for *all* expressions, whether complete or incomplete, and is specifically applied, in *Grundlagen*, to proper names. It is therefore a thesis whose content is *additional* to the principle of the incompleteness of concepts and relations; and it is, for that reason, fruitless to cite, as evidence that Frege continued to adhere to it, a passage that expressly concerns the notion of incompleteness or unsaturatedness. What would prove that he did so would be a remark to the effect that a proper name, an expression not requiring completion, had a sense or a reference only as occurring in the context of a sentence; but no such remark is cited by those who argue that Frege demonstrably retained the context principle. What is primarily at issue is whether, after Frege had assimilated sentences to complex proper names, as he did in his mature period, he did, or consistently could, maintain a principle that assigned a particular importance to the occurrence of an expression in a *sentence*. The difficulty does not arise so sharply for his late period, because, in the writings that survive from that period, the assimilation of sentences to proper names is barely touched on. For the mature period, the difficulty is more acute. It would resolve the matter in favour of the view that Frege retained the context principle, if there could be cited a remark that an incomplete expression

[1] P. 39.
[2] Op. cit., pp. 524–5.

whose completion was not a sentence, that is, a functional expression yielding, on completion, a complex proper name, had a sense or a reference, not merely when completed, but when occurring within a *sentence*. But, again, those who contend for the view fail to produce any such citation.

The position is, thus, that, neither in his mature nor in his late period did Frege either explicitly reaffirm or explicitly repudiate the context principle. The same could indeed be said of his definition of analyticity or of the principle concerning criteria of identity; but, according to the canons of exegesis proposed in Chapter 2, the presumption should be that both of these, as doctrines formulated and given prominence in *Grundlagen*, continued to be acceptable to Frege. The context principle, however, is in a different case, precisely because a cardinal thesis of Frege's mature doctrine, the thesis that sentences are, logically, just a particular kind of complex proper name, is, if not formally inconsistent, at least in great tension with a principle that accords a unique logical role to sentences. Now, as already observed, the fact is that Frege's theory of meaning cannot be made coherent without acknowledging the context principle, taken as a thesis concerning sense; but this means that it cannot be made coherent without recognizing that sentences form a distinct logical category, not a subdivision of the category of proper names. Hence, in default of any explicit statement by Frege after *Grundlagen* for or against the context principle as a thesis concerning sense, the most reasonable judgment is that he could not embody it in his official doctrine, but that it continued implicitly to guide his thinking, an influence he could not explicitly recognize without amending the doctrine.

This judgment accords well with the way in which Frege's logical theory is expounded in *Grundgesetze*, Part I. He continued to maintain a sharp distinction between the thought expressed by a sentence and the assertoric force attached to its expression, that is, between expressing a thought and asserting it. The assertion sign—what Frege called the 'judgment-stroke'—can be attached only to the name of a truth-value, i.e. to a sentence; this is even physically true, since it may figure only at the left-hand end of what in *Grundgesetze* was called the 'horizontal', and any well-formed expression beginning with the horizontal is a name of a truth-value. Here, then, we have what seems to be a radical distinction between sentences and other complete expressions. But, as previously noted, this distinction is virtually nullified by the treatment of the horizontal in *Grundgesetze* as capable of being attached to *any* proper name, thereby converting it into the name of a truth-value. Thus, as Frege points out in *Function und Begriff* (p. 23), if '2' is a proper name of the number 2 in the symbolism,

'———— 2' is well-formed and is a name of the False, and hence '——┬— 2' is also well-formed and a name of the True: we may therefore correctly make the assertion ' |——┬— 2'. This is a far-reaching departure from *Begriffsschrift*, where, as we saw, the distinction between sentences and (other) proper names, acknowledged as the distinction between expressions whose contents are 'judgeable', that is, can be judged to be true or false, and those whose contents are not judgeable, is reflected in the fact that the content-stroke can be attached only to the expression of a judgeable content. In *Grundgesetze* the distinction between sentences and other proper names has not vanished altogether; but it is a shadow of its former self.

A similar instance is provided by Frege's paragraph summarized, in the table of contents, as 'Every sentence of the formalism (*Begriffsschriftsatz*) expresses a thought', § 32 of *Grundgesetze*, vol. I. The paragraph is concerned with the notion of sense, and Frege begins by remarking that it has been shown[1] that the eight primitive names of the symbolism have a reference 'and hence that the same holds also for all complex names correctly formed from them'. 'However,' he continues, 'not only a reference, but also a sense, belongs to all names correctly formed from our symbols.' He does not, however, immediately explain in what this sense consists for an arbitrary such name, but states it only for names of truth-values, i.e. for sentences; he continues immediately as follows: 'Every such name of a truth-value *expresses* a sense, a *thought*. Namely, by our stipulations it is determined under which conditions it stands for the True. The sense of this name, the *thought*, is the thought that these conditions are fulfilled.' Later in the paragraph, he speaks of the senses of expressions that do not name truth-values; using the *Grundgesetze* terminology according to which every expression to which a reference can be ascribed is called a name, he says, 'Now the names, whether simple or themselves already complex, of which the name of a truth-value consists contribute to the expression of the thought, and this contribution of the individual constituent is its *sense*. If a name is part of a name of a truth-value, the sense of the former name is part of the thought expressed by the latter.' Here the whole thrust of the exposition is towards taking the senses of sentences, that is, thoughts, which may be true or false, as primary in the order of explanation, so that the sense of an expression smaller than a sentence is taken to be the contribution it makes to the thoughts expressed by sentences in which it occurs. That is to say, the passage has its most natural

---

[1] In §§ 28–31.

interpretation as in conformity with the context principle, understood as a thesis concerning sense. It is, however, so phrased as not to commit Frege to the context principle. He makes no general statement about what the sense of an expression other than a sentence consists in; he merely considers the case in which such an expression occurs within a sentence, and says that its sense contributes to the expression of the thought and is thereby a part of that thought. So far as this goes, no reason is given why just the same may not be said when the expression occurs as a part of a proper name which is not a name of a truth-value: indeed, it would be inconsistent for Frege to deny that, in this case, too, the sense of the part was part of the sense of the whole. The context principle is not merely to the effect that the senses of the constituent expressions within a sentence are parts of the thought expressed by the sentence as a whole; it involves that we can explain in what the sense of an expression other than a sentence consists only in terms of its contribution to the senses of sentences containing it. But, in this paragraph, Frege avoids saying in what, in general, the sense of an expression of his symbolism consists; he leaves that open. He says in what the sense of a sentence consists, and states the relation between the sense of a sentence and the senses of the constituent expressions. He does this, moreover, in a manner which points naturally towards an account of the senses of expressions other than sentences in conformity with the context principle: but he avoids actually asserting anything that would commit him to that principle.

a thesis about
reference We have now to turn to the context principle construed as a thesis concerning *reference*. Since, when writing *Grundlagen*, Frege did not as yet distinguish between sense and reference, he obviously could not distinguish, either, between applying the context principle to the *sense* of a word and applying it to its *reference*. We, however, in drawing that distinction, can see that, in *Grundlagen*, his principal concern was to apply the principle to the references of certain expressions. So interpreted, the principle lays down that, if a sense has been fixed for all possible sentences in which an expression may occur, then no additional stipulation is needed to confer a reference on that expression. From the standpoint of Frege's later, more systematic, account of sense and reference, it would be necessary first to ensure that the expression was genuinely a logically unitary one; as he remarked in the Appendix to vol. II of *Grundgesetze*, dealing with Russell's paradox, if it were merely a typographic component of one or more longer expressions each of which had a reference only as a whole, it would not be proper to ascribe a reference to it. Frege is discussing various alternative reinterpretations of class-terms that might be proposed in order to avoid the paradox, and, among them, he discusses the possibility of 'regarding class-names as pseudo-proper-names, which would therefore in fact have no reference'.[1] 'They would then,' he says, 'have to be regarded as parts of signs that would have a reference only as wholes. One may indeed consider it advantageous, for some purpose or other, to devise different symbols that are identical in some part, without thereby making them into composite symbols. The simplicity of a symbol indeed requires only that the parts that one can distinguish within it do not have a reference on their own (*selbständig*). In this case, even what we are accustomed to regard as a numeral (*Zahlzeichen*) would not really be a symbol at all, but only a dependent (*unselbständige*) part of a symbol. A definition of the symbol "2" would be impossible; one would have instead to define several symbols, which contained "2" as a dependent constituent part, but were not to be thought of as logically compounded out of "2" and another part.' The price of this would be, not only that numerals could not be thought of as possessing reference, nor, therefore, sense, but that they could not legitimately be replaced by variables. 'It would then be impermissible to allow such a dependent part to be replaced by a letter; for, in respect of the content, no compositeness would be present.' To have a reference and to be capable of replacement by a bound variable is one and the same thing.

When he is discussing the context principle in *Grundlagen*, however, Frege's attention is not directed towards this point. It would, indeed, be possible to view the remark just quoted from the Appendix to *Grundgesetze* as embodying an explicit rejection of the context principle, interpreted as a thesis about reference; but, although, as we shall note below, there is some warrant for understanding the context principle in a sense that would conflict with these later remarks, I shall not so understand it here, but assume that it is to be applied only to expressions that Frege would recognize as logical units. In any case, Frege is chiefly concerned, in *Grundlagen*, to apply it to proper names (singular terms). So applied, the context principle is closely allied to the point I made in disagreeing with the view formerly expressed by Geach:[2] granted that number-words stand for numbers, we establish that numbers are objects by establishing that number-words are proper names, not conversely. But the point is not quite the same. I was maintaining that we can first establish that a number-word is a proper name, and infer from that that what it stands for is an

[1] P. 255.
[2] *FPL*, pp. 56–7.

object; but the context principle is concerned with what justifies us in holding that number-words stand for anything at all, that is, in ascribing a reference to them.

According to the context principle, what justifies us in regarding an expression as standing for an object is, first, that it behaves like a proper name, and, secondly, that a definite sense has been provided for every sentence in which it may occur. What its behaving like a proper name consists in is something that Frege never troubled to spell out; I attempted to do so in Chapter 4 of *FPL*. On Frege's later view, any sentence containing a proper name should continue to have a sense when that proper name is replaced by any other proper name whatever. But in *Grundlagen* he had not yet arrived at so exigent a doctrine. He is prepared to allow that we may have introduced a certain range of proper names as capable of occupying only certain kinds of context, and have simply failed to provide for their occurrence in any other contexts. Thus, in § 65 he is considering the introduction of proper names of the form 'the direction of *a*' by means of a contextual definition that stipulates that a sentence of the form 'The direction of the straight line *a* is identical with the direction of the straight line *b*' is to be equivalent to 'The straight line *a* is parallel to the straight line *b*'; and he remarks that 'in order to justify our proposed definition of the direction of a straight line, we should have to show that it is possible, if the straight line *a* is parallel to the straight line *b*, to substitute "the direction of *b*" everywhere for "the direction of *a*". This task is simplified by the fact that we do not at the outset know of anything that can be predicated of the direction of a straight line other than that it coincides with the direction of another straight line. We should thus need to demonstrate the possibility of substitution only in such a statement of identity, or in contents which contain such identity-statements as constituent parts. Everything else predicated of directions would first have to be defined, and for these definitions we can lay down the rule that the possibility of substituting the direction of one straight line for that of another parallel to it must be preserved.' Here it is evident that we are to be allowed to introduce proper names for directions only in a restricted range of contexts, those, namely, for which we expressly provide by means of further contextual definitions. The only absolute demand that Frege makes is that a sense should be provided for every identity-statement connecting any two proper names. In § 62 he says, 'We have already settled that number words are to be understood as standing for self-subsistent (*selbständige*) objects. And that is enough to give us a family of sentences that must have a sense, those sentences which express recognition', by which he means statements of identity. A sense must be provided for every identity-statement, whatever the proper names standing on either side of the sign of identity: if directions are objects, then there must be a sense for 'England is the same as the direction of the Earth's axis' (§ 66); if numbers are objects, there must be a sense for a sentence of the form 'Julius Caesar is the number belonging to the concept *F*' (§ 56).

Suppose, then, that a given expression '*a*' passes the tests for functioning as a proper name (singular term), and, further, that we have provided a determinate sense for every sentence in which we wish to permit '*a*' to occur, including all identity-statements. We cannot, consistently with Frege's later views, say without more ado that '*a*' has a reference, since according to those views, sentences containing names lacking reference may still have a sense; but the context principle rules out the need for any further *philosophical* enquiry in order to determine whether or not '*a*' has a reference. On Frege's later view, a sentence containing an empty name lacks a truth-value; for '*a*' to have a reference, it is therefore sufficient that some one sentence containing it, whose sense is by hypothesis already fixed, should be established as either true or false. The enquiry is therefore no longer of a philosophical character: it belongs to whatever subject-matter sentences containing '*a*' relate to, for instance to arithmetic if '*a*' is a numerical term. If this test is thought to rely too heavily upon Frege's particular views concerning sentences containing empty names, we could say that what remained, in order to determine that '*a*' had a reference, would be that the sentence 'There is such an object as *a*' should be recognized as true; again, we are concerned, not, in general, with a philosophical question, but with one falling within the province to which those sentences containing '*a*' whose senses have already been laid down belong. Or, if this is thought too simple a formulation, we could say that what is required is to find a predicate '*F*' such that we can recognize the sentence '*a* is *F*, and only *a* is *F*' as being true if it has a truth-value at all, and then establish the truth of the sentence 'There is something which is *F*'. In the same way, any question as to what kind of object '*a*' stands for, or what object, in particular, it stands for, is to be answered, in so far as it is legitimate at all, by determining the truth-value of a suitable sentence containing '*a*'. A question of the form, 'Does "*a*" stand for a *G*?', is to be answered by determining the sentence, '*a* is a *G*', as true or false, if indeed we have provided a sense for that sentence. Likewise, a question of the form, 'Does "*a*" stand for *b*?', is to be answered by determining the truth-value of the sentence, '*a* is the same as *b*'; and such a question is always capable of a determinate answer, since we must have supplied a sense, that is, have laid down truth-conditions, for every identity-statement.

What Frege treats, in *Grundlagen*,[1] as the mistake most obviously due to a failure to appreciate the context principle is taking the reference, or the meaning, of an abstract term to be an idea (*Vorstellung*) or mental image. But what the context principle, interpreted as a thesis about reference, and applied to proper names, tells most immediately against is the conception that an expression can behave *exactly* like a singular term and yet be denied a reference. An expression might function in many respects like a singular term, and yet, because of some crucial difference in its behaviour, be denied the status of a singular term, and hence be held not to stand for any object. But to say that an expression behaves exactly like a singular term is to say that it has just the connections with the use of predicates, general terms and quantifiers that will render the denial of a reference to it incoherent. To say, for instance, that 'the number 27' does not stand for an object is to say that there is no such object as the number 27, or that there is no such number as 27; that 3 has no cube and 26 no successor. But this is absurd, since, by appeal to the sense we have provided for the sentence 'There is a number which is a cube of 3', we can easily demonstrate it to be true. We might try to escape the absurdity by allowing that '27' stands for a number, but denying that numbers are objects. But, from Frege's standpoint, such a position would be tantamount to banning the substantival use of number-words, and permitting them to occur only as adjectives: to continue to admit the use of '27' as a singular term, while denying that it stood for an object, would be to divorce the principles by which we categorize reality—the realm of reference—from those by which we categorize linguistic expressions. It is fundamental to Frege's whole philosophy that the two must match; and I argued in Chapter 12 that the linguistic categories are the key to the ontological ones, that is, have a certain priority in our understanding. At any rate, they must match: if an expression functions like a proper name, then it is a proper name, and hence, if it stands for anything, what it stands for is an object; to deny that it stands for an object (while allowing that it may occur in true sentences) is intelligible only if it embodies a thesis that it is not, or ought not to be, used as a proper name. Of course, if someone denies that '27' stands for an object, we cannot conclude at once that he is in disagreement with Frege: he might be using 'object' in a way that differs from Frege's, to apply only to a special class of what Frege calls

[1] P. x and § 106.

'objects'. But, if so, then he must be willing to admit the notion Frege expressed, from *Grundlagen* onwards, by the term 'object', and earlier, by the term 'individual thing', to mean anything that we use an expression functioning like a proper name to talk about.

'ξ is an object', as Frege uses it, is simply the most general first-level predicate, under which every sortal predicate such as 'ξ is a city', 'ξ is a planet', 'ξ is a direction', 'ξ is a number', etc., is subsumed. The fact that '27' behaves like a proper name shows in its interchangeability with 'what "27" stands for': it is one and the same thing to say that '27' stands for an object and to say that 27 is an object. To deny that '27 is an object' is true makes no sense unless it also be denied that '27 is a number' is true, and that can be denied only if the sentence is taken to be ill-formed, i.e. if it is held, after all, that '27' is not, or should not be, treated as behaving like a proper name. There is, indeed, one consequence of the utmost importance, which Frege held to flow from the categorization of any given range of entities, e.g. numbers, as objects, namely that they fall within the unique all-embracing domain assigned to every individual variable. This by no means immediately follows from the fact that expressions for such entities behave like proper names; it depends, in addition, on Frege's principle that every logical difference—every distinction the neglect of which will lead to the formation of sentences that fail to possess a sense—must reflect a difference of logical type. Without this principle, we could recognize distinct sorts of objects, forming disjoint domains over which distinct sorts of individual variables were to range: proper names of objects of different sorts would behave analogously, but would not be interchangeable without a destruction of sense. In *Grundlagen*, Frege had not yet drawn the full consequences of the principle: it is allowed that, if terms for directions were introduced by contextual definition, only certain predicates might be defined over directions, and the same would, by parity, apply to terms for numbers. On the other hand, the identity-sign may meaningfully stand between any two proper names, which would be unusual in a many-sorted logic; and it is implicitly assumed that all objects, including numbers, fall within the range of the individual variables, distinct sorts of which are not envisaged. Two doctrines, not distinguished by Frege, form vitally important ingredients of his mature theory: that what can intelligibly be said of any object can be intelligibly said of any other object, so that no logical differentiation of sorts is required; and that there is a single all-embracing domain of objects, so that no specification of the domain is needed. The second of these doctrines was the source of the Russell contradiction. But these are best regarded as theses that Frege held concerning objects, which may be, and, in the second case, must be, disputed, rather than as constitutive of the notion of an object. To deny that numerical terms have a reference would be to hold that they have significance only as parts of longer expressions that could be considered as having a reference only as a whole, as would be the case if they were allowed to occur only adjectivally, and every adjectival occurrence were convertible to the form 'There are just n . . .'. This is, in effect, what is proposed in § 55 of *Grundlagen*, and rejected by Frege in the following sections as inadequate to explain the substantival uses of number-words; moreover, as remarked in the Appendix to *Grundgesetze*, vol. II, such a view would render illegitimate the replacement of numerals by variables, since variables can stand only in place of expressions that have a reference of their own. To regard numerical terms as having a reference, but not as standing for objects, could only be to take them as expressions needing completion, and hence as replaceable by variables carrying one or more argument-places. In either case, the apparent form of arithmetical statements would have to be rejected as misleading; an analysis of the essential structure of such statements would reveal numerical terms as not being singular terms at all.

The context principle, considered as a thesis about reference, thus forbids us to treat numerical terms as proper names while denying that they stand for objects. Equally contrary to this application of the context principle is the view that they stand for objects, indeed, but that such objects only have being and not real existence. Such a conception introduces a special philosophical sense of 'exists', divorced from the existential quantifier: it compels us to say such things as that there is a number which is the third power of 3, but that no such number (really) *exists*. The whole point of the context principle is, however, to deny that there are any special philosophical notions of existence or of objects which are to be distinguished from those employed in the correct mode of expression of our thoughts. Not, indeed, that every sentence of ordinary language is to be taken at its face-value; but what is not to be so taken is either sense-less or can be re-expressed so as to reveal its structure more perspicuously, and there will then be no special philosophers' notion of existence distinct from the existence asserted in the sentences of such a purified language. A philosophical distinction between being and existence is tempting as a means of accounting for the intelligibility of singular terms which would ordinarily be said not to stand for anything. Meinong notoriously sought, by in effect extending the notion of reference, to explain empty names as after all standing for objects, though not for existent ones; Frege, by using the distinction between sense and reference, had a better explanation. But to distinguish, among terms that would ordinarily be said to stand for something, those that stand for objects which merely have being, and those that stand for objects which really exist, is to reject the context principle utterly, or else to overlook its entire point.

As we saw in Chapter 18, Sluga's comparison, in 'Frege as a Rationalist', between what he calls 'Frege's distinction between reality and objectivity' and Lotze's distinction between reality and validity appears to place him squarely among those who thus miss the point of the context principle as a principle concerning reference; indeed, to make of him one who misses the point of it so completely as actually to attribute a version of the opposition between existence and being, in the form of that between objectivity and reality, to Frege himself. Frege did indeed hold that numbers, and logical objects generally, are *objektiv* but not *wirklich*. *'Objektiv'*, as he used it, is certainly to be translated 'objective'; the question is what Frege meant by *'wirklich'*, and whether that word, in his employment of it, is properly to be translated 'real'. In 'Frege's Alleged Realism',[1] Sluga quotes three pairs of terms used by Lotze in his *Logik* to indicate the distinction expressed by Sluga by means of the words 'reality' and 'validity': *'Wirklichkeit der Dinge'* versus *'Objektivität'*,[2] *'Sein'* versus *'Gelten'*[3] and *'Realität'* versus *'Geltung'*.[4] He goes on to remark that how any of Frege's or Lotze's terms are to be translated into English is completely irrelevant to the argument, the argument, namely, that the two philosophers meant much the same by their respective distinctions. It would, indeed, be irrelevant to the argument were it being conducted in German or in Japanese; but, when the argument is being conducted in English, as by Sluga, it is highly germane, because the question at issue is precisely what Frege and Lotze respectively meant.

The word *'wirklich'* in German is a perfectly ordinary word for 'real'; but we know from other cases, such as the words *'Bedeutung'* and *'Begriff'*, that it is dangerous to trust common usage as a guide to Frege's intentions in using quite ordinary words adopted by him as quasi-technical terms. In the case of the word *'wirklich'*, there is no need for any uncertainty, because Frege indicates very clearly what he understands by it. In order to remove any possible doubt, let us collect some texts: in rendering these

[1] P. 232.
[2] *Logik*, p. 16.
[3] Ibid., p. 511.
[4] Ibid., pp. 517 and 519.

into English, I will follow the practice of Austin in the second edition of his version of the *Grundlagen*, and of Furth in his translation of Part I of *Grundgesetze*, by using 'actual' to translate '*wirklich*'; this will beg no questions. In *Grundlagen*, § 26, we find the following: 'I distinguish being objective from being manipulable, from being spatial and from being actual. The axis of the Earth and the centre of mass of the Solar System are objective, but I should not like to call them actual, as the Earth itself is. One often calls the equator an *imaginary* (*gedachte*) line; but it would be incorrect to call it a *fictitious* (*erdachte*) line: it was not created by thinking, as the product of a mental process, but only recognized, apprehended, by thinking. If coming to be recognized were to be created, we should not be able to predicate anything positive about the equator as relating to a time preceding this supposed creation'. The last sentence of *Grundlagen* asserts (contrary to the celebrated dictum of Kronecker) that positive integers are no more real, more *wirklich*, more tangible or more unmysterious than numbers of other kinds. In the same vein, Frege, commenting in § 85 on Cantor's *Grundlagen einer allgemeinen Mannichfaltigkeitslehre*, which had come out a year before his own book, expresses his concurrence with a remark of Cantor's involving the word *wirklich*. 'In a remarkable work', he says, 'G. Cantor has recently introduced infinite cardinal numbers. I thoroughly agree with his estimate of the opinion which allows only the finite cardinal numbers to count as *wirklich*. They are not, indeed, in space or perceptible by the senses; neither are fractions, or negative, irrational or complex numbers. If one calls *wirklich* that which acts on the senses, or which at least produces effects (*Wirkungen*) of which sense-perceptions may be near or remote consequences, then, admittedly, no number of any of these kinds is *wirklich*. At the same time, we have no need whatever for such perceptions as grounds for proving theorems. We can in our investigations use without reserve a name or symbol the manner of whose introduction was logically unobjectionable. Our cardinal number ∞_1 is therefore as justified as the number two or three'. '∞_1' is Frege's notation for the transfinite cardinal now denoted, following Cantor, by '$\aleph_0$'. Here the usage whereby only that which acts, directly or indirectly, upon the senses is to be called *wirklich* is that favoured by Frege himself; the word as used by Cantor corresponds, rather, to Frege's *objectiv*. The distinction between what is objective and what is actual plays a very small role in *Grundlagen*: there is further discussion of the objectivity of numbers, in § 61, but no other use of the term '*wirklich*'.

In the Preface to *Grundgesetze*, vol. I, there is considerable discussion of actuality and of objectivity, in opposition first to the formalists and then to psychologistic logicians such as Benno Erdmann. On p. xiii, Frege gives as one reason why his book may not be well received, 'the widespread inclination to acknowledge as existing (*vorhanden*) only what is perceptible by the senses'. Among objects not perceptible by the senses, Frege says, are the numbers, the objects of arithmetic; and he goes on to attack the attempt to get out of the difficulty by identifying the numbers with the numerical symbols, and investing these with the desired properties by creative definitions. On p. xviii he says, 'I recognize a domain of that which is objective but not actual, whereas the psychological logicians take what is not actual without more ado as subjective. And yet it is incomprehensible why that which subsists independently of a judging subject should have to be actual, i.e. capable of acting immediately or mediately upon the senses. Such a connection between these concepts is not to be discovered. One can indeed cite examples that show the opposite. One will not easily take, e.g., the number one to be actual, if one is not a follower of J. S. Mill. On the other hand, it is impossible to ascribe to each individual his own number one. . . Since the number one, as the same for everyone, stands over against (*gegenübersteht*) everyone in the same way, it can no more be investigated by means of psychological observations than can the Moon. Whatever ideas there may be of the number one in individual minds, they are to be distinguished from the number one just as much as ideas of the Moon are from the Moon itself. Because the psychological logicians fail to recognize the possibility of what is objective but not actual, they take concepts for ideas and assign them to psychology.' On p. xix he says, 'Some objective things are actual, others are not. "Actual" is only one predicate out of many, and concerns logic no more closely than, say, the predicate "algebraic" as applied to a curve.' And on p. xxv he remarks, 'Existence (*Existenz*) is confused by Herr B. Erdmann with actuality, which, as we saw, is also not clearly distinguished from objectivity. Of which thing are we really asserting that it is actual when we say that there are square roots of four? Of two or of —2? . . . If I wished to say that the number two acts or is active or actual, this would be false and quite distinct from what I wish to say by means of the sentence "There are square roots of four".'

In his brief article of 1895 in French, 'Le Nombre entier', Frege used the word '*réel*' as the equivalent of '*wirklich*'. When this is rendered 'actual', as before, the relevant passage runs: 'The theorems of arithmetic never relate to symbols, but to the things designated (*représentées*) by them. These objects are not, indeed, tangible, nor visible, nor even actual, if one calls "actual" that which can exert influence and be subject to it. The numbers do not change; for the theorems of arithmetic embody eternal truths. One may thus say that these objects are outside time, from which it is apparent that they are not perceptions or subjective ideas (*idées*), since such things constantly change in accordance with psychological laws'. In *Grundgesetze*, vol. II, § 74, Frege wrote, 'Without, indeed, meaning to give any exhaustive partition, we may distinguish between physical and logical objects. The former are actual, in the strict sense; the latter are not actual, but are no less objective on that account: they cannot, indeed, act upon our senses, but can be grasped by means of our logical faculties. Our cardinal numbers (*Anzahlen*) are logical objects of this sort; and it is probable that numbers of other kinds belong among logical objects also'. What Frege here states as probable is his own conviction; he cites it at this stage as merely probable, because he is here engaged in examining the views of others on real numbers, in this case Cantor's, and has not yet given his own. Finally, at the end of 'Der Gedanke', there is a discussion of the question whether thoughts are to be regarded as 'actual'. Frege says, 'Admittedly a thought is not something that one is accustomed to call actual. The world of the actual is a world in which this acts upon that, changes it and itself experiences reactions and is changed by them. All this is a process in time. We shall hardly recognize as actual that which is timeless and changeless. Now is a thought changeable, or is it timeless? The thought that we express in Pythagoras's Theorem is indeed timeless, eternal, unchangeable.'[1] Frege then goes on to argue, in his usual fashion, against the view that there are some thoughts which are true at one time and false at another, concluding, 'The same sequence of words may, as a result of the changeability of language, take on a different sense, express a different thought; but the change concerns only what is linguistic.' He continues, 'And yet! What value could the eternally unchangeable have for us, that could neither be acted upon (*Wirkungen erfahren*) nor act upon us? Something that was completely and in every respect inactive would not be in the least actual (*wäre auch ganz unwirklich*) and would not exist for us (*wäre für uns nicht vorhanden*). Even the timeless, if it is to be anything for us, must in some way be intertwined with temporality (*mit der Zeitlichkeit verflochten sein*). What would a thought be for me, that was never grasped by me? But through my grasping a thought, I enter into a relation to it, and it to me. It is possible that the same thought, that is today thought by me, was not thought by me yesterday. In this way the strict timelessness of the thought is, indeed, cancelled. But one is inclined to distinguish between essential and inessential properties, and

---

[1] 'Der Gedanke', p. 76.

to recognize something as timeless when the changes that it undergoes relate only to the inessential properties. A property of a thought that consists in, or follows from, the fact that it is grasped by a thinker, will be called inessential. How does a thought act? By being grasped and by being taken as true. This is a process in the inner world of a thinker, which may have further consequences in this inner world, consequences which, by invading the domain of the will, make themselves observable in the outer world also. If, for example, I grasp the thought that we express in Pythagoras's Theorem, the consequence may be that I recognize it as true, and, further, that I apply it, making a decision that brings about (*bewirkt*) accelerations of masses. In this way our actions (*Taten*) are usually prepared for by thinking and by making judgments. And hence thoughts can indirectly influence the motions of masses. The action of one person upon another is for the most part mediated by thoughts. One communicates a thought. How does that happen? One brings about (*bewirkt*) changes in the outer world common to all, changes which, when perceived by another, are meant to induce him to grasp a thought and to take it as true. Could the great events of world history have come about otherwise than by the communication of thoughts? And yet we are inclined to regard thoughts as not being actual, because they appear to be inactive (*untätig*) in events, whereas thinking, judging, uttering, understanding, every kind of doing in this connection is an affair of human beings. How actual a hammer seems, by contrast, compared with a thought! How different is the process of handing over a hammer from that of communicating a thought! The hammer passes from the control of one to that of another, it is gripped and thereby undergoes pressure, which alters its density and the disposition of its parts in places. Nothing of the kind occurs with a thought. By being communicated, the thought does not pass out of the control of the one who communicates it, for a human being has, after all, no control of it. By being grasped, a thought brings about (*bewirkt*) changes, in the first place only in the inner world of the one who grasps it; yet it remains itself untouched by this in the core of its being, since the changes which it undergoes affect only its inessential properties. Here there is lacking something which we recognize everywhere in natural processes: reciprocal action. Thoughts are not completely without actuality (*sind nicht durchaus unwirklich*), but their actuality is of a quite different kind from that of things. And their action is effected by what the thinkers do; without this, they would be inactive, at least so far as we can see. And yet the thinker does not create them, but must take them as they are. They may be true, without being grasped by a thinker; and, even in this case, they are not wholly without actuality, at least if they are capable of being grasped and thereby rendered active.'[1]

These passages, which I have quoted in full, comprise, to the best of my belief, all those in which Frege discussed in print the concept of actuality (*Wirklichkeit*), as he understood it.[2] The concept of objectivity plays a large part in Frege's writings: in many passages, he asserts it of concepts, senses and logical objects, while denying it to ideas and mental contents. But the concept of actuality does not play a major role in his philosophy; and, as can be seen from the passages quoted, his account of it was not fully worked out. In all the passages, being actual is associated with being in space and time and with being subject to being acted on; and, in all save that from *Grundlagen*, with being perceptible through the senses. Again with the exception of that from *Grundlagen*, all the passages make the connection between being *wirklich* (actual) and acting (*wirken*) on things, being active (*wirksam*) and giving rise to actions (*Wirkungen*), as well as being subject to the action of other things: that is, an object is *wirklich* if it is both an agent and a subject of casual effects. I have, as far as possible, attempted, in the above renderings, to preserve the association between cognate expressions, as did Furth in his translation of *Grundgesetze*, Part I, at the cost of smoothness of translation in some cases; except where otherwise indicated by the inclusion of the German in brackets, words like 'active', 'reaction', etc., signalize the use in the German of a word cognate with '*wirklich*'. Such a distinction between those objects which do, and those which do not, give rise to and are subject to causal effects is a natural way of distinguishing between concrete and abstract objects, and leads naturally to the idea that abstract objects are not the subjects of change, which Frege also uses as a criterion for not being *wirklich*; but, as is evident from the passage from 'Der Gedanke', these criteria are more easily stated than explained or applied, as I noted in Chapter 14 of *FPL*. In any case, it is apparent, from the remark in the Preface to *Grundgesetze*, that '*wirklich*' is just one predicate of objects out of many, and that Frege did not use this adjective to mean 'real' in the proper sense, that sense, namely, in which 'is not a real *F*' is synonymous with 'is not really an *F*'. In the passage from 'Der Gedanke', Frege is plainly using '*wirklich*' with an echo of its common meaning 'real', as when he says that what is totally inactive (*unwirksam*), that is, without effects, would be quite *unwirklich* and would not exist for us (or 'would not be present to us'); it is for this reason that he concludes that thoughts

[1] Ibid., pp. 76–7.
[2] See also 'Logik', 1897, *N.S.*, pp. 138, 149–50, *P.W.*, pp. 127, 137–8.

have a certain kind of actuality, though one very different from physical objects, whereas, at earlier periods, he would surely have said outright that they were not *wirklich*. But, in general, it is plain that Frege uses '*wirklich*' to refer to a particular character possessed by some objects and not by others, the class of those which are *unwirklich* including logical objects, senses and others, such as the Equator, that fall into neither category. There is not the slightest ground for taking him to be hinting, in those rare passages in which he employs the word '*wirklich*', that *unwirkliche* or abstract objects are devoid of reality or possess it in a diminished or diluted form, or that they may possess it so far as logic is concerned, the question whether they do being reserved for metaphysics. How else are we to interpret Sluga, despite the difficulties we have seen to arise in understanding him, save as asserting just that when he says that 'the doctrine of the objectivity of numbers, concepts and thoughts is not an ontological one for Frege'?[1] There is, of course, no *one* such doctrine: the thesis that numbers are objective is quite distinct from the thesis that thoughts are objective, and must be argued for separately; and both, in turn, are distinct from the thesis that concepts are objective. '*Wirklich*' is a predicate of objects only; no genuine predicate could apply univocally both to objects and to concepts. Hence not even a false interpretation of the word '*wirklich*', as Frege uses it, could be put to the purpose of arguing that Frege's thesis that concepts are objective is not to be interpreted 'ontologically': for numbers and for thoughts, such an argument can rest only on a false interpretation of that word, a determination to ignore the context principle as Frege employs it in *Grundlagen*, and a drive to minimize Frege's originality by assimilating his philosophy to such a philosopher as Lotze.

What justice is there in Sluga's comparison of Frege's distinction between objectivity and actuality and any distinction drawn by Hermann Lotze? Is Sluga right, as regards Lotze, in saying that 'it is obviously a mistake to regard' Frege's and Lotze's doctrines 'as ontological theories, at least according to the intentions of their authors'?[2] In 'Frege's Alleged Realism',[3] Sluga cites Lotze's distinction as first being drawn in his *Logik*, Book I, Chapter I, § 3. Lotze there speaks of a 'first operation of thought' which converts an *impression* into an *idea*.[4] By this operation, which consists in forming a name, an objectivity is accorded to the object of thought which falls short of reality (*Wirklichkeit*): 'when we speak of

[1] 'Frege's Alleged Realism', p. 236.

[2] 'Frege as a Rationalist', p. 29.

[3] Pp. 232–3.

[4] H. Lotze, *Logic*, trans. B. Bosanquet, Oxford, 1884, p. 11.

"pain", "brightness", "freedom", we do not imply that they could exist
if there were no person to feel, to see, to enjoy them, respectively'. Sluga
himself quotes the continuation, which runs in Bosanquet's translation:
'The logical objectification, then, which the creation of a name implies,
does not give an external reality to the matter named; the common world,
in which others are expected to recognize what we point to, is, speaking
generally, only the world of thought . . . It is quite indifferent whether
certain parts of this world of thought indicate something which has besides
an independent reality outside the thinking minds, or whether all that
it contains exists only in the thoughts of those who think it, but with
equal validity for them all.' Here Lotze expressly says that objectivity,
as he is using the term, is unaffected by whether that to which it attaches
does or does not exist independently of thought or experience. It would,
therefore, have been better called 'intersubjectivity', and it would seem
intelligible to say that it is not an ontological notion. But it plainly has
nothing to do with Frege's notion of objectivity, for which it is essential
that that to which it is rightly ascribed exists independently of whether it
is apprehended or referred to by any thinking subject. Evidently Frege's
distinction between *Objektivität* and *Wirklichkeit* is not to be compared
with that drawn by Lotze in this passage at all: the words used are the
same, the concepts expressed entirely different.

Sluga next refers to Book III of Lotze's *Logik*, of which he says that it
'seems to have been studied most closely by Frege',[1] and proceeds to
try to indicate the derivation of various of Frege's ideas from it. He compares Lotze's rejection of the correspondence theory of truth[2] to Frege's
rejection of it in 'Der Gedanke', and credits Lotze with giving, in his
§ 305, a version of Frege's regress argument against it.[3] This is incorrect.
Frege's regress argument is aimed at *any* general characterization of truth;
the conclusion is that truth is indefinable. Lotze's argument, which is
entirely different from Frege's, is aimed at establishing something like a
coherence theory: it is, essentially, that it is senseless to suppose that we could
compare our ideas with things as they are in themselves, external to us,
since 'It is . . . this varied world of ideas within us . . . which forms the
sole material directly given to us' (§ 306). This is a familiar idealist argument, found in one form or another in the writings of many philosophers,
and having nothing in common with Frege's grounds for rejecting the
correspondence theory of truth. Sluga now cites the distinction made by

[1] Ibid., p. 233.
[2] Book III, ch. 1, § 304.
[3] Sluga, op. cit., p. 234.

Lotze in Book III, Chapter II, § 316, between being (*Sein*) and holding (*Gelten*); on p. 232 he speaks of this as being the same distinction as that made by Lotze in § 3 between objectivity and reality (*Wirklichkeit*), though the terminology has changed; but on p. 233 he speaks of the later distinction as a wider one that replaces the earlier distinction. In any case, the new distinction, whether it coincides with or replaces the old one, is again to be compared with Frege's distinction expressed by the terms *objektiv* and *wirklich*. In fact, however, the distinction drawn by Lotze in his § 316 does not seem to be the same at all as that he drew in § 3; if it were, he would have switched terminology in a most confusing way. He says that that which is, we call real (*wirklich*), but that we call it so in different senses, according to its form, by which he means its logical type.[1] Thus *things exist* or have *being*; *events* do not exist, but *occur*; *relations* neither exist nor occur, but *obtain*; and *propositions hold* or have *validity*: each of these is the mode of reality proper to the entity in question. There is not here a dichotomy, as you would suppose from Sluga's exposition, but a manifold distinction. None of these distinctions has anything to do with Frege's distinction of objectivity from actuality (*Wirklichkeit*), nor with that drawn earlier by Lotze between objectivity and reality (*Wirklichkeit*): rather, he is not equivocating with his term *wirklich*, but drawing new distinctions, *within* the category of that which is *wirklich*, between different modes of *Wirklichkeit*. If these distinctions are to be compared with anything in Frege, they should be related to his distinctions of level and of logical type, which force a differentiation between the second-level property of the existence of an object falling under a given concept and the third-level property of the existence of a first-level concept falling under a given second-level one. It should be noted that, when Lotze speaks of a proposition as holding or being valid, he is *not* concerned with what Frege expressed by saying that a thought, true or false, exists objectively and independently of any thinker: he means simply that the proposition is true. (Sluga compounds confusion by adding in a footnote that he is deliberately ignoring Lotze's use of '*Wirklichkeit*' to cover both '*Geltung*' and '*Realität*'; 'the addition of this third term affects in no way Lotze's doctrines as I explain them here'. As far as I have noticed, Lotze does not employ the unqualified term '*Realität*' as equivalent with '*Sein*'; he speaks only of the reality of existence and the reality of thought, modes of reality. But this is a minor matter: the important point is that '*Wirklichkeit*' is not a third term, newly added; it is the same term as previously introduced by Lotze in

---

[1] Op. cit., p. 439.

§ 3. Sluga regards it as something new only because he has confused two quite separate distinctions of Lotze's, the initial one between objectivity and reality, and the later manifold one between different modes of reality.) The distinctions made by Lotze in his § 316 can hardly be reasonably denied to be ontological ones: they are distinctions of modes of reality, what others would call 'modes of being', the very stuff of ontological theories. We cannot use the phrase 'modes of being' in connection with Lotze, since he associates 'being' only with what he calls 'things', as opposed to events, etc.: this fact hardly justifies the denial that we are in the realm of ontology.

Sluga now refers to Lotze's discussion, in §§ 317–21, of Plato's theory of ideas. Lotze says that ideas (*Ideen*), as they are present in our minds, possess reality in the sense of an event, namely, they *occur* in us; but their contents, regarded in abstraction from our mental activity, cannot be said to occur, nor to exist as do things, but only to possess validity (*Geltung*).[1] This distinction he ascribes to Plato, though admitting that Plato had no terminology with which to express it; and, when we realize this, we can correct the misinterpretation that 'Plato . . . ascribed to the Ideas . . . an existence apart from things, and yet . . . of like kind with the existence of things', a misinterpretation originating with Aristotle.[2] While it is obvious what Lotze means by speaking of a proposition as being valid, namely that it is true, it is obscure, as he himself confesses, how this notion can be transferred to ideas, platonic or otherwise; and equally obscure, as he likewise confesses, what could be meant by the view that he is combating, that ideas have an existence of a like kind to that of things. However this may be, Lotze's conception of ideas as having validity does not strike me as affording any useful comparison with Frege's views (i) that logical objects are objective, (ii) that senses are objective, (iii) that concepts are objective, (iv) that logical objects are not actual or (v) that senses are not actual. Lotze at first (§ 316) refuses the demand for an explanation of the validity of ideas. Later he says (§ 321), in a passage to which Sluga refers, that propositions must be employed as examples to explain the meaning of validity as opposed to existence, and that the term can then be transferred to single concepts, but only with some degree of obscurity: 'we can only say of concepts that they *mean* something, and they mean something because certain propositions are valid of them, as for example that the content of any given concept is identical with itself.' Sluga comments that 'the similarity of this thesis to Frege's contextual principle

[1] Ibid., pp. 439–40.
[2] Ibid., p. 444.

needs no stressing'.[1] I doubt that there is any true analogy. Sluga, at least, who conflates the context principle with that of the extraction of functions, ought to doubt it, since, in § 8 of his *Logik*, Lotze says of 'the assertion that in logic the theory of judgment . . . must precede the treatment of concepts' that it is 'over-hasty', and argues that every judgment must be compounded out of ideas which were formed in advance of the judgment arrived at by combining them. 'Pure logic must place the form of the concept before that of the judgment.' Sluga can make it appear that Frege's philosophy was in part derived from Lotze's only by distorting both. The history of art deals with 'influences' based on vague resemblances; but in the history of philosophy superficial analogies reflecting no genuine correspondence of thought are worthless.

There is some excuse for mistaking Frege's intentions, not, indeed, in using the word '*wirklich*', but in enunciating the context principle; it is probable that, at the time of writing *Grundlagen*, he was not himself wholly clear about the matter. In the development of Frege's thought and of his terminology, *Grundlagen* is a transitional work. In *Begriffsschrift*, the term 'content', for that which an expression or a sentence conveys, is used, somewhat as a technical term, though without any precise explanation; it is qualified as judgeable (the content of a sentence) or unjudgeable (that of an expression less than a complete sentence), and also as conceptual or otherwise, the latter distinction corresponding to the later one between sense and tone. From 1891 onwards, the notion of content is replaced by the two notions of sense and reference, and that of judgeable content, in particular, by those of a thought and a truth-value. In *Grundlagen*, however, the term '*Inhalt*' (content) and the cognate verb '*enthalten*' (to have as content) are used in a quite untechnical manner, without the qualification 'conceptual'; the qualification 'judgeable' is used extremely sparingly.[2] In *Begriffsschrift* and other writings of the early period, Frege uses 'individual thing' for what a singular term stands for, whereas in *Grundlagen* the later term 'object' is firmly established. In *Begriffsschrift* itself the word 'concept' is not employed: Frege uses 'function', though not quite consistently, for an incomplete *expression*; for the content of such an expression, he uses 'property' and 'relation' (§ 10). 'Concept' appears, alongside 'property' and 'relation', in 'Booles rechnende Logik', complete with the terminology of 'falling under a concept' and 'subordination';[3] both it and 'object' are used in the unfinished 'Logik'

---

[1] Op. cit., p. 234.
[2] In the footnote to § 66 and in § 70.
[3] *N.S.*, p. 17–20, *P.W.*, pp. 16–18.

of the 1880s.[1] But neither in 'Booles rechnende Logik' nor in *Grund-lagen* is it restricted to the content of a *one*-place predicate, as it was from 1891 onwards: in the former[2] Frege uses the expression 'concept of a relation' (*Begriff einer Relation*), and in *Grundlagen*, § 70, he speaks of 'relation-concepts' (*Beziehungsbegriffe*), as he also does in the 'Logik', contrasting with the 'simple' concepts expressed by one-place predicates. This reflects the fact that Frege did not yet regard 'concept' and 'relation' as co-ordinate terms, as they were in the usage of his mature period; and that in turn reflects the fact that he had not yet drawn the sense/reference distinction. From 1891, a concept is always treated as the *referent* of a one-place predicate, a relation being that of a two-place predicate; but in *Grundlagen* the term 'concept' still carries some of its ordinary connotation of something belonging to the realm of sense. In such passages as § 70 and §§ 46–7, in the latter of which Frege is enunciating his thesis that the content of a statement of number is a predication concerning a concept (*eine Aussage von einem Begriffe*), and arguing that concepts are objective, 'concept' is evidently being used for what would later have been regarded as belonging to the realm of reference; in others, it is used in a more everyday manner, as when, in § 19, Frege discusses whether a geometrical concept of number would suffice for arithmetic, and when, in § 21, he asks whether the concept of number can be classed together with that of colour, and when, in § 29, he observes that the content of a concept diminishes as its extension increases. In reading *Grundlagen*, we must therefore be extremely wary of interpreting the vocabulary after the manner either of the earlier or of the later writings.

In *Begriffsschrift*, Frege employs a turn of phrase very similar to his formulation of the context principle in *Grundlagen*, and employs it to express almost the opposite idea. He says, in § 9 of *Begriffsschrift*, that 'The expression "every positive integer" by itself, unlike "the number 20", yields no independent idea (*selbständige Vorstellung*); it acquires a sense only in the context of a sentence.' Here we are evidently meant to understand that the meaning of a phrase like 'every positive integer' does not consist in its standing for a curious kind of thing, a universal positive integer; rather, it does not stand for anything, but its meaning is given by the way a sentence containing it is to be explained as a whole. It would be entirely wrong to interpret the context principle, as enunciated in *Grundlagen*, in the light of this passage from *Begriffsschrift*, for example as implying that, just as there is no universal positive integer, so there

[1] *N.S.*, p. 1, *P.W.*, p. 1.
[2] *N.S.*, p. 18, *P.W.*, p. 17.

are not really any (individual) numbers. On the contrary, it is absolutely plain that in *Grundlagen* Frege uses the context principle as a justification for saying that there are numbers, that numbers are objective, self-subsistent objects which we speak about just as we speak about cities and planets. Nevertheless, there remains in *Grundlagen* a definite trace of the earlier conception. When Frege introduces the context principle in § 60, he remarks that 'it suffices that the sentence as a whole has a sense; it is this from which its parts obtain their content also'; and he adds a footnote illustrating the remark by reference to a differential equation of the form 'd $f(x) = g(x)$ dx', saying that the point is to define the sense of such an equation as a whole, not to indicate an interval bounded by two distinct points whose length is dx. Here the thought seems to be that the expression 'dx', although it looks like a term standing for an (infinitesimal) number, does not really stand for anything at all and is not therefore really a singular term: the proper explanation of the sense of the equation belies its surface appearance. If so, it may be that Frege came to perceive that, beneath a single form of words, two inconsistent, indeed diametrically opposed, conceptions lay concealed, and that this was the decisive reason for his choosing never to employ that form of words in his subsequent writings. It is not quite clear, however, that he intended his footnote to be understood in just this way. At the end of his review of Hermann Cohen's *Das Prinzip der Infinitesimal-Methode*, which appeared in 1885, he says,[1] 'As far as the foundations of the differential calculus are concerned, one will, I believe, have to go back to the concept of a limit in the sense of analysis, . . . In my *Grundlagen der Arithmetik* (p. 72, fn. 1), I briefly indicated how, on a basis of this kind, one can even secure for the differential a certain self-subsistence (*Selbständigkeit*)'. Possibly, therefore, he saw a definition in terms of limits as guaranteeing a reference for 'dx', though not to an infinitesimal interval.

Just as we asked, of the context principle considered as a thesis concerning sense, whether Frege continued to maintain it after *Grundlagen*, so we must ask the same question about the principle construed as a thesis concerning reference. The answer appears to be much the same as in the previous case, and for the same reason. Frege's thinking is still implicitly guided by the context principle; but, because it will not tally with his classification of sentences, not as forming a logical category on their own, but as a subdivision of the logical category of proper names, he cannot explicitly affirm it as part of his official logical doctrine. There remains

the generalized principle

[1] P. 329.

a shadow of it, as a generalized principle to the effect that an expression has reference only as occurring in context; but Frege feels himself unable to treat occurrence within *sentences* in any special way. The closest he comes to a reiteration of the context principle, as a principle concerning reference, is in a passage in *Grundgesetze*, vol. II, § 97, to which my attention was drawn by Dr Matthias Schirn; there Frege says, 'One may ask about references only where the signs are constituents of sentences that express thoughts.' Taken out of context, this sentence indeed appears to embody an outright reaffirmation of the context principle; but, when we consider the section as a whole, it becomes hard to press the precise wording without confirmation from passages in which Frege is more directly concerned with what is necessary for an expression to have a reference. The section is one in which Frege is criticizing the formalist philosophy of mathematics as expounded by Thomae. In § 91, he observes that 'whereas in meaningful (*inhaltlichen*) arithmetic the equations and inequalities are sentences that express thoughts, in formal arithmetic they are to be compared to positions of chess pieces, which are transformed in accordance with certain rules without regard to any sense'. In § 97, he fastens on Thomae's concession that 'there are cases even in arithmetic in which a not merely formal reference (*Bedeutung*) attaches to numbers'; on this he comments that the formal standpoint cannot always be affirmed, since in the calculating game itself the reference of the signs cannot come into question. It is at this point that he says, 'One may ask about references only where the signs are constituents of sentences that express thoughts.' In the context, it is the natural thing to say: Thomae's concession concerns the occurrence of numerals in the statements of theorems which even he feels forced to acknowledge as expressing thoughts which are to be viewed as true or false, whereas the whole point of the formalist interpretation of arithmetic was to deny that arithmetical statements need to be so regarded. The passage shows, indeed, that Frege did still think along lines that accorded with the context principle; but it can hardly be used as a proof that he still accepted it as his official doctrine.

The passage in *Grundgesetze* which is crucial for the assessment of Frege's later attitude to the context principle, as applied to reference, is § 10 of vol. I, to which I alluded on pp. 196 and 645 of *FPL*, together with its coda, § 31. In these sections, Frege discusses what is required to secure a reference for value-range terms; since, apart from truth-values, value-ranges, including classes (extensions of concepts), form the only specific examples of the category of logical objects, the question which he here attempts to answer could be phrased, in the style of *Grundlagen*, as

'How are logical objects to be given to us?'. The resulting discussion is very much a piece of unfinished business. If the context principle is to be interpreted as proposed above, it may be asked in what way it actually applies to the final account of the senses of numerical terms as given in *Grundlagen*. From Frege's reiteration of the principle in the course of his recapitulation,[1] it is plain that he saw it as providing the correct answer to his question of § 62, 'How are numbers to be given to us?', not as suggesting a plausible answer that had failed to work out in practice. It appears, in the recapitulation, as an essential step in the argument; it leads directly to the need to fix the senses of statements of identity between numbers; and this leads in turn to defining numbers as extensions of concepts.[2] As a conclusion to the preceding discussion of 'other numbers' (negative numbers, rationals, complex numbers, etc.), Frege has again raised the question, 'How are fractions, irrationals and complex numbers to be given to us?',[3] and has likewise replied that we have to fix the senses of statements of identity between such numbers, drawing the conclusion that numbers of all these kinds must also be defined as extensions of concepts. He thus sees the context principle, as his Introduction suggests, as having guided his construction of arithmetic. But how has it guided it? He has ended by giving explicit definitions of cardinal numbers as extensions of concepts; and he proposes to do the same for numbers of other kinds. Surely, in giving an explicit definition of a term, one thereby assigns to it a determinate reference. If so, there will be no need to invoke the context principle to justify ascribing a reference to it: its having a reference does not need to be inferred from the fact that we have fixed the senses of sentences containing it, since we fixed them by laying down what its reference was to be.

This objection is conclusive if we assume that no problem arises over the reference of terms of the form 'the extension of the concept F'. If we know what such a term stands for, then, by defining a numerical term as equivalent to one of this form, we have associated a referent with it. But this does not tell us *how* we know what terms for extensions of concepts stand for; as Frege says,[4] 'we here presuppose the sense of the expression "extension of the concept" as already known'. By defining logical objects of one sort, cardinal numbers, as a subclass of logical objects of another sort, extensions of concepts, we contribute nothing towards an answer to the question how logical objects, in general, are to be given to us. At the conclusion of

[1] *Grundlagen*, § 106.
[2] Ibid., § 107.
[3] Ibid., § 104.
[4] Ibid., § 107.

Grundlagen, that question remains to be answered; and the indications are clear that Frege believed, when he wrote that book, that the answer lay in an appeal to the context principle. To understand his later attitude to that principle, the critical question we must ask is how, in *Grundgesetze*, he proposed to justify the ascription of reference to terms for extensions of concepts, or, more generally, value-ranges.

When he comes to discuss this question in vol. 1, § 10, Frege has laid down that the value-range of a function f is the same as that of a function g, in symbols, that $\dot{\varepsilon} f(\varepsilon) = \dot{\alpha} g(\alpha)$, just in case f and g have the same value for every argument, i.e. $\forall \alpha\, f(\alpha) = g(\alpha)$; this is the stipulation later to be embodied in Axiom V of the formal system. He now asks whether the stipulation is sufficient to determine uniquely the reference of every value-range term, and answers that it is not. The course of the discussion is somewhat tortuous, and is worth setting out in detail. First, Frege argues that we can, so far, recognize an object as being a value-range only when it is designated by a value-range term: for an object not given *as* a value-range, we have no means of deciding whether or not it is a value-range, nor, if it is, of what function it is the extension; nor, for an object given as a value-range, have we the means of deciding whether or not it has a given property, unless that property is expressible in terms of the function of which the value-range is the extension. This argument is exactly parallel to the complaint made by Frege in § 56 of *Grundlagen* that the definitions proposed in § 55 do not enable us to decide whether Julius Caesar is a number or not, that is, whether, for any concept F, he is the number belonging to that concept; and likewise parallel to the objection lodged in § 66 of *Grundlagen* to the contextual definition of 'the direction of ξ' proposed in § 65, namely that it does not enable us to determine whether England is the same as the direction of the Earth's axis, or, in general, the truth of any statement of the form 'The direction of a is the same as q', where 'q' is not of the form 'the direction of b'. The difference is that, in *Grundlagen*, it is assumed that we shall want every such sentence to come out false, whereas, in *Grundgesetze*, there is no presumption that an identity-statement having a value-range term on one side and a term of another kind on the other ought to come out to be false.

Frege now adds the following. Suppose that h is a permutation, i.e. a function whose values are always distinct for distinct arguments. Then '$h(\dot{\varepsilon} f(\varepsilon)) = h(\dot{\alpha} g(\alpha))$' will likewise always have the same truth-value as '$\forall \alpha\, f(\alpha) = g(\alpha)$'; provided that there exists a non-trivial such permutation h, one mapping at least one value-range on to an object other than itself, this shows that the stipulation of Axiom V by no means fully determines the references of value-range terms. On the face of it, this is an entirely different argument. One way of setting it out is as follows. Suppose that there is an assignment of referents to value-range terms that will satisfy Axiom V, and choose some one such assignment θ. Let h be a non-trivial permutation (of all objects), and consider the assignment $\varkappa$ to value-range terms such that, for any object q assigned by θ to any value-range term, $\varkappa$ assigns $h(q)$ to that term. Then $\varkappa$ will also satisfy Axiom V, and will be distinct from θ. Hence, if there is any assignment of referents satisfying Axiom V, there is more than one.

Having, on the basis of these two arguments, established that the stipulation of Axiom V does not uniquely fix the references of value-range terms, Frege asks how the indeterminacy is to be resolved. The answer he gives is, 'By determining for every function, as it is introduced, what values it shall have for value-ranges as arguments, just as for all other arguments.' He proceeds, accordingly, to consider the only three primitive functions that have, up to that point, been introduced, namely identity, the horizontal and negation. Negation can be neglected, since it makes no difference, given an object a, whether we take a itself or ——— a as argument of the negation function. The horizontal, however, may be reduced to identity. ——— ξ is a function that yields the True as value for the True as argument, and the False as value for every other argument: it is therefore extensionally the same as $\xi = (\xi = \xi)$. This leaves us with only identity to deal with. Frege proceeds to treat of this case, and does so rather laboriously. What we have to decide is the value of identity, considered as a function of two arguments whose values are truth-values, for all possible arguments. Axiom V determines its value when both arguments are value-ranges. We have, therefore, only to deal with the case when one of the arguments is given as a value-range, and the other in some other way. So far, however, Frege observes, 'we have introduced as objects only value-ranges and truth-values'. We have, therefore, to consider only the case when one argument is given as a value-range and the other as a truth-value. Now, if neither of the truth-values is a value-range, the value of identity when one argument is a value-range and the other a truth-value is automatically the False. If, on the other hand, each truth-value is the value-range of some specific function, then the stipulation embodied in Axiom V will likewise determine the value of identity when a truth-value is taken as one of the arguments, the other being given as a value-range.

At this point, Frege gives an argument to show two things: first, that

Axiom V is powerless to decide the question whether or not either truth-value is a value-range; and, secondly, that, without contradicting Axiom V, 'it is always possible to stipulate that an arbitrary value-range is to be the True and an arbitrary other value-range the False'. Without following Frege's somewhat tortuous manner of exposition, I will set out this argument in the same style as before. Let θ be, as before, an assignment of referents to value-range terms satisfying Axiom V. Let '$f(\xi)$' and '$g(\xi)$' be function-symbols denoting, respectively, two particular extensionally non-coincident functions, and let θ assign a to '$\acute{\varepsilon} f(\varepsilon)$' and b to '$\acute{\alpha} g(\alpha)$'. Let h be a function such that $h(a)$ is the True, $h(b)$ is the False, h(the True) is a and h(the False) is b, and, for every object x distinct from these, $h(x) = x$. Finally, let $\varkappa$ be an assignment to value–range terms related to θ as before, with respect to the particular permutation h just specified. Then, as before, $\varkappa$ will satisfy Axiom V.

Since we are free to stipulate that the True is to be identified with the value-range of any function whatever, and the False with that of any other extensionally non-equivalent function, Frege proposes to resolve the indeterminacy by making just such a stipulation: the True is to be identified with its own unit class, and the False with its unit class. This is highly reminiscent of a device adopted by Quine in his *Mathematical Logic*.[1] Quine achieves his effect by reinterpreting the membership symbol: '$x \varepsilon y$' is to be understood as meaning 'x is a member of y or is identical with y according as y is or is not a class', with the result that every object not intuitively a class is identified with its own unit class. In a footnote, Frege considers the possibility of extending his stipulation in just such a way, but rejects it as unworkable. His ground is that we could not, consistently with Axiom V, identify every object, including value-ranges, with its own unit class: the greatest generality we could achieve would be to stipulate that every object not given to us as a value-range should be identified with its unit class; and this, he says, would not be tolerable, since the way in which an object is given is not a property of the object, the same object being capable of being given in different ways. This is precisely parallel to Frege's objection, in *Grundlagen* § 67, to the proposal to resolve the analogous difficulty about terms for directions by stipulating that no object not given as a direction was to be taken to be a direction, thus automatically rendering 'the direction of a is identical with q' false if 'q' is not of the form 'the direction of b': Frege there objected that such a stipulation would falsely presuppose that an object can be given in only one single way.

[1] Harvard, 1947, § 22.

Having arrived at this point, then, Frege remarks that he has determined value-ranges to the extent that is so far possible. Whenever a new function is introduced that is not fully reducible to already known functions, it will be stipulated what values it is to have for value-ranges as arguments; this can then be regarded as being as much a determination of value-ranges as of the function in question. It should be noted that Frege does not incorporate the stipulation identifying each of the truth-values with its own unit class into the axioms when he comes to state them. In the same way, in § 11, he stipulates, for his description function \\ξ, both that its value for a unit class as argument shall be the sole member of that unit class, and that its value for any argument not a unit class shall be that argument itself; but, when he formulates the axiom of the system governing the description operator, Axiom VI, it embodies only the first of these two stipulations. For Frege, it is essential to guarantee a determinate interpretation for the system, and, for this purpose, to include, in the informal exposition, enough to determine the reference of every term; but it is unnecessary to embody in the formal axioms more of these stipulations than will actually be required to prove the substantial theorems.

This paragraph of *Grundgesetze* deserves close study. Let us begin by considering the problem from a modern standpoint. A modern logician might enquire whether Frege is concerned with giving a unique intended interpretation of his formal system, or only with characterizing intended models of it up to isomorphism. The solution he provides is a stipulation which, although not in fact embodied in the axioms, is expressible in the language of the system and might have been included in its axioms. But, by laying down the truth of one or more formulas of the system, we cannot possibly discriminate between isomorphic models; the best we could achieve would be a categorical theory, that is, one all of whose models were isomorphic. On the other hand, the way Frege poses the problem at the outset, as that of determining the references of value-range terms, suggests that he has it in mind to specify a unique particular model. This would be possible, but only by specifying outright, in the metalanguage, the references of the primitive expressions, the metalinguistic terms in which the specification is given being taken as already fixed and not up for interpretation: it cannot be done by the means Frege adopts, a stipulation expressible in the object-language.

Such a reaction runs counter to the context principle, according to which a set of stipulations sufficient to determine the truth-values of all formulas of the system is adequate for the determination of the references of its terms. A comparison may be made with the claim that the Peano axioms completely characterize our concept of 'natural number'. To this it may readily be objected, with Russell, that, if we do not assume 'o' and 'successor' as already understood, the Peano axioms yield only the abstract notion of what Russell calls a 'progression', i.e. a sequence of order-type ω; given the natural numbers as one model of the Peano axioms, we can form other distinct, though isomorphic, models from them, such as the odd numbers, 'o' being reinterpreted as standing for 1, and 'S' as standing for the operation of adding 2. But the hypothesis to be criticized is not that every sequence of order-type ω constitutes the totality of natural numbers. It is, rather, that the concept of 'natural number' is given to us as that of a term of a purely abstract sequence of that order-type, abstract in the sense of having no other characteristics whatever than that of being such a sequence; and, against that hypothesis, the observation that we may construct, in terms of the natural numbers, other sequences of the same order-type is quite devoid of force. The hypothesis is tenable only if it is also maintained that we are incapable of forming the conception of any sequence of order-type ω save by explicit or tacit appeal to the concept of 'natural number', but that, given the natural numbers as the prototype of such an infinite sequence, we can define others in terms of it. On this assumption, it becomes nonsensical to suppose that anyone could misinterpret the Peano axioms in terms of the wrong sequence of order-type ω, such as the odd numbers: our understanding of what the number 1 is is given in the first place, on this hypothesis, by the Peano axioms, namely as being the successor of 0, where 'o' and 'successor' are characterized by the axioms; there is therefore no possibility of our mistaking 'o', as it occurs in those axioms, as standing for 1.

Frege's first argument to show that the truth of Axiom V does not determine the references of value-range terms is that it does not settle whether an object that is not given to us as a value-range can be a value-range, or, if so, of what function. It would seem, therefore, that, without the need for any further discussion, this difficulty could be met by a stipulation concerning the identity-relation, such as Frege eventually provides as the solution to the problem; in fact, it is only after considerable further argumentation that he arrives at this stipulation. Care is needed in stating what the stipulation should do. We obviously could not require it to be laid down whether a value-range can be identical with an object that is not a value-range, since a negative answer to this question does not need to be stipulated. It might, therefore, seem natural to express the problem linguistically, as that of determining the truth-value of every identity-statement in which the sign of identity connects a value-range term with a term of some other kind. Frege rightly does not formulate it in this way. We are concerned not only with the references of those value-range terms that can be constructed in the formal language, but with the determination of the second-level function $\dot{\varepsilon}\,\varphi(\varepsilon)$, that is, of the reference of the abstraction operator '$\dot{\varepsilon}\,\varphi(\varepsilon)$': we need to determine the identity-relation between all those objects the existence of which is required by the axioms on the intended interpretation of the system, including the value-ranges of all first-level functions whose existence is so required. Frege therefore does not pose the problem in the linguistic mode; instead, he carefully states it as being that of determining the value of the identity-relation (the function $\xi = \zeta$) when one of its arguments is a value-range.[1]

In so far as Frege is justified in claiming that the only objects required by the system are value-ranges and truth-values, the problem reduces to the one he eventually meets by stipulation, namely whether a truth-value can be a value-range. The justice of the claim cannot be vindicated by inspecting solely the terms that can actually be constructed in the formal language: even when, as in Frege's theory, a description operator is present, the axioms of a theory may demand the existence of more objects than can actually be denoted by terms constructible in the language of the theory. Nevertheless, Frege is right: his theory, had it been consistent, would not have required the domain to include any objects other than value-ranges and truth-values. It is, all the same, somewhat odd, on first appearance, that Frege should appeal to this fact. In the informal exposition occupying Part I of *Grundgesetze*, he attempts no specification of the domain of the individual variables: the reader is left to understand

---

[1] In § 29, he is not so careful, saying that a name for a function of first or second level has a reference provided that the result of inserting in its argument-place a name of the appropriate type (proper name or name of a function of first level) is always a proper name having a reference, given that the name inserted in the argument-place has a reference. This linguistic formulation is adequate only if we tacitly add 'for any conceivable expansion of the formal language which does not require an extension of the domain of the individual variables'. By such an addition, we expressly invoke the domain of objects; the requirement would therefore be better framed directly in terms of values of the functions for arbitrary arguments from the relevant domain, rather than in terms of insertions of symbolic expressions in the argument-places of the function-names. For a proper name, Frege says that it has a reference provided that the result of inserting it into the argument-place of a name of a function of first level is always a proper name having a reference, given that the function-name has a reference—a direct statement of the generalized context principle. In § 30, he comments that these stipulations cannot be regarded as defining the phrase 'has a reference', on account of their recursive character: 'their application always presupposes that some names have already been recognised as having a reference'.

that they range over all objects whatever. If so, it seems obscure why the references of value-range terms are fixed by determining the relation of identity between value-ranges and just those two objects, not given as value-ranges, which Frege's axioms *require* to be in the domain: it seems that it ought to be necessary to determine the identity-relation as between a value-range and any other object of any kind. It is admitted that we have not yet determined for which object each value-range term stands; our stipulations do not yet settle whether, for example, any such term stands for the Moon. A complete determination of the reference of each such term ought, surely, to settle that question, one way or the other: the fact that the Moon cannot be referred to in the language of the system, or that it need not fall within the domain of a model of the axioms, appears irrelevant, especially if the Moon is meant, on the intended interpretation, to be included in the domain.

Frege does not proceed immediately to make the stipulation concerning the identity-relation by which his first argument could evidently have been met. Instead, he gives a second, more general, argument, the permutation argument, to show that Axiom V does not determine the references of value-range terms. In face of this more general argument, a general solution is demanded. As the basic principle governing any such solution, Frege states that the references of value-range terms will have been fixed when we have determined for every function, when it is introduced, what values it assumes for value-ranges as arguments. Stated generally, in respect of any range of proper names, rather than just of value-range terms, the principle is that the references of those names are fixed when it has been determined, for every (primitive) function, what the value of that function is to be for the referent of any of those names as argument or as one of the arguments. This is still not quite general enough, since, in the given case, we are, as noted above, concerned with every value-range, not just with those for which we can construct actual terms (proper names). The general form of the principle thus comes to be this. Given a primitive function (of any level), that function will have been determined if we have determined, for every primitive first-level function, what the value of the latter function is to be for a value of the former function as argument or as one of the arguments.

This is, in effect, a generalization of the context principle. It is a generalization, in that it allots no distinguished place to sentences (names of truth-values). We can here see very clearly how Frege's later assimilation of sentences to complex proper names has caused him to abandon the context principle in its original form: instead of requiring that a truth-value be determined for every atomic sentence formed by putting a value-range term in the argument-place of every primitive first-level predicate and relational expression, or, more generally, that every primitive first-level concept and relation be defined over all value-ranges, Frege feels that he is not entitled to make any distinction between primitive concepts and relations and other primitive functions, between primitive predicates and relational expressions and any other primitive functional expressions. He nevertheless retains the context principle—or what, in *FPL*,[1] I referred to as its echo—as far as can be done without distinguishing between sentences and other complex proper names, between concepts or relations and other functions. The resulting doctrine is not clearly coherent. Right or wrong, it is perfectly coherent to hold that it suffices to lay down determinate conditions under which each sentence is true or false, and that a reference is thereby determined for the proper names occurring in those sentences. But when sentences are deprived of their distinguished role, it becomes unclear what the doctrine is. It is required that every proper name should have a reference. In stipulating a reference for functional expressions, and so for the complex proper names formed by means of them, we must at some stage directly stipulate the references of some of these proper names. If this can be done for some of them, why cannot it be done for all? In what way is the reference of a proper name, when not directly stipulated, indirectly fixed by stipulations as to the reference of more complex proper names containing it? The rationale is clear for saying that a proper name, like every other expression, has significance only as occurring in a sentence, and that therefore all we need to know is its contribution to the truth-conditions of sentences containing it. But, when sentences are deprived of their unique status, all that remains is that a word or symbol has significance only as it occurs in some complete expression, i.e. proper name; its significance will then consist in its contribution to fixing the reference of a proper name of which it is a part. But if it is itself a proper name, it must have a reference in its own right: there seems neither ground nor explanation for the claim that, by fixing the references of proper names of which it is a proper part, we thereby fix its reference, considered on its own. The context principle, in its original form, is an intelligible doctrine; its echo is scarcely so.

Frege raises this problem at a stage at which he has not yet introduced all the primitive expressions of his system, and he therefore considers only the functions denoted by the three primitives, other than the abstraction

---

[1] P. 196.

operator, that he has introduced. As it happens, these functions are all either concepts or relations, that is to say, always take truth-values as values; the horizontal and negation functions are concepts and identity is of course a relation. This fact is not stressed by Frege, however, in his discussion; and, as remarked, the general principle that he has enunciated does not distinguish concepts and relations from other functions. Moreover, it so happens that Frege is able to reduce the case of the negation function to that of the horizontal, and that of the horizontal in turn to that of identity, so that, in the end, the question comes back to that of deciding whether objects not given as value-ranges are to be identified with value-ranges, which was all that Frege's first argument appeared to require. It remains that the general principle which, in this particular case, is found to be satisfied by such a stipulation, is not one specifically concerning identity, or even the context principle in the form in which it is stated in *Grundlagen*, but a generalization of that principle which no longer accords a distinguished role to sentences.

How far does Frege's stipulation, identifying the two truth-values with their own unit classes, achieve the intended effect of fixing the references of value-range terms? It was argued above that, in so far as the intended interpretation involves the inclusion of *all* objects, including ones which we can name in natural language, though not in the language of the formal system, in the domain of the individual variables, the stipulation appears to fail in its purpose, in that it fails to tell us, of such objects as the Moon or Copenhagen, whether or not they are to be identified with any value-ranges. In *Grundlagen* Frege complains, of certain proposed definitions, that they fail to determine whether Julius Caesar is a number or England a direction. The explicit definition of numbers and directions as extensions of concepts, i.e. as classes, is supposed to take care of that; the assumption must be that we know how to determine whether or not Julius Caesar and England are classes (Frege is obviously taking it for granted, in *Grundlagen*, that they are not). In *Grundgesetze*, numbers are again defined as classes, that is, as a particular type of value-range; but this does not determine whether or not Julius Caesar is a number unless we know whether or not he is a value-range. Indeed, the difficulty does not depend upon the assumption that the domain is all-inclusive and contains *all* objects. Suppose that it be agreed that the domain of the individual variables is to contain only such objects as are required to exist by the axioms of *Grundgesetze*, and thus only value-ranges and truth-values. We still do not know whether or not one of the value-ranges included in the domain may be Julius Caesar and another England. Frege assumes that it is sufficient to determine the identity-relation between objects given as values of functions expressible in the system. The context principle certainly implies that this would be adequate if the language of the system were the only language that we had. But it is not the only language that we have: we start with natural language, and it is natural language, supplemented, indeed, by technical terms Frege has explained in natural language, that serves as the metalanguage in which the interpretation of the system has been set out. In natural language, we can refer to the referent of a value-range term of the formal system, say the term '$\dot{\varepsilon}\,(\varepsilon = \varepsilon)$', by means of a phrase like 'the referent of "$\dot{\varepsilon}\,(\varepsilon = \varepsilon)$" in the system of *Grundgesetze*'; and, on Frege's own principles, the reference of this phrase has not been fully determined, since we have no way to decide the truth or falsity of, e.g., 'The referent of "$\dot{\varepsilon}\,(\varepsilon = \varepsilon)$" is Julius Caesar'. It seems a strange doctrine (stated in the metalanguage) that the reference of the expression '$\dot{\varepsilon}\,(\varepsilon = \varepsilon)$' of the object-language has been determined, but not that of the metalinguistic expression 'the referent of "$\dot{\varepsilon}\,(\varepsilon = \varepsilon)$" '.

Frege here by implication advances a thesis of the relativity of reference to language that does not appear to be entailed by the context principle as originally formulated. Suppose that the language of the system of *Grundgesetze* were expanded to allow the formation of singular terms of some new kind. Then, on Frege's principles, the referents of value-range terms in this expanded language would not have been fully fixed until we had stipulated the truth-value of each identity-statement connecting a value-range term with one of these new terms. But, if the references of value-range terms had already been fully determined in the original language, how could they become indeterminate by the mere expansion of the language? The problem did not arise in this form in *Grundlagen*, because Frege was not working with a formalized language, but within natural language, supplemented by the use of bound variables. But it seems natural to demand that whatever is deemed to fix the reference of value-range terms should provide in advance for the effects of introducing any possible new terms, in so far as we are now capable of formulating whatever specification we shall in fact give of the references of such new terms otherwise than by alluding to or quantifying over value-ranges.

These difficulties could be overcome in various ways. First, whether or not human beings and celestial bodies were to be taken from the outset as lying within the domain of the individual variables, we could, if there were enough of them, and we had some specific means of correlating objects of these two sorts with the functions required to exist by the theory, decree that the value-range of each function was to be identified with the person or heavenly body correlated with it. In something of the same way, Frege could, in the *Grundlagen*, have solved his problem concerning directions by arbitrarily choosing some point O as origin, and identifying the direction of any line a with the line through O parallel to a. (It is to be assumed that we know enough about England, and about lines, to be able to say that England is not a line.) When this method is adopted, there is no need to invoke the context principle to justify the ascription of a reference to the terms in question, terms for directions or for value-ranges. On the contrary, it represents a conception according to which we start with a domain of objects, which we grasp in advance of acquiring any notion of directions, in the one case, or of value-ranges, in the other. In the geometrical case, it would be natural to take this domain as consisting of points, lines and planes; for the system of *Grundgesetze*, it might be taken to consist of animals, celestial bodies and other familiar objects, material or otherwise. In each case, the operator in question, 'the direction of ξ' or the abstraction operator, is then introduced as standing for some one function, satisfying the stipulated condition, with values in the antecedently given domain; there will, in general, be many such functions (provided that there is any at all), but we are indifferent which function the operator is taken as denoting. Thus, in the *Grundgesetze* system, the abstraction operator is introduced as standing for some one mapping of first-level functions, defined over the given domain, on to objects in that domain, satisfying Axiom V. The values of the second-level function which effects this mapping, denoted by the abstraction operator, are thus not themselves abstract objects, but simply whatever familiar concrete objects—Julius Caesar, the Moon and the like—have been taken as included in the domain, just as, on the analogous conception, directions of lines are not objects of some *new* kind, but simply certain particular lines under a new guise. On this conception, therefore, it is value-range *terms*, not their referents, which are abstract. Axiom V does not, of course, decide for *which* mapping of functions on to objects the abstraction operator stands; it lays down conditions which, as Frege's permutation argument shows, if satisfied by any second-level function, are satisfied by many others. Nothing of importance in the theory depends upon which second-level function is chosen; but, if we feel it necessary to specify, we must do so by finding a suitable correlation of functions defined over the domain with objects in the domain.

In fact, of course, no mapping satisfying Frege's Axiom V can exist. If there are n objects in the domain, where n may be finite or transfinite, there are n^n extensionally distinct functions over the domain; Axiom V demands that extensionally distinct functions be mapped on to distinct objects, which is impossible since $n^n > n$ for $n > 1$. Frege's emendation of Axiom V in the Appendix to *Grundgesetze*, vol. II, does not help much, since it only reduces the number of functions having distinct value-ranges to n^{n-1}, and $n^{n-1} > n$ for $n > 2$. But, even if we prescind from the exact character of Axiom V, this first method is impracticable for value-ranges, though quite practicable for directions, since any reasonable axiom will require the existence of infinitely many value-ranges, if the construction of the natural numbers is to be possible, and of non-denumerably many, if that of the real numbers is to be possible; hence, not only do we lack a systematic means of correlating functions to antecedently given objects, but no sufficient supply of material objects is available.

A second method would be to scrap Frege's stipulation concerning truth-values, and simply to decree that every object not given as a value-range shall be deemed to be distinct from every value-range. This is the method considered, but rejected, by Frege in *Grundlagen*, § 67, as a means of overcoming the analogous difficulty concerning directions. The analogy is, indeed, very exact. The proposed contextual definition of directions, and the proposed contextual definition of numbers with which it is being taken as analogous, specify the condition for the truth of an identity-statement connecting two terms of the kind being introduced, namely, in the one case, terms for directions, and, in the other, numerical terms. Axiom V does the very same thing for value-range terms: it is in exact formal analogy with the proposed contextual definition of the operator 'the number of Φs'. The sole significant difference lies in the fact that neither Axiom V, nor the informal stipulation corresponding to it, is held to be, or to be part of, any kind of *definition*, as is emphasized in *Grundgesetze*, vol. II, § 146. And, in both cases, it is the same difficulty that arises as that which arises over value-ranges: the stipulation in question, contextual definition or axiom, does not suffice to determine the truth-value of an identity-statement connecting a term of the form under consideration with a term of another kind. In *Grundlagen*, the difficulty is met by adopting explicit definitions of 'the direction of ξ' and of 'the number of Φs', which identify directions and numbers with certain classes: this solution is obviously unavailable in *Grundgesetze*. The solution presently being considered, the second method stated above, amounts, in effect, to declaring that we have no way of referring to value-ranges save *as* value-ranges, so that an object may be recognized as not being a value-range from the mere fact of its not being given as a value-range. To admit this possibility seems wholly in the spirit of the context principle: value-range terms have reference because they behave as singular terms, and sentences containing them have determinable truth-conditions; it is unnecessary to secure a reference for them by using some other means of picking out the objects for which they are to stand.

A third possibility would be to generalize the stipulation that Frege makes concerning truth-values, by laying down that every object not given as a value-range is to be identified with its own unit class. This is the suggestion considered, and rejected, by Frege in his footnote to § 10 of *Grundgesetze*, vol. 1; and, as we saw, it is what Quine actually does. Quine is able to do what Frege considers impossible because he helps himself to the intuitive notion of a class. We are assumed to know in advance which objects are, and which are not, classes in the intuitive sense; and we appeal to this notion so as to redefine '$x \varepsilon y$' to mean 'y is a class and x is a member of y or y is not a class and $x = y$'. Given this reinterpretation, we can define 'y is a class' to mean 'Either, for every x, $x \notin y$, or, for some x, $x \in y$ and $x \neq y$': but it was only because we understood the notion in advance of its definition that we are able to understand the definition. But, were Frege to have assumed that we know from the outset which objects are value-ranges and which are not, he would have had no problem.

Now, as we already saw, in *Grundlagen* Frege rejected the analogue of the second method, and in *Grundgesetze* he rejected the third method, by appeal, in each case, to the same argument, namely that we should be wrongly making the way an object is given or presented into a characteristic of the object. What substance does this argument have? It amounts to saying that we cannot in general tell, from the fact that an object is not given as a value-range, that is, that it is being referred to by means of a term other than a value-range term, that we may not have to recognize it as being a value-range. And this is true. Within the system, there are terms formed by means of the description operator: there can be no general guarantee that we can immediately decide, for every definite description, whether or not we must take it as standing for a value-range. Outside the system, there are, e.g., terms for natural numbers and for real numbers, objects which in *Grundgesetze* are defined to be value-ranges of certain kinds; but we should not ordinarily understand terms for numbers of either kind as standing for value-ranges. In this case, too, we cannot tell in advance *which* objects logical analysis may compel us to recognize as being value-ranges. There may be some objects about which we may be fairly sure that this is not so, lobsters for example: but both the second method and the third require us to be able to say of every object whether or not it is *required* to be a value-range, in order to go on to make stipulations concerning all those that are not so required.

We seem to have reached an impasse. It appeared, earlier, that Frege's stipulations, restricted to truth-values, were insufficiently general, and we considered three methods of remedying this. The first was impracticable; and now it seems that Frege's objection to the second and third methods is sound. Perhaps our original line of argument was mistaken; perhaps we need to think again about our objections to Frege's implicit relativism concerning reference.

The right way of looking at the matter is surely as follows. Instead of regarding Frege's system, in the conventional way, as once for all bounded by the primitive symbols introduced, and axioms stated, at the outset, let us view it as something capable of growing by the addition of new vocabulary and new axioms. As such, it represents the beginnings of a reconstruction of the conceptual apparatus embodied in our language. What is given at the outset as primitive will remain primitive: but it is not determined in advance which new notions will be introduced, either by defining them in terms of the existing primitives or by adding them as new primitives, governed by new axioms. (I am, of course, still prescinding from the inconsistency of the system.) Now what we *know* is that the notion of a value-range is to be taken as primitive. At the outset, we do not know whether the notion of a cardinal number, of a point in space, or of a mountain-peak, will be introduced at all, or, if it is, how it will be introduced. Any such notion may be introduced by definition, e.g. as covering value-ranges of a particular kind; or it may be introduced by means of a new primitive, allowing the formation of new terms. If a new primitive is introduced, it is desirable that the new axioms should either be known to yield a proof within the system that the objects denoted by the new terms are or are not value-ranges, or else should allow us to demonstrate in the metalanguage that they do not require us either to identify them with or to discriminate them from value-ranges. In the latter case, we are free to make any stipulation we find convenient, as Frege was free to declare truth-values not to be value-ranges, had he so preferred. Definite descriptions, admittedly, do not satisfy this requirement: but, if the application of every predicate of the system has been rendered determinate under the intended interpretation, then the referent of each definite description has thereby been determined, so that no problem arises even when *we* cannot decide what the referent is.

On this view, the references of value-range terms do not depend upon our subsequent stipulations concerning other primitive expressions. We need to respect, not merely the priority of primitive expressions over defined ones, but also the order in which undefined expressions are introduced as the system expands: in this reconstruction of our conceptual apparatus, the notion of a value-range is not merely primitive, in the sense of not being defined, but basic, in the sense of being introduced at the outset. The reason for respecting the order of introduction is twofold. First, if the system, thought of as in growth, is really to represent a reconstruction of our conceptual apparatus, the order of introduction of the notions expressed by simple designations, defined or undefined, must be an order in which those notions can be acquired, not necessarily by one having no antecedent language, but at least by one who knows natural language. Hence any later stipulations, regarding new terms, as to whether their referents are or are not to be identified with value-ranges are to be regarded as going to fix the references of the new terms, not of the value-range terms we were presumed to understand at the outset.

Secondly, in order to grasp the intended interpretation of the system at each stage of its growth, it is necessary to have a clear conception of the domain; and this cannot be mediated, at any stage, by notions not yet expressed in the system. Thus, at the outset, we need not think of the domain as comprising all objects to which we can now refer in natural language: it need contain only those objects which our original set of axioms require to be included, viz. value-ranges and truth-values. As the system expands, it may or may not be found necessary to expand the domain. When the reconstruction is complete, the domain will, indeed, comprise all objects whatsoever; but, at that stage, all problems of identification between objects presented in different ways, i.e. referred to by terms of various forms, will have been resolved. Thus the notions expressed in natural language are not to be straightforwardly *identified* with the corresponding ones in the formal system. The latter are *reconstructed* ones, introduced in a different order, and by different means, from those of natural language. Hence we cannot, strictly speaking, mix the two languages. If we introduce the notion of a value-range into natural language, we introduce it into a framework in which we already have the conception of many different sorts of object, concrete and abstract; and then, to make the notion definite, we must do as Frege says, and indicate whether value-ranges are to be objects of a wholly new sort, or are to be identified with any of the objects to which we already refer in other ways. But, by speaking, in natural language, of the referents of the value-range terms of Frege's system, we mix the two languages, the unreconstructed and the reconstructed ones, in a manner that is, strictly speaking, illegitimate.

I do not myself believe that any such reconstruction could be attained within the confines of a single formalized language, precisely because it appears to me that the primary lesson of the paradoxes is that we cannot consistently assume an all-embracing domain of all objects whatever. Nor can I claim the authority of Frege for this interpretation; but I think it must approximate to his perspective. It is the closest I can get to an account which would justify his implicit relativism concerning reference, his treating the reference of terms of the formal system as relative to the language of the system, not to our total linguistic equipment. On such a view, it would not be strictly true to say that a value-range could be referred to only *as* a value-range. It could be referred to by means of a definite description; it could, given Frege's actual stipulation, be referred to as a truth-value; and it could, using a defined expression, be referred to as a cardinal number. What would be true is that it is not by appeal to the identification of a value-range with any object given otherwise than as a value-range that we grasp the reference of value-range terms, or that of the functional expression '$\grave{\varepsilon}\,\varphi(\varepsilon)$'. We understand value-range terms just by grasping the truth-conditions of sentences containing such terms, sentences of the language as it is when we first employ such terms, namely at the outset: that this is enough is precisely the content of the context principle.

The interpretation thus suggested does not, indeed, wholly fit everything that Frege says. In particular, it does not agree with his saying, at the end of § 10, that when new primitive functions are introduced, the specification of their values for value-ranges as arguments not only serves to determine those functions, but also to determine what value-ranges are; on the view just sketched, the references of those value-range terms that can be formed in the original notation of the system have been fixed once and for all, and any stipulations concerning functional expressions subsequently introduced serve only to fix the references of those functional expressions and of the terms formed from them. The present interpretation does, on the other hand, fit Frege's denial, in 'Logik in der Mathematik', that analytical definitions normally preserve unmodified the senses previously attached to the words defined. Against this may be set the fact alluded to in Chapter 2, that he does not represent the formulas of his logical notation as expressing thoughts not expressible in natural language; but we might explain this as relating solely to the use of the method of expression, by means of quantifiers, bound variables, sentential operators, etc., rather than to the specific formal language used in *Grundgesetze*. The fact of the matter probably is, however, that no firm opinion on these questions is to be ascribed to Frege: we have to consider different possible interpretations, without presupposing that some one particular one was his.

In any case, the present interpretation involves an enormously difficult conception. According to it, at the outset of the construction of the system of *Grundgesetze*, our grasp of the domain of the individual variables of the system is *not* mediated by any notions, given from without, that is, from our understanding of natural language, of different sorts of objects, e.g. material objects, notions which we as yet lack a means of expressing within the formal language. Rather, our initial grasp of the domain is acquired solely through our grasp of the notions, basic to the system, of value-ranges and of truth-values. We thus have to form, at the outset, a bare conception of a domain consisting of the two truth-values and of the values of a second-level function, the abstraction function, mapping first-level functions defined over that very domain into the domain (on to it, when we identify the truth-values with their own unit classes), that function being one that satisfies Axiom V (or, rather, some consistent replacement of it). Except for the two truth-values, these objects possess no characteristics save for their being the values of the abstraction function, that is, the value-ranges of certain first-level functions defined over them. On this conception, if, later in the development of the system, we either define certain objects, say numbers, as being particular value-ranges, or introduce new undefined primitives, the terms constructed out of which we stipulate informally to stand for certain value-ranges, we do not thereby make our original notion of a value-range, or our original grasp of the domain, more determinate. (It is at just this point that the conception I am expounding departs from what Frege says; but I cannot see how to defend what he actually asserts.) Our notion of a value-range, and our grasp of the domain, are not *filled out* by these subsequently introduced notions; if they were, there would have been something lacking in them before those notions were introduced into the system. When we introduce, by definition, the notion of cardinal number into the system, we are not, on this conception, *importing* into it our pre-existing, though unanalysed, notion of cardinal numbers: we are reconstructing that notion in terms of our notion of value-ranges. Likewise, if we were to introduce into the system, as new primitives, the means of referring to spatial points, and stipulated either that points were to be distinct from all value-ranges, or that they were to coincide with their own unit classes, we should be expanding the domain. But if we were to stipulate that they were to coincide with certain value-ranges whose existence was already required before the introduction of terms for spatial points, then, again, we should not be filling out our previous conception of those value-ranges by the importation of an already given notion of spatial points. We should, rather, be exploiting our previously attained conception of value-ranges in order to provide a reconstruction of the everyday notion of spatial points; our understanding of the reconstructed notion would not in principle depend upon our already having the everyday notion.

Even if the condition laid down by Axiom V were one whose fulfilment was a logical possibility, the idea that we could form so abstract a conception as this interpretation requires is hard to accept, and one of whose coherence it is difficult to feel assured. And yet, if the context principle, taken as a principle concerning reference, has any real substance, and if, so taken, it is sound, it appears to legitimize such a conception. It is important that, on this interpretation, the system is not to be thought of as one admitting distinct specific models: though its objects, the value-ranges, appear shadowy, with an impoverished supply of qualities, the context principle demands that we should recognize them as fully determinate. The analogy suggested earlier with the conception of the natural numbers as forming a prototypical sequence of order-type ω, having no other characteristics, is reasonably exact: the context principle would prohibit us from objecting that the Peano axioms *could* not serve to characterize the natural numbers uniquely, but can only be taken as exhibiting the structure of many distinct, though isomorphic, particular totalities; they *can* be so taken, but only *after* we have, by means of them, first attained the conception of the prototype. (This, of course, is not Frege's conception of the natural numbers: no more than an analogy is intended.) In favour of this interpretation, it may be asked how else we are supposed to attain a grasp of totalities of abstract objects of higher cardinalities. The first method, under which the domain was grasped in the first place as constituted by ordinary material objects, was impracticable, for the obvious reason that we have no reason to suppose it sufficiently large, or, indeed, even denumerable. We might, of course, appeal instead to our pre-systematic conceptions of natural numbers, real numbers, etc.: but still the question would arise how we came by those conceptions. This was the problem that was to occupy Frege at the very end of his life: how do we come by the conception of infinite totalities in general, or, in particular, of non-denumerable ones? In his last writings, he fell back on an appeal to geometrical intuition to supply an answer to this question.

It could be objected, not without justice, that this interpretation is unFregean. Dedekind said something at first sight like this, when he remarked that many will not recognize their old friends the natural numbers in the shadowy shapes in which he introduces them,[1] and Frege evinced little sympathy for his general view. This particular objection is unsound, for there is a crucial difference between Dedekind's viewpoint concerning the natural numbers and that which I have been using as an analogy for Frege's view of the value-ranges of his formal system, under the interpretation being considered. On the latter view, the Peano axioms characterize a single, determinate sequence of order-type ω, the natural numbers; other such sequences can be defined only in terms of that one, and a conception of them arrived at only after we first have the conception of the natural numbers. But Dedekind appeals to the psychological process of abstraction, invoked also by Husserl, Cantor and many others, and constantly inveighed against by Frege. Dedekind gives a general characterization of a 'simply infinite system', i.e. a sequence of order-type ω, and then remarks that 'if, in contemplating a simply infinite system N, ordered by a representation φ, we disregard entirely the particular character of the elements, retaining only the possibility of distinguishing them and considering only the relations in which they are placed by the ordering representation φ, then these elements are called *natural numbers*'.[2] In other words, for Dedekind we are able, *before* arriving at the notion of 'natural number', to conceive of many distinct sequences of order-type ω; we obtain the concept of 'natural number' by disregarding what differentiates such sequences, and thus attain to what is in common between them all. This is not at all an analogue for Frege's view, under the interpretation I am expounding.

Nevertheless, it may with a good deal more force be urged that Frege's criticisms of Hilbert's *Grundlagen der Geometrie* could hardly have been made by a man who thought in the manner I am suggesting. Frege remarked that Hilbert's axioms did not enable one to decide, of a given object, whether or not it was a point, and hence did not, as Hilbert claimed, contain an implicit definition of 'ξ is a point'.[3] Yet would Frege himself not be vulnerable to a similar criticism, that Axiom V, taken together with the additional informal stipulation, does not suffice to determine, of any given object, whether or not it was a value-range? Of course, on the interpretation suggested above, there would be an answer to this. *Within* the reconstructed language, of which the formal language of *Grundgesetze* represents the first stage, our notion of an object begins with value-ranges and truth-values, and, of any object presented in accordance with any

[1] *Was sind und was sollen die Zahlen?*, second edition, Brunswick, 1893, p. ix.
[2] Ibid., § 73.
[3] 'Über die Grundlagen der Geometrie', 1903, p. 370.

subsequent definition or expansion of the language, we must have made stipulations sufficient to determine whether or not it is a value-range. We cannot ask, at the initial stage, whether we can determine, of a given object, whether or not it is a value-range, save for asking this concerning the truth-values, the very point Frege resolves in § 10 of *Grundgesetze*, vol. I. We cannot ask this, because, within the reconstruction, it is via the notion of a value-range that we first grasp any domain of objects; before we have this notion, we cannot be given any object at all. This answer is available only if we take seriously the view of the formal system as the first stage of a total reconstruction of our conceptual apparatus and of our language: Frege could make the criticism of Hilbert's geometrical theory that he did only on the assumption that it was not to be part of any such reconstruction, but something to be added to natural language. But, if so, there is no trace of Frege's having made the relevant enquiry into Hilbert's intentions, or conceding that his criticisms would lose their force on a certain view of what it was that Hilbert was about. As already remarked, reflection on Frege's remarks on these matters fails to reveal, to me at least, a determinate conception that can with any confidence be ascribed to him of how abstract objects are to be introduced, in what our grasp of the references of abstract terms consists. Perhaps others can do better; or perhaps there is no solution to be found to the question what, precisely, it was that he thought.

At first sight, a strong ground against the correctness of the suggested interpretation is Frege's use of the permutation argument. That this argument to show that Axiom V does not determine the references of value-range terms really is distinct from the first argument to that effect is apparent from the possibility of considering the permutation as a non-trivial one defined over the whole domain, for which the two truth-values are fixed points. So considered, the permutation argument involves a rejection of the suggested application of the context principle. The thesis that the references of value-range terms are fixed by Axiom V, together with the additional stipulation concerning truth-values, is impugned by the permutation argument, since Axiom V and Frege's additional stipulation would both remain unaffected by a permutation of the kind mentioned. The parallel with the argument against the thesis that the Peano axioms characterize the concept of 'natural number' is very close. That argument denied that the Peano axioms can characterize for us any specific totality, on the ground that, given such a totality, we could describe, in terms of it, another model of the Peano axioms. The answer to it, in the light of the context principle, was that the argument fails to establish its conclusion, *if* no model of the Peano axioms, other than the natural numbers, can be described save by appeal to the natural numbers. This latter condition is plausible if it be supposed that a model whose elements are not themselves natural numbers can be described only as consisting of the values of a function defined by recursion over the natural numbers. Likewise, the permutation argument denies that Frege's stipulations concerning value-ranges can determine uniquely what each value-range term stands for, on the ground that, given any one interpretation, we can describe a distinct but equally sound interpretation by appeal to some permutation of the original referents. In the light of the context principle, a similar reply can be given: the argument fails if the only way to describe the alternative interpretation is in terms of a permutation defined with respect to the original interpretation.

Frege's use of the permutation argument is inconclusive against the suggested way of interpreting his thought on this matter for two reasons. First, not only does it conflict with the suggested application of the context principle; it is incompatible with the principle itself, on the most rudimentary understanding of it. Not only would Axiom V remain true under a permutation that left the two truth-values invariant, but the truth-value of every formula of the system would remain unaffected. At first sight, a permutation which interchanged the referents of what, in notation more familiar than Frege's, I will write as '$\{0, 1\}$' and '$\{0\}$', leaving all else invariant, would falsify the formal statement that $\{0, 1\}$ had two members and $\{0\}$ only one. But of course this is not so. The relation of class-membership, or, more generally, the application function, like every other concept, relation and function defined over value-ranges in Frege's system, is defined in terms of the function of which the value-range taken as argument is the extension. Specifically, '$a \cap u$' is defined to mean '$\backslash \grave{\alpha}(\exists \mathscr{g}\ (u = \grave{\varepsilon}\ \mathscr{g}\ (\varepsilon)\ \&\ \alpha = \mathscr{g}\ (a))$', where '$\backslash \xi$' is Frege's description operator, which acts on a unit class to extract its sole member; thus '$a \cap \grave{\varepsilon}\ f(\varepsilon)$' reduces to '$f(a)$', and, where '$F(\xi)$' is a predicate, '$a \cap \grave{\varepsilon}\ F(\varepsilon)$' reduces to '$F(a)$'. Hence, despite the permutation, which assigns to '$\{0, 1\}$' a class which 'really' has only one member, the formula saying that $\{0, 1\}$ has two members remains true, since it reduces to the statement that there are two objects satisfying the predicate '$\xi = 0$ or $\xi = 1$'. The permutation argument thus entails that the references of the terms may change even though no single sentence of the formal language undergoes any alteration in truth-value. This consequence is in flat contradiction with the context principle, unless the formal language is being thought of as embeddable in a richer language containing sentences whose truth-value *would* alter, or as an addition to, rather than a replacement for, natural language. If the context principle is sound, the permutation argument was therefore fallacious in the first place. It presupposes a connection between proper names and their referents that transcends what is required for a determination of the truth-values of sentences containing those proper names; but the context principle stigmatizes as spurious any such transcendent connection. According to the context principle, when the truth-values of all statements containing a proper name have been fixed, there is no further question as to *which* object it is that the name stands for; any supposition that the abstraction operator could be taken as standing, now for one mapping of functions on to objects, now for another, without altering the truth-value of any statement involving it, is therefore phantasmal.

Secondly, just for this reason, Frege's solution of the problem he raises gives not the slightest appearance of meeting the permutation argument. This applies both to his specific solution, by making the stipulation concerning truth-values, and to the general principle, the generalization or echo of the original context principle, which he enunciates concerning what is required to fix the references of value-range terms. Permutations remain as possible after the stipulation as they were before; if the permutation argument proved that the references of value-range terms were not fixed by Axiom V, it also proves that they are not fixed by the addition of the new stipulation, or by any that could be expressed in the formal language. It embodies, in other words, that view stated at the outset of this discussion as the view natural to a modern logician, that, by means of stipulations expressible in the formal language, one could not discriminate between isomorphic models. It is not to be objected that Frege is concerned with permutations as defined *within* the system rather than in the metalanguage. If '$h(\xi)$' is an expression of the formal language for the permutation which interchanges $\{0, 1\}$ and $\{0\}$, it is true that Axiom V will still hold when '$h(\grave{\varepsilon}\,f(\varepsilon))$' replaces '$\grave{\varepsilon}\,f(\varepsilon)$' and '$h(\acute{\alpha}\,g(\alpha))$' replaces '$\acute{\alpha}\,g(\alpha)$'; yet it will be possible to prove that the referent of '$h(\{0, 1\})$' has only one member. But, just for that very reason, no additional stipulation is needed to show that '$\{0, 1\}$' and '$h(\{0, 1\})$' have different referents: the problem arises only for a permutation defined in the metalanguage that respects the truth of every theorem. It is also no use to invoke permutations that might alter the truth-values of formulas neither provable nor refutable in the system. No doubt Frege would have claimed his axioms, taken together with the additional informal stipulations not embodied in them, as yielding a complete theory: to impute to him an awareness of the incompleteness of higher-order theories would be an anachronism.

For these reasons, we ought not to take the permutation argument very seriously as a guide to Frege's thinking: he states it as if valid, but makes no attempt to meet it on its own terms. It reveals, perhaps, a passing infirmity of grasp by him on his generalized context principle, a tendency to conceive of reference as a relation not necessarily reflected in linguistic practice; but, if so, the lapse was momentary. From his discussion in *Grundgesetze*, vol. 1, § 10, we can see very plainly how Frege stood, in his mature period, towards the context principle, taken as a thesis concerning reference. He appears to be advancing a view to which the context principle, in its original form, with sentences playing a distinguished role, is integral. However, this interpretation of his intentions is unsure; he is far from explicit, and there are things which he says that tell against it. He does not seem to have had a fully consistent, and certainly not an unwavering, view concerning how the references of abstract terms are to be fixed, generally or in his formal system; we are in the presence of ideas that have not been fully thought through. He comes as close as he can to actually formulating the context principle without admitting a distinction between sentences and other proper names as significant in this regard; and the result, as we saw, is a doctrine that is not clearly coherent. My claim that Frege's failure, in his later writings, to reiterate the original principle, was due to his assimilation of sentences to proper names, was not a mere deduction from a thesis ascribed to him by me, however reasonably ascribed. Rather, it is plain to see from this crucial discussion, in *Grundgesetze*, of the very point concerning which, in *Grundlagen*, the context principle was originally invoked, namely the determination of the references of abstract proper names.

For all that, it is natural to feel that, as a defence of the ascription of reference to terms for abstract objects, the context principle is unsuccessful. In general, the notion of reference is to be invoked in explaining the sense of a proper name, and hence of sentences in which it occurs: but here it seems that we are entitled to ascribe a reference to the name on the ground that the senses of such sentences have already been fixed. The connection between name and object must not, indeed, transcend the use of sentences containing the name, including recognition statements involving ostension; but, if the notion of reference is to be functional in the account of the senses of such sentences, the connection must allow of some procedure of identifying an object as the referent of the name. Now how are the senses of sentences containing numerical terms to be given? If they are explained by appeal to the notion of the reference of a numerical term, say in terms of the procedure of identifying some object as its referent, then the context principle cannot serve to justify ascribing a reference to such terms, since the context principle sanctions the ascription of a reference to an expression only in a case in which the senses of all sentences containing it have already been fixed. Hence, if Frege is entitled to invoke the context principle, as he does in *Grundlagen*, in order to justify ascribing a reference to numerical terms, that is, to justify taking them to stand for objects, the senses of sentences containing such terms must be given in a way that makes no use of the notion of the references of those terms. And this is precisely what Frege appears to envisage. In §§ 62 to 65 of *Grundlagen*, he discusses seriously the possibility of a contextual definition of numerical terms; although he eventually rejects the proposal, on the ground, already mentioned, that it would leave undetermined the truth-value of an identity-statement connecting a numerical term with a proper name of any other form, in § 63 he repudiates what is in effect an objection to contextual definitions as such. Actually, the proposed stipulation would not amount to a contextual definition save in the presence of assumptions guaranteeing the domain to be at least denumerable; but Frege manifests no awareness of this, and the corresponding contextual definition of terms for directions would involve no analogous difficulty.

Suppose, then, that the senses of sentences containing terms for directions were given by a set of contextual definitions which enabled us to transform any such sentence into one involving reference only to and quantification only over lines. We could then no longer claim that the sense of a term for a direction was given as a means of determining its referent, or that the determination of the truth-value of a sentence containing the term went via the referent. On the contrary, the most direct means of establishing such a sentence as true or false, that which corresponds, step by step, with the way in which the sense of the sentence is given, will consist in first transforming the sentence, in accordance with the contextual definition, into one about lines, and then establishing the truth-value of the latter sentence; in this way, the referent of the direction-term is bypassed altogether. Frege takes the possibility of giving an incontestably legitimate explanation, such as a contextual definition, of the senses of sentences containing terms of a given kind that behave like proper names as a justification for regarding those terms as standing for objects. But it is precisely in a case of this kind that other philosophers have seen the reduction, say of statements about directions to statements about lines, as affording us a dispensation from having to countenance such objects as directions, and hence from regarding terms for directions as having reference. Frege stresses the harmlessness of so regarding them; more parsimonious philosophers stress its superfluity.

The same will hold good of any stipulation that fixes the senses of sentences containing proper names of a given kind, say numerical terms, without appeal to the notion of reference for such names, whether or not it amounts to a contextual definition. If the stipulation is carried out in a logically unobjectionable manner, then no absurdity can arise from crediting those names with the property of standing for objects. It nevertheless remains that the notion of reference is not really *used* in the explanation of the senses of the terms in question; as applied to such terms, it has become non-functional, the theory of sense no longer resting upon the theory of reference. Numerical terms, if explained in such a way, would, as it were, be said to have a reference only by courtesy.

Viewed in this light, Frege's realism concerning abstract objects appears to reduce to little more than a form of words. It is for this reason that I said on p. 500 of *FPL* that there is a certain tension between the realism which informs Frege's whole philosophy and the context principle taken as a thesis containing reference, that is, as a justification for ascribing reference to abstract terms; there is, of course, no conflict between his realism and the context principle understood as relating only to sense. For there is no doubt about the form of words; numbers are objective, self-subsistent objects, belonging to the realm of reference but not to that of sense, which exist independently of us and whose objective properties and relations to one another render our statements about them true or false independently of our opinion or knowledge. The objectivity of truth for mathematical statements, taken as a whole, their being determinately either true or false, independently of us, must evidently be maintained in any philosophy of mathematics faithful to Frege's ideas: but a strong emphasis on the context principle, taken as a thesis about reference, must put it in doubt how far the conception of numbers as abstract, indeed logical, objects is to be taken at face-value.

As already remarked, it does not appear that Frege succeeded in thinking the matter through. Quite likely he was conscious of this; if so, this would have been a further reason for his not having reiterated the context principle after *Grundlagen*. It is impossible to elicit from his actual practice a coherent doctrine. In *Grundlagen*, an explicit definition is finally adopted, both for numerical terms and for terms for directions: this does not settle the matter either way, since both are defined as equivalence classes, of concepts and of lines respectively, so that we now have to ask how the sense of a class-term is given. This is, of course, discussed in *Grund-*

gesetze, after the fashion already reviewed. If we want to treat the notion of reference for abstract terms as genuinely analogous to that of proper names for concrete objects, we have to have some notion of the identification of an abstract object as the referent of a name; this may perhaps be attained by selecting, for each range of abstract objects, some canonical means of referring to them, as suggested on p. 499 of *FPL*. This is easily enough done for natural numbers, but obscure for classes or value-ranges in general; moreover, it has no warrant in Frege's writings. If we take the sense of a proper name of an abstract object to be given as a particular means of determining its referent, as presented in a canonical notation, the context principle will then play only a minor role in justifying the use of the notion of reference in connection with them and hence of speaking of abstract objects at all: it will serve only as a defence against the crude notion that an object must be capable of being immediately presented to us, independently of any concept expressible in language, that is, against epistemological atomism; and this, as we have seen, is not a thesis to be imputed to Frege even for concrete, *wirkliche* objects. If, on the other hand, the context principle is taken as a justification for ascribing reference to abstract terms in the strong sense that appears to be envisaged in *Grundlagen*, then the analogy between proper names of abstract objects and those of concrete ones reduces to the features of the employment of both kinds which constitute their behaving like proper names in the sense of Chapter 4 in *FPL*. In this case, sense and reference are not analogously related for proper names of the two kinds; and Frege's realism concerning abstract objects becomes more apparent than genuine. It seems useless to ask how Frege would have resolved the dilemma: he did not resolve it.

CHAPTER 20

Realism

metaphysics REALISM AND IDEALISM are metaphysical doctrines. So to say of Frege that he was a realist—or that he held views incompatible with realism—is to attribute to him a metaphysical position. Was Frege a metaphysician? It certainly seems that he did not consider himself one: he says, in the Preface to *Grundgesetze*,[1] 'I take it as a sure sign of a mistake when logic has need of metaphysics and psychology, sciences that themselves have need of logical principles.' We cannot, however, by appeal to some conception of metaphysics of our own, take this observation as decisive for the interpretation of Frege's doctrines, since metaphysics is the most ill-defined of all the branches of philosophy. It was, for example, one of the salient doctrines of logical positivism that metaphysics is impossible, and yet it would not be patently absurd to speak of the metaphysics of logical positivism. The obvious definition of metaphysics is that it is that branch of philosophy which is concerned with the most general features of reality, that is, of the world as it is in itself, rather than with our knowledge of or relation to the world. As such, it ought to be the apex of all philosophy, indeed of all knowledge: what can there be which we want to know more than that? And yet, when we tackle the questions that present themselves as part of such an enquiry, the other branches of philosophy conspire to rob metaphysics of independent existence. It is not, as the positivists thought, that metaphysics is a part of philosophy in which senseless questions are asked and senseless answers returned; it is, rather, that there do not seem to be any questions that fall specially within its province. Thus questions about the physical universe belong in part to the philosophy of perception and in part to the philosophy of science. The notion of cause obviously belongs to the latter domain, even if a good

[1] P. xix.

deal may be said about it without any detailed reference to science; and just the same is true of the notions of space and time, of which no adequate general account that neglects modern physics can possibly be given. Questions concerning the mental belong to the philosophy of mind; those concerning God to natural theology. What remains the business of metaphysics as such?

Perhaps we can at least retain ontology as a division of metaphysics that cannot be filched by any more specialized branch of philosophy: and, despite Sluga's strictures on ontological interpretations of Frege's doctrines, this seems to provide the best chance of claiming Frege as a metaphysician. Ontology is concerned to enumerate and characterize the most general categories of the things that exist: and Frege, with his classification of what exists into objects and functions of various types was surely concerned with ontology in this sense. He makes it plain that, in applying his notion of unsaturatedness not only to expressions and to their senses, but also to their referents, he is categorizing reality itself, and not just according to an accidental feature of the way we talk about it, but according to the very nature of what is talked of: as he says in *Function und Begriff*,[1] by our finding some device for treating of first-level functions in place of second-level ones, 'the distinction between functions of first and second level is not thereby banished from the world, because it is not made arbitrarily, but founded deep in the nature of things'.

Considered as an ontologist, however, Frege's categories are *very* general. He does, indeed, distinguish various kinds of object: logical objects; physical objects; ideas and other mental contents; rational beings; thoughts and other senses; truth-values; points, lines, surfaces and other geometrical objects in physical space. But he makes no profession of giving an exhaustive classification of all the different general kinds of object. Still less does he advance any comprehensive account of the nature of objects of all the kinds that he mentions. He has a doctrine of logical objects, of thoughts and senses, and of truth-values; he holds certain views concerning ideas and mental contents in general; and, for the rest, he makes occasional passing remarks, without putting forward any philosophical theory of, say, the constitution of material objects or the relation of mind and body. If Frege was a metaphysician, he was not much of one.

But, of course, Frege was not a metaphysician at all: he was a philosopher of mathematics and a logician, in that extended sense in which he used the term 'logic' to cover the theory of meaning or philosophy of language.

[1] P. 31.

And perhaps it is this thought which underlies Sluga's rejection of an 'ontological' interpretation of his notions of object, function, etc. For, if Frege was merely a logician, his doctrines must have been logical doctrines, not metaphysical ones, his distinctions purely logical distinctions: he cannot have intended them as a contribution to metaphysics. But to argue thus would be to maintain a rigid distinction between the different branches of philosophy in which the remark quoted above from the Preface to *Grundgesetze* provides the sole, flimsy, ground for supposing that Frege believed. The belief is a grossly implausible one, particularly in view of the propensity of other branches of philosophy to encroach on the domain of metaphysics. And, in Frege's case, such a belief is belied by his entire practice; it would go against the most basic principles of his philosophy. It would be quite contrary to the spirit of that philosophy to allow that something could exist in a purely logical, but not in a genuine or metaphysical, sense, or to allow that we are entitled, from a logical standpoint, to speak of certain entities which a metaphysical investigation may yet forbid us to speak about. Hence, if Frege had held that logical distinctions were quite unrelated to metaphysical or ontological ones, he would have drawn distinctions only between different types of linguistic expression and between different types of senses that they bear, not between the different types of thing for which they stand. We do not require assertions by Frege of the kind quoted above, that his distinctions were founded deep in the nature of things, to establish that his doctrines were meant to be understood ontologically, and that logic was a true guide to ontology. Since Sluga says so confidently and so repeatedly that I interpret Frege ontologically, he presumably means by 'ontological' something that fits my reading of Frege. It is in that sense that I am here affirming that Frege's doctrines are intended to be understood ontologically: namely that they are to be understood as relating, not only to expressions and their senses, but also to what there really is in the world. Even if Frege had not told us that the distinctions between objects and functions and between first- and second-level functions are founded deep in the nature of things, it would have been apparent in all that he says about them and about *Bedeutung* that they are distinctions between really existing things: any attempt to interpret him otherwise must pervert his entire philosophy.

He did not need to assert that his logical distinctions were founded in the nature of things: and it was slightly misleading of him ever to do so. It was quite sufficient for him to say, as he does repeatedly, that 'to this distinction among the signs there naturally corresponds one in the realm of references'.[1] It is not exactly that, for him, logical structure, the structure of thought and of its expression, provides a reliable clue to the structure of reality, as one might conjecture that the constitution of the human mind must conform particularly closely with the constitution of the physical universe for us to have discovered so much about that universe. Rather, it is that we cannot ask what fundamental types of thing there are in reality except by asking what types of thing we refer to: it is in this sense that reality is the realm of reference. The structure of language is the structure of thought; not merely because we are constrained by our nature to think in language, but because language is an instrument for the expression of thoughts. Whether or not we ever think thoughts that we do not express, even internally, in words, there cannot be an inexpressible thought: we do not have, besides the thoughts we convey to one another in speech, or embody in silent soliloquy, another range of thoughts that language cannot carry. It is because of this that the basic structure of thought is also the basic structure of reality, where 'basic structure' refers to the classification and characterization of the fundamental logical types. It would be simply senseless to ask whether there might not be other logical types of entity in reality of which we have no conception, or whether things we refer to by expressions of different logical type might not, in reality, be of the same type: the whole point is that we cannot separate the notion of the logical type of a thing from that of the logical type of the expression by means of which we refer to it, which is why the traditional doctrine of universals that can figure both as concepts or relations and as objects is incoherent. What we cannot in principle refer to does not exist for us: which is to say that it is not an intelligible thought that it exists. Logic is not a clue to metaphysics: if it were, one might complain that, in drawing metaphysical conclusions from his logical doctrines, Frege was stepping outside his proper sphere. But Frege does not draw metaphysical conclusions from his logical doctrines: the ontological ingredient of those doctrines is integral to them. Ontology of this very general kind is a part of metaphysics that is properly the territory of logic, just as other parts of metaphysics are properly the territories of other branches of philosophy. When logic is taken in the broad sense in which it comprises the theory of meaning, understood as a branch of philosophy, the idea of a logic that has no metaphysical, that is, no ontological, component is a delusion. There cannot be an aseptic logic that merely informs us how language functions and what is the structure

[1] 'Über die Grundlagen der Geometrie', 1903, II, p. 371.

of the thoughts which it expresses without committing itself to anything concerning reality, since reality is what we speak about—the realm of reference—and an account of language demands an account of how what we say *is* about reality and is rendered true or false by how things are in reality.

In just the same way, to describe Frege as a realist is not necessarily to represent him as trespassing over the boundaries of that area of philosophy with which he principally occupied himself. It does not entail so representing him if the metaphysical issue concerning realism is one that has its place within the theory of meaning. Now, on the face of it, there is not *one* issue concerning realism, but many. It does not appear sensible to classify a philosopher as a realist *tout court*. It is perfectly intelligible and consistent to adopt a realist view of some things and not of others: there hardly seems to be a coherent philosophical thesis which would compel one who held it to be a realist about everything. Hence the question concerning realism appears to split up into a multitude of different questions, each belonging to the appropriate branch of philosophy. Realism about the material world is to be evaluated by the philosophy of perception and the philosophy of physics; realism about mathematical objects by the philosophy of mathematics; realism about mental events and processes by the philosophy of mind; realism about the future and the past by the philosophy of time; realism about the theoretical entities of science by the philosophy of science. Such a segmentation of the problem corresponds rather badly, however, to the use of such epithets as 'realist' and 'idealist' in the histories of philosophy: it is common practice to describe philosophers as realists or as idealists of this or that variety, without restriction as to the subject-matter concerning which a realistic or idealistic view is being ascribed to them. This is due, in part, to a correct perception that the disputes concerning realism in regard to different subjects have a great deal in common: if we prescind from the specific topic, the forms of the arguments for and against realism display a very striking similarity. This would not be enough to justify the use of 'realist' and 'idealist' as unqualified descriptions of philosophical positions if there were not, to some extent, a connection between these different arguments as well as a structural similarity. Such a connection there actually is. For, although there is no conceivable argument to show that a realist attitude must be adopted towards each of the various disputed subjects, there are forms of argument to show that such an attitude *cannot* be adopted in any of them, as well as more specific arguments to show that it ought not to be adopted in this case or in that: in face of such a general form of argument against realism, one who wishes to adopt a realist view in any of the disputed cases will have to provide a general rebuttal. This rebuttal will not compel him to be a realist in every case: it will merely show that realism is, in general, possible, and leave him free to adopt it or to reject it in each specific case.

The crux of any dispute concerning realism is precisely where Frege what realism is locates it in the course of his attack, in the Preface to *Grundgesetze*, vol. I, on psychologism and on the idealism that is consequent upon it, namely in the relation between truth and our recognition of truth.[1] Frege's declarations that 'being true is something different from being taken to be true, whether by one, by many or by all, and is in no way reducible to it'[2] and that truth 'is for me something objective and independent of the one who judges'[3] are affirmations of his realist stance; and he puts his finger on the nub of the matter when he says that 'when I survey the whole question, the different conceptions of truth appear to me as the source of the dispute'.[4] If that is correct, then the general issue, whether realism is possible, will be a question belonging to the province of logic, in the broad sense which Frege gave to that term; it will be a question concerning the notion of truth, that notion which Frege regarded as both the starting-point of logic and as its subject-matter. As he says in the Preface to *Grundgesetze*, 'the conception of the laws of logic is necessarily decisive for the treatment of the science of logic; and that conception is in turn connected with how we understand the word "true" '.[5] One could, indeed, consistently accept Frege's views on the general issue, and yet reject realism concerning a particular subject-matter, for example adopting a formalist or constructivist view of mathematics: so, if the general issue is settled in favour of realism, there will still be a host of particular cases that remain to be decided. The strongest motivation for rejecting realism in particular cases will still be a negative decision on the general issue: if realism is never coherent, then one is compelled to find an alternative account in each specific case where the dispute arises. There is also a psychological impulsion, on the part of one favourably disposed towards realism in general because he regards the general arguments against it as fallacious, to adopt a realist attitude in the majority of disputed cases, just as Frege himself was not only a realist concerning the external world but a platonist in mathematics;

[1] Pp. xv–xviii.
[2] P. xv.
[3] P. xvii.
[4] P. xvii.
[5] Pp. xiv–xv.

this tendency provides further justification for the practice of characterizing a philosopher, as I think it right to characterize Frege, simply as a realist. In any case, if the general issue is really about the concept of truth, then it is another, and more important, example of a metaphysical issue which belongs to the theory of meaning, that is, to what Frege called 'logic'.

The primary tenet of realism, as applied to some given class of statements, is that each statement in the class is determined as true or not true, independently of our knowledge, by some objective reality whose existence and constitution is, again, independent of our knowledge. A realistic view of the past, for example, involves that the truth of a statement about the past does not depend upon whether there exist, in the present, any traces of the past state of affairs that would enable us to recognize it as true: if it is true, it is rendered true by what lies in the past, by how things were at the time to which it relates; and, since the past is determinate, it must either render the statement true or fail to do so. Likewise, a realistic view of mathematics, which is usually called a platonistic view, involves that the truth of a mathematical statement does not depend upon our having, or ever coming to have, a proof of it: it may be true even though it lies beyond our ability to prove it; and, again, it must either be true or not. Realism about the physical world entails that there is a determinate physical reality which renders true or false any statement we may make about material objects, independently of whether we can make any observations directly or indirectly confirming or disconfirming it; realism about mental processes and states entails that any specific such process either occurs or does not occur, any specific such state either obtains or fails to obtain, independently of whether there is any clue, from the behaviour of the person or organism concerned, to the occurrence of that process or the presence of that state. Realism about a given class of statements—statements in the past tense, mathematical statements, material-object statements, or the like—is thus a thesis about the appropriate notion of truth for such statements; and, because of the intimate connection between the notions of truth and of meaning, it is also a thesis about the kind of meaning that they have, that is, that we have succeeded in conferring upon them. That the appropriate notion of truth for the statements in question is of the kind that the realist supposes is possible only if it is integral to our understanding of those statements to conceive of them as rendered true or false objectively and independently of our knowledge or capacity for knowledge; our understanding must consist in an awareness of the condition for the truth of such a statement, a condition conceived of as determinately either obtaining or not obtaining. Realism thus involves a conception of the meanings of statements of the class in question as given in terms of the conditions for them to be true; and the general question whether realism is possible for any class of statements is the question whether a truth-conditional theory of meaning is feasible, that is, a theory of meaning of just the kind that Frege held. The general issue whether realism is possible is thus one belonging to the general theory of meaning, that is, to the branch of philosophy called by Frege 'logic'; to credit him with taking a position on this issue does not imply that he trespassed into some area of philosophy with which he had no right to be concerned.

According to a realistic view, every statement is determined either as true or as not true. There thus cannot be for the realist any objection in principle to introducing, for statements in that class of which he takes a realistic view, a classical negation operator, that is, one explained as yielding a statement 'Not A' which is false just in case 'A' is true and which is true in every other case. For a given range of statements, it may be that the language does not actually contain such an operator. There may be some operator—say 'Non'—which acts like classical negation for most statements, but, for statements in the given range, yields a statement which may in certain cases fail to be true even though the statement to which it is applied is not true either. If this is so, we shall be strongly inclined to apply the word 'false' to statements in that range in such a way that 'A' is deemed to be false just in case 'Non A' is true; and there will then be an apparent truth-value gap. But, from the realist's standpoint, there can be no objection to using the word 'false' in a different way, namely as equivalent to 'not true'; and, under *this* sense of 'false', the realist may be said to accept the principle of bivalence. The principle of bivalence may be stated as the thesis that every statement is, determinately, either true or false. The inclusion of the word 'determinately' in this formulation is essential. If it is not included, anyone who accepts the law of excluded middle and the equivalence thesis for both truth and falsity could claim to accept the principle of bivalence; and this would be much too weak. The law of excluded middle is the law that every statement of the form 'A or not A' is true; the equivalence thesis is the principle that, for every statement 'A', 'It is true that A if and only if A' and 'It is false that A if and only if not A' are both true. If, now, we equate asserting that 'A' is true with asserting 'It is true that A' and asserting that 'A' is false with asserting 'It is false that A', it will follow, for every statement 'A', that 'A' is either true or false. Notoriously, however, it is possible to subscribe to all these principles without accepting the principle of bivalence. Suppose, for example, that someone believes that there are various future possibilities which remain open, and that a statement about the future can be correctly asserted only if it holds whichever of these possibilities comes to be realized. He explains the sentential operators by means of the two-valued truth-tables, considered as relative to any one definite future course of events; and he accepts the equivalence thesis. If 'A' is a future-tensed statement whose verification depends upon the realization of one or more of those possibilities which are now open, he will not regard either 'A' or 'Not A' as assertable: but he will be willing to assert 'A or not A', and will therefore be prepared to say that 'A' is either true or false, since, in each definite future course of events, either 'A' or 'Not A' will hold, and hence 'A or not A' will hold in all of them. We may object that he is not using 'false' as the realist requires, namely as equivalent to 'not true'; but he declares that he is. The real difference is that he is not using 'true' absolutely, as the realist does, but only as relative to a definite future course of events; if he used 'true' to mean 'can be correctly asserted', we could then say that he was not using 'false' as the negation of 'true'. But he cannot use 'true' in this way without giving up the equivalence thesis. The example is in any case enough to show that the inclusion of 'determinately' is essential to the formulation of the principle of bivalence; and its function is to control the meaning of 'or' as it occurs in the statement of the principle. The force of 'Determinately, either A or B' is that 'or' is being used as subject to a quite unrestricted application of the rule of or-elimination: one may infer any statement 'C' that may be shown to follow both from 'A', together with any other statements accepted as true, and from 'B', together with any other statements accepted as true. This explanation is intended to capture the intuitive idea that it is determinately the case that either A or B if there is a definite answer to the question, 'Which?' (of course not, in general, excluding the answer 'Both'). This intuitive formulation is of little use in itself. If someone who believes in God asks what it means to say that there is a definite answer to a question, he may be helped by being told that it means that God knows what the answer is: 'Determinately, either A or B' implies 'Either God knows that A or God knows that B'. But even this explanation may be misunderstood, if the 'or' that occurs in the statement about God's knowledge does not itself admit the qualification 'determinately'; and, for someone who does not believe in God, this means of explaining the existence of a definite answer to a question is not available. To him, one can only say that there is a definite answer to the question, 'Which?', if one of the two statements is *true*: and this gets us no further forward, since the existential quantifier is likely to function in analogy with 'or'.

At this stage, it is tempting to *identify* realism concerning some class of statements with acceptance of the principle of bivalence for statements of that class; and this is a temptation to which I have sometimes, in the past, succumbed. But it should be resisted. For one thing, it tends to lead to the attempt to distinguish between 'serious' instances of a rejection of the principle of bivalence, which imply a repudiation of realism, and other instances of its rejection, which do not. For example, it may appear that the admission of truth-value gaps on the score that proper names lacking a reference render sentences in which they occur neither true nor false represents no genuine obstacle to a realist conception; and so one embarks on a futile search for a criterion for discriminating between 'serious' or 'deep' grounds for rejecting bivalence and shallow ones. Secondly, it prevents the classification of certain disputes concerning what has been labelled 'realism' as being about realism in the relevant sense, because the principle of bivalence is not involved: the most striking example is the dispute between realism and nominalism concerning universals. As recently as in the Preface to *Truth and Other Enigmas*,[1] I was still attempting to distinguish, in this fashion, between different senses of the word 'realism' (as opposed to different subjects in respect of which one may or may not be a realist); but I now regard this distinction as misguided.

The example of the neutralist concerning future-tense statements served to show that a willingness to assert that every statement is either true or false is not a sufficient condition for being a realist. But a very similar example shows that the principle of bivalence, as formulated with the qualification 'determinately', is not sufficient either. The example is that of a neutralist who has the very same view as before concerning the future, but who applies the words 'true' and 'false' differently: he calls a statement 'true' just in case it would be correct to assert it, i.e. if it is true *in* every definite future course of events, and 'false' if it is not true (and thus *not* only if it is false in every definite future course of events). Since for him every statement is objectively determined as true or false in this sense, he may claim to subscribe to the principle of bivalence: but he is obviously not a realist. If acceptance of bivalence is not sufficient for realism, however, it *is* necessary. Strawson's view that the occurrence in a sentence of a singular term lacking reference (relative to a given utterance of the sentence) results in its failing to convey a statement, true or false, as Frege holds to be the case with sentences of natural language, admittedly does not,

[1] P. xliv.

at first sight, appear to involve any departure from realism. But, if it does not, we are left with the problem how to discriminate between deviations from the principle of bivalence that are, and those that are not, incompatible with realism. We might think that the admission of truth-value gaps such that a statement is capable of being recognized to be neither true nor false falls into the latter category. In the same way, we might also so classify the replacement of a two-valued semantic theory by a finitely many-valued one, where the possession of a designated value is taken as the condition for a statement to be correctly assertable. So viewed, the multiple system of truth-values is introduced only in order to allow a more complicated means of determining the condition for a complex sentence to be correctly assertable than one that depends only on whether or not each of its subsentences is correctly assertable, but this makes no essential difference; all that matters, so far as the implications for realism are concerned, is that every possible assertion is objectively either correct or incorrect. This suggests that we should fasten upon the notion of correct assertability, rather than on that of truth. On this suggestion, a rejection of the principle of bivalence is to be regarded as inconsistent with realism just in case it involves rejecting also the assumption that the condition for a statement to be correctly asserted determinately either obtains or does not obtain; for example, the intuitionistic theory of meaning for mathematical statements entails denying realism in regard to mathematics, while a Strawsonian account of singular terms in no way conflicts with realism.

The example of the neutralist about the future shows this suggestion to be mistaken, however: in whatever way the neutralist prefers to construe the notions of truth and falsity, he does regard the condition for the correct assertability of any statement as being, objectively, either fulfilled or unfulfilled, and yet he plainly is not a realist about the future. The mistake in the suggestion lay, not in choosing the wrong criterion for distinguishing between types of ground for rejecting the principle of bivalence, but in seeking any at all. Even the belief in truth-value gaps due to failure of reference for singular terms represents a repudiation of realism in the relevant respect: it is opposed to realism concerning non-existent objects, as maintained explicitly by Meinong (and as implicit in a belief in the validity of the ontological argument).

The correct view is, I think, an extension of our earlier observation that, for a realist, classical negation must be intelligible: namely that *any* departure from two-valued semantics for the logical constants, whether or not it involves a deviation from classical logic, represents a divergence, extensive or slight, from realism. To this it may, with some reason, be objected that what marks a divergence from realism is not the use of non-two-valued logical operators, which might be wanted for a variety of innocent purposes, but the denial that it would be legitimate to introduce the two-valued ones. This objection should probably be admitted; but it should be admitted only with caution. If we allow it too much weight, we shall be back where we were before: anyone who admits that, for every statement, either the condition for it to be correctly asserted is fulfilled, or it is not, must to that extent allow that it would be possible to introduce the two-valued constants. In some cases, however, it would be entirely unnatural to introduce them; this may be seen by once more considering the neutralist about the future. Such a neutralist may not be prepared to introduce any logical operations which are not merely the product, over the set of possible future courses of events, of operations defined relative to each future course of events. But, if he is prepared to do so, then he will gain greater expressive power by introducing a single unary operation analogous to that expressed by the necessity operator than by allowing two-valued operations with respect to absolute truth and its absence. Where '*A*' is said to be absolutely true if it is true in all possible future courses of events, the introduction of two-valued operations will allow, e.g., a distinction between different kinds of disjunction: '*A* or *B*' will be absolutely true, and therefore assertable, just in case, in each possible future course of events, either '*A*' or '*B*' is true, while '*A* OR *B*', where 'OR' is two-valued, will be absolutely true only if either '*A*' or '*B*' is absolutely true. But, where '$\square$ *A*' is true in a given future course of events just in case '*A*' is absolutely true, its introduction will allow yet other combinations to be expressed, e.g. '*A* or $\square$ *B*', which is true in a given future course of events if and only if either '*A*' is true in it or '*B*' is absolutely true: there would be no warrant for introducing 'OR' and the other two-valued operators which would not also justify the introduction of the more expressive operator '$\square$'. This does not leave us with a very precise criterion: a theory of meaning will be realistic if it allows for the introduction of the two-valued constants, where one could not get the same or a better effect in a different way. I do not at present know how to improve the criterion: but, to a rough approximation, we may adhere to our original formulation, that a realistic theory of meaning must rest on the two-valued semantics as a base, while recognizing that, as thus stated, it makes somewhat too strong a demand.

Those deviations from realism which do not call in question either a truth-conditional account of meaning or the principle of bivalence seem to turn on the notion of reference: a nominalist opposes realism concerning universals because he does not regard general terms as standing for anything in reality. This also fits the case of empty singular terms: for a Meinongian realist, such terms are *not* devoid of reference, but stand for non-existent objects. Likewise, Frege is not a realist about vague properties. As he says in 'Ausführungen über Sinn und Bedeutung', an unpublished work of 1892–5, 'one must reject concept-words that have no reference. These are . . . those whose boundaries are vague. It must be determinate, for every object, whether it falls under the concept or not; a concept-word which does not satisfy this condition on its reference is devoid of reference'.[1] Frege's thought on this matter is surely in accord with that which I expressed in 'Wang's Paradox' by saying, 'the notion that things might actually *be* vague, as well as being vaguely described, is not properly intelligible'.[2] I should like now to withdraw this remark. There does not appear to be any a priori reason why the world should be such that, for every vague predicate, there exists a completely sharp predicate corresponding to it; it might be that, for a given predicate, we could, beyond a certain stage, find no way to eliminate a residual vagueness of application. The prejudice that this must be due to our own limitations is extremely strong: it is natural to us to conceive of physical reality as, in itself, capable of description in absolutely precise mathematical terms, a description upon which any other would be supervenient even if imprecise. This inclination does not, however, appear to be more than a prejudice; at least it is hard to construct any a priori justification of it. It is not apparently absurd to suppose the contrary, namely that the physical world is in itself such that the most precise description of it that even omniscience would yield might yet involve the use of expressions having some degree of vagueness. The question remains obscure, as does almost everything concerning the important topic of vagueness. In particular, if, in the sense here suggested, realism concerning vague properties and relations were to be justifiable, it would be a form of realism that would not fit the proposed criterion according to which realism demands an acceptance of a classical two-valued semantics. On the contrary, a theory of meaning for a language containing vague expressions cannot assume that every statement is determinately either true or false, but must employ a more complicated semantic theory as its base: it is just for this reason that Frege was *not* a realist about vague properties. Realism about vague properties has more affinity with various forms of anti-realism than it does with the corresponding forms

[1] *N.S.*, p. 133, *P.W.*, p. 122.
[2] *Truth and Other Enigmas*, p. 260.

of realism, in that it allows that reality may in certain respects be indeterminate; it is for this reason a signally untypical case.

A characterization of realism in terms of reference would be more traditional than one in terms of truth; but it certainly would be less illuminating, and would fit fewer cases. It would not fit realism concerning the past or the future, which do not diverge from the corresponding forms of anti-realism by asserting the referentiality of any terms (certainly not of temporal adverbs) nor would it be apt as a characterization of platonism as a philosophy of mathematics, since the issue between platonism and constructivism is not whether there are mathematical objects, and is only misleadingly described as relating to the character of mathematical objects. At the same time, unless we take reference into account, we shall not succeed in including under our general characterization of realism every philosophical doctrine that has traditionally been so labelled. The solution lies to hand. Full-fledged realism concerning a given class of statements consists in the acceptance, for those statements, of a truth-conditional theory of meaning taking as its base a completely unmodified classical two-valued semantics. Such a semantic theory embodies not only the assumption that each of the statements in question is determined, by the reality to which such statements relate, either as true or as false, but also a detailed conception of the manner in which those statements are so determined. One ingredient of that conception is the appeal to the notion of reference: the semantic role of a singular term occurring in a statement of the given class is to stand for some particular object within that domain which gives the range of the expressions of generality. This thesis must, for present purposes, be understood as governed by the principle that sense determines semantic value, that is, in this case, reference. It is not merely that, for the sake of a semantic theory sufficient to yield a suitable notion of the interpretation of a logical formula, and hence a suitable notion of validity, the semantic value of a singular term may be taken to be an element of the domain: the semantic theory is here a base for the theory of meaning as a whole, and hence the sense of the singular term must be given as a means of determining its referent, and the determination of the truth-value of a sentence containing it must go via that referent. Another ingredient of classical semantics is the principle that the truth-value of every complex sentence depends, in a definite manner, on the truth-values of certain atomic sentences which may be viewed as its constituent subsentences. This applies not only to the sentential operators but also to the quantifiers or equivalent expressions of generality. The truth-value of a quantified sentence is determined by the truth-values of its instances, just as the truth-value of a sentence formed by means of a sentential connective is determined by those of its two immediate subsentences: the truth-value of the quantified sentence is a truth-function of the truth-values of its instances, although, if the domain is infinite, an infinitary truth-function. The truth-value of a universally quantified sentence is the logical product of the truth-values of its instances, that of an existentially quantified one their logical sum. These possibly infinitary truth-functions are conceived of as having a value in every case: the application of a quantifier to a predicate that is determinately true or false of each object in the domain will always yield a sentence that is itself determinately either true or false. Thus, on the semantic level, universal quantification amounts to possibly infinite conjunction, existential quantification to possibly infinite disjunction, though this is not true at the level of sense, since to know the sense of a quantified sentence it is not necessary to know the senses of all its instances, but only to grasp the domain of quantification in some general way. That part of the semantic theory which relates to the sentential operators and the quantifiers is, of course, concerned with how the senses of complex sentences are given, that is, how we conceive of their truth-values as being determined. The truth-values of complex sentences depend on, and only on, the truth-values of atomic ones; and it is to the part of the theory that relates to atomic sentences that the notion of the reference of singular terms belongs.

If realism is characterized as the acceptance of a truth-conditional theory of meaning resting on an unmodified two-valued semantic theory, it becomes perplexing indeed how it could be questioned that Frege was a realist. He is the very archetype of a realist, precisely because he exhibited an unwavering adherence to a two-valued classical semantic theory, and was, indeed, the first to set out such a theory systematically and to indicate the place that a semantic theory should have in a theory of meaning as a whole by means of his doctrine of sense and reference. It is, indeed, only in respect of language as it *ought* to be that Frege held a realistic theory of meaning. Natural language fails to accord with a two-valued semantics in a great many ways, by containing singular terms lacking reference, vague predicates and predicates that are not everywhere defined; but for just that reason, natural language requires improvement before we have an instrument adequate for arriving at truth. He was, therefore, not a whole-hearted realist in respect of natural language: he did not regard proper names and definite descriptions as in every case having a reference, if sometimes to non-existent objects, nor did he think that there were any concepts to serve as the referents of vague predicates. But, in relation to a properly constructed language, he was not merely a realist: he supplied us with the very picture of what it is to be a realist. There had, of course, been many realists before Frege: but, with him, the conception of realism came into sharp focus for the first time in the history of philosophy.

As Frege showed himself aware, one frequent motive for rejecting realism in favour of idealism, constructivism, behaviourism or the like is the desire to narrow the gulf between what makes a statement true and that by means of which we recognize it as true. The opponent of realism for some given class of statements claims that the only legitimate notion of truth for a statement of that class is one under which it is true only if we have established it as true; or only if we either have done so or shall do so at some future time; or only if we have some procedure which, were we to carry it out, would establish it as true; or, at least, only if there exists something, of the sort that we normally take as a basis for the assertion of a statement of that class, such that, if we knew of it, we should treat it as a ground for the truth of the statement. In critical cases, a conception of truth of any of these kinds will undermine bivalence: in other words, the realist's insistence on bivalence compels him to make the relation between truth and our recognition of it more remote. In *Grundlagen*, § 47, Frege shows himself so anxious to preserve the distinction between the two that he risks making the relation between them too remote even for the most convinced realist. He is arguing that a statement of subordination, such as 'All whales are mammals', is not about animals, but about concepts; its content is that the concept of a whale is subordinate to that of a mammal, this being an objective, factual statement, since concepts are objective. 'Even supposing that a whale is before us, our sentence still asserts nothing about it. One could not infer from it that the animal before us was a mammal without adding the proposition that it is a whale, about which our sentence contains nothing.' He concludes by making the general observation that 'however much our sentence is capable of being justified only by the observation of individual animals, this proves nothing as to its content. Whether it is true or not, or on what grounds we hold it to be true, is irrelevant to the question what it is about.' Frege appears here to have gone too far in distinguishing between what makes a statement true, as determined by what the statement is about, and that on the basis of which we judge it to be true; he comes close to sundering the content of the sentence even from what makes it true when it is true. We may grant that the sentence 'All whales are mammals' is about concepts, in Frege's sense, rather than about individual animals without agreeing that the mode of verification of the sentence is irrelevant to its content. Frege's argument depends in part upon his particular logical analysis of such a sentence, namely as a universally quantified hypothetical, where the quantification extends over all objects. So viewed, the statement is not, logically considered, about individual whales any more than it is about other objects: but there is a reasonable sense in which it is about individual objects, saying of each of them that it satisfies the predicate 'if ξ is a whale, ξ is a mammal'. Perhaps his exaggeration in this passage is due to the fact, already noted in Chapters 18 and 19, that in *Grundlagen* Frege had not yet attained a clear distinction between a concept, thought of as belonging to the realm of reference, and the sense of a concept-word, as shown by the uneasy combination of the thesis that a statement about a concept asserts something factual and the thesis that concepts do not belong to the external world.

According to Frege's mature views, our grasp of the sense of a sentence consists in our conception of how its truth-value is determined in accordance with its composition. Frege does not himself employ the notion of what *makes* the thought expressed by a sentence true, perhaps because he wants to avoid the conception of a fact or state of affairs as belonging to the realm of reference; but it is a natural notion for a realist to appeal to, and need not be interpreted in terms of an ontology of facts: the notion relates, rather, to the *sense* of the sentence. When a sentence is true, the notion of that which makes it true must be understood in terms of our conception of how it is determined as true, in a manner corresponding to its structure, this conception constituting our grasp of its sense. There must be some sentences for which we are able to perceive or apprehend that which makes them true, that is, to perceive or to recognize directly that they are true, since otherwise it is hard to see how we could ever establish the truth of any sentence. This does not apply only to reports of observation, but equally (say) to numerical equations stating the result of a computation. But disputes concerning realism arise chiefly because, in other cases, the notion of what makes a sentence true comes apart from that on the basis of which we recognize it as true. The most obvious example is a sentence involving quantification over an infinite totality. What, on a platonist view, makes 'Every natural number is the sum of four squares' true is the joint satisfaction, by each natural number, of the predicate 'ξ is the sum of four squares'; and the point of saying this is that it represents the way that, on a classical theory of meaning, the sense of the universal quantifier is given to us, namely in terms of how the truth-value of a universally quantified sentence is determined. What, in turn, makes the predicate 'ξ is the sum of four squares' true of a given number, say 23, is the truth of some one equation of the form exemplified by '$3^2 + 3^2 + 2^2 + 1^2 = 23$'. But, though we can recognize the truth of '23 is the sum of four squares' by checking through the finitely many relevant equations, we cannot come to recognize the truth of Lagrange's Theorem itself in a manner that similarly corresponds to what we take as making it true, since we cannot inspect each member of an infinite totality; we are therefore forced to rely on an indirect means of recognizing the universally quantified sentence as true—one that does not mirror the sense of the sentence as given in terms of its structure—namely in this case, a relatively complicated proof. One who holds that, on the contrary, it is the proof that makes the theorem true must equate the truth of a mathematical statement with the existence of a proof. He must then explain the sense of the universal quantifier in a different way, namely in terms of what is required to prove a universally quantified statement; and he then no longer has a ground for regarding every such statement as being either true or false.

A harsh critic of Frege might connect his view of senses as immutable entities independent of being grasped with his realism. I have connected it with his desire to safeguard the objectivity of sense in face of what he took to be the irredeemably subjective character of the mental. For him, to grasp a sense is a mental act, but senses are not mental contents: that which is grasped lies outside the mind and is independent of it. In Chapter 16, I represented Wittgenstein's dictum that 'understanding is not a mental process' as his solution to a problem with which Frege grappled. But it is hardly, in itself, a solution, only a rejection of a false account: for the solution, we must look to Wittgenstein's positive account of understanding. There is, of course, no brief slogan that encapsulates this: we might cite the following. 'The grammar of the word "knows" is evidently closely related to that of "can", "is able to". But also closely related to that of "understands". ('Mastery' of a technique.)[1] ' "It's as if we could grasp the whole use of a word in a flash". — . . . we sometimes describe what we do in these words. But there is . . . nothing queer about what happens. It becomes queer when we are led to think that the future development must in some way already be present in the act of grasping the use and yet isn't present—For we say that there isn't any doubt that we understand the word, and on the other hand its meaning lies in its use'.[2] 'To understand a sentence means to understand a language. To understand a language means to be master of a technique.'[3] Now in fact Wittgenstein's

senses

---

[1] *Investigations*, I-150.

[2] Ibid., I-197.

[3] Ibid., I-199.

arguments for denying that understanding is a mental process are essentially the same as Frege's arguments for denying that senses are mental contents. Why, then, did Frege not arrive at a conception of understanding similar to Wittgenstein's? A hostile critic might reply that Frege could not take understanding to reside in a practical ability, the mastery of a technique, without endangering his realism, since an ability to use the language may embody a capacity to recognize a sentence as true, but, when the two diverge, cannot embody a knowledge of what makes the sentence true. Hence, according to such a critic, Frege took refuge in the idea of sense as an objective inhabitant of a realm accessible to our minds, though not through the sense-organs: our grasp of sense guides our use of the expression, and indeed determines the whole of its use in advance, without having to be exhaustively manifested by that use. I record this view, but I do not share it: as I already observed in Chapter 3, this would lay Frege open to the same attack as that which he made upon psychologism, and fails to tally with his claim that it is an ascertainable matter which sense another speaker associates with a given expression.[1] But it should be acknowledged that we have here a point, and one indeed of the greatest importance, concerning which the interpretation of Frege must remain uncertain: he says too little on this crucial matter for it to be possible to ascribe to him one view or the other. We do best to note that there are elements of his thought which point in one direction, and others which point in the opposite one.

naive realism   The theory of meaning determines what makes a statement true, if it is true; it belongs to epistemology to judge whether we are able to recognize what makes a statement true as obtaining, or whether we are able to establish the truth of the statement only indirectly. Disputes concerning realism thus acquire an epistemological component as well as a logical one: and, in traditional discussions of the question, realism has often been characterized as involving an epistemological doctrine. The way this comes about is as follows. The fundamental thesis of realism, as we have been considering it so far, is that we really do succeed in referring to external objects, existing independently of our knowledge of them, and that the statements we make about them carry a meaning of such a kind that they are rendered true or false by an objective reality the constitution of which is, again, independent of our knowledge. This is a thesis concerning the theory of meaning. A theory of meaning must, however, do much more than simply present a semantic theory, a theory of reference

[1] 'Über Sinn und Bedeutung', pp. 29–30.

in Frege's terminology: it must, that is, do more than simply analyse the way in which a sentence is determined as true, when it is true, in accordance with its composition. It must also explain in what the senses of expressions consist, and how those senses determine the references of the expressions. Its account of sense may be given directly in terms of the use of the expressions, their role in the practice of speaking the language; or it may be given in terms of the speakers' mastery of those expressions, their ability to engage in that practice as it relates to the expressions in question. For Frege, a mastery of an expression consists in a grasp of its sense, and we saw in Chapter 5 that, for him, to grasp a sense was to know something: sense is for him a cognitive notion, as I remarked repeatedly in *FPL*. So conceived, part of the function of a theory of meaning is to say what it is that a speaker knows when he grasps the sense of an expression of the language, and to explain how the sense grasped by the speakers determines the expression as having that reference which it has, its reference being that whereby it contributes to determining the truth or falsity of any sentence in which it occurs. A realistic theory of meaning must take a truth-conditional form: it must, as Frege did, equate a grasp of the thought expressed by a sentence with a knowledge of the condition that must obtain for that sentence to be true. It has, therefore, to explain in what a speaker's knowledge of that condition consists.

Now we cannot, in general, presume that there will always be an informative answer to the question what makes a given statement true, if it is true, or what, in general, makes a statement of some given class true, when it is true. A trivial answer to the question what makes a statement *A* true, if it is true, is one that consists, actually or in effect, of simply repeating the statement; and a trivial general answer to the question what makes any statement of a certain class true, when it is true, is one that amounts to no more than saying, 'That statement's being true'. In some instances, an informative answer may be given to the question what makes a given statement, or any statement of a certain class, true if it is true; but, in others, nothing better than a trivial answer may be available. It sometimes happens that the disagreement between a realist and his opponent is of such a nature that, for the opponent, there is an informative answer to the question, as applied to the class of statements in dispute, while the realist can offer only a trivial answer. For example, a constructivist has an informative answer to the question, 'What, in general, makes a true mathematical statement true?', namely, 'The existence of a proof of that statement'. One who adopts a realistic interpretation of mathematical statements, on the other hand, that is to say, a platonist, can give no answer to the question, 'What makes Lagrange's Theorem true?', save 'Every natural number's being the sum of four squares', which is simply to formulate Lagrange's Theorem. To the general question, 'What makes a mathematical statement true, if it is true?', the platonist can do no better than to reply, 'The constitution of mathematical reality'; but since mathematical reality is composed of mathematical facts, this reply amounts to saying that each true mathematical statement is rendered true by the fact which it states, and is therefore quite uninformative. That is not to say that it is constitutive of realism concerning a given class of statements to hold that only a trivial answer can be given to the question what, in general, makes such a statement true when it is true; we might use the label 'naive realism' for a version of realism that incorporates such a thesis, which is a type of irreducibility thesis. It is true that the enunciation of a reductive thesis is very often a prelude to advancing a non-realistic interpretation of the statements to which the reduction is to be applied. A reductive thesis may take the form of proposing a translation of statements of one class into statements of another, or the weaker form of holding that statements of the former class can be true only if suitable statements of the latter class are true; here statements of the latter class are thought of as intelligible independently of those of the former class, but not conversely: rather, a grasp of the relation between them expressed by the reductive thesis is essential to an understanding of statements of the former class. Very often, a reductive thesis is expressed, rather vaguely, by saying that statements apparently about things of one kind are really about things of another kind. For instance, statements ascribing sensations may be held to be reducible to statements concerning behaviour, or statements in the past tense to statements about present evidence: both these reductive theses would provide a basis for the adoption of an anti-realistic view of sensations or of the past. Because a reductive thesis is very often the first step towards a rejection of realism, there is a temptation to equate anti-realism with reductionism. This is a mistake, however: a rejection of realism need not embody any reductive thesis; and, more importantly for our purpose, certain reductive theses are quite consistent with realism. What is called central-state materialism embodies a reductive thesis, to the effect that a psychological statement can be true only in virtue of some state of the central nervous system: but, so far from calling realism concerning psychological statements in question, it tends to reinforce it, because of the plausibility of the principle of bivalence for statements about the central nervous system. Realism of such a kind may be called sophisticated realism, in contrast to the naive variety.

epistemological
component

As we saw, given Frege's conception of grasping the sense of an expression as consisting in a piece of knowledge, it is part of the task of a theory of meaning to explain in what a speaker's knowledge of the condition for the truth of a sentence consists. When it is possible to give a non-trivial answer to the question in virtue of what a sentence of a certain form is true, if it is true, whether by appeal to some reductive thesis or in the light of some logical analysis of the expressions contained in it, we already have an explanation of what a speaker must know in knowing the condition for a sentence of that form to be true. But, even when no non-trivial answer can be given, there must be a non-trivial answer to the question in what our knowledge of the condition for such a statement to be true consists. The simplest way in which this latter question can be answered will be by attributing to the speaker a capacity, in favourable circumstances, to recognize the condition as obtaining or not obtaining. Just because we cannot state informatively what will render the sentence true, when it is true, the faculty of recognition thus attributed to the speaker will be a faculty of *unmediated* recognition; neither the speaker nor the meaning-theorist can say *whereby* he recognizes the condition as obtaining. That which renders the sentence true is the very thing of which we are directly aware when we recognize it as being true.

It is in this way that epistemology enters the question, for the claim that we possess a faculty for the direct recognition of a condition of a certain kind is evidently an epistemological one. Realism is a metaphysical doctrine, but one whose principal content belongs to the theory of meaning, or so it has been argued in the present chapter. The theory of meaning cannot, however, be kept sterilized from all epistemological considerations; especially is this so when sense is taken, as Frege takes it, to be a cognitive notion, the sense of an expression being what a speaker must know if he is to grasp its sense. For this reason, the phrase 'naive realism' has usually been understood in a stronger sense than that allotted to it above, as requiring an epistemological thesis as well as a semantic one: the thesis, namely, that we have a direct knowledge of the states of affairs which render true or false statements in the given class. For instance, a realistic interpretation of statements about the past involves regarding them as determinately true or false, independently of whether we know their truth-values or, in a particular case, have any means of knowing. On a realist view of past-tense statements, no reductive thesis concerning them has any plausibility; there will therefore be no non-trivial answer to the question what, in general, renders a statement in the past tense true if it is true. By the criterion stated above, a realistic view of statements about the past should therefore be classified as naively realistic; but this does not accord with accepted terminology. What would ordinarily be required, in addition, of naive realism about the past is the view that we can be directly acquainted with past states of affairs, memory affording us a direct contact with them.

In holding that our knowledge of the past in memory is direct, the naive realist is not merely making the true observation that a report of memory is not ordinarily the conclusion of an inference. For the same observation may be made about knowledge based on testimony; in asserting something which I have been told, I am not, in the standard case, expressing the conclusion of an inference from the premiss that my informant is usually reliable about such matters. Without its being ordinary practice to take what other people tell us to be true, we could not have a language; part of what a child has to learn, in learning language, is to accept and act on what other people say. If I were to call in doubt the truth of everything for which I have only the authority of others, I should simply know too little about the world to be able to judge, on an inductive basis, of the reliability of what others said to me. No one would say, however, that we have direct knowledge of what we know on the basis of testimony. The direct knowledge which the naive realist invokes is therefore not merely non-inferential knowledge: it is knowledge which excludes Cartesian doubt and which presents the object of knowledge to us as it really is in itself. If my knowledge of the past, in memory, is the outcome of a direct contact that I now make with the past event, Cartesian doubt becomes impossible: it must be *senseless* to suppose that I should have this memory even though the past event did not occur. For the naive realist, the connection between that which renders a statement true and our knowledge of its truth, when this is direct knowledge, becomes an intimate one, just as it is for the anti-realist. Because he is a realist, the naive realist believes that any statement of the given class must be determinately either true or false, whether or not we are able to recognize its truth-value, directly or indirectly; but it is our capacity, in favourable cases, to perceive directly that which renders true statements of that class that constitutes our understanding of what it is for any statement of that class to be true. Knowing what it is like to have direct knowledge of the truth of such a statement, we grasp what it is for any statement of the class to *be* true.

Without a grasp of this conception of direct knowledge, it is hard to understand empiricist epistemology. Locke, for instance, says, of colours, that they 'are nothing in the objects themselves but powers to produce various sensations in us'.[1] Ayer, having quoted this statement of Locke's, then attributes to him the view that 'colour is nothing in the object itself', without adding the phrase 'but powers to produce various sensations in us'.[2] At first sight, this is as unwarranted as if someone, accused of being nothing but a snob, should say, 'He said that I was nothing': if colours, in the objects, are powers to produce sensations, then presumably they are in the objects, though indeed only as powers. Yet Ayer is not misrepresenting Locke, who later says that colours are not really in the bodies.[3] How does it come about that he makes this seemingly unjustifiable transition from his own doctrine as originally stated? The answer is that Locke is attracted to naive realism, though wishing to depart from it in respect of secondary qualities. A naive realist about the physical world supposes that, in perception, we are in direct contact with physical objects: we know them as they really are. When, under normal conditions, I perceive an object, then, given my perceptual state, it would be senseless to suppose that the object was not present or was otherwise than I perceive it to be; mistakes occur only because perception does not always take place under normal conditions. My ability to judge the truth of material-object statements on the basis of observation constitutes, for the naive realist, my knowledge of what has to be the case for those statements to be true, my grasp of their truth-conditions: so the very meaning of an ascription of perceptible qualities to an object is given by reference to the process of perceptual recognition of those qualities, and can only be so given. A disposition, on the other hand, is not a quality of which we can be directly aware in such a way. On Locke's analysis of the word 'colour', a colour is a disposition, and is really in the object. But, on the naive realist's understanding of the word 'colour', a colour cannot be a disposition, for then perception, under normal conditions, would not be an immediate awareness of the object as it really is: so, as he understands 'colour', Locke's view entails that objects do not have colours. It is the conflation of these two conceptions of what the word 'colour' means that produces Locke's contradictory modes of expression.

The thesis of direct knowledge, considered as a component of naive realism, serves many purposes. Epistemologically, it is a means of defeating scepticism by rendering it senseless. From the standpoint of a theory of meaning, it provides an account of our grasp of the truth-conditions, and thereby of the senses, of sentences of the given class. Metaphysically,

[1] *Essay concerning Human Understanding*, bk. II, ch. VIII, § 10.
[2] *The Central Questions of Philosophy*, London, 1973, p. 85.
[3] Ibid., § 17.

it embodies a doctrine concerning the character of things as they are in themselves. The question how things are in themselves is, as already observed, the fundamental question of metaphysics. What we seek is a characterization of reality not dependent, for its truth or for its intelligibility, on our particular position in the world, our particular faculties of perception and intellectual capacities and spatiotemporal perspective. To the attainment of such a characterization of reality in absolute terms—or to the recognition that it is unattainable—the issues regarding realism concerning the various classes of statements in dispute are highly relevant, and, in particular, the correctness or incorrectness of reductive theses that enter into disputes concerning realism. Nevertheless, we should not construe realism or the rival doctrines advanced by those who reject this or that form of realism as embracing an entire metaphysical theory: realism, as such, is a doctrine concerning the relation between our thought, as expressed in language, and the reality about which we think, not an all-embracing theory of the constitution of that reality. Frege's contributions to epistemology are sparse: in particular, he expressed no views concerning the character of the knowledge that is not arrived at by inference and is not a priori; and he neither defended nor opposed the conception of direct knowledge which I have here taken to be a component of naive realism. It is possible that those who resist the description of Frege as a realist are moved by precisely this consideration. But, if so, they are mistaken. The thesis about direct knowledge is not a necessary ingredient of realism as such: it is an ingredient of *naive* realism, and it is perfectly possible to be a realist while rejecting either that thesis or the irreducibility thesis which I have here treated as characterizing naive realism.

the context principle

As we saw in Chapter 19, there is one place where Frege's realism appears to falter, namely when the context principle, as a thesis concerning reference, is invoked to justify the ascription of reference to abstract proper names. When applied in this way, the context principle appears to presume that the senses of sentences containing proper names of the abstract objects in question are given in advance and independently of the ascription of reference to those proper names, and that the means of fixing their senses is appealed to in justification of our ascribing a reference to them. If this is so, then the notion of reference will not be employed in the theory of meaning, as it relates to those sentences: the truth-conditions of such sentences will be represented as given in some other way. This is most easily seen for the case in which their senses are given by means of some contextual definition, a procedure which, in *Grundlagen*, Frege takes the context principle as warranting. A contextual definition for sentences of a certain kind, e.g. sentences containing numerical terms, is, in effect, a strong form of reductive thesis, offering an actual translation. As we have noted, a reductive thesis is not in itself inconsistent with realism, but merely guarantees that the realist must be sophisticated rather than naive. But the reductive thesis remains consistent with realism only if it preserves the logical structure of the sentences to which it applies; if, for example, the singular terms occurring in those sentences are treated as genuine singular terms standing for objects, even if objects characterizable in a quite different way. For instance, central-state materialism, earlier given as an example of a reductive thesis that does not impugn realism concerning psychological states, does not analyse out expressions for psychological states; it merely treats them as standing for states of the central nervous system. But the type of contextual definition envisaged in *Grundlagen* will convert sentences containing numerical terms into ones containing no corresponding terms at all: it does not explain numerical terms as standing for objects of a kind we should not at first sight take them as standing for, but explains sentences containing them as equivalent to sentences containing no proper names at all. A reduction of this kind is not compatible with realism. The sense of a sentence containing numerical terms is thus to be explained by appeal to the given method of translation into sentences containing no such terms; the notion of reference, as applied to numerical terms, plays no part in the account of the senses of such sentences, nor, therefore, of numerical terms themselves. It is, of course, true that Frege, having toyed with the idea of so explaining numerical terms, rejected it in favour of an explicit definition of them as classes of concepts. But that only leads to the question with which Frege grappled in *Grundgesetze*, vol. I, § 10, namely how the senses of sentences containing class-terms, or, more generally, value-range terms, are given, and what role the notion of the reference of such terms plays in our grasp of their senses.

In 'Frege as a Realist', I remarked[1] that 'if . . . we are justified in taking abstract names at their face-value and ascribing reference to them simply on the ground that we have provided determinate truth-conditions for sentences containing them, then the means by which such truth-conditions were laid down cannot itself have involved any appeal to the notion of reference for such names'; and I commented that 'whether this was what Frege intended . . . is far from clear, since he does not achieve, in *Grund-gesetze*, a means of stipulating the truth-conditions of sentences containing

---

[1] P. 458.

names of value-ranges in terms that do not presuppose that we know what, in general, value-ranges are'. Sluga quotes this comment, and retorts, 'That, of course, is something that Frege found out only in 1902 and cannot have been a reason for his supposed abandoning of the contextual principle in 1891.'[1] The point is not, however, that the system of *Grundgesetze* was inconsistent, but that, as I stated in 'Frege as a Realist',[2] 'for the stipulations to be successful, we must already take the individual variables as ranging over a domain including value-ranges (or at least over an equally large domain)'. Frege should have been aware of this in writing *Grundgesetze*, and of the analogous point concerning numerical terms in writing *Grundlagen*: it does not depend upon the fact that the domain for the system of *Grundgesetze* was required to be impossibly large. Suppose that we start with some theory, whose interpretation we shall assume to be unproblematic, allowing higher-order quantification, and with a domain for the individual variables comprising concrete objects of some kind, say animals or stars. Within this theory we can define 'There are just as many Φ's as Ψ's' in terms of the existence of a relation effecting a one-to-one mapping, where the argument-places indicated by 'Φ' and 'Ψ' are to be filled with predicates of the theory, defined over the domain of the theory. We may now, if we wish, introduce a new form of sentence, 'The number of Φ's = the number of Ψ's', defined contextually as equivalent to 'There are just as many Φ's as Ψ's'; and we may also introduce a new sort of individual variable, namely numerical variables, where 'For every u, $A(\mathit{u})$' is contextually defined as equivalent to 'For every f, A(the number of f's)'. So long as we keep the new numerical variables quite distinct from the original individual variables of the theory, we have here genuine contextual definitions; sentences containing numerical terms formed by means of the new operator 'the number of Φ's', and ones containing bound numerical variables, can be transformed into equivalent sentences of the original theory. We may therefore either think of the numerical variables as ranging over a domain distinct from the original domain over which the ordinary individual variables range, and of the numerical terms as standing for elements of this new domain, or regard reference to and quantification over numbers as a mere façon de parler, a means of expressing statements already expressible in the original theory. But the status of our means of introducing numerical terms and numerical quantifiers as a system of contextual definitions remains unimpaired only so long as we restrict the application of the operator 'the number of Φ's'

[1] 'Frege's Alleged Realism', pp. 240–1.
[2] P. 458.

to predicates defined only over the original domain; as soon as we allow that we may insert in its argument-place a predicate defined over numbers, that is, over the new domain containing the referents of numerical terms, we have lost the means of transforming sentences containing numerical terms and numerical variables into ones not containing them.

Now, in *Grundlagen*, Frege labours to persuade his readers that it is necessary to regard numbers as objects. Taking them as objects belonging to some domain quite distinct from that of the ordinary individual variables would not, for him, have been to treat them as genuine objects at all, but as some kind of pseudo-objects; it is implicit in his use of the term 'object' that whatever is recognized as an object belongs to that domain over which all individual variables are to range. This is not merely consonant with his general philosophy, but essential to his conception of numbers; in the Appendix to *Grundgesetze*, vol. II,[1] he speaks of the necessity of being able to speak of the number of numbers of a given kind (for instance, the number of solutions of an equation or the number of primes less than a given number). Not merely is it essential to his conception of numbers, but it is crucial for his derivation of the fundamental laws of number theory from purely logical principles: the proof, in *Grundlagen*, §§ 79–83, of the infinity of the series of natural numbers, namely that every natural number has a successor, depends upon being able to apply the operator 'the number of Φ's' to the predicate 'ξ belongs to the series of natural numbers ending with n', i.e. to the predicate '$\xi \leq n$'. For this proof to be given, it was therefore essential that the numerical operator should be introduced in such a way that the terms formed by its means were taken as standing for objects lying in the domain of the individual variables of the theory; there was thus no possibility, from the outset, of introducing it by means of a genuine contextual definition, where it is taken as essential to a definition that one has a means of replacing sentences containing the defined term by equivalent ones not containing it. Either the domain must, from the outset, be conceived as including numbers, or, at least, it must have been conceived as large enough for the numerical terms to be assigned elements of it as their referents, that is to say, as being at least denumerable. There is here, of course, no question of inconsistency: it is just that, quite apart from the objections Frege raises in §§ 66–7 of *Grundlagen* to the manner of introducing the numerical operator proposed in §§ 62–3, that way of introducing it would not really have constituted a contextual definition; it would, rather, have

[1] P. 255.

been an axiom governing a primitive operator. It is thus far from clear that we should, even on that way of introducing it, have a means of fixing the senses of sentences containing numerical terms that did not invoke the notion of reference for such terms; and equally unclear that we could really justify the ascription of reference to them by appeal to the context principle.

In *Grundgesetze*, we have what is expressly presented as an axiom governing a primitive operator, the abstraction operator which yields terms for value-ranges; otherwise, save for the inconsistency of the system, indeed not known to Frege until 1902, the situation is exactly parallel. If value-range terms were thought of as denoting elements of a domain distinct from that over which the ordinary individual variables ranged, and if a special sort of variable were to be used to range over value-ranges, then Axiom V would, in effect, embody a contextual definition, and would be quite consistent; in that case, we could regard reference to and quantification over value-ranges as only a manner of speaking, and it could be said without a qualm that a statement of the identity of value-ranges expressed precisely the same sense as the statement that the functions had the same values for every argument. In fact, things stand quite differently: value-ranges are to be taken as belonging to the domain of the one sort of individual variable, and the abstraction operator can be applied to expressions for functions defined over value-ranges. It would thus be quite wrong to say that an equation between value-ranges expressed no more than the thought expressed by the universal quantification of an equation between the values of the functions for the same argument, as Frege was disposed to claim in *Function und Begriff* but ever afterwards avoided saying. It would also be untrue to say that we had a means of fixing the senses of symbolic formulas containing value-range terms that did not appeal to the notion of reference for such terms: to understand the formulas, we must know over what domain the variables are intended to range, and we have no way of grasping that without knowing that it must be a domain closed under the operation which carries a first-level function, defined over the domain, into its value-range. We thus do not have in Frege's work any genuine, or at least straightforward, instance of a justification of an ascription of reference to abstract terms by appeal to the context principle. The suggestion, in *Grundlagen*, that such a justification would be sound provides a hint that Frege's realism concerning abstract objects is more rhetorical than genuine: but it is no more than a hint, since his actual practice never allows for such a justification. It may be argued, by some, that, in the end, Frege does not have a coherent doctrine concerning abstract objects, that is, a coherent account of how the senses of sentences about them are given. If they are right, it naturally becomes impossible to say for certain whether Frege's realism about abstract objects was genuine or not: what is certain is that he professes himself a realist concerning them.

Taken as a thesis concerning reference, the context principle appears to run counter to realism; but it may be argued that this is true in a profounder sense than we have yet envisaged. It does not apply only to terms whose sense is given by means of a way of fixing the senses of sentences containing them that does not appeal to the notion of reference for such terms: rather, on this view, it applies even where we do appeal to the notion of reference. Donald Davidson argues[1] that, although the notion of reference is indispensable for any systematic account of the way in which the truth-conditions of the sentences of a language are determined, the connection between that part of a theory of meaning for the language which supplies such an account and our actual practice in speaking the language relates only to the notion of truth, not to that of reference: 'it is the notion of truth, as applied to closed sentences, which must be connected with human ends and activities.'[2] The reason is that 'words have no function save as they play a role in sentences: their semantic features are abstracted from the semantic features of sentences, just as the semantic features of sentences are abstracted from *their* part in helping people achieve goals or realize intentions.'[3] We therefore need to connect the notion of truth, as employed by the theory of meaning, with the actual employment of sentences; but we need no account of that in which the relation of reference consists, such as, for example, the causal theory of reference purports to provide. The role of the concepts of satisfaction and reference is theoretical; that is to say, they have their place solely *within* the recursive characterization of the truth-conditions of sentences of the language, and are not themselves to be connected with any features of linguistic practice: it suffices that we can so connect the truth-conditions of sentences with their employment in speech.

This thesis is evidently derived from the context principle, taken simultaneously as a principle concerning sense and reference. If it is correct, then it implies that a fully-fledged realism, as it has been characterized in this chapter, is always mistaken; at least, if that characterization be read as involving that the notion of reference employed by the theory of

a theoretical notion?

---

[1] 'Reality without Reference', *Dialectica*, vol. 31, 1977, pp. 247–58.
[2] Ibid., p. 254.
[3] Ibid., pp. 252–3.

meaning can be directly explained in terms of some feature of linguistic practice, rather than remaining a mere theoretical tool in the specification of the truth-conditions of sentences. It also implies that, in so far as Frege continued to adhere to the context principle, he was *not* a fully-fledged realist. He may have been a realist in respect of the main structure of his semantic theory, as a classical two-valued semantics governed by the assumption of bivalence, and in respect of the fundamental character of his theory of meaning, according to which to grasp the sense of a sentence is to apprehend the condition for it to be true. He may also have used realistic language in talking about the referents of expressions: but this language is not to be taken at face-value, since, for him, the notion of reference 'plays no essential role in explaining the relation between language and reality',[1] but is a purely theoretical notion functioning as an auxiliary in a theory to be judged solely by its representation of the senses of whole sentences.

Can it be that it is on the basis of such an interpretation of Frege that Sluga, who believes that I underestimate the importance of the context principle in Frege's philosophy, has denied that Frege was a realist and that his doctrines are to be interpreted ontologically? It is hard to find a hint in Sluga's text that this was his meaning; but, if it was, he is surely mistaken, if not about the realism, then about the ontology. For, as Davidson says,[2] a theory of the kind he is recommending 'does not . . . explain reference, at least in this sense: it assigns no empirical content directly to relations between names or predicates and objects. These relations are given a content *indirectly* when the T-sentences are', the T-sentences being those which state the truth-conditions of the sentences of the object-language. 'The theory gives up reference, then,' he continues, 'as part of the cost of going empirical. It can't, however, be said to have given up ontology. For the theory relates each singular term to some object or other, and it tells what entities satisfy each predicate. Doing without reference is not at all to embrace a policy of doing without semantics or ontology.' That is to say, such a theory really does say that, for example, 'Prague' stands for a specific city, 'Jimmy Carter' for a specific man, etc.; it is just that it offers no direct justification for its saying this, but only an indirect justification relating to the use made of whole sentences containing the names 'Prague' and 'Jimmy Carter'. A theory of this kind therefore does not eliminate ontology; and it deviates from realism only in so far as it is taken as essential to realism to assume that a direct explana-

[1] Ibid., p. 258.
[2] Ibid., pp. 255–6.

tion of the relation of reference can be given. If we do not assume this, then surely abstract terms are as good as any other. We suppose otherwise, because we think that there is a special difficulty, in their case, in saying in what the relation of reference consists. The correct answer is that we do not need, and should not try, to say in *any* case in what the relation of reference consists; it is only because we wrongly suppose both that we ought to, and that we can, say in what the relation consists when the proper names stand for concrete objects that the context principle appears as a justification for ascribing reference to abstract proper names in particular.

The general principle to which Davidson is appealing, namely that a theory of meaning may legitimately make use of theoretical notions with no direct empirical content, is surely sound. Suppose, for example, that some finitely many-valued semantic theory is found to afford a neat method of systematizing the manner in which the truth-conditions of complex sentences depend upon the subsentences. There will obviously be no need to justify the use of the many-valued truth-tables by appeal to anything of which the speakers are aware, or may readily be made aware, or to any feature of their use of the subsentences save their treating the complex sentences as true in and only in such-and-such cases. But can reference itself be a purely theoretical notion of this kind? Davidson's idea is that it is a mere auxiliary, although an indispensable one, in devising a finitely axiomatized theory from which we can derive the truth-conditions of all sentences of the language. For instance, if the object-language has a singular term 'XIII' and a predicate 'Py(ξ)', it may be that we shall need one axiom stating that 'XIII' stands for 13 and another stating that, for each x, x satisfies 'Py(ξ)' iff x is a natural number and, for some $n \geqslant 1$, $x = 8n - 3$; from these, together with a general axiom relating to atomic sentences, we shall be able to derive that 'Py(XIII)' is true iff, for some n, $13 = 8n - 3$. There will be no need to give any empirical content to the proposition that 'XIII' stands for 13; all that is required is to give empirical content to the proposition expressed by the T-sentence ' "Py (XIII)" is true iff, for some n, $13 = 8n - 3$' and other like propositions. But what empirical content is to be given to this proposition? What is it for the speakers to treat a given sentence as having a certain truth-condition? Davidson's remark, quoted earlier, that the semantic features of words are abstracted from the semantic features of sentences is surely correct. But this means that any plausible account of what it is to treat an atomic sentence as having a certain truth-condition must manifest, in the behaviour which constitutes so treating it, an articulation, corresponding to the structure of the sentence: we shall be able to indicate a common feature of the use of two or more sentences containing the same singular term, and a different common feature of the use of two or more sentences containing the same predicate. Indeed, it is hardly thinkable that we can isolate that item of our linguistic behaviour which constitutes treating some individual sentence as having a certain truth-condition: the justification for saying that we so treat it will depend in part of our use of other sentences related to it in various ways, including the occurrence of the same singular term and that of the same primitive predicate. That is to say, to assert that a given sentence is treated as having a certain truth-condition is to appeal to a discernible pattern in the use that we make, not only of it, but of other sentences structurally related to it: and the description of this pattern must invoke the inner composition of the sentences. Davidson argues that the attempt to provide a semantic theory by means of a direct explanation of the semantic features of proper names and simple predicates, 'often called the Building-Block theory, . . . has often been tried. And it is hopeless.'¹ He ascribes such a theory to the British empiricists, citing Berkeley, Hume and Mill. It should give us pause that Frege, the author of the context principle upon which Davidson's whole argument is based, himself used the metaphor of building-blocks. What is hopeless is what the empiricists attempted to do, namely to explain the meanings of proper names and simple predicates otherwise than as relating to the sentences in which they occur. It does not follow that an account of the use of such sentences will not display common features in the uses of sentences containing the same proper name or the same predicate, nor that it will make no appeal to the composition of the sentences. It is, indeed, virtually impossible to see how it can avoid doing so. If we concentrate only on the necessity of arriving at a statement of the truth-conditions of sentences, it will be natural to see reference and satisfaction as merely auxiliary devices for attaining that end. But the task of a theory of meaning is far from completed at that point; it has also to explain what it is to assign a given truth-condition to a sentence, and it is hardly thinkable that it can do so without taking further account of the inner structure of the sentence.

The context principle certainly rules out any account of the relation of reference which, like a crude interpretation of the causal theory of reference, makes the question whether the relation obtains between a proper name and an object independent of what the speakers would

¹ Ibid., p. 252.

recognize as settling the truth of sentences containing the name. It also rules out an account of that relation which, like more sophisticated versions of the causal theory, allow for an explanation of the relation in terms which do not allude to the use of sentences containing the name. But, even when we aim to give a direct description of the connection between the truth-conditions of sentences and our linguistic practice as it relates to those sentences, it does not rule out an appeal, in the course of that description, to the notion of reference. The form that that appeal must take is clearer when the language contains demonstratives and the proper name can occur in recognition statements, which is why the problem arises whether the notion of reference can really play the same role in our theory of meaning as applied to terms for abstract objects as it does when applied to names of concrete ones. But it is a mistake to think that, even when the proper name is capable of occurring in recognition statements, the account of the relation of reference is utterly straightforward and uncomplicated: on the contrary, it involves a description of the use of the most basic layer of language, that in which demonstratives play an essential role, which, as we have seen, is itself a complex matter; we cannot explain what it is to treat a name as standing for an object of a certain kind without explaining what it is to identify an object of that kind. This conclusion is reinforced when a grasp of the sense of a sentence is thought of as Frege does, namely as something that the speaker knows. Here the understanding of the sentence, which is something cognitive, an act of the mind, mediates between the semantic features of the sentence, in the strict sense, that is, its structure and the references of its constituents, and the actual employment of the sentence. For Frege, a speaker grasps the sense of a sentence only by apprehending its truth-value as being determined in a certain way corresponding to its structure, the senses of the constituents determining their referents and hence the truth-value of the whole. The conception of the references of the parts of the sentence therefore enters into the speaker's grasp of the thought it expresses: without this conception, we cannot explain what it is for him to know the condition that must obtain for it to be true.

Sluga calls my characterization of realism 'crude', and questions whether it will coincide with the notion of realism as traditionally employed.[1] Part of the point of the characterization is to bring out the similarities between philosophical disputes concerning many different kinds of subject-matter. If one interprets 'realism' as opposed only to idealism, it becomes

anti-realism

---

[1] 'Frege's Alleged Realism' p. 236.

impossible to do this. One cannot then see behaviourism as a rejection of realism concerning mental states, or neutralism as a rejection of realism about the future; one will find difficulty in the description of David Lewis as a realist concerning possible worlds; since instrumentalism may spring from a naive realist view of the physical world, one will be confused how it may also be a rejection of realism concerning the theoretical entities of science; and one will regard the realism of the scholastics, realism concerning universals, as wholly unrelated to the realism of modern philosophy. But it may still be objected that my characterization of realism is too generous; that notorious idealists such as Berkeley will come out, under it, as realists, even if highly sophisticated ones. But I think it no great objection if there are some at first sight counter-intuitive results of this kind. There has been a persistent tendency to confuse realism with the rejection of reductive theses. The confusion is understandable, since, as previously observed, the enunciation of a reductive thesis is very often the first step towards the adoption of an anti-realist position, though it is not essential for such a position. But it is a confusion, nevertheless; acceptance of a reductive thesis does not necessarily involve the rejection of realism, although, under the definition here given, it necessarily entails repudiating naive realism. It depends upon the character of the reductive thesis, and the conception adopted of the meanings of the statements to which the reduction is made, whether the resulting view is an anti-realist one or only a species of sophisticated realism. If this distinction has not always been clear to those who have loosely used the term 'realism', it remains an important distinction; and, whether the result is crude or not, I believe I have made a more determined attempt than have most people to give the term 'realism' a precise sense. As for Berkeley, it is probably true that he ends up in a position describable as a sophisticated realism about the material world. His initial arguments are reductive ones, which appear to lead to a decidedly anti-realist view, phenomenalism. But he has further arguments, which lead him to think that the truth of the question cannot be stated without reference to God. Most of his admirers are not prepared to follow him into this second phase of his discussion of the subject, and so his principal interest has been felt to be as an early proponent of phenomenalism; but that entails no conclusion about how Berkeley's own final position ought to be described. Frege, on the other hand, rejected even the first steps that lead in the anti-realist direction; and he did so because, although he had no philosophical account to offer of the nature of material objects, his logic, that is, his theory of meaning, demands realism.

Sluga hazards the view that 'Frege's position must be akin to' Kant's.[1] There is no need to speculate what Frege's view of Kant was; he tells us a great deal about it in *Grundlagen*. In a long footnote to § 27, he says that it is because Kant associated both the subjective and the objective meaning with the word 'idea' (*Vorstellung*) that 'he gave his doctrine a highly subjective, idealistic complexion'. In § 88 he criticizes Kant for underestimating the value of analytic judgments, for defining analyticity too narrowly, and for thinking of concepts as determined only by the conjunction of characteristics, 'one of the least fruitful methods of concept-formation'. In § 89 he rejects Kant's assertion that without sensibility no object would be given to us. He then piously remarks that he must call attention to the points on which he agrees with Kant, which outweigh his disagreements, 'in order not to incur the reproach of picking petty quarrels with a genius to whom we must all look up with grateful awe': he lists the distinction between synthetic and analytic judgments, the existence of synthetic a priori ones, and the recognition that geometrical truths are of this nature, despite the mistake of believing the same about arithmetical ones. This seems rather a thin crop for one whom Sluga believes to have been so close to Kant in philosophical outlook; and the remark from the footnote to § 27 hardly suggests that it was the idealist strain in Kant that Frege admired. But does not Frege's acceptance of the synthetic a priori commit him to a substantial endorsement of Kantian thought? It does not do so, because, just as Frege's explanation of 'analytic' differs from Kant's, so does his explanation of 'a priori'. According to Frege, the characterization of a truth as analytic, synthetic a priori or a posteriori relates to the ultimate justification for holding it to be true (*Grundlagen*, § 3); not the actual ground we may have for believing it, but the type of justification that is to be found. An analytic truth is one that can be derived from general logical laws, appealing only to logical principles of inference and to definitions. An a posteriori truth, Frege says, is one that cannot be proved 'without appeal to facts, that is, to truths that are not provable and lack generality, having as their content statements about particular objects'. A synthetic a priori truth is, then, one that can be proved without appeal to 'facts' in this sense, but is derived solely from general laws, although those laws are not exclusively logical in character. Both analytic and synthetic a priori truths are thus ones derivable from general laws, laws of which Frege says that they 'neither need nor admit of proof'; such laws are classifiable into those that are fundamental laws

[1] Ibid., p. 237.

of logic and those that are of a different kind. In the second footnote to § 3, Frege remarks that 'we must admit that there are such basic laws' of a non-logical kind, 'if we recognize general truths at all, . . . because from mere individual facts nothing follows save on the basis of a law'. As an example, he gives 'the general proposition that the method' of induction 'can establish the truth or at least the probability of a law', since otherwise there would be no justification for accepting that which was arrived at by the inductive method. Now although, in the first footnote to § 3, Frege professes not to be assigning a new sense to 'analytic' and 'a priori', but only to hit on what earlier writers, and Kant in particular, have meant, in § 88 he is quite willing to say that Kant defined 'analytic' too narrowly, and that, 'on the basis of his definition, the division of judgments into analytic and synthetic is not exhaustive', and to speak of 'the wider concept' of analyticity which he himself has used. All that we can say, therefore, is that he recognized a threefold classification analogous to Kant's, but drawn somewhat differently. In particular, he admitted the existence of general laws which, even though not laws of logic, we can recognize a priori as true, and which include the principles underlying geometry; but there is no ground for ascribing to him any thesis about what enables us to recognize such truths a priori. Indeed, the fact that, in saying what he can, in § 89, in favour of Kant, he does *not* say that Kant's explanation of the existence of synthetic a priori truths is correct serves to suggest that he did not share it.

Sluga remarks that 'throughout his life Frege held to the Kantian thesis that space and time are *a priori* intuitions and that geometrical and temporal propositions are, therefore, synthetic *a priori*'.[1] Now at the very end of his life Frege wrote an article, 'Erkenntnisquellen der Mathematik und der mathematischen Naturwissenschaften',[2] and began another, 'Neuer Versuch der Grundlegung der Arithmetik',[3] in which he propounded a geometrical foundation for the whole of mathematics. In these, he distinguishes three fundamental sources of knowledge, sense-perception and the logical and geometrical sources, with which he couples the temporal one. Mathematics requires no appeal to sense-perception, and there are no objects given by logic alone; so even arithmetic must derive from the geometrical source of knowledge, which alone can yield the infinite, and from which the axioms of geometry spring. In the second of the two articles, Frege refers to *Grundgesetze*, vol. 1 p. 1, which opens

[1] Ibid., p. 236.
[2] *N.S.*, pp. 286–94, *P.W.*, pp. 267–74.
[3] *N.S.*, pp. 298–302, *P.W.*, pp. 278–81.

with the observation, 'In my *Grundlagen der Arithmetik* I sought to make it probable that arithmetic is a branch of logic and needs to draw neither from experience nor from intuition any ground of proof', and retracts this, so far as intuition is concerned; and he explains that 'I understand by intuition the geometrical source of knowledge'. Friedrich Kaulbach states that this remark seems to indicate that the geometrical source of knowledge is closely connected with the 'sensible a priori intuition of which Kant spoke and which he designated as one of the "sources" from which flows the knowledge not only of geometry but also of arithmetic'.[1] It is true that Kant uses the term 'sources of knowledge';[2] and it may be that, in using the word 'intuition' in this connection, Frege is meaning to echo Kant:[3] but it seems more likely that he uses it precisely because he is engaged in saying by which of the opening remarks of *Grundgesetze* he now stands and which he now rejects. Frege does not use the word 'intuition' in the other of the two articles; and in neither does he tell us much about the character of the geometrical and temporal source of knowledge. For want of more detailed information, it is natural to think of a Kantian interpretation; but that is by no means certain, and, in any case, there can be no argument from these late works to Frege's earlier views, since he is quite consciously propounding a philosophy of mathematics wholly at variance with that of his mature period.

Sluga's confident assertion that Frege adhered, throughout his life, to a Kantian conception of space and time as *a priori* intuitions gives a sharp outline to his philosophy of geometry that does not accord with the cloudiness that in fact enfolds it. It is, indeed, certain that, throughout his life, Frege denied that geometry rests upon a purely logical foundation. He remarks that, in contrast to arithmetic, to assume the opposite of the axioms proper to geometry involves, from a purely logical standpoint, no contradiction;[4] the axioms of geometry relate to what is spatial, while arithmetic governs whatever can be an object of thought.[5] In speaking, in this connection, of the axioms of geometry, Frege presumably intended to refer to those of Euclidean geometry, which he continued throughout his life to regard as true, and as known by us to be true, under the primary senses of the geometrical primitives; he was never prepared to allow non-Euclidean

---

[1] *N.S.*, p. xxxi.

[2] *Critique of Pure Reason*, B55.

[3] He is certainly doing so in his letter to Marty of 1882, when he speaks of 'a source of knowledge like spatial intuition or sense perception' (*BW*, p. 164, *P.M.C.*, p. 100).

[4] 'Über formale Theorien der Arithmetik', 1885, p. 94.

[5] Ibid., pp. 94–5.

geometries a status equal to that of the Euclidean theory. But, although he affirmed these beliefs, he never attempted any clear explanation of the basis of our knowledge of the axioms of Euclidean geometry. He did, indeed, in a few passages, allude vaguely to intuition as the source of this knowledge. In 'Über formale Theorien' he remarks[1] that spatial intuition cannot form a basis for the knowledge of arithmetical truths, without saying positively that it is a basis for the knowledge of geometrical ones. His doctoral dissertation of 1873, 'Über eine geometrische Darstellung der imaginären Gebilde in der Ebene', opens with a declaration that 'the whole of geometry rests ultimately on axioms which derive their validity from the nature of our intuitive abilities'; this makes it problematic how we may speak of imaginary points of intersection of a circle with a straight line, or, in projective geometry, of points at infinity, which do not occur in the space of our intuition. In his *Habilitationsschrift* of 1874 the contrast between arithmetic and geometry is already clearly drawn. 'There is a remarkable distinction between geometry and arithmetic,' Frege wrote, 'as regards the basis of their fundamental principles. The elements of all geometrical constructions are intuitions, and geometry appeals to intuition as the source of its axioms. Since the object of arithmetic is not intuitable, its fundamental principles cannot spring from intuition.'[2] The dissertation itself is concerned with the concept of magnitude, one so comprehensive and abstract that, Frege claims, it clearly cannot be an intuition. 'That the concept of magnitude is capable of application in various ways in the realm of intuition suffices to assure us that we are not losing ourselves in empty speculation. This is the only use which we need to make of intuition.'[3] These references to intuition are obviously very unspecific. One could read 'perception' for 'intuition' without doing any violence to the texts; indeed, in the 'Logik' of 1897, Frege speaks of intuition (*Anschauung*) as arising out of present sensations,[4] and the English translators render *Anschauung* as 'perception'.[5] Plainly, one cannot elicit from these passages any particular philosophical doctrine, other than the negative assertion that geometry does not rest on logic alone; to attribute to Frege a specifically Kantian view of spatial intuition is to read that view into what he says, not from it, while temporal intuition receives no mention at all before 1924. The word '*Anschauung*' is in fact used very sparingly

[1] Ibid., p. 95.
[2] *Habilitationsschrift*, p. 1.
[3] Ibid., pp. 1–2.
[4] *N.S.*, p. 142.
[5] *P.W.*, p. 131.

in Frege's writings, and usually in no very precise manner, at least as far as can be ascertained from his text. There is only one work of his in which it occurs fairly frequently, and in which there is any explicit discussion of it, namely the *Grundlagen*; and it is also only in that work that he engages in any extended consideration of the doctrines of Kant. To it, therefore, we must return if we are to discover with any greater exactitude what he thought about these matters before he abandoned his life's ambition to found arithmetic securely upon logic.

The word 'intuition' occurs in the *Grundlagen* principally where Frege is criticizing the views of others, particularly Kant, and seldom in the course of any positive assertion. In § 5, Frege cites Kant's view that numerical equations are unprovable and synthetic, and asks how, if not by means of a proof, they are seen to be true, since they are not self-evident. Kant, he says, 'wishes to call upon the intuition of fingers or of points for support'; but 'whatever the intuition of 37863 fingers may be, it is certainly not a pure one', and, in any case, we have no such intuition. For if we did have the relevant intuitions, the correctness of a given equation would be immediately obvious, 'at least as applied to fingers'. It is difficult to see here any deep respect for Kant's notion of pure intuition. In § 12, Frege takes the matter up once more, remarking that Kant regards arithmetical laws as synthetic a priori. 'In that case,' he says, 'there remains nothing left other than a pure intuition to invoke as the ultimate ground of our knowledge, although it is hard to say whether it is spatial or temporal or something else again'. But, just as in his *Habilitationsschrift*, he objects, this time to Hankel, that 'the expression "pure intuition of magnitude" gives us pause. If we consider all the different things that are called magnitudes, . . . it is easily understood how they can all be subordinated to a *concept* of magnitude; but the expression "intuition of magnitude", and, still worse, "pure intuition of magnitude", cannot be admitted as appropriate.' In general, he remarks, 'we are all too ready to invoke inner intuition whenever we cannot cite any other ground'. He goes on to comment on the difference in the use of the word 'intuition' in Kant's *Logic* and in the *Critique of Pure Reason*. In the *Logic*, the sense given to the word is wider: an intuition is defined as an individual idea, as opposed to a concept, which is a general idea; but an intuition in that sense cannot serve as a ground for our knowledge of arithmetical laws. It is only in the *Critique* that intuition is connected with sensibility, when Kant says (B33) that 'it is through the medium of sensibility that objects are given to us' and that it is sensibility alone that furnishes us with intuitions. It is only intuition thus conceived as connected with sensibility that can, according to Frege, serve as the principle of our knowledge of synthetic a priori judgments. In the wider sense of 'intuition' as used in the *Logic*, 100,000 might perhaps be called an intuition, since it is certainly not a general concept; but, in the sense of the *Critique*, which is that relevant to synthetic a priori truths, it cannot be allowed that there is an intuition of 100,000. In §§ 89 and 104, Frege comes back to the question, again denying, at least in general, that we have intuitions of numbers; in § 89, he rejects Kant's statement (B75) that without sensibility no object would be given to us, hazarding the guess that Kant uses the word 'object' in a sense different from his own, one under which it will not apply to numbers, and remarks that, in that case, he has allowed no place for numbers, since they are not concepts, and even of a concept Kant requires that we should attach its object to it in intuition.

Of the scattered remarks made by Frege of his own accord about intuition in the *Grundlagen*, several seem to bear out Sluga's contention that he consistently regarded spatial intuition as supplying the ground of our knowledge of the truth of geometrical axioms. As noted above, he appears, in § 12, to allow that a knowledge of synthetic a priori truths must rest upon pure intuition. In § 13, he emphasizes the difference between arithmetic and geometry. One such difference is that each number has its own individual character, whereas a geometrical point, line or plane, considered in itself, cannot be distinguished from any other of its kind: 'it is only when several points, lines or planes are simultaneously comprehended in a single intuition that one distinguishes them.' Hence, he says, 'if in geometry general propositions are derived from intuition, the points, lines and planes that are intuited are not really particular at all and hence are able to count as representatives of their whole kind'. The antecedent of this conditional is not actually asserted; but he seems to look favourably upon it. He goes on, in § 14, to draw the contrast between the two branches of mathematics in much the same way as in 'Über formale Theorien', delivered as a lecture the year after the publication of *Grundlagen*. Geometrical truths govern the domain of what is spatially intuitable, whether actual or merely imagined. But the basis of arithmetic lies deeper than that of empirical science or even of geometry. Arithmetical truths govern all that is countable, and this domain is more comprehensive, since it comprises not only what is intuitable but everything that is even thinkable. It is true that, even in dealing with geometrical conceptions, conceptual thought is able to leave the ground of intuition behind, when, for example, it postulates a space of four dimensions or of positive curvature. For purposes of conceptual thought we can postulate the contrary of this or that geometrical axiom, without involving ourselves in any consequential contradiction. From the consistency of non-Euclidean geometries Frege here concludes that the axioms of (Euclidean) geometry are independent, not only of one another, but of the laws of logic, and that they must therefore be synthetic: by contrast, an attempt to deny any of the basic principles of arithmetic induces confusion. Later, Frege was to argue against the possibility of demonstrating the consistency of non-Euclidean geometries or the independence of the geometrical axioms. In any case, in investigating non-Euclidean geometries, we have left the ground of intuition behind: we have an intuition only of Euclidean space. In the same spirit, Frege speaks in § 90 of the axioms of intuition, and of the synthetic as resting on intuition, although he discouragingly remarks that we cannot compile a complete set of the axioms of intuition from which all mathematical proofs may be derived by means of logical laws; and in § 91 he congratulates himself on having, in his arithmetical proofs, borrowed no axiom from intuition.

All this would go quite well with an acceptance of Kant's view of geometry, although it falls far short of implying it. But when we look at the section of *Grundlagen* in which Frege sets out most explicitly his positive views on the matter, § 26, we receive a quite different impression. Anyone who commits himself to the Kantian thesis that space and time are a priori intuitions, Sluga tells us, 'commits himself to something like the belief that objects, in the normal, empirical sense, are mere appearances and do not exist apart from cognition';[1] and Frege held to that Kantian thesis throughout his life. There is, however, no need to rely on deductions: in § 26 of *Grundlagen* Frege sets out his attitude to such ideas with complete clarity. 'Space, according to Kant, belongs to appearance,' he says; 'to other rational beings it would be possible for it to present itself quite otherwise than to us'—a point on which, in fact, Kant expresses himself as agnostic (B72). As far as intuition goes, Frege is prepared to go further: 'we cannot even know whether it appears the same to one human being as to another: for we cannot lay the spatial intuition of one alongside that of another in order to compare them.' But that does not prove that space belongs to appearance. On the contrary, 'there is something objective contained in it; all recognize the same geometrical axioms, even if only by their behaviour. . . What is objective is what is subject to laws, what can be conceived and judged, what can be expressed in words. That which belongs to pure intuition is not communicable.' Later he reiterates, 'I understand by objectivity an independence from our sensations, intuitions and ideas.' On the view that Frege is here expressing, there is an objective

---

[1] 'Frege's Alleged Realism', p. 236.

world, with an objectively spatial character, governed by the axioms of (Euclidean) geometry. It is only the objective properties of that world that we can express in words and convey to one another by means of words: it is only to such objective properties that our *thoughts* relate. Precisely what, in this passage, Frege is denying is that to which Sluga says that he was committed; or, rather, what, with characteristic caution, he says is something like that to which Frege was committed.

It may be objected that what Frege says in § 26 is inconsistent with the view expressed, in the other passages in *Grundlagen* and elsewhere, that intuition forms the basis of our knowledge of geometrical truths. For, in § 26, the laws of geometry, which, Frege there says, one must acknowledge if one is to be able to find one's way about the world, are cited as determining the objective character of space; and what is objective is expressly stated to be independent of intuition. The objectivity of the geometrical axioms does not, in itself, conflict with their being synthetic, nor with our having some special source of knowledge, namely of fundamental laws of a non-logical character, on the basis of which we apprehend their truth; but it does appear to conflict with the derivation of this knowledge from intuition. In so far as different rational beings may intuit space differently, that difference would not be expressed in different geometrical axioms, and, in fact, could not be expressed by anything they could say. A possible means of resolving the apparent conflict would be to take Frege as holding, first, that it is intuition that prompts our recognition of the general laws embodied in the axioms of geometry, but, secondly, that these laws relate only to the general structure of our spatial intuition, and that this is constant under all variations in spatial intuition possible for rational beings. The *structure* of our intuition may seem to be what Kant meant by 'the pure form of sensibility' (B34); this he asserted to be a pure intuition, meaning thereby one 'in which nothing is met which belongs to sensation'. Frege does not, however, suggest that what underlies our recognition of geometrical axioms is a pure intuition in this sense. More importantly, as against Kant's denial that space is objective (B64), Frege asserts that it is objective in regard to those features we are capable of expressing in words or grasping in thought: he thus does not think that the structure of our spatial intuition is due to our constitution rather than to that of objective reality. In the one passage of his writings in which he confronted the Kantian view that space belongs to appearance, Frege repudiated it: to argue that he cannot have been a realist because he was, throughout his life, committed to a thesis that entailed such a view, or something like it, is special pleading indeed.

There are, of course, Kantian elements in Frege's thought. There are Kantian elements in the thought of virtually every philosopher after Kant. This is particularly true of philosophers of mathematics: although they clashed head on, both Hilbert and Brouwer were, in different ways, Kantians. But the presence of some such elements does not justify the description of Frege as a transcendental idealist. Still, even if the gulf between Frege's views and those of Kant is much wider than Sluga supposes, it is a reasonable challenge to ask, as he does, whether my criterion of realism 'can distinguish between realism and transcendental idealism': how does Kant come out on such a characterization of realism as that given above? It looks at first as though he must be a realist, even if a highly sophisticated one, because of the noumenal realm: and certainly it was, notoriously, the elimination of things in themselves that gave to post-Kantian philosophy its unmistakably idealist character. In any case, Kant's starting-point is not a question about the kind of meaning that our statements about the world that we experience have; it is an epistemological question, how synthetic a priori knowledge is possible. But the answer to this epistemo-logical question takes the form of saying what makes our synthetic a priori judgments, and all other judgments concerning the phenomenal world, true; and a doctrine about what makes some range of statements true is, in virtue of the intimate connection between truth and meaning, neces-sarily also a doctrine about the kind of meaning that they have. It follows that Kant's position is to be assessed as realist or anti-realist: but it does not follow whether he is to be classified as a sophisticated realist or as rejecting realism. Sluga remarks that he did not reject the law of excluded middle. But we cannot conclude directly from this that, on my criterion, he must count as a realist. For one thing, to accept the law of excluded middle is not necessarily to accept bivalence; for another, plenty of phil-osophers who have adopted anti-realist positions that cut the ground from under the principle of bivalence have failed to notice that their metaphysical views have natural consequences for logic. As I pointed out in 'Realism',[1] this is historically true even of most phenomenalists, who weakened their own position by failing to observe that their view of physical reality entailed similar consequences for the logic governing statements about it as those which Brouwer saw followed, for mathematical statements, from constructivism. A philosopher who, like McTaggart, believes that time is unreal, but holds that there really are order relations which we misperceive as temporal, may most reasonably be classified

---

[1] *Truth and Other Enigmas*, pp. 158–9.

as a sophisticated realist concerning time: our judgments concerning temporal precedence are rendered true or false by an objective relation obtaining, or failing to obtain, between things as they are in themselves, even if this relation does not have the character we ordinarily take it as having. But Kant's doctrine, if I have understood him correctly, is not of this kind. He does not hold that there are, between things in themselves, relations which we incorrectly apprehend as spatial, temporal or causal, so that our statements, expressed in phenomenal terms, may be regarded as rendered true or false by the constitution of the noumenal realm. And, if he does not hold this, then he is not a realist concerning statements so expressed or judgements so expressible. So far as I can see, he can have no reasonable ground for maintaining the principle of bivalence as governing such statements: the notion of truth for such statements cannot be explained or conceived in accordance with classical two-valued semantics. Just how it is to be explained or conceived, in accordance with such a philosophy, I shall not attempt to consider, nor whether the resulting conception would or would not enable us to retain classical logic, and, with it, the law of excluded middle. But I see no reason to doubt that the question whether Kant's philosophy is properly to be classified as a form of idealism or a sophisticated form of realism is most fruitfully asked in the terms I have proposed; it matters very little how those who have attempted to give no very precise meanings to those terms have been disposed to answer it.

As was earlier remarked, many philosophers start off by propounding views which may naturally lead in an idealist or other anti-realist direction, and finish up by adopting positions best described as a sophisticated realism: we may say that they have idealist thoughts without, in the end, embracing idealism. Frege was not one of these. He had an abhorrence of idealism, and resisted taking the first step which he saw as leading him along that path. But the service which, in this respect, he did for philosophy did not lie so much in his advocacy of realism, but in his making it possible for us to achieve a more exact conception and formulation of what realism is; this is a contribution for which even the most determined opponent of realism must be grateful to him. He provided us with an absolutely sharp picture of what it is to be a realist: it is a pity when this picture is blurred by interpretations making him out not to have been a realist at all.

Appendices

IN THE FOLLOWING three appendices, I discuss certain works which first appeared, or first came to my attention, when this book was already in proof: David Bell's book *Frege's Theory of Judgment* (Oxford, 1979); two further contributions to the controversy in *Inquiry* concerning Frege's realism, one by Gregory Currie called 'Frege's Realism' (*Inquiry*, vol. 21, 1978, pp. 218–21) and the other by Michael Resnik ('Frege as Idealist and then Realist', *Inquiry*, vol. 22, 1979, pp. 350–7); Hans Sluga's book *Gottlob Frege* (London, Boston and Henley, 1980); and the Preface to the edition in book form of Saul Kripke's *Naming and Necessity* (Oxford, 1980). No doubt other articles and even books bearing directly on the matters that have been discussed in this volume will appear before it does: it hardly seems possible to publish a book that is up to date in any field in which others are actively working. But, while it was still possible, since this book was only at the galley-proof stage, it seemed a pity to leave it seriously incomplete by omitting mention of these highly relevant works. I have discussed Sluga's views so extensively, on the basis of the articles he has published on the subject, that it would have been unfair both to him and to readers to include no discussion of his book when that was possible for me. In his book, he had an opportunity to develop some of his views at greater length than he had had space to do in his articles. I have nevertheless found it difficult to revise the main text of this book to take account of Sluga's; and so I decided to put my discussion of his book, as opposed to his articles, in an appendix. The reason is that, while, indeed, some points made in the articles are given a more expanded treatment in the book, others, that were heavily stressed in the articles, play a diminished part; there seems to be some change of view, and certainly of emphasis. Kripke's Preface is short; but it contains his first response to my criticisms. The response is brief, not to say curt; but I have felt it worth while to try to point out why it is inadequate. Since he did not think fit to go into detail, I have had to do so; but I have been glad of the opportunity. Kripke's ideas on rigid designation and metaphysical necessity have had an enormous impact. It is not, of course, that I hold them to be completely mistaken or think that there are no genuine insights underlying them; but I believe that, in his expositions of them, some error is mixed with truth, and I believe also that, presented as he has presented them, they are apt to tempt those impressed by them into philosophical blind alleys. I thought that I had written clearly, and fairly accurately, on the topic in *FPL*; but I did not succeed in dimming the allure of these very seductive notions. I have therefore been glad to attempt, in Appendix 3, to provide what I hope is a balanced estimate of the degree of truth and of falsity in Kripke's apparatus of rigid and non-rigid designators, and a faithful account of its true relation to the notion of scope. I have not sought to go thoroughly into the notion of metaphysical necessity or the conception of possible worlds; that would have taken longer, and would have led too far away from what is relevant to Frege. The theory of rigid designation, however, contains a criticism of Frege's conception of sense which Kripke has more than once made explicit; in discussing the theory here, I have had my eye upon whether any valid critique of that conception is to be based upon it.

It frequently happens in philosophy that certain ideas for a time gain a grip on the thinking of all the members of a particular philosophical school or of certain university departments, who accept them as the indispensable stock in trade of the subject. Just as neo-scholastic philosophers cannot conceive of philosophy without the notions of form and matter or act and potency, so, for a considerable era, analytical philosophers were incapable of calling in question the legitimacy, and the sharpness, of the analytic/synthetic distinction or the assumption that all necessity derives from linguistic conventions: so much of their work rested on these ideas that they could not imagine themselves functioning philosophically without them. That is why Quine was right to characterize the analytic/synthetic distinction as a dogma, and why the first attacks on it, by him and others, seemed to many analytical philosophers shocking and even threatening. Once someone has extricated himself from ideas that once had such a grip on him, he may look back with amazement on his former captivity; but he may fall into the grip of other, equally constrictive, ideas, like someone recovering from an unhappy love affair, liable to be caught on the rebound. Like Alice's recitations, some philosophical ideas turn out to have been wrong from beginning to end. Most prove to have some truth in them; but practically none do all that was hoped of them when they were first introduced. Real creativity in philosophy consists in the production of radically new ideas. Such ideas are always, on first encounter, compelling. What, then, is the right response to them? It certainly is not the romantic response voiced in William Blake's lines, 'I must Create a System or be enslav'd by another Man's. I will not Reason & Compare: my business is to Create'. It is folly to bar one's mind against the ideas of others; but even that is a more fruitful response than to be enslaved by them. Discipleship is to be avoided in philosophy at all costs; one ought to strive neither to have disciples nor to be one. The disciple's thought is forced along narrow channels; he seldom produces anything that needs to be added to the work of his leader, and his efforts succeed, if at all, only in bringing about a climate in which it is hard to question ideas that need to be questioned. Indeed, the truly great philosopher would be he who was not enslaved even by his own ideas; but, although Wittgenstein did contrive to break free from one net that he had woven, I doubt whether the philosopher has yet been born who could do that consistently. Our business is neither to be enslaved nor obstinately to resist, but, precisely, to reason and compare. Knowing that even the best idea is likely to prove no more than a half-truth, we best serve philosophical progress neither by being dazzled by the glamour of new ideas nor by dismissing them as tinsel, but by attempting patiently to discover where they apply and where they fail, which of the claims made for them are secure and which collapse.

Bell's book differs somewhat from the other writings on Frege I have discussed at length: it neither advances any strong criticism of my own interpretation of him nor puts forward a radically new one. As I have explained in Appendix 1, I think that on particular points Bell has failed to understand Frege correctly; but these, though often important, may be described as points of detail: he does not, as do several of those I have discussed, propose to interpret in a novel manner Frege's most basic doctrines. For that reason, I considered leaving his book undiscussed; I have not, after all, had the intention of writing a conspectus of the whole secondary literature on Frege, which is why I have not mentioned a number of interesting pieces of writing about him. But Bell's book is not only stimulating, but bears directly on some of the topics treated in detail in this one, and I therefore thought it worth while to discuss it fairly briefly.

Appendix 1: Bell

'I USE THE word "thought",' Frege wrote, 'roughly in the sense of "judgment" in the writings of the logicians . . . It seems to me that a sufficient distinction has not hitherto been made between a thought and a judgment'.[1] For him, a thought is that to which, in their primary application, truth and falsity may be ascribed. It is that which is expressed by a complete assertoric sentence, where a complete sentence is one for which the truth-value depends only on the senses of the component words and not on the particular context of utterance; the thought expressed by a complete sentence is, indeed, to be identified with its sense. But a thought is not, for Frege, a mental content. It does not depend, for its existence, upon our grasping it, expressing it or even having the ability to express it; it exists objectively and independently of us. It is timeless and unchangeable; it was not brought into being by being grasped, and it is incapable of the least alteration. A volcano may change, and even a mountain; but a thought cannot change in the least degree, and still remain the same thought, which is why nothing changeable can be part of a thought. Grasping a thought is a mental act; but it is one in which the subject stands in relation to that which is outside his mind. But even the act of grasping the thought, let alone the thought itself, must be distinguished from the further act of judging it to be true; and likewise the expression of the thought must be distinguished from assertion, which is the communication of the judgment, since the same thought which may be asserted may also be expressed without being asserted, for instance by a constituent clause in a disjunctive sentence or by an interrogative sentence employed to ask whether the thought expressed is true.

As David Bell remarks on the first page of his *Frege's Theory of Judgment*, the 'theory of judgment' no longer has the pre-eminence that it once had. But it had this pre-eminence in the writings of those who failed to make the sharp distinction on which Frege insisted between thoughts and judgments; and much of what they took to belong to the theory of judgment he would have regarded as part of the theory of thoughts, or, more generally, of sense. It is therefore somewhat dubious whether, given the distinction that he drew, he is to be credited with having had a *theory* of judgment at all, though he did have a certain amount to say about it. 'This process'—that of grasping a

---

[1] 'Der Gedanke', p. 61, fn. 1, and p. 62, fn. 3.

thought—'is perhaps the most mysterious of all,' he wrote, 'but just because it is mental in character, we do not need to concern ourselves with it in logic;'[1] and if this is true of thinking—grasping thoughts—it must be equally true of judging. Frege indeed had a theory of sense, and thus a theory of *thoughts*, which are the objects of the mental acts of thinking and judging; but he did not claim to have a fully worked out account of the nature of those mental acts.

A thought is essentially complex; and Frege's theory of sense deals with the analysis of thoughts into their constitutent senses. The traditional type of theory of judgment likewise concerned itself with this; but Frege, distinguishing between thoughts and judgments, held emphatically that a theory of judgment, properly so called, had no business to do so. 'Many people who have tried to explain what a judgment is . . . have hit upon compositeness,' he remarked;[2] but 'the act of judging did not make the thought or set its parts in order; for the thought was already there'—and, he goes on, was already there before it was even grasped. From this standpoint, an explanation of the complexity of the thought belongs to the theory of sense; judgment is to be conceived as a mental act directed at a thought that is already a unity, built up from its constituent senses. A theory of judgment could therefore be for him only an account of the character of the mental act which consists in coming to recognize a thought as true. Since Frege's time, only a few philosophers have proffered a theory of judgment which does not take it as directed towards a unitary, though complex, object, a thought or a proposition, but requires explicit reference to its constituents; one such theory was Russell's, and another that of Peter Geach, in his book *Mental Acts*. On Frege's view, any theory of this kind is wholly misconceived.

It thus appears that the content of Bell's book must be rather thin. That this is not so is due to his reckoning to Frege's theory of judgment not only what he would have regarded as properly belonging to such a theory, but also the whole of his theory of sense. Now the theory of sense may be said to form a large part—though not the whole, as Frege himself made clear—of what is now called the theory of meaning. This subsumption is not in conflict with Frege's view, despite his thinking that senses exist independently of our grasping or expressing them. For Frege, it is not contradictory to conceive of beings capable of grasping the same thoughts as we do but without clothing them in sensible form; but *we* can grasp a thought only via its linguistic or symbolic expression, and so our only access to senses is as the meanings, or ingredients in the meanings, of words or symbols. Thus it is

[1] 'Logik' (1897), *N.S.*, p. 157, *P.W.*, p. 145.
[2] 'Die Verneinung', pp. 150-1.

plausible that an account of the mental act of thinking, if not of that of judging, must take explicit notice of the complexity of the thought. Thinking is grasping a thought, and a thought is the sense of a sentence; we can grasp a thought only *as* the sense of some sentence. To grasp the sense of an expression is to understand that expression; and it is plausible that meaning, which includes sense, can be explained only at the same time as understanding, i.e. that an account of sense must simultaneously yield an account of understanding. This seems to run counter to Frege's argument cited above: the thought was already there before it was grasped. But the point is not really whether the thought was antecedent to the judgment that it was true, but whether, if we had an account of thoughts, we could explain what judgment was without explicit reference to the components of the thought: and it is plausible that we cannot explain what it is to grasp a thought save in terms of an apprehension of its structure, or to understand a sentence save in terms of an understanding of its component words. Whether or not Frege equivocated on this point, Bell does not. For him, a theory of sense, or, more generally, of meaning, is unequivocally a theory of understanding. He barely argues this, but takes it more or less for granted, as when (p. 60) he introduces a discussion of the senses of proper names by asking when I may be said to understand the name 'Julius Caesar'. He does, indeed, remark (p. 53) that Frege introduces the notion of sense in a slightly different way, namely as the mode of presentation of the referent; but he immediately dismisses this, as a general account of the notion, on the score of doubts concerning the ascription of reference to expressions other than names.

Frege's theory of sense is inseparable from his theory of reference. Bell correctly perceives that there were two ingredients in Frege's notion of reference; in fact, he overstates the case by saying (p. 42) that he had two notions of reference. One of these notions he characterizes, correctly enough, as that of the 'extra-linguistic entity with which the expression has been correlated or which it picks out'. In characterizing the second, however, he makes a crucial error. He says that it is that property of the expression which renders it capable of being used in a sentence possessing a truth-value. He is of course right in saying that, for Frege, the lack of a reference by a component expression deprives a sentence of truth-value; but it is enough to show Bell's characterization inadequate that a change of truth-value consequent upon the replacement of one expression by another requires us to distinguish their references. Bell concurs with Frege that the lack, by a singular term, a 'proper name' in Frege's sense, of an extra-linguistic correlate robs of truth-value a sentence of which it is the subject; but he spends much time attacking Frege's requirements, on predicates and functional expressions, for them to have a reference in the second sense. These require-ments are that they be sharp, not vague, and that they be defined for all objects; and Bell very unfortunately follows Frege in failing to make a clear distinction between these two requirements, which makes it much easier for him to criticize the doctrine; he fails to consider, in any serious way, whether vague expressions can be fitted into Frege's doctrine, or whether, if not, this reveals an inadequacy in Frege's doctrine, or, as Frege thought, shows that all vagueness must be eliminated from a language apt for scientific purposes. Bell is so keen to deny the possibility of a predicate's having sense but not reference, in the second sense of 'reference', that he will not consider, as a candidate, a predicate such as '( ) saw a moon of Vulcan', containing a proper name without reference; he states (p. 75) that 'Hegel saw a moon of Vulcan' is *false*, without reflecting that this either conflicts with his previous agreement with Frege (p. 64) that a proper name without reference deprives a sentence of truth-value, or requires a quite unFregean distinction between subject-position and other positions in a sentence. Bell therefore rejects Frege's application of his second notion of reference to incomplete ex-pressions; but he also insists (pp. 48–9) that there is no argument from this second notion to the first: Frege has no legitimate ground to ascribe extra-linguistic correlates to incomplete expressions. With this, the whole of Frege's theory of reference for predicates and functional expressions is dismantled.

It is true enough that Frege's demand that all predicates be everywhere defined is highly dubious, and his arguments for it unconvincing. It is also arguable that we need a semantic theory for vague expressions, and cannot rest content with dismissing them as part of the pathology of natural language. But Bell's mistake lies in the way he characterizes the 'second notion' of reference. The reference of an expression is not merely a property which it must have if any sentence containing it is to have a truth-value; it represents the contribution which it makes to determining what the truth-value of any such sentence is. The theory of reference is a theory of the manner of determination of the truth-value of any sentence in accordance with its composition. It is for this reason that Frege cannot conceive that reference is not to be ascribed to the expressions of any genuine logical category. If we understand the notion in this way, we shall not see him as having had two distinct, though conflated, notions: there are two ingredients in *one* notion. One ingredient, that just stated, tells us what Frege wanted the notion of reference *for*; the other tells us how he thought that it applied to the various categories of expression. An implausibility in Frege's account of what it is for, say, a predicate to lack a reference may point to some defect in his account of what the reference of a predicate is; but, viewed in this way, it cannot call into question the idea that predicates, in general, possess reference. It is true that, from this standpoint, one can still argue that the reference of a predicate consists in its being true or false of each object (or of each object for which it is defined), rather than in its standing for some *one* entity, a concept; and Bell quotes with approval (p. 48) my remark that the role of a predicate is not to pick out a concept. But, as I see it, the proper response is not to deny that there are concepts, or to say, for example, that predicates have reference but not referents, but simply to note where the analogy with the reference of proper names holds and where it fails; if second-level quantification is admitted as intelligible, then the assertion that there is something for which '( ) is a horse' stands can scarcely be questioned.

Bell's mistake in rejecting outright the notion of reference for incomplete expressions inevitably leads to error in his discussion of Frege's notion of sense. The two are very tightly connected by the principle that the sense of an expression is the way in which its reference is given to us; but, as remarked above, Bell is forced to reject this, as a general account, in view of his rejection of the notion of reference as generally applicable (p. 53). He wrongly sees such an account of sense as a rival to the view of sense as correlative with understanding, whereas it is plainly compatible with it. It is his failure fully to understand how Frege's notions of sense and reference were related that leads him to complain (p. 52) that the reference of a sentence (or other complex expression) is overdetermined, on the ground that it is determined both by the references of its parts and by its own sense, which in turn depends on the senses of its parts: there is no overdetermination here when sense is construed as Frege intended, namely as that component in meaning which determines reference. The result is that Bell does not succeed in giving a clear or accurate account of Frege's notion of sense; and so he makes it difficult for the reader to evaluate his proposal that we should replace what he calls Frege's 'mundane' account by a 'transcendental' one (p. 78). By a 'transcendental' account he means one which, in Wittgensteinian fashion, assumes the existence of a linguistic community whose use of language is integrated with other, non-linguistic, activities (p. 79). But a comparison of the two is rendered even harder by the thinness of Bell's exposition of a transcendental account of the sense of a predicate, namely as 'a rule for the collection of objects of a certain sort or type', a grasp of which will be manifest in, but not only in, an ability to make true judgments that the predicate applies to specific objects. Such an account does not obviously appeal either to the existence of a linguistic community or to non-linguistic activities to any greater extent than did Frege's, and suffers from the additional defect of being exceedingly vague. Must the rule be an effective one? When is a false judgment compatible with a grasp of the sense of the predicate? In what other ways does someone manifest his grasp of it? (I am afraid, too, that the use of the term 'collection' has its home in a bad old tradition of writing about these matters of the kind that Frege constantly ridiculed: Bell is not really meaning to allude to the activities of collectors.)

On pp. 54–5 Bell commits himself to the view that, while we can refer to the sense of an expression, we cannot say what it is. I do not believe that Frege's theory requires us to adopt such a view, but a great deal of it is consistent with it; as Bell rightly remarks, the view certainly does not imply that there are no such things as senses. But, because of his failure to relate the notions of sense and reference correctly, this leads Bell into difficulties about how we can ever convey the sense of an expression. The natural answer is that, although we cannot state what its sense is, we can *show* what it is by choosing a particular way of laying down what its reference is to be; Bell is therefore quite wrong to object (p. 46) that merely stipulating a reference does not provide an expression with a sense.

Anyone who engages to write about Frege's theory of meaning must treat of his notion of incompleteness or unsaturatedness. Bell makes a big point of this in his Introduction (pp. 8–10); as he rightly remarks, the notion represents Frege's solution to the problem of the unity of the proposition. Bell states (pp. 13–14) as a main aim of his book 'to offer an interpretation and, with some modification, a defence' of this doctrine of Frege's. With his rejection of the notion of the reference of incomplete expressions, he naturally cannot defend it at the level of reference. This leads him to make rather heavier weather of Frege's corollary, that a saturated or complete expression such as 'the colour blue' cannot stand for the same thing as an incomplete one such as the predicate '( ) is blue', than he might otherwise have done. He criticizes my observation[1] that we can come by the notion of a relation only via that of a relational expression by remarking (pp. 80–1) that this is true only of the *general* notion of a relation, whereas we may 'introduce a specific relation by means of entirely non-relational expressions'. The remark is true, but misses the point. Our language does indeed allow us to frame such a definition as 'Congruence is similarity combined with equality of length, area or volume'. But this does not show Frege to be wrong, for two reasons. First, the definition would not be a definition *of a relation* unless it were taken as fixing the sense of the expression '( ) is congruent to ( )' rather than of the term 'congruence'. And, secondly, the thesis that the abstract noun 'congruence' is to be understood as standing for

---

[1] 'Frege on Functions: a Reply', *Philosophical Review*, vol. LXIV, 1955, p. 106; reprinted in *Truth and Other Enigmas*, p. 84.

the very same thing as that for which '( ) is congruent to ( )' stands is not semantically usable unless accompanied by a recipe for converting every sentence containing the abstract noun into one containing, instead, the relational expression; the thesis can have no content save that such a transformation can always be effected. It is odd that Bell should offer this objection, since, in an earlier passage, he had rejected it, and for approximately the right reason. He says (p. 38) that if, in 'Drunkenness is undesirable', 'drunkenness' is construed as referring to a concept, the sentence must be analysed as stating that it falls within a second-level concept, and explains this as requiring the reading 'ξ *is drunk* is a concept which ought to have no instances'. In using an italicized predicate, complete with argument-place, to refer to a concept, Bell is following Frege's example in *Grundgesetze*; but the practice is incoherent on Frege's own principles. An expression for a concept or function should always carry with it its argument-place; we therefore have to treat the 'ξ' in the above sentence as capable of being replaced by a name of an argument, whereas such a replacement would produce obvious nonsense. The reading that we want is 'It is undesirable that, for some x, x is drunk (that anyone should be drunk)'; and now all appearance that we have a *term* standing for a concept has vanished.

Unable to defend Frege's doctrine at the level of reference, Bell observes, quite correctly, that Frege applied the saturated/unsaturated distinction also to the *senses* of expressions (pp. 72–3); and it is at this level that he wishes to defend it. One might feel misgivings at such an approach, since there is a temptation, to which many have succumbed, to suppose that Frege meant that the sense of a predicate is incomplete in the same way that a function is, i.e. that it is itself a function. This interpretation cannot, however, be generally correct, since it conflicts with the Fregean doctrine that the sense of the part is part of the sense of the whole; a function is no part of its value for any given argument, and Frege quickly came to see that it had been an aberration for him ever to have written as though it were. The incompleteness of the sense of a functional expression consists, rather, in its being understood as standing for a function; and this is an explanation that Bell cannot give, in view of his repudiation of the notion of reference for such expressions. For all that, he does not adopt the mistaken (indeed incoherent) interpretation mentioned above.

His final account of the matter is to be found in the last chapter, which is by far the most interesting and valuable of the four of which the book consists. The matter is delicate, because it is one Frege never fully thought through. In connection with his Begriffsschrift, Frege emphasized that a concept or function is extracted from a complete content of judgment by a process of omitting the content of one or more occurrences of some term (or of imagining it as replaceable in different ways). For such a complex predicate, it is at least coherent (even if not quite correct) to regard its sense as a function mapping the sense of a term in the argument-place to the sense of the completed whole, since it is not to such a predicate that the thesis that the sense of the part is part of the sense of the whole applies; as Frege states in *Begriffsschrift*, the decomposition into function and argument has nothing to do with the content itself, but only with our way of looking at it. Indeed, the only point of such a decomposition appears to be as a means of understanding sentences involving generality, for which, as Frege says, the occurrence of the complex predicate does represent the intrinsic constitution of the content; in the later terminology, the sense of the predicate is then genuinely a constituent of the thought. If, however, this account, according to which, as Bell remarks (p. 5), judgments are prior to concepts, were taken as yielding the full content of the doctrine of the incompleteness of the senses of predicates and functional expressions, it would *not* provide us with an explanation of the unity of the proposition. The thought that the Earth spins has, as constituents, the sense of the name 'the Earth' and that of the predicate '( ) spins'. We cannot say that it splits up into these two constituents just according to our way of looking at it: not only is the analysis immediate from our mode of expressing the thought, but we can form no conception of a grasp of that thought involving no apprehension of its complexity. Hence, if we are to account for the unity of the thought—the fact that the sense of the name and of the predicate cohere to form a thought—we must regard the sense of the predicate as having an incompleteness that does not consist either in its being a function from the senses of names to thoughts or in its being extracted from a thought grasped in advance of any grasp of it. Such a notion of incompleteness can be provided in terms of its being the sense of an expression with an incomplete reference: to understand the predicate is to take it as standing for a function from objects to truth-values. But, as remarked, Bell does not have this explanation available to him.

As we saw in Chapter 16, Frege himself showed an awareness of the difficulty when he wrote, in about 1880, that 'if the expression of a judgeable content is to be analysable . . . , it must already be articulated', and inferred that 'the properties and relations which are not further analysable must have their own simple designations'; but he insisted that, even in this case, they are not grasped in advance of judgments involving them, but 'arise simultaneously with them'.[1] This 'simultaneously' presents a dilemma Frege never

---

[1] 'Booles rechnende Logik', *N.S.*, pp. 18–19, *P.W.*, p. 17.

faced. Roughly, I know what 'That tree is green' means by knowing, among other things, what 'is green' means; but my knowledge of what 'is green' means consists in my knowing what it means to say, of any specific object, that it is green. A grasp of the thought involves a grasp of the sense of the predicate, and a grasp of that involves an understanding of its contribution to the thought expressed by any sentence containing it: it does not seem that either can precede the other.[1] At least this much is clear, that even Frege does not wish to explain the matter by claiming that the thought or judgment is, in a case of *this* kind, prior to the concept. A grasp of the sense of a complex predicate is subsequent to a grasp of the sense of a sentence containing it. A grasp of the sense of a simple predicate introduced by definition may precede the understanding of any sentence in which that simple predicate occurs. 'A case of this kind' means one in which the predicate is both simple and primitive.

Bell considers the picture theory of Wittgenstein's *Tractatus*, according to which every elementary proposition consists entirely of names. On such a theory, as he says, the sense of a sentence is not compounded out of the senses of its constitutents; the unity of the proposition cannot be explained in terms of the slotting of saturated constituents into the argument-places of unsaturated ones. Nevertheless, predicates, of any number of arguments, can be extracted from such an elementary proposition by the process described by Frege: even if we remove *all* the constituent names, to arrive at a pure logical form (proto-picture), we still have something of conventional significance—not an expression, even one with gaps in it, but a form of arrangement determining the sense of any proposition exemplifying it in accordance with a rule of projection (pp. 132–3).

Bell can hardly here be arguing merely that there is room, even on the picture theory, for a Fregean conception of predicates, as propositional functions in the most literal sense. What there is still room for is a notion corresponding to that of a *complex* predicate, and also, in the as yet un-analysed forms of everyday speech, to that of a superficially simple but definable one. What the picture theory eliminates is anything like simple primitive predicates, and, with them, the problem of explaining in what their incompleteness consists. It therefore seems natural to understand Bell as actually advocating the picture theory as part of his explanation of propositional unity.

---

[1] In this connection Bell very aptly quotes, on pp. 5 and 135, Wittgenstein's *Tractatus*, 3.263: 'The meanings of primitive signs can be explained by means of elucidations. Elucidations are propositions that contain the primitive signs. So they can only be understood if the meanings of those signs are already known.'

This interpretation of Bell is put in doubt, however, by a remark he makes on p. 133. Having just explained how it is still possible to apply to Wittgenstein's elementary propositions Frege's process of extracting predicates, he observes that 'just the same account can be given of the more familiar predicate expression ['( ) is between [ ] and { }'] and its role with respect to the sentence "B is between A and C" ', and claims that 'Wittgenstein himself makes this point at 3.1432'. This reads like a claim that one can have the advantages of the picture theory without actually subscribing to it; but, if so, Wittgenstein is very unlikely to have acknowledged this, since it would have destroyed his ground for advancing the picture theory. *Tractatus* 3.1432 reads, 'Instead of, "The complex sign '*aRb*' says that *a* stands to *b* in the relation *R*", we ought to put, "*That* '*a*' stands to '*b*' in a certain relation says *that aRb*" '. I take this remark to express *one* of two distinct theses which constitute the picture theory, the thesis, namely, that 'the propositional sign is a fact' (3.14). Frege held that what stands for an object, a proper name, is itself an object, a complete expression. What stands for something incomplete, a function, is itself incomplete: a predicate is not really a detachable part of a sentence, but may be viewed as a common property of certain sentences, or as a function whose values are those sentences. There is thus a congruence in logical type between the referents of expressions and the expressions themselves. Regarding sentences as complete expressions, as themselves objects, Frege took their referents, truth-values, to be objects, and the sentences themselves therefore to be a kind of complex proper names. As Wittgenstein said, 'in a printed proposition, for example, no essential difference is apparent between the propositional sign and a word. (That is what made it possible for Frege to call a proposition a complex name.)' (3.143). (The word standardly rendered 'proposition' by translators of Wittgenstein is simply *Satz*, meaning 'sentence'.) But at this point Wittgenstein diverged from Frege. What a proposition or sentence does is to present a state of affairs as obtaining; and so, in conformity with the Fregean principle of the congruence of logical type between symbol and what is symbolized, the proposition must, contrary to superficial appearance, itself be a state of affairs, a fact. 'Only facts can express a sense, a set of names cannot' (3.142). This is the first ingredient of the picture theory.

The second thesis which goes to make up the picture theory is that, upon analysis, every proposition is resolved into a truth-function of elementary propositions, the constituents of elementary propositions being simple names. It is to this ingredient of the picture theory that Bell appeals, as going, in part, to resolve the problem of propositional unity: but with this, as I read it, 3.1432 has nothing to do. 3.1432 relates to the first thesis, that propositions are facts; it says that this thesis holds good as much for the un-analysed propositions of natural language as for what emerges from analysis. It follows, indeed, that Frege's process for extracting predicates can be applied to sentences of natural language, as they stand, as well as to the elementary propositions of which they are in fact truth-functions. That, however, was not what Bell needed to establish. It is not the legitimacy of Frege's extraction process which is in question, but how far it applies. It seems that it is only complex predicates at which we can arrive in this way, but that our language requires simple primitive predicates if we are to be able to form any sentences at all. The picture theory would resolve this difficulty by denying the existence of simple primitive predicates; but the part of the theory that has this effect is the second thesis. Unless that thesis is actually accepted, there is no solution to be had by adverting to the picture theory, which Wittgenstein would never have propounded if he had thought he could have all its advantages without believing in it.

Even if Bell does mean to endorse the picture theory, it does not fully resolve the problems: there remains that of the relative priority of a pro-position and its constituents, which arises as much when the constituents are names as when they are simple incomplete expressions. In some extremely compressed pages (133-9), Bell argues that this problem can be solved if the *Tractatus* requirement of the determinateness of sense is replaced by Wittgenstein's later account of fundamental rules as embodied solely in a practice for which no justification can be given or required. He adds that to substitute such an (eclectically) Wittgensteinian account for that of Frege compels us to abandon Frege's realism for 'an anti-realist account of human thought and language' (p. 138). Though sympathetic to the anti-realist con-clusion, I believe the picture theory to have been radically mistaken; and, as just explained, I do not believe that, without it, Bell has a solution. I cannot therefore pretend to find his line of argument convincing; but I shall not here examine it further. In any case, this is without doubt the most stimulating and challenging section of his book.

In opposing Frege's realism, Bell appeals not only to Wittgenstein but to Kant (p. 122). He rightly observes that a principal motive for Frege's taking thoughts to be independent, timeless entities was to safeguard the objectivity of sense, and comments, equally rightly, that it is neither necessary nor sufficient for the purpose. For sense to be objective, we must be able to determine what sense someone else attaches to his words; Frege was not unaware of this, but it is a weak point in his thought. Bell concludes (p. 123) that the hypostatization of thoughts is unnecessary. The word 'hypostatiza-tion' should, I think, be eschewed by philosophers; it tends to blur distinctions, and it does so here. We should do right to reject a claim that a religion can exist without ever being believed or practised; but language would be crippled if we were not allowed to refer to Christianity or the Christian religion, but were compelled to speak only of people's acting or believing Christianly. In the same way, we may well look askance at Frege's claim that a thought exists independently of any means of expressing it or any minds to grasp it; but it does not follow, as Bell seems to suppose (p. 121), that we ought no more to speak of an object of judgment (that which is judged to be true) than of an object of leaping. He is here commenting on Frege's remark[1] that we do best to understand the word 'judgment' as meaning 'an act of judging', as a leap is an act of leaping, and has seized on the fact that, while 'leap' is an intransitive verb, Frege takes 'judge', like 'grasp', as transitive. He rightly stresses that, for Frege, a thought is not a content of consciousness: but he does not see the force of this contention, one carried further by Wittgenstein when he said that understanding is not a mental process, but dismisses it as merely a misguided way of safeguarding the objectivity of sense. Frege may, no doubt, be criticized for exaggerating the incommunicability of mental contents; it remains that it is impossible to give a coherent account of thought as an inner process, as we should be forced to do if we understood 'think', either in the sense of grasping thoughts or in that of judging them to be true, as a straightforwardly intransitive verb like 'leap'. Bell fails to indicate in any way *how* he proposes to dispense with objects of thought.

When Frege restricts himself, as he usually does, to sentences involving no significant demonstrative or indexical features, his notion of sense may, as we have seen, be equated with the main ingredient in linguistic meaning. But when we consider sentences which do have these features, his insistence that a thought is true or false absolutely, not relatively to a person or a time, compels a distinction between sense and linguistic meaning. Bell is convinced that no unitary notion of sense can do all that Frege required of the notion (pp. 112–18); but his discussion is remarkably hasty. He distinguishes 'input sense' (linguistic meaning) from 'output sense' (the thought expressed, considered as true or false absolutely), remarking that several contemporary philosophers have argued the need for such a distinction and citing three, among whom, very oddly, he does not include Strawson. The linguistic meanings of the constituent words go to compose the input sense; but Bell simply declares, what is very far from obvious, that subsentential expressions do not have output sense. The only argument he gives for saying

[1] 'Die Verneinung', p. 151, fn. 10.

this is that he has *defined* 'output sense' to be the thought expressed, for instance by saying on one day 'It is cold today' and, on the next, 'It was cold yesterday'; and, to this extent, it is not merely obvious, but utterly trivial, that words and phrases do not have output sense. But the serious question is whether the output sense may be considered to have constituents, as the input sense, that is, the linguistic meaning, has constituents. On Bell's account, the linguistic meaning (input sense) of a sentence is determined by the linguistic meanings of its constituent words; and this linguistic meaning, taken together with the context, determines the thought expressed by—the output sense of—any particular utterance of the sentence. According to this picture, we need to advert to the linguistic meanings of the constituent words only in order to grasp the linguistic meaning of the sentence, considered as a type; once we have grasped the linguistic meaning of the sentence as a whole, we can then advert to the context in order to determine the thought expressed by a specific utterance of it. This becomes an enormously implausible picture as soon as we consider how the linguistic meanings of demonstratives and indexicals are given to us: we grasp the linguistic meanings of those words, and so the linguistic meaning of a sentence in which they occur, considered as a type, only by mastering the principle whereby the context goes to determine a referent. The context thus bears directly upon these words, and not just upon the sentence-type, taken as a whole.

This is not, of course, a criticism of the distinction between input sense and output sense as such, as exemplified, for instance, in Strawson's celebrated distinction between the meaning of a sentence and the statement made by means of a particular utterance of it. Strawson would acknowledge a parallel distinction between the meaning of a referring expression and the referent on a particular occasion of utterance; the criticism just made was directed only at the contention that output sense has no constituents, in particular none that correspond to the particular words contained in the sentence uttered. To hold that the output sense has constituents is not, however, to resolve the question in Frege's favour. The original question was whether we can find *one* notion of sense which will do all that Frege requires of it; and that is indeed problematic. The natural way to think about the word 'I', for example, is that it has a linguistic meaning which consists in a principle for determining its reference from the context. This does not provide any application for Frege's notion of sense as expressed by an utterance of this word. The linguistic meaning is obviously not a Fregean sense, since a sentence containing 'I' does not, considered as a type, express any determinate thought. But the referent cannot be part of the thought, either.

'That part of the thought which corresponds to the name "Etna" cannot be Mount Etna itself; it cannot be the reference of this name. For each individual piece of frozen, solidified lava which is part of Mount Etna would then also be part of the thought that Etna is higher than Vesuvius. But it appears to me absurd that pieces of lava, even pieces of which I had no knowledge, should be parts of my thought,' Frege wrote to Jourdain.[1] The mountain cannot be part of the thought, since, otherwise, whenever the mountain changed, the thought would change. If someone repeatedly had, throughout his life, the thought, 'I am the son of a great philologist', he could not himself be a part of that thought; for, if he were, the thought would change as he grew older, grew a beard, or went to live elsewhere, whereas it remains the same thought that is always pressing on him. The cognitive character of Frege's notion of sense comes out strongly in his remark that pieces of lava of which he had no knowledge could not be part of his thought; that is, of a thought which he had grasped, since, as he says elsewhere, the thought itself is not really *his*. The sense which a speaker attaches to a word or which is a constituent in someone's thought can include only what is known to him; it goes to constitute his grasp of what it is that he is saying or thinking, in so far as this relates to what determines it as true or false.

It is not enough, then, for Frege, that a word should have a linguistic meaning, which the speakers grasp, and which determines the referent from the context. Rather, he wants the linguistic meaning and the context jointly to determine a sense, which in turn, without any further appeal to the context, determines the referent. If someone uses that word to express a thought, to himself or to others, then its use on that occasion must represent a particular way in which he picks out the referent. Just as someone may communicate a thought to others by using a proper name whose sense he does not know, so, presumably, it is conceivable that someone might, by the use of an indexical, convey a thought, even though he himself did not by its means pick out a referent: an example might be a frightened man saying in the dark, 'I know you're there.' In such a case, he does not really have a thought, though, if there really is someone there, he may take the speaker's words as expressing one. But, if someone has a genuine thought, expressed by means of an indexical, if he really grasps that thought, as opposed to uttering a form of words that expresses a thought to others, then what determines that thought as the thought it is cannot be any feature of the context unknown to the speaker or thinker; it must be something in the

[1] *BW*, p. 127, *P.M.C.*, p. 79.

context from which he determines who or what it is that he is speaking or thinking about. That must be so, if it is to be a definite thought and, at the same time, his thought, a thought he really grasps. If he has a thought about someone, then there must be a way of identifying the person of whom he is thinking, or else the thought is not a definite one with definite truth-conditions; and it must be *his* way of identifying that person, or else it is not his thought.

This reasoning is, I think, sound; but it is insufficient to establish Frege's conclusion. Given that the speaker or thinker must have a means of identifying or picking out the referents of his words, or of the corresponding thought-constituents, it by no means follows that this means must be independent of his particular perspective on the world at the time of speaking or thinking. For Frege, the 'I' of soliloquy, as used by Dr Lauben, must be associated with the unique manner in which Dr Lauben is given to himself. In a sense, it is, since Dr Lauben's grasp of the linguistic meaning of the word 'I' is shown, in part, by the fact that it is on the basis of the pain that *he* feels and the blood that is pouring from *his* leg that he thinks, 'I have been wounded.' Frege wants, however, to conceive of the way in which Dr Lauben is given to himself as independent of the fact that it is *he* who is having the thought. It must be a way of identifying a particular person that would lead anyone who had it to Dr Lauben, even though it happens to be a way of doing so that only Dr Lauben can have. It is dubious whether such a conception is even coherent. For the 'I' of communication, there is an argument for holding that the means of identification of the referent associated with it must be independent of the particular perspective of the speaker. When Dr Lauben says, 'I have been wounded,' those he is addressing must be able to grasp the thought he is expressing; so 'I' must serve, in that utterance, to pick out Dr Lauben in a manner that is independent of the identity of whoever grasps the thought expressed. Frege thought, therefore, that, in such a case, the thought must incorporate a reference to some feature of the context apprehended, and in the same manner, by everyone so situated as to be able to grasp the thought at all (perhaps the direction of the voice). Even here, the conclusion does not plainly follow: there is no absurdity in the idea that the linguistic meaning of 'I' may be such that everyone identifies the referent of a particular utterance of it in a manner that depends essentially upon his own perspective on the world, and hence differs from the means of identification used by anyone else.

It is, thus, indeed doubtful whether we either need, or can have, any notion that does all the work which Frege wanted his notion of sense to perform. The issue is, however, both complex and deep: it is not to be resolved, as Bell attempts to do, by merely defining technical terms in such a way as to make it impossible, by means of them, to express such a notion.

Bell makes numerous sound and interesting points in the course of his book; I welcome, in particular, his refusal to ascribe to Frege a 'description theory' of proper names (pp. 55–6) and his recognition, contrary to what is often said, that thoughts must, for Frege, be objects (p. 110). The last of his four chapters, already discussed in detail, is certainly the most interesting and original; the third, on assertion, the closest, in a sense, to the theme announced in the title of the book, is not altogether satisfactory. It was maintained by V. H. Dudman[1] that Frege gave two inconsistent accounts, which he failed to distinguish, of his judgment-stroke. One of these accounts had, according to Dudman, been fastened on by Max Black and used by him to criticize Frege's theory.[2] This is that a sentence, as such, is merely a name, and so, by itself, *says* nothing: the judgment-stroke is needed 'to restore . . . its truth-claiming aspect', in Black's phrase. Dudman remarked that this account, as stated, is only to be found after the introduction of the sense/reference distinction. One that is somewhat like it is met with in *Begriffsschrift*, where the judgment-stroke is called 'the common predicate of all judgments' in the symbolic language:[3] this common predicate can be rendered 'is a fact', where the result '————A' of prefixing the content-stroke to a sign 'A' for a judgeable content is read by means of a substantival phrase like 'the violent death of Archimedes at the capture of Syracuse'. However, as Dudman pointed out, this idea is not exactly the same as the account extracted by Black from the writings from 1891 onwards. Frege later stressed that *no* predicate—not even 'is true'—can guarantee that the speaker is claiming the sentence he utters to be true, since any sentence containing the predicate can still be uttered without assertoric force, e.g. as one half of a disjunction.[4] That is why Frege insists that the judgment-stroke is not a functional expression, but is *sui generis*.[5] He had been wrong, in *Begriffsschrift*, to represent it as converting a substantival phrase into a declarative sentence: rather, it confers assertoric force on what is already a declarative sentence.

The second of Frege's accounts, according to Dudman, was that the judgment-stroke serves merely to mark a difference that is already there,

[1] 'Frege's Judgment-Stroke', *Philosophical Quarterly*, vol. 20, 1970, pp. 150–61.

[2] *A Companion to Wittgenstein's Tractatus*, Cambridge, 1964, p. 227.

[3] *Begriffsschrift*, § 3.

[4] 'Der Gedanke', p. 63; 'Meine grundlegenden logischen Einsichten' (1915), *N.S.*, pp. 271–2, *P.W.*, pp. 251–2; 'Über Sinn und Bedeutung', p. 34.

[5] *Function und Begriff*, p. 22n.; *Grundgesetze*, vol. I, § 26.

the difference between asserted and unasserted occurrences of a sentence; it is thus 'an index of assertion'. This second account Dudman associates with Peter Geach[1] as the basis on which he defended Frege's theory. The difference, according to Dudman, from Black's interpretation, is that, for Geach, the judgment-stroke does not alter the semantic status of that to which it is attached, which, even without it, already expressed something capable of being held true: it merely signals that it is in fact being advanced as true. Dudman believed that both accounts were to be found in Frege's mature writings; that he failed to distinguish them; that they are incompatible; and that that which he identifies as Geach's interpretation is the only tenable one.

All this I take to be a mistake. Dudman was, indeed, quite right to object to the formulation in *Begriffsschrift*, for just the reasons, already noted, which led Frege to abandon it. For the rest, however, it is wrong to hold Frege to have confused two distinct accounts: he had a single, coherent account. It is a feature of natural language that the very same form of words—a declarative sentence—can be used, now as having assertoric force, now as lacking it. For Frege, this was another of the defects of natural language: the attachment of the assertoric force ought to be made explicit. When this is done, as in his symbolic language, a sentence in that language without the sign for assertoric force becomes strictly incomparable with any expression of natural language. We cannot equate it with anything but a declarative sentence; but we also cannot equate it with a declarative sentence of natural language, since the latter *can* be used as having assertoric force, while the symbolic sentence, as it stands, cannot. The judgment-stroke, as used in the symbolic language, does not, therefore, merely mark a distinction that would already be present if it were omitted, as on the account Dudman attributed to Geach: it makes a vital difference to the significance of a formula. The difference is not, indeed, to transform something incapable of being held to be true into something capable of being so held: if that to which the judgment-stroke is attached were incapable of being held to be true, the result of attaching it would be nonsense. The difference is that between something that serves merely to express a thought and something that conveys an assertion: without the judgment-stroke, one could not, in the symbolic language, convey that or any other assertion.

Bell's treatment of the topic is rather similar to Dudman's, though independent of it; but he goes further, claiming (p. 104) to have discerned seven distinct uses to which Frege suggests, in one passage or another, that the judgment-stroke may be put. One of these is precisely what Dudman

---

[1] 'Assertion', *Philosophical Review*, vol. LXXIV, 1965, pp. 449–65, reprinted in *Logic Matters*, Oxford, 1972.

calls its use as an index of assertion. Bell remarks (pp. 88–9) that some philosophers have mistakenly explained the meanings of declarative sentences as necessarily incorporating assertoric force, and that, among these, some have then produced bizarre theories to account for non-assertoric occurrences of them. But in the end he reduces the distinction between assertoric and non-assertoric occurrences to the logical distinction between exportable and non-exportable ones (p. 104): 'A' occurs assertorically in 'Φ(A)' if the truth of 'Φ(A)' entails the truth of 'A', which accordingly occurs assertorically in 'A and B' but not in 'A or B'. This misses the point of Frege's proposed reform of language, whereby a sentence without the judgment-stroke has no assertoric force, and hence cannot be used, by itself, to make an assertion. Frege distinguished, as separate ingredients in the conventional significance of a declarative sentence of natural language, the determination of its truth-conditions, the thought which it always expresses, and the force, which is only sometimes present, whereby the speaker is understood as asserting those truth-conditions to be fulfilled. He wanted, in his symbolic language, to attach these two types of significance to distinct signs. This involved stripping the verb or predicate of the assertoric force it sometimes carried, so that, in the symbolic language, the sentence, by itself, served *only* to determine the truth-conditions. Connectives like 'or' and 'and' contribute to determining the truth-conditions: so they must operate upon unasserted sentences. If, then, the judgment-stroke is attached to the whole complex sentence, it must be attached to it as a whole; it cannot be taken to attach to any subsentence, even when the asserted complex sentence would logically justify the assertion of some subsentence. The judgment-stroke does not mark a deductive relation. Rather, it conveys an essential ingredient in the conventional significance of a large range of utterances, an ingredient which, in natural language, is not cleanly separated from the ingredient which corresponds to Frege's sense, the determination of the specific truth-conditions.

Bell's attitude to the *Begriffsschrift* account seems ambiguous. He first objects to it as redundant (pp. 86–7): there is no need first to convert a sentence into a substantival phrase by means of the content-stroke, and then re-convert it into a sentence by means of the judgment-stroke. But later (pp. 92–4), discussing the presentation of the matter in Frege's mature writings, he surprisingly revives the *Begriffsschrift* account, saying that a formula of the form '———Δ' is best represented by a substantival phrase. As already remarked, such a formula cannot be represented faithfully in natural language at all; natural language does not work like Frege's symbolic language, and its failure to do so was his complaint against it.

As yet another distinct use for the judgment-stroke, Bell presents (pp. 94–8) what is, I believe, the true account, and the only one intended by Frege. Even here he has difficulty with the distinction between the external act of assertion and the internal act of judging. The judgment-stroke of course serves only to effect the external act: but Frege left it obscure how, if at all, that act is to be characterized, and, in particular, whether the notion of assertion or of judgment has the priority. To say that the notion of judgment is prior is to say that assertion is to be characterized as the expression of a judgment (rather than judgment as an internalized assertion). Whichever we decide, we ought not to put expressing or grasping a thought on the same level as assertion or judgment. Frege of course frequently remarked on the need to distinguish the first two from the second two: but this does not mean that expressing a thought is a linguistic act comparable to assertion. On the contrary, it is involved in a great many different types of linguistic act, since such acts—say asserting that something is so and asking whether it is so—have in common a thought as their content: but an expression of the form '——— A' merely expresses this common content, and effects no linguistic act, since *no* force, assertoric or otherwise, has yet been attached to it. It is therefore a mistake, to which some of Frege's turns of phrase tempt us, to identify grasping a thought with adopting it as a hypothesis, wondering whether it is true, or the like; and equally a mistake to treat '——— A' as serving to advance a hypothesis, to pose a question or to express wonderment or uncertainty. Bell proposes this interpretation of it (pp. 100, 102–3). But he then observes (p. 105) that '——— A' may also be taken as expressing the common content of distinct linguistic acts, in which case it does not itself serve to effect any particular such act; to convey wonderment, we should need a distinct kind of force-indicator (p. 106). This last is the correct account; but Bell has no warrant for accusing Frege of confusion (pp. 85, 104)—it was simply that Bell's first interpretation did not accord with Frege's intentions. Bell complains that there is a gap in Frege's list:

1. grasping a thought—thinking;
2. recognizing the truth of a thought—judging;
3. communicating this judgment—asserting.[1]

The gap of which Bell complains (p. 102) is the external manifestation of (1); it is in fact quite easily filled, namely by 'expressing a thought'. Since, however, expressing a thought is *not* a linguistic act, it is never done on its own,

---

[1] 'Der Gedanke', p. 62.

but always as part of some linguistic act, whose content may be the thought in question or may be one of which that thought is a constituent. Bell therefore has no ground for accusing Frege of thinking that 'such activities as wondering or grasping a thought are ineluctably interior: private to the person who performs them' (p. 103), or for suggesting (pp. 85, 95) that Frege's theory of assertion was psychologistic in a way that conflicted with his own strictures on psychologism. Indeed, if assertion is to be explained as the expression of judgment or of belief, assertoric force requires a psychological explanation. But this is a point which Frege did not elucidate; nor, for the matter of that, does Bell.

Appendix 2: Sluga

HANS SLUGA'S BOOK, *Gottlob Frege*, naturally advances a broadly similar line to that propounded in his articles on the subject; but, surprisingly, only broadly similar. It is, for this reason, most easily discussed separately from them, as in this appendix. The historical background is treated in greater detail, and the historical thesis is argued at greater length. The denial that Frege was a realist is integral to this thesis, and is still maintained, though not greatly clarified; but several things associated in Sluga's articles with that denial are missing from the book. It contains, for example, some discussion of the context principle and of the thesis of the priority of judgments over concepts, the two being virtually identified with each other by Sluga; but the thesis that we apprehend thoughts, in the first instance, as structureless units, which in the articles appeared as a principal component of the priority thesis, is no longer maintained or even mentioned. In the articles, Sluga opposed the identification of the *Bedeutung* of a proper name with its bearer, and rebuked me for failing to adopt Ernst Tugendhat's interpretation of Frege's notion of *Bedeutung*, according to which the *Bedeutung* of a proper name is only dubiously an entity at all, and, at best, an abstract one, nothing like a man, a planet, a mountain or a city as we normally conceive of such objects. But, in the book, Sluga does not himself adopt Tugendhat's interpretation. Tugendhat himself receives only the briefest mention, and it is impossible to discover from his book that Sluga now takes the *Bedeutung* of a proper name to be anything other than its bearer, that is, the object we should normally take ourselves, in using the name, to be talking about. Sluga had maintained, in his articles, that to construe the *Bedeutung* of a proper name as its bearer entailed ascribing epistemological atomism to Frege; but practically nothing is said in the book concerning epistemological atomism. These ideas were linked, in the articles, with the contention that to interpret Frege's theory of *Bedeutung* in the light of subsequent classical semantics or model theory is to distort Frege's views; but this thesis is not developed in the book. It is therefore impossible to equate Sluga's interpretation of Frege, as set forth in his articles and as discussed in the main body of the present work, with his interpretation of him as expounded in his book and as discussed in this appendix. This observation is not meant as a criticism, but only as a warning to readers who overlook the differences; there is obviously nothing wrong with a change of mind. It is true that, in one or two passages, some of the ideas which I have here listed as absent from Sluga's book make a shy appearance, either as the result of an insufficiently thorough revision of an earlier draft or as an indication that he still subscribes to them but preferred not to develop them here; I shall discuss these passages in later sections.

Historical perspective

Sluga's book aims to set Frege in historical perspective. Though he provides brief concluding sections on Russell, Carnap and Wittgenstein, he is principally concerned with Frege's relation, not to those who came after him, but to his contemporaries and predecessors. Sluga had formerly described Frege's celebrated theories of sense and reference as 'an appendix to a philosophy of mathematics'; we might therefore expect a comparison of Frege's work in the foundations of mathematics with that of his contemporaries Dedekind and Cantor and with the remarkable pioneering work of Bolzano, who died in the year that Frege was born. There is, however, no such detailed comparison: Bolzano is mentioned only twice, and Dedekind three times, both in passing; and though Cantor appears a little more frequently, not much more is said about him than that he 'wished to create the numbers by abstraction' (p. 98). Sluga is interested in Frege's philosophy of mathematics only in respect of its logical foundations; what concern him are Frege's general philosophical views, not the applications that he made of them in that specialized branch of the subject, and Sluga's comparisons are therefore primarily with the professional philosophers. Here, again, however, we receive a surprise. One might expect, of such a project, an extensive comparison of Frege's ideas with those of Brentano,

Husserl and Meinong, who, of all his contemporaries, and certainly of those writing in German, appear the closest to his outlook. But this is not at all what Sluga supplies: Brentano is accorded only one page, devoted entirely to his inaugural lecture at Vienna; and Meinong is not mentioned once. Even Husserl, by far the most influential of these three philosophers, receives rather scant attention; Sluga admits that the comparison between him and Frege 'is inviting', but explains that 'because of the difficulty of Husserl's views and the insufficiently understood historical relationship between them, it falls outside the scope of the present study' (p. 41). On the contrary, it falls squarely within the scope of such a study; to clarify the historical relationship between these two important philosophers is just what one might look to it to do.

Brentano, Husserl and Meinong are usually represented as heading a realist revolt against the dominant idealism of the German philosophical schools; the description of Brentano and Meinong as realists is certainly correct, although Husserl's thought underwent so complex an evolution that it is possible to attach the label to him only in a certain phase. This explains Sluga's lack of interest in comparing Frege with this group: he wishes to combat the interpretation of Frege as a realist. His aim is, first, to give a picture of the philosophical scene in Germany during Frege's lifetime; secondly, in the light of this picture, to advance a hypothesis concerning the philosophical influences upon Frege; and, finally, on the strength of that hypothesis, to propound a new interpretation of Frege's philosophy.

On the last page but one of FPL_1, I spoke of Frege's philosophy as possibly having played some part in the overthrow of Hegelian idealism. Sluga objects that Hegelianism had little influence at the time when Frege's creative work began; and I now think that, in this, he is quite right. The important question is how much bearing this has upon the interpretation of Frege. In other passages of *FPL*, I spoke of Frege as being a realist, in opposition to the dominant idealism of his day, without specifying any particular version of idealism. Sluga denies both halves of this contention: he denies that Frege was a realist; and he also says that 'idealism had ceased to be a real power in German thought by about 1830' (p. 9). Now, of course, the term 'idealism' may be used with varying degrees of breadth; and the remark just quoted might be defended by taking 'idealism' to refer specifically to post-Kantian idealism of the kind espoused by Hegel and Fichte. But, if so, though it controverts my remark about Hegelianism, it does nothing to contradict the more general observation that idealism was dominant in the contemporary German philosophical schools. At least, it does not do so when 'idealism' is understood in the broader sense in which it is normally used; and it must be so understood if, as Sluga wishes, Frege is to be made out to have been an idealist rather than a realist. For Sluga does not wish to maintain that Frege was anything like a Hegelian; it is to Kant that he wishes to compare him in this respect, regarding him as a transcendental idealist of Kant's type. According to Sluga himself, neo-Kantianism was the dominant philosophy in Germany from 1870 until at least the end of the century; so idealism, of just the kind he wishes to represent Frege as having adhered to, was the most powerful influence from about the moment (1869) that Frege entered university. Except by an irrelevant equivocation upon the word 'idealism', therefore, Sluga does not succeed in showing anything wrong with speaking of the dominant idealism of Frege's day. For all that, his interpretation of Frege might be correct; that depends upon whether he was opposed to or sympathetic with the prevailing tendency.

It makes little difference to the argument whether Sluga's own historical picture is accurate or not; the principal argument must depend upon the exegesis of Frege's writings. The fact remains that Sluga's picture does not seem to me to be accurate. He manifests an awareness of the difficulty of fitting schematic pictures to an untidy reality, both because not everyone swims with the tide and because a lifetime is longer than a generation. Nevertheless, he advances his picture of the history of nineteenth-century German philosophy with a good deal of confidence. This picture, as set out in the first two of his six chapters, is that the grip of post-Kantian idealism was abruptly broken in about 1830; that 'roughly from 1830 to 1870' (p. 32) the dominant influence was naturalism, that is, a rather crude scientific materialism; and that from 1870 onwards there took place a revolt against naturalism, which principally assumed a neo-Kantian form. Of this revolt, Frege formed a part; it was to naturalism, not to idealism, that he was principally opposed, and he should, in effect, be considered as a member of the neo-Kantian movement which, from 1870 onwards, formed the leading philosophical school in Germany, despite dissidents such as Husserl and the positivist Mach.

Sluga's exposition of this historical thesis contains accounts of some little remembered philosophers such as Czolbe which are unquestionably interesting and agreeably written; nevertheless, the picture seems to me distorted. The influence of Hegel certainly did not die, with Hegel, in 1831. It was extremely strong upon the Left Hegelians such as Feuerbach, whom Sluga groups with the scientific materialists, and, of course, Marx and Engels. These indeed converted Hegelianism into a materialist system; but there were also Right Hegelians who preserved its idealist character. Sluga surely exaggerates when he says that Schelling's Berlin lectures of 1841 'found almost no audience' and that he 'quickly faded from the scene' (p. 14). According to Copleston, the lectures started with some éclat and a large audience, which admittedly shrunk;[1] Schelling did not retire until 1846, at the age of seventy-one. The idealist tradition was also continued by men like C. H. Weisse (1801–1866) and the younger Fichte (1796–1879). The idealist heirs of Hegel and Fichte in the 1840s and 50s may have been philosophers of relatively small stature; but it was they who occupied the chairs of philosophy at the universities. As Passmore observes, speaking of the year 1855, 'in Germany, . . . with its State-controlled universities, there was an "official" philosophy—at this time a watered-down version of Hegelianism'.[2]

As for the naturalists, they were none of them professional philosophers, but scientists. Scientific materialism made an impact, and undoubtedly affected the intellectual climate; but it at no time dominated academic philosophy, not even for a decade, let alone four. It was a philosophy of non-philosophers: as Passmore also remarks, it 'had a considerable impact upon the development of philosophy, just as the existence of an underworld affects the lives of respectable citizens who never venture into it'.[3] There had been contemporaries of Hegel, such as Herbart, who disliked his views; but the strong reaction against him began in the 1850s, when Schopenhauer first gained a general celebrity with the publication of his *Parerga and Paralipomena* in 1851. Schopenhauer was of course a bitter opponent of Hegel, but no less of an idealist.

The influence of Kant himself had never died out. Sluga remarks that 'one of the strongholds' of neo-Kantianism 'was Frege's own university, Jena' (p. 37). That is true; and the man who established that tradition there was J. F. Fries, who died in 1843 and had been the originator of psychologism. Sluga maintains that psychologism, which Frege vehemently attacked, was the offspring of scientific materialism (p. 18). It was perhaps a natural ally of materialism, or at least of a thoughtless scientism. It is certainly not an essential ingredient of idealism, which is why, in *FPL*, I described the idealism of Frege's day as 'entangled with an irrelevant psychologism'.[4] Sluga is right to maintain, with Lotze, that it is a misunderstanding of Kant to attribute to him a psychologistic view of logic

---

[1] F. Copleston, S.J., *A History of Philosophy*, vol. VII, *Fichte to Nietzsche*, London, 1963, p. 97.

[2] J. Passmore, *A Hundred Years of Philosophy*, London, 1957, p. 33.

[3] Ibid., p. 46.

[4] *FPL*, p. 470.

(p. 53). Nevertheless, it was from an effort to interpret Kant in psychological terms, rather than from any kind of scientism, that psychologism was originally born. Lotze was another philosopher opposed to Hegelianism but deeply influenced by Kant; according to Sluga, he had a profound influence upon Frege, but he does not fit Sluga's temporal scheme at all. He published a *Metaphysik* in 1841 and the first version of his *Logik* in 1843, and his philosophical activity continued unabated until his death in 1881. Kuno Fischer, another Kantian, likewise published his *System der Logik und Metaphysik* in 1852, and was professor of philosophy at Jena when Frege was a student there; he was succeeded by Rudolf Eucken, the last of those who practised philosophy in the grand manner of the post-Kantian idealists.

If a date is to be given for the emergence of neo-Kantianism as a *movement* (though a far from unified one), it should probably be 1865 rather than 1870: it was in the former year that Liebmann coined the slogan 'Back to Kant!', as Sluga notes (p. 36), and in that year also that Trendelenburg engaged in controversy with Fischer about the interpretation of Kant; Lange's *Geschichte des Materialismus* appeared in the following year. But the movement was not primarily, as Sluga represents it, a reaction against materialism; its leaders wanted to get back to Kant behind Schopenhauer, Fichte and Hegel. The amount of attention paid to materialism by Lotze is shown by the fact that, in his article 'Philosophy in the last Forty Years' of 1880, he did not even mention it. Idealism, in one form or another, post-Kantian or neo-Kantian, did dominate German philosophy, at least as practised by the professional academic philosophers, throughout the century.

Influences on Frege

None of this proves much, one way or the other, about how Frege is to be interpreted. We cannot presume that Frege was in opposition to, or that he was in accord with, the dominant philosophy of his day; we have to read what he wrote. Even if we could make such a presumption, it would matter little which school of philosophers was dominant before 1870. The philosophy Frege encountered at Jena was that of the Kantian Kuno Fischer, and, at Göttingen, that of the idealist Hermann Lotze; on Sluga's own showing, neo-Kantianism was dominant from 1870 onwards. Certainly Frege's university experience would have inclined him to regard it as such; he would hardly have received the impression from his university studies that naturalism dominated the philosophical schools. The thesis of Frege's alignment with the neo-Kantians receives little enough support from his overt references to them. His *Grundlagen* of 1884 contains a bitterly hostile reference to Kuno Fischer;[1] and in 1885 he published a strongly critical review of a book by Hermann Cohen, the leader of the Marburg school of neo-Kantians.

Sluga lists, as the four 'great philosophical influences on Frege', Leibniz, Kant, Herbart and Lotze (p. 40). Frege does once refer, favourably, to Herbart;[2] but since Sluga mentions him only on one page, and makes no case for including him in the list, we need not enquire more closely into his alleged influence. Of the influence of Leibniz and of Kant, there can be no doubt; Frege treated them as great philosophers, worthy of much respect, as he would have been a fool not to do; and he expressly acknowledged his debts to both. With Lotze it is quite otherwise. Frege never once mentions him; yet, according to Sluga, he owed to him several of his leading ideas. Even if we rate Frege a singularly ungenerous man, this cannot be accounted for by the fact that Leibniz and Kant were dead, since Lotze, too, died before the *Grundlagen* was published. We have to presume that Sluga is more perspicacious in detecting the sources of Frege's ideas than was Frege himself. Sluga also assigns an important influence on Frege to Trendelenburg, to whom Frege refers in the Preface to his *Begriffsschrift* as expounding Leibniz's idea of a *lingua characteristica*; but, since the influence proves to amount to no more than the transmission to Frege of this idea of Leibniz's, it need not detain us.

All this discussion of influences overlooks the eccentric character of Frege's career. He studied mathematics at both Jena and Göttingen, taking a few courses in chemistry, physics and philosophy on the side; and he spent his entire professional life in the mathematics department at Jena. He entered philosophy by a side-door: he surely did not foresee, at the outset, how much he would have to engage himself with it. He set himself to write a definitive work, establishing number theory and analysis upon their true foundations: from 1879 to 1903, almost everything he wrote was directed towards that end. Fortunately for all of us—since he was a philosophical genius—this took him, in the event, deep into philosophy. It remains that he was not by training a philosopher, but a mathematician; though a well educated man, I do not believe that he was well read in philosophy by the standards of a professional. He studied whatever he thought necessary for his purpose: but, even on philosophical points, he quotes mathematicians and logicians as frequently as pure philosophers. In the *Grundlagen*, he

[1] P. iii.
[2] *Grundlagen*, p. iii again.

quotes Kant, Mill, Jevons, Herbart and Kuno Fischer from editions of their works, but Descartes, Hobbes, Spinoza, Newton, Locke, Berkeley and Hume solely from a collection by Baumann of original writings on space, time and mathematics: Leibniz he quotes from both types of source. He evidently studied Baumann's collection very carefully: it is difficult to feel any confidence that he knew the work of the philosophers in the second list from any other source. He acknowledged his debt to Leibniz for the idea of a *lingua characteristica* (though not its execution), and for the principle known as 'Leibniz's law' (of identity). But, as Sluga himself remarks, apropos of Frege's alleged debt to Trendelenburg, Frege took from other writers ideas of value to him, ignoring the doctrine in which they were embedded (p. 52); contrary to what Sluga thinks, this appears to me to be the case in regard to Leibniz also. As for Kant, Frege's engagement with his ideas was much deeper, as surely must have been that of anyone writing about philosophy in Germany in the last two decades of the nineteenth century: but we know rather precisely what his stance was towards them, since he was at pains in the *Grundlagen* to make it quite explicit.

Realism, idealism, rationalism, empiricism

Perhaps more important than whom Frege took himself to be agreeing with or following is the question whom he regarded as his opponents. By identifying the errors that he saw himself as combating, we may hope to discern how he meant the doctrines he offered in their place to be understood. This, at least, is Sluga's idea; and it is one of much greater merit than the search for unrecognized influences. Certainly it is hard to grasp Frege's positive philosophy of mathematics without setting it against the background of his opposition to empiricism, psychologism and formalism. His opposition to these trends does not need to be *discovered*: he was a great polemicist, and constantly attacked them, vehemently and at length. What is important for us is to see these attacks, not as merely clearing the ground for his own logicist and platonist philosophy of mathematics, but as arguments in its favour: we see what numbers must be by seeing what they cannot be. Natural numbers and real numbers are not mere symbols, as the formalists hold; nor are they given in experience, as the empiricists believe; nor are they creations of the human mind, as psychologism would have us suppose. Because formalism is wrong, there is, for mathematical symbols as for terms of other kinds, a distinction between the sign and that which it designates, and so they must be objects. Because psychologism is wrong, they must be objective; and because both it and empiricism are wrong, they must be given neither in sensation nor in intuition, but to the reason alone, and so they must be logical objects.

What, then, did Frege see as the enemies against which his general philosophical doctrines were barricades? In this area, he did not so frequently preface his positive account by a critique of rival theories; but we can certainly again say that he was opposed to empiricism and to psychologism. Since Sluga regards the latter as arising from naturalism, he views Frege as part of the neo-Kantian movement which he takes to be primarily a reaction against naturalism, and concludes that he should be interpreted, not as a realist, but as an idealist of Kant's type. The difficulty here is that, whenever Frege mentioned idealism, as he did in 'Über Sinn und Bedeutung' and in the Preface to the *Grundgesetze*, he mentioned it with hostility; his ground of attack upon psychologism was not that it originated in materialism, but that it led to idealism. By contrast, he spoke unfavourably of realism only when it assumed a form that degenerated into idealism.

Sluga's explanation of this consists in an appeal to two types of idealism distinguished by Kant: empirical idealism, as exemplified by Berkeley, which he claimed to have refuted, and transcendental idealism, which he advocated. According to Sluga, Frege was, like Kant, a transcendental idealist; when he criticized what he described as 'idealists', without qualification, what he meant were empirical idealists. This does not seem to me, in the circumstances, very plausible. Frege indeed specifically criticized Berkeleyan idealism; but the term 'idealism' was, in current German philosophical usage, far more often employed in allusion to Kantian and post-Kantian idealism than to the empiricist variety, and he would have been inviting misunderstanding if he had used it, without qualification, to refer to the latter as opposed to the former. Especially does Sluga's interpretation strike me as implausible in view of the footnote in Frege's *Grundlagen* in which he says that Kant's theory took on a subjective and idealist tinge which obscured his true opinion.[1] When Frege spoke generally of idealism, he was surely referring to what is in common between all varieties of philosophy to which that label is attached. Without doubt there are great differences between the various forms of idealist philosophy. It is, however, a mistake to think, as Sluga apparently does, that the term 'idealism', as applied to all of them, is purely equivocal: one who believes this will be taken by surprise on reading, for example, G. E. Moore's 'Refutation of Idealism' of 1903,[2] which is directed against Bradley

[1] *Grundlagen*, p. 37n.
[2] *Mind*, 1903, reprinted in G. E. Moore, *Philosophical Studies*, 1922.

rather than Berkeley, but is devoted to disproving the thesis that *esse* is *percipi*.

When we look more closely, something appears amiss with Sluga's whole perspective. He tends to associate rationalism with idealism as both being part of 'the classical German tradition' of philosophy (p. 50), descending from Leibniz through Kant to Lotze, within which he locates Frege. Rationalism he admits to be compatible with a Platonic realism (p. 60), though not, we must infer from his silence, with realism concerning the physical world; but 'a strong argument' is required to prise rationalism away from the transcendental idealism which is its natural matrix. In fact, the association between them is not a natural one at all. The disagreement between rationalists and empiricists is over epistemology; that between idealists and realists, on the other hand, is primarily metaphysical. Rationalists believe that human reason can, by itself, lead to the knowledge of substantial truths: those of arithmetic, geometry, metaphysics, natural theology and other branches of mathematics and philosophy; perception, for it, is either a more confused mode of rational apprehension, or an exercise of the reason assisted by the senses to attain knowledge not exhaustively explicable in terms of experience. For empiricists, all genuine knowledge is derived from experience: we represent and summarize our experience in our thought and our language, but these are significant only in so far as they can be interpreted experientially, and are justified only in so far as they are backed by experience. Plainly these are not the only possible alternatives: we may have modes of knowledge neither experiential nor ratiocinatory. Kant, for instance, was neither an empiricist nor a rationalist. For him, we have substantial knowledge which, as a priori, is not derived from experience, and, as synthetic, is not attained by mere ratiocination. Frege, who said that having visual impressions is necessary but not sufficient for seeing things, was certainly no empiricist; as one who believed that the recognition of analytic truths may be a substantive extension of knowledge, he was more of a rationalist than Kant; but, as one who accepted that we have synthetic a priori knowledge, he was still not a pure rationalist.

Idealism, in the strict sense of the word, stands opposed to materialism. Materialists believe that all reality is ultimately material, idealists that it is ultimately mental or spiritual: obviously there is no need to belong to either party. In any case, this is a metaphysical dispute. Frege, who believed in the existence of immaterial objects of various kinds, such as numbers and thoughts, was obviously not a materialist; and it hardly seems likely that, insisting that neither logical objects such as numbers nor even thoughts and their component senses depend, for their existence, upon any thinker, and distinguishing sharply between an idea of the Moon and what 'the Moon' stands for, he was yet an idealist in the correlative sense. Idealism often appears, however, as contrasted with realism; and it is this contrast with which Sluga is concerned. Opposition to realism does not always take an idealistic form, which is why I have usually preferred the more general term 'anti-realism'; but the issue still belongs to metaphysics rather than to epistemology. The question is what it is that renders our judgments (thoughts, statements) true or false: in other words, what constitutes reality, or at least that reality of which we speak or about which we think. For a realist, our judgments are true or false in virtue of a reality that exists objectively and independently of our knowledge. For an idealist, we cannot so much as conceive of that which goes beyond our capacity to know it. More exactly, this is the general anti-realist response, which need not assume an idealist guise; behaviourism, for example, is a characteristic anti-realist reaction to realism about mental events. Anti-realism takes an idealist form when it is held that reality is in some way constituted by our apprehension of it. Considered as relating to our intellectual scope, the question concerns the range of thoughts we can apprehend or express, rather than of those to a knowledge of whose truth we can attain; it nevertheless naturally becomes entangled with epistemology, since the notion of knowledge enters into its formulation. A realist will admit a large range of questions we can intelligibly ask, but to which we are unlikely ever to know the answer; and he can consistently hold that there are many to which we can never, in principle, discover the answer. He can do so because he does not explain our grasp of thoughts, or the meanings we give to our statements, in terms of that on the basis of which we judge them to be true. But in practice those who restrict the range of what we can know are likely to restrict also the range of what we can intelligibly think; and that is why empiricism is always liable to lead to idealism, as with Berkeley. The Kantian path to idealism is quite different, but also has an epistemological base; it arises from Kant's account of the source of our synthetic a priori knowledge. For Kant, this knowledge rests upon our own nature: we impose certain forms upon our perception and apprehension of empirical reality, and therefore we know a priori that it must exhibit those forms. For this reason, Kant conceived of us as contributing much to the constitution of empirical reality; and it is this which made him, what he professed to be, a transcendental idealist.

The relations between these various currents of thought are very complex, both theoretically and, even more, historically; in particular, Kant's philosophy, standing at the intersection of several lines of thought, could be developed in various directions, which is why neo-Kantianism was not a unified movement. Even stronger than Sluga's inclination to associate rationalism and idealism is his tendency to blur the distinction between realism and materialism. 'The naturalists . . . were committing themselves to a strict ontological realism and materialism' (p. 18); the neo-Kantians 'tended to think of the naturalists as epistemologically naive because of their realism and materialism' (p. 36); until Mach, psychologism was 'tied exclusively to the realism and materialism of the scientific naturalists' (p. 38). In so far as realism is assimilated to materialism, it becomes very easy to maintain that Frege was not a realist, since he was obviously no materialist. Plainly, however, realism about physical objects does not imply materialism; and it does not do to equate naturalism with realism. Naturalism may be aggressively materialist, but it may also assume an empiricist form which readily slips into idealism, as Frege was very well aware. It could even take on a Kantian tinge, as it did in the writings of the scientist Helmholtz, of one of whose essays Frege wrote in 1903, 'Hardly ever have I come across anything more unphilosophical than this philosophical essay.'[1] Realism is not, of course, a single doctrine; one can be a realist about some things but not about others. Material objects, mental events, theoretical entities, mathematical objects, the meanings of sentences, the objects of propositional attitudes, universals, the past, the future, possible objects, possible worlds: all have been the subject of disputes between realists and anti-realists, and probably there are few philosophers who have been realists about them all or anti-realists about them all. But these disputes have a strong formal resemblance to one another. There is therefore a tendency, though no more than a tendency, for a philosopher who takes the realist side in any one such dispute to take it also in another, and conversely. The reason, although Sluga would appear to deny it (p. 161), is that realism rests upon a general attitude to the way we give meaning to our sentences, and anti-realism upon an opposed attitude. In no one specific dispute does either attitude entail that one takes up the corresponding side in that dispute; but it inclines one towards doing so. Sluga notes this phenomenon in the case of the early Russell and Moore, but offers no explanation of it (p. 176). In general, he is inclined to treat realism about material objects quite separately from realism about thoughts and about mathematical and logical objects, although the latter two are in fact as distinct from one another as from the first. He denies that Frege was a realist about any of these things; but he considers them as unconnected issues, or, at least, does not exhibit the connection. His

[1] *Grundgesetze*, vol. II, § 137, fn. 2.

principal ground for holding that Frege was not a realist about logical objects or about thoughts is that he denied that these are *wirklich*, which Sluga is still disposed to translate as 'real'. Physical objects, on the other hand, were for Frege a prime example of what is *wirklich*; and so he has to be denied to be a realist about them on different grounds.

As already remarked, psychologism was not 'tied exclusively' to scientific naturalism, but was launched by Fries, a follower of Kant. In a passage Sluga quotes from me (p. 9, quoting from *FPL*, p. 684), I pointed out that idealism does not entail psychologism; but it should be obvious why it is liable to slip into psychologism, which in turn can provide a path to idealism. Frege's attack on psychologism in the Preface to the *Grundgesetze* is simultaneously an attack upon idealism, in fact upon psychologism on the ground that it leads to idealism. There is, indeed, a certain equivocation in the word 'idealism', according as it is opposed to 'materialism' or to 'realism'. All who reject realism on idealist grounds reject also materialism, but the converse does not hold. Leibniz, for example, was an idealist in the sense in which that is the opposite of being a materialist, but he cannot be said to have been an anti-realist; an inclination to think otherwise is due to the error of supposing that realism must always assume the form of what is called 'naive realism', whereas there can be sophisticated versions. But, as already remarked, there is no equivocation in applying the word 'idealist' both to phenomenalists and to post- or neo-Kantian idealists: these are idealists in the same, anti-realist, sense, although they arrive at their positions by different routes.

It should now be clear why it is also a mistake to link idealism with rationalism. The realist has to explain how we can reach out in thought to that which transcends our experience; he is in a stronger position to do this if he holds that our knowledge is not derived solely from experience. Of course, if he is to maintain his realism, he must still hold, against Kant, that our knowledge is of things as they are in themselves; and rationalism is one way of making this out. Rationalism is therefore a natural ally of realism. Stress the dependence of our knowledge on experience too heavily, and you may fall into idealism of the phenomenalist variety; insist that we bring to experience the forms which it must assume, and you find yourself an idealist of a Kantian type. It would therefore be no reason for doubting Frege's realism to suppose him to have been deeply influenced by the rationalism of Leibniz, as Sluga does; I simply see no ground for thinking that to be true.

Sluga's position is inherently unstable. He wants to deny that Frege was a realist, and represent him as a kind of transcendental idealist; and he therefore wants to exploit what was surely a mistake on my part in supposing

Hegelianism still to be influential at the beginning of Frege's career, a mistake to which he repeatedly adverts (pp. 8–9, 14, 176). But the correction of this error would have no probative force unless it were also denied that other versions of idealism were prevalent; that is why Sluga contends that idealism was not a real power in German thought after 1830, and repudiates my characterization of it as dominant in Frege's day (pp. 9, 45). If this were left unqualified, we should have the amazing picture of Frege as the reviver of Kantianism in a realist environment; so it is modified to allow that neo-Kantianism superseded naturalism at just about the time Frege began his studies. Unfortunately, this undercuts the original argument: idealism, though not, indeed, Hegelian idealism as such, was, after all, the dominant philosophical force in Frege's time. Sluga is then left with the problem of showing that Frege was not against it but for it.

'Since Frege is opposed to Hegelian idealism, Dummett reasons, he must clearly be a realist,' Sluga once wrote, as part of an account of *FPL*.[1] I did not, of course, deduce that Frege was a realist from any such historical premiss, let alone that one; I found realist views expressed in his writings. Sluga's interpretation of Frege as an idealist, on the other hand, depends very critically upon historical arguments. It is apparent that his *general* historical argument, concerning the course of German philosophy during the nineteenth century, achieves nothing in this regard. We have, therefore, to turn to the specific arguments, involving comparisons with Kant and Lotze. I do not think that Sluga would maintain that Frege's idealist opinions are clearly expressed in his writings in such a way as to be apparent to anyone unfamiliar with Kant and with Lotze. His view seems to be, rather, that, if you know those philosophers, you can infer what Frege meant, and what he must have believed, but did not explicitly or at least unmistakably say; that is why his interpretation depends so heavily upon the historical comparisons he makes, in a manner in which my own did not, and was not meant to, depend upon any historical contrasts. It is these comparisons, therefore, which have now to be examined.

Frege and Kant

Once we have disentangled idealism from rationalism and realism from materialism, how does Frege come out? Sluga's argument that Frege was not a realist in respect of physical objects is based on an assimilation of his views concerning space to those of Kant. This was extensively discussed in Chapter 20; and, in this regard, Sluga's views appear to have changed little

---

[1] 'Frege and the Rise of Analytic Philosophy', *Inquiry*, vol. 18, 1975, p. 477.

from those expressed in his articles, and his evidence to have remained the same, so that the matter may here be dealt with quite briefly. It is without doubt that Frege was influenced by Kant; but his observation, quoted above, that Kant's theory took on a subjective and idealist tinge which obscured his true opinion, renders it unlikely that this influence was in an idealist direction. Frege indeed believed in the existence of synthetic a priori truths, and praised Kant for recognizing their existence; and he included in this category the truths of geometry. Sluga interprets this to mean that 'Frege held a Kantian view of space and hence a transcendentally subjective view of the objects that occupy it', that is, of material things (p. 45). This is the plainest example of the dependence of Sluga's interpretation of Frege upon historical deduction. We have no discussion, in Frege's writings, of the nature of material objects, nor, with two exceptions, of the nature of space;[1] we have only the reiterated assertion that geometrical truths are synthetic a priori, and a number of vague allusions to intuition. Without a knowledge of Kant, one would gain no clue from these remarks that he took a transcendental idealist view of material objects. It may, indeed, be argued that Frege was, in using Kantian terminology, presupposing a familiarity with Kant's doctrines; but Sluga's conclusion follows only if we presume that he intended to endorse all that Kant said about intuition and the synthetic a priori. But, as we saw in Chapter 20, there is no ground for such a presumption. Frege does not, in *Grundlagen*, simply employ these terms as having a well-established meaning: he explains explicitly how he understands the terms 'synthetic' and 'a priori',[2] and comments upon Kant's employment of the term 'intuition'.[3] Although Frege thought that there are synthetic a priori truths, his explanation of how we know such truths does not resemble Kant's. For Frege, there are certain fundamental laws which neither need nor admit of proof. Some of these are of a logical character, and the truths derived from them are analytic; others are non-logical, and the truths inferred from them as premisses are synthetic a priori. We can consistently describe, but cannot imagine, a world in which the synthetic a priori truths, for instance those of geometry, fail.[4] These fundamental laws are obviously a surd in Frege's theory; notoriously, his only reply to one who would question them was, 'We have here a hitherto unknown type of mad-

---

[1] The two exceptions are § 26 of the *Grundlagen*, and the essay-review 'Über das Trägheitsgesetz' of 1891, containing a very interesting, but, as it seems to me, quite unKantian, discussion of the Newtonian concept of absolute space.

[2] § 3.

[3] § 12.

[4] *Grundlagen*, § 14.

ness.'[1] The important point is, however, that Frege does not concur with the Kantian explanation of our knowledge of the fundamental laws as representing the necessary conditions for our perceiving and apprehending the world. He is explicit about this in respect of the fundamental laws of logic. 'The question why and with what right we acknowledge a law of logic to be true, logic can answer only by reducing it to another law of logic. Where that is not possible, the question must remain unanswered. Stepping away from logic, one may say: we are compelled to make judgments by our own nature and by external circumstances, and, when we judge, we cannot reject this law—e.g. that of identity—but must acknowledge it, unless we wish to bring our thought into confusion and finally renounce all judgment. I do not wish either to dispute or to endorse this view; I wish only to observe that we do not here have a logical deduction. What is given is not a ground for the law's being true, but for our taking it to be true. Moreover, this impossibility of rejecting the law, which holds for us, does not in the least prevent us from supposing beings who do reject it; but it prevents us from supposing that such beings are right to do so; and it also prevents us from doubting whether it is we or they who are right.'[2] Frege is here, indeed, speaking of a fundamental law of logic, rather than of those fundamental non-logical laws he supposes to underlie synthetic a priori truths; but it is unthinkable that he should say for the latter what he so firmly dismisses for the former.

For Kant, the fact that we cannot but take synthetic a priori judgments as true is sufficient ground for their truth, since their truth extends only to the phenomenal world; it is just that which makes him a transcendental idealist. But, in the Preface to *Grundgesetze*, from which the passage just quoted is taken, Frege is operating with the sharpest possible distinction between being true and being taken to be true: 'being true,' he says, 'is different from being taken to be true . . . and in no case is to be reduced to it',[3] and, in saying this, expresses what appears to me to be the nub of the opposition between realists and idealists. He neither disputes nor endorses the view that we cannot but acknowledge the truth of the fundamental laws, but insists that, even if that is so, it does not render them true. We have no ground for the fundamental laws—they are not capable of proof,[4] which is what makes them fundamental; we acknowledge them as true, and perhaps cannot do otherwise, but our acknowledging them as true is quite a different

[1] *Grundgesetze*, vol. I, p. xvi.
[2] *Grundgesetze*, vol. I, p. xvii.
[3] *Grundgesetze*, vol. I, p. xv.
[4] *Grundlagen*, § 3.

matter from their being true, that is, from their being what we acknowledge them to be. In drawing his distinction between being true and being taken to be true, Frege hits the very centre of the issue concerning realism. Is our notion of truth, as applied to the statements we can make and comprehend, to be explained in terms of what we treat as grounds for judging such statements true, and of our reasons for doing so when grounds are lacking, or do we have a conception of what it is that renders them true, if they are true, which is independent of our means of judging them? One who gives the former answer is an anti-realist, and, quite likely, an idealist. One who gives the latter answer is a realist; and Frege emphatically gives the latter answer. There could not be a clearer general declaration of Frege's adherence to what I understand by 'realism' and what, I believe, has usually been understood by it in philosophical discussion. Frege's distinction between being true and being taken to be true is drawn in the course of an attack upon the psychologistic logician Benno Erdmann, whom he condemns as an idealist. It seems unlikely that, in 1893, he was using the word 'idealist' in some quite different sense from that in which, in 1884, he had deprecated the idealist tinge in Kant's theories; if he was, he was uncharacteristically confused.

Frege's firm opinion that the truths of geometry are synthetic a priori thus yields no ground whatever for Sluga's conclusion that he held a transcendental idealist view of space and its material occupants. Much the same holds good for Frege's occasional allusions to intuition, of which notion, indeed, he nowhere attempts a clear account. Sluga quotes him as saying in 1874 that geometry points to intuition as the source of its axioms (p. 47, quoting from *Rechnungsmethoden*, p. 1); this is echoed in some of his very late unpublished writings, and certainly has a Kantian ring. But, as we saw in Chapter 20, in the only passage in which Frege deals with the matter at length, a very different doctrine is advanced.[1] Having remarked that, according to Kant, space belongs to appearance (that is, to the merely phenomenal world), he observes that spatial intuitions are incommunicable. 'Nevertheless,' he says, 'there is something objective about space all the same; everyone recognizes the same geometrical axioms, and must do so if he is to find his way about the world. What is objective about it is what is subject to laws, what can be conceived and judged, what is expressible in words. What is purely intuitable is not communicable.' He concludes by saying that 'by objectivity I understand independence from our sensation, intuition and imagination'. Here the axioms of geometry, and all concerning it that we can express in words, are objective and hence do *not* rest upon

[1] *Grundlagen*, § 26.

intuition. They are not, for that reason, analytic. Frege has already made clear that he considers them synthetic a priori; there therefore could not be a plainer statement that he does not accept Kant's account of synthetic a priori truths or of the relation of the truths of geometry to intuition, pure or otherwise.

Frege's notion of objectivity

Just as Sluga's conclusion that Frege held an idealist view of material objects rests on his assimilation of his views about space to those of Kant, so his argument that he was not a realist in respect of logical objects such as numbers, or in respect of thoughts and their component senses, is based on a comparison with Lotze. As in his articles, the premiss of his argument is Frege's distinction between objectivity and *Wirklichkeit*: Sluga claims that Frege took the notion of objectivity from Lotze's *Logik* of 1874, in which the notion is likewise distinguished from that of *Wirklichkeit* (p. 118). He now hedges somewhat over whether *wirklich*, in Frege, is to be translated as 'real' or 'actual', remarking that either is a legitimate translation of the word as normally used (pp. 118, 195); Frege was, however, prone to use ordinary German words, such as *bedeuten*, in rather special ways.

Sluga argues, from the alleged affinity between Frege and Lotze, that 'it seems plausible to hold that Frege's doctrine of objectivity, like Lotze's, was intended as an epistemological thesis and that he was a critical rather than a dogmatic thinker' (p. 120). What, then, is the epistemological thesis that he takes Frege to be advancing and to have been misinterpreted as an ontological thesis? Frege says that logical objects, like physical ones, are objective, but, unlike them, are not *wirklich*; thoughts are also objective, but at best dubiously *wirklich*. Sluga would like to understand *wirklich* as meaning 'real', and to conclude that, in calling numbers and thoughts objective, Frege was not asserting an ontological thesis. Now, as 'real' is ordinarily understood, a sentence in which it occurs as an adjective can always be transformed, without change of content, into one containing the adverb 'really': 'A termite is not a real ant' means 'A termite is not really an ant', and 'Prospero was not a real man' means 'There was not really any such man as Prospero'. It is only when the word 'real' is used so as to admit such a transformation of the sentence that we deny an ontological thesis by denying reality to something. Sluga must, therefore, be ascribing to Frege a belief either that there are not really any such objects as numbers and thoughts, or that numbers and thoughts are not really objects, but something else. If so, the former presumably represents his intention, since he stresses

Frege's classification of numbers and classes as logical objects, and is surprisingly emphatic that, for Frege, a thought is an object, going so far as to say that it was a 'paradigmatic object' (p. 122). If, then, the content of Frege's doctrine that numbers are not *wirklich* is, in this way, the denial of an ontological thesis, his other doctrine, that numbers and thoughts are objective, can hardly be meant as an ontological assertion; and this leaves it open that it may be intended as an epistemological thesis. But, in such a case, we must ask again: *what* epistemological thesis does it express? The extraordinary fact is that Sluga makes virtually no attempt to answer this question. We are being offered a radically novel interpretation of Frege, but its author, though supplying some reasons for rejecting the interpretation he opposes, forgets to say what his own is; he tells us that it is epistemological in character, and leaves us to work it out for ourselves.

The only help he gives us, apart from the reiteration of the negative characterization ('not a dogmatic metaphysical claim', p. 120), is a string of four rather difficult quotations from Frege. The second and third of these are two passages, indeed rather similar, from *Grundlagen* and 'Der Gedanke' respectively. In the first, Frege says that 'in arithmetic we are concerned with objects . . . that are immediately given to the reason', or, in Sluga's rendering, 'immediately given to Reason';[1] in the second, that 'neither logic nor mathematics has the task of investigating minds and the content of a consciousness whose bearer is an individual human being', but that 'one might, rather, represent their task as that of investigating mind—mind, not minds'.[2] Sluga justly remarks on the Kantian ring of these passages, but puts no specific interpretation on them. He does, however, gloss the first of his quotations, which is the continuation of that cited above from *Grundlagen*, § 26, in which Frege explains 'objectivity' as meaning independence from sensation, intuition and imagination, but not, he goes on, independence from reason, 'for to answer the question what things are independently of reason would be as much as to judge without judging, to wash the fur without wetting it'. Sluga explains this cryptic remark as meaning that 'it is incoherent for us to try to say what things are in themselves, independent of our judgments'. This does not elucidate the matter greatly; but I take him to interpret Frege's remark to mean that something that is objective exists independently of our perceiving or imagining it, but not of our thinking about it. A little later he says, expounding Frege, that 'the objective is not something alien or external to the mind, but constitutive of it' (p. 121). This comment is still not quite to the point, which is not whether certain

[1] *Grundlagen*, § 105.
[2] 'Der Gedanke', p. 74.

objects constitute the mind, but whether, according to Frege, the mind constitutes the objects. Nothing is clearer in Frege than that what he calls objective is *not* constituted by our minds or by our thinking of it; not even a thought is constituted by our thinking it. 'In order to be true, thoughts— e.g. natural laws—do not need to be recognized by us as true; they do not even have to have been thought by us at all. A natural law is not invented by us, but discovered. And just as a desolate island in the Arctic Ocean was there long before anyone had set eyes on it, so laws of nature, and likewise those of mathematics, have held good at all times and not just since they were discovered. We can gather from this that thoughts are not only true independently of our recognizing them to be so (in the cases when they *are* true), but that they are altogether independent of our thinking.'[1] A thought is devoid of truth-value if the objects to which it purports to relate do not exist; so, if an arithmetical law exists and is true independently of our even thinking it, the numbers of which it treats must likewise exist independently of our thinking of them. This is why it may be said of the mathematician, as of the natural scientist, that he 'cannot create things at will, any more than the geographer can; he too can only discover what is there and give it a name.'[2] Sluga's interpretation of the passage from *Grundlagen*, § 26, runs counter to the passage he himself cites from 'Der Gedanke': if the objects of logic and mathematics depended upon our thinking, or constituted or were constituted by our minds, then minds, in the plural, would be the ultimate field of investigation for those sciences. I do not, indeed, feel wholly sure what Frege intended in speaking as he does of 'reason' in the two passages from *Grundlagen*. In § 26, reason appears, alongside sensation, intuition and imagination, as one of *our* faculties; he may intend no more than that what is objective remains subject to the laws of rational thought. His remark in § 105 may hark back to the question he had posed in § 62, 'How are numbers to be given to us, if we can have no idea or intuition of them?', a question that he had there answered without invoking the vague conception of their being 'given to the reason', but in such a way as to justify calling numbers 'logical objects'. If more lies behind these two remarks, it seems irrecoverable now, since there is no echo, let alone elucidation, of them in any other place. If the remarks from the *Grundlagen* sound faintly Kantian, the isolated sentence from 'Der Gedanke' could be viewed as Hegelian;[3] while it is clear what Frege is denying, it is obscure what he is

---

[1] 'Logik', 1897, *N.S.*, pp. 144–5, *P.W.*, p. 133.

[2] *Grundlagen*, § 96.

[3] The task of logic and mathematics is said to be *die Erforschung des Geistes, des Geistes, nicht der Geister*.

asserting. But, whatever it was precisely that he intended by these rare and uncharacteristic passing remarks, it is certainly not what Sluga ascribes to him, a view he repeatedly and emphatically rejects.

Sluga supports his interpretation by a fourth quotation, again from 'Der Gedanke': 'What I hold in my hand can indeed be regarded as the content of my hand, but is the content of my hand in quite a different way from the bones and muscles of which it consists, . . . and is far more alien to it than they.'[1] 'If we take this analogy seriously,' Sluga comments, 'it seems to imply that Frege does not hold that thoughts are in the mind as the bird is in the hand, but rather as the muscles and bones are in the hand' (p. 121). He has got it exactly the wrong way round. Frege consistently held that thoughts are not mental contents. In the passage to which is appended the footnote from which the quotation is taken, he has been expounding just this view, though without using the word 'content'. In the footnote, he points out that the word 'content', in any case metaphorical, can be taken in two ways. It is in one of these that Frege wishes to deny that a thought is a mental content, unlike a mental image, namely that in which a mental content is in the mind as the muscles are in the hand: the thought does not go to constitute the mind, nor does the mind constitute it. If, on the other hand, when I grasp a cricket ball, the ball were said to be the content of my hand, then a thought might, in a comparable sense, be said to be a content of my mind; for Frege favours the use of the verb 'to grasp' as a metaphorical expression for the relation of the thinker to the thought. The reason is, as he says, that what is grasped exists independently of him who grasps it, or of its being grasped at all. We do not need to go outside 'Der Gedanke' to confirm this: 'When one grasps or thinks a thought, one does not create it, but only comes to stand in a certain relation to what already existed beforehand' is only one of many similar remarks to be found there.[2] He had held this view before he adopted the term 'thought', but was speaking of 'judgeable contents': 'a judgeable content . . . is not the result of an inner process or the product of a mental act which men perform, but something objective . . . just as the Sun, say, is something objective.'[3]

If thoughts are independent of our thinking, it can hardly be expected that numbers will be dependent on it: the mistake of supposing them to be so is diagnosed by Frege in the Preface to *Grundgesetze* as stemming from the belief that only what is *wirklich* can be objective. That brings us back to what Frege meant by *wirklich*. As we saw in Chapter 20, there is no mystery

[1] 'Der Gedanke', p. 74n.
[2] 'Der Gedanke', p. 69n.
[3] 'Logik', early 1880s, *N.S.*, p. 7, *P.W.*, p. 7.

about this: he explained it clearly when he wrote '. . . to be *wirklich*, i.e. to be capable of acting directly or indirectly on the senses'.[1] The verb used here for 'to act' is *wirken*, cognate with *wirklich*. If an object has causal effects, then it can act, at least indirectly, upon the senses; but to some objects, such as numbers, it is impossible to ascribe causal effects, and they are therefore properly described as not *wirklich*. For all that, they are just as objective, as independent of us and of our thinking about them, as physical objects. Given that Frege used the word *wirklich* in this way, it obviously invites confusion to translate it as 'real', rather than as 'actual', which most translators have adopted and which preserves the relation with 'acting'. Of course, the point is not so much how it should be translated as how it should be understood. Frege did not intend it to be understood as meaning 'real' in that sense of the word in which alone a denial of reality is a repudiation of an ontological claim, although, indeed, other German writers use *wirklich* in just this sense. Sluga's continued misunderstanding of Frege's use of the term, in the face of the quite explicit explanations of it that Frege gave, involves him in an extensive misinterpretation of Frege's thought.

Currie

Sluga considers it a necessary, but not a sufficient, condition for Frege to have been a realist concerning objects of a given kind that he should have recognized them as *wirklich*; his denial of *Wirklichkeit* to logical objects shows him not to have been a realist in respect of them, though his ascription of it to physical objects is compatible with his having viewed them in a transcendental idealist light. In his intervention in the dispute between Sluga and me about Frege's realism,[2] Currie takes the opposite view: for him, Frege's classification of a range of objects as *wirklich* is a *sufficient* ground to consider him a realist concerning them. Hence, since, as he points out, in 'Der Gedanke' Frege allows *Wirklichkeit* even to thoughts, he concludes, contrary to Sluga, that Frege was a realist in regard to them. In the light of Frege's consistent employment of the word *wirklich*,[3] both he and Sluga are wrong; whether objects of a given kind are or are not *wirklich* is irrelevant to whether a realist view of them is correct. It must be conceded

[1] *Grundgesetze*, vol. I, p. xviii.

[2] G. Currie, 'Frege's Realism', *Inquiry*, vol. 21, 1978, pp. 218–21. Discussion of the intervention of Michael Resnik will be postponed until after consideration of Sluga's views on the context principle, which figures prominently in Resnik's article.

[3] In *Grundlagen*, § 85, Frege characterises the *wirklich* as 'that which affects our senses or at least produces effects which may cause sense-perceptions as near or remote consequences'.

that, in 'Der Gedanke', there is a hint of the interpretation of *wirklich* as 'real' when Frege says that 'something wholly and in every respect inactive (*unwirksames*) would also be quite *unwirklich* and would not exist for us'.[1] Frege's difficulty is that it appears that, if something gives rise to no effects, we could have no knowledge of it; it would be for us as if it did not exist. This train of thought has appeared, in recent writings on the philosophy of mathematics, as a difficulty for platonism, and, in epistemological discussions, as an objection to causal accounts of knowledge. If numbers are abstract objects, possessing no causal powers, how can we have any knowledge of them? Alternatively: since we have knowledge of numbers, which are abstract objects, how can knowledge depend upon a causal connection between the object of knowledge and the subject? Versions of platonism which ascribe to us an intuitive faculty, analogous to perception, yielding us knowledge of abstract objects, can evade this difficulty; but Frege held that intuition played no role in our arithmetical knowledge. It is hardly to be imagined that, at the stage when he still believed in logical objects, he would have admitted the *general* argument embodied in the sentence quoted above as showing them, too, to possess a degree of *Wirklichkeit*; but, when he wrote 'Der Gedanke', he had most probably already abandoned any belief in logical objects.[2]

The requirement of a causal connection between the object of knowledge and the subject is proposed as a means of distinguishing knowledge properly so called from well-grounded belief which is nevertheless only accidentally true. For this purpose, it is sufficient to require the ground of acceptance of the proposition to correspond with what in fact renders it true; it is implausible that, in all cases, such a correspondence should entail a causal connection. In any case, Frege, in 'Der Gedanke', is not concerned with what differentiates knowledge proper from any more uncertain species of awareness. The objection to platonism can be generalized: if numbers possess no causal powers, they can in no way affect what happens, and hence

---

[1] *wäre . . . für uns nicht vorhanden*; 'Der Gedanke', p. 76.

[2] Frege's category of logical objects is wider than that of what, in *FPL*, p. 503, I called 'pure abstract objects', since, for him, all classes (and all value-ranges) are logical objects, even when they have empirical objects as members. For all that, it is hardly to be supposed that logical objects comprise all those that are not *wirklich* and do not belong to the realm of sense; for instance, the axis of the Earth and the centre of mass of the Solar System, which, in *Grundlagen*, § 26, are cited as not being *wirklich*. In *Grundgesetze*, vol. II, § 74, Frege expressly allows that the classification into physical and logical objects is not exhaustive. The same must presumably be said of the division of reality, in 'Der Gedanke', into the outer and inner worlds and the 'third realm' of senses; or, if not, the outer world must contain some *unwirkliche* occupants such as the Earth's axis.

cannot be invoked in any explanation of what happens; how, then, can we have any ground for believing in their existence? An answer to this can be given if it can be shown that the applications of mathematics in, say, physics turn only on mathematical propositions that can be stated without invoking the existence of the real or complex numbers; in such a case, formulations of those propositions which do invoke the existence of the numbers may be regarded as a convenient *façon de parler*. This would certainly not have been Frege's response; he was of the opinion that the mathematical truths to which physics appeals would not hold good unless there in fact exist objects satisfying the axioms for the field of real numbers. But, in his mature period, the difficulty would surely not have impressed him. It is, perhaps, acute for a platonist who regards reference to the real numbers as more than a *façon de parler*, eschews intuition as the source of our knowledge of them, and denies that mathematical laws are logical truths; but one who held, like Frege, that the truths of arithmetic and analysis are analytic was not in the same dilemma. If the existence of the real numbers is an analytic truth, we cannot intelligibly suppose them not to exist, and so cannot argue that everything would happen just the same if they did not exist. Our awareness of their existence then rests only on that faculty, namely our reason, by which we are able to apprehend the truth of logical laws. No causal efficacy needs to be ascribed to them in order to explain this: they are given to us neither in sensation nor by intuition, but as the referents of certain terms in sentences whose sense we grasp in grasping their truth-conditions, and whose truth we acknowledge on purely logical grounds. For the Frege of the *Grundlagen* and of the *Grundgesetze*, our awareness of the existence of numbers could supply no ground for attributing *Wirklichkeit* to them.

We can be aware of objects of a given kind if we can grasp thoughts about them. A thought is about an object if it has a component which refers to it. To transpose the context principle to the mode of sense, such a thought-component exists only *as* a component of that and other thoughts; but our apprehension of the thought itself cannot be explained in the same manner, since its primary manifestation is by using a sentence expressing the thought rather than a phrase referring to it. The denial that 'the thought first comes into existence as a result of thinking or is constituted by thinking',[1]

---

[1] 'Logik', 1897, *N.S.*, p. 149, *P.W.*, p. 137. Frege continues, 'As I do not create a tree by seeing it, and as I do not cause a pencil to come into existence by taking hold of it, so I also do not generate a thought by thinking. Far less does the brain secrete it as the liver secretes bile.' The last sentence is a repudiation of the ludicrous dictum of the materialist Karl Vogt, and could therefore have been quoted by Sluga as evidence of Frege's opposition to materialism.

the conception of thoughts as objective and unchanging, were features of Frege's philosophy from its earliest phase; but it is from 1897 onwards that he started to put great emphasis on it, and from then also that he treats our ability to grasp thoughts as mysterious.[1] In explanation of this, he says, in 'Der Gedanke', only that 'to the grasping of the thought there must correspond a particular mental faculty, the power of thinking' (p. 74) and that 'although the thought does not belong to the content of the thinker's consciousness, yet something in his consciousness must be aimed at the thought' (p. 75). It remains that thoughts do influence events, in virtue of their being grasped and judged to be true and hence motivating the actions of human beings. And so he says in the unpublished 'Logik' of 1897 that 'if one wishes to speak of thoughts as having a *Wirklichkeit*, this can be done only in the sense that the knowledge that someone has of, e.g., a natural law acts on his decisions, which can have as a consequence the motions of masses. The acknowledgment of a law would then be construed as its acting upon the one who acknowledges it, and this is perhaps possible, in a manner similar to that in which we regard the seeing of a flower as the flower's indirectly acting upon the one who sees it'.[2] In the same way, he asks, in 'Der Gedanke', 'How does a thought act?', and replies, 'By being grasped and taken to be true ... If, e.g., I grasp the thought which we express by Pythagoras's theorem, the consequence may be that I acknowledge it as true and, further, that I apply it, making a decision that effects (*bewirkt*) accelerations of masses ... Thus thoughts can have indirect influence on accelerations of masses ... And yet we are inclined to regard thoughts as *unwirklich* because they appear to be ineffective in regard to events' (pp. 76–7). His conclusion is that 'thoughts are not altogether *unwirklich*, but their *Wirklichkeit* is of quite a different kind from that of things' (p. 77). The difference lies in the fact that, although in a certain manner they act on us, we do not act on them. 'No essential alteration is effected (*bewirkt*) in the thought' by our grasping it; 'hence if it is perhaps possible to speak of the thought as acting on human beings, there can be no question of human beings acting on the thought'.[3] The reason is that we have 'to distinguish between essential and inessential properties and to regard something as timeless if the changes to which it is subject affect only the inessential properties. One will call a property of a thought inessential when it consists in or follows from its being grasped by a thinker.'[4] Perhaps, then, a better

[1] 'Logik', 1897, *N.S.*, p. 157, *P.W.*, p. 145.
[2] *N.S.*, pp. 149–50, *P.W.*, p. 138.
[3] 'Logik', 1897, *N.S.*, p. 150, *P.W.*, p. 138.
[4] 'Der Gedanke', p. 76.

way of drawing the distinction between what is *wirklich* and what is *unwirklich* is according as it is or is not capable of being acted on, rather than whether it does or does not act on other things; in that case God, whom Frege never considers in this connection, would come out as *unwirklich* instead of supremely *wirklich*. Sluga's comment on Currie's contribution is that 'Frege is not saying that thoughts themselves are real, but that they are real only in so far as they are grasped or can be grasped. It is our ideas of thoughts that are strictly speaking real' (pp. 195–6). It should be apparent that none of this discussion has any tendency to call in question Frege's realism concerning thoughts or any bearing on whether, in the customary sense of 'real', he regarded them as real.

Frege and Lotze

There is something suspiciously like a circularity in Sluga's principal argument: because we know Frege to have been a follower of Lotze, we must interpret his writings to agree with Lotze; and because Frege agreed so much with Lotze, we can infer that he was a follower of his. In fact, however, as we saw in Chapter 19, Lotze did not say, concerning objectivity and *Wirklichkeit*, what Sluga construes him as saying and hence interprets Frege as saying. In Book I of his *Logik*, Lotze speaks of a 'first operation of thought' which converts an impression into an idea, and is effected by the formation of a name.[1] Sluga's comment on this runs: 'Some insight into how the notion of objectivity'—i.e. Frege's notion of objectivity—'is to be understood can be derived from the fact that Frege took it from Lotze's *Logik*. In that work Lotze says explicitly that objectivity "does not in general coincide with the *Wirklichkeit* that belongs to things". And he maintains that the objective is that "which is the same for all thinking beings and which is independent of them"' (p. 118). This is a very tendentious piece of quotation. Lotze indeed says that, by means of his first operation of thought, an objectivity is accorded to the object of thought which falls short of reality (*Wirklichkeit*), as stated in the first phrase Sluga quotes from him.[2] But he immediately goes on to explain this by denying that such objectivity involves independence from thinking beings: 'when we speak of "pain", "brightness", "freedom", we do not imply that they could exist if there were no person to feel, to see, to enjoy them, respectively.' He proceeds to elaborate the point that objectivity, as he uses the term, is unaffected by whether that to which it attaches does or does not exist independently of thought or experience in a passage

[1] H. Lotze, *Logik*, §§ 1–3.
[2] *Logik*, § 3.

which runs in Bosanquet's translation as follows: 'The logical objectification, then, which the creation of a name implies, does not give an external reality (*Wirklichkeit*) to the matter named; the common world, in which others are expected to recognize what we point to, is, speaking generally, only the world of thought; what we do here is to ascribe to it the first trace of an existence of its own and an inward order which is the same for all thinking beings and independent of them: it is quite indifferent whether certain parts of this world of thought indicate something which has besides an independent reality (*Wirklichkeit*) outside the thinking minds, or whether all that it contains exists only in the thoughts of those who think it, but with equal validity for them all.'[1] It is apparent that, for Lotze, the objective is indeed that which is 'the same for all thinking beings', but that it is not necessarily 'independent of them'; he is in fact going out of his way to stress that it need not be independent of them. He says that, in ascribing objectivity to something, we are attributing to it only 'the first trace' of an independent existence. Sluga, by omitting 'the first trace', and all the rest of the passage, has contrived to represent Lotze as saying the very opposite of what he here says quite plainly; only so is he able to claim of Lotze that 'he endorses all three of Frege's assertions about the objective' (p. 118).

It is thus plain that Lotze did *not* mean by 'objective' what Frege meant by it, which corresponds, rather, to *wirklich* in Lotze's usage. Sluga now proceeds to discuss Lotze's comments on Plato's theory of ideas (pp. 118–20). He does not, as he had done in his articles, equate the notion of validity which Lotze deploys in this connection with that of objectivity; but he does not explain the background to it, either, without which it is hard to understand Lotze's discussion of Plato. The background is a distinction which Lotze makes, *within* the general notion of *Wirklichkeit*, of several subordinate notions. That which is, he says, we call *wirklich*, but in different senses, according to its form, meaning by the latter what we are accustomed to call logical type. Thus things *exist* or have *being*; events do not exist, but *occur*; relations neither exist nor occur, but *obtain*; and propositions *hold* or have *validity*: each of these is the mode of reality proper to the entity in question.[2] Frege of course recognized, without emphasizing it, a systematic shift in the sense of the (existential) quantifier as it governed variables of different types, but did not acknowledge distinct logical types either for events or propositions (thoughts); it should be noted that, for Lotze, the analogue for a proposition of the existence of a thing is its validity, i.e. its holding true, a most unFregean conception.

[1] Ibid.
[2] *Logik*, § 316.

It is only in the light of this doctrine that we can understand Lotze's comments on Plato, which Sluga cites. Lotze argues that Plato had intended to ascribe reality to the ideas only in the sense of their validity; they represent truths which hold independently of whether there are any minds to recognize them or of whether they are manifested in the external world.[1] He has been misinterpreted as holding that the ideas *exist* in the way that things exist, although apart from things. Such a doctrine is not only a misinterpretation of Plato, but absurd in itself, a kind of category confusion in fact, since it is only to things that existence can, properly speaking, be ascribed. Sluga summarizes this by saying that Lotze takes Plato's theory of ideas 'as an epistemological, rather than an ontological, theory' and that 'therefore he is an epistemological rather than an ontological Platonist' (p. 119). The justice of this is unclear to me; he after all allowed that 'this world of ideas is the permanent and inexhaustible treasure-house from which the things of the external world draw all the diverse and shifting attributes they wear'.[2] Perhaps his position is too subtle to be caught by such simple philosophical dichotomies. Sluga goes on to suggest that 'Frege, like Lotze, was an epistemological, and not an ontological, Platonist' (p. 120). There seems little enough resemblance between what Lotze says about Plato and anything that Frege held. Asked whether numbers or thoughts exist in the same sense as do material things, Frege would have had only one criterion for judging, namely whether numbers, or thoughts, are objects. Numbers he very emphatically rated as objects; and Sluga himself, as already noted, insists that, for Frege, thoughts are objects, too. Frege would have admitted no further consideration as telling against saying that numbers and thoughts exist in the very same sense as physical objects; for him, existence is a second-level concept, and a purely logical one at that, and involves no reference to changeability or the occupation of space. The difficulty is that Sluga has given his account of Lotze's commentary on Plato without first explaining his background distinction between existence, occurrence, validity, etc.; the reader therefore gains only the haziest impression of what Lotze was saying. It is at this stage that Sluga claims that 'on the basis of these affinities, it seems plausible to hold that Frege's doctrine of objectivity, like Lotze's, was intended as an epistemological thesis', and argues for this from the four passages from Frege that we considered in the last section but one.

We there had some difficulty in understanding what epistemological thesis it was that Sluga meant to ascribe to Frege. Possibly his previous explanation of what he meant by calling Lotze an epistemological rather than

[1] *Logik*, §§ 317–18.
[2] *Logik*, § 318.

an ontological Platonist was intended to supply the answer. 'That is to say,' Sluga writes, 'he (Lotze) believes with Plato that empirical knowledge of temporal, changing things presupposes some knowledge of non-temporal, non-changing things' (p. 119). It is difficult to see how one could hold this epistemological thesis without also holding an ontological one; for, if there were no non-temporal, non-changing things, how could one have any knowledge of them? At any rate, nothing is plainer than that Frege did believe that there are such things, and that they in no way owe their existence to our knowledge of them, nor, in the case of thoughts, their truth either.

As remarked, we can tell what Frege's views were concerning Kant, because he was at pains to state them; but it would seem, from the absence of any express reference by him to Lotze, that we have, in this case, to rely on indirect arguments. In fact, this is not so. Among Frege's posthumous papers is a curious fragment consisting of seventeen numbered aphorisms on logic, one of the very few of his papers that survived the War not merely as a typescript but as a photograph of his manuscript.[1] As observed by the editors of his *Nachgelassene Schriften*, internal evidence suggests a date for it in the period 1880–3; but what went unnoticed by them, by the English translators and by Heinrich Scholz, the original custodian of Frege's papers, is what the fragment is. It is more surprising that this should not have been noticed by Sluga, who insists very strongly upon the influence of Lotze on Frege; for a comparison between the fragment and the Introduction to Lotze's *Logik*, first published in 1874, with a second edition in 1880, shows unmistakably that it is a series of comments by Frege on Lotze's Introduction. Thus Lotze speaks of a combination of ideas (*Verknüpfungen von Vorstellungen*), and of making a distinction of value (*Werthunterschied*) between them in respect of truth and untruth:[2] Frege comments (no. 1) that 'the combinations (*Verknüpfungen*) that constitute the essence of thinking are essentially different from associations of ideas (*Vorstellungensassociationen*)' and (no. 3) that 'in thinking it is not really ideas (*Vorstellungen*) that are combined (*verknüpft*), but things, properties, concepts, relations'. Lotze says that ordinary linguistic usage ascribes general validity and truth to those combinations of ideas which it looks to thinking to produce, and attempts to characterize the notion of truth so ascribed, namely as conformity with those relations between the contents of the ideas which are the same for every consciousness which has the ideas.[3]

---

[1] 'Siebzehn Kernsätze zur Logik', *N.S.*, pp. 189–90; 'Seventeen Key Sentences on Logic', *P.W.*, pp. 174–5.

[2] § II.

[3] § III.

Frege comments (no. 4) that 'a thought always contains something that reaches out beyond the particular case, whereby this comes into consciousness as falling under something general'; (no. 6) that 'it may serve as an external criterion for a combination that constitutes a thought (*denkende Verknüpfung*) that, for it, the question whether it is true or untrue has a sense: associations of ideas are neither true nor untrue'; and (no. 7) that 'what truth is I hold to be indefinable'. Lotze contrasts human thought with the approach made to it by animals, identifying the difference as being that a human being justifies the combination of ideas by appeal to the dependence of the particular upon the general;[1] he goes on to say that what thinking contributes, over and above the mere current of ideas, consists in the auxiliary thoughts (*Nebengedanken*) which add the ground of justification (*den Rechtsgrund . . . hinzufügen*) for the combinations of ideas, and comments that it is in this that there lies the peculiarity of thinking (*Eigenthümlichkeit des Denkens*). Frege replies (no. 2) that the distinction[2] between a thought and an association of ideas to which he had referred in no. 1 'does not merely consist in an auxiliary thought (*Nebengedanken*) which adds the ground of justification for the combination (*der den Rechtsgrund für die Verknüpfung hinzufügt*)', and observes (no. 5) that 'the linguistic expression for the peculiarity of the thought (*Eigenthümlichkeit des Gedankens*) is the copula or the personal inflection of the verb'. In § X, Lotze declares that even if our ideas are subject to the laws of a psychic mechanism, 'still logic itself first begins with the conviction (*beginnt die Logik selbst erst mit der Ueberzeugung*) that the matter ought not to rest there, that between the combinations of ideas . . . there obtains a distinction of truth and untruth[3], that there are forms to which these combinations are *supposed* to correspond, laws which they are *supposed* to obey'. Frege writes more pithily (no. 12), but this time in agreement, that 'logic first begins with the conviction that a distinction holds between truth and untruth' (*die Logik beginnt erst mit der Ueberzeugung, dass ein Unterschied zwischen Wahrheit und Unwahrheit bestehe*); Sluga quotes part of Lotze's sentence (p. 54), without noticing the resemblance to Frege's. Lotze goes on to allow the possibility of a psychological investigation (*psychologische Untersuchung*) aimed at explaining the origin of this law-giving consciousness in us, but points out that the results of such an enquiry could be measured only by the standard set up by that consciousness; Frege writes (no. 17), more plainly, that 'the laws of logic cannot be justified by means of a psychological investigation (*psychologische*

---

[1] § VI.

[2] *Unterschied* (cf. Lotze's § II cited above).

[3] *ein Unterschied der Wahrheit und Unwahrheit stattfinde*.

Untersuchung)'. Lotze ends by explaining[1] that Book I of his *Logik* will be divided, in the traditional manner, into treatments of concepts, judgments and inferences, as indeed it is; Frege comments (no. 14) that 'the theories of concepts and of judgments serve only as a preparation for the theory of deduction', having said, in no. 13, that only deduction is the subject-matter of logic.

The coincidences are too many and too exact to allow any doubt that what we have here is a set of comments on the Introduction to Lotze's book, especially when we take account of the otherwise puzzling divergences from Frege's accustomed terminology and of the rather strange assortment of remarks. We may therefore conclude with certainty that Frege did read Lotze, or at least a few pages of him, since there seems no especial reason to assume that he went on to read the rest of the book. We are thus not without direct evidence concerning what Frege thought of Lotze; and it will be seen from the foregoing that, although he was in agreement with him on certain points, he does not seem to have been deeply impressed. Sluga pushes his thesis of Lotze's influence on Frege very hard indeed: a great many of Frege's leading ideas appear, in Sluga's book, as having been derived from Lotze. With respect to the notion of objectivity, this results in a far-reaching misinterpretation of Frege's thought, as well as of Lotze's. In most cases, however, it is only Lotze who suffers the misinterpretation, which has the effect of detracting from Frege's originality, but not of distorting his ideas. Thus Frege is said by Sluga to have borrowed from Lotze the idea that arithmetic can be reduced to logic, and consists of analytic truths (pp. 57–8, 104). In fact, while Lotze makes some scattered remarks suggesting that mathematics in its entirety is part of logic (which, of course, Frege did not think), the extensive discussion at the end of his *Logik* makes it plain that he thought arithmetical equations, like the laws of geometry and mechanics, to be synthetic a priori. Thus he declares himself 'in entire agreement with Kant . . . in maintaining the pure or a priori intuition of numerical quantity',[2] a thesis derided by Frege.[3] He says, of the equation '$a - a = 0$', that 'no mere logical analysis can possibly inform us' that it holds, that we learn this solely through intuition and that it is therefore 'a synthetic assertion of identity'.[4] He includes equations among 'synthetic truths . . . which . . . possess a validity guaranteed . . . by their own self-evidence . . . which, if we insist on grounding all logical truth on the

[1] In § XI.
[2] *Logik*, § 353.
[3] *Grundlagen*, §§ 5, 12, 104.
[4] *Logik*, § 361.

principle of identity, must no longer be called logical but aesthetic';[1] I suppose the alternative is to admit that logic itself consists in part of synthetic a priori truths. Again, referring to § 322 of Lotze's *Logik*, Sluga speaks of Frege as having 'revived' a thesis of Lotze's that the genesis of knowledge is irrelevant to its justification (p. 56). Frege indeed maintained that thesis, emphatically and in full generality. Lotze, on the other hand, does not reject the genetic method of enquiry, when applied to 'particular' beliefs, as a means of ascertaining their truth, saying, rather, that it has undoubted advantages in that case. He maintains its unavailability only when we raise philosophical questions about the truth of human knowledge in general; his concern is to argue for the necessity of some basic metaphysical assumptions. One of the gravest examples of Sluga's distortion of Lotze we already looked at, in Chapter 19, in connection with his articles. He claims that Frege's argument for the indefinability of truth was repeated 'almost literally' from Lotze (p. 114). Sluga's criteria for literal repetition must be exceedingly weak; as we saw, the point of Lotze's argument is in fact quite different from that of Frege's. Lotze's argument is the standard idealist one that we cannot compare our ideas with external things, since 'it is . . . this varied world of ideas within us . . . which forms the sole material directly given to us'.[2] Frege's argument, on the other hand, is expressly directed against *any* characterization of truth, and is an argument by infinite regress; there is no suggestion of any regress in Lotze's argument, and the conclusion is much weaker, namely that it is not in terms of correspondence with external reality that truth is to be explained. We have, indeed, noted above Frege's affirmation of the indefinability of truth, in the so-called '17 Kernsätze', in *opposition* to what Lotze says in his Introduction.

Sluga's methodology

The historical emphasis in Sluga's book is very heavy. Only two of the fifteen sections comprising the first two chapters are primarily devoted to Frege; some later ones contain as much about contemporaries of Frege as about Frege himself (notably, § 2 of chapter III and § 5 of chapter IV). Sluga does not explain this as simply the result of his having hit upon important clues, in the writings of his contemporaries, to Frege's true meaning; rather, it exemplifies the proper method to be adopted in interpreting any philosopher. Frege was 'the first analytic philosopher' (p. 2; cf. p. 176). But 'analytic philosophy misinterprets its own history' in general and Frege in

[1] *Logik*, 364.
[2] *Logik*, § 306.

particular (pp. 4–6, 176–81, 186). It is a familiar, and plausible, charge that philosophers of a given school misinterpret one of its founders by assimilating his ideas too closely to their own; but Sluga's principal accusation is the paradoxical one that analytic philosophers misinterpret Frege just because they are too faithful to his ideas. Analytic philosophy is fundamentally anti-historical in outlook (p. 2). But it turns out that this is an inheritance from Frege himself, and one of which Sluga profoundly disapproves. He quotes Frege as saying that 'for the logical concept there is no development, no history' and that ' "the elementary concepts are not given at the outset of the scientific enquiry", but . . . must first be discovered by the work of logical analysis . . . What comes first logically and in the nature of the case is not what is psychologically and historically first' (pp. 132 and 133 respectively, quoting from 'Über das Trägheitsgesetz', pp. 158 and 161). It is their adherence to the type of anti-historical and 'logically oriented philosophy of language that originated with Frege' (p. 186) that renders analytic philosophers incapable of understanding him aright. Frege was 'one of the origins of the [analytic] movement and Moore and Russell another'; Sluga's aim has been to display 'the peculiar combination of German and British, rationalist and empiricist, elements that characterize the whole [analytic] tradition from its beginning to the present day' (p. 176). The key to its history is that 'Frege thought he had banished radical empiricism', but in fact analytic philosophy has been 'forced to make greater concessions to the claims of empiricism as it has developed' (p. 186). It has not yet, however, come to terms with the radical empiricism implicit in the thought of Wittgenstein, but instead has tried to assimilate his thought to the 'logically oriented philosophy' which is Frege's baleful legacy. Wittgenstein's work in fact demands that 'the abstract theory of meaning must give way . . . to the examination of actual historical discourse' (ibid.). 'No meaning analysis of the kind offered by analytic philosophers from Frege through Tarski and Carnap to Dummett can recover the actual historical meaning' of a philosophical statement; 'that requires historical analysis of the kind provided in this study . . . Only then can the limits of the "objective" unhistorical kind of meaning analysis conducted by analytic philosophers be overcome' (p. 181). *FPL* can, in fact, 'serve as a paradigm for the failure of analytic philosophers to come to grips with the actual, historical Frege' (p. 3). We are thus evidently meant to see Sluga's book as the first Wittgensteinian examination of Frege's thought; Fregean approaches to it, as intrinsically unhistorical, cannot but get it wrong.

The approach Sluga adopts to the interpretation of Frege is thus presented as an example of a whole new method for arriving at an understanding of a philosopher of the past, one which ought to replace the 'objective' analysis of the meaning of his writings favoured by analytic philosophers. This is nonsense. In interpreting a philosopher, there can be no substitute for thinking through, rigorously and in detail, what his arguments are and how they are supposed to work, what hidden assumptions must hold good if they are to be cogent, what answers could be given to objections, what relation one thesis has to another, in short, for subjecting his work to logical analysis. This is not in the least to deny the importance of the historical context. We need to recognize which theses a given philosopher took to be familiar and which new, which uncontroversial and which contentious; we need to catch his allusions; we need to identify what he conceived himself as opposing. But historical comparisons do not provide an alternative, or preferable, path to the same goal as logical analysis: they are of use only as going to inform such analysis.

Sluga's methodological claims introduce the book and conclude it; if what came between formed an impressive piece of exegesis, they might have acquired some substance. Unfortunately it does not. A good, though partial, test for the perceptiveness of any exposition of the thought of a great philosopher may be had by asking how interesting the result would be, simply as a piece of philosophy, for someone who had neither read that philosopher nor felt any special curiosity about the correct way of interpreting him. Something that passes this test may nevertheless represent a thorough misunderstanding of the philosopher in question; but anything that fails it is bound to fall far short of being an adequate account of his thought. In my opinion, Sluga's book signally fails the proposed test. Frege's thought seldom comes into sharp focus in Sluga's book: Sluga appears to have little sympathy for the rigour and exactitude at which Frege aimed and for which he is celebrated, and, in consequence, his book fails even to convey the flavour of Frege's thinking, let alone to offer exact or plausible accounts of his doctrines. There is a pervasive vagueness in much of what Sluga writes. Not only does he persistently hedge, instead of making outright assertions,[1] but he is much given to merely labelling theses that he wishes to ascribe to Frege or to other philosophers instead of actually stating them, by means of adjectives like 'epistemological' or 'ontological'.[2] Sluga's adherence

---

[1] 'the implication seems to be . . .', p. 94; 'it is implausible to conclude . . .', p. 95; 'That seems to imply that . . .', p. 106; 'it seems plausible to hold . . .', p. 120; 'The point seems to be that . . .', p. 120; 'it seems to imply . . .', p. 121.

[2] We have already noted one instance of this tendency, the characterization on p. 120 of Frege's thesis that numbers are objective as 'epistemological', without further explanation. Another example occurs on p. 95, where I am accused of having rejected the 'supposed epistemic implications' of the context principle, without its being stated what these are. (I cannot account for the occurrence of the word 'supposed' in this phrase.)

to a historical mode of discussion frequently makes his writing resemble art history, with its talk of influences and tendencies, more than philosophy.

Sluga is so keen to discover sources for Frege's ideas, and so imprecise in distinguishing one idea from another, that he fails to convey what was great about Frege and what was new in his work. Sluga does not pose the question what Frege did that his predecessors had not done; and a reader previously unfamiliar with Frege would find it hard, from Sluga's book, to answer that question, save in respect of formal logic. He would, indeed, gather that Frege was one of the founders of a whole school of philosophy; but Sluga makes no attempt to explain what it is that distinguishes analytic philosophy from other schools, or what it was that Frege propounded that accords him the rank of an originator of a new philosophical movement. Even from a strictly historical standpoint, this is a grave omission; but it also points to an exegetical weakness. In expounding a philosopher, one has of course to report the theses which he held in common with his contemporaries or borrowed from his predecessors; but what makes him interesting will usually be the ideas that were original with him. Emphasis on the historical background will often be useful in making the original ideas stand out prominently from the derivative ones; but the historical method, as Sluga employs it, makes it hard to see what was original about Frege at all.

Sense and reference

The distinction between sense and reference is undoubtedly the most celebrated of Frege's ideas in philosophical logic. Whether or not it was the most profound or the most important, almost everything that he wrote on logical topics, after he had introduced the distinction, is formulated in terms of that distinction or of one of his two notions of sense and of reference. It is therefore incumbent upon anyone writing about Frege's general philosophy to give a clear account of these notions. No doubt an excellent book on Frege might be written by someone who thought the distinction incoherent; but it would have to explain just what the theory was and how it was supposed to work, and then to demonstrate in detail why it did not work. Sluga fails to provide such an explanation; he appears anxious to play down both the importance and the merit of the notion of sense, on which Frege himself laid such stress. He connects the sense/reference distinction almost exclusively with the explanation of identity-statements. The distinction indeed first appeared in Frege's published work as an answer to a natural objection to construing the equals sign as expressing strict identity.[1] Frege thus re-

[1] *Function und Begriff*, 1891, p. 14.

placed his earlier account of identity, and of how identity-statements can be informative, by the doctrine that the condition for their truth is that the references of the two sides coincide, and the condition for their informativeness is that the senses of the two sides differ. Sluga commends Frege for having borrowed his earlier account, given in *Begriffsschrift*, from Lotze (p. 151), and chides him for having abandoned it (p. 153). He admits certain difficulties in the *Begriffsschrift* account, but assures his readers that it might have been modified to meet them, without informing them what this modification would have been (p. 152). He considers, quite implausibly as it seems to me, that Frege's introduction of the notion of sense represented his adoption of a Kantian thesis (p. 154). In any case, he deplores the change: Frege's argument for it 'is peculiar because it contains nothing that [he] had not been fully aware of' when he gave his earlier account, 'and that earlier account actually appears more plausible' (p. 153). Frege's notion of sense represents a 'conflation of semantics with epistemology', Sluga says, and promises to enquire whether that was a happy move to have made (p. 154). This is true only if the word 'semantics' is used rather loosely; more strictly used, a semantic theory corresponds to Frege's theory of reference, which it was the object of his mature theory to distinguish from, and relate to, the theory of sense. It is true enough, however, that the notion of sense is a cognitive one, and therefore represents the insertion of a cognitive element into the theory of meaning, to use a non-Fregean phrase. It is at least arguably in place there if understanding is taken to be knowledge of meaning, and meaning is held to be explicable in terms of understanding.

The relation of the three notions of meaning, understanding and knowledge is, in fact, one of the most interesting unresolved problems in the philosophy of language; and the reader will therefore look forward eagerly to Sluga's promised discussion of Frege's conflation of semantics with epistemology. But, when it comes, it is exceedingly disappointing. All that the reader is told is that, in *FPL*, I pursued such a conflation further than anyone else, but that my development of Frege's idea does not 'necessarily represent Frege's own thoughts' (p. 161); the reader presumably knows that it does not *necessarily* do so, but wants to be told whether it does or does not, and what reasons there are for thinking one or the other. It is then added that, because of the alleged complexity of my account, 'one might prefer a sharp separation of epistemology and semantics', and Kripke is briefly commended for separating them. Again, it is obvious that one might prefer to separate them: what we expect from a book such as this is some discussion of whether one would be *right* to do so.

Although Sluga has little liking for the sense/reference distinction, he nevertheless assigns it a vital role as a basis 'for the proof that value-ranges are logical objects' (p. 130). His argument is extremely hard to follow. Value-ranges were indeed essential to Frege's reduction of arithmetic to logic, since it was as value-ranges that he defined numbers of all kinds; and they were introduced by a stipulation embodied, in the formal system, in the notorious Axiom V, from which sprung Russell's contradiction. It appears at first that the reason Sluga regards the sense/reference distinction as essential in this connection is that Axiom V takes the form of a (generalized) identity-statement, and the truth of an identity-statement requires the coincidence only of the references, not of the senses, of the two sides (p. 150). It then emerges, however, that Sluga believes Frege to have held the two sides of Axiom V to coincide in *sense* (p. 156). If this were so, it would be one of the identity-statements which can be explained without appeal to the distinction between sense and reference: the content of both sides would be the same, on a quite undifferentiated understanding of 'content'.

One might argue that Frege must regard the two sides of Axiom V as coinciding in sense in the following way. For Frege, an axiom must not only be true, but self-evident.[1] For a sentence to express a self-evident thought, it is necessary for anyone who grasps its sense to recognize it as true. But, if the truth of an identity-statement is evident to anyone who grasps the senses of the two sides, that can only be because they have the same sense. After all, Frege's criterion for two sentences' having the same sense is that anyone who grasps their senses immediately recognizes their equivalence;[2] the same criterion can hardly fail for expressions other than sentences. Such an argument is not employed by Sluga; but it is highly worthy of attention. As a general argument, it is unconvincing. In the particular case, it cannot withstand the intuitive objection that, in Sluga's words, 'the sentence on the left side makes a statement about functions and the sentence on the right side is about value-ranges' (p. 149). Why should it not be held that the use of the abstraction operator represents an integral feature of the sense of the right-hand side, and that a grasp of its sense involves a knowledge of the criterion for the identity of value-ranges, as expressed by the left-hand side, while it is also held that one may grasp the sense of the left-hand side although devoid of the conception of value-ranges? But, if so, Frege's criterion for coincidence of sense is amiss. One needs to demand, not merely that anyone who grasps the senses of both sentences recognizes them as equivalent, but that anyone who grasps the thought expressed by either must grasp that expressed by the other, without necessarily understanding the *sentence*

---

[1] 'Über die Grundlagen der Geometrie', 1903, I, p. 319.
[2] 'Kurze Übersicht meiner logischen Lehren', 1906, *N.S.*, p. 213, *P.W.*, p. 197.

expressing it. (The ambiguity in Frege's phrase 'grasp the sense of . . .' here becomes important.)

The matter remains puzzling, since, if it is not claimed, with Sluga, that Frege thought the two sides of Axiom V to express the same sense, it is unclear how he ever came to think it a logical axiom; and it is of immense importance, not only because of the contradiction, but because he reduced the introduction of all logical objects to the introduction of value-ranges. Sluga's case for his claim is nevertheless extremely weak. He refers to a passage in *Grundlagen* where Frege, speaking of a principle formally quite analogous to Axiom V, claims that the two sides coincide in content (p. 156, quoting *Grundlagen*, § 64, 'We carve up the content in a way different from the original one'). In *Grundlagen*, Frege was operating with a single undifferentiated notion of content, not having yet distinguished between sense and reference. Sluga says that content corresponds to what Frege later called 'reference' (pp. 151, 156). This is wrong: Frege said that the distinction between sense and reference was made *within* his earlier notion of content.[1] Where proper names are concerned, the earlier notion of content did amount to what he later called 'reference'; but what stand on the two sides of Axiom V are expressions for second-level relations. It is therefore likely that, in speaking of content in the *Grundlagen* passage, he meant what he would later have expressed by 'sense'. The passage on which Sluga principally bases his claim is one from *Function und Begriff* in which Frege does indeed assert that one side of the law 'expresses the same sense' as the other, 'but in a different way' (p. 156, quoting *Function und Begriff*, p. 11). But in the *Grundgesetze*, where much space is devoted to justifying the introduction of value-ranges, the assertion is not repeated. It is well known that Frege admitted, in his Introduction, that Axiom V could be disputed;[2] if both sides had had the same sense, no dispute would have been possible. The remark in *Function und Begriff* is surely a residue from his earlier style of thought, before sense and reference had been distinguished; when he had reflected further on the new distinction, he realized that he could not sustain the claim. If the claim is, as Sluga thinks, to be taken seriously, we are owed some account of the notion of sense that would make it at least plausible and reconcile it with the other things Frege says regarding that notion; Sluga makes no attempt to provide us with any such account.

If we want a motivation from the philosophy of mathematics for Frege's distinction between sense and reference, it is sufficiently provided by its use to defend his insistence that mathematical equations are identity-state-

[1] *Grundgesetze*, vol. I, p. x.
[2] *Grundgesetze*, vol. I, p. vii.

ments. But it is a mistake to link the notion of sense as tightly as Sluga does with that of identity. Frege indeed introduced the notion in this connection; and it is easy to see why this was a good heuristic strategy. His puzzle about how an identity-statement can be informative can in fact be reproduced for any atomic statement. In this general form, however, it would not have had the same impact, since, when we have only an undifferentiated notion of content, we more naturally take the content of a predicate to be, not what Frege understood to be its reference, but, rather, its sense. A generalized form of the argument would therefore require a prior demonstration that the sense of a predicate is not the true analogue of the bearer of a name. Frege therefore started with identity-statements, for which the point is intuitively obvious; but, once introduced, the notion of sense played a much more general role, as can be seen from its extensive use in his 'Logical Investigations'.[1]

One might try to justify Frege's extension of the sense/reference distinction from complete to incomplete expressions as needed to explain *generalized* identity-statements, and this would be a natural strategy for Sluga to adopt; but in fact he does not so much as discuss this extension. The relation between the sense of a 'proper name' in Frege's use of that term and that of a sentence is somewhat obscure on Sluga's account. We are told that, although in his exposition Frege dealt first with proper names and then with sentences, the interpretation according to which he began by distinguishing sense and reference for proper names, and then moved on to do the same for sentences, assimilating them to proper names, is unsatisfactory (p. 159). The ground Sluga gives for deeming it so is that Frege defined 'proper name' at the outset in such a way as to include sentences (p. 160). This makes it appear that Sluga is claiming that Frege's initial explanation of the notion of sense already clearly applied to sentences as well as to singular terms. Now Frege's initial explanation was that the sense is the mode of presentation of the referent; such a claim would therefore require that the notion of reference applies unequivocally to sentences. It turns out, however, that Sluga cannot be making so strong a claim; for he says that, when Frege moved from discussing the sense and reference of referring expressions (singular terms) to the sense and reference of sentences, he did 'not give a

[1] In his 'Einleitung in die Logik' of 1906, Frege gives two distinct arguments for differentiating between the sense and the reference of a proper name *before* citing the argument from identity-statements: that an object such as Mont Blanc cannot be part of a thought (*N.S.*, pp. 203-4, *P.W.*, p. 187); and that our belief that 'Odysseus' has no reference does not make us deny that sentences of the *Odyssey* containing it express thoughts, while our abandonment of that belief would not change those thoughts (*N.S.*, p. 208, *P.W.*, p. 191).

compelling reason for saying that thoughts are the senses of sentences and truth-values are their references' (p. 160). It thus appears that all that Sluga can be claiming is that Frege had from the start an intention of applying the sense/reference distinction to sentences; this, I think, no one has ever denied. Sluga here fails to observe that the question what, specifically, the sense and the reference of a sentence are has no clear content unless we have some general characterization of the notions of sense and of reference, a characterization which Sluga does not attempt to provide. Here, as elsewhere in the book, some rival interpretation is, with some bravura, pronounced to be mistaken; but the promised alternative fails to materialize, or, at best, reduces to a banality.

Nevertheless, Sluga appears to be under the impression that he has scotched a false interpretation and replaced it by a true one; for, in the immediately preceding passage, he has spoken of the assumption 'that Frege's doctrine is meant primarily as a theory about referring expressions' as an 'erroneous interpretation', and has gone on to commend Tugendhat for setting us on the right track (p. 158). This is the only passage in the book in which Tugendhat's name occurs, and Sluga says, of him, that he is right to hold 'that the semantics of sense and reference is primarily a semantics of whole sentences and not of sentence parts' (pp. 158–9). He cites in support a passage in which Frege says that 'the fact that we concern ourselves at all with the *Bedeutung* of a part of the sentence is a sign that, in general, we recognize and demand a *Bedeutung* for the sentence itself, too'. 'Why do we want every proper name to have, not only a sense, but a *Bedeutung*?,' Frege goes on to ask, and answers, 'Because, and in so far as, we are concerned with the truth-value' of the sentence.[1]

Frege's thought in the quoted passage is perfectly clear. He is leading up to identifying the *Bedeutung* of a sentence as its truth-value. As part of an argument to that conclusion, he is observing that it is indifferent, for whether a sentence expresses a thought, whether any part of that sentence has a *Bedeutung*; but the latter question becomes crucial as soon as we enquire whether the sentence is true, or whether it has a truth-value at all. But the thought Sluga means to express by saying that 'the semantics of sense and reference is primarily a semantics of whole sentences and not of sentence parts' is far from clear. If we try to construe the sentence as meaning 'The semantics of sense and reference is primarily: a semantics of whole sentences and not of sentence parts', we obtain nonsense. A semantic theory can only be a theory that relates both to whole sentences and to their parts: it explains the contribution of the parts to the determination of the truth of

[1] 'Über Sinn und Bedeutung', p. 33.

the whole. If we suppress the part of the theory that deals with the parts, we have no theory left, save, possibly, one that operates at the level of sentential logic and explains the way subsentences contribute to the determination of the truth or otherwise of a complex sentence; and subsentences are hardly to be called 'whole sentences', since they are sentences functioning as sentence-parts. The same goes for a theory of sense: if we set aside that part of it which explains how the sense of a sentence is determined in accordance with its composition, we have no theory. We have, therefore, to construe Sluga's sentence as meaning, 'The semantics of sense and reference is a semantics that is primarily of whole sentences, and not primarily of sentence parts.' Even this would leave a very vague impression on anyone not familiar with the thesis of the primacy of sentences. In the light of that thesis, we may interpret it as probably meaning that, while the theory of sense and the theory of reference will treat of sentence-parts, sentences will play a distinguished role. This is, of course, quite correct, both in itself and as an interpretation of Frege. The general notion of semantic value can be explained only by mentioning sentences: the semantic value of an expression is that feature of it which goes to determine any sentence in which it occurs as true or otherwise; and I argued in *FPL* that we could understand Frege's general notion of *Bedeutung* only as that of semantic value, as it is construed in a particular semantic theory. It does not, of course, follow that one cannot state what one takes the *Bedeutung* of a particular expression, or of a whole category of expressions, to be without mentioning sentences; in 'Über Sinn und Bedeutung', Frege had already done precisely that, for proper names, before, on p. 32, he raised the question of the *Bedeutungen* of sentences. What we cannot do is to ask whether we have characterized the *Bedeutung* of any expression *correctly*, without adverting to the general notion of semantic value, and so to the distinguished role of sentences; without doing so, any such characterization is a mere stipulation. The same goes for the general notion of sense, which is distinguished from tone by being that ingredient in a speaker's mastery of an expression which is relevant to the determination of the truth-value of a sentence in which it occurs. Interpreted in this manner, therefore, Sluga's observation is perfectly correct; but it is stated in a fashion that leaves its intended interpretation somewhat in doubt.

Sluga does not develop his observation in this way. Instead, he proceeds immediately to remark that 'the claim that after 1891 the name/bearer relationship is the paradigm of Frege's semantics and that his theory of sense and reference is primarily meant as a theory of referring expressions has the effect of assigning a basic role to empirical objects'. I am uncertain at whom this remark is directed. If at me, I remain unrepentant about considering the name/bearer relation to be a basic ingredient in Frege's notion of *Bedeutung*, though I am not happy with the phrase 'the paradigm of Frege's semantics'. The second part of the claim, that the 'theory of sense and reference is primarily meant as a theory of referring expressions', looks tautological at first sight, at least in regard to the theory of reference; but the explanation is that Sluga unhappily uses 'referring expression' in a Strawsonian sense, to mean essentially 'singular term'. So understood, I cannot recognize the claim as anything I have propounded. Since the mention of this claim comes upon the heels of the observation that 'the semantics of sense and reference is primarily a semantics of whole sentences and not of sentence parts', the claim must surely be understood as contradicting that observation. If the observation is to be interpreted as I suggested above, I certainly should not want to contradict it, and have not ever done so; if the observation is to be interpreted in some other way, I cannot think what that should be.

Having stated that to claim Frege's theory of sense and reference to be meant primarily as a theory of referring expressions means assigning a basic role to empirical objects, Sluga proceeds to argue that 'it seems doubtful that such objects could ever have played an important role in Frege's thought'. It is difficult to know how to respond to so vague a remark. Frege admittedly did not have much to say about empirical objects in his philosophical writings; but the topic in hand is his notion of *Bedeutung*, which he certainly often introduced by citing proper names of such objects. Sluga now goes on to insist that Frege did 'not regard empirical objects as items of acquaintance that can be simply named or described'. The reader unfamiliar with Sluga's articles may be perplexed by this remark; he may be helped by the reference Sluga goes on to make to Frege's statement, in 'Der Gedanke', that sensory impressions are insufficient for perception, but this surely will not dispel his bewilderment altogether. Frege did not deny that we can be acquainted with empirical objects, nor that we can use simple proper names to refer to them, still less that we can describe them. Those who have read Sluga's articles will, however, recognize in this sentence a hazy formulation of the denial that Frege was an epistemological atomist. The thesis that epistemological atomism follows from taking the *Bedeutung* of a proper name to be its bearer was discussed in Chapter 18; from exactly what doctrine Sluga is claiming, in the present passage, that epistemological atomism follows, his text is too imprecise to allow us to judge. The passage is, however, the only one in the book in which epistemological atomism makes any overt appearance, and the only one in which doubt is cast upon the identification of the referent of a name with its bearer; this is remarkable, in view of the stress Sluga laid upon these points in his articles.

Sluga's discussion of Frege's salient ideas of sense and reference thus leaves the reader with a very confused impression. Frege invoked the distinction principally in explanation of identity-statements; but he did not need it for this purpose, having an adequate explanation of them already to hand. His main motive for introducing it, very well concealed, was to give a justification of Axiom V of the *Grundgesetze*. Sluga does not explain how this justification is supposed to work, that is, on what account of sense it could be claimed that the two sides of the axiom have the same sense; presumably he holds Frege's justification to be wholly spurious, since there would plainly be no chance of offering a parallel justification in terms of the *Begriffsschrift* account of identity, which Sluga prefers. Although Frege first introduced the distinction in connection with singular terms, he intended it primarily as a theory about sentences; but he did not succeed in making out that it should be extended to sentences in the way that he claimed. The most surprising omission is Sluga's failure to discuss the application of these notions to incomplete expressions. One of the first questions that comes to the mind of anyone reading Frege's mature works for the first time is what right he has to apply the notion of reference to predicates and functional expressions; but Sluga, by placing his discussion of concepts and functions (ch. v, §§ 4 and 5) *before* his account of sense and reference (ch. v, §§ 7 and 8), is able to skate round the question entirely. This accords badly with the attention he pays, in this connection, to Frege's Axiom V, since what, in that axiom, are connected by the identity-sign are expressions for second-level relations.[1] There is lacking any discussion of what, in general, the sense of an expression is supposed to be, or of what, in general, its reference is supposed to be, or of what role these notions play in Frege's theory of meaning otherwise than in the explanation of identity-statements. No one, reading Sluga, could suppose that the reason why, as he says, 'the Fregean doctrine of sense and reference has been the predominant focus of attention in the philosophical study of his work' (p. 159) is that it is a powerful theory which has been found extremely compelling; he would think, rather, that it was just the kind of ill-developed and confused idea one might expect to find in the writings of a disciple of Lotze.

The context principle and the priority thesis

Rightly or wrongly, Sluga does not think highly of the sense/reference distinction; it may therefore be objected that his discussion of it does not

---

[1] Sluga says, incorrectly, that they are sentences (p. 149); this is to overlook the fact that the italic function-letters are really variables bound by an initial universal quantifier.

provide the best test of his new, historical method of philosophical exegesis. It is his treatment of Frege's context principle, that a word has meaning only in the context of a sentence, and of his priority thesis, that judgments are prior to concepts, that he expressly challenges his readers to compare with 'the "objective" unhistorical kind of meaning analysis conducted by analytic philosophers', to the disadvantage of the latter.[1] His account of these doctrines should therefore provide the crucial test for the superiority of his own approach.

Sluga certainly establishes that the opinion was widespread in nineteenth-century Germany that judgments are prior to concepts (pp. 23, 30, 55). He is, however, wrong to ascribe that view to Lotze and to suggest that it was through his influence that 'the doctrine also reached Frege' (pp. 55, 119). On the contrary, Lotze took the other side in this dispute, stigmatizing 'the assertion that in logic the theory of judgment . . . must precede the treatment of concepts' as 'overhasty', and arguing that every judgment must be compounded out of ideas which were formed in advance of the judgment arrived at by combining them.[2]

There is no doubt that Frege subscribed to the doctrine; especially in his early writing, he frequently made statements like the following from 1919: 'I do not start from concepts and compound the thought or the judgment out of them, but I arrive at the parts of the thought by decomposing it.'[3] It indeed seems quite likely that Frege adopted this way of expressing himself just because the question whether concepts or judgments have the priority was actively canvassed, judgments and terms or concepts being the two topics with which logic traditionally had to deal before reaching inference or the syllogism. More important than whether other people said that judgments are prior to concepts before Frege did is, however, the question what the statement means, and whether Frege meant the same by it as others did; for, after all, the sense of the statement is by no means immediately apparent. The fact is that, as Frege understood the doctrine, it is a prime example of what he meant when, in 1906, surveying what remained of his work after Russell's contradiction had defeated the attempt to reduce arithmetic to logic, he wrote, 'Almost everything is connected with the

---

[1] P. 181; 'the history of Frege's dictum', i.e. the context principle, 'is instructive as showing how a doctrine that is at one moment of great significance in a philosophical tradition can be lost or change its meaning. When that has happened, no meaning analysis of the kind offered by analytic philosophers . . . can recover the actual historical meaning of the statement. That requires historical analysis of the kind provided in this study'.

[2] H. Lotze, *Logik*, § 8.

[3] 'Aufzeichnungen für Ludwig Darmstaedter', 1919, *N.S.*, p. 273, *P.W.*, p. 253.

Begriffsschrift',[1] that is, with his logical notation and the analysis of logical form embodied in it. No one has attempted to deny, of Frege's formal logic, that it was utterly original and owed nothing to his predecessors. But, whatever others may have meant by speaking of the priority of judgments over concepts, what Frege meant by it was intimately connected with his analysis of logical form; no one who did not subscribe to that analysis could have subscribed to the thesis that judgments or thoughts are prior to concepts in the sense in which Frege understood it, because his idea can be explained only in terms of that analysis.

Frege's reiteration of the priority thesis in his brief summary of his doctrines made for Darmstaedter in 1919 is important, because he there also reiterates another leading idea, namely that a thought is built up out of constituents which are the senses of the words making up the sentence expressing it.[2] As we saw in Chapter 15, the two doctrines thus stated within a page or two of one another appear, on the face of it, to be in conflict; to state their content is therefore evidently a delicate matter. Sluga displays no delicacy in his approach to the matter. He briefly mentions the doctrine of the senses of words as thought-constituents (p. 161), but makes no attempt to explain it, let alone to reconcile it with the priority thesis, on which he lays such emphasis; he does not even note the apparent conflict between them. This may be seen as a symptom of his general failure to come to grips with the notion of sense.

His treatment of the priority thesis is badly at fault in a second respect: he assimilates it to the context principle, which is in fact a quite different doctrine. The priority thesis concerns only concepts and functions, or, more exactly, their linguistic expression; the context principle applies to words of all kinds, and is expressly invoked by Frege as applying to abstract singular terms. The priority thesis enjoins us to regard a predicate or functional expression as, in general, extracted from a sentence or complex singular term by the omission of one or more occurrences of some constituent expression, rather than as directly built up out of its component words. Such a thesis properly applies to *complex* predicates and functional expressions; it is what makes it possible for Frege to explain the sentential operators only for the case when they are applied to complete sentences, even though they do not occur only as so applied, and analogously for the quantifiers. Frege invited misunderstanding by failing to make clear—possibly by not himself being wholly clear—that the thesis could not in the same way be applied

---

[1] 'Was kann ich als Ergebnis meiner Arbeit ansehen?', August 1906, *N.S.*, p. 200, *P.W.*, p. 184.

[2] *N.S.*, p. 275, *P.W.*, p. 255.

to *simple* predicates; but he never made the least suggestion that it applied to complete expressions such as proper names.

The context principle, on the other hand, is not concerned with how an expression is formed, but with what it is for it to have a sense and a reference, even though, when Frege stated it in the *Grundlagen*, he had not yet distinguished sense from reference. If we interpret it as a principle concerning sense, it embodies the doctrine of the primacy of sentences, to which Frege certainly adhered in his early period, though he did not then express it in this way. The doctrine lays down that the sense of a subsentential expression consists in its contribution to the senses of sentences in which it may occur: we cannot grasp the sense of such an expression save as that of something capable of forming part of a sentence. We could not in the same way say that the sense of a sentence consists in its contribution to the sense of an entire speech or paragraph in which it might occur: the sentence expresses a thought, which can be grasped on its own; even if, in order to express that thought, the particular sentence depends on external features of the context, including what was said previously, the same thought could always be expressed by means of a complete sentence which would convey that thought independently of the context; or so, at least, Frege believed.

In the *Grundlagen*, however, the only one of Frege's works in which the context principle is expressly stated, it is, in effect, employed as a principle concerning reference. So used, it lays down that, if an expression behaves logically as a proper name or singular term, and if a sense has been provided for every sentence in which it might occur, then it has a reference, and we may legitimately speak of that to which it refers. Suppose that these conditions have been fulfilled for an abstract singular term such as 'the number 2'. Then any legitimate question as to what, in particular, the term refers to, for instance whether it refers to the class of all two-membered classes, or to Julius Caesar, can be expressed by asking after the truth-value of an identity-statement, such as 'The number 2 is the class of all two-membered classes' or 'The number 2 is Julius Caesar'. By hypothesis, a sense must have been given to such sentences, because, according to Frege, we cannot prohibit the formation of an identity-statement connecting any two singular terms. In conferring a sense upon those statements, we have determined the conditions under which they are true or false; we have thereby determined the answers to all legitimate questions concerning the reference of the given term. If any questions be asked concerning its reference which cannot be expressed in this way, they are illegitimate, and may be ignored. Such a principle is intended as a defence against objections to the ascription of reference to abstract terms, and so to the recognition of abstract objects, and is expressly used by Frege for that purpose. When, in the *Grundgesetze*, Frege defends his introduction of abstract objects in the form of value-ranges, there is an echo of this context principle. He does not there explicitly formulate it as a general principle, however, and it is not apparent how he could coherently have done so in that setting, since by that time he had come to classify sentences as just a special case of complex singular terms, namely as those standing for truth-values; this impeded him from giving due recognition to his earlier insight into the quite special, and fundamental, semantic role to be assigned to sentences.

Sluga repeatedly refers to the context principle, and is right to lay great stress on it, since, under both its aspects, it is crucial to a consideration of Frege's philosophy. He nevertheless leaves his readers with only a very hazy impression of the content of the principle. In his first reference to it, he expressly characterizes it as a form of the priority thesis, as supposedly derived by Frege from Lotze (p. 55). He next gives a slightly woolly explanation of the priority thesis, as presented in *Begriffsschrift* (pp. 85–7); it is doubtful whether a reader who did not already grasp its importance would do so from this account.[1] In a subsequent section headed 'The priority of judgments over concepts' (pp. 90–5), Sluga explains that the priority thesis, as he understands it, 'implies at least four different things' (p. 92). These are: (1) that the contents of judgments are epistemically primary; (2) that concepts are always reached through the analysis of judgments, which are not composed of previously given constituents; (3) that concepts are incomplete or unsaturated; and (4) that the parts of a sentence of natural language may have a meaning only in context, but signify nothing on their own. Of these four theses, stated by Sluga himself to be distinct, only (2), which he explains very vaguely, is clearly to be identified with the priority thesis. Thesis (3) is the predicative nature of concepts, of which Sluga says that Frege derived it from Kant (pp. 55, 93). It was emphatically held by Frege, and can indeed be ascribed to Kant; but, though it is connected with the priority thesis, it is by no means to be *identified* with that thesis. The reason is that one could obviously maintain the predicative nature of concepts while denying the priority thesis. The priority thesis is connected with thesis (3) in that it serves as an *explanation* for the incompleteness of predicates that have been arrived at be extraction from sentences. Simple predicates cannot be

---

[1] Sluga pauses, on p. 86, to call in question my statement that only from 1891 did Frege identify concepts and relations as special kinds of functions, on the irrelevant ground that in 1879 he used the word 'function' to mean an incomplete *expression*; when 'function' is taken to mean what Frege later meant by it, the remark is quite correct, as is evident from the distinction between judgeable and unjudgeable contents.

regarded as having been arrived at in this way; and so, although they must still be regarded as unsaturated, the priority thesis does not provide an explanation of their having such a character. As we saw in Chapter 16, Frege paid inadequate attention to this point; but, in stating thesis (2), which is simply the priority thesis itself, Sluga contrives to quote one of the few passages where Frege does show such awareness, namely one in which he says that *simple* concepts and relations originate *at the same time as* the first judgments involving them.[1] Without noticing the difference, Sluga immediately goes on to say that 'concepts are always reached through the splitting up of judgments'; if this were true, their attainment would always be *subsequent* to the judgment. This would make it impossible for Sluga to account for Frege's later insistence that the sense of a sentence is compounded from the senses of its constituents, and that we understand a sentence because we grasp the senses of its component words, save as a radical change of view; but he deals with the difficulty by ignoring this feature of Frege's thought. That will not suffice to solve the reader's problems. Whether or not he knows that Frege himself emphasized the fact, the reader is likely to think that it is by knowing the senses of the words that we are able to understand sentences we hear, including new ones. He will therefore want to know how, in the face of this apparently indisputable fact, the thesis that concepts are always arrived at by the analysis of a judgment is to be understood. He will not receive any help from Sluga, to whom the need for an explanation does not seem to occur.

Sluga's citation of thesis (4) as a component of the priority thesis embodies the most serious confusion. The thesis has to do exclusively with natural language, and is based by Sluga on two passages, from 1879 and 1896 respectively, which in fact themselves make distinct points. He associates these passages with the priority thesis, which he equates with the context principle, because of a verbal resemblance with the latter, having previously claimed it as having demonstrably been held by Frege throughout his career (p. 55). In point of fact, the contents of the two passages he cites are quite different from the context principle; they are therefore good evidence that, at those two dates, Frege either did not hold that principle or at least would not have expressed it in the same way.

The 1896 passage comes from Frege's published letter to Peano.[2] In it, Frege lays it down that every word ought to have both a sense and a reference that is independent of the context of its occurrence. This might look like a flat repudiation of the context principle, but that is not in fact so. Frege is

---

[1] Sluga, p. 92, quoting 'Booles rechnende Logik', 1880–1, *N.S.*, p. 19, *P.W.*, p. 17.

[2] 'Lettera del sig. G. Frege all'editore', pp. 55–6.

here demanding that each word should have the *same* sense and the *same* reference in every context. The context principle, on the other hand, is not concerned to vindicate the possibility of (systematic or unsystematic) variations of meaning, but with what is required for us to be entitled to ascribe a meaning to an expression at all. In this passage, Frege goes on to complain that, in natural language, his demand is frequently violated. This is obviously so; and it can readily be admitted that variation of sense is a defect of natural language, tempting us to make fallacious inferences, though this is not nearly so clear with systematic variations of reference. When Frege says, however, that the individual words of natural language do not merely vary in sense and reference, but lack a sense or a reference of their own altogether, the sentences in which they occur having a sense only as a whole, he appears to be scolding too severely. We should, indeed, be puzzled to say what the word 'upside' meant by itself, though we know perfectly well what 'upside down' means; but, if natural language were like this through and through, how should we know what sense to attach to any given sentence?

It is easy to understand how, given his view that a concept not sharply defined is no concept at all, Frege came to be guilty of this exaggeration; but the present point is that what he is saying in this passage has no resemblance to the context principle, let alone to the priority thesis. The context principle is concerned to state a sufficient condition for a word to have a meaning; here he is talking about the quite different requirement of constancy of sense and of reference, and denying that we can properly ascribe a sense or a reference to a word that does not satisfy that requirement. The other passage cited by Sluga in support of his thesis (4) comes from the *Begriffsschrift*[1] and is also directed against natural language. Contrasting '20 is the sum of four squares' with 'Every positive integer is the sum of four squares', Frege says that it is an illusion generated by language to regard 'is the sum of four squares' as a function which now takes the argument '20' and now the argument 'every positive integer'; the latter, unlike the former, yields no independent idea, but acquires a meaning only from the context of the sentence. When these are expressed in the logical symbolism, the illusion vanishes. Frege is here warning his readers against considering 'every positive integer' as standing for some composite entity of which being the sum of four squares is predicated. Saying that 'every positive integer' has a meaning only in the context of a sentence here conveys that it should not be taken as standing for any kind of object, or as functioning like a name. In the *Grundlagen*, on the other hand, the observation that a word is required to

[1] § 9.

have a meaning only in the context of a sentence is used as a justification for regarding a term like 'the number 2', which does function like a name, as standing for an object; the point being made, in similar language, is wholly disparate. The observation in *Begriffsschrift* differs equally from that made in the 1896 passage. Frege is not saying, in *Begriffsschrift*, that 'every positive integer' lacks a meaning, but only that it is an expression of a different level from 'the number 2'. Sluga, however, is oblivious to these distinctions. He even states Frege's point in *Begriffsschrift* misleadingly by saying that 'Frege argues that it is a mistake to consider the expressions "the number 20" and "every positive integer" as the subjects of their respective sentences' (p. 94): there is in fact nothing wrong with so considering 'the number 20'.

Having thus expounded the priority thesis as an amalgam of these four distinct components, Sluga immediately goes on to refer to the context principle, as stated in *Grundlagen*, as a form of the same thesis, a form 'meant . . . primarily as a methodological principle for the analysis of sentences of ordinary language'. This is presumably to be explained by Sluga's reading it in the light of the passages he has quoted in support of thesis (4); but it is quite mistaken. The passage in the letter to Peano does not propose a means of analysing sentences of natural language, but roundly condemns it as too unsystematic to allow of analysis, and as therefore 'not designed for the carrying out of proofs'. If this had been the content of the context principle, it could not have served as a justification of anything, nor as supplying a method of analysis, but only as a warning to avoid the forms of natural language. Aware that this is not the role it plays in Frege's argument, Sluga feels constrained to add that 'the implication seems to be that there is a priority of sentence meaning over word meaning for every language, including a logically perfect one'. The only explanation he offers for this is that 'in this stronger sense the principle would amount to the reaffirmation of the Kantian doctrine of the priority of judgments over concepts' (pp. 94–5). As we have already noted, this is quite wrong: the *Grundlagen* principle is not confined to concepts or predicates, but is applied particularly to abstract terms as standing for abstract objects.

In much of Frege's writing there is a sharp contrast drawn between natural language, with its manifold defects, and the type of perfected instrument for the expression of thought to which Frege's logical symbolism was meant as an approximation. But in *Grundlagen* this opposition is in no way stressed, at least in part because it was designedly written without symbolic notation. In the constructive sections of the book, we should certainly take what Frege says as applying to a logically correct language as well as to natural language in so far as the latter is not logically defective. We therefore do not need to ask what 'the implication seems to be'; Frege says just what he means. The context principle indeed involves a 'priority of sentence meaning over word meaning', but in a specific respect, which Sluga fails to state. One cannot ask, 'Is sentence meaning prior to word meaning, or the other way about?', and expect an unequivocal answer; the question has no unique sense, and one could only reply, 'Prior in what order?'

Sluga thus not merely conflates the priority thesis and the context principle, but fails to give a clear account of either; and his treatment of these doctrines, which he himself has claimed as a triumph of the historical method, serves to display its inadequacy, at least as employed by him. Instead of a precise exposition, we are presented with a melange of disparate doctrines, none of which is clearly explained. The historical method, as Sluga conceives it, is in part directly responsible for this. Frege's thought probably shows greater continuity than that of any other philosopher; even so, Sluga is anxious to exaggerate it, and so interprets passages which say quite different things as saying the same. He is also, of course, eager to identify Frege's ideas with those of his predecessors; and this, too, leads to imprecision and misinterpretation. Sluga's poor opinion of the notions of sense and reference does particular damage. One is not always bound to prefer a philosopher's later thoughts to his earlier ones; but when he has struggled to win through to a clarification of what he saw as imperfections in his earlier work, we must pay serious attention to his claim to have succeeded. Both the priority thesis and the context principle were formulated before Frege had arrived at the sense/reference distinction. But Frege believed that, by means of that distinction, he had improved substantially on his earlier work; hence, in considering the earlier doctrines, we must at least envisage the possibility that they cannot be satisfactorily explained without invoking that later distinction. This is particularly true of the context principle, which one can hardly discuss profitably without distinguishing its use as a principle concerning sense and as one concerning reference. A clear example of two of these defects is given by Sluga's characterization of the context principle as applied to a logically perfect language as a 'reaffirmation of the Kantian doctrine'. All that can be attributed to Kant is a recognition of the predicative nature of concepts. This may be regarded as a *part* of the context principle, that is, an application of it to predicates, when that principle is taken as relating to *sense*. It is only part of the principle, even then; and it has nothing to do with the principle, conceived as one governing *reference*. But the historical method, as used by Sluga, leaves nothing clear; the despised procedures of logical analysis are set aside, and all that emerges is a hazy blur.

The epistemic content of the context principle and modern semantics

The priority thesis, as stated by Frege in 'Booles rechnende Logik' of 1880–1, was said by Sluga to imply 'at least four different things'. Of these, thesis (2) is the priority thesis itself, as actually stated in the passage Sluga quotes, while theses (3) and (4) are those we have just examined. Thesis (1), on the other hand, was the thesis that 'the contents of judgments are epistemically primary'. Sluga leaves the purport of this thesis highly mysterious. Since it is supposed to be something *different* from thesis (2), which is concerned with the formation of concepts, or, as he would later have preferred to say, how we come to grasp them (more exactly, to grasp the senses of predicates), we gain no help from the two quotations from Frege Sluga gives in connection with thesis (1). One is the passage from the notes for Ludwig Darmstaedter of 1919 which I quoted above; another is a passage from a letter of Anton Marty of 1882, in which Frege speaks explicitly of 'the formation of concepts'.[1] These two quotations ought, therefore, to have been cited in connection with thesis (2); and, since Sluga gives no further explanation of thesis (1) in that section of his book (p. 92), we are left uncertain what he takes this first component of the priority thesis to amount to.

The idea that the priority thesis has an epistemic component nevertheless appears to play a leading role in his thought. As we have seen, having identified the context principle as a form of the priority thesis, Sluga distinguishes between what is primarily meant by it, namely a doctrine about natural language, and a 'stronger sense' that only seems to be implied, namely one applying to all languages. He immediately goes on to criticize me for holding that 'the principle must be interpreted weakly' (p. 95). In view of the distinction just drawn, one might take this as suggesting that I thought that the context principle applied only to natural language, not to a logically perfect one. But this proves not to be Sluga's meaning. The limitation I am accused of putting on the principle is that of 'rejecting its supposed epistemic implications'. 'In the context of [Frege's] philosophical outlook', Sluga tells us, the meaning of the context principle 'is not exhausted by the weak interpretation which Dummett has given of it.'

The epistemic implications which Sluga takes me to have rejected are presumably the doctrine embodied in component (1) of the priority thesis; the difficulty is to know what this doctrine is. The only other passage of Sluga's book which promises to throw light on this riddle is the section devoted to Carnap in the last chapter. Here Carnap's *Meaning and Necessity*

---

[1] *Das Bilden der Begriffe*; *BW*, p. 164, *P.M.C.*, p. 101.

is described as giving 'the first detailed account of Frege's semantic doctrines, treating them as a special version of the compositional theory of meaning that he was developing in accordance with Tarski's semantic methodology' (p. 181). Sluga comments that Carnap makes no reference to the context principle, and holds it to be unclear 'how a semantic theory of the Tarski type could be developed with that doctrine in mind'. He then turns to me. Having remarked that my 'interpretation of Frege as a precursor of modern semantics may be due in part' to Carnap's book,[1] he observes that 'unlike Carnap, Dummett is aware of the significance of Frege's maxim'. However, he continues, 'since, like Carnap, his purpose is to present Frege's views in the context of the developments initiated by Tarski, he reduces the significance of that principle to merely expository importance'. I should not know to what Sluga was here referring did he not go on to quote from me the remark that 'in the order of explanation the sense of the sentence is primary, but in the order of recognition the sense of a word is primary'.[2] This slogan was not, of course, intended to convey that the context principle was a mere expository device, not a genuine premiss in Frege's argument. It was meant to epitomize the way I hoped to reconcile that principle, taken as one relating to sense, with the thesis that the sense of a sentence is built up out of the senses of the words. This is a difficulty which faces most readers of Frege. In speaking of 'the order of explanation', I did not mean that the context principle was only a means of explanation rather than a substantial doctrine, but that it was a doctrine *about* how something is to be explained, namely, what, in general, it is for a word to have a sense. The thesis that a thought is compounded out of parts comes into apparent conflict, not only with the context principle, but also with the priority thesis; but Sluga takes no notice of either conflict. As we have seen, the resolution of the second conflict is already indicated in *Begriffsschrift*, where Frege distinguishes between an analysis that corresponds to the actual composition of the judgeable content and one that merely reflects the way we choose to look at it. Sluga quotes this passage (pp. 86–7); but he fails to see its significance, because he has not recognized the difficulty which it points the way to removing.

Sluga's misunderstanding of my slogan about the order of explanation is

---

[1] This is a bad guess. Misled by Ryle's hostility to Carnap, I did not study him until quite late, and, when I did, it was the earlier works that I read; I had not read *Meaning and Necessity* when I wrote *FPL*. I mention this only because it impairs my confidence in Sluga's numerous pronouncements concerning what Frege must have read and have been influenced by.

[2] *FPL*, p. 4.

not, however, the principal clue to his thought, which is given, rather, by his allusions to Tarski and modern semantics. These echo Sluga's earlier diagnosis of my alleged weak interpretation of the context principle, 'rejecting its supposed epistemic implications'. 'The evidence seems to contradict . . . Dummett's claims,' he had written; 'his attempt to associate Frege with contemporary (recursive) model-theoretic semantics appears to be his only reason for' adopting this weak, non-epistemic interpretation (p. 95). We may therefore seek in Sluga's aspersions on interpretations of Frege in the light of modern semantics for a clue to what he takes the epistemic implications of the context principle to be, and hence to the content of the first of his four components of the priority thesis. We ought also to find the clue to his contention that analytic philosophers in general have lost the meaning of the context principle, which can be recovered only by historical analysis of the kind Sluga provides, a contention that immediately follows his critical remarks concerning Carnap and myself (p. 181).

It is presumably his adoption of the historical method which accounts for the prevalence, already noted, of phrases like 'the evidence seems to contradict . . .'. For Sluga, the interpretation of a philosopher does not depend upon discovering which propositions are entailed by or depend on a given proposition, enquiries characteristic of the unhistorical method of logical analysis deriving from Frege; rather, it depends on amassing pointers from the work of that philosopher and others he may be supposed to have read or heard, and getting from them a feel for the general direction they indicate. Exegesis is a historical enquiry, and so demands, not logical reasoning, but *evidence* on which is based an estimate of what seems plausible. Sluga's remarks about modern semantics show this historical method at its worst. 'Semantics as it has developed from Tarski's work,' he says, 'is strongly committed to philosophical assumptions that are antithetical to Frege's . . . Tarski's philosophical views are indebted to the reism of Kotarbinski, which sees the world merely as an arrangement of objects. This philosophical viewpoint is, however, completely alien to Frege' (pp. 180–1). Tarski of course played an important part in the development of contemporary semantic treatments of formal systems. However strong the connection may have been in Tarski's mind between his work in this field and Kotarbinski's reism, it does not follow that there is any genuine logical connection between them; still less does it follow that the use of semantic theories by others depends upon reism of any kind. Only if it does is there any objection to appealing to such theories to throw light on Frege; but whether it does or not can be established only by logical analysis.

In *FPL* I indeed suggested that Frege's theory of reference becomes clearer if we compare it with classical two-valued semantics for logical formulas. Without this, it is perplexing why Frege ascribes reference to sentences and to incomplete expressions; almost everyone, on first reading Frege's mature writings, is puzzled why he discusses what we should take the reference of such expressions to be, without, usually, even raising the question whether they can be said to have a reference at all. Sluga does not raise this question; he does not even ask why the apparent implausibility of ascribing a reference to sentences did not prevent him from classifying them as proper names. If we regard the notion of reference as playing the role of that of semantic value under the intended interpretation, the difficulty is resolved. The reference of an expression then becomes that feature of it which goes to determine each sentence in which it occurs as true or as false; the theory of reference is seen as a theory about the determination of the truth-values of sentences in accordance with their composition.

There are several different theses the relations between which need to be grasped; it may, for once, help to attach labels to them. Let us refer to the interpretation of reference as semantic value as *Sem*, and to the context principle as *Con*, specifying Con_S or Con_R according as it is taken as relating to sense or to reference. There is also Frege's conception of the sense of an expression as being that in our understanding of it which determines its reference—the particular way in which its reference is given to us in virtue of our understanding of it; let us label this thesis *Giv*. Sluga maintains that *Sem* conflicts with *Con*. It certainly does not conflict with Con_S, which embodies the primacy of sentences, that is, the principle that the sense of a word can be explained only in terms of its role within sentences. On the contrary, *Sem* and *Giv* together imply Con_S. The sense of a word is the manner in which its reference is given; its reference is that which goes to determine the truth-values of sentences containing it; and so we can explain its sense only in terms of its use in sentences. Is *Sem* incompatible with Con_R? Suppose that, in stipulating the intended interpretation of some formal language, we have said that a primitive constant 'o' is to stand for the number zero. Nothing is thereby presupposed about how we should explain what taking a symbol to stand for that number involves; it is assumed as known what it is to take it so. Con_R, applied to this case, takes it as a hypothesis that we have found some way of fixing the senses of all sentences in which 'the number zero' occurs, and then, in view of that expression's behaving logically like a proper name, licenses us to regard it as having a reference. In that case, we shall know what is conveyed by stipulating, of the term 'o', that it is to stand for the number zero; we shall construe the senses of formulas containing 'o' as being fixed in the way we fixed the senses of sentences containing 'the number zero'. The stipulation of the semantic value of 'o' remains neutral as between rival accounts of what it is to take a symbol to have a given reference. To hold that the references of the symbols composing a formula jointly determine its truth-value says nothing about what having a reference involves, and is therefore compatible with Con_R and with its denial. What *is* in conflict with Con_R is *Giv*, not *Sem*. If Con_R is needed to justify ascribing a reference to certain terms, then their senses cannot have been given as a manner of determining their references, or otherwise no justification would be required; the truth-conditions of sentences containing them must, rather, have been fixed so as to supply a means of determining their truth-values which does not go via the references of the terms. This conflict cannot be used to discredit any particular interpretation of Frege, since it is between two theses unquestionably advanced by him. In their full-fledged forms, *Giv* was stated only from 1892 onwards, while *Con* was propounded only in 1884. We do not need to assume that Frege ever became completely clear about the matter to see this as telling strongly against Sluga's belief that Frege adhered to *Con* to the end of his life.

It must be presumed, from the few hints that he gives us, that Sluga sees the connections differently. He appears to associate classical model theory with the meaning-theoretic thesis that the reference of a word is always directly given to us, without the mediation of a sense, or with the epistemo-logical thesis that objects are directly presented to us. If so, it would indeed be ridiculous to interpret Frege's thought in the light of it; but a semantic theory, as employed by logicians, is free of any such presuppositions. It is for philosophers to determine what relation a theory of meaning or of under-standing has to a semantic theory in the strict sense, and how the theory of meaning is related to the theory of knowledge. The term 'interpretation', as used in model theory, is a technical one; it should not be taken as correlative with 'understanding'. But, if this is the right way to construe Sluga's aspersions on the approach of analytic philosophers to the context principle, the epistemic implications of that principle, which I am accused of rejecting, are presumably those which disprove epistemological atomism, which thus makes a second, even more covert, appearance in the book. Hence it seems likely that Sluga's component (1) of the priority thesis, the epistemic primacy of the contents of judgments, is intended to be something entailing the falsity of epistemological atomism. Usually, when it is said that A's are epistemologically prior to B's, it is meant that one could come by the concept of a B only if one had first grasped that of an A. It is, however, unlikely that Sluga means that the general concept of a concept is so related to the general concept of a judgment: the priority thesis concerns the extraction of a specific concept from a specific judgment or range of judgments. The doctrines which make Frege an opponent of epistemological atomism are, in fact, that proper names have sense, that the sense of a proper name always involves a criterion of identity, and that awareness of an object must involve the apprehension of a sense; the context principle plays only a minor role in this connection, and the priority thesis none. A reader who did not know of Sluga's remarks, in his articles, concerning epistemological atomism will surely find the thesis of the epistemic primacy of judgeable contents exceedingly opaque; even with that help, it is difficult to attach a precise meaning to it.

Resnik

As its title indicates, Michael Resnik's article attempts to effect a compromise between Sluga's views and my own concerning Frege's attitude to realism.[1] Resnik agrees with me that, in his mature period, Frege took up 'a thoroughly realist stance' (p. 351). He believes, however, that Sluga has given 'an extremely plausible and well-supported view of Frege's *Grundlagen*', although, unfortunately, some of Frege's pronouncements during that period 'cloud this interpretation of him as a non-platonic transcendental idealist' (pp. 351, 352). It is impossible 'to eradicate all the tension in Frege's views', but the interpretation which reduces this tension to a minimum places him as 'an ontological platonist and an objective idealist' (p. 353).

In arguing thus, Resnik is wholly concerned with Frege's attitude to 'numbers, sets, and the like' (p. 350), that is, to what he regarded as logical objects; he pays no attention to Sluga's thesis that Frege also took a transcendentally idealist view of material objects. He explains an ontological platonist as one 'who recognizes the existence of numbers, sets, and the like as on a par with ordinary objects and who does not attempt to reduce them to physical or subjective mental entities'. More reasonably than Sluga, he regards epistemological platonism as a *stronger* doctrine than the merely ontological variety; an epistemological platonist is an ontological platonist 'who also believes that our knowledge of mathematical objects is at least in part based upon a direct acquaintance with them which is analogous to our perception of physical objects' (ibid.). It will be recalled that, in his book, Sluga classifies Lotze as 'an epistemological *rather than* an ontological Platonist' (p. 119; my italics), explaining an epistemological Platonist as one who thinks that we have 'knowledge of non-temporal, non-changing

[1] M. D. Resnik, 'Frege as Idealist and then Realist', *Inquiry*, vol. 22, 1979, pp. 350-7.

things', and that he goes on to suggest that it is plausible to categorize Frege in the same way (p. 130). Sluga thus thinks it possible to hold that we have knowledge of non-temporal things without supposing that they really exist, whereas Resnik does not; Resnik believes the Frege of the *Grundlagen* to have been an ontological platonist but not an epistemological one, while Sluga believes the exact opposite. There seems no doubt that he was an ontological platonist in Resnik's sense.[1] He was also an epistemological platonist in Sluga's sense, since he certainly believed that we have knowledge concerning logical objects. Whether he was one in Resnik's sense is more obscure, since Resnik demands 'direct acquaintance' with numbers and classes. Certainly Frege credits us with no special faculty of mathematical intuition whereby we apprehend, say, the natural numbers; for him, the faculty whereby we know of them is our reason, in accordance with their being *logical* objects. In a passage which has already given us trouble, and which Resnik also quotes, he says that real and natural numbers are 'objects . . . which are immediately given to the reason and which, as being its very own, it can see right through'.[2] If one may intelligibly ask whether our knowledge of logical objects amounts to direct acquaintance, this passage appears to return as affirmative an answer as could be given; but possibly the analogy between perception and this use of our reason is insufficiently close for Frege to count as an epistemological platonist on Resnik's definition.

By 'objective idealist' Resnik means the same as 'transcendental idealist'. An objective idealist could be an ontological or even an epistemological platonist by holding 'that Mind or Reason constructs the whole world of mathematical objects prior to our "experiencing" it'; 'the effect of this,' he says, 'would be to make such a world *objective* in the sense of being 'independent of our sensation, intuition and imagination . . .", but still not a world of things in themselves' (p. 351). I am afraid that this doctrine remains highly opaque to me. In *FPL* I held it to be a consequence of a sound interpretation of Frege's conception of criteria of identity that reality does not come to us already articulated into discrete objects, but that, by choosing to employ certain (sortal) concepts where we might have employed others, we slice it up into objects in one particular way out of many possible ones;[3] this is an expression of the falsity of epistemological atomism. Ought we to say, in consequence, that we 'construct' empirical reality and that

---

[1] See, for instance, *Grundlagen*, §§ 60–1, to which Resnik alludes.

[2] *Grundlagen*, § 105; I have here abandoned Austin's beautiful translation for a ploddingly literal one.

[3] *FPL*, p. 577.

empirical objects are not things in themselves? Surely not. We have adopted a particular way of describing reality, and might have adopted a different one; but, from a realist standpoint, it remains the case that the statements we make, using that mode of description, are objectively true or false, and that what renders them so is, in general, independent of the means we have for recognizing them as such. It is perhaps likewise true that we might have interested ourselves in different mathematical structures from those with which, in fact, our mathematics is concerned; but, from a platonist standpoint, the mathematical objects which interest us no more sprang into existence as a result of our acknowledging them than did rivers as a result of our grasping the concept of a river or giving proper names to rivers. Transcendental idealism is the doctrine that certain propositions hold good only of the world as we experience it, not of the world as it is in itself, and that the only ground of their truth is that we are incapable of apprehending anything save as conforming to those propositions. Frege held that arithmetic, unlike geometry, holds good for everything thinkable. But he surely did not mean, even in the *Grundlagen*, that it holds good only in virtue of our thinking in this way and our inability to think otherwise, and that therefore it holds only of reality as we think of it and not as it is in itself. Such an interpretation can derive only from an exclusive concentration on Frege's conception of numbers as logical objects, neglecting his awareness of arithmetical truths as capable of being *applied*. In the *Grundlagen*, cardinal numbers are classes of concepts; but the concepts to which they belong (which are members of them) include those under which empirical objects fall. It was a prime concern of his logical construction of the theory of cardinal numbers, as of his unfinished construction of the theory of real numbers in vol. II of *Grundgesetze*, to render their application—natural numbers for counting, real numbers for measuring—as direct as possible, so that the application of an arithmetical truth appears as the instantiation of a logical one. Arithmetic, as an extension of logic, is applicable to every sector of reality. Hence to hold that arithmetic does not describe the realm of logical objects as it is in itself would entail holding that, in so far as we take all reality to be subject to the laws of arithmetic, we are describing it only as we have, at least in part, constructed it, and not as we have any reason to suppose it to be in itself.

This is an utterly unFregean doctrine. It has already been noted that, although Frege accepts the Kantian trichotomy of a posteriori, synthetic a priori and analytic, he does not adopt Kant's explanation of our knowledge of synthetic a priori truths or of what makes them true. To regard him as a transcendental idealist concerning arithmetical truths is, in effect, to attribute to him an explanation of analytic truth very similar to Kant's explanation of synthetic a priori truth, with reason replacing intuition. Such a way of reading him appears little less than perverse.

It makes no difference to the argument just given that, in *Grundlagen*, Frege prefers not to speak of arithmetical laws as directly applicable to the external world. 'What they apply to,' he says, 'are judgments that hold of things in the external world: they are laws of the laws of nature' and 'assert a connection, not between natural phenomena, but between judgments.'[1] But the connections which they assert are those to which we must conform if we are to arrive at true judgments, about the external world as about other things. 'The laws of logic are nothing but an unfolding of the content of the word "true"', he wrote, probably shortly before composing the *Grundlagen*; change 'is contrary to the essence of a logical law, because it conflicts with the sense of the word "true", which excludes any reference to the knowing subject'.[2] If we are to make true judgments about the external world, or about anything else, we must make them in conformity with the laws of arithmetic. If those laws were constructed by us, rather than holding good independently of our thinking and judging, then, to that extent, the external world would have been constructed by us. To be a transcendental idealist about logical objects would entail being one about all objects whatever.

The impulse to consider Frege an idealist may spring from a disposition to expect realism to take a fairly crude form. But to argue that his platonism can be viewed only as a form of realism, not of idealism, however attenuated, is not to deny that it is sophisticated; and Resnik gives a good account of this sophistication. He explains Frege's saying that numbers are given directly to the reason as resting on the context principle; in this he is surely right. 'The elements of reason are judgments, since we do not reason with words but rather with sentences and in so doing make judgments,' he says (p. 353). In order to determine what number-words mean, we must therefore ask after the senses of sentences containing number-words. One of the passages cited by Sluga as showing Frege to have been a transcendental idealist was that in which he says that what is objective is 'not . . . independent of the reason', since 'to answer the question what things are independently of the reason would be to judge without judging'.[3] Sluga interpreted this to mean that 'the claim that something is objective is not a dogmatic metaphysical claim', since we cannot coherently 'say what things are in themselves, independent of our judgments' (p. 120). Resnik interprets it as

[1] *Grundlagen*, § 87.
[2] 'Logik', perhaps about 1882, *N.S.*, pp. 3, 5, *P.W.*, pp. 3, 5.
[3] *Grundlagen*, § 26.

another form of the prohibition on asking after the meaning of a word in isolation: 'asking what numbers are like independently of judgments . . . is to ask what they are like independently of the reason', and 'to answer that would be to "judge without judging"' (p. 353). This is a plausible interpretation of the passage; but, unless it is added that numbers would not be what they are, or, perhaps, would not exist at all, if we did not make the judgments that we do, or were not around to make them, the conclusion that Resnik wants, that Frege was 'an objective idealist' concerning numbers, does not follow.

Resnik notes the effect of Frege's use of the context principle to justify ascribing references to number-words; but he overstates it. 'It could be argued,' he says, 'that Frege aimed at giving a non-referential truth-value semantics for arithmetic, that is, a semantics in which sentences receive truth-values directly and the "references" of their parts are construed as abstractions or a *façon de parler*' (p. 352). Resnik does not himself accept such an interpretation, since in the end 'no such semantics is given for number-words in the *Grundlagen*', but, instead, they are defined explicitly (p. 353). The trouble with this is that the proposed interpretation arrives at too strong a conclusion, while the rejection of this conclusion, in the light of Frege's explicit definitions, makes it appear that, in the end, the context principle plays no role in his final account. This is certainly not how Frege saw the matter. The last four sections of the *Grundlagen* summarize the argument of the entire book. In the course of this summary, Frege says, 'We next laid down the fundamental principle that the meaning of a word is to be explained, not in isolation, but in the context of a sentence; only by adhering to this can we, I believe, avoid a physicalist view of number without slipping into a psychological one.'[1] He then immediately goes on to discuss his method of giving a sense to statements of identity between numbers. In the next section, he explains the difficulty which led him to treat this explanation as less than adequate as a definition, namely that *any* identity-statement, even one connecting a numerical term with one not of that form, 'must . . . always have a sense'; for this reason it was necessary to adopt the explicit definition of numbers as extensions of (second-order) concepts. The context principle does not here appear as merely suggesting what proved to be an unsuccessful line of attack, which it would be if the explicit definition rendered an appeal to it unnecessary. Rather, it figures as an essential step in the argument, the only pilot that will steer us between the Scylla of physicalism and the Charybdis of psychologism.

Frege's appeal to the context principle indeed suggests that he has a

[1] *Grundlagen*, § 106.

means of giving sense to sentences containing number-words that does not go via any method of assigning references to them. But, where many would conclude that to speak of numbers was a mere *façon de parler*, Frege does not. The context principle fully licenses us, in such a case, to ascribe a reference to number-words; the whole point of the context principle is that, for a word to have a reference, nothing more can be demanded. Hence, even if Frege had rested context with contextual definitions for number-words, it would be wrong, from his standpoint, to draw the conclusion Resnik thinks would follow, that he was not even an ontological platonist. But, even if the context principle legitimates contextual definitions, this does not exhaust its force. If we fail to acknowledge the principle, we shall overlook the entire realm of logical objects, and recognize only physical objects and mental ones. Directions, shapes, perhaps even colours considered as objects, are in a like case;[1] though they cannot be defined in purely logical terms, they, too, are logical objects, since they are to be defined as extensions of concepts.[2] The phrase 'extension of a concept', Frege wrote, 'itself indicates that we are not here dealing with something spatial and physical, but with something logical. By means of our logical faculties we lay hold upon the extension of a concept, by starting out from the concept.'[3] The explicit definitions merely reduce the notions of number, direction and shape to that of the extension of a concept; it was obviously Frege's opinion that we cannot clearly comprehend the character of extensions of concepts and the possibility of referring to them unless we acknowledge the context principle. That is why extensions of concepts are so readily confused with the results of physical aggregation. At the time of writing *Grundlagen*, Frege was still uncertain about this notion;[4] but he was clear enough that, whatever the precise form of the required explicit definition of numbers, an appeal to the context principle would be needed in order to be sure that, by means of that definition, a reference had indeed been accorded to number-words.

Resnik agrees with me that Frege abandoned the context principle in his mature period, and associates this with his alleged change of mind from objective idealism to full-fledged realism. One reason that he gives for Frege's abandonment of the context principle is incorrect. He rightly says that the doctrine of incomplete or unsaturated expressions represented Frege's solution to the problem of the unity of a thought (p. 356). Less plausibly, he sees the context principle as having, at an earlier period, served

---

[1] *Grundlagen*, § 68.

[2] 'Über Schoenflies', 1906, *N.S.*, p. 197, *P.W.*, p. 181.

[3] See the end of § 107.

[4] *Grundlagen*, § 106 and footnote.

the same purpose; the introduction of the notion of unsaturatedness, which did not occur until 1891 (p. 355), therefore rendered the context principle superfluous. Unfortunately, the historical premiss is mistaken. The metaphor of unsaturatedness occurs already in Frege's letter to Marty of 1882.[1]

Resnik offers three grounds for thinking Frege to have abandoned the context principle. With the first and third of these I fully agree. The first is that, from 1891 onwards, Frege admitted no distinction of type between sentences and proper names; and the third is the demand, in the published letter to Peano, that each word have a sense and a reference independent of context. It will be recalled that, as Resnik remarks, Sluga actually cited this passage as evidence of Frege's continued adherence to the context principle; Resnik rightly observes that the characterization of natural language contained in the passage is intended as a *criticism* of it (p. 354). As we saw earlier, however, Resnik is wrong to read the passage as expressly denying the context principle. Rather, the argument is more indirect: if Frege had still adhered to the context principle, he would hardly have expressed a demand in fact consistent with it in terms that look like a flat contradiction of it.

The second of Resnik's three grounds is not convincing, namely the thesis that a thought is compounded of parts corresponding to the parts of the sentence; it is a misinterpretation of the context principle to construe it as incompatible with this thesis. Resnik rightly points to the occurrence in Part I of the *Grundgesetze* of a 'trace' of the context principle, namely in the discussion of the references of value-range terms, and rightly refuses to admit it as more than a trace. He also discusses Frege's use of the term *wirklich*, about which he concludes, as I have done, that it did not serve to mark a 'contrast between the real and the ideal' (p. 355). Resnik's reading of Frege does not seem to be far away from mine; but I differ from him in thinking that he has provided no convincing grounds for supposing Frege to have been any kind of idealist, even when he wrote the *Grundlagen*.

Appendix 3: Kripke

KRIPKE'S THREE LECTURES on 'Naming and Necessity', which were discussed extensively on pp. 110–51 of *FPL*, have now been issued in book form. The text is unaltered, but a new Preface has been added; it is that which will be discussed here.

[1] *BW*, p. 164, *P.M.C.*, p. 101.

In this Preface, Kripke is concerned to defend his notion of rigid designation, and to argue that a knowledge of the rigidity of a rigid designator is an essential ingredient of a full understanding of such a term. On p. 6 he says, of the statement 'Aristotle was fond of dogs', that 'a proper understanding of this statement involves an understanding both of the (extensionally correct) conditions under which it is in fact true, *and* of the conditions under which a counterfactual course of history, resembling the actual course in some respects but not in others, would be correctly (partially) described by' it (his italics). The thesis is explicitly enunciated only for this one specific sentence; but it would have no plausibility whatever unless it were meant to sustain fairly wide generalization. We thus have it that, perhaps for *every* sentence, or perhaps just for each member of some large, though unspecified, class of sentences, a proper understanding of a statement made by uttering it involves understanding two distinguishable things; possibly more, but at least these two. We are not told whether the understanding of the statement *consists* in understanding these two things, or these two together with others, or whether it is something distinct from the understanding of these two things, but from which the understanding of them *flows*. No doubt Kripke's argument is independent of the answers to these questions.

The first of the two things which we must understand if we are to have a proper understanding of the statement is the condition under which the statement is in fact true. Some philosophers, including Frege, have wished to *identify* a grasp of the thought expressed by a particular utterance of a sentence, that is, of the sense of the sentence as then uttered, with an understanding of the condition for the statement thereby made (the thought thereby expressed) to be true. Whether that identification be accepted or rejected, it is in the highest degree plausible that an understanding of a sentence, as uttered on a given occasion, *involves* grasping what determines the statement made by uttering it as true. Let us say, then, that someone who grasps this has a *grade-one* understanding of the statement.

Now does a grade-one understanding amount to a full (or what Kripke calls a 'proper') understanding of it? Kripke maintains that a proper understanding involves understanding a second thing: understanding whether the statement would be true in certain counterfactual courses of history. Let us say that someone who understands both these things concerning the statement has a *grade-two* understanding of it. Kripke leaves it open whether a grade-two understanding is sufficient for a proper understanding; but he says expressly that it is necessary for it.

Let us now ask whether a grade-one understanding entails a grade-two understanding: does someone who understands under what conditions the statement is in fact true thereby also understand whether it would be true in hypothetical courses of world history? From the italicization of the 'and' in Kripke's formulation of his thesis, we should naturally suppose not. What he wishes to make out is that a grade-two understanding of 'Aristotle was fond of dogs' requires an implicit grasp of the rigidity of the term 'Aristotle', something which is not required for a mere grade-one understanding. If we give an explanation of the conditions under which the statement is *in fact* true, we do not need to mention the fact that 'Aristotle' is a rigid designator. Indeed, we cannot, in such terms, explain what it is to be a rigid designator: that feature of the term relates only to truth in counter-factual courses of history. So a mere grade-one understanding, one that does not include a grade-two understanding, is at least in principle con-ceivable; and one who has it has only an attentuated understanding of the statement: he does not yet 'properly' understand it. According to this thesis, Frege was guilty of overlooking an essential ingredient in our grasp of a thought.

The gap between a grade-one and a grade-two understanding with which Kripke is concerned relates entirely to the subject-term, in his example 'Aristotle', and not at all to the predicate. Kripke is supposing, for the sake of argument, that the reference of the name 'Aristotle' is fixed as being the same as that of the definite description 'the last great philosopher of antiquity'. He is concerned to explain the difference in our understanding of the sentences 'Aristotle was fond of dogs' and 'The last great philosopher of antiquity was fond of dogs'. On the supposition he is making for the sake of argument, a grade-one understanding will not differentiate between the two sentences; the difference comes to light only when we advance to a grade-two understanding, which involves grasping that 'Aristotle' is a rigid designator and 'the last great philosopher of antiquity' is not, although, according to the supposition, their references are fixed in the same way. The supposition is, unfortunately, highly implausible; and this makes it difficult to think clearly about the matter, since one is required to hold firmly in place a deeply unrealistic assumption.

Why has Kripke adopted such an assumption at all? He is not, in this passage, concerned to argue against the description theory of proper names, or against what is in fact the more general thesis that proper names with the same reference may have different senses; he is concerned solely with a distinct way in which he holds that their linguistic behaviour diverges from that of definite descriptions, namely in their being rigid designators. In *FPL*, I distinguished (pp. 111, 135) between these two Kripkean theses: that proper names are rigid designators, and that they lack senses. One might think, indeed, that I did not emphasize the distinction strongly enough. The two theses contrast proper names with definite descriptions in two different respects: the thesis about rigid designation relates to their denotations in other possible worlds, whereas the denial that they have senses concerns how their reference in the actual world is determined. The former thesis does not imply the latter: a proper name could function as a rigid designator even if the description theory gave a correct account of the way in which its actual reference is fixed. Indeed, it is only because no such implication holds that Kripke is able to claim that, to have a proper understanding of a statement, one needs to know something *more* than how its truth-value is actually determined: if, from knowing the latter, one thereby knew something which entailed that a proper name used in making the statement was a rigid designator, and hence entailed the conditions under which the statement was true with respect to other possible worlds, it would be quite misleading to say that one needed to know something more in order properly to understand it. It is, indeed, arguable that Kripke's two theses about proper names are not wholly independent: it is plausible that a name lacking sense, but having a referent, would necessarily behave as a rigid designator in modal contexts.[1] Precisely for that reason, however, such a name would be useless as an example for the line of argument Kripke develops in the passage of his Preface which we are considering. This is an argument to the necessity for the notion of rigid designation from an intuition that a full or proper understanding of a sentence containing a proper name is not provided by an account of the manner in which its actual truth-value is determined. For such an argument to go through, it is strictly necessary to consider a proper name for which its being a rigid designator cannot be thought to follow from the way its actual reference is fixed; and it is preferable to consider one whose reference is taken to be fixed in just the same way as some other term, such as a definite description, which is not a rigid designator.

An argument for the need to admit the notion of rigid designation that was based upon a sentence containing a proper name lacking a sense, and

[1] Whether this is really so or not depends on some obscure questions. If Kripke's causal theory were correct, would it really be true that proper names lacked senses? If so, would a hypothetical proper name, phonetically the same as an actual one, and connected by the speakers with the same beliefs about its bearer as are actually held, but attached by a chain of communication to a different individual, be the same proper name as its actual homonym? If the answers to both questions are affirmative, then, at least for Kripke, there can be no absurdity in the conception of proper names as lacking senses but behaving as flexible designators: in that case, neither of the two theses would follow from the other.

therefore incapable, or not obviously capable, of functioning as a flexible designator, would have quite a different form. It could not use as an intermediate step any claim that a grasp of the way the actual truth-value is determined falls short of a proper understanding; there could not be, or could not obviously be, another sentence agreeing with the given one in this respect but differing from it in its truth-value with respect to certain possible worlds. The conclusion of such an argument would be weaker, too. The conclusion would be merely that the proper name in question would *be* a rigid designator, in Kripke's sense of denoting the same object in every possible world, not that we need expressly to grasp that feature of it in order to understand and use the sentence containing it.

This is not to say that Kripke's two theses about proper names are unconnected. In 'A Puzzle about Belief',[1] he connects them by ascribing to a proper name the 'Millian' character that 'it *simply* refers to its bearer, and has no other linguistic function' (pp. 239–40).[2] From this he infers that 'proper names of the same thing are everywhere interchangeable not only *salva veritate* but even *salva significatione*: the proposition expressed by a sentence should remain the same no matter what name of the object it uses' (p. 240). Now 'whether a sentence expresses a necessary truth or a contingent one depends only on the proposition expressed and not on the words used to express it', he goes on to say: hence 'any simple sentence should retain its "modal value" (necessary, impossible, contingently true, or contingently false)' when one proper name is replaced by another having the same reference, 'since such a replacement leaves the content of the sentence unaltered' (p. 241). That proper names lack senses obviously follows from the thesis that they are Millian, i.e. have no linguistic function other than their reference: here we have a deduction from their Millian character to the conclusion, not specifically that they are rigid designators, nor even directly to a doctrine concerning the truth-values with respect to possible

---

[1] In A. Margalit (ed.), *Meaning and Use*, Dordrecht, Boston, London and Jerusalem, pp. 239–83; see pp. 239–41.

[2] Kripke here follows the Mill of legend, not of history. Mill does *not* say that the name is directly connected with the object. Rather, he says the contrary; 'we put a mark, not indeed upon the object itself, but, so to speak, upon the idea of the object' (J. S. Mill, *System of Logic*, bk. I, ch. II, § 5). 'A proper name,' he continues, 'is but an unmeaning mark which we connect in our minds with the idea of the object.' It is left obscure whether different people can have the same idea of an object, and whether one person may have different ideas of the same object, without necessarily knowing that they are of the same object. If the answer to both questions is affirmative, the doctrine, despite its psychologistic formulation, is not far removed from Frege's conception of the sense of a proper name. No doubt the Mill of legend is a more interesting figure than the Mill of history.

worlds of sentences containing them, but at least to the possession by such sentences of the modal values which the semantic doctrine of rigid designation is intended to explain. This does not, however, imply that, from the thesis that proper names are rigid designators, we may infer that they lack senses. Without trying to decide whether the converse inference would be valid, we may say that, if proper names were flexible designators, that would be one respect in which their linguistic function went beyond their (actual) reference; and, if they were rigid designators, but possessed senses, that would be another. Hence, if they are altogether Millian, they cannot have either feature: but from this it does not follow that the absence of one feature entails the absence of the other.

For the sake of his argument, then, it is essential for Kripke to use an example of a sentence containing a proper name which has a sense but functions as a rigid designator: and he elects to do this by pretending that this is true of the name 'Aristotle'; true, that is, even when 'having a sense' is equated with 'satisfying the description theory'. This name is to be treated as the precise equivalent of the phrase 'dthat the last great philosopher of antiquity', where 'dthat' is the operator invented by David Kaplan for converting any definite description into a rigid designator, its actual reference being determined exactly as before.[1] The conception that such an operator is possible is, of course, precisely the conception that being a rigid designator is a feature of a term which need not depend upon its lacking a sense.

Since, as remarked, the equivalence of 'Aristotle' with 'dthat the last great philosopher of antiquity' is so unrealistic an assumption, it will assist thought if we replace the example by one for which the corresponding assumption is not implausible. Let us, then, take as our example the name 'Deutero-Isaiah', understood as standing for the author of the prophecy embodied in chapters 40 to 55 of the Book of Isaiah. I do not mean to treat this term as a mere abbreviation for the definite description 'the author of the prophecy embodied in chapters 40 to 55 of the Book of Isaiah'; I am supposing that its reference is fixed by means of that definite description, but that it has been introduced as a proper name, and hence as to be used in the manner proper to what Kripke calls a 'rigid designator'. The example, therefore serves a similar purpose to that of the name 'St. Anne', as used in *FPL*, pp. 112–32. The latter has, however, the disadvantage, for present purposes, that, according to Kripke, the Blessed Virgin could not have had a different mother, since no one with a different mother would have

<hr />

[1] David Kaplan, 'Dthat', in P. Cole (ed.), *Syntax and Semantics*, vol. 9, *Pragmatics*, New York, 1978, pp. 221–43.

been she. I shall assume that the analogue does not apply to literary works such as the second part of the Book of Isaiah. I shall assume, that is, that we should be wrong to claim that, if Shakespeare had not written *Macbeth*, but someone else had, in about 1605, written a play word for word the same, that play would still not have been *Macbeth*. The predicate may be anything the understanding of which may be taken to be unproblematic, say 'had five sons', or 'was fond of dogs' if one likes: our problem concerns solely what is involved in understanding the name (and the corresponding definite description).

Now much of the apparent power of Kripke's argument, as formulated in the passage of his Preface under consideration, for the notion of rigid designators depends upon the ambiguity of the phrase 'the (extensionally correct) conditions under which [the statement] is in fact true'. On the one hand, it looks as though Kripke is identifying a lacuna in Frege's account of the sense of an utterance of a sentence as consisting in the manner in which the (actual) truth-value of the thought expressed is determined: that, he is telling us, is only *part* of what we must grasp if we are to have a proper understanding of it. On the other hand, what it is that he claims that we must know in addition looks so obviously required that the reader accepts his claim without hesitation. To be said to understand a statement, it is not enough that one who hears it is able to determine whether or not it is, in the actual circumstances, true. He must also know what would be required for its truth if the circumstances were different in any of many conceivable ways; and this, it may well seem, is just what Kripke is saying that he must, in addition, understand. But to read the argument in this way is to miss the point; for, to use our alternative example, it does not differentiate between 'Deutero-Isaiah had five sons' and 'The author of the prophecy had five sons' (where 'the prophecy' refers to that embodied in the second part of the Book of Isaiah). To be said to understand the latter statement, too, one would have to be able to say whether it would be true in any sufficiently specific set of hypothetical circumstances; as far as the reference of the subject-term is concerned, this involves grasping the principle governing the determination of its referent. In order to know an extensionally correct condition for the actual truth of the statement, it would be sufficient if, by some fluke, one were to take the definite description as referring to an individual who as a matter of fact composed the prophecy, even though one did not understand the words 'author' and 'prophecy'; but this would not suffice for a genuine understanding of the statement. The improbability of such a partial understanding in a case of this kind is beside the point; it is clear that, to be said to understand the statement, one must know the principle according to which the subject-term is taken as referring to whoever satisfied a particular condition. In this regard, however, the statement, 'Deutero-Isaiah had five sons', stands no differently. For 'Deutero-Isaiah' is, as 'Aristotle' is being taken for the sake of argument to be, a proper name which carries a Fregean sense, on which its reference depends, indeed a name for which the description theory holds. Its referent is determined in exactly the same way as that of 'the author of the prophecy'; just as, on the assumption which Kripke makes concerning the name 'Aristotle', its referent is determined in exactly the same way as that of 'the last great philosopher of antiquity'. To understand the statement, one must know what, in all possible circumstances, would make it true; to know this, one must know what would make an individual the person about whom we, by using the name 'Deutero-Isaiah', were speaking. This is, however, the very same thing as makes someone the referent of 'the author of the pro-phecy'; and so no difference between the two statements emerges from looking at them in this light.

If it were right to take the contrast as being between one who has merely got the reference of the term—proper name or definite description—right, and one who grasps the principle according to which, as we use the term, its reference is determined, then there would be no ground for seeing it as pointing to any defect in Frege's account. The whole point of Frege's application of the sense/reference distinction to proper names is that he did not think a correct identification of the referent sufficient for a grasp of a thought expressed by a sentence containing the name: whenever one can speak of the way the reference is fixed, or of the principle according to which it is determined, that will, for Frege, constitute the sense of the name, a grasp of which is essential to the apprehension of any such thought. An under-standing of the condition for the truth of the statement must, then, be taken to involve a knowledge of the sense of the subject-term, of the way in which the reference of that term is fixed. If it is so taken, however, the ground disappears for thinking that knowing the condition for the statement to be true in hypothetical circumstances involves knowing any more than the condition for its actual truth. In Kripke's phrase, 'the . . . conditions under which [the statement] is in fact true', the expression 'in fact' does not really jibe with the word 'conditions'. One may be in a state of merely knowing whether or not a sentence, as uttered on a given occasion, *in fact* expresses a truth: but if one knows the *condition* that must hold for it to do so, one thereby also knows the condition that would have to hold for it to do so were the circumstances different. Of course, one may speak of knowing a (not 'the') condition which, in virtue of some contingent circumstances, is *in fact* necessary and sufficient for the truth of the statement; but just this is the interpretation we have already rejected as inadequate to pick out what is in common between an understanding of the statement involving the proper name and that of the one involving the definite description, or to characterize Frege's conception of the grasp of a thought. To know *the* condition for the truth of a statement, in the relevant sense, is to know the condition required simply by the way we use the words in which it is stated. Hence, if one knows this, one thereby knows the condition required in all circumstances, provided only that those words are used in the same way; for it is the very same condition.

What Kripke wants to do is to pinpoint that which differentiates our understanding of, say, 'Deutero-Isaiah had five sons' from our understanding of 'The author of the prophecy had five sons'. The difference in question arises, on his account, solely from the fact that 'Deutero-Isaiah' is a rigid designator and 'the author of the prophecy' is not; and it is our apprehension of this difference which is the ingredient of a grade-two understanding absent from an understanding which is only of grade one. This ingredient has nothing to do with how we should determine the truth-value of the statement were the circumstances obtaining when it was made other than they are; for, provided that we continued to use the words involved in the same way as in fact we do, we should take the references of 'Deutero-Isaiah' and of 'the author of the prophecy' to be determined in exactly the same way as we now do, and therefore in the same way as one another. If we use the terminology of possible worlds, we may say that these statements, which are made in the actual world, are also made in some possible worlds; here 'making a statement' is to be equated with 'expressing a thought' rather than with 'making an assertion'. In saying this, we mean merely that the same statements might be made in circumstances different from the actual ones; this would happen if, for example, the same sentences were uttered (by the same speakers and at the same times, if that is relevant), and the words composing them were all used and understood in the way we use and understand them. Expressed in this terminology, then, the present contention is that the ingredient distinguishing a grade-two from a grade-one understanding does not depend upon the truth-values which the statements are correctly judged to have in those possible worlds in which they are made; in other words, upon the truth-values which they would be correctly judged to have if the circumstances were different. No semantic theory needs to lay down anything about this. The additional ingredient depends upon something quite different: namely, upon the truth-values relativized to possible worlds which a semantic theory ascribes to the statements we actually make in order to explain our use of modalized statements.

There is here a contrast between a semantic theory for temporal discourse and one for modal discourse. In a semantic theory for temporal discourse, time enters in two ways.[1] On the one hand, utterances of sentences, to which truth-values are ascribed, must be indexed by a speaker and a time; on the other, the truth-values of such utterances must be relativized to times. More exactly, such relativization is required if tenses and temporal adverbs and adverbial phrases are represented, in the regimented language to which the semantic theory directly applies, by sentential operators in Prior's tense-logical style. It is an essential part of our understanding of sentences of natural language that we grasp the way in which the truth-value of an utterance, and the references of terms and the application of predicates contained in the sentence uttered, all depend systematically upon the time of utterance: this is represented in the semantic theory by indexing utterances by times. Relativization of truth-values to times, on the other hand, is needed to explain the temporal operators: it would still be needed if we were constructing a theory adequate to explain only utterances made at some one specific time. As well as the relativized truth-values, we want a notion of the absolute truth or falsity of an utterance: these are connected by the principle that an utterance $\langle S, x, t \rangle$, where S is the sentence uttered, x the speaker who utters it and t the time of utterance, is true absolutely just in case it is true with respect to t. To a considerable extent, the relativization of truth-values to times will agree with the variation of absolute truth-value according to the time of utterance: that is, for a great many sentences S, $\langle S, x, t \rangle$ will be true with respect to t' just in case $\langle S, x, t' \rangle$ is true absolutely, i.e. is true with respect to t'. But expressions of natural language like 'here' and 'now' may be treated in the semantic theory as temporally rigid designators; and, if they are, their presence in a sentence S will produce exceptions to this principle. For instance, let S be the sentence 'It is noisy here', where the semantic theory treats 'here' as temporally rigid. Then $\langle S, x, t \rangle$ is true with respect to t' just in case it is, at t', noisy at the place where x is at t; whereas $\langle S, x, t' \rangle$ is true absolutely just in case it is, at t', noisy at the place where x is at t'. It is in just this respect that 'here' differs from the flexible designator 'where I am'. If S' is the sentence 'It is noisy where I am', it obeys the general principle violated by S: $\langle S', x, t \rangle$ is true with respect to t' just in case it is, at t', noisy where x is at

---

[1] This was perhaps first clearly pointed out by Hans Kamp in his 'Formal properties of "now"', *Theoria*, vol. 37, 1971, pp. 227–73; I am grateful to Professor David Kaplan for drawing my attention to this article.

t', and hence just in case $\langle S', x, t' \rangle$ is true absolutely. It is for this reason that the regimented versions of utterances, by the same speaker at the same time, of 'It is always noisy here' and of 'It is always noisy where I am', may come out as having different truth-values.

A semantic theory for modal discourse, framed in terms of possible worlds, will, if it treats some terms as modally rigid designators, display a similar phenomenon. An utterance involving a modally rigid term may be true with respect to a possible world, even though, considered as made *in* that world, it is false. If 'Deutero-Isaiah' is treated as a rigid designator, then 'Deutero-Isaiah had five sons' might be true with respect to a certain possible world in which a different individual, whom we may call 'Johanan', composed the prophecy, because, in that world, the man who actually composed the prophecy had five sons. But if, in that world, the name 'Deutero-Isaiah' were used according to the principles which, as things are, govern its use, it would, as used in that world, serve to refer to Johanan; hence if, in that world, Johanan were childless, the utterance in that world of 'Deutero-Isaiah had five sons' would state a falsehood. It is this which has the result that sentences regimented as 'Necessarily: A(Deutero-Isaiah)' and 'Necessarily: A(the author of the prophecy)' may have different truth-values.

So far, then, the modal case resembles the temporal one; but, of several respects in which they differ, the one important for our purpose is that, in the semantic theory for modal discourse, we do not need to consider utterances as indexed by possible worlds. We do not require of the theory that it contain any part explicitly laying down when an utterance, taken as made in some other possible world, is true or is false: it need deal only with utterances considered as made in the actual world. That is not to say that it applies, or could be construed as applying, only to actual utterances: for every sentence S, speaker x and time t, it must assign a truth-value to $\langle S, x, t \rangle$, without our having to know, in general, whether or not x uttered S at t. The reason why we do not need the theory to lay down the truth-conditions of utterances considered as made in other possible worlds, and so do not need to index utterances by worlds, is not that we are indifferent to what truth-value an utterance would have had if the circumstances had been different, but, rather, that the theory, if adequate at all, will be adequate to tell us this without any special mechanism for doing so. Suppose that we have a semantic theory for some language containing no modal expressions. The theory will lay down the principles determining the truth-value of any utterance of a sentence of the language in a manner that depends, in general, on how, in certain respects, things are in the world; but the theory will not itself state how things are in those respects. For this reason, we can use the theory just as well to say what truth-value an utterance would have had in certain hypothetical circumstances as we can use it to say what truth-value it has in the actual circumstances, once we have established what those are: we use the theory in exactly the same way to do both things, and it is irrelevant that the theory itself contains no apparatus of possible circumstances. The semantic theory is, in this regard, just like any other theory: a theory of celestial mechanics will enable us to determine how the planets would move if the Sun's mass were a tenth as great again as it is just as easily as it enables us to determine their orbits given the true mass of the Sun. A theory represents the easy case for explaining the truth or correctness of counterfactuals: a counterfactual is judged correct or otherwise in just the same way as a prediction is judged as being in accordance with the theory or otherwise; it is just a matter of the values we plug in to the parameters, and the theory is indifferent to which of those values are the true ones. It makes not the slightest difference when the theory happens to be a semantic theory for modal discourse. In that case, it may work by relativizing the truth-values of utterances to possible worlds; but it still needs no special machinery to explain what the truth-values of those utterances would have been had a different possible world been the actual one. It does not, after all, tell us which possible world is the actual one, that is, which utterances are in fact true; if it did, a modal logician who knew the theory would be omniscient.

What someone who has only a grade-one understanding of a statement lacks is not, therefore, a knowledge of what would have to hold for it to be true if the circumstances were different. That is something which he does know; what he lacks is the quite distinct knowledge of the condition for the truth of the statement *with respect to* any particular possible world. At least, that is what we have to take a grade-one understanding to be if its possessor understands all that is to be understood about the sentences 'Deutero-Isaiah had five sons' and 'The author of the prophecy had five sons' except what differentiates them. One with a grade-one understanding of a singular term understands how its reference is fixed; but he does not know whether it is a rigid or a flexible designator, that is, how its denotation is determined with respect to possible worlds or hypothetical circumstances. This may be because, possessing no modal vocabulary, he does not so much as have the conception of hypothetical circumstances and of truth with respect to them; or he may have that conception, but simply be unaware how the term in question behaves when in the scope of a modal operator. In the same way, what someone who knows everything about a term save whether or not it is temporally rigid does not know is what it denotes *with respect to* times other than the time of utterance; this is quite different from the variation of its reference in accordance with the time of utterance, which is something he does understand. Suppose, for example, that we introduce the term 'Thatcherabouts', related to 'where Mrs Thatcher is' as 'here' is related to 'where I am'; and assume a semantic theory which accounts for this difference by construing 'Thatcherabouts' as temporally rigid and 'where Mrs Thatcher is' as temporally flexible. Then one who understands everything about these expressions except what differentiates them will know that the sentence, 'It is noisy Thatcherabouts', uttered at noon tomorrow, will convey an (absolutely) true statement just in case it is, at noon tomorrow, noisy at the place where Mrs Thatcher is at noon tomorrow, and that the same holds good of the sentence, 'It is noisy where Mrs Thatcher is'. What he will not know is what are the references of the two expressions with respect to times *other* than the time of utterance; ignorant of this, he will not know how to determine the truth-values of certain sentences containing temporal operators like 'always', nor, therefore, understand the difference in the truth-conditions of an utterance of 'It is always noisy Thatcherabouts' (true, for example, when said as Mrs Thatcher stands beside Niagara Falls) and of 'It is always noisy where Mrs Thatcher is' (true only if Mrs Thatcher is surrounded by a hubbub wherever she goes).

It is far from clear that Kripke sees the argument of his Preface in this light. Thus he says (p. 6) that 'there is a certain man—the philosopher we call "Aristotle"—such that, as a matter of fact, (1) is true if and only if *he* was fond of dogs'; here '(1)' denotes the statement 'Aristotle was fond of dogs'. 'The thesis of rigid designation', he continues, 'is simply . . . that the same paradigm applies to the truth conditions of (1) as it describes *counter-factual* situations.' And he says further (p. 7) that 'the actual truth conditions of (3) agree extensionally with those mentioned above for (1), assuming that Aristotle was the last great philosopher of antiquity'; (3) is the statement 'Exactly one person was last among the great philosophers of antiquity, and any such person was fond of dogs'. It seems, then, that Kripke identifies an understanding of the actual truth-conditions of the statement 'Aristotle was fond of dogs', that is, a grade-one understanding of it, with knowing, of a particular man, that the statement is true if and only if the predicate 'fond of dogs' is true of him. To know the actual truth-conditions of (1), it is enough, so far as the name 'Aristotle' is concerned, to get its reference right; at least, this is what Kripke appears to be saying, although it is surprising that he should apply the same doctrine to the statement which uses the corresponding definite description, especially when, as in (3), the sentence is expanded in Russellian fashion. It is, however, essential to his argument that what he calls 'the actual truth conditions' should be unaffected by whether we use the proper name or the definite description; at the level of a grade-one understanding, the two statements are indistinguishable. All this suggests that what is needed, in order to attain a proper, or grade-two, understanding is a grasp of the general principle governing the way the reference of the name or of the definite description is fixed; and it is just because of this suggestion that the reader is likely to assent so readily to Kripke's claim about the two grades of understanding. But, if Kripke was construing his claim in such a way—something hard to decide from his text—he was confusing two different things: one that Frege would have counted as part of the senses of the two terms, and that does not differentiate them; and that element, not included in a grasp of the sense as Frege thought of it, with respect to which the proper name differs from the definite description. It is this element, which consists in recognizing the term in question as a rigid designator or as a flexible one, which Kripke has to take as converting a grade-one understanding into one of grade two if his argument is to go through: and, when it is so taken, it is not at all so evident that he is right to claim it as an ingredient of a 'proper understanding' of the statement.

*

What merit is there in the claim? If there were a language which did not contain modal expressions, its speakers would presumably have only a grade-one understanding of the statements that could be made in it, since they would not so much as have the idea of counterfactual courses of world history. Would they be lacking a proper understanding of their own language? Or would it be, rather, that their sentences possessed only an impoverished, grade-one type of sense?

How does a speaker manifest a grade-one understanding of a statement? He does so by the way he sets about deciding or discovering whether it is in fact true, by what he says and does in response to the statement as made by someone else, and by the effect that accepting it as true has on his behaviour. In certain cases, problems arise over whether he can, by these means, fully manifest a grasp of the condition for the truth of the statement, when this is conceived, as Frege conceived it, as a condition that determinately either obtains or does not obtain, independently of our knowledge or our capacity to know. It would be out of place, however, to raise these problems in the present connection: Kripke is prescinding from them, and so shall I. We may, for present purposes, treat the conception of a speaker's grasp of what determines a statement as true or not true as being, at least in simple cases, unproblematic: it is manifested by how he decides whether it is true and by how he acts if he takes it to be true.

How, then, does a speaker manifest his possession of that ingredient of a grade-two understanding of such a statement as 'Aristotle was fond of dogs' or 'Deutero-Isaiah had five sons' which goes beyond his grade-one understanding? There is no means by which he can manifest it otherwise than by the judgments he makes concerning various counterfactual conditionals and other modal statements. Someone who has a language which lacks subjunctive conditionals and modal operators cannot express such judgments, and may be supposed incapable of the thought of counterfactual courses of history. It follows, therefore, that one whose language is of that kind cannot attain to a grade-two understanding of any statement. One who has a language containing modal expressions manifests his grade-two understanding of a given statement by his assessment of statements involving such expressions. If the given statement, with his grade-two understanding of which we are concerned, is of the kind chosen by Kripke to illustrate his argument, namely one like 'Aristotle was fond of dogs', then it does not itself contain any modal expressions. This is a point to which Kripke himself goes out of his way to call attention, remarking (p. 11) that both this statement and 'The last great philosopher of antiquity was fond of dogs' are *simple* sentences, of which neither contains modal or other operators. It follows that a speaker's grade-two understanding of such a sentence will not manifest itself in any statement he makes by uttering that sentence on its own, or any response he makes to a statement so made by another; for a grade-two understanding can be manifested only by the use of sentences containing modal expressions. His grade-two understanding of 'Aristotle was fond of dogs' will not be shown by his use of *that* sentence on its own, but by his use of other sentences represented, in the regimentation of natural language, by the result of applying a modal operator to that sentence: sentences like 'Aristotle may have been fond of dogs' and 'If Aristotle had lived in Syracuse, he would have been fond of dogs'.

In just the same way, a speaker cannot manifest his grasp of the condition for the truth with respect to a time other than the time of utterance of a statement made by means of such a sentence as 'It is noisy here' or 'It is noisy Thatcherabouts' by the use he makes of that sentence on its own, that is, uttered as a complete sentence. He does in just that way manifest his grasp of the dependence of the condition for the truth of the statement upon the time of utterance of the sentence used to make it; but his grasp of the condition for the truth of the statement with respect to some *other* time will be shown only by the use he makes of more complex sentences. The more complex sentences which are relevant to this are ones like 'It is always noisy here' and 'It will be noisy Thatcherabouts at noon tomorrow'. Such sentences contain temporal operators, or, more exactly, their regimented versions do; in this they differ from those like 'It is noisy here' and 'It is noisy where Mrs Thatcher is', which are, in the relevant respect, simple sentences.

A grade-two understanding of a modally simple sentence, which Kripke claims as an essential part of a proper understanding of it, is therefore manifested, not by the use that the speaker makes of it on its own, but by the use he makes of other regimented sentences in whose regimented versions it figures as a subsentence. When the understanding of a subsentential expression is in question, what is at issue is the contribution made by that expression to the meanings of all sentences in which it can significantly occur. There is no other way of regarding the matter, since the expression cannot be used on its own, but only as part of some sentence. When it is the understanding of a *sentence* that is in question, however, we must distinguish, as was stated on pp. 446–7 of *FPL*, between two levels of understanding. Because the sentence *can* be used on its own, we may concern ourselves solely with that understanding which is sufficient for comprehending it when it is so used. Where the sentence is an assertoric one, this amounts to grasping the content of an assertion made by uttering the sentence on its own, and was referred to in *FPL* as 'knowing the content' of the sentence. Since, on the other hand, the sentence may, instead, form part of a more complex sentence, we may also consider it as if it were a subsentential expression, and enquire what is needed to grasp its contribution to the content of any sentence of which it is a constituent. Understanding the principle governing this contribution was called in *FPL* 'knowing the ingredient sense' of the sentence. A grasp of the ingredient sense of a sentence always includes a grasp of its content, whereas the converse does not, in general, hold. A grasp of the ingredient sense may therefore be contrasted with a grasp of the content as constituting a full understanding, as opposed to a partial one. On the other hand, it is a grasp of the content of a sentence that is the primary notion. When it is said, following Frege, that the notion of sentence-meaning has a certain primacy over that of word-meaning, it is the content of sentences, their meanings when used on their own, rather than as parts of other sentences, that is regarded as primary. This is because meanings can be ascribed to subsentential expressions only in so far as they contribute to the meanings of sentences used on their own, that is, as they contribute to determining the content of sentences in which they occur. In the same way, whatever more, beyond the content of a sentence, that we need to know in order to grasp its ingredient sense is required only for a grasp of the content of complex sentences containing the given one as a constituent. For this reason, the first step towards an account of what meaning is consists in characterizing correctly what grasping the content of a sentence amounts to. The subsequent steps are not determined by this first one; but they cannot be right unless the first one is right. We cannot deduce, from knowing what is involved in understanding a sentence as used on its own, just what contribution is made to its meaning by the subsentential expressions that compose it; but we know that their meanings must be explained as making such a contribution.

Kripke's thesis of the two ingredients in a proper understanding seems to contradict Frege's account of what it is to grasp the sense of a sentence, since this amounts only to what Kripke regards—or ought to regard, if his argument is to have a chance of working—as a mere grade-one understanding of it. It has now appeared, however, that the additional ingredient that would convert a grade-one understanding into one of grade two relates solely to the use of the sentence as a constituent in a complex modal sentence. It follows that Frege's main tenet is not contradicted at all. His main tenet was that a grasp of what I am calling the content of a sentence consists in knowing what condition must hold for the thought expressed by an utterance of it to be true. Kripke's remarks in his Preface give the appearance that he is contending that this forms only *half* of what goes to make up an understanding of the sentence and that there is another equally important ingredient. But this appearance is illusory. When his argument is freed of misleading suggestions, it does not appear as supporting a claim that there is anything more than Frege supposes that is involved in understanding a sentence as used on its own; it supports only the claim that we need to know something further about the sentence if we are to be able to understand modal sentences in whose regimented versions it occurs as a constituent. Even this claim is at variance with Frege's theory; not with its main tenet, however, but only with a subsidiary one. Frege does not draw the distinction drawn here between content and ingredient sense. He does not need to do so because he holds a subsidiary tenet: namely that, in a logically correct language, a constituent sentence will contribute to the determination of the truth-value of a complex one in which it occurs only via its own truth-value. Given this subsidiary tenet, ingredient sense will coincide with content, and there will be no need to distinguish them. Now, indeed, if modal auxilaries and adverbs are to be represented as sentential operators, this subsidiary tenet must be relinquished, whatever the specific semantic theory adopted; the same holds good if we adopt a tense logic and construe temporal reference as effected by sentential operators. But the tenet is only a subsidiary one: repudiation of it is quite consistent with maintenance of the principal tenet, that a grasp of the content of a sentence, as used on its own, consists wholly in an understanding of the condition required for its truth.

*

The question whether what differentiates a grade-two from a grade-one understanding of a sentence relates only to its ingredient sense or to its content is entangled, in Kripke's discussion, with the much more special question whether the mechanism of scope is adequate to replace that of rigid designation.

Since Frege, philosophers engaged on logical analysis have usually proceeded, as he did, in two stages. The first stage is to transform sentences of natural language into what Quine calls a 'regimented' form; the second is to construct a semantic theory whose direct application is to the regimented language. The semantic theory states how each sentence of the regimented language is determined, in accordance with its composition, as true or as false; it indirectly assigns truth-conditions to sentences of natural language in virtue of the mapping of those sentences on to regimented ones.[1] The entire analysis is to be judged successful or unsuccessful by whether the truth-conditions thus indirectly assigned to sentences of natural language accord with our intuitive understanding of those sentences. The regimentation cannot be judged correct or incorrect in isolation: it has no significance on its own, but only as supplying the syntactic forms to which we formulate the semantic theory as applying.

Virtually all such regimentations involve the use of quantifiers and bound variables to express generality, as introduced by Frege. In the present case, we are tacitly assuming that, in the regimented sentences, modality will be expressed by means of sentential operators such as the '$\Box$' and '$\Diamond$' of modal logic. In talking about rigid designation, we are also tacitly assuming something about the semantic theory: namely, that it will involve a structure of possible worlds, sentences in the regimented language bearing truth-values

---

[1] Strictly speaking, we should continue to speak, not of a sentence, but of an utterance of it by a particular speaker at a particular time, or of the statement made by means of that utterance, as true or false; but, for ease of exposition, we may in this connection ignore indexicality.

relativized to those possible worlds. It remains the aim of the theory to explain what determines each such sentence as true or false absolutely; the absolute truth-value of any sentence will coincide with its truth-value relative to the actual world.

In relativizing to possible worlds the truth-values of sentences, we necessarily likewise relativize the application or satisfaction of predicates. If in the regimented language there are definite descriptions, treated as genuine terms, this will carry with it also the relativization to possible worlds of the denotation of a term. Likewise, if the language admits functors such as 'the wife of x', it is intuitively plausible that complex terms formed by means of them should have different denotations in different worlds. However we regard simple terms (proper names), it will also be intuitively natural to allow them to lack denotations in certain worlds. If the language allows quantification into the scope of modal operators, we cannot circumvent these problems by choosing to regard the domains of different worlds as disjoint. '$\exists x \Diamond A(x)$' will be true with respect to a world w iff there is in the domain of w some object i such that, for some world v possible relatively to w, '$A(x)$' is true of i with respect to v. We therefore need the notion of a predicate's being true, with respect to some possible world, of an object in the domain of another world. The easiest way to obtain such a notion is by identifying objects in the domains of different worlds; and there is nothing to be gained by refusing to make such identifications.

Since this is so, the notion of the scope of a term is available to us if we wish to use it. We may, that is, distinguish between a sentence of the form '$B(t)$', where 't' is a term, and one of the form '$\{\lambda x.\ B(x)\}\ (t)$', in which '$t$' stands outside the scope of any operators occurring in '$B(x)$'. If 't' denotes an object i in w, '$\{\lambda x.\ B(x)\}\ (t)$' will be true with respect to w iff '$B(x)$' is true of i with respect to w. If '$B(x)$' contains no modal operator, this will also be the condition for the truth, with respect to w, of '$B(t)$'; but, if some modal operator occurs within '$B(x)$', it may not. Suppose, for example, that '$B(x)$' is '$\Diamond A(x)$'. Then '$B(t)$' will be true with respect to w just in case, for some world v possible relatively to w, '$A(t)$' is true with respect to v, and hence provided that 't' denotes some object j in v such that '$A(x)$' is true of j with respect to v. The condition for the truth with respect to w of '$\{\lambda x.\ B(x)\}\ (t)$', on the other hand, is that there should be some world u possible relatively to w such that '$A(x)$' is true of i with respect to u. According to the way the term 't' behaves, this condition may not be equivalent to that for the truth of '$B(t)$' with respect to w. Suppose, for example, that i is not identical with j, where 't' denotes j in v. If there is no world u possible relatively to w in which 't' denotes an object of which '$A(x)$' is true with respect to u, then '$\Diamond A(t)$' is false with respect to w. But if '$A(x)$' is true of i with respect to v, '$\{\lambda x.\ \Diamond A(x)\}(t)$' will be true with respect to w.

We have here violated what may be called the fundamental principle concerning predicates, namely that a predicate is true of an object just in case any sentence that results from inserting a term denoting that object in the argument-place of the predicate is true. Frege would have abhorred any violation of this principle, since, in accordance with his principle of the extraction of functions, he believed the sense of a sentence to be given in advance of the sense of a complex predicate from which it was extracted: the fundamental principle concerning predicates constituted, for him, the explanation of what it is for a complex predicate to be true of an object. But a possible-worlds semantics involves, of itself, a considerable departure from Frege's own two-valued semantic theory; we should therefore be unsurprised that it supplies a rationale for a violation of the fundamental principle. It is, perhaps, inappropriate to use the λ-notation to construct predicate abstracts which do not satisfy the principle of λ-conversion, which is just a form of the fundamental principle concerning predicates; but this is only a point of notational etiquette.

Now consider the sentence 'The author of the prophecy died in infancy', where 'the prophecy' is understood as before. Let us agree that it is impossible for an infant to compose a prophecy, or for anyone to compose one after he is dead. Let us assume further that the phrase 'the author of the prophecy' is represented in the regimented language by a genuine singular term, which we may abbreviate as 't', and that the denotation of 't' in different possible worlds is such as to bring out true, with respect to any world in which 't' has a denotation, the regimented version of 'The author of the prophecy composed the prophecy'. Then the regimented version of 'The author of the prophecy died in infancy', which we may abbreviate as '$D(t)$', will be false with respect to every world in which 't' has a denotation. Accordingly '$\Diamond D(t)$' will come out as false absolutely.

Does this accord with intuition? If we take '$\Diamond D(t)$' as the regimentation of 'The author of the prophecy might have died in infancy', we get an equivocal verdict (or a hung jury). Kripke, like most of us, would regard such a sentence as ambiguous. Taken one way, it is false, since the author of the prophecy must have lived long enough to compose a prophecy; and, so understood, it is properly regimented as '$\Diamond D(t)$'. But, understood another way, it is true; for the man who in fact composed the prophecy was, as an infant, as liable as any other to fatal disease or accident. So understood, therefore, it must be regimented differently; for instance as '$\{\lambda x.\ \Diamond D(x)\}(t)$'. If '$t$' denotes i in the actual world, there is a possible world v such that

'$D(x)$' is true of i with respect to v; hence this sentence of the regimented language is true, and our conflicting linguistic intuitions are both vindicated.

Now what is our intuition concerning the sentence 'Deutero-Isaiah might have died in infancy'? One may think it ambiguous in just the same way as 'The author of the prophecy might have died in infancy'; one may hold that to say, 'Deutero-Isaiah could not have died in infancy, since someone who composed no prophecy would not have been Deutero-Isaiah', is to express, not conceptual confusion, but an intuition as worthy of respect as that voiced by Kripke in saying that someone with different parents would not have been Socrates. In *FPL*, I argued for just such a position, with regard to the sentence 'St. Anne might not have been a parent' (p. 113). For present purposes, however, let us adopt Kripke's view that 'Deutero-Isaiah might have died in infancy' is unambiguously true. How is our theory to account for this?

Two strategies are possible. One is to appeal once more to the mechanism of scope. On this account, the expression 'Deutero-Isaiah' is, like 'the author of the prophecy', to be represented in the regimented language by the term 't', whose denotation in possible worlds we have already considered. The regimented versions of 'Deutero-Isaiah died in infancy' and of 'The author of the prophecy died in infancy' will then be the same, namely '$D(t)$'. This is not to say that 'Deutero-Isaiah' and 'the author of the prophecy', considered as expressions of natural language, behave, on this account, in exactly the same way. Sentences containing 'Deutero-Isaiah' demand to be understood in such a way that, in regimenting them, the term that represents 'Deutero-Isaiah', namely 't', is given the widest possible scope. Hence 'Deutero-Isaiah might have died in infancy' must be regimented as '$\{\lambda x.\ \Diamond D(x)\}(t)$', which is true; it does not admit the regimentation '$\Diamond D(t)$'.

Alternatively, we may represent 'Deutero-Isaiah' by a distinct term 'd' of the regimented language, which is stipulated in the semantic theory to be a rigid designator, i.e. to denote in every possible world the object identical with the actual referent of 'Deutero-Isaiah' (or of 't'). In this case, 'Deutero-Isaiah might have died in infancy' may be regimented as '$\Diamond D(d)$'; as Kripke remarks, this sentence will have the same truth-conditions as '$\{\lambda x.\ \Diamond D(x)\}(d)$'.

Which of these two analyses ought we to prefer? Linguistic intuition will not help us here, at least in so far as it relates to the truth-conditions of sentences of natural language, since both analyses ascribe exactly the same truth-conditions to such sentences. If 'Deutero-Isaiah' denotes i in the actual world, then, on both analyses, 'Deutero-Isaiah might have died in infancy' will be true just in case, for some world v, '$D(x)$' is true of i with respect to v; and this is in both cases a direct, rather than a remote, consequence of the stipulations of the theory. If the linguistic phenomena with which an analysis is required to accord are our intuitions concerning the conditions under which a statement made in natural language is true or false, neither analysis can have any advantage over the other.

The choice between them may seem important, however. On the second analysis, the regimentation '$D(d)$' of 'Deutero-Isaiah died in infancy' is true with respect to any possible world v such that '$D(x)$' is true of i with respect to v. In such a world, 't' will not of course denote i, but may denote some other object j of which '$D(x)$' is not true with respect to v. On the first analysis, however, the regimentation of 'Deutero-Isaiah died in infancy' will be '$D(t)$', and this will be false with respect to v. We ought not, strictly speaking, to describe sentences of natural language, but only their regimentations, as being true or false with respect to possible worlds; but if, as is very natural, we do so, the two analyses will in this way attribute to the simple (unmodalized) sentence 'Deutero-Isaiah died in infancy' different relativized truth-conditions. Moreover, we may well be disposed to follow what may be called 'the modal involvement principle', namely that a sentence of natural language is *possibly true* just in case '$\lozenge P$' is true absolutely, where 'P' is the regimentation of that sentence. If we do, then, on the second analysis, 'Deutero-Isaiah died in infancy' will be possibly true, since '$\lozenge D(d)$' is true absolutely. On the first analysis, however, the regimentation of 'Deutero-Isaiah died in infancy' is '$D(t)$', and '$\lozenge D(t)$' is false. This is so despite the fact that 'Deutero-Isaiah might have died in infancy' is true, since the latter sentence is not to be represented as '$\lozenge D(t)$'; hence the simple sentence of natural language is not, on the first analysis, possibly true, although it is on the second. Thus the choice between the two analyses will affect the modal status we assign to unmodalized sentences of natural language.

Does this provide a ground for preferring one or the other analysis? It would do so only if our intuitions concerned the modal status of sentences as well as their truth-conditions; but they do not, or, if they do, they give conflicting testimony. Kripke himself acknowledges two types of modal status, epistemic and metaphysical, to explain this apparent conflict; it is hardly to be claimed that this distinction is clear to unreflective intuition. In ordinary discourse, we seldom assign modal status at all, that is, use predicates applying to sentences or statements; instead, we use modal auxiliaries or adverbs to form sentences over whose truth-conditions the two analyses, as we have seen, do not differ. Indeed, modal status is here being explained in terms of the truth of a modalized sentence by appeal to the modal involvement principle. The principle could not be applied directly to natural language without, in some cases, giving equivocal results: we could not decide the modal status of 'The author of the prophecy died in infancy' by reference to the truth-value of 'The author of the prophecy might have died in infancy', because of the ambiguity of the latter sentence. The principle applies, in the first instance, to sentences of the regimented language; so it cannot help us to choose between alternative analyses, since its outcome depends upon which analysis has been selected.

In his Preface, Kripke says (p. 10), 'it seems to me to be wrong to suppose that *all* our intuitions can be handled' in terms of scope. In discussing this question, we must distinguish between intuitions as to the truth-conditions of sentences of natural language and intuitions as to other matters. In respect of the former, it seems demonstrable that the mechanism of scope is adequate to the purpose. To treat a term, say 'd', as a rigid designator is to take it as denoting, in each possible world, the object i which it denotes in the actual world, provided i is in the domain of the possible world. This has the effect that, for any predicate '$C(x)$', '$C(d)$' is true with respect to a world v iff '$C(x)$' is true of i with respect to v. But, if 't' is any term whose actual referent is i, then, no matter what t denotes in v, '$\{\lambda x.\ C(x)\}(t)$' will likewise be true with respect to v iff '$C(x)$' is true of i with respect to v; so '$C(d)$' and '$\{\lambda x.\ C(x)\}\ (t)$' will be strictly equivalent. Kripke must, therefore, be speaking of intuitions that bear on something other than the conditions under which what we say is true.

What, then, are these other intuitions? Having remarked that not all our intuitions can be handled in terms of scope, Kripke continues (pp. 10–11), 'I dealt with this question rather briefly, on page 62' of *Naming and Necessity*[1] 'and in the accompanying footnote 25, but the discussion seems to have been overlooked by many readers. In the footnote I adduce some linguistic phenomena that, I think, support the rigidity intuition as opposed to an explanation in terms of scope'. In the footnote, he remarked that one may truly say that the teacher of Alexander might not have taught Alexander, and, in that case, would not have been the teacher of Alexander, although it is untrue that Aristotle might not have been Aristotle; even if he had not taught Alexander, he would still have been Aristotle. I am not one of those who overlooked Kripke's discussion: I commented on it on pp. 113–14 of *FPL*, citing both that page and the accompanying footnote. I explained how the ambiguity of 'The teacher of Alexander might not have been the teacher of Alexander' could be resolved by appeal to scope, and cited Kripke as

[1] P. 279 of the original article.

having said the same himself on that very page. This example could not easily be handled in terms of rigid and flexible designation, for two reasons. First, the sentence is ambiguous, whereas a stipulation that an expression is a rigid designator leaves no room for ambiguity; and, secondly, 'the teacher of Alexander' could not be treated as a rigid designator in both occurrences. The most we could say was that, in its second occurrence, it was understood as a flexible designator, but that the first occurrence could be taken as flexible or as rigid, locating the ambiguity in the *term* and not, as on a scope explanation, in the construction; but this would be an obviously unhappy solution.

Why, then, does Kripke claim all this as an intuitive ground for an explanation in terms of rigid designation? The argument is that, if 'Aristotle' were a flexible designator, 'Aristotle might not have been Aristotle' would be ambiguous and capable of being construed as true, whereas it is neither. Rigid designation is not, however, itself a linguistic phenomenon: it is a device of semantic theory to explain certain linguistic phenomena. It would be quite wrong to deny that proper names behave differently in certain ways from definite descriptions; the fact that, in particular, expressions of the two kinds behave differently when they follow verbs such as 'to be' and 'to become' is specifically noted in *FPL*, pp. 131–2. In the present context, we are, for the sake of argument, assuming that Kripke is wholly right about these differences, to the extent of granting that 'Deutero-Isaiah might have died in infancy' is *unambiguously* true. What is at issue is not the linguistic phenomenon, but whether the mechanism of scope is adequate to explain it. Reliance on this mechanism involves understanding the use of proper names in natural language as governed by a convention requiring us to represent sentences containing them so as to accord them the widest scope. Such a thesis is quite sufficient to explain why 'Aristotle might not have been Aristotle' is unambiguously false, namely as saying, of the referent of 'Aristotle', that he might not have been identical with himself: the question relates to the truth-conditions of that sentence, concerning which, as already remarked, the two rival analyses agree. There is, indeed, more to be said on this subject; I shall revert to it below.

When, in his Preface, Kripke addresses himself particularly to my observations in *FPL*, he raises a different point. On p. 11, he states my view as being that 'the doctrine of rigidity simply *is* the doctrine that natural language has a convention that a name, in the context of any sentence, should be read with a wide scope including all modal operators'. 'This latter idea,' he comments, 'is particularly wide of the mark; in terms of modal logic, it represents a technical error.' His basis for this charge is that

'Aristotle was fond of dogs' and 'The last great philosopher of antiquity was fond of dogs' are simple sentences in the sense that neither contains modal operators; there is therefore no room for any scope distinctions. 'No scope convention about more complex sentences affects the interpretation of *these* sentences. Yet the issue of rigidity makes sense as applied to both. My view is that "Aristotle" . . . is rigid, but "the last great philosopher of antiquity" . . . is not. No hypothesis about scope conventions for modal contexts expresses this view; it is a doctrine about the truth conditions, with respect to counterfactual situations, of . . . *all* sentences, including *simple* sentences' (pp. 11–12).

This argument leaves it obscure at which level it is intended to apply: at that of our intuitions concerning sentences of natural language, or at that of our regimentations of those sentences and the semantic theory we present as governing them. At the latter level, it is certainly correct. Let v be a world in which the individual who in fact composed the prophecy died in infancy, but in which someone else composed the very same prophecy. Then, on the first of the two analyses discussed above, 'Deutero-Isaiah died in infancy' is represented by a regimented sentence '$D(t)$' which is false with respect to v, whereas, on the second analysis, it is represented by a sentence '$D(d)$' which is true with respect to v. Hence, if we accept the modal involvement principle, 'Deutero-Isaiah died in infancy' is necessarily false under the first analysis, but possibly true under the second. Kripke's argument is irrelevant if it is concerned only to make this point, which is indeed a 'technical' one. It has force only if it be held that, among the linguistic intuitions to which a logical analysis is to be held responsible, there are ones which bear, not upon the absolute truth or falsity of what we say, but upon its truth or falsity with respect to hypothetical circumstances, or upon its modal status.

We do, indeed, have (faltering) intuitions as to the truth or falsity of modalized sentences of natural language; but these are not here to the point, since both analyses rate 'Deutero-Isaiah might have died in infancy' as true. Truth or falsity with respect to possible worlds is a very different thing from the truth or falsity of counterfactual conditionals. For one thing, a sound judgment that, if Jones had attended the meeting, he would have proposed a vote of censure on the chairman, does not amount to a judgment that it would have been *impossible* for Jones to attend the meeting without proposing a vote of censure; its truth therefore does not demand that 'Jones proposed a vote of censure' is true with respect to every possible world with respect to which 'Jones attended the meeting' is true. For another thing, we may judge a counterfactual statement to be correct without committing ourselves to accepting the antecedent as stating a genuine possibility. The notion of truth-value with respect to possible worlds is a technical one, which may or may not admit a coherent explanation, but belongs to semantic theory rather than to that understanding of our own language which is the datum for such theory. The same holds good for modal status. We have no intuition that 'Deutero-Isaiah died in infancy' is possibly true other than our intuition that 'Deutero-Isaiah might have died in infancy' is true; as already noted, the latter intuition is supported by both analyses. We hardly use such expressions as 'possibly true' in ordinary discourse, and, to the extent that we do, not in so firm a way as to provide support for one analysis as against the other. Indeed, it would be quite a natural thing to say that 'Deutero-Isaiah died in infancy' could not possibly be true. Kripke would account for this by conceding that, though possibly true, the sentence is false a priori; but he can scarcely hope to ground so subtle a distinction on untutored intuition. In any case, the most obvious intuitive reason for claiming the sentence as possibly true is an appeal to the modal involvement principle, that is, to an explanation of modal status in terms of the truth of modalized sentences.

We have here, in effect, the same point as that involved in the discussion of an understanding of grade one and grade two. A grade-two understanding of a simple sentence relates, as does the thesis that it contains a rigid designator, to its truth-conditions with respect to counterfactual situations (possible worlds). But Kripke fails to ask for what purpose we need to consider the truth-value of a sentence with respect to a counterfactual situation. The answer is that we need the notion only in order to explain the contribution of that sentence to the content of more complex sentences of which it is a constituent; it serves, on a particular type of semantic theory, to explain the ingredient sense of the sentence, and is quite irrelevant to the content of the sentence when used on its own. We can, if we like, say of someone who has only a grade-one understanding of a simple sentence that he does not know the truth-conditions of the sentence with respect to other possible worlds. We can point out that this is a feature of *that sentence*, a sentence which contains no modal expression. But all this is a kind of empty rhetoric, so long as we can point to no deficiency in his understanding of the sentence as used on its own. If his failure to grasp the truth-conditions of the sentence with respect to other possible worlds is manifested only in his inability to grasp the content of sentences in which the given one occurs as a constituent, then that is what he does not understand; to make any more sweeping claim is just playing with words.

If anyone doubts the correctness of these conclusions, a simple thought-experiment is available to him. Kaplan's expression 'dthat' serves, as already explained, to render any term to which it is prefixed a rigid designator. If the notion of rigidity has an intuitive base, then this explanation does not represent merely the employment of a particular semantic theory to determine the truth-conditions of sentences of English supplemented by the word 'dthat', but encapsulates the implicit understanding that we should, as ordinary speakers, have of that word. Now the use of the notion of rigid designation does not deprive us of the notion of scope. The conception of modal expressions as requiring to be regimented as sentential operators makes the notion of scope available, since it is intrinsic to linguistic operators to have scope; and, as we have seen, the necessity to relativize the denotations of terms to possible worlds will, in general, involve that the truth-conditions of a sentence will be affected by whether a term stands within or outside the scope of a modal operator. We may therefore intelligibly imagine the addition of another word, 'dthis', to English; when prefixed to a term, 'dthis' leaves the denotation of the term, in any possible world, unaffected, but serves to signal that the term is to be construed as lying outside the scope of any modal operator. The sentences 'Dthis the author of the prophecy died in infancy' and 'Dthat the author of the prophecy died in infancy' are now related exactly as are the two analyses of 'Deutero-Isaiah died in infancy'. Since no modal operator occurs in the sentence, 'Dthis the author of the prophecy died in infancy' has exactly the same semantic properties as 'The author of the prophecy died in infancy'; it will be false with respect to the world v mentioned above, and will be regimented as '$D(t)$'. 'Dthat the author of the prophecy died in infancy', on the other hand, will be true with respect to the world v, and will be regimented as '$D(\theta t)$', where 'θ' represents 'dthat', so that 'θt' is equivalent to 'd'. However, 'Dthis the author of the prophecy might have died in infancy' and 'Dthat the author of the prophecy might have died in infancy' will both be unambiguously true. The former will be regimented as '$\{\lambda x. \Diamond D(x)\}(t)$' and the latter as '$\Diamond D(\theta t)$'; but these will have the same relativized truth-conditions. Now, if Kripke is right, 'dthat' and 'dthis' would have intuitively distinct meanings; English speakers who had attained to a proper understanding of the language would apprehend the difference between them. If I am right, on the other hand, there would be no difference between the two words, considered as expressions of natural language; the apparent difference arises only because we have chosen to adopt different mechanisms for explaining identical linguistic phenomena. It appears to me that nothing could be more evident than that no fact of actual linguistic usage would correspond to this difference in explanatory mechanism; no linguistic intuition is available to decide which is the right mechanism to invoke to account for the facts of linguistic practice.

*

The decision between the mechanisms of scope and rigidity must therefore be made on grounds of convenience. One such ground in favour of rigidity is the greater notational simplicity: we do not have to employ predicate abstracts. This may seem untrue, since, when there is ambiguity in the natural-language sentence, we shall have to resolve it by appeal to scope, unless we are willing to say that the same singular term may function now as a rigid designator, now as a flexible one. To illustrate the notion of scope, Russell imagined someone saying, 'I thought your yacht was larger than it is', and receiving the facetious or testy reply, 'Of course it is not larger than it is.' In a similar manner, if someone says, 'Suppose that Venice had been founded ten years later than it was', he might receive the rejoinder, 'How could any city be founded ten years after its foundation?'. To express the first speaker's meaning, we must understand him as supposing, of the year in which Venice was founded, that Venice should have been founded ten years after it. But, so long as such ambiguities arise only in connection with definite descriptions, or what can be represented as such, we can, by adopting Russell's theory of descriptions, remove them from the scope of any operator without employing predicate abstracts. More generally, however we handle definite descriptions, we know that questions of scope will arise for them, unless, like Frege, we guarantee them a reference: it therefore seems natural to invoke the notion of scope in connection with them, but far less natural to invoke it in connection with proper names. Nevertheless, whenever it is open to question whether or not a name has a referent, the notion of scope becomes applicable to it; and no theory can plausibly guarantee an ordinary name a reference in every possible world.

Against the greater notational convenience of the rigidity mechanism stands its lack of suppleness. By deeming a term to be a rigid designator, we rule out the possibility of ambiguity: one who says that Deutero-Isaiah could not have died in infancy has to be condemned as mistaken or confused. More exactly, he must be understood as using 'could' in a different sense, to express epistemic rather than metaphysical possibility: 'Deutero-Isaiah lived long enough to compose a prophecy' expresses a truth of the kind characterized by Kripke as a priori though contingent. Its a priori character is, however, something of which the semantic theory can give no account. Metaphysical necessity satisfies a modal involvement principle: 'P' is metaphysically necessary just in case '$\Box P$' is true. By contrast, there is no sentence of the (regimented) object-language to which the semantic theory applies whose truth is equivalent to the a priori truth of 'Deutero-Isaiah lived long enough to compose a prophecy'. If we employ the scope mechanism, on the other hand, and regiment the sentence as '$L(t)$', its a priori truth becomes equivalent to the truth of '$\Box L(t)$, and its contingency to the truth of '$\{\lambda x. \neg \Box L(x)\}(t)$'. Both the intuition underlying the contention that Deutero-Isaiah might have died in infancy, and that underlying the contention that he could not have done, receive expression in the regimented language if we adopt the mechanism of scope.

*

Let us say that a term so understood that its referent is taken to be the unique object satisfying a certain condition is a *signifying* term, leaving it open whether or not all singular terms are in this sense signifying ones. Then, for any signifying term, there are two natural ways in which its denotation in possible worlds may be fixed. (i) If it is a flexible designator, its referent in a world v will be that object, if any, which in v satisfies the condition in question. (ii) If it is a rigid designator, its referent in v will be that object which in the actual world satisfies the condition. Suppose, now, that the condition is one which is uniquely and necessarily satisfied by any object which satisfies it. Then, whether we apply principle (i) or principle (ii), the term will denote the same object in every possible world in which it denotes any. We may call it a *modally neutral* designator, neither rigid nor flexible.

On Kripke's definition, such a term would be rigid: why alter the terminology? The reason is that, if the only signifying terms whose denotations did not vary from one world to another were modally neutral ones, we should need no *doctrine* of rigid designation: the same semantic principle (i) could be taken as governing all signifying terms. To specify a particular possible world, we should have to stipulate the truth, with respect to it, of a large number of unmodalized sentences. The possible world so specified is taken to provide a model of this set of sentences. But not just *any* model: the sentences are not treated as uninterpreted formulas, but as carrying their ordinary meanings. If one of the sentences is 'All sheep are blue', then, in that world, animals of the kind we call 'sheep' will have the colour we call 'blue'. Hence, for us so much as to form the conception of a possible world, we must presume that most words used in specifying it will be subject to a generalization of principle (i): something will, with respect to that world, satisfy the predicate 'x is blue' just in case it would correctly be called 'blue' by someone in that world who used the word 'blue' on the same understanding of it as governs our use. It is the deviations from this general principle, such as rigid designators, for which we need to make special stipulations. No such stipulations are required for neutral designators.

This is why, in alluding to the temporal analogue, I did not cite as temporally rigid designators terms like 'Mrs Thatcher' or 'Trafalgar Square', but ones like 'here' and 'Thatcherabouts'. The question whether a signifying term is modally rigid or flexible arises only if the associated condition is satisfied by different objects in different possible worlds. In an analogous way, the question whether a term is temporally rigid or flexible arises only if its reference varies systematically with the time of utterance, that is, if it is temporally indexical: if its reference, with respect to the time of utterance, does not vary with that time, it is temporally neutral. If it is indexical, its reference with respect to the time t of utterance will be a certain function of t, say $\psi(t)$. There will then, again, be two possibilities concerning its reference with respect to a time t other than the time of utterance. (i) If it is temporally flexible, like 'where I am' or 'where Mrs Thatcher is', its reference with respect to t' will be $\psi(t')$. (ii) If it is temporally rigid, like 'here' or 'Thatcherabouts', its reference with respect to t' will be $\psi(t)$ (t being the time of *utterance*). That is why, although 'It is noisy Thatcherabouts' and 'It is noisy where Mrs Thatcher is', if uttered at the same time, must agree in truth-value, 'It will be noisy Thatcherabouts tomorrow' and 'It will be noisy tomorrow where Mrs Thatcher is' may well differ.

Just as a modally neutral term is one whose reference is fixed by means of essential properties of the object, so we may regard a temporally neutral term as one whose reference is fixed by means of permanent properties of the object. If we understand such a term, we shall know that its reference will not vary according to time at all. If all terms were temporally neutral, we should have no need to introduce the idea that, in evaluating the truth-value of a sentence with respect to a time, we must evaluate the denotation with respect to that time of a term occurring in it; the denotations of all terms would be constant over times. Since some terms are temporally flexible, we shall need, if we interpret temporal indicators as sentential operators, also to consider denotation as relativized to times; but we shall not need to introduce a special semantic doctrine concerning temporally neutral terms. Having learned how the denotation of a temporally neutral term is fixed, we shall already know that it is invariable; it is not a further feature of the use of that term of which we need to become aware, as one who understood 'here' as used in sentences involving no temporal operators might have still to become aware of its behaviour in their presence. The notion of rigidity was introduced by Kripke in connection with modality; and its application to temporal discourse is a matter of analogy. If we understand, of a modally neutral term, how its actual reference is fixed, we cannot take it as having a denotation that varies from one possible world to another; the question of variable denotation does not arise for such a term. If we were to follow Kripke in labelling modally neutral terms 'rigid designators', it would be senseless to enquire whether the linguistic phenomenon so accounted for could be explained in terms of scope. There would be no effective difference made by assigning a different scope to a term that could not intelligibly be regarded as a flexible designator, and hence to one which could not be taken to have a denotation varying with worlds (or times). But, for just that reason, we could not claim that rigidity provided a better explanation of the relevant phenomenon: there would be no linguistic phenomenon to be explained. That is why I have not here chosen to regard proper names and terms like 'the founder of the Sung dynasty', devoid of indexicality, as temporally rigid designators.

In a different respect, indeed, the analogy with modally rigid designators does apply, in the temporal dimension, to proper names. Kripke insists that, if a proper name is introduced by means of a definite description, it nevertheless does not have the same meaning as the definite description, since the latter is flexible while the name is rigid; the description represents merely the way in which the reference of the name is fixed. This applies temporally as well as modally. If the meteorologist responsible for naming hurricanes announces, 'The hurricane approaching the coast of Florida will be known as "Charlie"', no one takes him to mean that, in future parlance, the name 'Charlie' will be interchangeable with the phrase 'the hurricane approaching the coast of Florida'. The denotation of the latter phrase varies with time: but the stipulation is not understood as transmitting this feature to the newly introduced name. It was with this point that I concerned myself in Chapter 9 and in the Preface to my *Truth and other Enigmas*.[1] In this sense, therefore, the name 'Charlie' might be said to be temporally rigid: this is a genuine analogy with a feature Kripke has heavily emphasized in discussing the modal rigidity of proper names.

As already remarked, it is not this sense of 'temporally rigid' which has been used here; for the reasons explained, the analogy has here been drawn in a different way. What is not intended to carry over to a name introduced by means of a definite description is the indexicality of the latter, and, in

[1] London and Cambridge, Mass., 1978, pp. xlvi–xlviii.

particular, its temporal indexicality; and indexicality is a feature shared by what have here been called temporally rigid and temporally flexible designators. The phrase 'the hurricane now approaching the coast of Florida' has been rendered temporally rigid, in the terminology here used, by the insertion of the word 'now': in a complex sentence, its denotation with respect to any time would depend, not on that time, but solely on the time of utterance. The addition of the word 'now' would not, however, make the slightest difference to the point made above concerning our understanding of the name 'Charlie', namely as having a denotation altogether independent of time. 'Charlie' is, in the terminology here used, a temporally neutral term.

What would be the strict analogue of the non-transmission of temporal indexicality to the proper name from the definite description used to introduce it? The name 'Deutero-Isaiah' would exhibit the strictly analogous property if it were true of it that speakers in other possible worlds used it in the same way as we do but always to refer to the man who in the actual world composed the prophecy, even if he did not do so in those worlds. How, in that case, *could* they be using it in the same way as we do? It would have to be that they regarded the name as having been introduced in *our* world, but on the understanding that the manner of fixing its reference was to be taken as relative to our world and not to different worlds inhabited by other speakers. All this is, of course, nonsense, and illustrates the absurdity of regarding 'actual' as an indexical or utterances as having to be indexed by worlds.

*

It was argued earlier that Kripke is mistaken in thinking that there being an acceptable sense for 'The teacher of Alexander might not have been the teacher of Alexander', but none for 'Aristotle might not have been Aristotle', favours an explanation in terms of rigid designation rather than one in terms of scope: the difference can be explained equally well in either way. What it does appear to show is that there is a difference, to be accounted for in one way or the other, between definite descriptions and proper names. Now if the condition associated with a signifying term is one necessarily possessed by the bearer, then the term is modally neutral; and, if there are non-signifying terms, they are presumably modally neutral also, since their reference is not mediated by a condition which might have been satisfied by a different object. 'Deutero-Isaiah' is a signifying term. If someone says, 'If Deutero-Isaiah had died in infancy, he would not have been Deutero-Isaiah', there is an obvious objection, namely that it would not then have been Deutero-Isaiah who died in infancy. But the same objection can be lodged against saying, 'If the teacher of Alexander had refused the post, he would not have been the teacher of Alexander'. Hence, even if there is no acceptable sense for 'Deutero-Isaiah might not have been Deutero-Isaiah', we can grasp the sense that the speaker intended to convey. If someone were to say, 'Aristotle might not have been Aristotle', however, it seems that we could not even do that: it is not merely that he would have expressed himself wrongly, but that we should gain no idea what he was trying to express. This is because we find it hard to say what is the condition someone must satisfy to be the referent of the name 'Aristotle' as we use it. Should we say, then, that 'Aristotle' is not a signifying term, and that it is therefore modally neutral? If so, we shall need no explanation, by appeal either to a scope convention or to a semantic rule that the name is to be treated as a rigid designator, for the absurdity of 'Aristotle might not have been Aristotle'. It is here that the connection between Kripke's two theses about proper names makes itself felt; it is a great merit in his work to have reopened the question what is the nature of the connection between name and bearer. The thesis that even when, like 'Deutero-Isaiah', a proper name is a straightforwardly signifying term, it is still a rigid designator relates, however, to an altogether distinct question: by discussing examples under the *pretence* that a name like 'Aristotle' is of this kind, Kripke makes it hard to separate the two issues.

In Chapter 10 it was contended that Kripke's observations about the way in which the references of proper names are actually fixed do not tell against Frege's thesis that proper names have senses, taken as involving no more than that there be some condition which an object must uniquely satisfy for it to be the referent of a given name. It may seem that Kripke's view is not that there need be no such condition at all, but only that the condition is often one that cannot be stated without express allusion to the name itself, whereas, to ascribe sense to a name, one would have to assume a condition involving no such allusion. This can hardly be the correct interpretation, however. If, when my garage tells me that there is something wrong with the gasket of my car, I pass this information on to someone else, I, not knowing what a gasket is, cannot be said to be using the word 'gasket' to mean more than 'that part of a car which is called a "gasket" '. It is not impossible that one speaker should so use the word: what is impossible is that all who use it should use it with that meaning, for, if they did, there would be no part of a car that was called a 'gasket'. Likewise, it could not be that all speakers used the word 'sheep' to mean 'one of the animals called "sheep" ', or the name 'Socrates' to mean 'the man called

"Socrates"'. The argument is not that, if all speakers used 'sheep' and 'Socrates' in that manner, those words would lack Fregean senses: it is that it is unconditionally impossible that they should do so. A speaker may be said to use a word derivatively if he employs it with the intention that it be understood in accordance with its accepted use in the language, but does not have a full knowledge of what that use is. For it to be possible to use a word derivatively, there must be speakers who use it autonomously. Such speakers may still hold themselves responsible to the accepted use of the word, in that they will acknowledge what they say to have been mistaken if it is shown to conflict with that use; but they can convey, without reference to other speakers, what they take its accepted use to be.

This principle applies as much to proper names as to other words: the chain of communication must terminate in speakers who use the name to refer to a particular object, where their doing so does not depend upon anyone else's use of it. Only because people came to call the island 'Madagascar', wrongly believing that their use of the name conformed to that of those from whom they had acquired it, was it possible for the name to be transferred to the island from a part of the mainland. We could not understand one of Kripke's initial introductions ('baptisms') if we did not already understand the use of a name as referring to an object of the relevant kind. This does not show that derivative uses of a proper name, or other word, may not need to be mentioned in an account of its use in our language: for it is possible that all now use it as ultimately derivative upon its use in the past. Nor does it show that a proper name must have a Fregean sense: the argument does not rule it out that the autonomous use is purely referential. It shows only that derivative uses of the name cannot, of themselves, determine it as having a reference; to know what connects the name with its referent, we must look to the autonomous uses of it.

How can we decide whether a proper name, say 'Rouen', is purely referential? One ground might be that, by uttering a sentence containing it, a speaker evinces what on p. 325 was called predicative knowledge, often called *de re* knowledge, or expresses a predicative belief or, more generally, thought. That there is predicative or *de re* thought, belief and knowledge is not to be called into question. If Albert has said, 'Rouen is a beautiful city', we have a licence, when, without knowing it, he is driving through the outskirts of Rouen, to describe him as being in a city he has declared to be beautiful. To regard the name 'Rouen' as purely referential might be warranted if, by his utterance, Albert expressed an *irreducibly* predicative thought. This would be one a knowledge of the truth of which did not rest on any piece of propositional (*de dicto*) knowledge: the ascription of the predicative knowledge would constitute a complete characterization of that piece of knowledge. We saw that Frege is to be interpreted as rejecting the notion of irreducibly predicative knowledge; this is the foundation for his holding that no name or other word can be purely referential, having reference but no sense. The argument would be circular if we could not conclude that there can be no irreducibly predicative knowledge in advance of deciding that a proper name cannot be purely referential. Happily, we can show that, if irreducibly predicative knowledge is impossible, we can recognize it to be so without invoking any premiss concerning the linguistic function of proper names.

To show this, it is sufficient to show that, if there were irreducibly predicative knowledge, there would be a way of expressing it without using a proper name. Suppose there were not; and suppose Marie does not know the name 'Rouen'. Then either she can have irreducibly predicative knowledge about Rouen which she has no means of expressing, or she cannot, as yet, have such knowledge; since the former is grossly implausible, we may assume the latter. By the same token, we may assume that, by learning the name 'Rouen', she gains the ability to express irreducibly predicative knowledge about the city, since otherwise she will never be able to express such knowledge. Now either, in order to acquire the use of the name 'Rouen', she has to come to know, of the city, that the name stands for it, or she does not need to know anything about the name. The former is itself a piece of predicative knowledge. If it is not irreducibly predicative, then the name has a sense, and is not purely referential; knowledge that she expresses by uttering a sentence containing the name will then be propositional knowledge not tantamount to the corresponding predicative knowledge. If her knowing, of the city, that 'Rouen' stands for it is irreducibly predicative, then she was able, without having previously known the name, to acquire a piece of irreducibly predicative knowledge about Rouen, viz. one relating to the name; it is therefore unintelligible why she should not have been able to gain some other irreducibly predicative knowledge about it. If, finally, to acquire the name, she need learn nothing connecting it with the city, no utterance of hers involving the name will express any predicative knowledge about Rouen at all. Although there *is* such a connection, i.e. although Rouen *is* called 'Rouen', Marie, in saying, 'Rouen is a beautiful city', displays only that she knows that the city called 'Rouen' is beautiful, but does not show herself to know, of Rouen, that it is beautiful, or to know that Rouen is beautiful. Thus, in all cases, if Marie could not express irreducibly predicative knowledge about Rouen before she learned the name 'Rouen', she cannot express it when she does learn it, either.

A believer in irreducibly predicative knowledge is likely to propose, as being a means of expressing it, a sentence like 'This is a beautiful city' containing a demonstrative. Frege would not accept the subject of such a sentence as purely referential: even in such a case, the referent is given in a particular way. Not only is it given *as a city*, that is, as an object whose identification on different occasions is subject to a particular constraint, but it is given as that city in which the speaker then is, which presumably Frege would not object to describing as a way in which it could not be given to him when he was elsewhere. If even this is not to count as an expression of an irreducibly predicative thought, the conception of such a thought becomes unintelligible: there could be no thought about an object not involving its being picked out in some particular way.

That there can be no irreducibly predicative thought does not imply that there can be no purely referential terms. When an individual speaker utters, assertorically, a sentence containing the name 'Rouen', he will always be expressing a propositional belief, the complete characterization of which cannot be achieved by ascribing a predicative belief to him. In some cases, his grasp of how the name is used may not be firm enough to allow us to express his belief otherwise than as that something holds good of the city called 'Rouen'. In all other cases, there must be some connection between the name and the city of which he is aware or which he supposes to obtain; this will be embodied in a full characterization of what it is that he believes. It does not follow that the connection need be the same for all sufficiently informed speakers, i.e. for all who may be said to use the name autonomously. This is the case envisaged by Frege in which different speakers attach different senses to the name, though agreeing on its reference, which would then be its only function in the common language. There would then be no one condition to be satisfied by a city for it to be the referent of 'Rouen', and hence no thought even incorrectly expressed by 'Rouen might not have been Rouen'.

'Deutero-Isaiah might not have been Deutero-Isaiah' expresses, even if incorrectly, the thought that someone satisfied the condition for being the referent of 'Deutero-Isaiah', but might not have satisfied that condition. Would it make sense to suppose that someone other than Solomon might have satisfied the condition for being the referent of 'Solomon'? Yes: suppose that the baby born to Bathsheba had, unknown to her, been exchanged by the midwife just after birth for another baby, and that the changeling had then been given Solomon's name and had grown up to lead just the life that Solomon in fact lived. We should, in such a case, use the name 'Solomon' just as we now do, and Solomon's contemporaries would have used its

Hebrew equivalent in the same way as in fact they did: one cannot legislate that the difference of reference would have made the name different or the way it was used different. The sentence 'Solomon might not have been the referent of the name "Solomon" ' thus expresses unexceptionably a thought not only intelligible but true. To express it by 'Solomon might not have been Solomon' would indeed be incorrect: this is a case in which a name '*N*' is not interchangeable with 'die Bedeutung des Namens "*N*" ', just because the latter is a definite description. There *is*, nevertheless, a condition for being the referent of the name 'Solomon', although one of a very different kind from that for being the referent of 'Deutero-Isaiah'; which is to say that the name is *not* 'purely referential'. The former condition is altogether more diffuse; to obtain an absolutely clearcut case in which Solomon failed the condition for being the referent of 'Solomon', we had to imagine one in which almost everything in fact true of Solomon was true of someone else. Since such a case can be imagined, it is not to the present purpose to debate just how much *need* be true of someone for him to satisfy the condition. The name of a city poses further problems, since no other actual city could have been the referent of 'Venice', and we have no sharp criterion for saying in which hypothetical cases it would be a different city that occupied the site actually occupied by Venice. If the date of foundation is taken as an essential property of a city, we can then describe circumstances in which the referent of 'Venice' would not have been Venice, and perhaps conversely; but we have no clear idea what the essential properties of a city may be. It remains that an employment of a name as literally purely referential is an unintelligible fantasy. If speakers are to be able to employ a name with the same reference, they must not only intend to do so, but be able to discover whether they are doing so; since there is no irreducibly predicative knowledge, this means that the use of the name in the common language must rest on more than common reference.

*

In devising a semantic theory for temporal discourse, we may represent temporal indicators either as additional arguments for the predicates or as indices of sentential operators. Whichever we do, it is natural to frame our theory in terms of particular times, since the natural-language sentences we have to regiment contain overt references to such times, whatever philosophical analysis of the notion of a time (moment or interval) we may subsequently want to give. When modal discourse is in question, there is little obvious alternative to representing modal expressions as operators on sentences or predicates; but it is far from evident that our theory is to be framed in terms of particular possible worlds. We do not come already equipped with a conception of such possible worlds, which must therefore be introduced in the course of formulating the semantic theory; explaining it gives rise to considerable difficulties. If, despite these difficulties, we do frame our theory in terms of possible worlds, we shall need to invoke scope distinctions in regimenting sentences of natural language. We may wish also to incorporate the device of rigid designation into our semantic theory. It has here been argued that the mechanism of scope is capable of entirely replacing that of rigid designation; whether or not we choose to employ the latter is a question of pure convenience. It was noted above that Kripke stigmatizes as a technical error my saying, on pp. 127–8 of FPL_1, that the notion of rigid designation reduces to that of having wide scope. The observation he is criticizing does not appear as a technical one: it is prefaced by the remark that to speak of possible worlds is to use a metaphor, and the reduction is said to result from removing the metaphor. What concerned me was not how the semantic theory works, *given* possible worlds and the notion of denotation with respect to them, but how possible worlds and relativized denotations are to be introduced and explained. Much of the discussion in Kripke's Preface blurs this vital distinction and that between sentences of natural language and the regimentations to which we subject them. I think, however, that the passage of FPL_1 to which Kripke objects also blurs these distinctions, and is, in consequence, at best very misleading; and so I have altered it in FPL_2. In particular, the remark on p. 128 of FPL_1 that, if to be a rigid designator is to have wide scope, to be a flexible designator must be to have narrow scope, was especially liable to mislead. I was not, indeed, ascribing to Kripke the view that definite descriptions always have narrow scope in modal contexts, but expressly emphasized, on that page and elsewhere, that he took them as sometimes having wide scope. The point was, rather, that, to give a uniform account using the notion of rigid designation, we should have to eschew appeal to scope altogether; in that case, definite descriptions would have to be viewed as sometimes rigid and sometimes flexible. To invoke scope in some cases and rigid designation in others is to explain by different means similar linguistic phenomena. But the manner of expression obscured the fact that, considered as semantic devices, scope and rigid designation are quite different, even if, in explaining them, we shall have to appeal to the same intuitive notions.

Let '*a*' and '*b*' be terms whose actual reference coincides and is fixed in the same way. If '*a*' is stipulated always to have widest possible scope, and '*b*' to be a rigid designator, the significance of such stipulations depends ultimately only upon their effect on the conditions for the absolute truth of sentences containing the terms. Let '*A*' and '*B*' be any two sentences differing only in that '*b*' occurs in '*B*' where '*a*' occurs in '*A*'. Then not only will the absolute truth-values of '*A*' and '*B*' coincide, but the manner in which they are determined will be explained in the same way, namely as depending on whether or not a certain predicate is true with respect to the actual world of the common actual referent of '*a*' and '*b*'. If that predicate contains a modal operator, then, to determine whether or not it is true of the object with respect to the actual world, we shall have to consider whether or not some simpler predicate is true of that object with respect to other possible worlds; but at no step will it make a difference whether we are concerned with '*A*' or with '*B*'. Especially when they do *not* contain a modal operator, those two sentences may themselves differ in truth-value with respect to certain possible worlds, because '*a*' may be stipulated by the theory to denote different objects in those worlds; but since '*a*' must always be taken as having widest possible scope, these relativized denotations are an idle part of the machinery, with no practical effect on absolute truth-values. To say that a term is a rigid designator is not to say the same thing as that it always has wide scope; but it is very clear in what sense it amounts to saying the same thing.

Kripke unquestionably established a negative point concerning counterfactual suppositions about a named individual. Let '*b*' be a proper name such that there is some condition by means of which we fix its reference ('*b*' might be 'Deutero-Isaiah'). Then Kripke showed that, if we say, 'Suppose that *b* had done so-and-so', we are not, in general, supposing that some individual uniquely satisfied the condition and also did so-and-so. What, then, are we supposing? Our understanding of temporally rigid designators is grounded upon our grasp of identity across time; we attach a sense to 'The murder took place just here' because we know what it is for the location of a past event to be the same as the speaker's present location. In the modal case, Kripke repudiates a parallel explanation: our understanding of the use of proper names in modal contexts does not rest upon a prior or independent grasp of the criteria for transworld identity. We simply use the names in specifying the hypothetical circumstances, or possible world, we have in mind. In what way, then, does our use of them contribute to specifying those circumstances? Other words, such as 'hairy' and 'breathe', used in specifying them must retain their normal meanings, since otherwise a possible world becomes in effect a model of a set of uninterpreted sentences. The way in which the reference of a proper name is fixed is not, for Kripke, a part of its meaning, so it will not retain that; but, if it retains *nothing*, the specification of the possible world must be unaffected by our selecting one proper name rather than another. It might reasonably be said that 'Deutero-Isaiah' means 'the individual who in (actual) fact composed the prophecy'; but to assume that the name retains *this* meaning does not help us at all, since it leaves it unexplained what it is to specify a hypothetical individual to be the one who in fact did such-and-such, save if we have a condition for identity across possible worlds to appeal to. If proper names are purely referential, then what they must retain is their reference. To say that they retain nothing would be to say that, in specifying possible worlds which differed only in that all that, in one, was true of Aristotle was, in the other, true of Plato, and conversely, one would not really be specifying *distinct* possible worlds. To say that they retained their references, and nothing else, would be to say that two such worlds would indeed be distinct: the difference would just consist in its being *Aristotle* of which, in one, certain things were true, and its being *Plato* of whom they were true in the other. Indeed, there would be nothing to prevent our considering two worlds related to each other in the same way vis-à-vis, not Aristotle and Plato, but, say, Aristotle and Mt Everest.

Kripke does not, of course, occupy so absurd a position. Individuals are supposed to possess essential properties, which impose constraints on what may be specified as holding of a named individual. It may still be asked whether the totality of an individual's essential properties are jointly constitutive of its being that individual. Suppose that we are specifying a possible world, and that, to some as yet unnamed individual, we ascribe each of Saul Kripke's essential properties, perhaps without realizing that we have done so. Shall we then still be describing a *possible* world if we go on to specify that that individual is *not* Saul Kripke? If so, there is a further question: should we, by specifying the given individual not to be Saul Kripke, really be specifying a *distinct* possible world from that we should have specified had we said that he was Saul Kripke? If we say that the possibilities are not genuinely distinct, there is a plain sense in which we did not *need* the name 'Saul Kripke' to specify the circumstances we had in mind. If, on the other hand, these are distinct possibilities, the principle of distinction is mysterious. In *Naming and Necessity*, Kripke mocks the notion of 'bare particulars',[1] and the objection that this notion is involved in using proper names to specify hypothetical situations unless they are assumed to be eliminable in favour of a purely qualitative description; but, in the case here supposed, the particulars have become disquietingly bare.

[1] P. 52 (p. 272 of original). Much that philosophers have written about bare particulars indeed deserves mockery.

The alternative is that, by ascribing all Saul Kripke's essential properties to some individual, we have debarred ourselves from going on to specify that he[1] is not Saul Kripke; in this case, by proceeding to identify him as Saul Kripke, we shall be no further circumscribing the possible state of affairs than we have already done. If this is how things stand, then, if we know how to discover what Saul Kripke's essential properties are, we have, after all, a criterion for his identity across possible worlds. We may not know, and may fail to discover, those essential properties, since, according to Kripke, essence is often discovered empirically; by the same token, we cannot always know whether we have specified a possible state of affairs. In this case, we shall be unable to apply the criterion; our only way of ensuring that it is Saul Kripke we are talking about will be to mention him explicitly. Nevertheless, we are here concerned with a philosophical problem, not a practical one: what is involved in identifying an individual in hypothetical circumstances as Saul Kripke. If our notion of an essential property is sharp enough to make it determinate what his essential properties are, and if they are jointly constitutive of his being Saul Kripke, then the use of his name in modal contexts can be explained in those terms, and is in principle, though not in practice, dispensable. The criterion of transworld identity so obtained may depend upon the identification of other individuals, e.g. Saul Kripke's parents, and so be far from 'purely qualitative'. We might then consider the set consisting of Saul Kripke and all individuals his relations to whom are essential properties of his, and ask whether the essential properties of this set are jointly constitutive of its identity. If not, we have the same problems as before; but, if so, it will be interesting to ask whether, by iterating this procedure, we shall eventually arrive at a set none of whose essential properties involve reference to any individual not in the set.

If we already have a conception of identity across possible worlds, then we can, by appeal to it, give substance to the thesis that proper names are modally rigid designators. If, alternatively, we already grasp a non-trivial condition for an individual, described solely in terms of what is true of it in some possible world, to be the referent in that world of a given proper name, then to say that proper names are rigid designators fixes the condition for identity across possible worlds. But if we start from neither base, what substance does the thesis have? It gains some substance from the doctrines concerning essential properties. In imagining Kant in some hypothetical situation, we are at least imagining someone with all Kant's essential

---

[1] Or, perhaps, she: I do not know whether someone's sex is one of his or her essential properties.

properties in that situation; perhaps that is all that we have to be doing, perhaps not. This would not help at all if the notion of essential properties remained purely programmatic; in the presence of particular theses about what they are, it yields specific claims. But this is not yet anything resembling a philosophical analysis until we have some account of the principle by which a property is to be classified as essential or accidental or of the point of so classifying it. Kripke substitutes for such an account an appeal to intuition, which he defends as the most conclusive evidence one can have.[1] 'Intuition', in this connection, may refer to one of two things. One is linguistic intuition, our judgments as to the truth-conditions of various forms of sentences of natural language. With allowance for occasional confusion, this must be respected. If we are devising a semantic theory, the linguistic phenomena by its accordance with which it is to be judged correct or incorrect are our judgments as to the truth or falsity of statements of natural language, to which our opinions about how we should judge in hypothetical cases are excellent guides. 'Intuition' may also refer to the inclinations, which everyone has, to come out with various philosophical observations. A philosophical notion, like that of metaphysical necessity, cannot be based on intuition, in this sense, because the most that such inclinations may show is that there is some possibly coherent notion there, not what it is.

We are left, then, with the task of giving a systematic account of the use in natural language of counterfactual conditionals and modal sentences, and, in particular, of those which contain proper names. Suppose that the role of proper names in such sentences can be satisfactorily accounted for by a more detailed classification of properties into essential and accidental ones. We might still find ourselves in the position of failing to see what point there was in having in our language forms of sentence whose truth-conditions depended upon that classification. If we were not in that position, we should probably be able to say something explicitly to explain the point of it; or possibly it would at that stage have become so obvious as not to need stating. But, in advance of arriving at one position or the other, appeals to intuition are no substitute for elucidation: we have no clear conception of what metaphysical necessity and essential properties are, and no defence against the suspicion that, if modal discourse does rest on those notions, then it is in fact pointless.

My own belief is that there is no clear notion of essential properties to be attained, and that that of metaphysical necessity is in even worse condition. This belief is not groundless, though of course perhaps mistaken; I shall argue it elsewhere. The publishers' blurb to *Naming and Necessity*

---

[1] *Naming and Necessity*, p. 42 (p. 266 of the original).

speaks of 'today's thriving essentialist metaphysics' as largely owing its impetus to Kripke's article. They are doubtless right in holding Kripke responsible for a whole generation of philosophers talking about zygotes under the impression that they are doing metaphysics; but, though aware that I may be making a massive misjudgment, I cannot see this development as more than a diversion into a cul-de-sac.

If it is essential properties that give substance to Kripke's doctrine concerning the use of proper names in modal contexts, why talk about them as rigid designators? The notion of a rigid designator is *explained* in terms of identity; it acquires substances if we go on to explain transworld identity. Just that is what Kripke refuses to do: we need no such explanation, but simply stipulate, by using a proper name, that we are talking about the very object for which the name in fact stands. But, if our conception of identity across possible worlds is mediated solely by our use of proper names in modal contexts, it plays no effective role in explaining that use; the characterization of proper names as rigid designators is emptied of content if our notion of its being the same object that we are talking about springs solely from our using the same name.

The answer is that, although he declines to explain either, Kripke rightly perceives that our intuitive notion of the identity of objects across distinct possible states of affairs is linked with our use of proper names in modal contexts. That we have such a notion is evident from our use of sentences demanding the attribution of wide scope: if I say, 'The man I'm pointing at might have been in Rome', I do not invite the retort, 'How could you point at him if he were in Rome?'. Now it was argued earlier that, for *every* name 'N' having a genuine use (and not only for ones like 'Deutero-Isaiah'), there is a condition for being the referent of 'N'; but it is natural to say that this is not the same as the condition for being N, and that it is the latter condition with which we are concerned when we use 'N' in modal contexts, whereas the condition for being the referent of 'the teacher of Alexander' *is* the condition for having been the teacher of Alexander. A definite description occurring after 'to be' or 'to become' has narrow scope, since, as Geach observes, it functions more as a predicate than as a term. We can still explain the behaviour of a proper name 'N' in this position by ascribing wide scope to it; but for the difference in scope conventions, it may then be taken as interchangeable with 'the referent of "N"'. Someone not in fact the referent of 'the teacher of Alexander' might have been the teacher of Alexander. But, though someone not in fact the referent of 'Aristotle' might have been the referent of 'Aristotle', such a person could not have been Aristotle. We may explain this as its being true to say, of Aristotle, that no such person could have been he, just as, in the earlier example, I am saying, of the man I am pointing at, that he might have been in Rome. Nothing goes wrong with our theory if we give this explanation. But the explanation violates our inclination to take the complement of the verb 'to be' as a position occupied only by an expression with narrow scope. The inclination is strong; and it is here reinforced by that close link between proper names and identity on which Frege insisted. Together, these make it more natural, once the notion of rigid designation has been introduced, to adopt this account rather than one framed entirely in terms of scope, which is why Kripke claims the absurdity of 'Aristotle might not have been Aristotle' as giving intuitive support to the former. It provides no sort of proof; the scope explanation remains perfectly workable, as we have seen that it must: but it helps to explain why the rigid/flexible distinction may seem so compelling.

Whether the mechanism of rigidity be adopted or that of scope made to do all the work is not of primary importance. It is of course the case that taking names to be rigid designators makes it superfluous also to regard them as having wide scope: it already has the same effect, so that, by according them wide scope, we should make no difference to the truth-conditions. What is of primary importance is the common root in terms of which both mechanisms are to be explained: the application to an actual individual of a counterfactual predicate. We have such forms of expression in our language, embodying a conception of the identity of an actual individual with one in hypothetical circumstances. Reference to these forms of expression does not, of itself, in the least explain what that conception is; it shows only that we have it. If the hypothetical circumstances are sufficiently close to the actual ones, the identification of actual individuals as involved in them is unproblematic: the question is whether there are uniform general principles governing such identifications in all cases, and, if so, what they are. Merely remarking that, in ordinary discourse, we do not make explicit appeal to such principles, but take them for granted, gives no ground for an affirmative answer to the first half of the question, and is no substitute for a detailed answer to the second. My own belief, as already indicated, is that there are no uniform general principles.[1]

---

[1] The foregoing appendix was written before I became aware of the late Gareth Evans's article 'Reference and Contingency' (*The Monist*, vol. 62, 1979, pp. 161–89). In this, although not sharing my conviction of the superfluity, in principle, of the rigid/flexible distinction, he arrived at very similar conclusions concerning its bearing on a Fregean account of sense. He accepts (with an acknowledgment) my distinction between the assertoric content and the ingredient sense of a sentence, specializing it, for the case where only modal operators are involved, to that between the content and the proposition expressed (pp. 176–8); here a 'proposition' is a function from possible worlds to

truth-values. In a passage highly reminiscent of Frege's remarks concerning the identity of thoughts (p. 176), he very rightly observes that it is the content, not (in this terminology) the proposition, to which a propositional attitude such as belief relates. He nevertheless controverts (p. 161) my remark, on p. 121 of *FPL*, that something must be amiss with arguments, such as Kripke's, that lead to the conclusion that one can, by making some stipulation, for instance of a standard of measurement, learn a contingent fact about the world. This he does by drawing a distinction between the 'deeply contingent' and the 'superficially contingent'. A deeply contingent statement is one for which there is no guarantee that there is any state of affairs which makes it true (p. 185), where what makes a statement true is related to its content, not to the proposition it expresses (p. 181); a statement true a priori cannot be deeply contingent (p. 161). Evans's deep contingency thus corresponds with what, on p. 117 of *FPL*, I called 'ontic contingency', and, on p. 121, distinguished from Kripke's metaphysical contingency on precisely the ground that it did not allow for a class of contingent a priori statements, though one might well question Evans's use of the term 'guarantee' in this connection. A superficially contingent sentence 'Q', on the other hand, is for Evans one such that 'It is possible that not Q' is true (p. 185); this property depends upon the proposition it expresses, not on its content, which is why it may be known to be true a priori. Evans is thus defining superficial contingency by appeal to what in the foregoing appendix was called a modal involvement principle, which, for sentences containing terms recognized as rigid designators, yields a notion of possibility divergent from the epistemic one correlative to a priori truth. The distinction between deep and superficial, or between ontic and metaphysical, contingency is indeed of great importance. The application of the modal involvement principle, and hence the extension of the predicate 'superficially (metaphysically) contingent', will depend heavily upon whether the semantic theory employs the mechanism of rigid designation or not; the principle cannot be applied directly to natural language, in terms of 'might not have' instead of 'it is possible that not', if determinate results are to be obtained: a specific mode of regimentation must be assumed. Whether the notions of superficial or metaphysical contingency and necessity have any source other than the doctrine of rigid designation is an important question left undiscussed in the foregoing appendix.

I also regret having been unable, in my comments on Gregory Currie in Appendix 2, to take into account his 'Frege on Thoughts' (*Mind*, vol. LXXXIX, 1980, pp. 234–48). In this, he is less concerned than in his *Inquiry* article with whether Frege was a realist, but discusses at greater length the ascription, in 'Der Gedanke', of *Wirklichkeit* to thoughts; he continues misleadingly to translate Frege's term as 'reality', but correctly emphasizes its connection with causal efficacy. He cites the 1897 'Logik' as containing a 'tentative' statement of the same view, but fails to note the caveat in Frege's summary that it is only in a special sense that a thought is something *wirklich* (*N.S.*, p. 138, *P.W.*, p. 127), a caveat echoed in 'Der Gedanke' by the remark that 'thoughts are not altogether *unwirklich*, but their *Wirklichkeit* is of a quite different kind from that of things' (p. 77). Currie wrongly claims, on the strength of § 85, that Frege uses '*wirklich*' inconsistently in *Grundlagen*. This is a genuine instance of a failure to appreciate the historical context. Cantor was opposing the conception according to which negative numbers and the like are 'ideal' in a sense in which the positive integers are not. This conception, though enshrined in the phrase 'imaginary number' and in the algebraic use of the noun 'ideal', is now quite dead, but was still alive when Cantor and Frege were writing. Cantor, in saying that other numbers are no less real (*wirklich*) than the positive integers, was repudiating that conception; in agreeing with him, Frege made a concession to his terminology. The point was not to ascribe *Wirklichkeit* to numbers of all kinds, but to deny that there was any distinction in this regard between natural numbers and those of other kinds; Frege immediately went on to explain that he himself would prefer to use the term '*wirklich*' in such a way as not to apply to numbers of any kind.

Currie suggests that the context principle was intended, not as a doctrine about meaning at all, but as a formulation of the thesis—which we may call thesis *K*—that knowledge of objects always consists in knowing something about them, that is, in knowing the truth of thoughts concerning them; Frege's failure to reiterate the context principle in its original form was due, according to Currie, only to his realization that it was misleadingly framed as if it concerned meaning or reference. Thesis *K* indeed follows from the context principle, and Frege certainly subscribed to it. In formulating the context principle, however, he never mentioned knowledge, and always used the word '*Bedeutung*' or '*bedeuten*': it is therefore altogether unlikely that he never intended by it anything about meaning. In thus reducing the principle to one of its consequences, Currie goes against the obvious sense of Frege's words; the drive to find a new interpretation should not overpower the need to settle on a credible one.

Currie explains that thesis *K* made it unnecessary for Frege to ascribe *Wirklichkeit* to abstract objects other than thoughts, since it is sufficient that we grasp thoughts about them; he adds that thesis *K* cannot be applied to thoughts themselves (for otherwise we should be involved in an infinite regress of thoughts about thoughts). Both observations are entirely reasonable. The first squares badly, however, with Frege's remark in 'Der Gedanke' that 'something altogether and in every respect inactive would also be quite *unwirklich* and would not exist for us' (p. 76); but, in my view, he could have written that only after he had ceased to believe in logical objects. Currie thinks that Frege supposed thoughts to have a genuine causal operation upon those who grasp them, and opposes this view by an analogy with computing machines; the actual working of the machine, he says, does not involve the propositions represented upon its output tape, being describable without appeal to the method of representation. The analogue may, he thinks, hold for human beings. I cannot see that, in arguing thus, he is denying anything affirmed by Frege, who held that we can grasp thoughts only as clothed in linguistic or symbolic form. In 'Der Gedanke' Frege ascribed *Wirklichkeit* to thoughts inasmuch as our actions are influenced by our grasping them and judging them to be true, just as, in 'Logik', he said that one can speak of their *Wirklichkeit* 'only in the sense that the knowledge that someone has of, e.g., a law of nature influences his decisions' (*N.S.*, p. 149, *P.W.*, p. 138). That observation is compatible with thinking that human actions are causally explicable without appeal to the meanings of the words in which we think, and equally compatible with thinking that they are not; for the former view should not lead one to *deny* that our beliefs influence our decisions. It is also compatible with the intermediate view that an adequate causal explanation of human actions, though not of the operation of a computer, would necessarily display what gave the words and symbols their meanings, without needing explicitly to invoke the notion of meaning: no judgment on these issues is, in my opinion, to be extracted from Frege's writings.

Currie ends by arguing that a belief in abstract objects of any kind can be defended only if they are taken as having effects ('upon us', he says at the end, or 'on real things', he says on p. 247), on the ground that, if they had no effect upon our mental and physical world, 'then nothing in that world would be different if they did not exist'. This runs counter to Currie's previous explanation why Frege did not need to ascribe *Wirklichkeit* to abstract objects other than thoughts, namely that it is sufficient that we have thoughts about those objects and are influenced by those thoughts; there is then no need to ascribe causal influence to the objects. The validity of this explanation remains unaffected even if, for the reasons advanced by Currie or for others, thoughts themselves are deemed not to be causally effective or *wirklich*. Currie is here also ignoring the fact that numbers were, for Frege, logical objects the existence of which is an analytic truth. For such objects, the argument that we can have no ground for believing them to exist, since, if they did not, we should not notice the difference, is devoid of cogency: it is not by noticing that things are not as they would be if numbers did not exist that Frege supposes us to come by our knowledge of their existence, and he regards the supposition that they do not exist as self-contradictory, so that we cannot even sensibly make that supposition.

Currie's line of thought has affinities with that of Hartry Field in his interesting *Science Without Numbers* (Oxford, 1980). Currie views any claim that it is useful to treat mathematical objects as existing as an acknowledgment of their causal efficacy. This is once more to overlook his own defence of Frege's denial of *Wirklichkeit* to them. It would be useful to treat them as existing if, by doing so, we could make inferences from empirical statements to other empirical statements that we could not otherwise make; the objects themselves need play no causal role in our making those inferences. This was undoubtedly Frege's view of the application of a mathematical theory, even *within* mathematics; he argued that we cannot derive a theorem about real numbers from one about complex numbers, for instance the formulas for the sines and cosines of multiples from De Moivre's theorem, unless we can affirm the existence of complex numbers (*Grundlagen*, § 101, 'Über formale Theorien der Arithmetik', pp. 102–3). Field is more subtle than Currie. He first observes that, if a mathematical theory S is analytically true, it must be conservative over a physical theory N, in the sense that any statement expressible in N which is a consequence of the union of N and S is a consequence of N alone. This is indubitable if 'consequence' is understood in a semantic sense. Since, however, it would be idle to question the existence of the objects of S if S were analytically true, Field assumes that it is *not* analytically true but that it *is* conservative, on the ground that it could hardly have been held to be analytic were it not even conservative. The conservativeness of S is irrelevant to the existence of its objects if N itself refers to them; even if it does not, S is not rendered useless by being conservative over it. If S is conservative only in the semantic sense, it may be that we can *draw* consequences from $S + N$ that we cannot draw from N alone. Even if S is conservative in the proof-theoretic sense, it might be that we could conclude that it was so only by assuming it to be true; this is in effect Frege's view. Hence Field attempts to show that we can formulate physical theories without quantification over real numbers or other mathematical objects so as to preserve their empirical strength, reckoned proof-theoretically, but not the ease with which we are able to derive consequences from them. This last distinction reveals a way in which S may be useful without being true; contrary to Currie's view, it may be useful to speak of mathematical objects as existing without there being any ground for believing them to do so. Even if Field's claim is excessive, his line of enquiry is illuminating: if we can say at just which points the assumption of the existence of a mathematical structure becomes important for applications, we thereby attain a clearer grasp of what is involved in making that assumption.

Bibliography

Abbreviations used in footnotes and bibliography

(a) *Modern editions and collections*

B.a.A. G. Frege, *Begriffsschrift und andere Aufsätze*, ed. I Angelelli, 2nd edn., Hildesheim, 1964

BLA G. Frege, *The Basic Laws of Arithmetic*, trans. and ed. M. Furth, Berkeley and Los Angeles, 1964

BW G. Frege, *Wissenschaftlicher Briefwechsel*, ed. G. Gabriel, H. Hermes, F. Kambartel, C. Thiel and A. Veraart, Hamburg, 1976

C.N. G. Frege, *Conceptual Notation and Related Articles*, trans. and ed. T. W. Bynum, Oxford, 1972

EF E. D. Klemke (ed.), *Essays on Frege*, Urbana, Chicago and London, 1968

FG G. Frege, *On the Foundations of Geometry and Formal Theories of Arithmetic*, trans. and ed. E.-H. W. Kluge, New Haven and London, 1971

K.S. G. Frege, *Kleine Schriften*, ed. I. Angelelli, Hildesheim, 1967

LI G. Frege, *Logical Investigations*, trans. and ed. P. T. Geach and R. H. Stoothoff, Oxford, 1977

N.S. G. Frege, *Nachgelassene Schriften*, ed. H. Hermes, F. Kambartel and F. Kaulbach, Hamburg, 1969

P.M.C. G. Frege, *Philosophical and Mathematical Correspondence*, ed. B. McGuinness, trans. H. Kaal, Oxford, 1980

P.W. G. Frege, *Posthumous Writings*, trans. P. Long and R. White with the assistance of R. Hargreaves, Oxford, 1979

SF M. Schirn (ed.), *Studien zu Frege/Studies on Frege*, three vols., Stuttgart and Bad Canstatt, 1976

T.F. P. Geach and M. Black (ed. and trans.), *Translations from the Philosophical Writings of Gottlob Frege*, Oxford, 1952, 1960, 1980

(b) *Journals in which Frege published*

BPI *Beiträge zur Philosophie des deutschen Idealismus*
DL *Deutsche Literaturzeitung*
JDMV *Jahresbericht der Deutschen Mathematiker-Vereinigung*
JL *Jenaer Literaturzeitung*
JZN *Jenaische Zeitschrift für Naturwissenschaft*
ZPK *Zeitschrift für Philosophie und philosophische Kritik*

Frege's writings

Unpublished works are indented. Works mentioned in the text are starred.

(i) Early period (to 1891)

*1873 Über eine geometrische Darstellung der imaginären Gebilde in der Ebene, Jena, 1873. Reprinted in K.S., pp. 1–49

*1874 Rechnungsmethoden, die sich auf eine Erweiterung des Grössenbegriffes gründen, Jena, 1874. Reprinted in K.S., pp. 50–84

1874 Review of H. Seeger, Die Elemente der Arithmetik, für den Schulunterricht bearbeitet, in JL, vol. I, 1874, no. 46, p. 722. Reprinted in K.S., pp. 85–6

*1874–80 'Siebzehn Kernsätze zur Logik', in N.S., pp. 189–90. Trans. in P.W., pp. 174–5

1877 Review of A. von Gall and E. Winter, Die analytische Geometrie des Punktes and der Geraden und ihre Anwendung auf Aufgaben, in JL, vol. IV, 1877, no. 9, pp. 133–4. Reprinted in K.S., pp. 87–8

1877 Review of J. Thomae, Sammlung von Formeln, welche bei Anwendung der elliptischen und Rosenhainschen Funktionen gebraucht werden, in JL, vol. IV, 1877, no. 30, p. 472. Reprinted in K.S., p. 89

1878 'Über eine Weise, die Gestalt eines Dreiecks als komplexe Grösse aufzufassen', in JZN, vol. XII, 1878, supplement, p. xviii. Reprinted in K.S., pp. 90–1

*1879 Begriffsschrift, eine der arithmetischen nachgebildete Formelsprache des reinen Denkens, Halle, 1879. Reprinted in B.a.A., pp. vii–xvi, 1–88. Trans. in C.N., pp. 101–203, and in J. van Heijenoort (ed.), From Frege to Gödel, Cambridge, Mass., 1967, pp. 5–82

*1879 'Anwendungen der Begriffsschrift', in JZN, vol. XIII, 1879, supplement II, pp. 29–33. Reprinted in B.a.A., pp. 89–93. Trans. in C.N., pp. 204–8

1880 Review of Hoppe, Lehrbuch der analytischen Geometrie, in DL, vol. I, 1880, pp. 210–11. Reprinted in K.S., pp. 92–3

*1881 'Booles rechnende Logik und die Begriffsschrift', in N.S., pp. 9–52. Trans. in P.W., pp. 9–46

1882 'Über den Briefwechsel Leibnizens und Huygens mit Papin', in JZN, vol. xv, 1882, supplement, pp. 29–32. Reprinted in B.a.A., pp. 93–6

*1882 'Über die wissenschaftliche Berechtigung einer Begriffsschrift', in ZPK, vol. LXXXI, 1882, pp. 48–56. Reprinted in B.a.A., pp. 106–14. Trans. in C.N., pp. 83–9

1882 'Booles logische Formelsprache und meine Begriffsschrift', in N.S., pp. 53–9. Trans. in P.W., pp. 47–52

*1882 Letter to Anton Marty, in BW, pp. 163–5. Trans. in P.M.C., pp. 99–102

*1880–3 'Dialog mit Pünjer über Existenz', in N.S., pp. 60–75. Trans. in P.W., pp. 53–67

*1883 'Über den Zweck der Begriffsschrift', in JZN, vol. XVI, 1883, supplement, pp. 1–10. Reprinted in B.a.A., pp. 97–106. Trans. in C.N., pp. 90–100

1884 'Geometrie der Punktpaare in der Ebene', in JZN, vol. XVII, 1884, supplement, pp. 98–102. Reprinted in K.S., pp. 94–8

*1884 Die Grundlagen der Arithmetik, Breslau, 1884. Reprinted Breslau, 1934, and Darmstadt and Hildesheim, 1961. Reprinted with English trans. by J. L. Austin, Oxford, 1950, 1953

*1882–8 'Logik', in N.S., pp. 1–8. Trans. in P.W., pp. 1–8

*1885 Review of H. Cohen, Das Prinzip der Infinitesimal-Methode und seine Geschichte, in ZPK, vol. LXXXVII, 1885, pp. 324–9. Reprinted in K.S., pp. 99–102

1885 'Erwiderung', in *DL*, vol. VI, 1885, col. 1030. Reprinted in *K.S.*, p. 112

*1886 'Über formale Theorien der Arithmetik', in *JZN*, vol. XIX, 1886, supplement, pp. 94–104. Reprinted in *K.S.*, pp. 103–11. Trans. in *FG*.

*1888–90 'Über den Begriff der Zahl', in *N.S.*, pp. 81–95. Trans. in *P.W.*, pp. 72–86

*1891 'Über das Trägheitsgesetz', in *ZPK*, vol. XCVIII, 1891, pp. 145–61. Reprinted in *K.S.*, pp. 113–24. Trans. by R. Rand in *Synthese*, vol. XIII, 1961, pp. 350–63, and by H. Jackson and E. Levy in *Studies in the History and Philosophy of Science*, vol. II, 1971–2, pp. 195–212

(ii) *Mature period (1891–1906)*

*1891 *Function und Begriff*, Jena, 1891. Reprinted in *K.S.*, pp. 125–42. Trans. in *T.F.*, pp. 21–41

*1891 Letter to Husserl, in *BW*, pp. 94–8. Trans. in *P.M.C.*, pp. 61–4

*1892 'Über Sinn und Bedeutung', in *ZPK*, vol. C, 1892, pp. 25–50. Reprinted in *K.S.*, pp. 143–62. Trans. in *T.F.*, pp. 56–78

*1892 'Über Begriff und Gegenstand', in *Vierteljahrsschrift für wissenschaftliche Philosophie*, vol. XVI, 1892, pp. 192–205. Reprinted in *K.S.*, pp. 167–78. Trans. in *T.F.*, pp. 42–55. Draft in *N.S.*, pp. 96–127, trans. in *P.W.*, pp. 87–117

1892 Review of G. Cantor, *Zur Lehre vom Transfiniten*, in *ZPK*, vol. C, 1892, pp. 269–72. Reprinted in *K.S.*, pp. 163–6. Draft in *N.S.*, pp. 76–80, trans. in *P.W.*, pp. 68–71

*1893 *Grundgesetze der Arithmetik*, vol. I, Jena, 1893. Reprinted Darmstadt and Hildesheim, 1962. Trans. of Part I in *BLA*

*1892–5 'Ausführungen über Sinn und Bedeutung', in *N.S.*, pp. 128–36. Trans. in *P.W.*, pp. 118–25

*1894 Review of E. Husserl, *Philosophie der Arithmetik*, in *ZPK*, vol. CIII, 1894, pp. 313–32. Reprinted in *K.S.*, pp. 179–92. Trans. by E.-H. W. Kluge in *Mind*, vol. LXXXI, 1972, pp. 321–37

*1894–6 Correspondence with Peano, in *BW*, pp. 176–98. Trans. in *P.M.C.*, pp. 108–29

*1895 'Le nombre entier', in *Revue de métaphysique et de morale*, vol. III, 1895, pp. 73–8. Reprinted in *K.S.*, pp. 211–19. Trans. by V. H. Dudman in *Mind*, vol. LXXIX, 1970, pp. 481–6

1895 'Kritische Beleuchtung einiger Punkte in E. Schröders *Vorlesungen über die Algebra der Logik*', in *Archiv für systematische Philosophie*, vol. I, 1895, pp. 433–56. Reprinted in *K.S.*, pp. 193–210. Trans. in *T.F.*, pp. 86–106

1895 Letter to Hilbert, in *BW*, pp. 58–9. Trans. in *P.M.C.*, pp. 32–4

*1896 Lettera del sig. G. Frege all'editore, in *Rivista di Matematica*, vol. VI, 1896–9, pp. 53–9. Reprinted in *K.S.*, pp. 234–9. Trans. by V. H. Dudman in *Southern Journal of Philosophy*, vol. IX, 1971, pp. 31–6

*1897 'Über die Begriffsschrift des Herrn Peano und meine eigene', in *Berichte über die Verhandlungen der Königlich Sächsischen Gesellschaft der Wissenschaften zu Leipzig, Mathematisch-Physische Klasse*, vol. XLVIII, 1897, pp. 361–78. Reprinted in *K.S.*, pp. 220–33

*1897 'Logik', in *N.S.*, pp. 137–63. Trans. in *P.W.*, pp. 126–51

*1897–8 'Begründung meiner strengeren Grundsätze des Definierens', in *N.S.*, pp. 164–70 (probably intended as a draft for *Grundgesetze*, vol. II, as remarked by the translators). Trans. in *P.W.*, pp. 152–6

*1899 *Über die Zahlen des Herrn H. Schubert*, Jena, 1899. Reprinted in *K.S.*, pp. 240–61

1898–1902 'Logische Mängel in der Mathematik', in *N.S.*, pp. 171–81 (probably intended as a draft for *Grundgesetze*, vol. II). Trans. in *P.W.*, pp. 157–66

*1899–1900   Correspondence with Hilbert and Liebmann, in *BW*, pp. 60–79, 147–51. Trans. in *P.M.C.*, pp. 34–51, 90–4

*1903   'Über die Grundlagen der Geometrie', in *JDMV*, vol. XII, 1903, pp. 319–24, 368–75. Reprinted in *K.S.*, pp. 262–72. Trans. by M. E. Szabo in *Philosophical Review*, vol. LXIX, 1960, pp. 3–17, and in *EF*, pp. 559–75. Also in *FG*.

*1902–4   Letter to Huntington, letter to Jourdain and correspondence with Russell, in *BW*, pp. 88–90, 111, 211–51. Trans. in *P.M.C.*, pp. 57–9, 73, 130–70

*1903   *Grundgesetze der Arithmetik*, vol. II, Jena, 1903. Reprinted Darmstadt and Hildesheim, 1962. Appendix trans. in *BLA*, pp. 127–43. §§ 56–57, 86–137, 139–44, 146–7 trans. in *T.F.* (1952 and 1960, pp. 159–233; 1980, pp. 139–213)

*1904   'Was ist eine Funktion?', in *Festschrift L. Boltzmann gewidmet zum sechzigsten Geburtstage*, Leipzig, 1904, pp. 656–66. Reprinted in *K.S.*, pp. 273–80. Trans. in *T.F.*, pp. 107–16

1903–5   Notes to Hilbert's *Grundlagen der Geometrie*, in *N.S.*, pp. 183–8. Trans. in *P.W.*, pp. 170–3

1899–1906   'Über Euklidische Geometrie', in *N.S.*, pp. 182–4. Trans. in *P.W.*, pp. 167–9

*1906   'Über die Grundlagen der Geometrie', in *JDMV*, vol. XV, 1906, pp. 293–309, 377–403, 423–30. Reprinted in *K.S.*, pp. 281–323. Trans. in *FG*.

*1906   'Über Schoenflies, *Die logischen Paradoxien der Mengenlehre*', in *N.S.*, pp. 191–199. Trans. in *P.W.*, pp. 176–83

(iii) *Late period (from 1906)*

*1906   'Was kann ich als Ergebnis meiner Arbeit ansehen?', in *N.S.*, p. 200. Trans. in *P.W.*, p. 184

*1906   'Einleitung in die Logik', in *N.S.*, pp. 201–12. Trans. in *P.W.*, pp. 185–96

*1906   'Kurze Übersicht meiner logischen Lehren', in *N.S.*, pp. 213–18. Trans. in *P.W.*, pp. 197–202.

1906   'Antwort auf die Ferienplauderei des Herrn Thomae', in *JDMV*, vol. XV, 1906, pp. 586–90. Reprinted in *K.S.*, pp. 324–8. Trans. in *FG*

*1906   Letters to Husserl, in *BW*, pp. 101–6. Trans. in *P.M.C.*, pp. 66–71

1908   'Die Unmöglichkeit der Thomaeschen formalen Arithmetik aus Neue nachgewiesen', with Schlussbemerkung, in *JDMV*, vol. XVII, 1908, pp. 52–6. Reprinted in *K.S.*, pp. 329–33. Trans. in *FG*

*1912   Notes to P. E. B. Jourdain, 'The Development of the Theories of Mathematical Logic and the Principles of Mathematics: Gottlob Frege', in *Quarterly Journal of Pure and Applied Mathematics*, vol. XLIII, 1912, pp. 237–69. Reprinted in *K.S.*, pp. 334–41. German original of 1910 in *BW*, pp. 116–24

*1914   Letters to Jourdain, in *BW*, pp. 126–33. Trans. in *P.M.C.*, pp. 78–84

*1914   'Logik in der Mathematik', in *N.S.*, pp. 219–70. Trans. in *P.W.*, pp. 203–50

*1915   'Meine grundlegenden logischen Einsichten', in *N.S.*, pp. 271–2. Trans. in *P.W.*, pp. 251–2

*1917   Correspondence with Dingler, in *BW*, pp. 29–45. Trans. in *P.M.C.*, pp. 16–30

*1918   'Der Gedanke: eine logische Untersuchung', in *BPT*, vol. I, 1918–19, pp. 58–77. Reprinted in *K.S.*, pp. 342–62. Trans. by A. and M. Quinton in *Mind*, vol. LXV, 1956, pp. 289–311, and in *EF*, pp. 507–35. Also by P. T. Geach in *LI*

*1918   'Die Verneinung: eine logische Untersuchung', in *BPI*, vol. I, 1918–19, pp. 143–57. Reprinted in *K.S.*, pp. 362–78. Trans. in *T.F.* (1952 and 1960), pp. 117–35, and in *LI*

1918   Letter to Zsigmondy, in *BW*, pp. 269–71. Trans. in *P.M.C.*, pp. 176–8

*1919 'Aufzeichnungen für Ludwig Darmstaedter', in *N.S.*, pp. 273-7. Trans. in *P.W.*, pp. 253-7

*1923 'Logische Untersuchungen, dritter Teil: Gedankengefüge', in *BPI*, vol. III, 1923-6, pp. 36-51. Reprinted in *K.S.*, pp. 378-94. Trans. by R. Stoothoff in *Mind*, vol. LXXII, 1963, pp. 1-17, and in *LI*

*1923 'Logische Allgemeinheit', in *N.S.*, pp. 278-81. Trans. in *P.W.*, pp. 258-62

1924 Tagebuch. From this are excerpted in *N.S.*, pp. 282-3, three entries concerning the concept of number. Trans. in *P.W.*, pp. 263-4

*1924 'Zahl', in *N.S.*, pp. 284-5. Trans. in *P.W.*, pp. 265-6

*1924-5 'Erkenntnisquellen der Mathematik und der mathematischen Naturwissenschaften', in *N.S.*, pp. 286-94. Trans. in *P.W.*, pp. 267-74

1924-5 'Zahlen und Arithmetik', in *N.S.*, pp. 295-7. Trans. in *P.W.*, pp. 275-7

*1924-5 'Neuer Versuch der Grundlegung der Arithmetik', in *N.S.*, pp. 298-302. Trans. in *P.W.*, pp. 278-81

1925 Letter to Hönigswald, in *BW*, pp. 85-7. Trans. in *P.M.C.*, pp. 54-6

Works by other writers

The only items here listed are those quoted or alluded to in this book. Standard texts are not included.

Angelelli, I.:
Studies on Gottlob Frege and Traditional Philosophy, Dordrecht, 1967
Anon.:
Review of *FPL* in *Times Literary Supplement* for 30 November, 1973
Anscombe, G. E. M.:
An Introduction to Wittgenstein's Tractatus, London, 1959
'The First Person', in S. Guttenplan (ed.), *Mind and Language*, Oxford, 1975, pp. 45-65
Anscombe, G. E. M., and Geach, P. T.:
Three Philosophers, Oxford, 1961
Ayer, A. J.:
The Central Questions of Philosophy, London, 1973
Bell, D.:
Frege's Theory of Judgment, Oxford, 1979
Black, M.:
A Companion to Wittgenstein's Tractatus, Cambridge, 1964
Blackburn, S., and Code, A.:
'The Power of Russell's Criticism of Frege: "On Denoting",' pp. 48-50, *Analysis*, vol. 38, 1978, pp. 65-77
Brentano, F.:
Psychologie vom empirischen Standpunkte, Leipzig, 1874; 2nd edn., ed. O. Kraus, 1924. Trans. by A. C. Rancurello, D. B. Terrell and L. L. McAlister as *Psychology from an Empirical Standpoint*, ed. L. L. McAlister, London, 1973
Carnap, R.:
Meaning and Necessity, Chicago, 1956
Church, A.:
'On Carnap's Analysis of Statements of Assertion and Belief', *Analysis*, vol. 10, 1950, pp. 97-9
Copleston, F.:
A History of Philosophy, vol. VII, *Fichte to Nietzsche*, London, 1963
Currie, G.:
Review of *FPL*, *British Journal for the Philosophy of Science*, vol. 27, 1976, pp. 79-92

'Frege's Realism', *Inquiry*, vol. 21, 1978, pp. 218–21
'Frege on Thoughts', *Mind*, vol. LXXXIX, 1980, pp. 234–48

Davidson, D.:
'Reality without Reference', *Dialectica*, vol. 31, 1977, pp. 247–58; reprinted in M. Platts (ed.), *Reference, Truth and Reality*, pp. 131–41
'The Method of Truth in Metaphysics', in P. A. French, T. E. Uehling, Jr., and H. K. Wettstein (eds.), *Studies in the Philosophy of Language*, vol. II of *Mid-West Studies in Philosophy*, Morris, Minnesota, 1977, pp. 244–54

Dedekind, R.:
Was sind und was sollen die Zahlen?, Brunswick, 1888, 1893. English trans. by W. W. Berman in R. Dedekind, *Essays on the Theory of Numbers*, Chicago, 1901

Dudman, V. H.:
'*Bedeutung* for Predicates', in *SF*, vol. III, pp. 71–84

Dummett, M.:
Truth and other Enigmas, London and Cambridge, Mass., 1978 (abbreviated *TE*)
Review of *T.F.*, *Mind*, vol. LXIII, 1954, pp. 102–5
'Frege on Functions: a Reply', *Philosophical Review*, vol. LXIV, 1955, pp. 96–107; reprinted in *EF*, pp. 268–83, and as 'Frege on Functions' in *TE*, pp. 74–84
'Note: Frege on Functions', *Philosophical Review*, vol. LXV, 1956, pp. 229–30; reprinted in *EF*, pp. 295–7, and as Postscript to the foregoing in *TE*, pp. 85–6
'Nominalism', *Philosophical Review*, vol. LXV, 1956, pp. 491–505; reprinted in *EF*, pp. 321–36, and in *TE*, pp. 38–49
Article on Frege, Gottlob, in Paul Edwards (ed.), *The Encyclopedia of Philosophy*, vol. III, New York, 1962, pp. 225–37; reprinted as 'Frege's Philosophy' in *TE*, pp. 87–115
'Platonism', in *TE*, pp. 202–14
'The Social Character of Meaning', *Synthese*, vol. 27, 1974, pp. 523–34; reprinted in *TE*, pp. 420–30
'The Philosophical Basis of Intuitionistic Logic', in H. E. Rose and J. D. Shepherdson (eds.), *Logic Colloquium '73*, Amsterdam, 1975, pp. 5–40; reprinted in *TE*, pp. 215–47
'Frege', *Teorema*, vol. V, 1975, pp. 149–88; English version as 'Frege's Distinction between Sense and Reference' in *TE*, pp. 116–44
'Frege as a Realist', *Inquiry*, vol. 19, 1976, pp. 455–68

Evans, G.:
'Reference and Contingency', *The Monist*, vol. 62, 1979, pp. 161–80
'Understanding Demonstratives', in H. Paret and J. Bouvresse (eds.), *Meaning and Understanding*, Berlin, forthcoming (proceedings of conference at Cerisy-la-Salle, 1979)

Field, H. H.:
Science Without Numbers, Oxford, 1980

Føllesdal, D.:
'Brentano and Husserl on Intentional Objects and Perception', *Grazer philosophische Studien*, vol. 5, 1978, pp. 83–94
'Husserl and Heidegger on the Role of Actions in the Constitution of the World', in E. Saarinen, R. Hilpinen, I. Niiniluoto and M. Provence Hintikka (eds.), *Essays in Honour of Jaakko Hintikka*, Dordrecht, 1979, pp. 365–78

Geach, P. T.:
Reference and Generality, Ithaca, N.Y., 1962, 1968, 1980
Logic Matters, Oxford, 1972 (abbreviated as *LM*)
'Russell on Meaning and Denoting', *Analysis*, vol. 19, 1959, pp. 69–72; reprinted in *LM*, pp. 27–31
'Assertion', *Philosophical Review*, vol. LXXIV, 1965, pp. 449–65; reprinted in *LM*, pp. 254–69

'Ontological Relativity and Relative Identity', in M. K. Munitz (ed.), *Logic and Ontology*, New York, 1973, pp. 287–302

Review of *FPL*, *Mind*, vol. LXXXV, 1975, pp. 436–49

'Names and Identity', in S. Guttenplan (ed.), *Mind and Language*, Oxford, 1975, pp. 139–58

'Existential or Particular Quantifier?', in P. Weingartner and E. Morscher (eds.), *Ontology and Logic*, Berlin, 1979, pp. 137–51

See also Anscombe, G. E. M., and Geach, P. T.

Grossmann, R.:

'Frege's Ontology', *Philosophical Review*, vol. LXX, 1961, pp. 23–40; reprinted in *EF*, pp. 79–98

Reflections on Frege's Philosophy, Evanston, 1969

Heidelberger, H.:

Review of *FPL*, *Metaphilosophy*, vol. 6, 1975, pp. 35–43

Hilbert, D.:

Die Grundlagen der Geometrie, as part of *Festschrift zur Feier der Enthüllung des Gauss-Weber-Denkmals in Göttingen* (with E. Wiechert), Leipzig, 1899; 2nd (separate) edn., 1903. 1st edn, trans. by E. J. Townsend as *The Foundations of Geometry*, London, 1902; 10th edn. trans. by L. Unger, revised by P. Bernays, La Salle, Ill., 1971

Kamp, H.:

'Formal properties of "now" ', *Theoria*, vol. 37, 1971, pp. 227–73

Kaplan, D.:

'Dthat', in P. Cole (ed.), *Syntax and Semantics*, vol. 9, *Pragmatics*, New York and London, 1978, pp. 221–43

Kluge, E.-H. W.:

'Reflections on Frege', *Dialogue*, vol. IX, 1970, pp. 401–9

'Frege et les termes sans référence', *Dialogue*, vol. XIV, 1975, pp. 254–80

'Freges Begriff des Logischeinfachen', in *SF*, vol. II, pp. 51–66

Review of *FPL*, *Dialogue*, vol. XVI, 1977, pp. 519–33

Kripke, S.:

'Naming and Necessity', in G. Harman and D. Davidson (eds.), *The Semantics of Natural Language*, Dordrecht, 1972, pp. 352–5; reprinted, with newly added Preface, as *Naming and Necessity*, Oxford, 1979

'A Puzzle about Belief', in A. Margalit (ed.), *Meaning and Use*, Dordrecht, Boston, London and Jerusalem, 1979, pp. 239–83

Lotze, R. H.:

Logik, Leipzig, 1874, 1880. Trans. by B. Bosanquet as *Logic*, Oxford, 1884

Marshall, W.:

'Frege's Theory of Functions and Objects', *Philosophical Review*, vol. LXII, 1953, pp. 374–90; reprinted in *EF*, pp. 249–67

'Sense and Reference: a Reply', *Philosophical Review*, vol. LXV, 1956, pp. 342–61; reprinted in *EF*, pp. 298–320

Mates, B.:

'Synonymity', *University of California Publications in Philosophy*, no. 25, Berkeley, 1950, pp. 201–26; reprinted in L. Linsky (ed.), *Semantics and the Philosophy of Language*, Urbana, 1952, pp. 111–36

McDowell, J.:

'On the Sense and Reference of a Proper Name', *Mind*, vol. LXXXVI, 1977, pp. 159–185

Moore, G. E.:

'The Refutation of Idealism', *Mind*, vol. XIII, 1903, pp. 433–53; reprinted in G. E. Moore, *Philosophical Studies*, London, 1922, pp. 1–30

Noonan, H. W.:
Objects and Identity, The Hague, Boston and London, 1980
Passmore, J.:
A Hundred Years of Philosophy, London, 1957
Perry, J.:
'Frege on Demonstratives', *Philosophical Review*, vol. LXXXVI, 1977, pp. 474–97
Quine, W. V. O.:
Mathematical Logic, Cambridge, Mass., 1947
Review of P. T. Geach, *Reference and Generality, Philosophical Review*, vol. LXIII, 1964, pp. 100–4
Ramsey, F. P.:
The Foundations of Mathematics, ed. R. B. Braithwaite, London, 1931; 2nd edn., *Foundations*, ed. D. H. Mellor, London and Henley, 1978
Reichenbach, H.:
Elements of Symbolic Logic, New York, 1947
Resnik, M. D.:
'The Context Principle in Frege's Philosophy', *Philosophy and Phenomenological Research*, vol. XXVII, 1967, pp. 356–65
'Frege's Context Principle Revisited', in *SF*, vol. III, pp. 35–49
'Frege as Idealist and then Realist', *Inquiry*, vol. 22, 1979, pp. 350–7
Russell, B.:
'On Denoting', *Mind*, vol. XIV, 1905, pp. 479–93; reprinted in B. Russell, *Logic and Knowledge*, ed, R. C. Marsh, London, 1956, pp. 41–56, and in B. Russell, *Essays in Analysis*, ed. D. Lackey, London, 1973, pp. 103–19
'Mr. Strawson on Referring', *Mind*, vol. LXVI, 1957, pp. 385–9; reprinted in B. Russell, *Essays in Analysis*, ed. D. Lackey, London, 1973, pp. 120–6
Searle, J. R.:
'Russell's Objections to Frege's Theory of Sense and Reference', *Analysis*, vol. 18, 1957, pp. 137–43; reprinted in *EF*, pp. 337–45
Shwayder, D. S.:
'On the Determination of Reference by Sense', in *SF*, vol. III, pp. 85–95
Sluga, H.:
Gottlob Frege, London, Boston and Henley, 1980
'Frege and the Rise of Analytical Philosophy', *Inquiry*, vol. 18, 1975, pp. 471–87; embodies a review of *FPL*
'Frege as a Rationalist', in *SF*, vol. I, pp. 27–47
'Frege's Alleged Realism', *Inquiry*, vol. 20, 1977, pp. 227–42
Strawson, P. F.:
Individuals, London, 1960
'On Referring', *Mind*, vol. LIX, 1950, pp. 320–44; reprinted in P. F. Strawson, *Logico-Linguistic Papers*, London, 1971, pp. 1–27
Tugendhat, E.:
'The Meaning of "Bedeutung" in Frege', *Analysis*, vol. 30, 1970, pp. 177–89. German version, 'Die Bedeutung des Ausdrucks "Bedeutung" bei Frege', in *SF*, vol. III, pp. 51–65, with newly added Postskript, pp. 65–9
Wells, R. S.:
'Frege's Ontology', *The Review of Metaphysics*, vol. IV, 1951, pp. 537–73; reprinted in *EF*, pp. 3–41
Wittgenstein, L.:
Tractatus Logico-Philosophicus, trans. D. Pears and B. F. McGuinness, London and New York, 1961
Philosophical Investigations, trans. G. E. M. Anscombe, Oxford, 1953

Lectures on the Foundations of Mathematics, ed. C. Diamond, Hassocks and Ithaca, N.Y., 1976

Remarks on the Foundations of Mathematics, revised edn., ed. G. H. von Wright, R. Rhees and G. E. M. Anscombe, trans. G. E. M. Anscombe, Oxford, Cambridge, Mass., and London, 1978

Index

DATE DUE